Family breakdown and pensions

To Baroness Hollis,
without whom it is unlikely that the current improvements in
the ways that pensions can be dealt with on divorce would exist.

Family breakdown and pensions

Second edition

Robin Ellison
Chairman, Pensions Group, Eversheds

Maggie Rae
Partner, Clintons

with a chapter on insurance by

Keith Popplewell
Managing Director, The Divorce Corporation

Butterworths
London, Edinburgh, Dublin
2001

United Kingdom	Butterworths, a Division of Reed Elsevier (UK) Ltd, Halsbury House, 35 Chancery Lane, LONDON WC2A 1EL and 4 Hill Street, EDINBURGH EH2 3JZ
Australia	Butterworths, a Division of Reed International Books Australia Pty Ltd, CHATSWOOD, New South Wales
Canada	Butterworths Canada Ltd, MARKHAM, Ontario
Hong Kong	Butterworths Hong Kong, a division of Reed Elsevier (Greater China) Ltd, HONG KONG
India	Butterworths India, NEW DELHI
Ireland	Butterworth (Ireland) Ltd, DUBLIN
Malaysia	Malayan Law Journal Sdn Bhd, KUALA LUMPUR
New Zealand	Butterworths of New Zealand Ltd, WELLINGTON
Singapore	Butterworths Asia, SINGAPORE
South Africa	Butterworths Publishers (Pty) Ltd, DURBAN
USA	Lexis Law Publishing, CHARLOTTESVILLE, Virginia

© Reed Elsevier (UK) Ltd 2001

A CIP Catalogue record for this book is available from the British Library.

ISBN 0 406 91310 2

Typeset by Doyle & Co, Colchester
Printed and bound by Bookcraft (Bath) Ltd, Midsomer Norton, Avon

Visit Butterworths LEXIS direct at: www.butterworths.com

Preface

This book has been written with the practising lawyer, independent financial adviser, accountant and now pension scheme manager and adviser in mind. It is based on the considerable efforts of others, including at one time the Pensions Management Institute and Law Society Working Party on Pensions and Divorce, and on the studies done by many other academics and practising lawyers. Credit has been given for the work of others wherever possible; apologies for any that have been overlooked. Special thanks are due to the staff of Butterworths, our agent Micheline Steinberg, and partners and colleagues as well as (in the first edition) the advice and counsel of Claire Meltzer and the constructive remarks of reviewers of the first edition. We are alone responsible for errors and omissions. Suggestions for the improvement of any future edition are always welcome, and should be addressed to the publishers.

The text has been written with less time than we would have liked, thanks to the late publication of many of the regulations. Accordingly, there has been less time for reflection and discussion with colleagues than is usual and, with the extraordinary complexity of many of the regulations, our conclusions may need revision in due course. The drafting of the law on pensions and divorce is an object lesson on how not to do it; other countries manage it in just a few pages and in relatively simple language. One day the draftsman will be prevailed upon to legislate with economy and simplicity, but we may have some time to wait.

To solve some of these issues we have arranged with the publishers to maintain a website with news of later developments, contents of amending regulations (of which there will be no shortage), points of practice and new cases as they appear. It might even develop into some kind of bulletin board. In due course most of these improvements will be compiled into any third edition, and acknowledgements made.

The law is stated as at 1 April 2001.

Robin Ellison (ellisor@eversheds.com)
Maggie Rae (maggie@clintons.co.uk

> To enable readers to update their knowledge of the subject, the secondary legislation is included on a website at the following address:
>
> http://www.butterworths.com/corporate/products/publications/index.htm
>
> The necessary password is: pensions

Contents

Chapter Nine   Implications for pension scheme practice

Appendices

Table of Statutes

References are to numbered headings. Those prefixed 'S' refer to headings in the Summary and those prefixed 'A' refer to headings in the Appendices. References in **bold** indicate where the legislation is set out in part or in full.

Table of Statutory Instruments

References are to numbered headings. Those prefixed 'S' refer to headings in the Summary and those prefixed 'A' refer to headings in the Appendices. References in **bold** indicate where the legislation is set out in part or in full.

Table of Cases

References are to numbered headings. Those prefixed 'S' refer to headings in the Summary.

List of acronyms

Legislation

AA 1955	Army Act 1955
AFA 1955	Air Force Act 1955
FA 1989	Finance Act 1989
FA 1999	Finance Act 1999
FL(S)A 1985	Family Law (Scotland) Act 1985
FLA 1996	Family Law Act 1996
FPR 1991	Family Proceedings Rules 1991
FSA 1986	Financial Services Act 1986
HRA 1998	Human Rights Act 1998
ICTA 1970	Income and Corporation Taxes Act 1970
ICTA 1988	Income and Corporation Taxes Act 1988
IH(PFD)A 1975	Inheritance (Provision for Family and Dependants) Act 1975
LAA 1774	Life Assurance Act 1774
LPA 1925	Law of Property Act 1925
MCA 1973	Matrimonial Causes Act 1973
MFPA 1984	Matrimonial and Family Proceedings Act 1984
MHA 1967	Matrimonial Homes Act 1967
MWPA 1882	Married Women's Property Act 1882
NDA 1957	Naval Discipline Act 1957
PA 1995	Pensions Act 1995
PAA 1867	Policies of Assurance Act 1867
PSA 1993	Pension Schemes Act 1993
SSA 1986	Social Security Act 1986
SSPA 1975	Social Security Pensions Act 1975
WRAPA 1999	Welfare Reform and Pensions Act 1999

Other

IRNICO	Inland Revenue National Insurance Contributions Office
PSO	Pension Schemes Office (of the Inland Revenue)
GMP	Guaranteed Minimum Pension
SERPS	State Earning Related Pension Sheme
S2P	State Second Pension *(not SSP)*

Summary

S.1 Introduction

Pensions benefits can in many cases be the most significant financial element in divorce proceedings. These notes explain:

- Briefly how pensions work in the UK.
- How to obtain the necessary valuations of the value of pension rights.
- How to negotiate in relation to those values.

It is now required (Matrimonial Causes Act 1973 (MCA 1973), s 25B) that pension rights should be taken into account by advisers and the court when reviewing division of matrimonial property on divorce. There are two main problems in practice:

- first, whether the statutory valuation is appropriate in the circumstances; and
- secondly, once the valuation is agreed, which method of settlement is appropriate.

The question of settlement method is a relatively new one; for cases in which petitions were issued before 1 July 1996 there was only one method. Then there were two, and from 2 December 2000 there are three. They are as follows:

- **Set-off** As before, readjusting the division of matrimonial assets to take account of pension rights.
- **Earmarking** Ie an order of the court directing that part or all of any lump sum or pension arising at retirement be paid to the other spouse.
- **Sharing** Ie an order of the court directing the pension scheme to allocate part or all of the pension rights to be awarded to the other spouse at divorce. This is provided for in amendments made by the Welfare Reform and Pensions Act 1999 (WRAPA 1999).

This note looks at whether and how these choices might be exercised, and the practical options available to the parties. Before looking at the choices, and how to exercise them in practice, it may be useful first to examine the UK pension system.

S.2   Simple guide to pensions

S.2.1 *State benefits*

There are two state pension arrangements:

- **The basic state pension** This provides a maximum of around £67.50 pw for a single person, provided he has a full employment record. Since this is payable as a social security benefit, and the courts have no jurisdiction over social security, it is not normally taken account of in divorce matters. In any event, a divorced former wife (although not a divorced former husband) can use a former husband's earnings record to enjoy a pension in her own right. The basic state pension is therefore in practice ignored in divorce arrangements.
- **The additional state pension** The State Earnings Related Pension Scheme (SERPS) provides around 20% of earnings up to around £28,000 pa. On divorce, however, the spouse cannot use the earner's track record to enjoy a parallel state benefit; it is therefore lost to the spouse.
    The benefits can either be provided:
    – by the state (in which case the scheme is 'contracted-in'); or
    – privately by an employer's pension scheme (in which case the scheme is 'contracted-out') or through an individual's personal pension (in which case it is an 'appropriate personal pension').

In this guide the SERPS benefits are not dealt with separately. The level of benefits can be ascertained by asking the DSS (see form BR19, available from the DSS). If the benefits are provided through a company or personal pension scheme, they are conventionally included in the ordinary valuation and not separately identified.

SERPS is being phased out over the next five years to be replaced by a State Second Pension (S2P).

S.2.2 *Occupational and personal pensions*

Pensions can either be provided:
- individually, either –
    – by the individual making contributions to a personal pension scheme (perhaps with an insurance company or bank or building society) with or without contributions from the employer; or
    – by an employer making contributions to a company scheme, (perhaps with contributions by the employee); or
- collectively, by the employer providing benefits as set out in a 'defined-benefits' scheme, with contributions made preponderantly or solely by the employer, sometimes with contributions, or added contributions, by the employee.

S.2.3 *Money purchase and final salary*

When dividing pension rights, it is essential to determine just what those rights are:

- **Defined contribution schemes** In some schemes ('defined-contribution' or 'money-purchase' schemes) the benefits are merely what can be provided by a sum of money accumulated over time. The accumulated sum is used at retirement to buy a pension. The value depends on what annuity rates are at that time, and whether the value of the accumulated sum is affected by for example a fall or rise in the stock market at the time it is cashed in to buy an annuity.
- **Defined benefit schemes** In other schemes (which must be employer-related), the amount of money in the scheme is not relevant; the promise is of a benefit, perhaps related to salary. For example the promise by the employer may be to provide half-salary or two-thirds salary. The promise is built up over years, perhaps at $^1/_{60}$ of salary for each year of employment, so that after 40 years employment the employee will be entitled to $^{40}/_{60}$ of his salary at retirement (ie two-thirds). Such benefits may be index-linked, and with additional benefits sometimes at the discretion of the scheme's trustees. At one time, there was no need to have such promises by an employer supported by financial guarantees. From April 1997 the law required such promises to be supported by funds in a pension scheme.

From October 2001, employers with five employees or more are required to offer 'stakeholder pensions', which are technically occupational schemes, but regulated for tax purposes as personal pensions. Employers do not, however, have to make contributions to such schemes.

S.2.4 Funded and unfunded schemes

While money-purchase schemes are by definition funded, defined benefit schemes often do not have enough funds to pay all benefits if the schemes were closed tomorrow. There are many good reasons for this:

- The assets may have fallen in value at the time the scheme was closed, although in normal circumstances they would have been sufficient.
- Interest rates had fallen at the time although that was not reasonably expected, or promises had been made that would have been paid for over the years, but not enough time had passed.

In addition:

- it is not normally tax effective to provide assets to support promises for pensions in respect of income over the 'cap', currently around £91,800 pa.
- many perfectly proper pension schemes are not funded; these include many schemes in the public sector (among them, the Civil Service, teachers, police and firemen). It is calculated that the Civil Service scheme would have had to find around £500m per year of money it does not have if it were required to pay capital sums to divorced spouses on divorce.

S.2.5 Discretionary and indexed benefits

In final-salary or salary-related systems, some benefits are available as of right (subject to sufficient assets being available), and others may or may not be available, depending again on resources and the views of the trustees or managers. When valuing benefits it is not always clear whether these discretionary benefits (which may include for example benefits on ill-health, early-retirement benefits or inflation-protection) are to be included or not.

S.3   Valuation

S.3.1   Introduction

In practice, one of the major difficulties is the valuation of both the member's and the spouse's rights. Both need to be valued separately.
   Valuing has its problems:

- **Member's valuations**   The value of a member's or an employee's rights in a money-purchase pension system is (theoretically) relatively easy to identify; it is (except as below) the value of the assets standing to his credit. The value of an employee's interests in a final-salary scheme is more difficult to define, since it involves the application of actuarial techniques, identifying the value of the underlying guarantee, and the impact of the imprecise value of discretionary benefits. There is, however, a standard valuation technique, called a 'cash-equivalent', based on recommended actuarial guidance, which is used by the regulations. This is discussed below.

- **Spouse's valuations**   The value of a spouse's rights is a proportion of a member's rights.
      But a spouse's interest is in several parts, particularly in respect of salary-related schemes:
   - the survivor's rights, which will disappear by virtue of any divorce, and
   - the interest in the member's rights which he will enjoy once the benefit is in payment.

There will be some actuarial interest in discretionary or contingent benefits; but lump sums (except as a means of future payment) are only a different way of expressing a pension benefit (this is slightly different in the case of some public sector schemes).
   The interest will be affected or can be affected by a number of elements including:

- The life expectancy of the member; if that is impaired, the spouse's interest will be greater.
- The difference in ages of the spouses; if the spouse is much younger, her interest could be greater.

It is often convenient to express a spouse's rights as a percentage of a member's rights.

S.3.2   Methods available

There are many ways of valuing a member's interests.

In money-purchase cases the value of the account is often easy to determine. But even here, there may be a different value depending on whether the funds are left with the investment manager or insurer (the 'fund value') or whether the policy is to be paid up or surrendered (the 'surrender value'), which could be very substantially less.

In defined-benefit cases, as well as the problems of what benefits to take into account, and the variability of the personal factors, there are problems of assumptions. There are two main assumption problems:

- First, the fact that assumptions as to future interest rates, income rates and annuity rates can be difficult to agree. Few can guess as to future inflation rates for example; and low future inflation could double the value of a benefit compared with high future inflation. Different actuaries will have different expectations about these future rates, and small differences in assumptions can have a major differences in valuations. It is sensible to use mid-range assumptions, regardless of whether the valuation is prepared for the petitioner or the respondent, but in particular cases these may not be appropriate.
- Secondly, the fact that defined-benefit schemes often contain reserves designed to cope with the fact that a member may continue in employment with the company and that he may enjoy salary increases and career progression increases. If the member leaves before they come into play, those reserves are no longer required.

It is therefore possible to value the same pension rights in many different ways; it may be helpful to refer to just three:

- Past service reserves, which include the reserves mentioned above.
- Transfer values (or sometimes cash equivalents) a statutory minimum valuation, which does not take into account these reserves.
- Share of fund, which, if there is a significant surplus in the fund, may be higher than the first two (or lower, if there is a deficit in the fund).

S.3.3   *Cash equivalent transfer value*

The regulations (Pension Sharing (Valuation) Regulations 2000, SI 2000/1052) require that the valuation method used in the proceedings is the cash equivalent transfer value (CETV). It was the method recommended by the Pensions Management Institute/Law Society Working Party Report of 1993. Its advantage is that it is cheap or free to the parties and readily calculable by pension schemes.

But where the parties have been married for some time, or the earnings are higher, such a valuation can be misleading, sometimes by a factor of four or five. In such cases it is crucial and prudent to use a different system, perhaps the past service reserve approach, which may be more appropriate. It certainly enables the solicitor to give proper advice on which method of settlement should be employed.

The CETV used is not identical to that used to calculate transfers when leaving a scheme; it is reduced by the value of the survivor's benefit.

S.4   Powers of the court

Since 1 July 1996 the court has had power to make an order in respect of pensions. In relation to petitions issued before July, although it was settled law that the court could take pensions into account when considering financial arrangements on divorce (and in Scotland had to consider pensions), in practice the law throughout the UK was constrained by the fact that the courts had no authority to direct pension scheme managers and trustees to allocate one spouse's interests or part of them to another. In practice, there were two main problems:

- That the court had no power to make an order in relation to a member's pension rights.
- That it was difficult in some cases for a spouse's advisers to obtain the information.

S.4.1   Protective trusts

There were three main reasons for the court's previous difficulties:

- First, the Inland Revenue require as a condition of approval of the scheme that it contains a clause against 'alienation', prohibiting a member charging or alienating his acquired pension interests to anyone else.
- Secondly, the Inland Revenue rules as set down in statute and in practice notes prohibit the allocation of a member's pension rights to a spouse.
- Thirdly, almost all occupational schemes and an increasing number of personal pensions contain 'protective trusts' or 'spendthrift trusts' which operate a form of 'Catch-22' system. It operates so that where a court makes an order against a member's rights in a scheme, they will be forfeit, and the trustees then decide to whom to make payments – which can include the member himself. In practice, it makes it all but impossible to obtain garnishee orders against such payments, so that to all intents and purposes the protective trust mechanism is effective as protection. From 1 July 1996 the court has power to overcome these trusts in relation to divorce matters.

S.4.2   Obtaining information

It is now much easier than before to obtain information about pension arrangements. A member should normally disclose in his Form E (or if not should be asked about them) details of all pension arrangements.

Once that information is available, it is normally possible to obtain the necessary further information to value the member's interests by one of the following methods:

- Under the Pensions on Divorce (Provision of Information) Regulations 2000, SI 2000/1048 and the Pension Schemes Act 1993 (PSA 1993), s 133, under which a spouse has rights to some of a member's pensions information.

- Under an order under the Family Proceedings Rules 1991 (FPR 1991) , SI 1991/1247, r 2.63 for a production order.
- Under the Pensions on Divorce (Provision of Information) Regulations 2000 which oblige pension schemes to provide information to the member, the member's spouse and the court.

S.4.3 *Making the spouse a scheme member – the Brooks case*

There has been some confusion about the relevance of the decision in *Brooks v Brooks* [1996] AC 375, [1995] 3 All ER 257, HL. This suggests that the court may in some case have jurisdiction under the Matrimonial Causes Act 1973 to reallocate pension rights between husband and wife. The House of Lords decision seems to apply only in relatively infrequent cases:

- In the absence of protective trusts.
- Where an order would not affect third party rights, ie where the only member is the respondent.
- Where the scheme is in surplus.
- Where the spouse was employed by the same employer.
- Where the scheme was established under trust (not always the case in personal pension arrangements).

In practice, it seems limited to certain rare small self-administered pension schemes, a special form of pension scheme appropriate to small family companies. In any event, the impact of MCA 1973, s 25B suggests that such orders would not normally be considered by the courts and WRAPA 1999 now makes it unavailable as a remedy.

S.4.4 *The changes*

It was recommended by the Pensions Management Institute/Law Society report in May 1993 and the Goode Committee Report on pensions law reform in September 1993 that the law be reformed to allow the court to grant in some cases a 'Pensions Adjustment Order' directing the trustees or managers to reallocate pensions interests. The reform suggested was of 'pensions splitting' (ie division at divorce) rather than 'earmarking' (ie orders to take effect at retirement).

The law was changed following substantial pressure for reform during the passage of the Pensions Act 1995 (PA 1995), which introduced the concept of earmarking to MCA 1973. In particular, ss 25B–25D gave the court power:

- to award a periodical payments order against the pension when in payment; and/or
- to compel a member to take such commutation of pension rights as is available and transfer some or all of it to the spouse; and/or
- to require scheme trustees to pay part or all of any death-in-service lump sums to the spouse, overriding any nomination letters.

The periodical payments orders come to an end on the death of either of the parties or on remarriage of the spouse.

The principles underlying the earmarking regulations were set out in a summary paper issued by the Lord Chancellor's Department in June 1996.

Sharing, formerly known as splitting, was introduced as a remedy by WRAPA 1999; it is dealt with in more detail below.

S.5   Valuation and offsetting

Obtaining the CETV for both the member's and the spouse's pensions interests is only part of the process, but is the only value that must be provided in the documents available to the court (usually the Form E); it will not usually be the right value to be used in advising clients whether to seek a set-off or an earmarking order. Nor is it the right value to use in deciding what level of settlement to advise in either case.

The reason for the inadequacy of the CETV is set out below; in carrying out the negotiations on behalf of the client the following will be taken into account.

S.5.1   *Variability of valuations*

A valuation is a matter of art rather than of science; for example:

- In a money-purchase scheme, the CETV uses the surrender value of the policy; this can in practice be very much less than the fund value and misleading in particular circumstances.
- In a defined-benefit scheme the figure will vary according to the assumptions made, the method of valuation, the importance of any discretionary and contingent benefits and the extent of the spouse's interest. The CETV assumes that the member will leave the scheme at the time of divorce; this will give a much lower valuation than using an assumption that he will stay in the scheme until retirement. Furthermore the CETV does not take into account death benefits or discretionary benefits.

Accordingly, it is usually sensible to obtain a further independent valuation on the basis that the member will continue in service; the correct figure to use in negotiations will therefore be somewhere between the two extremes.

S.5.2   *Negotiating a set-off*

When deciding whether to seek a set-off solution rather than an earmarking solution, the following will normally be considered:

- **Tax** Whatever is agreed as the member's value, and then whatever is agreed as the spouse's percentage of that value, the agreed figure should be adjusted to take account of the fact that it will be settled without any tax obligation; normally pensions bear tax of between 10% and 40%, although sometimes some of it can be commuted tax-free.
- **Discount for cash** A spouse may also wish to give a further allowance for the fact that a benefit is being acquired in cash, rather than later in the form of pension.
- **Discount for early payment** A spouse may also wish to give a further allowance for the fact that a benefit is being acquired now rather than some years in the future.

- **Discount for risk** A spouse may also wish to give a further allowance for the fact that a benefit is being acquired which is certain, rather than subject to the vagaries of risk to the investments of the funds, the risks of death of either the member or the spouse or both, the risks of tax changes and other risks.
- **Setting off of own pension arrangements** Spouses will be aware that whatever applies to a member's pension rights will also apply to their own.
- **Pensions for house** In the past, the practice has often been to adjust a spouse's interest in the proceedings of the matrimonial home in lieu of being able to settle the pension rights. This practice will no doubt continue (even after the reforms), but spouses will be aware that sometimes there is insufficient equity in the house to do this. In the case especially of lower-earners with significant pension rights, it may even now be appropriate to defer a divorce until the pension is in payment, and then obtain a maintenance order rather than seek an earmarking order.

S.5.3 Earmarking

Earmarking allows the court to make an order addressed to the trustees or managers of a pension scheme directing them at the time the member begins to draw benefits:

- To pay some or all of any lump sum (such as a death-in-service benefit, or a commutation of a part of the pension) to the spouse; an order can require a spouse to commute.
- To pay some or all of any pension to the spouse as periodical payments.

The lump sum payments are treated as capital payments and thus survive the death or remarriage of the spouse. The pension payments do not survive death of either party or remarriage of the spouse.

The order can be made in percentage terms or in money terms. Orders will need to accommodate the fact that the tax is paid by the member before payment, that tax rates may change, and that life expectancies or the desire to remarry will affect the decision. The use of the CETV, in deciding whether cash adjustments or earmarking is preferable, will be misleading.

In any event the spouse will need to consider insuring the member against death before the spouse, since the pension payments will cease on the member's death. In addition, pension arrangements will need to be considered for the spouse. In due course, it is expected that non-earners will be able to make contributions to pension schemes. Such contributions are, however, not presently possible.

S.5.3.1 Tax

It is necessary to consider tax; the rules which currently apply to pensions will need to be revised by the Inland Revenue, especially in relation to inheritance tax.

S.5.3.2 *Tracing*

It is crucial that a spouse keeps track of a member's rights after the divorce. The scheme will send notices to the last known address, but must therefore be aware of that address. This will in practice be a problem where the member transfers his rights at some future date. The Pensions Registry is not suitable for this purpose.

S.5.3.3 *Unfunded arrangements*

Many higher earners now enjoy unfunded arrangements. There are no guides on how to value such rights, although orders can be made against an employer to take effect at retirement, somewhat like a garnishee order. It is thought that these could pose significant difficulties in practice

S.5.3.4 *Avoidance techniques*

Many observers are now considering avoidance techniques, ie to escape the jurisdiction of the court; one currently being discussed, for example, suggests making all benefits discretionary. The effectiveness and practicality of this and several other techniques (including income withdrawal) has yet to be tested.

S.6   The present system in practice

S.6.1 *Earmarking and pre-Pensions Act divorces*

The earmarking provisions apply to petitions for divorce, judicial separation or nullity filed on or after 1 July 1996, where the prescribed notice of application has been filed on or after 1 August 1996 (Pension Act 1995 (Commencement) (No 5) Order 1996, SI 1996/1775). Where the petition was issued on or after 1 July 1996 and the prescribed notice of application has been filed before 1 August 1996, the notice of application could be amended on or after 1 August 1996 so as to include provision under MCA 1973, ss 25B or 25C (Pensions Act 1995 (Commencement) (No 5) Order 1996, art 4; Family Proceedings (Amendment) (No 2) Rules 1996, SI 1996/1674, r 3). Leave is not required for such an amendment. Where the petition for divorce, nullity or judicial separation was issued before 1 July 1996, PA 1995, s 166 does not apply to any answer or cross-petition filed in the proceedings (Pensions Act 1995 (Commencement) (No 5) Order 1996, art 4(2)).

If a scheme member issued a petition immediately before 1 July 1996 in order to pre-empt the spouse from invoking the new earmarking provisions, a spouse could consider issuing a further petition and leave is not required. The court may order consolidation (Hallam 'Earmarking – avoiding the 1 July 1996 barrier' [1997] Fam Law 267).

A spouse who issued his or her own petition before 1 July 1996 could apply to have the petition dismissed, although it could be argued that it would be an abuse of process.

S.6.2 Earmarking orders available

The court may make an order that:

- The pension scheme trustees or managers pay all or part of the member's pension to his spouse as a periodical payment order. Such an order will come into effect only when a party with pension rights takes his pension. It comes to an end when the pension scheme member dies. The court cannot direct when the scheme member should retire.
- The scheme member commutes his pension benefits up to the lump sum maximum allowed by the pension scheme on retirement and that the scheme pays all or part of that benefit to the former spouse.
- The pension scheme pay all or part of the death benefits to the other party.

These are varieties of periodical payments order and lump sum orders and unless otherwise provided have the same characteristics. Earmarking orders are only effective where there are benefits to meet them. They cannot be made so that the scheme has to pay more than is available for payment to an individual pension scheme member.

S.6.3 Application for an earmarking order

The court cannot make an order of its own motion, and an application must be made (FPR 1991, r 2.70(3)). The petition should include a claim for the usual forms of ancillary relief, and a specific claim for an earmarking order. The application should be made on Form A.

The application must be served on the pension scheme trustees or managers. They must also be provided with the following information:

- an address to which any notice which the trustees or managers are required to serve under the Divorce etc (Pensions) Regulations 2000, SI 2000/1123 is to be sent;
- an address to which any payment which the managers or trustees are required to pay the party without pension rights is to be sent; and
- if that address is a bank or building society or the Department of National Savings, sufficient details to enable payment to be made into that account.

S.6.4 After the order is made

The person in whose favour the order is made must serve it on the trustees or managers of the pension scheme. This applies also to orders amending or revoking earmarking orders. The spouse who is in receipt of an earmarking order needs to keep the pension scheme managers and trustees informed of changes of addresses and bank details (Divorce etc (Pensions) Regulations 2000, SI 2000/1123). Where the details supplied earlier have ceased to have effect because the spouse with the order has remarried or for other reasons, the recipient of the earmarking order has to give notice to the trustees or managers of pension schemes within 14 days of the event taking place.

Where it is not reasonably practicably for the pension scheme trustees to make the payment under the order because the details have not been given or kept up to date, the pension scheme must make the payment to the person with pension rights. The trustees are then discharged from their liability to make the payments under the order. The beneficiary is not able to recover payments from the scheme, but must attempt to claim them from the scheme member.

If the payments are made in error because the party without pension rights has failed to notify the pension scheme trustees or administrators of, for example, her remarriage, the pension scheme is absolved of liability if the payments were made in good faith and the pension scheme member will need to try to recover the payments made in error from the spouse.

Pension schemes must notify beneficiaries of transfers of pension benefits by the scheme member to another scheme and must give a copy of the order and details about payments to the new scheme. Schemes must also inform the beneficiaries of the earmarking order of any event likely to result in a significant reduction in the benefits payable under the scheme. These are not defined, but will include, for example, early retirement.

Consent orders An earmarking order may be made by consent but an application must be made on Form A or a draft order must be lodged. The pension scheme must be served with the notice or draft order.

Variation and duration of order Orders can be varied, including orders for the payment of lump sums. An order for the payment of lump sum death-in-service benefits does not lapse on remarriage unless specifically provided for but cannot be varied after the death of either of the parties (MCA 1973, s 31(2)(dd), 31(2)(2B)).

S.6.5 Drafting the order

The court must, since 1 December 2000, make the order as a percentage of the benefit payable.

S.6.6 Earmarking and the Inland Revenue

Periodical payments under an earmarking order from a pension scheme are regarded for tax purposes as deferred maintenance. Such payments for income tax purposes are regarded as the income of the scheme member and are not taxable in the hands of the payee (ie the former spouse).

Income tax will, however, be payable by the payer, since the pension payments are regarded as part of his income.

S.6.7 Earmarking and the clean break

Earmarking does not sit comfortably – or at all – with the principle of the clean break. The injunction in MCA 1973, s 25A towards clean break solutions has not been amended by PA 1995, or WRAPA 1999.

If a clean break solution is agreed which contains an earmarking order for periodical payments, the order in relation to the period between date of the order and the date of the husband's retirement could be expressed in one of three ways:

- A nominal order for periodical payments for the spouse.
- No order for periodical payments for the spouse.
- A non-extendable (nominal) term order expressed to be subject only to the earmarked order for periodical payments.

S.6.8 Earmarking and offsetting

A combination of earmarking and offsetting may be helpful where some assets are available immediately by way of an offset, but a clean break is not possible.

S.6.9 Earmarking and bankruptcy

Personal pensions The benefits under a personal pension policy (or retirement annuity) effected by a bankrupt before his bankruptcy, but which become payable after his discharge do not amount to property which was acquired after his bankruptcy. The benefits are 'choses in action' which comprise property belonging to the bankrupt at the commencement of the bankruptcy and therefore vest in the trustee in bankruptcy. On retirement, they are payable to the trustee in bankruptcy and not to the discharged bankrupt (*Re Landau* (1997) Times, 1 January) (per Ferris J). In *Lesser v Lawrence* (CA) [2001] Ch 76, [2000] 37 Pensions Benefits Law Reports (www.pensionslaw.com) *Landau* was confirmed, although there are still issues outstanding. From 29 May 2000 all pensions have been protected in the same manner as occupational schemes. It is not clear whether 'protective trusts' (see below) are effective in personal pension schemes, it being suggested that they might fall foul of the general principle that an individual cannot contract out of the insolvency legislation.

Occupational schemes In general, members of occupational schemes are protected by 'protective trusts' which provide that on bankruptcy the member's benefits are forfeited and held on discretionary trusts for a class of beneficiaries consisting of the bankrupt, the spouse and dependants. Normally, the trustees of the scheme will pay any benefits to the spouse until discharge and then recommence payments to the former bankrupt. The trustee in bankruptcy will not therefore even be able to obtain pension payments made before the discharge. Now that WRAPA 1999, s 11 is in operation there is a general principle in force that pension rights do not form part of a bankrupt's estate.

S.6.10 Earmarking and publicly funded cases

If the award from the pension scheme to the assisted person is in the form of an order for deferred earmarked maintenance, such payments are exempt from the statutory charge. The position in relation to orders for payment of lump sums remains unclear (see 6.3.1 and Appendix IX).

S.6.11 Frequency of earmarking orders

It is reported that few earmarking orders have been made since they became available. It is possible that problems with valuation, the conflict with the clean break principle, the absence of any widow's provision on death of the member and the prospect of a spouse's remarriage affecting the order all have a bearing. Orders however for lump sums do survive a spouse's remarriage, unless the order contains a proviso for lapse on remarriage (as well as on the spouse's death prior to the member's retirement) (*Legrove v Legrove* [1995] 1 FCR 102, [1994] 2 FLR 119, CA).

Furthermore, the court cannot compel the member to retire. Earmarking survives the introduction of pension sharing.

S.7   Pension sharing

Pension sharing (formerly known as splitting) now enables the court to split a pension at the time of divorce so that the spouse either becomes a member of the pension scheme in her own right ('internal transfer') or take a transfer of a designated amount into his or her own pension scheme ('external transfer'). External transfers are not possible from unfunded public schemes, which are treated differently.

The Family Law Act 1996 (FLA 1996), s 16 provided in theory for sharing, but it operated by amending the earmarking provisions of MCA 1973, s 25B which were regarded as defective law-making because that section only permits the making of financial provision orders, and no jurisdiction (or even definition) to make 'pension adjustment orders' was referred to FLA 1996. It was, however, never implemented. Politicians of all parties accepted the principle of pensions sharing as set out in the White Paper 'Pension Rights on Divorce' in February 1997. After an abortive Pensions Sharing Bill in 1998, sharing was enacted by WRAPA 1999, which introduced new provisions into MCA 1973. These provide that:

*   Retrospective implementation does not apply.
*   Pensions sharing does not apply to judicial separation.
*   Pensions sharing applies only to those overseas pensions which are subject to United Kingdom jurisdiction and where a court order could be enforced abroad.
*   Pensions sharing applies to SERPS rights but not the basic state pension.
*   Pensions sharing applies only to the rights which have accrued to the date of the divorce order, although the order may grant the spouse a higher percentage of the pension to deal with the loss of prospective benefits.
*   The valuation used is the CETV; in Scotland, the valuation applies only to the pension accumulated during the period of the marriage.
*   Earmarking continues as an option.
*   The division may include all rights involved in the pension scheme, including for example AVCs. Different percentage splits may apply to different pension schemes of the member.
*   There is a new category of former spouses within occupational schemes.
*   A spouse who receives pension rights under a pension-split takes the pension at his or her own normal retirement age.

Pension sharing is available in cases where the petition for nullity or divorce was filed after December 2000.

S.8   Advising the client

Clients need to be advised, in writing, that:

- An order for earmarked periodical payments does not survive the remarriage of the spouse.
- An order for earmarked periodical payments ceases on the death of the member; it does not entitle the beneficiary unless a clause has been inserted specifically providing to the contrary.
- An order for periodical payments or a lump sum or both from a pension scheme does not come into effect at all if the pension scheme member dies before retirement. Only an order for the payment of death-in-service benefit will operate in these circumstances
- If the beneficiary of an earmarking order does not keep the pension scheme informed of bank details and current address and as a result the scheme is unable to make payments under the order, it is entitled to make all the payments due to the beneficiary to the member. The beneficiary under the order would then have to try and claim the money back from the member, which might prove difficult.
- The spousal beneficiary of an earmarking order is obliged to notify the pension scheme of any changes, eg remarriage, which would mean that the order should not be paid. If she does not do this and payments are made in error, the pension scheme is not liable to the pension scheme member. The member will, however, have to reclaim the overpaid benefits from the former spouse.
- Earmarking orders, whether periodical or lump sum, may be varied. However, an order for the payment of any death-in-service benefits cannot be varied after either of the parties dies unless a specific provision is made in the order. If the beneficiary dies before the member, the member will not be able to vary the order. If the member dies before retirement, the lump sum due under the order will be paid to the spouse's estate.
- The legal aid statutory charge normally applies to lump sums acquired or preserved as a resulting of earmarking orders.
- A sharing order is based on the CETV, which may not reflect the true value of the pension rights.
- A spouse may not have a right to an internal transfer when a pension sharing order is made, even if this is preferable.
- Costs of sharing could be significant, so that any remedy chosen should bear in mind the costs of implementation.

S.9   Conclusion

When giving client advice, practitioners will bear in mind:

- Whether set-off, earmarking or sharing is appropriate, and if earmarking, whether a lump sum or periodical payments order is preferable.

- That obtaining the CETV will be satisfactory in standard cases; but in many, if not most, cases a separate valuation (on the basis that the member will be staying in the scheme) will enable better advice to be given.
- That worrying about the date of the valuation (about which the regulations are much exercised) is not normally relevant; a difference of a year or two is usually not material.
- That a letter setting out the options to the client should invariably be written, and a copy preserved on file, since with hindsight many clients will find they have made the wrong decision, blame their adviser for not telling them about the downsides of their decision and seek redress.
- That, where an earmarking order is made, a letter to the client should be kept on file recording the advice that a spouse should write annually to the pension scheme with a note of the address; the regulations make it clear that it is not the scheme's job to keep track of the spouse, and if they cannot find the spouse, they will pay the member instead.
- That many clients will prefer the cash set-off at divorce, rather than an earmarking or sharing order, but will need to recognise that the cash sum may be reduced to take account of the fact it is tax-free, paid immediately rather than in the future, and is certain rather than contingent.
- That, in earmarking cases, the spouse will need to consider insuring the member against death before the spouse, since the pension payments will cease on the member's death.

Chapter One

Introduction

'. . . in no circumstances can a man divorce his wife simply because, through no fault of her own, she has deteriorated physically. Quite apart from the cruelty of deserting a person at the very time when she most needs sympathy, they think that, if this sort of thing were allowed, there'd be no security whatever for old age, which not only brings many diseases with it, but is really a disease in itself.'

Thomas More, *Utopia*

Note *In the interests of simplicity this book uses the following conventions: 'member' is the person who has acquired pension rights and 'spouse' is the person without pension rights. In many cases, of course, parties will enjoy both statuses in respect of their own pension rights and those of their partner. 'Pensions' is also frequently used instead of the rather cumbersome 'retirement benefits' so as to include all retirement benefits including commuted sums, death-in-service benefits and other benefits available under a scheme.*

In addition, we use the term 'earmarking' to indicate attachment of pension rights introduced under PA 1995; this has become a term of art in the field, although in practice and in the regulations it means nothing more than simple attachment.

Finally, to achieve further shorthand we have used the words 'pension scheme' to replace the cumbersome phrase used in the legislation namely 'person responsible for pension arrangements', a term which is intended to cover scheme trustees, managers and providers.

As this book went to press, the Inland Revenue announced that the work of the Pension Scheme Office would be carried out from 1 April 2001 by the Inland Revenue (Savings, Pensions and Share Schemes Business Stream). It has not been possible at this stage to change the frequent references to the PSO in the text.

1.1 Background

It is now a cliche that pension rights, for many people, are more important in financial terms than their interest in a home – especially after some years of negative equity. For example, in individual terms, although many commentators suggest that pensions as an asset rank after the matrimonial home, the evidence indicates that pension rights often considerably exceed that value, certainly in the case of employees in the public sector. Today, a senior civil servant might earn £100,000 pa. Although the benefits would not be drawn in the same way, he would be entitled to the equivalent of a two-thirds salary pension after 40 years service of around £67,000 pa, index-linked, with a similar survivor's pension of two-third's that. It is not unreasonable to place a capital value on the benefits at retirement age of around £1.5m; there are few such employees with a house of that value, even in the London area. In a long marriage, the spouse's interests may be worth perhaps one-third to one-half of that, say £600,000–£750,000.

The spouse's loss is, of course, usually not limited merely to the share of the member's retirement pension. Most pension arrangements include a matrix of other benefits too. The right to a survivor's pension, the protection of death-in-service life cover, ill-health early-retirement pensions and five-year pension guarantees if the member dies shortly after retirement are also lost when a couple divorce.

All this would not be a problem except for the fact that most couples do not enjoy equivalent pension provision. It is hardly surprising therefore that there has been so much interest in what should happen to pension rights on family breakdown. Family law practitioners have, however, faced several problems when attempting to deal with pensions:

- Pensions can be complex.
- The pension system, especially that part of it involving company pension arrangements, is not designed to cope with family breakdown. It is based on principles established by the Inland Revenue in the 1920s when divorce was rare.
- Many pension arrangements include clauses specifically constructed to oust the jurisdiction of the court.
- Pensions are contingent assets and are difficult to value; and, more recently.
- The options made available to divorcing spouses are so varied that it is difficult to advise which is the preferred one in individual circumstances.

Nevertheless, however difficult the task, it is clear that family lawyers have an obligation to deal with pension rights on divorce, nullity and judicial separation. This obligation has been highlighted by the separate reforms which took place in 1996 and 1999. But even before those enactments it was clearly potentially negligent to ignore the effect of divorce on pension benefits. In *Griffiths v Dawson & Co* [1993] 2 FLR 315, for example, a firm of solicitors was held not to have considered the pensions issue carefully enough and was ordered to compensate Mrs Griffiths for the consequences of its failure so to do. In that case Mrs Griffiths' solicitors allowed her husband to obtain a decree absolute before the financial arrangements had been settled. As a result, Mrs Griffiths lost her entitlement to a survivor's pension under her husband's pension scheme. The court held that in those circumstances her solicitors should have objected to a decree on the basis that she would suffer hardship and that they were negligent not to have done so (see 1.5).

Now the choice available to divorcing couples and to practitioners, and the advice which is needed, is much wider – and the opportunities for getting it wrong much greater. PA 1995 (and accompanying regulations) gave the courts new powers to make orders for the payment of periodical and lump sum payments directly from pension funds. WRAPA 1999 gives the courts the power to share (or 'split') pensions. The majority of these reforms operate by amending MCA 1973, and introducing a raft of regulations.

The three main options available are therefore:

- **Offsetting** The option, as was always the case, of rearrangement of the other matrimonial assets to enable the recipient spouse to have appropriate provision for retirement.
- **Earmarking** The powers now contained in MCA 1973, ss 25B and 25C which enable the court to instruct pension fund trustees and providers to pay all or some of the benefits arising *on retirement* to the other spouse.
- **Sharing** The powers contained in MCA 1973, s 24 to divide in any proportion the court thinks fit, the transfer values *on divorce or nullity* between one party and the other. Some pensions were already capable, in a limited way, of being shared as a result of the decision in *Brooks v Brooks* [1996] AC 375, HL. That option no longer exists where pensions sharing is available (see 6.10).

The reforms raise a number of issues in practice: valuation of pension rights, obtaining information as to those rights and, most crucially, advising on which of the options is best in particular circumstances – as well as dealing with the state arrangements. These and other issues pose problems (and opportunities) for advisers and divorcing couples.

1.2 Pensions in the United Kingdom

Pension funds are now a major economic force: UK pension fund assets are estimated at around £900 billion. This compares with a GNP of around £345 billion, or assets in mortgage banks of around £200 billion.

In consequence, the government has a significant interest in the affairs of pension funds – and has introduced extensive legislation to control them. This legislation was driven, initially largely by the Inland Revenue, to limit the benefits of (and hence the tax-relief on) pensions. At the same time, the DSS is deeply concerned about a demographic profile (ie more older people and fewer children) which means significantly increased state pension costs, with fewer contributors available to pay for them. This accounts for recent and likely future changes to the state pension scheme.

One of the less appealing features of the system for matrimonial lawyers is its complexity. The state system is complex, especially the State Earnings Related Scheme (SERPS), and the UK has a large (perhaps excessive) variety of forms of private pension. This makes it difficult for matrimonial lawyers and others to give clear, simple, advice to clients. It also makes it difficult to draft simple, clear legislation relating to the allocation of pension rights between the parties on divorce.

1.3 What was wrong with the former system

In many divorce cases, pensions matters were not given sufficient attention by practitioners. In itself that did not necessitate a change in the law, simply changes in perception and the attitudes of the courts and practitioners. Where pensions were properly taken into account, and there were sufficient free reserves, the pensions issue could be accommodated by, for example, awarding a greater share of the proceeds of other assets to compensate for loss of expected pension benefits. This is commonly referred to as *offsetting*.

In a perfect world, on a divorce, if it thought it proper or the parties wanted to, the court could simply divide the pension rights between the parties, and tell the pension provider how much and to whom to pay. But this was not usually possible because:

- Most pension schemes contained 'protective trusts' (sometimes known as spendthrift trusts) which excluded the jurisdiction of the court; these trust clauses in scheme deeds protect members' rights by arranging for the rights to be forfeit if a court order is made against them. Their effectiveness was tested in *Edmonds v Edmonds* [1965] 1 All ER 379n and found valid (see 3.3.1). There are similar protective, statutory trusts in forces and services pension arrangements. They do not apply in the Civil Service Pension Scheme, or other unfunded schemes where there are no funds available to charge.
- Pension rights resemble Solomon's baby; cutting them up may destroy the thing it is intended to preserve. This is likely to emerge as an issue with sharing pensions. It arises because dividing a pension reduces its value in such a way that the two halves do not add up to the value of the whole.
- Granting pension rights to the spouse would affect the tax approval of the scheme, which would seriously affect the scheme member's position as well as that of other members of the scheme.
- It was not always clear quite what a pension right was. Family lawyers, indeed all lawyers, are comfortable with conventional property rights – the home, the building society account, even the furniture. Pension rights are in fact usually contingent choses in action – scheme members only get it if they live (and they may not), spouses only get a spouse's pension if the other spouse dies and if a scheme member dies before retirement he will get nothing.

The usual way to make provision for retirement was therefore to offset the loss of pension arrangements against other assets. This was far from satisfactory in many cases. In practice there were two main difficulties. First, there was no quick easy and cost-effective mechanism for valuing pension rights. Second, where there were insufficient free reserves, there was no way in which pensions could be divided between the scheme member and his spouse.

Where offsetting was not possible, there was often no satisfactory solution and a great deal of dissatisfaction. This was particularly so where members earned modest incomes but enjoyed good pension schemes. Typical examples are firemen, policemen, teachers and civil servants.

1.4   The prelude to reform

After several years of dissatisfaction the pressure for reform became intense. Reform proposals came in several steps:

- The Law Commission reviewed the issue as far back as 1969 in its *Report on Financial Provision in Matrimonial Proceedings* (HMSO, 1969), pointing out that once the divorce took place, the spouse could no longer become a widow and enjoy a widow's pension. Once the divorce law changed to allow an 'innocent wife' (ie on the basis of having been separated for five years) to be divorced against her will, this resulted in a possible hardship so great as to be unconscionable. The Commission recommended that there should be reform; but failed to conclude what type of reform was required. Indeed, it concluded, the problem was incapable of a full solution. In any event, there was no urgency, it added, since the terms of the Matrimonial Homes Act 1967 (MHA 1967), the introduction of an earnings-related pension in 1978 and the possibility of objecting to a divorce on the grounds of grave financial hardship (see 1.11 and 6.11 below) all served to mitigate any injustice. No recommendation was made.

- In 1976, the now disbanded Occupational Pensions Board (OPB) reviewed the question of equal status of men and women in pension schemes, and incidentally looked at what happened on divorce. It recommended that courts be given powers to enable them, in the course of making financial provision on divorce, to order that a survivor's pension which is automatically provided under the rules of a scheme should be able to be paid in whole or part to a divorced spouse. This conclusion was very much ahead of its time. Furthermore, said the OPB, any such order should be capable of applying to state pensions, at least the second state pension (SERPS, see 2.6 below). Finally, schemes were to be encouraged to be more flexible in allocating personal pensions or apportioning pensions between different beneficiaries. It needed additional powers to modify schemes (which were requested by the OPB) and consequent changes to Inland Revenue rules. No changes occurred.

- A second study by the Law Commission one year later in 1977 again concluded that something should be done. Particularly in relation to longer marriages, it was thought, there should be power for the court to have access to pension payments. But curiously, and against the thinking that developed later, it considered that the move away from life-long support for divorced wives should also apply to pensions. In other words, in most cases there would be no need to make any special provision.

- In 1985, the Lord Chancellor's Department proposed that only older spouses should be able to claim and that the question of quantum should be left until retirement. Only then could the situation of the parties be reviewed. At the time the solution was widely ridiculed, mainly because it ran contrary to the principle of the clean break. With hindsight it appears to offer some significant advantages, although of course it offers neither certainty nor a clean break. It may be, however, that pensions matters do not respond best to being treated as other assets. In any event, the consultation paper failed to make any progress.

- Matters rested until 1990, when the Labour Party proposed splitting pension rights on divorce. It was a short paper and lacked any analysis of the problems with splitting SERPS benefits (see 6.4.11 below). It was based on the assumption that pensions were not taken into account on divorce already.

- In 1991, the Law Society Family Law Committee returned to the subject with a range of proposals, most notably that the court should have power to split all pension rights (including armed services rights) and recommended that courts be given the power to make pensions adjustment orders and that husbands should be given power to make contributions into a personal pension arrangement for a wife.

- The major catalyst for reform, however, was the report of the Pensions Management Institute/Law Society Working Party in May 1993. It recommended that the court be given a power to make a pensions adjustment order, directing, where appropriate, the splitting of pension rights at divorce. This met the clean break requirements of divorce policy and retained the court's discretion in deciding the appropriate split (rather than setting down automatic terms). There was a wide consensus for its adoption, both because it left open the flexibility of using valuations of pension rights where appropriate (rather than the statutory use of cash equivalents – see below) and because the recommendations emerged from a working party whose members included lawyers, actuaries, the pensions industry and academics. It had also benefited by enjoying the presence of the Inland Revenue and the DSS as observers – and it was clearly written and argued.

- Some six months later, the Pensions Law Review Committee, under the chairmanship of Professor Goode, endorsed the PMI/Law Society conclusions in broad terms but suggested that further research needed to be carried out before they were implemented.

- In June 1994, the White Paper on pensions law reform broadly accepted the conclusions of the PMI/Law Society paper and the Goode Report, but considered that the appropriate place for reform was not in the the then forthcoming Pensions Bill but in a Matrimonial Causes Act or Administration of Justice Act – and that only after further research. The need for reform, and the need for its urgent implementation, was recognised.

It was expected that the matter would rest for a year or two while the research was completed. However, a combination of circumstances – the fact that the Bill started in the House of Lords rather than the Commons and a tiny government majority – conspired to bring reform earlier than expected. In the Lords, Baroness Hollis proposed an amendment to the Pensions Bill which introduced sharing. The then government eventually conceded the principle of reform, but sought a compromise by suggesting an arrangement (later known as *earmarking*) which would give the courts power to make an attachment order on benefits arising at retirement rather than divorce. In due course this was implemented as PA 1995, s 166 (s 167 for Scotland).

A period of consolidation was expected until the regulations were published and the Act brought into force. But Baroness Hollis seized on another opportunity presented by the fact that the Family Law Bill was also introduced first through the Lords. The Lords agreed to an amendment introducing the principle of pensions sharing and it became part of FLA 1996. The pension sharing provisions of that Act were in fact never implemented (and are now repealed), but the broad sweep of its intent was repeated in WRAPA 1999 to take effect in the year 2000 (see *Pension Sharing on Divorce: reforming pensions for a fairer future* (DSS, June 1998)). The consequence was that instead of either earmarking or sharing (called until 1998 'splitting') the reforms included both.

1.4.1 The two reforms

The pensions reforms broadly follow the principles of divorce law reform generally. The object of the divorce law system is less to adjudicate on the breakdown of marriage but where money and property are concerned, to provide some form of equitable distribution of family assets. Since it is common for one spouse to be dependent on the other for some if not all of the marriage, it is often appropriate to transfer assets from one spouse to another.

In practice, one spouse (historically the wife) has enjoyed much lower pension rights because she has stayed at home, more frequently works part-time, or enjoys generally lower earnings on which pension rights are based. The reforms were intended to acknowledge that, where there is a divorce, the anticipated reliance on the higher earner's pension fails. In practice, the most complex financial position is often that of the pension rights. Now and in the future the position of private pension arrangements, ie through occupational or personal pension provision, is becoming even more important because of the anticipated fall in the relative level of state retirement provisions.

1.4.1.1 Earmarking: the Matrimonial Causes Act 1973 and the Pensions Act 1995

PA 1995 introduced amendments to MCA 1973 and in particular gave the courts the power to make orders requiring sums to be paid directly by pension funds to non-pension scheme members. These orders are collectively known as earmarking or attachment orders. Orders can be made in respect of three types of pension benefits:

- **Pension lump sums payable at retirement** The court can order the pension scheme member to commute the lump sum available under the pension to the maximum permitted under the scheme and the pension scheme to pay all or a specified percentage of it to the scheme member's former spouse. Prior to 1 December 2000, this sum could be expressed as a figure or a percentage.
- **Pensions payable during retirement** The court can order the pension scheme to pay all or a specified amount of the pension in payment to the former spouse. This sum could be expressed as a fixed amount, but where the order was made after 1 December 2000, it must be expressed as a percentage of the sum due.
- **Death in service benefits** The court can order that all or a percentage of any benefits payable when a scheme member dies before retirement can be paid to a former spouse. As with the other earmarking orders, those made after 1 December 2000 must be expressed as a percentage of the sum due.

Earmarking only applies to cases where the petition was issued after 1 July 1996, and the first orders requiring pension schemes to make periodical payments to a spouse who was not a member took effect only from April 1997. The provisions apply to petitions for divorce, nullity and (unlike sharing) judicial separation. The strengths and weaknesses of earmarking and the operation of the procedures in practice are discussed in detail in Chapter 6.

Earmarking operates by continuing the member's pension rights in the scheme, but allowing part of the pension or commuted lump sum to be earmarked for the spouse, payable to the former spouse from the same date as the member's own benefits. The position differs in Scotland, where no earmarking order can be made against the member's pension. Orders may also be made in relation to any lump sum death benefit, in which case the sum due becomes payable on the death of the member or pensioner.

There are disadvantages to earmarking, both in principle and in implementation. First, payment of an earmarked pension depends on the member's survival. If the member dies before pension age, no earmarked pension is payable to the former spouse. Secondly, the court has no power to make orders concerning survivor's pensions. Thirdly, spouses need to track where benefits have come to rest when members change jobs and transfers occur. Fourthly, earmarking breaches the 'clean break' objective of UK divorce policy. Fifthly, there are differences between the law in England and Wales and the law in Scotland (namely the inability to earmark pensions in Scotland, even though consistent with Scots divorce law). Finally, there have been practical problems; the courts and practitioners have found it difficult to draft and implement orders, and pension schemes have not always had systems that can cope with recognising orders.

1.4.1.2 *Sharing: the Matrimonial Causes Act 1973 and the Welfare Reform and Pensions Act 1999*

After two false starts, first with FLA 1996 and then with a draft Pensions Sharing Bill in 1998, the power to share pensions was introduced by WRAPA 1999. It was presaged by an unprecedented series of consultation documents and White Papers. Its main features are:

*   There is a statutory power to share pension rights where a petition for divorce or nullity is filed after 1 December 2000. The provisions do not apply to petitions for judicial separation. If a pension is subject to an eamarking order it cannot be shared.
*   Pensions sharing is an additional, rather than a replacement, remedy, and fits into the general operation of the factors contained in MCA 1973, s 25. Thus, sharing is not appropriate in every case and where it is, the proportion of the pension to be given to the spouse will vary depending on all the circumstances of the case.
*   The value to be given to the pension rights is the CETV as is the case generally (see Chapter 5).
*   The power to share pension rights extends to SERPS benefits (see 2.6), but not the basic state pension.
*   External transfers from unfunded public sector schemes are not permitted (for reasons of public expenditure). Other schemes may choose the internal or external option.
*   It is open to the trustees or managers of occupational pension schemes to decide whether or not to offer scheme membership to spouses without pension rights who have been given part of a split pension.
*   Where pension rights are shared, all pension benefits are shared in the same proportion, so that if a spouse receives 25% of her husband's pension rights she will receive 25% of the accrued pension and 25% of any lump sum entitlement that exists.
*   Pensions in payment may be split.
*   A spouse who receives a shared pension is able to take the pension when she retires and not when the member does.
*   The scheme member's benefits are valued and split at the time of divorce, so that two distinct pension entitlements arise. If both parties' rights are kept within the scheme, the ex-spouse is in some respects similar to a

deferred pensioner (the internal scheme option). If a transfer is made to another pension scheme or arrangement outside the scheme, there is no further liability within the scheme itself (the external scheme option).

- There is no retrospection – it can only apply in proceedings on divorce and annulment (not judicial separation) begun *after* 1 December 2000.
- Pension sharing is not compulsory. Offsetting, earmarking and other mechanisms remain as options (see Chapter 6).
- Pension sharing is available where rights exist under:
  - an occupational scheme;
  - a personal pension;
  - SERPS;
  - second state pension (when introduced);
  - stakeholder pensions; and
  - other pension arrangements (eg insurance contract or retirement annuity premium)

  but NOT the basic state pension.
- A member in respect of whom a court has made a sharing order is subject to a pension debit; his or her spouse receives a corresponding credit. The member's rights are calculated on a cash equivalent basis, but it is open to spouses to argue before the court that a higher percentage of the cash equivalent is appropriate (see 5.4).
- The question whether or not discretionary benefits are to be taken into account requires a decision from the trustees: in practice, they invariably decline to include such benefits.
- Schemes may charge the reasonable costs of sharing to the individuals concerned.

In certain cases it had already been possible to share pensions, either by agreement or by a court order varying the pension if the scheme were held to be an ante- or post-nuptial settlement. The circumstances where this is likely to be both possible and desirable are limited, and the option is not available to petitions filed after 1 December 2000. This variation on sharing is discussed in slightly more detail at 6.10.

1.5 The adviser's duty

When advising clients practitioners must now bear the following in mind:

- MCA 1973, s 25B(1) specifically requires the court to take pensions into account on divorce; advisers must therefore do so when giving advice.
- MCA 1973, ss 25B and 25C gives power to the court to make an earmarking order in relation to pension payments, whether periodical or lump sum and including lump sums payable on death in service when they fall due. It is not possible to make a pension sharing order and an earmarking order in respect of the same pension (see 6.4.4). This may present problems where an earmarking order is sought in relation to death-in-service benefits in order to safeguard the payment of periodical payments in the event of the payer's death, but where a pension sharing order is also sought (see 6.4.4).
- MCA 1973, ss 24B–24D gives power to the court to make a sharing order in relation to accrued pension rights. Advisers will have to consider

whether such provision is appropriate or whether a claim is best dealt with in some other way.
- The decision in *Griffiths v Dawson & Co* [1993] 2 FLR 315 made it clear that it is a solicitor's duty to protect clients from the loss of pension rights where appropriate. The decision in *T v T* [1998] 1 FLR 1072 makes it clear that pension interests are assets to be considered in every case.

There is serious exposure to professional liability allegations in relation to dealing with pensions. Practitioners will, unless they have protected themselves carefully, find that with hindsight their client would have wished to adopt a different solution to that actually adopted – and blame their adviser for their disadvantage. Potential exposure to liability exists in several discrete areas:

- Valuations: although the regulations only require Form E to disclose the value of pension rights based on one form of valuation (the 'cash equivalent'), in practice it will be all but impossible for an individual to know which is the preferable remedy without knowing the alternative forms of valuation, in particular the past service reserve valuation.
- Options: there are at least three remedies available: offsetting, earmarking (in two forms) and sharing. Which is the better for any particular client will very much depend on their particular circumstances. For example, most spouses choose offsetting, if available, since it provides ready cash. But that may not be the best value. First, the Community Legal Service may have a statutory charge on it (which it might not in other remedies), which might make it less valuable. Second, if the scheme member lives or is likely to live a fair while, the earmarking order could offer substantially better value. Earmarking of a pension can (or should) be very attractive – unless the ex-spouse remarries, in which case it fails. Few people consider remarriage during their divorce, but many may change their minds some years later.
- File instructions: few solicitors have as much experience in taking instructions in relation to pensions as they have in other areas of family law. However, they will need to be meticulous, since some clients will invariably complain in hindsight that they were not advised of the pros and cons of each of the remedies and their application to the particular situation. Files will need to reflect the practice of independent financial advisers so that they record the advice given (since any silence is likely to be interpreted against the adviser) in full detail.
- The duty to take pensions into account: it is insufficient merely to record the value of a pension amongst all the other assets of the couple. As the decision in *Griffiths v Dawson* indicated, there is now a duty on advisers to take pensions into account when advising on a settlement, and with the reduction in the importance of state pensions and the concomitant increase in the relative importance of private pension arrangements that duty becomes ever more important.
- The burden of proof: the problem with pension claims by clients is that the burden of proof will fall on the adviser to show that proper advice was given, not on the client to show that the advice given was negligent.
- In practice there will be certain areas which will give rise to more claims than others. In many cases there will be no death-in-service cover in many orders – a benefit which only emerges in rare cases, but when it

does it is very much welcome and missed if not thought about in the court order. A further issue is whether any of the orders for earmarking in particular are protected, if possible, by some form of maintenance protection cover. This may not be available at a reasonable price – but the advice file should record it was raised, even if only to be dismissed. Finally, the particular circumstances of the case will need exploration: the difference in the age of the parties (making certain benefits very attractive in the long term) is one, and there will be others, such as the relative health of the spouse, the financial expectations of the former spouse and the aspirations of the client him or herself, taking into account the chances of future remarriage, the health of the client, the expectation of future interest rates, house values and annuity rates.

In practice, most lawyers will need to maintain immaculate files, use external advice wherever possible (and at a reasonable cost) and ensure that there is no come-back on what, for very modest fees, could amount to very substantial claims.

1.6   Investigating pensions

In every case, the lawyer should investigate the pension position of his client and his or her spouse; many of the issues have been mentioned above. Not to do so is clearly now negligent. In any event the court will require details of the parties' pensions as well as their objectives and future expectations.

In some cases, of course, pensions will not be important. It is, however, impossible to categorise these; for example:

- **Low earners** If a spouse is a low earner, it might be thought that pensions are unlikely to be an important part of the financial arrangements. That will be true in many cases. However, paradoxically, where the other assets are of very little value, pensions can be relatively more important. In the case of public servants (teachers, firemen, hospital workers and the like) the state-backed, index-linked pensions can be highly significant. And in some rare cases, for example, the prospective loss of pension rights has been used to object to the grant of a divorce (see 6.11).
- **Short marriages** Similarly, it is improbable in short marriages that pensions will be a crucial financial element. But a marriage late in life, even if short-lived, could result in the acquisition of high contingent pension rights.

Where pensions are unlikely to be important, perhaps because both parties have equivalent pension arrangements or they are de minimis, they should not be pursued, in order to avoid spending unnecessary costs on matters which are not material.

1.7   Obtaining the information

The law imposes a duty on all applicants and respondents to a claim for ancillary relief to make complete disclosure of their financial position. This specifically includes details of pension rights. The regulations lay down specific requirements as to what must be disclosed in relation to pensions and what information must be provided by those responsible for pension arrangements (see 4.3.3.3).

The rules state that parties must provide the court with all the information they have in their possession, power or control regarding any policies in a pension scheme which they have or are likely to have. This must include the most recent valuation furnished by the trustees of the pension scheme under the Occupational Pension Schemes (Disclosure of Information) Regulations 1996, SI 1996/1655, or the Personal Pension Schemes (Disclosure of Information) Regulations 1987, SI 1987/1110, or as a result of a request made after matrimonial proceedings have been commenced under the Pensions on Divorce etc (Provision of Information) Regulations 2000, SI 2000/1048, which replicate most of those provisions in divorce matters. The Disclosure Regulations provide that scheme members or holders of personal pension plans must be furnished with a valuation of their pension rights every year unless the pension is due to come into payment within two years. Regulation 3 of the Pensions on Divorce etc (Provision of Information) Regulations 2000, SI 2000/1048 imposes a further obligation on pension schemes to provide a CETV of a member's interest where there are matrimonial proceedings, and the information has not already been provided for the proceedings or the court has ordered the scheme member to obtain the information. The details are complex and are set out in Chapter 4.

1.8   Valuation

There are several ways to value pension rights. The simplest and cheapest method, in most cases, is to use the CETV as required by the regulations.

However, in cases where the parties have been married for many years, and one at least enjoys a substantial income, the CETV may not provide enough information to enable the spouse or her advisors to decide which solution is best. This is because the CETV gives the value of pension rights for a person leaving a scheme, not the cost of buying someone into a scheme (or even staying in the scheme) and the two values can be very different, sometimes by as much as a factor of five. Moreover, the CETV does not always include discretionary benefits. Nor does it take account of the particular features of each case, eg if there are dependant children or the spouse is much younger than the member.

Where the sums involved are greater, despite the requirement to use statutory values, it may be necessary to obtain a further valuation on other bases. The valuation costs can be considerable if instructions are not defined tightly at the outset; additional 'what-if' requests can prove expensive, as can the provision of expert evidence if the case goes to trial. It is important to evaluate the costs to be incurred in the valuation exercise in comparison with the amounts in issue and the significance of loss of pension benefits.

Even where the CETV is considered adequate, by itself it will not offer sufficient information to enable either the adviser or the parties to decide which is the most appropriate remedy, or combination of remedies. Several external companies now offer services which report on the options, and these can offer comfort and advice where the choice is confusing.

1.9   The state pension scheme

The state scheme is diminishing in importance as time goes by; this is one of the reasons for the growing relative importance of private arrangements. The basic state pension was approximately 22% of national average earnings in 1975; it should fall to about 6% by 2020 (see Fry and Smith, *Pensions and the public purse* (1990) IFS Report Series No 36). This book deals only briefly with the pension provisions of the state scheme.

The basic state scheme copes well with divorce matters, since spouses can use the earnings record of the contributor for payment of benefits even after divorce (see 2.8). It is not possible for the court to make any orders adjusting, transferring or otherwise dealing with the basic state pension on divorce or judicial separation.

So far as the second state pension (SERPS) is concerned, this is normally treated as a private pension – even where it is paid by the state. It can be made the subject of a pension sharing order but not an earmarking order.

If the basic state pension of a person whose marriage ends by divorce or annulment does not reach the full rate, the contribution record of the former spouse can be substituted for all the tax years in the claimant's working life, either:

- until the end of the tax year in which the marriage ends, or before the one in which the claimant reaches state pension age; or, if more favourable,
- from the beginning of the year in which the claimant married the former spouse until the end of the one in which the marriage ends or before the one in which the claimant reaches state pension age.

The rule applies in the case of a person whose marriage has ended and who has not remarried before reaching state pension age (before 6 April 1979, this applied to women only) and, since 6 April 1979, in the case of a person whose marriage ends when he or she is over state pension age (Social Security Pensions Act 1975 (SSPA 1975), s 20; Social Security (Widow's Benefit and Retirement Pension) Regulations 1979, SI 1979/642, reg 8, Sch 1).

1.10   Tax approval

Pension schemes cannot usually operate efficiently without Revenue approval. To gain approval they must comply with Inland Revenue rules (administered by its Pension Schemes Office). These rules are based on principles largely established in the 1920s and which even now largely do not cater for earmarking or sharing.

In relation to earmarking, the Revenue rules impinge only slightly; in particular it is not certain whether a court order directing trustees to pay a lump sum on death to a spouse brings the lump sum into the deceased's estate for inheritance tax (IHT) purposes. At the time of writing, the Inland Revenue has indicated that inheritance tax will not be levied in such cases. At present, such payments are exempt if they are paid under the trustees' discretion, but not exempt if paid under external direction. However, the Revenue have said that the existing permissible arrangements which ensure that lump sum benefits do not form part of a member's estate would not be affected by a court order directing the scheme trustees to pay all or part of the lump sum to a former spouse.

In relation to sharing, the Revenue rules were changed to allow non-employees to become members of schemes. The Revenue rules always allowed for pension rights to be given to former wives – but only:

- where they are dependent (see Inland Revenue Practice Notes IR12); and
- at the discretion of the scheme trustees

so that the former wives could not rely on enjoying any benefits, even if the member wrote to the trustees notifying them of his wish to support his former spouse. A member can decide to allocate part of his pension as a dependant's pension (provided it does not exceed his own pension). The problem with relying on the dependency route (which is still available) is that it is unreliable because dependency needs to be proved to the satisfaction of the trustees and, even if it is, they can exercise their discretion not to pay.

1.11   The pension scheme as a defence – grave financial hardship

MCA 1973, s 5 allows a respondent to plead as a defence to a petition based on five years' separation that she will suffer grave financial or other hardship as a result of a divorce. Section 5(3) provides that hardship includes the loss of a chance of acquiring any benefit which the respondent might acquire if the marriage were not dissolved; the hardship must result from the dissolution of the marriage, rather than its breakdown.

The defence has normally been invoked to deal with the loss of pension benefits on divorce. The courts have shown themselves reluctant to allow the defence to succeed, particularly where the petitioner offers a reasonable alternative. However, *K v K* [1997] 1 FLR 35 (see 6.11) indicated that the use of earmarking does not necessarily compensate a wife for the loss of a widow's pension.

1.12   Scotland

Scots law is not covered by this book; however a brief outline is set down below to assist advisers in England and Wales who are faced with the prospect of Scottish proceedings. The provisions on division of matrimonial property on divorce are set out in the Family Law (Scotland) Act 1985 (FL(S)A 1985), ss 8–17. A court in Scotland has power to make four main types of order for financial provisions, namely:

(a) An order for the payment of a capital sum. (Under s 12 a capital sum order may be deferred or payable by instalments. Under the same section, it is provided that on application by either party to the marriage on a material change of circumstances, the court may vary the date or method of payment of the capital sum.)
(b) An order for the transfer of property by one party to the other. (Under s 12 a transfer of property order may come into effect at a future date and, on application by either party to the marriage on a material change of circumstances, the court may vary the date of transfer of the property.)
(c) An order for periodical allowance.

(d) An incidental order (for example, an order for the sale or valuation of property, or regulating occupancy of or liability for expenditure on the matrimonial home).

In making orders for financial provision on divorce, the court must apply certain principles set out in s 9. These are that:

(a) the net value of the matrimonial property should be shared fairly between the parties to the marriage;
(b) fair account should be taken of any economic advantage derived by either party from contributions by the other, and of any economic disadvantage suffered by either party in the interests of the other party or of the family;
(c) any economic burden of caring, after divorce, for a child of the marriage under the age of 16 years should be shared fairly between the parties;
(d) a party who has been dependent to a substantial degree on the financial support of the other party should be awarded such financial provision as is reasonable to enable him to adjust, over a period of not more than three years from the date of the decree of divorce, to the loss of that support on divorce; and
(e) a party who at the time of divorce seems likely to suffer serious financial hardship as a result of the divorce should be awarded such financial provision as is reasonable to relieve him of hardship over a reasonable period.

Fair sharing of the matrimonial property means equal sharing or sharing in such other proportions as are justified by special circumstances (s 10). The net matrimonial property is valued as 'at the relevant date'. The relevant date is the earlier of:

(a) the date on which the parties ceased to cohabit (not taking into account short periods of reconciliation thereafter as defined in sub-s (7)); and
(b) the date of service of the summons in the action for divorce.

The matrimonial property is defined for the purposes of ss 10 and 11 as:

'. . . all the property belonging to the parties or either of them at the relevant date which was acquired by them or him (otherwise than by way of gift or succession from a third party) –
(a) before the marriage for use by them as a family home or as furniture or plenishings for such a home; or
(b) during the marriage but before the relevant date.'

Before being amended by PA 1995, s 10(5) provided expressly that the proportion of any rights or interests of either party under a life policy or occupational pension scheme or similar arrangement, which is referable to the period during the marriage but before the 'relevant date' was to form part of the matrimonial property.

Section 11 provides for various factors to be taken into account in making certain orders for financial provision, such as the existence and age of children, the age, health and earning capacity of the party claiming, etc. The remaining sections deal with specific aspects of capital sum orders, orders for periodical allowance, incidental orders, variation of agreements reached between the parties by court order, and the application of divorce provisions to nullity.

1.12.1 Earmarking: PA 1995, s 167

PA 1995, s 167 amended the FL(S)A 1985 materially so that s 10(5) provides:

> 'The proportion of any rights or interests of either party
> (a) under a life policy or similar arrangement; and
> (b) in any benefits under a pension scheme which either party has or may have (including such benefits payable in respect of the death of either party),
> which is referable to the period to which subsection (4)(b) above refers [ie the period during the marriage but before the relevant date] shall be taken to form part of the matrimonial property.'

The expressions 'benefits under a pension scheme' and 'pension scheme' are expressly defined. The amendment makes it clear that the relevant proportion of benefits under a pension scheme of, for example, the husband, may include a widow's pension and thus form part of matrimonial property and vice versa. This reverses the effect of certain recent cases in Scotland, such as *Brooks v Brooks* 1993 SLT 184; *Welsh v Welsh* 1994 SLT 828; and *Crosbie v Crosbie* 1996 SLT 86, Sh Ct.

Regulations can make provision (s 10) for:

> '(a) the value of any benefits under a pension scheme to be calculated and verified, for the purposes of [FL(S)A 1985] in a prescribed manner;
> (b) the trustees or managers of any pension scheme to provide, for the purposes of [FL(S)A 1985], information as to that value, and for the recovery of their administrative expenses of providing such information from either party.'

A court, where it makes a capital sum order in circumstances where the liable party's pension benefits form part of the matrimonial property and those benefits include any lump sum payable to him or in respect of his death, may make a separate order requiring the trustees or managers of a pension scheme to pay the whole or part of such lump sum to the other party (FL(S)A 1985, s 12). Any such payment is treated as a payment towards the amount due under the capital sum order.

The court may also make various orders (FL(S)A 1985, s 12), not only where the lump sum is payable to the party liable to pay the capital sum order but also where the liable party dies before the pension comes into payment or shortly thereafter, so as to ensure that the other party can benefit from the lump sum payable in respect of the death of the liable party.

These provisions extend only to the case where the pension benefits include a lump sum payable to the liable party or in respect of his death. They do not enable the court to order the trustees or managers of the pension scheme to pay a proportion of the liable party's pension direct to the other party. This is because it was thought that this would not fit in to the concept of having a clean break at divorce. Any payment of periodic allowance by one party to the other party is not intended to extend beyond any temporary period required for readjustment.

Regulations:

(a) require notices to be given in respect of changes of circumstances relevant to the orders the court may make under s 12A(2) or (3); and
(b) make provision for the recovery of the administrative expenses of complying with such orders from the liable party or the other party.

The regulations provide for the value of benefits under a pension scheme to be calculated and verified in a prescribed manner for the purpose of divorce proceedings. This is intended to encourage uniformity of approach to the valuation of pensions. The manner is not, however, the same for all pension arrangements and also differs for pensions already in payment.

In most cases, particularly in occupational and personal pension schemes, the prescribed method of valuation of pensions will be based on a calculation of the CETV of the pension, which will be provided by the trustees or managers of the scheme member's pension scheme.

The adoption of CETV in Scotland as the prescribed manner of pension valuation represented a change from the method more commonly adopted by the Scottish courts in recent times of valuing pension rights on the basis of the liable party continuing in service. That is, the valuation is a reflection of what the pension might be at the point of retirement, assuming continuing membership of the scheme. For example in *Bannon v Bannon* 1993 SLT 999, the husband's pension rights on a continuing service basis (ie assuming continuance in the police service until retirement on full pension) were valued at £46,000. The alternative and lower leaving-service value of £34,270 was rejected because the husband had not left the police service. It was also suggested in this case that the 'transfer value' approach did not take into account the fact that pension contributions made before separation provide cover for a future pension just as much as contributions afterwards do. Conversely, in *Park v Park* 1988 SCLR 584, Sh Ct, where the continuing-service value was £2,652 and the leaving-service value zero, the sheriff adopted a broad brush approach and valued the right at £900 on the assumption that the husband would remain in employment for a further ten years.

Either of the divorcing spouses may well be a member or former member of more than one scheme. In this case, a calculation of the CETV would have to be obtained from the trustees or managers of each scheme of which either spouse is a member or former member. Only a period of membership falling between the date of the marriage and the relevant date is taken into account.

1.12.2 Date of valuation

The net matrimonial property is valued as 'at the relevant date'. When the liable party requests a pension valuation for the purposes of divorce proceedings, this is calculated as if the person had left the scheme at the relevant date. Where the liable party left the pension scheme before the relevant date, acquiring deferred benefits under the scheme, the valuation of those benefits should be as at the relevant date under the law of Scotland.

1.12.3 Proportion of pension referable to the period of the marriage

Unlike English law, under the FL(S)A 1985, the matrimonial property to be divided is that which accumulated during the marriage and before the relevant date (referred to as 'the period of the marriage'). Therefore, the benefits under a pension scheme to be taken into account will be those which accumulated during the period of the marriage. While under the regulations the pension scheme managers or trustees simply have to provide the valuation of the benefits on the CETV basis (including, where applicable, disaggregation into component parts), it is for the court to decide in accordance with the regulations what proportions of that value was referable to the period of the marriage. It is proposed that the regulations should prescribe that such proportions should bear the same relationship to the total value of the pension benefits as at the relevant date as the period of the marriage does to the period during which the liable party has been a member of the scheme in question. For example, if the husband was the liable party and has been a member of the scheme for 15 years, and the marriage had lasted for five of those 15 years, the court would count one third of the value of the pension benefits as matrimonial property.

As in England and Wales, the provisions of PA 1995, s 167 enable a court in Scotland, in making a capital sum order against one party in a divorce, to bind a pension scheme to pay the capital sum to the other party, when the pension benefits come into payment. In Scotland such orders can only be made in respect of capital sums, and not periodical payments as in England and Wales, since there is no concept of deferred maintenance in Scotland.

1.12.4 Sharing

The principles of sharing in Scotland are broadly those applying in England and Wales, although there is specific provision for a 'qualifying agreement' under which the parties can agree to share their pension rights. There are also differences in terminology (see The Pensions on Divorce (Pension Sharing) (Scotland) Regulations 2000, SI 2000/1051 and the Divorce etc (Notification and Treatment of Pensions) (Scotland) Regulations 2000, SI 2000/1050). The main advantage is that they are much shorter and comprehensible.

1.13   Using this book

This is intended as a practical book; it is structured in a practical form. First, it explains the pensions system, how pensions work and their salient features; it then looks at the pension issues arising on divorce and separation, the procedures to be followed, the orders that can be made and the ways in which the pension issue can be dealt with, and the role of insurance.

The Appendices contain the relevant legislation, specimen orders and other materials of practical use to the practitioner as well as a glossary of pension terms.

While the book is intended primarily for use by family lawyers attempting to deal with the pensions aspects of marital breakdown, it also aims to act as a guide to pensions professionals intending to consider the impact of changes in divorce law on the design of their schemes and to independent financial advisers counselling their clients on the options available.

Chapter Two

The pensions system

INTRODUCTION

2.1 Background

Britain has one of the most complicated arrangements for retirement provision in any country of the world. Compared with our fellow Europeans, for example, the UK system offers some stark contrasts:

- Relatively modest (and diminishing) state provision.
- As a consequence, perhaps, a private pensions' sector which is more developed than anywhere else in Europe. This has resulted in a large variety of pension arrangements and a great deal of supervision and control by government and regulatory bodies.
- Most of the private arrangements are funded, ie there are funds to back the pension promises made. However, that is not always the case and the existence of the fund does not necessarily mean the existence of an asset which can be split between the parties.

2.2 The purpose of a pension

In discussion of the detail surrounding pensions it is all too easy to lose sight of the reason for the establishment of pension arrangements. Very simply, it is to give protection and security in old age (as compared with, for example, life assurance which gives protection to those dependent on someone who dies).

The first pensions were established by paternalistic employers towards the end of the first phase of the industrial revolution. By 1908, the first state pension was introduced as a universal benefit designed to overcome the extreme poverty which emerged when people became too old to work. There was at that time no concept of a retirement age – people who had no capital worked until they could work no more. At that time even private pensions were seen as a form of social security, rather than an asset. In time, possibly by the 1950s, pensions began to be seen as property.

Defining pensions as property, as will be seen, has its problems. They are a contingent asset, since if the individual beneficiary does not live he may receive nothing. Derived benefits, such as survivors', dependants', widow's and widower's benefits, are even more contingent. Not only that, but in general they cannot be traded or assigned or mortgaged.

Some have suggested that the asset can be represented by the funds underlying the promise. While this may work to some extent in money-purchase type systems (such as personal pensions) where there is a certain analogy with a building society account, it fails quite badly in benefits-related systems such as the final-salary schemes offered by many occupational schemes, the Civil Service or unfunded private systems, where there may be no funds backing the promise.

2.3   State and private

It is normally convenient to divide pension arrangements into state arrangements, statutory arrangements and private arrangements. Each is dealt with separately.

2.3.1 State

There are two main state pension arrangements:

- The basic state scheme.
- The supplementary state scheme, commonly known as SERPS. The benefits under this scheme can, where appropriate, be provided by the private sector.

Because the benefits provided by the state arrangements are modest even when SERPS benefits are included (and will decline in real terms in the future), the private sector is becoming increasingly important.

2.3.2 Statutory

Special pension arrangements are provided by the state through Acts of Parliament (hence the use of the word 'statutory') for its own employees; they can be unfunded (like the Civil Service), notionally funded (like the teachers' pension scheme) or fully or partially funded (like the local authority schemes). For many years it has been argued that there is no need to fund statutory pension schemes since the benefits are guaranteed by entities that cannot fail to provide, unlike private employers.

2.3.3 Private

There are several ways of providing pensions privately:

- Through an employer (known as occupational schemes). Such schemes can provide benefits in a variety of ways, either linked to contributions, or linked to target benefits.
- Individually, where the benefits are linked solely to the contributions made, and the performance the consequent investments have enjoyed.

Each of these arrangements is described in more detail below.

STATE ARRANGEMENTS

2.4 Introduction

For the matrimonial lawyer, the role of state benefits impinges in two areas:

- First, the existence of the benefits makes a difference to the income of the parties in due course.
- Second, the nature of the benefits affects the jurisdiction of the court. The court has no direct jurisdiction over social security benefits. They are not an 'asset' of the parties which can be allocated by the court and the court cannot direct the government to pay one party's social security benefits to another party. But some state benefits can in fact be paid by private schemes, or are regarded as private for some purposes. For example, guaranteed minimum pensions are paid by private schemes, but replace the SERPS benefits otherwise paid by the state. Depending on who pays the benefits, therefore, such benefits could be regarded as 'state' or 'private' and thus subject to jurisdiction or not.
  - They cannot be made the subject of an earmarking order (see 6.6.1); but
  - SERPs benefits can be made the subject of a sharing order.

2.5 The basic state scheme

The basic state pension is the one that every working member of the community eventually draws. It is contributory in that entitlement is dependent on the payment of National Insurance contributions. Where both parties to a marriage work, each is entitled to either:

- a 'Category A' pension paid at a flat rate (conditional upon the pensioner fulfilling certain contribution conditions); or
- a 'Category B' pension (based on the earnings record of the husband) which includes the flat rate for Category A recipients, and an earnings-related component based on SERPS (see para 2.6 below).

Special extra pensions are payable to older people who by and large will be outside the scope of this survey: a 'Category C' pension is payable to all men and women who were over state retirement age on 5 July 1948; and a 'Category D' pension is payable to certain persons over 80 who do not have a full state pension.

The normal pension age under the state scheme is currently 65 for men and 60 for women. PA 1995 provides that the state pension age for women will increase in monthly steps for those retiring between 6 April 2010 and 6 April 2020. After that date both men and women will be entitled to receive the state pension at 65. There is no provision for early retirement under the state scheme.

2.6 The additional state scheme

The additional state pension scheme, also known as SERPS, the State Earnings-Related Pension Scheme, provides an additional element of state pension. It is paid in relation to earnings under about £91,800 pa (for 2000/01).

For many employees it will prove a substantial part of their retirement income. It can, however, be provided not only by the state, but by any employee who is not in an occupational scheme. Such an employee can receive a reduction in his rate of National Insurance contributions in exchange for assuming the state's obligations. This additional pension changes its name, depending on who provides the pension.

If it is provided:

- By the *state*, through paying full National Insurance contributions, it is called 'SERPS'. The maximum pension is 25% of earnings between the prescribed lower and upper earnings limits. For 2000/01 the lower earnings limit is £67 pw and the upper earnings limit £535 pw.
- Through a *company pension scheme*, it is called a 'Guaranteed Minimum Pension', and the scheme is called 'contracted-out'. This pension was phased out for future accruals after April 1997 (being replaced by a similar benefit called 'requisite benefits'), and the value of future rights is now much reduced. Requisite benefits means that the pension scheme does not have to match the SERPS pension, but promise a minimum formula for benefits (around $1/80$ of salary for each year of service).
- Through a *personal pension scheme*, where there is no guaranteed level of pension, and which is called an 'appropriate personal pension'. People who agreed to go private on SERPS in the last few years received a government incentive to do so.

SERPS is due to be phased out within a few years, and replaced by a 'State second pension' (S2P) expected to come into operation from 2005. It will provide:

- 40% of earnings between the lower earnings limit and £9,000, with low earners treated as earning at least £9,000;
- 10% of earnings between £9,000 and £18,500; and
- 20% of earnings between £18,500 and the upper earnings limit of around £26,000.

This pension together with the basic state pension will together provide around £110 pw, somewhat more than the minimum income guarantee of around £75 pw. It will, however, take time to build up. It is likely to result in confusion for many people, since it will be difficult to know whether to leave the scheme to qualify for the S2P. It is complicated – and in due course is bound to be merged with the basic pension, since it is pointless for the state to run two flat-rate pension systems at once.

2.7 Contracting-out

For reasons which now no longer apply, when the SERPS scheme was introduced, the government allowed employers to undertake its provision in exchange for the payment of a reduced National Insurance contribution. If an employer agrees to ensure its pension fund will provide such pensions, it has undertaken to 'contract-out', ie contract-out of the state pension scheme. For example, for an employee earning between £67 pw and £535 pw in 2000/01 the employer will pay National Insurance contributions of 7% of salary if the scheme is not contracted out. If it is, the employer will pay either 4% or 5.6% depending on whether the scheme is a contracted-out salary-related scheme (4%) or a contracted-out money-purchase scheme (5.6%). The employee's contribution also changes from 8.4% for those contracted out to 10% for those who are not.

Any employer who has undertaken this obligation through its pension scheme has its pension arrangements supervised by the Inland Revenue National Insurance Contributions Office (IRNICO), but only to ensure there is enough money to meet the state pension arrangements.

Individuals can also decide to 'contract-out', provided they were not in an occupational pension scheme, through their personal pension if they had one. These are called 'appropriate' personal pensions. The level of the pension will depend on the earnings of the pension fund investments over the years, and is unpredictable.

A company scheme can achieve contracting-out through a final-salary arrangement, in which case the benefits are salary-related (and the scheme known as a contracted-out salary-related scheme – COSR); alternatively it can be done through a money-purchase scheme (known colloquially as a COMP – a contracted-out money-purchase scheme). The difference between salary-related and money-purchase is discussed later, and is important from a divorce viewpoint. To add to the confusion, there are also contracted-out mixed-benefit schemes (COMBs).

In the case of a personal pension which is 'contracted-out' (an appropriate personal pension scheme) 'protected rights' must be provided. These include a pension for the member, and a pension for the surviving spouse. Surviving spouse does not include a divorced wife, although the contract may provide for benefits to be paid to an ex-wife if there is no lawful widow.

Loss of that expectation may of course prove a grave financial hardship to a surviving spouse, but the legislation does not require any protected rights to be reserved for ex-wives, even where there is no current widow. It is, however, possible to provide a benefit on death for any dependent at the date of death. Normally, where there has been a clean break capital and income settlement at the time of the divorce, the widow will not be a dependant at the date of death.

2.8 Married women and the state scheme

Although in theory in times of equality there should be no difference between the positions of married men and women, in practice these differences are significant. Even the DSS admit that the way in which married women are treated in relation to the state retirement pension is complicated. To receive a full state pension in her own right, a woman needs to have paid sufficient National Insurance contributions. Women need 39 qualifying years (this will change following the change in the state retirement age for women to 65 phased in over the next 20 years) to be able to claim a full state pension when they reach 60. The age at which the state retirement pension will be payable to women will eventually rise to 65. At present, a woman has the start of the tax year in which she reaches 16 to the end of the tax year before the one in which she reaches 60 to acquire the qualifying years, ie a tax year during which she has paid enough National Insurance contributions to count towards pension entitlement.

Women who are married, however, can claim a pension either on their own National Insurance contribution record, or on their husband's or on a combination of the two, although they may only claim a pension on their husband's contribution record when he claims his own pension. This does not apply to divorced men, who can only rely on their own National Insurance record.

Some pension is payable even without a full record, pro rata to the number of qualifying years. Whatever the level, the pension paid may consist of several elements:

- The basic pension, depending on the number of qualifying years built up during the working life.
- An additional pension SERPS based on the married woman's own earnings.
- Graduated retirement benefit (based on graduated National Insurance contributions paid during 1961 to 1975). This benefit is usually minimal. *less*
- contracted-out deductions, where the married woman has been a member of a contracted-out company scheme or contributing to an appropriate personal pension.

A married woman who married before 12 May 1977 has the option of paying reduced National Insurance contributions, but they do not count towards a pension. The reason for the option is that married women have the right to use both their own and their husband's contribution record, provided he has claimed his own pension. However, National Insurance credits are available to those drawing unemployment benefit and certain other benefits – including Home Responsibilities Protection. In summary:

- A divorcee can elect to have her own contributions record substituted by that of the former spouse, if this is beneficial. The substitution can begin from the start of the working life until the termination of marriage or for the duration of the marriage.
- If the parties at divorce are over retirement age, and one of the parties receives a full Category A pension with the partner receiving Category B, the ex-spouse can then claim the full Category A pension from the date of divorce – although no additional pension based on her former partner's contributions to SERPS.
- A divorcee cannot claim any 'graduated retirement benefit' (a pension benefit based on an earlier state scheme) using a former spouse's contribution record.
- Married women, widows and widowers can establish an entitlement to a Category B pension based on their spouse's contributions; divorced pensioners, however, cannot claim a Category B pension on the basis of a former spouse's contribution record.
- Category C and D pensions are not normally affected by divorce, since they are personal to the claimant and his or her own contributions record.

Married women are therefore in a uniquely privileged position in relation to the acquisition of credits under the state scheme; it may be that this special position will be eroded over time following the European Union drive towards equality in social security provision, despite dispensations under the various social security equality directives. Details are set out in the Benefits

Agency publications Information Pack, The State Retirement Pension and Married Women (WRP 4).

2.8.1 Retirement Benefit Forecasts

The Benefits Agency provides a retirement benefit forecast up to four months before pensionable age if a request is submitted on Form BR 19, available from local Social Security Offices (and see Appendix VII). The forecast will provide the following information:
About basic pension entitlement:

- The amount of basic state pension already earned.
- The amount of basic pension a person can expect at state pension age based on contributions already made and likely future contributions.

About the additional state pension and contracted-out schemes:

- The amount of additional pension already earned.
- The amount of anticipated additional pension that can be expected at state pension age based on payments already made and what additional amount might be earned before retirement.

About graduated retirement benefit (GRB):

- How many units of GRB have been acquired and their worth.

About the state pension available to divorced women:

- The amount of pension that can be obtained using a former spouse's National Insurance contributions, if this will give a better pension.

The Benefits Agency say that it usually takes about 17 working days to provide the forecast after receipt of the form. The forecast for divorced people takes longer – up to about 40 working days.

2.9 Statutory schemes

Many public sector employees are in statutory schemes (ie schemes set up by Act of Parliament). They are invariably final-salary schemes, and are governed not by trust deeds and trustees (as is usually the case with private sector pension schemes) but by statutory and statutory instrument provision, much of it of unimaginable complexity.

Despite the fact that the courts have sometimes regarded them as social security systems, they are invariably regarded by their users as private arrangements and can now be made the subject of pension sharing and earmarking orders. As privatisation increases, the number of employees in such schemes is diminishing; but they still cover teachers, the police, the judges and local government employees. In addition, civil servants are covered by a similar scheme.

There are three kinds of statutory schemes:

- **Unfunded** For example, the civil service scheme, where benefits are paid out of the consolidated fund, ie direct from the Treasury. The promise is made by the employer to pay the pension on retirement, but no funds are set aside during the employees' working years to meet the promise of a pension. There are deep concerns about the future management of schemes with substantial liabilities such as the fireman's scheme, since the pensions promises consume a disproportionate element of the fire service budget.
- **Funded** For example, publicly-owned industries and local government schemes, which operate very largely like private schemes, and which set aside reserves each year to meet the eventual cost of the pension.
- **Notionally funded** For example, teachers. Such schemes operate as though there were funds invested by way of reserves, and calculate contributions into the scheme on the performance of the notional investments, but in fact no assets are set aside. If the notional investments perform well, the contributions can be reduced, and vice versa. This mechanism therefore influences the level of contributions paid by the employer and employee.

2.9.1 Service pensions

Service pensions are also based on statutory schemes. Service pensions are those pensions granted through employment in the military services. They have presented particular problems to matrimonial lawyers because of the provisions of their governing statutes. This at one time led to a considerable amount of litigation, particularly in relation to their protective trusts. PA 1995 rectified this as far as matrimonial proceedings are concerned (see 3.3–3.5).

PRIVATE ARRANGEMENTS

2.10   Private pensions

Private pensions have been a static part of pensions provision in recent years, but are expected to grow as the role of state pensions diminishes. They are generally divided into:

- Occupational pension schemes.
- Personal pension schemes.

2.11   Occupational pension schemes

Occupational schemes are regulated by:

- The Inland Revenue (through its Pension Schemes Office – PSO), to ensure schemes are not overfunded.
- The Inland Revenue (through its National Insurance Contributions Office – IRNICO), where schemes are contracted-out, to ensure there is adequate money in the scheme to meet SERPS-equivalent benefits.
- The Occupational Pensions Regulatory Authority, whose duty in part is to ensure that there is enough money in each pension fund.
- Their governing instrument (invariably a trust deed) and their trustees, whose function is to act as guardians of the assets protecting the employer's promise to provide pension benefits.

They are also subject to burgeoning legislation reflecting the conflicting objectives of government. The Treasury want to limit the tax breaks of pension schemes, whilst the DSS wish to see a growth in private pensions to relieve the load on the state. There are several contrasting elements in schemes, and some of the more important are set out below.

2.11.1 Payments into occupational schemes

Many employers pay all their employees' contributions towards their pensions. The Government Actuary's 9th Survey of Occupational Pension Schemes in 1991 showed that 15.2% of private sector employees in pension schemes made no contribution to their pensions, whilst at the other end of the scale 10.2% paid 100%.

2.11.1.1 Money purchase and final salary

Final salary (also called defined benefit) Most employees in company schemes are in 'final-salary' schemes. According to the 21st Annual Survey of Occupational Pension Schemes published by the National Association of Pension Funds (NAPF), 93% of occupational scheme members were members of final-salary schemes. This figure includes public schemes, 100% of whose members were in such schemes. Two per cent of members only belonged to money-purchase schemes. The figures are based on a survey conducted by the NAPF which covers about 4.1 million out of approximately 10 million scheme members. However, indications are that new schemes and new members of existing schemes will be members of money purchase or hybrid schemes.

In a final-salary or defined-benefits scheme the benefits are determined in advance, and accrue year by year. For example, a man earning £10,000 pa would earn $1/60$ of that salary as a pension for each year of service, with a maximum (imposed by the Inland Revenue) of 40 such years. As salary increases year-by-year (and the pension is calculated as a fraction of the employee's final salary (hence the name)), there is an element of inflation protection built in. There are drawbacks to these schemes: transfer values can be inadequate; they are complex to administer; and they can be expensive to fund (for employers). But for most employees, despite the problems, final-salary schemes are very attractive.

Money purchase (also called defined contribution) Simpler to understand is the money-purchase arrangement. This can be seen as a piggy-bank into which pre-arranged contributions are paid, eg 5% of salary. The advantage is that at any time one can see the value of the accumulated savings. The bad news is that benefits are unpredictable. At retirement the fund is used to buy an annuity which provides the pension. This means that the level of pension benefits depends on the state of the financial markets at the date of retirement. If retirement takes place when the stock market is low and/or annuity rates are low, benefits will be low. In addition, administrative charges, especially when compared with company schemes, can be disproportionately high.

Company pension schemes can be either money-purchase or final-salary – or a hybrid of the two, where (as is often the case in smaller companies) there is an intention to pay final-salary benefits, but the promise to do so is limited by the actual amount in the fund at the date of retirement. The reason for this is that smaller employers may find it more difficult to guarantee a final-salary benefit but want to use their best endeavours so to do.

2.11.1.2 Additional voluntary contributions

Pension scheme members are able to make additional voluntary contributions (AVCs) to bring their benefits up to the maximum permitted by the Inland Revenue. Some final-salary schemes have arrangements under which AVCs can be used to buy additional years of pensionable service. Some AVC payments are made into the company scheme but scheme members may choose to make AVC payments to outside providers. In this case they are known as Free Standing AVCs (FSAVCs).

2.11.1.3 Insured and self-administered

Company pension schemes can invest their assets in almost anything, and can appoint or sub-contract others to manage the investments or administration:

*   If they hand them to an insurance company to manage, they are commonly described as 'insured', and the scheme is invested by and administered by an insurer.
*   In other cases, usually the larger funds, the scheme is 'self-administered', where responsibility for investments and administration is retained by the employer. These days, part or all of the investment management, administration, actuarial work, accounting, Revenue approval and other tasks will commonly be sub-contracted to a variety of experts, including merchant bankers, pensions consultants, administrators or other professionals.

In either case, however, the scheme will have trustees, who are ultimately responsible for the safe custody and management of the scheme. Trustees can either be individuals or corporations or a combination of the two. Increasingly, members of pension schemes have involvement in the selection and appointment of trustees. PA 1995 gives members the right to select one-third of pension scheme trustees. Pension schemes are usually established under trust, partly because of Inland Revenue pressure and partly because trusts are an appropriate legal vehicle for this purpose.

2.11.1.4 Unfunded, funded and partly-funded

Money-purchase type schemes are 'funded' by definition. In other words, there are accounts maintained in respect of each contributor.

Final-salary schemes do not have the same obligations to maintain backing funds. In the past the majority of pension schemes in the private sector were 'funded'; that is, funds were set aside to meet pension liabilities as they arose. But there was no obligation to do so, and some schemes had either no funds or insufficient funds.

Since April 1997 there has been a statutory requirement which ensures that sufficient money is set aside to meet the pension promises made by employers.

This requirement does not apply to statutory schemes many of which remain unfunded.

Certain unapproved schemes may also be totally unfunded. Earners over £91,800 pa (2000/01) may have pension benefits promised by the company which are not contained in the company's pension scheme. It is crucial to discover whether this is the case, since in some cases the benefits may be considerable. They are not however guaranteed by segregated funds, so there is a greater risk they will not be paid, especially if the company becomes insolvent (see 5.4).

Some schemes are 'underfunded', ie there are insufficient assets in the scheme to meet the full liability to pay benefits. If the scheme were wound-up, benefits would have to be curtailed, and even where the scheme is continuing, transfer values are reduced if people wish to withdraw their pension rights.

2.12   Personal pensions

Personal pensions are simply money-purchase schemes available to:

* the self-employed; and
* employed persons who are not members of occupational schemes.

They have been available since 1988. Before that, self-employed people could make pension provision through the purchase of Retirement Annuity Contracts, commonly known as section 226 policies because the legislation concerning them was originally contained in the Income and Corporation Taxes Act 1970 (ICTA 1970), ss 226–228.

Anyone under the age of 75 with taxable income from employment or self-employment can make contributions to a personal pension scheme. However, individuals cannot be members of both an occupational scheme and a personal pension scheme where contributions are from the same source of earnings unless:

* the occupational scheme only provides a lump sum benefit on death-in-service or pensions for spouse and/or dependants; or
* the personal pension is to be used by a member of a contracted-in occupational pension scheme for the sole purpose of contracting out of SERPS (see 2.6).

Payments to personal pension schemes attract tax relief. Where the contributions are made by employed (as opposed to self-employed) people, they are made net of basic rate tax. Higher rate taxpayers can reclaim the additional amounts due from the Inland Revenue. Self-employed contributors must pay the contributions gross and reclaim the tax.

If contributions in any tax year are less than the maximum amount permitted by the Revenue, the balance could be carried forward as 'unused relief', for usually any one of the following six tax years. This has been abolished from April 2001 and from that date tax reliefs must be used in the year in which they arise.

Personal pensions are usually provided by an insurance company, but can be provided by a bank, building society, unit trust manager or a variety of other providers. They operate more like a savings plan than a true pension system. Their value can be difficult to determine. For example, their true value is usually much lower than the contributions would indicate, since they often suffer very high management charges in the early years. On divorce, therefore, there will be uncertainty as to whether they should be valued at 'fund value' (the amount stated by the manager as its value) or at 'surrender value' (the amount if contributions ceased at the date of divorce) (see Table 2.1 for an example of how different these two figures can be).

Assume
- 25 year pension contributions contracted with the XYZ insurance company at £2,000 pa
- Insurance company overheads at industry average
- Contract has run 10 years

then

If request for fund value:

Contributions	10 x £2,000 = £20,000
Add growth, say	£10,000
Fund value	**£30,000**

If request for cash equivalent:
However, if contract discontinued, then the statutory cash equivalent is the surrender value, ie the fund value, *less* expenses commission and profits as follows:

• 10 years past at say £600 pa	£6,000
• 15 years future at say £400 pa	£6,000
	£12,000

Surrender value £30,000 – £12,000 .... **£18,000**

Table 2.1   Difference between surrender value and fund value

The Inland Revenue imposes certain controls on pension schemes:

- It limits how much can be paid in. The contributions which can be paid into a personal pension are limited to a proportion of earnings (technically, 'net relevant income'). Higher amounts can be paid in by older people.

Age on 6 April	Personal pension scheme	Retirement Annuity policy
35 or less	17.5%	17.5%
36-45	20%	17.5%
46-50	25%	17.5%
51-55	30%	20%
56-60	35%	22.5%
61 and over	40%	27.5%

Table 2.2   Permitted maximum contributions to personal pensions and retirement annuity contracts

- It limits how much income is pensionable. The amount of income that is pensionable is limited to the 'earnings cap' (£91,800 in 2000/01). Tax relief is not given in relation to contributions on income above that level – indeed, the pension provider is not permitted to accept such contributions. The cap does not apply to Retirement Annuity Contracts.
- It limits where the contributions can be invested. In most schemes the contributions are invested in insurance contracts (somewhat similar to unit trust contracts), which in turn invest in stocks and shares, government securities, property and cash.

   Some forms of personal pension schemes, known as SIPPs (self-invested personal pensions), allow the investor to indicate the investments in which he would like his contributions invested. These can include, for example, property to be occupied by the family business. The value of the scheme will thus reflect the value of the property, which may be worth more (eg if it enjoys planning permission) or less (eg if the company is going out of business or no one wishes to buy or rent it). In particular, some of these investments might not be able to be converted into cash immediately and paid to a spouse.
- It limits the amount of the fund which can be taken as a tax-free lump sum at retirement to 25% of the total fund in the case of personal pensions. The same limits do not apply to Retirement Annuity Contracts and the amount available will have to be calculated in each case, usually best done by the insurance company. The sum available will normally be about 30% of the fund.

The benefits available to members of personal pension schemes are limited to those available to money-purchase schemes, and are dependent on the value of the fund at the date of retirement. There is also no element of cross-subsidy with other members of the scheme, since each scheme stands alone for the individual members who cannot therefore benefit from reserves held generally for the scheme. In addition to providing a pension they may also provide dependants' benefits. These vary a great deal and reference needs to be made to each scheme for these details.

Before 30 June 1995, the annuity which was purchased to buy the pension had to be purchased at retirement regardless of the state of the annuity market at the time. Since then it has been possible to purchase the annuity in stages if the following conditions are met:

- Generally income withdrawals cannot be made before the scheme member reaches 50 or after he is 75.
- The amount withdrawn must be within a range calculated according to tables published by the Inland Revenue.
- Once withdrawals are made, no further contributions may be made or transfers made to or from the personal pension.
- If the member dies during the deferral period, the surviving spouse or dependant may continue to make income withdrawals until aged 75 or may purchase an annuity or take the fund as cash (this is however subject to a 35% tax charge).

2.12.1 Group personal pensions

Group personal pension schemes are particular forms of personal pensions usually organised for people employed by the same employer. They can achieve economies, for example, in administration charges which make them more cost effective than individual arrangements.

2.12.2 Stakeholder pensions

From October 2001 all employers must provide access to a 'stakeholder' pension if they do not have a suitable occupational or group personal pension scheme in place. Individuals, whether employed or not, can also make contributions to such schemes, perhaps offered by insurance companies. These schemes are treated for regulatory purposes as an occupational scheme (and therefore monitored by the Occupational Pensions Regulatory Authority), but for tax purposes as a personal pension. One feature unique to stakeholder pensions is that individuals may contribute regardless of whether they have any taxable earnings against which to set payments. In practice it is likely that few of the target employees (the government intends this to apply mostly to employees earnings around £20,000 or less) will take advantage of the facility. Conversely, it is likely to be used by higher earners to provide pensions for spouses and children; indeed carers, the unemployed and housewives can in theory make contributions to stakeholder pensions.

2.12.3 SSASs and SIPPs

Small self-administered pension schemes (SSASs) and self-invested personal pension schemes (SIPPs) are commonly used as pension vehicles for the higher-paid. They offer substantial advantages of wider investment powers and reduced overhead charges and are increasingly common. It is in matrimonial matters more sensible to value such schemes on a different basis than that used in the legislation, the CETV (qv), because the possibility for example of making use of surpluses in SSASs is much greater. And in SIPPs the ability to purchase property may affect the valuation since the property might be occupied by the business or become unsaleable or illiquid (and therefore affect the value of the pension rights).

2.13   The management of occupational and personal schemes

Company schemes are managed by a trustee or set of trustees (see 2.18.7); personal schemes can now be managed by a company, an insurer, a building society, bank or unit trust manager. Whatever the arrangement, the scheme can provide a menu of benefits, including cash lump sums, pensions, death cover, survivor's benefits and others, or a combination of all or some of them. In particular, there is no obligation to provide any particular benefit, and for divorce purposes, there is in particular no obligation to provide a survivor's pension.

2.14 The legal structure

The legal structure of private pension arrangements has never been very clear. In recent years, the theory has developed that, in final-salary schemes at least, the assets in a pension fund belong, if they belong to anyone, to the employer. The reason is twofold. First, in balance-of-cost schemes (ie where the employee pays a fixed amount or percentage and the employer pays the balance, whatever that may be) the liability for any deficit is purely the employer's (PSA 1993, s 164). Secondly, the promise of a pension is made under the contract of employment, and the sums set aside are simply to guarantee that promise in case the company fails in business and cannot meet its pension promises some years in the future. No funds are needed, for example, to guarantee the Civil Service pension arrangements because the state will always be able to pay. Accordingly, the conventional view that the assets of a trust belong to the beneficiaries seems inappropriate. It must follow that the structure is one of contract.

This is supported by the increasing prevalence of unfunded pension arrangements for the higher paid; these are promises by the employer to pay a certain pension after retirement age, but the strength of the promise depends on the employer continuing in business and being able to pay when the time comes (see 2.20).

2.15 The benefit structure of private pensions

Although pension arrangements bear a resemblance to savings arrangements (in particular, money-purchase schemes) on the one hand and insurance policies on the other, they do not fit either analogy comfortably. They are really a species of financial arrangement sui generis; this has not prevented attempts, especially by the courts, to relate them to more simple financial structures.

Their objective is to protect the subscriber and those for whom he is responsible against poverty in old age. Unlike savings, therefore, the benefits only arise if the contingency arises; and unlike insurance, the benefits do not crystallise on an event, but persist throughout an event.

Schemes vary enormously in their structure and benefit levels, to meet the very varied needs of their members and the different resources available. There are usually common themes to most structures, imposed if for no other reason than by the tax regime. Pension schemes which are approved by the Inland Revenue enjoy significant tax advantages.

2.16 Common features in approved pension schemes

Without tax relief, most pension schemes, at least funded schemes, would not exist. Such schemes would not be an efficient way of providing pension benefits. In fact, for many years, especially around the turn of the century, most schemes were unfunded and relied on the goodwill and financial viability of the employer to meet the expectations of the members. Such schemes, however, offered limited security to scheme members.

Today therefore, almost all pension arrangements (except in respect of higher earners with earnings over £91,800 in 2000/01) are established so as to be approved by the Pension Schemes Office of the Inland Revenue. The PSO set out complex criteria for the approval of such schemes, specifying maximum benefits, maximum funding and documentary requirements. Some of these requirements are very complicated indeed.

The requirements of the Inland Revenue dictate the nature of the benefits that can be provided as well as the contributions that can be made.

2.16.1 Pension benefits

The most common feature, obviously, is the provision of a pension for the member. The maximum (in a final-salary system) is two-thirds of the employee's final salary. The definition of final salary can and does vary from scheme to scheme within Inland Revenue limits. For example, it can be the employee's salary at retirement or average earnings over a fixed period before retirement. The rate at which the entitlement to a pension can be acquired is limited, so that it must be acquired over at least 20 years' service. In some cases the benefit is generous; in others it could be modest. For lower earners, for example, it could be merely replacing the SERPS benefit, in which case it might be small. Pensions are usually available as of right on reaching a specified age (commonly today 65 for both sexes) or earlier (subject to a reduction for early retirement) or on ill-health. In some cases this earlier retirement may be subject to checks such as medical certificates or trustees and/or employer's approval.

2.16.2 Spouse's benefits

Occupational schemes almost always provide spouses' pensions which are paid on the death of the contributor; there is, however, no legal requirement to do so (other than in relation to any SERPS replacement). Personal pensions often do not provide such pensions, since to do so would involve a reduction in the contributor's benefit. It is not unknown for a member of an occupational pension scheme to elect, as is his right, to arrange a transfer of his cash equivalent or transfer value to a personal pension with no spouse's benefit. The maximum survivor's pension is two-thirds of the member's pension (ie four-ninths of the member's salary in a final-salary scheme).

2.16.3 Dependant's benefits

In addition, most occupational schemes make provision for dependants such as children and more commonly these days 'significant others', whether married or not, or whether of the same sex or not. The essential difference from a spouse's pension is that eligibility depends on dependency, although different schemes may have weaker or stronger tests of dependency.

2.16.4 Lump sums

Most schemes make provision for lump sums, some in a variety of ways including:

- The provision of the right to 'commute' part of the pension (ie exchange it) for cash. This is tax effective, since a pension bears income tax when paid, while a commuted lump sum does not. The amount which can be commuted is limited by the Pension Schemes Office (broadly 1.5 x final salary, or 25% of the cash value of a personal pension and usually a little more in the case of Retirement Annuity Contracts). The commutation option is just that – an option. There is no requirement for the member to exercise it. There is, however, now statutory jurisdiction under MCA 1973, s 25B to order a commutation of part of the pension up to the limit allowed under the scheme rules and for all or part of that sum to be paid to the other spouse (see Chapter 6).
- The provision of a guarantee of at least five years' worth of pension benefits on retirement; in other words, if the member dies having enjoyed less than five years' worth of pension, the balance will be paid to the estate;
- The provision of a tax-free lump sum of (depending on the promise made in the scheme) up to four times salary on death in service. This, in order to be tax efficient, is payable at the discretion of the trustees, and is therefore not normally available as an asset for disposal. It also, of course, requires the death of the member. This too can be made the subject of an order under MCA 1973, s 25C (see Chapter 6), where the court can override the trustees' discretion and order the earmarking of such a lump sum.

2.16.5 Children

Most schemes nowadays provide for benefits for dependent children. They are normally quite modest.

2.16.6 Cohabitation

A few more schemes now make provision for unmarried couples, whether heterosexual or homosexual. The acquisition of such benefits is still often, however, at the discretion of the trustees and will often require a proof of dependency, usually financial dependency. The effect of cohabitation on pension rights is outside the scope of this book.

2.17 The regulatory structure

2.17.1 Regulatory areas

The regulatory structure affecting pension schemes, even before the Maxwell scandal, was notoriously complex. It broadly divides into three areas:

- Social security, involving equal treatment, transfer rights, revaluation requirements, and preservation (ie the right not to have rights confiscated or reduced merely because of leaving employment), membership, information and many other areas including the relationship with the SERPS scheme.

- Taxation, involving constraints on benefits, transfers, accrual rights, contributions and funding (especially surpluses). The Inland Revenue rules and requirements are based on the misguided principle that pension funds enjoy substantial tax-breaks. In reality, pension arrangements are in fact broadly tax neutral (there is relief on the money put in, but tax to pay when it is withdrawn except for tax-free lump sums).
- Investments, where most pension fund trustees are required under the Financial Services Act 1986 (FSA 1986) to delegate the day-to-day investment management to authorised persons. The FSA also imposes controls on the marketing of personal pensions.

2.18 Social security obligations

There is a large body of social security law governing the operation of occupational pension schemes. The principal legislation is set out in PSA 1993, PA 1995 and WRAPA 1999.

2.18.1 Equal treatment

Following a series of cases in the European Court of Justice, it is now established that pension benefits must be equal for men and women. This is reflected in the legislation, which also now provides for equal pension ages in the state scheme to be phased in by 2020. Equal eligibility for men and women to join pension schemes has been required for many years.

2.18.2 Preservation

Pension rights cannot be confiscated when an employee leaves employment once he has completed at least two years' employment. This rule, known as preservation in the UK and vesting elsewhere in the world, makes it illegal to discriminate in the provision of benefits between members who stay in employment with the employer and those who leave.

2.18.3 Transfers

A scheme member has the right to move his accrued benefits from one scheme to another scheme, or to a personal pension scheme, provided the receiving scheme will accept the benefits.

2.18.4 Information

A scheme member has the right to certain information about his scheme, including scheme accounts, deeds and rules, actuarial reports, and personal benefits. Under the provisions of PA 1995, which came into force in April 1997, there are penalties for failure to provide such information (see 9.6.5.1).

2.18.5 *Funding*

Since April 1997, final-salary pension schemes (other than certain public sector schemes and unapproved schemes) have had to meet minimum funding requirements. This does not guarantee that all pensions will be paid in full, nor that there are sufficient assets to meet all benefits, but it does underpin most of the expected pension benefits.

2.18.6 *Compensation fund*

A compensation fund makes good any losses in company pension funds caused by fraud and misappropriation where there is no company or employer to pick up the losses. Personal pension schemes seem less well protected.

2.18.7 *Trusteeship*

There is no requirement that pension scheme trustees be qualified, but since April 1997 the work of trustees has been regulated by OPRA (see 2.11) and one-third of trustees in schemes with more than 100 members must normally be employee-elected. When employers go out of business, the law requires an independent trustee to be appointed to balance the interests of the members against those of the insolvency practitioner. Trustees are entitled to paid time-off for training.

2.18.8 *Accounting*

Since almost all company schemes are established under trust, the normal principles of trust law apply. In addition, the scheme must keep full records, be audited, ensure advisers report to the scheme and consult with employers on investments.

2.18.9 *Benefits*

There is no requirement to provide any particular benefit, although there are limits on the maximum benefits that can be paid in approved schemes (see 2.12, 2.16 and 2.19). All approved pension schemes now have to provide limited price indexation (LPI) on all pension payments made in relation to pensionable employment carried out after 5 April 1997 and many did so before. The LPI requirements do not apply to personal pensions because the amount paid under those depends on the performance of the financial markets at the time the pension annuity was purchased. Nor do they apply to benefits derived from the payment of AVCs. The LPI increase is 5% or the increase in the RPI, if less. Increases granted in excess of the minimum required may be offset against the increase due in the following year.

2.18.10 *Contracting-out*

The DSS requires schemes which have undertaken to pay benefits which would otherwise be payable by SERPS to undergo special supervision to ensure that the funds are there to back the promise. In particular, actuarial reports must be regularly filed and there are special restrictions on the kinds of investments that such schemes can make, particularly in relation to employer-related investments (eg shares of the employer, or loans to the employer). Oddly, the responsibility for supervision has been transferred to the Inland Revenue, although not to its Pension Schemes Office, but its National Insurance Contributions Office.

2.19   Taxation

A scheme without tax approval is expensive to run:

- Contributions by the employee would not receive tax relief.
- Contributions by the employer would not enjoy tax relief.
- Income on the investments of the pension scheme would not enjoy tax relief.

Without tax relief, it would be more efficient for employers merely to offer unfunded pension benefits at retirement, unsecured by pre-funded arrangements. To obtain tax relief, the Pension Schemes Office of the Inland Revenue insist that there are controls. These are set out in the legislation (Income and Corporation Taxes Act 1988 (ICTA 1988)), regulations, and in Practice Notes (IR12, issued in loose-leaf form, available on the web at www.inlandrevenue.gov.uk). Controls include:

- In relation to final-salary type schemes, limits on the benefits that can be offered. These include a pension of no more than two-thirds of final salary, the right to commute part of that pension (but no more than one-and-a-half times the final salary), the right to offer life insurance on death-in-service (no more than four times salary) and a number of other benefits.
- In relation to personal pensions, while there are no limits on the benefits, there are limits on the amount put in rather than the amount taken out. The general limit is 17.5% of income as contributions (with higher amounts for older contributors: see Table 2.2, above). There is a limit of about 25% of the fund on the amount available at retirement for commutation.
- In relation to pensionable salary, only the first £91,800 (2000/01) is pensionable. Pension may be paid in relation to salary over that level by employers, but no tax relief is offered on such arrangements. Accordingly, in these cases it is common to be offered unfunded arrangements, subject always to the risk that the employer's promise will not be met if it goes out if business.
- In relation to investments there are few controls, except that:
  - In relation to small, self-administered pension schemes (SSASs), the Revenue insist on the appointment of a Revenue-approved trustee (a 'pensioneer trustee') to inform them if anything goes wrong; the restriction on investments (excluding residential property, for example); and limiting the funds paid into such schemes. A SSAS is a pension scheme normally established for a small, director-owned company with fewer than twelve members. Because such employers can determine their own salaries (and hence pensions) the

Revenue impose additional controls. The trustees of these schemes are also in an unusual position: they are often simultaneously employer, employee, director, shareholder, scheme member and trustee. In addition, the trustees (ie directors) usually invest the money themselves (ie self-administer) rather than buy insurance policies (ie insure).

- In relation to self-invested personal pensions (SIPPs), which are similar arrangements to SSASs but are personal pensions for the self-employed, the Revenue also restrict the investments (excluding residential property, for example).

2.20   FURBS, UURBS and SUBURBS

Before the Finance Act 1989 (FA 1989), employers could only provide their employees with pension benefits through approved schemes. On the other hand there was no cap on the earnings from which pension contributions could be made. FA 1989 introduced a cap on earnings for benefits from approved schemes, but also allowed unlimited benefits to be provided through unapproved arrangements without affecting the tax status of approved schemes. Accordingly, there has been a considerable growth in unapproved schemes for high earners since 1989. Such schemes may be funded (where they are known as 'funded unapproved retirement benefit schemes' or FURBS), unfunded (where they are known as 'unfunded unapproved retirement benefit schemes' or UURBS) or secured (where they are known as 'secured unapproved retirement benefit schemes' or 'SUBURBS'). SUBURBS are unfunded but are secured against the company's assets by way of a first charge. The tax treatment of these unapproved schemes varies according to whether they are funded or not. Because they do not have Inland Revenue approval, they are treated quite differently from approved schemes. The most important features are:

- The scheme's investment income and capital gains (if any) are subject to tax.
- Income tax is payable by the employee on the contributions made or the benefits received and in some cases both. If the scheme is funded, income tax will be payable on the contributions as they are made, since they are treated as benefits received by the employee. Pensions when paid are taxable in the recipient's hands as income. Income tax is not payable on a lump sum payment. If the scheme is unfunded, no contributions will have been made prior to the payment of a pension or lump sum and both will bear tax when they are paid. The whole fund can be paid as a lump sum (unless the rules require it to be paid as a pension).

Such arrangements are often not contained in the form normally used for setting out pension details, but in employment contracts or letters from the employer to the employee. Notwithstanding this, the obligation to disclose such arrangements in matrimonial proceedings is the same as for any other interest in a pension scheme. This may not necessarily be appreciated by the employer or his advisers, so it may have to be specifically raised when discussing disclosure with clients or evaluating the disclosure provided by the other spouse.

2.21   Investments

There are few restrictions on the investments of pension funds, except as mentioned above. However, in smaller schemes, especially those that invest in company property for example, there may be liquidity problems when attempting to pay unexpected benefits. Such schemes frequently insure large benefits to cover the problem. However, with the exception of SSASs and SIPPs, schemes need authorisation under FSA 1986 to make their own day-to-day investment decisions, and hence normally delegate the management to authorised persons, such as fund managers.

2.22   Regulatory bodies

There are three main governmental organisations involved with pensions:

- The Occupational Pensions Regulatory Authority (OPRA), Invicta House, Trafalgar Place, Trafalgar Street, Brighton, East Sussex, BN1 4DW (01273 627600). It controls equal treatment, information to members, transfers, preservation, payment of contributions, repayment of surpluses, scheme modifications and whistle blowing as well as general overall regulation, including control of trustees.
- The Inland Revenue National Insurance Contributions Office, Contracted-out Employment Group, Newcastle upon Tyne, NE98 1YX (0645 150150) ensures that the assets are sufficient in the fund to meet the quasi-state benefits promised where schemes are contracted-out. It acts to protect the interests of the government, who have permitted lower National Insurance contributions to be paid to the state, provided the obligation of paying SERPS benefits is met by the employer and pension fund.
- The Inland Revenue Pensions Schemes Office, St Nicholas Court, Castle Gate, Nottingham, NG1 7AR (0115 924 0000). This controls the assets going into schemes, to limit the tax reliefs, and limits many of the benefits.

In addition, funds can be regulated by:

- The Financial Services Authority (or one of its as yet still self-standing affiliates, IMRO, PIA and others), 1 Canada Square, Canary Wharf, London E14 4AB (020 7538 8860). These authorities are appropriate where schemes manage their own investments.
- The Data Protection Registrar, Wycliffe House, Water Lane, Wilmslow, Cheshire, SK9 5AF (01625 545745).
- The Pensions Ombudsman, 11 Belgrave Road, London SW1V 1RB (020 7834 9144).

There are also a number of other ombudsmen and regulatory bodies, including the Office of the Pensions Advisory Service (OPAS) at 11 Belgrave Road, London SW1V 1RB (020 7233 8080).

So far as matrimonial matters are concerned, few of these bodies wish to be involved. The Revenue is only concerned that tax reliefs are not widened further than they are available at present; the Occupational Pensions Regulatory Authority will on occasion help enforce the production of information. That aside, the authorities prefer to let the family lawyers and the parties resolve matters amongst themselves.

2.23 Disputes

Disputes between pension schemes and their members do arise. They are dealt with by using:

* schemes' internal procedures; or, if that fails,
* the Office of the Pensions Advisory Service; or, if that fails,
* the Pensions Ombudsman; or, if that fails,
* the conventional jurisdictions, usually the County Court or the Chancery Division of the High Court.

Complaints can also be made to OPRA which will supervise the proper enforcement of transfers and disclosure of information. It cannot award damages, but can penalise a scheme and its trustees and employers for deliberate breach of the rules.

Chapter Three

Pensions issues on separation, nullity and divorce

3.1   Introduction

For divorcing and separating spouses, pensions are often a very important consideration. As has already been seen, pensions are often the most valuable potential asset that a family has. They may have been built up over a long time and both spouses will have looked forward to being able to rely on them in retirement. Just as importantly, in the event of one spouse dying either before or after retirement, the pension will often provide security for the surviving spouse either through a death-in-service benefit or a widow's pension.

The pension provision of both spouses is rarely equal, often as a result of a family decision to allocate responsibility for earning and child care. One spouse may have stayed at home to bring up the family and to look after the house. She (for it is usually the wife) will not have accrued as large a pension (or possibly no pension at all) as her husband.

Typical scenarios include cases where the wife has worked for a few years and acquired a small pension through her employment. She may then stay at home looking after the children for perhaps 15 years before going back to work. For those 15 years she has not accrued any pension entitlement, whilst her husband has added to his pension rights every year.

Even when both spouses work, their pension provision may not be equal, and differences in life expectancy will of themselves produce different pension provisions from the same contributions made by husband and wife.

Example 3.1

In a defined contribution scheme a pension with a fund value of £10,000 at age 60 might produce a pension of £750 per annum for a man but only £650 per annum for a woman reflecting life expectancies of 18 and 22½ years respectively. However, a defined benefit scheme would provide the same benefits for men and women (indeed it must do so now).

Of equal importance for many households is the fact that there may be no adequate pension provision at all, and separation and divorce make the financial position of both spouses much more difficult. This is particularly so if the available capital now has to provide for two households rather than one, with the result that capital that would have been available to help fund the family in retirement has been depleted or spent.

The debate about pensions and divorce has largely centred on those families where the pension provision is unequally spread between the spouses. The principal difficulty has been that the courts have not been able to make orders directly affecting pension schemes or pensions themselves.

To effect justice, the courts have had to try to re-order the rest of the assets to compensate the spouse who has no pension, or only a small pension, for the loss of pension benefits. This is usually called offsetting. Earmarking orders did not really provide a solution to this problem, as reflected in the fact that very few have been made. The problem caused by the inability to split pensions has now been tackled with the introduction of pension sharing, available in cases where a petition for divorce or nullity (though not judicial separation) was filed after 1 December 2000 (see 6.4). Offsetting continues to be available, and it should not be assumed that because pension sharing is available it will be the solution or indeed the only answer in every case (see 6.5).

There is also an argument that pension rights should be considered as joint family assets in very much the same way as the family home is often regarded today. This reasoning leads to the conclusion that each spouse should come out of the marriage with the same pension provision or its equivalent. This is very close to treating pensions as if they were part of a community of property regime. This, however, is not the basis of English law (see, however, the decision of the House of Lords in *White v White* [2000] 3 WLR 1571 discussed at 6.2). There is no doubt that many spouses see pension provision as an entitlement but for some time this was undecided by the courts. However, in *T v T* [1998] 1 FLR 1072, Singer J held that there was no automatic entitlement to compensation for pension loss. He said that a pension was an asset that must be taken into account in the discretionary exercise set out in the Matrimonial Causes Act 1973, s 25, like other assets. The court must consider first whether an order for periodical payments, secured provision or a lump sum is appropriate and, second, how pension considerations should affect the terms of any such order. The answer to the second question might be 'not at all'. The impact of this decision and that in *White v White* is considered in more detail in Chapter 6.

When reordering family assets on divorce the court has to have regard to the provisions of MCA 1973, s 25, which imparts a large element of discretion into its deliberations. The court must also consider and, where possible, effect a clean break. The previous inability to make orders directly affecting pensions must, in many cases, have prevented the court from making clean break orders in circumstances where it would otherwise have wished so to do.

Pressure for reform resulted in first 'earmarking' and now pension sharing being introduced. This gives the court more flexibility (see 6.1). Earmarking, however, creates a continuing financial relationship between the divorced spouses and therefore does not help to facilitate a clean break. Relatively few earmarking orders have been made, probably because most couples wish to bring an end to their financial interdependence. The government believes that pension sharing will prove more attractive and estimates that as many as 50,000 pension sharing orders will be made each year.

This chapter considers the issues surrounding pensions which have so far proved complex and difficult for divorce lawyers.

3.2 The problem with pensions

Pensions present a number of different problems for divorce lawyers. The first has been the courts' inability to make orders directly affecting pension assets in the vast majority of cases. This has been addressed by the introduction of first earmarking and now pension sharing.

Strictly speaking, the law did not prevent a court making an order in relation to a pension. Indeed, not only did the court have an obligation to take pensions into account when resolving financial settlements on divorce, it has also had the power, at least in principle, to direct the split of pension arrangements under:

- its inherent jurisdiction; and
- the power contained in MCA 1973, s 24(1)(c), which enables the court to vary ante- or post-nuptial settlements, as was done in the case of *Brooks v Brooks* [1995] 3 All ER 257, [1995] 2 FLR 13.

The courts have exercised that power rarely because in most cases:

- To do so would affect the Revenue's approval of the pension scheme, loss of which would impose very high costs on employers and employees as well as on third parties (see further Chapter 2).
- It would adversely effect the interests of third parties generally, since, for example, it might rank spouses higher in any order of priorities in a pension scheme wind up.
- It would be subject to the provisions contained in the protective trusts which are written into the rules of most pension schemes.

3.3   Protective trusts

Protective trusts are to be found in almost all occupational pension schemes and an increasing number of personal pension arrangements.

A protective trust is usually set out in a clause in the pension scheme which aims to remove trust assets from the court's jurisdiction. It normally provides that if the scheme member or policy holder becomes bankrupt or a court order is made against the scheme member's interest in the pension, his right to pension benefits from the scheme are forfeit.

The clauses were not inserted into pension schemes to prevent spouses being assigned part of their husbands' pension rights on divorce, but to prevent pension scheme members assigning the benefit of their pension assets to a third party. This was most likely to arise where a pension scheme member in financial difficulty saw the pension as something that could be used to raise money and tried to assign or charge it to do so. For that reason the trusts have also been known as spendthrift trusts.

3.3.1 *Edmonds v Edmonds*

Edmonds v Edmonds [1965] 1 All ER 379n made it clear beyond doubt that a protective trust would operate to defeat an order made in matrimonial proceedings.

Mrs Edmonds was granted a decree of divorce in 1962. She applied for a maintenance order. Mr Edmonds lived abroad. He took no part in the proceedings and did not even file an affidavit of means. The court made a maintenance order which was served on Mr Edmonds' bank manager, who said it had been forwarded to Mr Edmonds. Despite that, Mr Edmonds did not pay and arrears accumulated under the order. Mrs Edmonds sought an attachment of earnings order against a pension that Mr Edmonds was being paid in relation to his previous employment. The court held the pension to be earnings for the purposes of making an attachment of earnings order, and made an order against the trustees of the pension fund requiring them to pay the amounts due to Mrs Edmonds directly to her from the pension payments.

The trustees appealed and asked the court whether in those circumstances the pension ceased upon the making of the order, since the rules of Mr Edmonds' pension scheme contained a protective trust. The clause itself read:

'If a member, or other beneficiary under the fund, shall become bankrupt or shall at any time assign or charge or purport to assign or charge any such pension or any sum receivable by him or her from the fund or shall do or suffer anything whereby such pension or income would but for this clause become vested in or payable to any other person, then such member's or other beneficiary's interests in such pension or sum shall cease and determine and in that event the trustees may, in cases of hardship, hold, apply or pay the pension or sum or any part thereof to or for the benefit of any one or more of the following persons namely the person originally entitled thereto, his wife or widow, children and other dependants or any of them as the case may be in such manner and in such proportions as the trustees shall think proper.'

The court held that the making of the attachment order brought this clause into operation. The court order was therefore ineffective because, by the very act of making it, the pension payments had become forfeit and Mr Edmonds was no longer entitled to receive the money. However, the trustees of the pension scheme retained a discretion to pay the pension or hold the pension on behalf of Mr Edmonds in the case of hardship. As it was in the trustees' discretion, it could not be made the subject of an order.

3.4   Provisions ousting the jurisdiction of the court ('ouster clauses')

Many statutory pension arrangements (see 2.9), particularly those governing the armed forces, contain statutory protective trusts. The Army Act 1955 (AA 1955), s 203, the Air Force Act 1955 (AFA 1955), s 203 and the Naval Discipline Act 1957 (NDA 1957), s 128 all prohibit the assignment of a pension, including a gratuity payable on leaving the service. These provisions prevented the courts from making orders that affect a pension benefit directly. They also prohibit any court order being made which will prevent a person receiving a benefit which he cannot assign.

These clauses have been the subject of judicial consideration on a number of occasions in the past:

• In *Ranson v Ranson* [1988] 1 WLR 183, CA, the court held that it could not make an order under the Matrimonial Causes Act equal to 20% of an eventual military gratuity, even where it was not expressed to be paid from the prospective gratuity.
• Once the gratuity had been paid, however, the court could make the order even though the payment would have to be made from the gratuity. Once

the gratuity has been paid it ceases to lose its significance as part of the pension scheme and becomes cash in the pension scheme member's hands (*Happé v Happé* [1991] 4 All ER 527, CA).
- Similar principles were held to apply to naval and marine pensions in *Legrove v Legrove* [1994] 2 FLR 119, CA.

The provisions of the Pensions Act 1995 rendered such clauses ineffective in matrimonial proceedings (see 3.5).

3.5   Protective trusts now

Provisions contained in PA 1995, s 91 (for private pensions) and PA 1995, s 166 (for service schemes) PA 1995 render the operation of protective trusts and 'ouster' clauses ineffective as far as matrimonial proceedings are concerned.

Section 166 provides that the following provisions shall not apply to a court exercising its powers under the Matrimonial Causes Act 1973, s 23 in respect of pension benefits:

- **Army Act 1955, s 203(1) and (2), Air Force Act 1955, s 203(1), Naval Discipline Act 1957, s 128G(1) and (2) or Pension Schemes Act 1993, s 159(4) and (4A)** These sections prevented both the assignment of pension benefits and the making of effective court orders which would restrain a person from receiving anything which he is prevented from assigning.
- **Pensions Act 1995, s 91** This imposes restrictions on the assignment, surrender and alienation of accrued rights under a pension scheme. It operates like a protective trust.
- Any provision in any Act which contains provisions corresponding to those contained in the statutes referred to above. This covers clauses included in statutory pension schemes (see 2.9).
- Any similar provision in any pension scheme.

Thus courts dealing with matrimonial cases brought under MCA 1973, s 23 can now make orders directly affecting pension schemes without any protective trusts or statutory prohibitions having any effect.

3.6   What is being lost when parties divorce

The nature and value of the pensions loss on divorce poses a difficult question for family lawyers. The position is made more complex by virtue of the fact that not all pension schemes pay the same kinds or levels of benefits (see 2.15). This and the wide discretion contained in s 25 make it impossible to say that the pension benefits will be relevant in every case. As Singer J said in *T v T*, there will be cases where pension benefits will not at all affect the orders made in matrimonial proceedings. (For a more detailed discussion of this see 6.2.) Practitioners should check exactly what benefits are provided under each pension scheme and not just rely on passing observation or their general knowledge (see 4.2).

In practice, there are two classes of benefits lost to a spouse on divorce: survivor's benefits and the spouse's interest in the scheme member's benefits.

3.7 Survivors' (ie widows' and widowers') benefits

Most occupational schemes and some personal pension schemes pay survivors' pensions where scheme members die in service as well as after retirement. These often amount to about half that which would have been paid to the scheme member. Some schemes calculate survivors' benefits on the pension rights that have accrued at the time of the scheme member's death. Others may add years of service to that.

Example 3.2

An occupational scheme provides for a pension of two-thirds ($^{40}/_{60}$) final salary on retirement after 40 years' service. A member dies at age 40 after 20 years membership on a salary of £30,000. His spouse might receive an immediate pension of half the member's accrued pension eg $^{1}/_{2}$ x $^{20}/_{60}$ x 30,000 = £5,000 pa or, more commonly, a pension of half the member's prospective pension at retirement age, say 60, eg $^{1}/_{2}$ x $^{40}/_{60}$ x 30,000 = £10,000 pa.

Some schemes also pay benefits to dependants other than the surviving spouse, whilst others do not pay survivors' benefits to surviving spouses who were separated at the time of death of the other spouse.

In some cases an ex-spouse may also enjoy pension benefits based on the breadwinner's pension rights, but only on proof of dependency and then invariably at the discretion of the trustees of the scheme.

On divorce a widow will automatically lose the right to widow's benefits, since to be a widow a woman must be married to the man at the date of his death (see *Re Norman's Will Trusts, Mitchell v Cozens* (1940) 84 Sol Jo 186).

The value of the spouse's benefit can be calculated according to a number of formulae, of which the best known is that published in *At A Glance* (see Appendix VI). It should be remembered that this method of calculation does not calculate the loss to the surviving spouse of her/his opportunity of sharing in the member's pension.

An earmarking order does not necessarily compensate for the loss of a spouse's pension, because it will not, for example, pay a survivor's pension to the former spouse of a deceased scheme member (see, for example, *K v K* [1997] 1 FLR 35 discussed more fully at 6.11).

Pension sharing orders offer a spouse the advantage of acquiring a pension of her own which will be paid until she dies, regardless of what befalls her former spouse.

Example 3.3

John and Jane divorce. She obtains an earmarking order requiring John's pension scheme trustees to pay her one-third of his pension payments. John dies four years after retirement. At that point, Jane's entitlement under the order ceases. If she had obtained a pension sharing order she would receive a pension of her own on her retirement which would last until her death and would be unaffected by John's death.

Finally, survivor's benefits are not, of course, paid to a former spouse but will be paid to a surviving spouse, regardless of any earmarking order.

Example 3.4

If John marries Sue after his divorce from Jane and he dies four years after retirement, Jane's earmarking order, if she had one, comes to an end. If Jane had obtained a pension sharing order, that would be unaffected by his death. Sue will receive a widow's pension from John's pension scheme of up to two-thirds of his remaining pension, depending on the benefits paid under the scheme. If Jane has obtained a pension sharing order, this will have resulted in a reduction to John's pension and therefore to Sue's widows' pension, unless John had been able to rebuild his pension rights following the making of the pension sharing order (see Chapter 6).

3.8   The spouse's interest in the scheme member's benefits

It is not only widow's or widower's benefits which are lost. A spouse has an expectation of an interest in the member's own benefits which she will lose on divorce or, sometimes, on separation. These benefits include:

*   The spouse's interest in the member's pension. If the marriage had continued the spouse would have enjoyed an interest, even if indirect, in the member's pension. Given that in a final-salary scheme (see 2.11.1.1) a member's pension can be as much as two-thirds of his final salary, the loss can be considerable.
*   In many occupational schemes a wife also has an interest in the benefits received if the scheme member dies in service, ie before he has reached pensionable age or taken retirement. These benefits, the beneficiaries of which are at the discretion of the trustees, can be up to four times the scheme member's salary on death (see 2.16.4). Loss of these benefits can now be compensated through an earmarking order under MCA 1973, s 25C, although this is not possible if a pension sharing order has been made in relation to the same pension (see Chapter 6).
*   A dependant's pension for minor children. These benefits are normally modest.

3.9   The law

3.9.1 The position before the Pension Act 1995

Until the PA 1995 came into force, pensions rated only a passing mention in s 25. Section 25(2)(h) provided that the court was to have consideration when exercising its powers to make financial orders to:

> '. . . the value to each of the parties to the marriage of any benefit (for example a pension) which, by reason of the dissolution or annulment of the marriage, such party will lose the chance of acquiring . . .'

The absence of pensions benefits in the section as a whole, coupled with the difficulties in dealing with them, meant that in practice they were often ignored. Where attempts were made to take them into account they were often disregarded because they were not going to be paid in the foreseeable future.

This arose because s 25(2)(a) provided that only '. . . the income, earning capacity, property and other financial resources which each of the parties has or is likely to have in the foreseeable future' could be taken into account. The words 'in the foreseeable future' meant that pension benefits which would not come into payment in the near future would usually be ignored. In *Milne v Milne* [1981] 2 FLR 286, CA, the court held that a benefit paid in more than ten years' time was not payable in the reasonably foreseeable future. In *Roberts v Roberts* [1986] 2 FLR 152, the court held that the longest period a court was likely to adjourn an application for capital provision where a party was likely to have a financial resource in the foreseeable future was four or five years.

These decisions made it difficult to advise a client as to whether or not a claim would be dismissed or diminished if it relied on claiming against pension benefits.

One way of attempting to get round this problem was to apply to adjourn claims. This is now unlikely to be a problem because of amendments made to the MCA 1973 (see below) which removed the test that pension benefits must be payable in the foreseeable future if they were to be taken into account, the availability of earmarking orders and, more particularly, pension sharing.

3.9.2 The current position

PA 1995, which introduced earmarking (or attachment as it is now called in some of the legislation) on 1 July 1996, amended the provisions of MCA 1973, s 25 in the following ways:

- **It made pensions more central to the exercise of the court's discretion** Three amendments were made to s 25 which gave pensions a more central role in the s 25 balancing exercise than hitherto. They are:
  - When considering the income, earning capacity, property and other financial resources which each of the parties to the marriage has or is likely to have, the court must now take into account any benefit under a pension scheme (MCA 1973, s 25B(1)(a) inserted by PA 1995).
  - The requirement that such resources can only be taken into account if they are to become available in the foreseeable future is specifically disapplied in the case of pensions (MCA 1973, s 25B (1)(b)), although not to any other assets.
  - When considering benefits which will be lost on divorce or nullity (but not judicial separation), the court must consider any benefits under a pension scheme which, because of the dissolution or annulment of the marriage, one of the spouses will lose the chance of acquiring (MCA 1973, ss 25(2)(h) and 25B(1)(b)).

That is of considerable importance. For example:

Example 3.5

Mr and Mrs Smith divorce. They are both aged 35. Mr Smith has a substantial pension entitlement, which he can exercise when he reaches 50 if he chooses. Mrs Smith has no pension. She met Mr Smith when they were both students and she married him and had their first child immediately after graduating. She has never worked outside the home. Under the previous law, a claim by her which asked the court to take into account her husband's future pension entitlement would probably have been dismissed because it would have failed the 'foreseeability' test. Now, the fact that the pension will not be paid for at least 15 years should not prevent it being considered, although whether the court will take it into account when making the order will depend on all the circumstances of the case (see Chapter 6).

- **Payments can be ordered to be made from pension funds by pension trustees to the spouse without pension rights** In any proceedings for a financial provision order where either party has or is likely to have a benefit under a pension scheme, the court must consider whether it should make an order for the payment of a lump sum or periodical payments by the pension fund to the party without pension rights (MCA 1973, s 25B (see 6.6)). This gets round the difficulty posed by protective trusts and similar statutory provisions whose operation in relation to matrimonial proceedings has now been rendered ineffective (see 3.3, 3.5).
- **The court can order a pension scheme member to commute part of his pension to a lump sum and order the trustees to pay all or part of it to the spouse** The court can also oblige a pension scheme member to commute part of his pension to a lump sum up to the maximum allowed by the pension scheme. This may be less than the maximum amount allowed by law (see 2.16.4) as some schemes do not permit members to commute to the maximum allowed. The court can also order that all or part of the commuted lump sum be paid to the other spouse; these can involve large sums, since a lump sum paid in a defined-benefits scheme can be up to one-and-a-half times the member's final salary and in a personal pension scheme up to one-quarter of the pension fund value on retirement.
- **The court can make orders in relation to death benefits** The court can make an order that requires the pension scheme to make payments of death-in-service benefits to the former spouse (MCA 1973, s 25C).

3.10   Sharing

Pension sharing under statute is available in cases where a petition for divorce or nullity (not judicial separation) was filed after 1 December 2000. The law was introduced by the WRAPA 1999, which amends MCA 1973. Originally, it was contained in the FLA 1996. That legislation, however, was considered defective and has not been brought into force.

Sharing, long advocated as the best solution to the pension problem by divorce lawyers, can only be effected by a court order even if the parties have agreed (for a detailed account of pension sharing see Chapter 6).

3.10.1 Sharing through variation of ante- and post-nuptial settlements

The case of *Brooks v Brooks* [1996] AC 375, HL (see 6.10) raised the prospect of pensions being considered as nuptial settlements and therefore susceptible to variation by the court under the provisions of MCA 1973, s 24(1)(c) . This option is specifically excluded by the pension sharing legislation (see the amended MCA 1973, s 21(2)(c) and (d)). This means that it is not available in cases where the petition was filed after 1 December 2000, although it will still be available where the petition was filed before that date. The use of this technique is discussed in more detail at 6.10.

3.11 Separation v divorce

From a pensions point of view there is usually a significant difference between judicial separation and divorce. The court can make the whole range of financial orders on separation, including earmarking orders, but not pension sharing orders. If spouses are judicially separated, the spouse who is not a scheme member usually, but not always, remains a potential survivor so that if the scheme member dies she will usually receive the survivor's benefits. This needs to be checked in each case as it does not apply in every scheme. Some schemes, for example, do not pay survivor's benefits to a separated spouse. In some schemes, this restriction applies if the spouses have been separated for more than a specified period even though there may have been no court proceedings.

3.12 Void and voidable marriages

In many pension schemes, survivors' pensions are discontinued on their remarriage and are not reinstated even if the survivor's second marriage is ended by divorce.

A particular problem arises in relation to marriages that are annulled. Both void and voidable marriages can be annulled by the grant of a decree of nullity. However, the effect of the decree is not quite the same in each case. A void marriage is in law void from the outset and once the decree is granted is deemed never to have existed, except that a spouse is able to apply for the usual range of financial relief.

A voidable marriage is held to have subsisted from the date of the marriage until the date of the pronouncement of the decree (MCA 1973, s 16).

This had unfortunate consequences for Mrs Ward, the widow of an army officer. After her husband's death she remarried. The marriage was a disaster from the outset and almost immediately after it had taken place Mrs Ward successfully petitioned for a decree of nullity on the ground of non-consummation. The army pension scheme paid Mrs Ward a survivor's pension which ceased on her remarriage. The pension was not recommenced on the granting of a decree of nullity as it was argued that as the marriage was valid until the date of the decree, the pension scheme rule providing for the discontinuance of the pension on remarriage applied. This decision was upheld by the court (see *Ward v Secretary of State for Social Services* [1990] FCR 361).

The court can make the full range of financial orders on granting a decree of nullity, including earmarking and pension sharing orders.

3.13 Polygamous marriages

Polygamy, although not permissible under English law, can be recognised by English law if it was celebrated in accordance with the laws of the country in which the marriage took place. It can present difficulties for pension schemes: if more than one wife is recognised under English law, how is the scheme to divide or decide how, if at all, the survivors' benefits should be allocated? What is now clear is that pension schemes are not obliged to follow the decision of the state in allocating pensions in such cases. This problem arose in the case of *R v Department of Health, ex p Misra* [1996] 2 FCR 464.

Dr Misra had died leaving his widow entitled to a state widow's pension and a pension under the National Health Superannuation scheme. But he left two wives. The Social Security tribunal decided that there had been no second marriage and therefore awarded the whole of the state pension to the first wife. The occupational pension scheme, in this case the National Health Superannuation Scheme, held that the findings of the tribunal should be taken into account but were not binding. The scheme concluded that both women were widows and that the widow's pension should be divided equally. The High Court held that the decision as to the state pension was not binding in respect of the superannuation scheme although the principles and issues arising for consideration were no different.

3.14   Conclusion

The courts and family lawyers now have a number of different ways of dealing with pension assets at the time of divorce, nullity or judicial separation – these include offsetting, earmarking and pension sharing. Which of these is appropriate depends on the circumstances of each case. There may well be cases where none of these options is right and where practitioners will need to look at other alternatives. These are explored more fully in Chapter 6.

Chapter Four

Information: procedure and discovery

4.1 Introduction

UK pension provision is complex:

* There are many different kinds of schemes.
* Different schemes provide different benefits.
* An individual may have several different kinds of pension interests.
* An individual may be entitled to other benefits under contract and contained in separate documentation.

Example 4.1

Mr Evans was employed as a miner until 1984 and was a member of the mineworkers pension scheme. In 1984 he was made redundant and received a generous redundancy payment. He used this to set up a business selling garden plants and equipment. He used some of his redundancy payment to purchase a Retirement Annuity Contract in 1986 and two personal pension plans in 1990. In 1996 he sold his business and obtained employment in the parks department of his local authority, where he still works. He is therefore a deferred member of the former mineworkers' scheme, has a Retirement Annuity Contract and two personal pension plans. He is also a member of the local authority's superannuation scheme, in relation to which he may be paying Additional Voluntary Contributions (AVCs) or Free Standing AVCs (FSAVCs). He has also been paying National Insurance contributions towards his state pension.

Practitioners need to bear these points in mind when embarking on discovery in relation to pension schemes – and to remember to remind clients that under the general rules of discovery (eg those contained in the Family Proceedings Rules 1991 (FPR 1991), SI 1991/1247, see 4.3.1 and Appendix I.7), parties to ancillary relief applications are obliged to make full disclosure of all their assets and liabilities. Some specific duties concerning pension schemes have now been added to this general duty.

The Family Proceedings Rules provide that parties to an application for ancillary relief must provide full details of their property and income including all information in their possession, power or control concerning any benefits under a pension scheme which they have or are likely to have, including the most recent valuation provided by the trustees or managers of the scheme under the pension disclosure regulations.

The ancillary relief procedure introduced on 5 June 2000 sets out what is to be produced and requires that this be presented in a standard form (Form E), a sworn document. Form E prescribes the information that must be supplied about pension interests (see Appendix III). The different types of schemes and the different types of benefits mean that care is needed to ensure that all the necessary information is obtained in relation to each pension interest. Even this prescriptive arrangement is not usually enough to show the benefits available under each pension scheme or plan as the examples below demonstrate.

This chapter looks at the procedure to be followed in cases where either or both spouses have pension interests, the discovery provisions generally and at the specific rules relating to pensions. It also offers practical guidance as to the type of information that should be sought.

4.2   What sort of pensions do people have?

The following three, not untypical, examples show the different types of situation that can exist.

Example 4.2

Mr Arkwright works in the health service and has done so since he left university 30 years ago. Recently, he has made payments to a free standing additional voluntary contribution scheme (FSAVC, see 2.11.1.2). He has five years to work before retirement and can expect the following types of benefits:

- A lump sum from his occupational scheme.
- A pension from his occupational scheme.
- A pension or return of his contributions less tax from his FSAVC.

Mrs Arkwright can expect:

- To share in his pension benefits at and after retirement.
- Death-in-service benefits from Mr Arkwright's occupational scheme if he dies before retirement.
- A widow's pension if he dies before or after retirement.

Example 4.3

Mrs Jones worked as a teacher for ten years before giving up work to look after her family. After a gap of 15 years she started work as a self-employed private tutor. She has a small pension from her years as a teacher and a personal pension plan she started in 1988. She will receive the following types of benefits on retirement:

- A small pension from her teacher's pension scheme.
- A lump sum from that scheme.
- A pension from her private pension plan, part of which she may convert into a lump sum.

Before any divorce Mr Jones could expect:

- A tiny widower's pension from her teacher's pension scheme if he survives her.
- To participate in Mrs Jones' pension benefits whilst they are both alive.
- A possible survivor's benefit from Mrs Jones' personal pension plan if Mr Jones survives her.

Example 4.4

Mr Green is a highly successful businessman aged 54. Until ten years ago he ran his own business and purchased a retirement annuity contract (see 2.12). He then sold the business and was employed as an executive by Greengross plc, which has provided him with a funded unapproved retirement benefit scheme (a FURB, see 2.20). Subsequently, he also enjoyed an unfunded unapproved retirement benefit (an UURB, see 2.20) from a second company he was involved with.

Mr Green can expect:

- A pension from his retirement annuity contract, some of which could be converted into a lump sum.

- A pension from his FURB, which would be taxable. He may be able, however, to take some or all the benefits as a tax-free lump sum depending on the terms of the scheme.

- A pension from the UURB, provided the employer remains solvent. Tax is payable on all pension benefits received from the UURB.

These three examples illustrate some of the variety of pension provision. They also show that many people do not just have one pension scheme to which they belong throughout their working lives. Career breaks and changes in employment are increasingly frequent today and are likely to result in growing numbers of people being members of more than one pension scheme and of more than one type of scheme. This has considerable impact on the types of questions that practitioners need to ask their clients and sometimes, their opponents.

Before proper questions can be asked, practitioners also need to know what pension benefits are likely to be received by their clients and their spouses. These are discussed in detail in Chapter 2.

4.3 The law

The discretionary system contained in MCA 1973, s 25 means that the court needs to have an accurate picture of the parties' financial circumstances before it can exercise its powers (see *Livesey v Livesey* [1985] 1 All ER 106, HL).

For the same reason, even though most cases settle without the need for court adjudication, it is unwise and may be negligent for practitioners to advise their clients to settle without adequate disclosure of both parties' assets. They run the risk of being sued subsequently by a dissatisfied client.

The discovery process consists of the following distinct stages:

- **Disclosure by each party** Each party should make full disclosure of their financial position, including pension arrangements. This means every pension in which that person has an interest, including AVCs and other top up benefits. Under the new procedure this is made on Form E (see Appendix III).
- **Further disclosure regulated by the court** The court can limit the amount of further information required and make orders compelling the production of documents or disclosure of further information.

- **Obtaining information from pension schemes and provider** In appropriate cases information can be obtained from pension schemes or providers by means of a request by the scheme member or his/her spouse or by court order. Retirement benefit forecasts for state pensions including SERPS can be obtained from the DSS using form BR19 (see 2.8.1).

4.3.1 Procedure: making the application and other preliminary matters

Applications for pension sharing or earmarking orders must be made in the petition, as well as an application on Form A or B. Those applying for financial orders will neither know at the outset whether or not they wish to apply for a pension order, nor have enough information to enable them to draft the application correctly. Frequently, therefore, a claim for a pension order will need to be made after initial discovery, and this is specifically dealt with in the rules. However, the court cannot make earmarking or pension sharing orders of its own motion and an application on Form A or B must be made and the service provisions described below must be complied with.

Applications for ancillary relief are governed by the provisions of FPR 1991. These have been amended notably to take account of the new ancillary relief procedure introduced on 5 June 2000 and to introduce new provisions dealing with the treatment to be given to pensions. A consolidated version of the relevant part of the Rules is contained in Appendix I.7.

Since 5 June 2000, all applications for ancillary relief orders or notices of intention to proceed with a claim in a petition for an ancillary relief order must be commenced by filing Form A with the court (see Appendix III.1). Applications for the court to consider the financial position of the respondent after a decree of divorce are made on Form B. In the Rules, unless the context otherwise requires, references to Form A are to be read as if they were also references to Form B (FPR 1991, r 2.45). An applicant who wishes to apply for an attachment/earmarking order or a pension sharing order must indicate this in the relevant section of Form A.

Once the application is lodged, the court fixes a date for the first appointment. This is heard by the court on a date not less than 12 and not more than 16 weeks after the application is filed, and specifies the terms of the order sought (FPR 1991, r 2.61A(3)).

The applicant must then serve the application and notice of the first appointment on the respondent within four days of the application being issued. If the application asks for an attachment or pensions sharing order, the applicant must serve a copy of the Form A on the person responsible for the pension arrangement. In many cases the applicant will not have the details of the respondent's pension interests at the time s/he makes the application for financial orders. Often the applicant will not know whether s/he wants to make an application until s/he has seen the other spouse's disclosure. In that case, service should be effected when the claim for a pension order is added (FPR 1991, r 2.70(6) and (7)).

4.3.2 Special provisions where an earmarking order is sought

Additionally, where the claim includes a claim for an earmarking/attachment order, the applicant must also serve the person responsible for the pension arrangement or arrangements concerned with the following:

- an address to which the pension scheme should send any notices it is required to send to the beneficiary of an attachment order. These notices are set out in the Divorce etc (Pensions) Regulations 2000, SI 2000/1123 and are considered further at Chapter 6;
- an address to which any payment due under an attachment order is to be sent; and
- if that address is a bank, building society or the Department of National Savings, sufficient details to enable payment to be made into the applicant's account (FPR 1991, r 2.70(7)).

If the application includes an application for an earmarking order the person responsible for the pension arrangement may ask to be provided with a copy of that part of the Form E which deals with the applicant's pension interests. The request must be made within 21 days of being served with the application and if a request is made, the relevant part of Form E must be provided within 21 days of being requested or the date by which Forms E have to be filed with the court, whichever is the later. The person responsible for the pension arrangement may, within 21 days of receipt of paragraph 2.16 of Form E, send a statement in answer to the court and can be represented at the first appointment. A copy of the statement must also be sent to the applicant and the respondent (r 2.70(8), (9) and (10)).

4.3.3 *The provision of initial financial information*

Both applicants and respondents to ancillary relief applications must complete, swear and exchange statements of Financial Information at least 35 days before the first appointment. The Forms E must also be filed with the court. There are particular provisions regarding the provision of information about pension interests which are additional to the duty to make full, frank and continuing disclosure of relevant circumstances. In addition, the law imposes specific obligations on those with pension interests and those responsible for them to provide information. The time limits are critical and should be strictly observed (see below).

Forms E must contain the information required by the Form and have attached to it the documents specified (FPR 1991, r 2.61B).

All pension interests should be disclosed and the information requested on page 10 of Form E provided in relation to each. Today, people may have several different pension interests and it is important that each is disclosed, including AVCs (see 2.11.1.2 and 4.2) where appropriate and pensions administered overseas.

4.3.3.1 *SERPS and state pensions*

Form E specifically provides that details of SERPs benefits must be given. This information should be sought from the DSS using Form BR 19, available from DSS offices and reproduced at Appendix VII.

It is good practice to obtain a pension benefit forecast from the DSS to show the entitlement to the basic state pension and whether a substitution of the spouse's contribution record would provide a more advantageous entitlement (see 2.8).

In addition, specific obligations are imposed on the Secretary of State for Social Security, to provide information to scheme members and their spouses in relation to SERPS benefits. (See the Sharing of State Scheme Rights (Provision of Information and Valuation) (No 2) Regulations 2000, SI 2000/2914).

The client's National Insurance number is needed for both requests. For a retirement benefits forecast the client's spouse's National Insurance number is also required. Since 1 December 2000 these must be provided on Form E, so that if a client does not know his/her spouse's number, s/he will be able to locate it once his/her Form E has been served. S/he can then make the application to the DSS, although at best s/he will only have five weeks in which to do this before the first appointment. If the information is important and it is hoped that the first appointment will be treated as an FDR, it may be sensible to ask the other side for the number prior to the exchange of Forms E.

4.3.3.2 Documents to be attached to Form E

Form E also requires that confirmatory evidence of the value of pension interests be attached to the Form. If that information is not available, a copy of the letter requesting the information should be attached to the Form. This emphasizes the need to begin to seek information at the earliest possible stage and, in any event, requests for specific information should be made to the pension provider(s) within seven days of receiving notification of the date of the first appointment. Failure to do so may lead to wasted costs orders being made.

Form E should also have attached to it any other documents which are necessary to explain or clarify the information contained in the Form and specifically any documents provided to the deponent by the person responsible for the pension arrangement either following a request under r 2.70 or as part of a 'relevant valuation' (FPR 1991, r 2.61B). A relevant valuation is a CETV (see 5.3) which has been calculated within the 12 months preceding the date of the first appointment, whether for the purpose of matrimonial proceedings or under the pensions legislation (FPR 1991, r 2.70(5)).

That part of Form E which deals with pension interests (page 10) is reproduced at Appendix III. It should be completed for each pension interest the deponent has. It is good practice to send a photocopy of the relevant page of the Form to each pension provider with the client's signed authority and ask the provider to complete the form and return it together with a letter or other documentary evidence to confirm the veracity and accuracy of the information supplied. This should be done within seven days of receiving notification of the date of the first appointment since some of the information that is needed for completion of Form E must also be requested within this time and it is sensible to make just one request (see paragraph below).

4.3.3.3 Requesting information from pension schemes and providers

The scheme member

The rules provide that the following information should be sought by each party from those responsible for each of their pension arrangements within seven days of receipt of the notice of the first appointment:

- A valuation of their pension rights or benefits. The valuation must be provided within three months of the request or six weeks if the member notifies the pension scheme that the valuation is needed in connection with matrimonial proceedings or proceedings brought under Pt III of the Matrimonial and Family Proceedings Act 1984 (MFPA 1984) (see Chapter 5). If the information required does not include a valuation, the scheme must supply it within one month.
- A statement summarising the way in which the valuation has been calculated.
- The pension benefits included in the valuation.
- Whether or not the person responsible for the pension arrangement offers scheme membership to the recipient of a pension sharing credit (see Chapter 6) and if so, what types of benefits are available to pension credit members.
- The charges that will be levied for the provision of this information (FPR 1991, r 2.70(2) and Pensions on Divorce etc (Provision of Information) Regulations 2000, SI 2000/1048, regs 2 and 3, see 4.5.2 below).

Apart from the valuation, the other information should be provided within one month of the request being made (Divorce etc (Provision of Information) Regulations 2000, reg 2(6)).

No request needs to be made where the scheme member has received an equivalent valuation under parallel legislation (FPR 1991, r 2.70(4)) within the 12 months preceding the date of the first appointment. There seems to be a flaw in the drafting, since conventional statements of CETVs do not include the other information specified in the Divorce Information Regulations, although in any event the spouse of the member is entitled to this information herself (see below).

The information must be sent to the other party within seven days of its receipt, together with the name and address of the person responsible for the pension arrangement. This should arrive before the first appointment and is important if a pension sharing order is being considered (see Chapter 6) or the parties wish to treat the first appointment as an FDR appointment (see 4.3.1).

The scheme member's spouse

The scheme member's spouse also has the right to be given on request certain information from her/his spouse's pension scheme in connection with ancillary relief proceedings. The information s/he can require is the same as that available to the scheme member except that s/he is not entitled to receive a valuation of the pension interest, but instead is entitled to be told that a valuation will be provided if requested by the scheme member or ordered by the court. Where the scheme member's spouse has requested the information listed above, this should be provided within one month of the request being received.

Whilst the valuation is almost certainly the most important piece of information required, the significance of the other information which the scheme member's spouse can obtain for him/herself under these Regulations should not be underestimated, particularly when s/he is evaluating the desirability or otherwise of asking the court to make a pension sharing order (see Chapter 6).

In many cases the scheme member's spouse will have received the relevant information from her spouse as set out above. If not, then s/he will be able to request the information set out above in sufficient time to have it available for the first appointment. This may be of considerable importance in those cases where the parties wish to treat the first appointment as an FDR hearing.

Similar provisions exist in relation to the provision of information regarding state scheme rights. These are contained in the Sharing of State Scheme Rights (Provision of Information and Valuation) (No 2) Regulations 2000, SI 2000/2914.

4.3.4   *The obligations on pension schemes once they have been notified that a pension sharing order may be made*

Once pension schemes have been notified that a pension sharing order may be made, they must provide certain information to the member or the court. The importance and relevance of this information is discussed in more detail in the section on pension sharing in Chapter 6.

The information is:

- The full name and address of the scheme or provider to which a pension sharing order should be sent.
- If the scheme is an occupational pension scheme, whether it is winding up and if so the date on which the winding up began and the name and address of the trustees who are dealing with the winding up.
- Where the CETV would be reduced because the scheme was underfunded. This will only apply to occupational schemes.
- Whether the person responsible for the pension arrangement is aware that the member's rights are affected by an existing pension sharing order, an earmarking order, a forfeiture, bankruptcy or sequestration order.
- Whether the member's rights include non-shareable rights.
- Whether the person responsible for the pension arrangement requires the charges or a proportion of them to be paid before the implementation period.
- Whether the pension provider may levy additional charges and, if so, the level of charges likely to be made.
- Whether the member is a trustee of the pension arrangement.
- Whether the person responsible for the pension arrangement may request details of the member's health if a pension sharing order was made.
- Whether the person responsible for the pension arrangement requires further information before implementing a pension sharing order.

The pension provider must provide this information to the member within 21 days of being notified that a pension sharing order might be made or on a date ordered by the court (Pensions on Divorce (Provision of Information) Regulations 2000, SI 2000/1048, reg 5.) The scheme can provide this information to the scheme member, his/her spouse or to the court.

Similar provisions exist in relation to the provision of information regarding state scheme rights. These are contained in the Sharing of State Scheme Rights (Provision of Information and Valuation) (No 2) Regulations 2000, SI 2000/2914.

4.3.5 *Procedure after Forms E have been exchanged and the first appointment*

After Forms E have been exchanged each party should produce a combined list of any further documentation sought and questions they wish to be answered. A concise statement of the issues in the case should also be produced. The new procedure requires that the combined request for documents and information should be linked to the concise statement of issues. So, if the statement of issues makes no reference to anything connected with pensions but the questionnaire does, the court is likely to want to know why. It is sensible therefore to establish the issues in dispute and then compile the request for documentation and the questionnaire, rather than the other way round. Now that spouses of scheme members are now able to ask for more information directly from pension schemes, this should limit the amount of further information needed.

At the first appointment, the court can order the pension scheme to provide any of the information that can be provided either to the scheme member or his/her spouse or any information relevant to an application brought under MCA 1973 or MFPA 1984, Pt III and which is not available under the Pension Disclosure Regulations (see 4.3.3 and Appendix I). The information should be provided within one month of receipt by the pension scheme of the order, except where the court orders a valuation of pension benefits, in which case it can order the valuation to be provided within a shorter time (Pensions on Divorce etc (Provision of Information) Regulations 2000, reg 2(5) and (6)). Where an application is made for an earmarking order, the court can also order the scheme member to request a valuation (FPR 1991, r 2.70). Once the first appointment has taken place neither party can call for information from the scheme without a court order (r 2.61D(3)).

4.4 When to seek additional information

4.4.1 Generally

If the provisions of FPR 1991 and the Pensions on Divorce etc (Provision of Information) Regulations 2000, SI 2000/1048 have been complied with there should usually be no need to ask for further information. However, consideration will need to be given in every case as to whether all the necessary information has been supplied. The following checklist may be helpful:

- Have details of all pension interests been disclosed including pensions from previous employment, old retirement annuity contracts, SERPS, all AVCs and pension benefits, eg FURBS (see Chapter 2 generally and 2.20 in particular) which may not be contained in the normal type of pension scheme, any supplemental provision promised in contracts of employment or side letters?
- For each pension disclosed, have the following been provided?
  - The CETV or other value if a CETV is not available (see Chapter 5).
  - Details of all benefits provided under the scheme.
  - Where appropriate, documentary evidence of the state of the scheme, benefits, etc (see Chapter 6).

Where an actuary or pension adviser is to be used, it is sensible to show him the information disclosed before finalising any request for further information. This will help to avoid having to make further requests for information, a practice frowned on by the courts (see *Evans v Evans* [1990] 2 All ER 147) and specifically discouraged under the new procedure (see 4.3).

4.4.2 Particular cases

In certain cases, specific requests for information should be made which are not covered by the disclosure regulations. These include:

* Pensions administered overseas.
* Where the CETV does not provide enough information to enable an accurate assessment of what should be sought, for example the fund value of a personal pension (see 5.3).
* Where a pension scheme member is entitled to draw down his pension in stages. These arrangements have evolved because members of money purchase or money purchase occupational schemes are now permitted to take their pension in stages. This option is normally exercised when annuity rates are low, so as to conserve the capital in the pension scheme until annuity rates improve. This option does not exist for members of final salary schemes. Where such arrangements could be available, it is sensible to enquire whether an income withdrawal scheme is in operation by the member. If such arrangements are in place and some payments are already being made, it is important to ask for a valuation of the capital reserved rather than just the annuity payable.
* Unfunded Unapproved Retirement Benefit Schemes (UURBS, see 2.20) and SUBURBS (ibid). The terms of these schemes are often found in service contracts and agreements rather than the conventional trust deed or booklet. Copies of the complete documentation are needed.
* Where employees have left pension schemes and bought personal pensions in their place as a result of government incentives to do so, or even if they had stayed in their scheme but bought FSAVCs instead of AVCs, the scheme member may be entitled to compensation. Details should be requested.

4.5   Non-disclosure of pension scheme details

There are a number of circumstances in which the pension scheme details will not be provided. The usual reasons will be that the pension scheme member is indolent or obstructive or has simply disappeared. This can now be dealt with directly by the court (see 4.3 above).

4.5.1 Production appointments

Production appointments were introduced by FPR 1991. Any party to an application for ancillary relief can apply to the court for an order that anyone, including a third party, attend an appointment and produce any document which appears to be necessary for the fair determination of the application or for saving costs (FPR 1991, r 2.62(7)). Production appointments are, in reality, an accelerated form of subpoena duces tecum which brings forward the time at which a witness may be required to attend court with a document. In *B v B (No 2)* [1995] 1 FLR 913, Thorpe J held that an application for a production appointment should normally be made inter partes, giving notice to the other spouse but not to the body who is to produce the documents. If there is a genuine fear that notice may lead to the destruction or disappearance of the document, the application may be made ex parte.

The person against whom the discovery is sought may be legally represented at the appointment (r 2.62(9)). If he or she is successful in opposing the application, it is likely that indemnity costs will be awarded against the party applying for the order (see *Frary v Frary* [1993] 2 FLR 696, CA).

In relation to pensions, the use of a production appointment is likely to be restricted to obtaining details from pension providers and trustees which cannot be obtained because the pension scheme will not provide them. Before resorting to a production appointment, it is important that the scheme is asked to provide the information it is required to provide under the regulations discussed above and that if that is unsuccessful, an order is obtained from the court requiring the information to be supplied.

4.5.2 *Charges*

Schemes, but not the state scheme, are entitled to charge for providing information as long as the parties are notified of the intention to charge, the level of those charges and that they are not items of information for which no charge may be made, for example an annual valuation. The information for which a charge may be made and that which must be provided free of charge is listed in the Pensions on Divorce etc (Charging) Regulations 2000, SI 2000/1049 (see Appendix I.10).

If schemes wish to charge for providing information, they must notify the parties at the outset or they will not be able to levy charges.

4.6   Schemes not covered by the regulations

Schemes not otherwise specifically covered are in fact subject to the general rules on disclosure. The fact that a particular scheme is not covered by the disclosure regulations does not mean that the obligation to disclose is in any way lessened. In extreme cases, if a scheme refuses to disclose information it may be necessary to resort to a subpoena or a production appointment as appropriate. Foreign pension providers may not be obliged to provide information to an English court. However the benefits should not be forgotten, nor ignored. The legislative provisions in the countries where the pension scheme is based should also be considered. Sometimes, as in Switzerland for example, the wife of a Swiss resident wherever she divorces will still be entitled to a part of her husband's Swiss pension on his or her retirement.

4.7   Avoidance of disposition

Applications for pension sharing orders are specifically included in the provisions of MCA 1973, s 37, which enables the court to make an order preventing the dissipation or removal of assets, If, for example, a spouse applied for a pension sharing order the spouse might attempt to transfer the pension rights to a scheme to which an order could not attach because it was a pension scheme not covered by pension sharing regulations, for example, a pension scheme administered outside the jurisdiction or one which although administered within the UK could not be made the subject of a pension sharing order because it was already subject to an earmarking order (see Chapter 6). An order could be sought preventing the transfer of the pension interest (WRAPA 1999, Sch 3, para 9).

Chapter Five

Valuing pensions

5.1 Introduction

Once the information has been obtained, the value of the pension needs to be considered. This has proved to be a complex business for divorce lawyers.

Valuing pensions is not something that only concerns divorce lawyers. Pension schemes and their members also need to know the value of pension rights.

Pension scheme members may have to transfer their pension rights from one pension scheme to another for one of three reasons:

- They may want or choose to do so. Every pension scheme member has the right to transfer his pension rights from one scheme to another, as long as there is a scheme willing to accept them. To do this, however, it is necessary to put a value on the rights to be transferred.
- The employer may sell or have his business acquired by someone else who transfers the pension scheme to the new employer. Again, a value will need to be put on the pension rights which are being transferred.
- The employer may reorganise his pension scheme.

In all these cases, the pension scheme will have to put a value on each member's pension.

Since the passing of the Social Security Act 1986 (SSA 1986), pension schemes have been obliged to offer a member who leaves an occupational scheme a transfer value in respect of accrued rights. That value is to be calculated as the cash equivalent, commonly referred to as the transfer value or CETV. It represents the value of the alternative preserved benefits to which the member would otherwise have been entitled. Members of personal pension plans and those with Retirement Annuity Contracts are also able to transfer their pensions, and pension schemes are obliged to give transfer values to their members.

Although the CETV is not the only method used to determine the value of a member's interest in a pension, it is the one most frequently used by the pensions industry when dealing with scheme members.

The position in relation to valuing pensions for divorce has been much less certain and there was little consistency in the method of valuation to be used until 1996, when regulations made it plain that the CETV is that which must be provided on disclosure (see 5.3).

In the absence of any guidance, a number of other valuation methods have been used, including future fund projections.

The use of such projections was considered by Thorpe J in *H v H* [1993] 2 FLR 335. In that case, the husband and wife were 39 and 42 respectively.

The husband was a doctor and had 13 years' membership of a pension scheme. At the time of the hearing, the husband's entitlement was to a pension of £3,200 per annum together with a lump sum of £9,600 on retirement and a widow's pension of £1,600. The wife's lawyers produced a projection of future benefits from a firm of accountants, prepared on the basis that the husband remained in employment, became a consultant in about four years' time and continued to work until he was 60 or 65. The figure this exercise produced was not given in the published report of the case, but was doubtless very large. The judge, however, rejected that approach and held that:

'. . . in deciding what weight to give to pension rights it is more important in this case to look at the value of what has been earned during cohabitation than to look at the prospective value of what may be earned over the course of the 25 or 30 years between separation and retirement age.'

Following that decision, the Law Society produced a note for guidance in 1994 which said that the decision backed up the PMI's view, as set out in its report, *Pensions and Divorce*, published May 1993 (see 1.4) that the best way to value pensions was by using transfer values ((1994) L S Gazette, 6 July).

It was, therefore, hardly surprising that when the government came to specify a method for valuing pensions within divorce proceedings, it specified the use of the CETV.

The CETV has the advantage of being cheap and easily available. Its uniform use gives some consistency to the valuation of pensions in divorce proceedings. However, there are cases where it may not of itself give a fair result.

This chapter looks at the CETV valuation method, the alternatives and when it may be appropriate to use them.

5.2   Valuation requirements

FPA 1991, r 2.61B, as amended by the Family Proceedings (Amendment No 2) Rules 1999, SI 1999/3491, stipulates that each party to an ancillary relief application must exchange completed Forms E giving details of their financial circumstances at least 35 days before the First Appointment. Form E has a section specifically devoted to pensions (reproduced at Appendix III) which specifies, inter alia, that the CETV must be provided for each pension (see Chapter 4). Who may calculate the CETV depends on the type of pension scheme or plan being valued. It will usually be an actuary or the scheme itself (see the Pensions on Divorce etc (Provision of Information) Regulations 2000).

The value of the pension to be used by the court should be that calculated on a date specified by the court, which should be no earlier than one year before the date of the petition and no later than the date on which the court makes the order (The Divorce etc (Pensions) Regulations 2000, SI 2000/1123, r 3).

In addition, the pension scheme must provide:

* a statement summarising the way in which the valuation has been calculated. This is, in particular, useful for advisors to examine whether discretionary benefits have been included (see Chapter 2), what assumptions have been used to come to the valuation and, most importantly, whether the scheme

is underfunded and the valuation reduced accordingly (see Pension sharing, Chapter 6);
• the pension benefits included in the valuation;
• whether or not the person responsible for the pension arrangement offers membership of the scheme to a person with a pension credit and, if so, the types of benefits available to members under that arrangement (see 6.4.2); and
• the charges which the scheme will levy (see 4.5.2 and Appendix VIII).

This information is important to enable a party to decide whether or not s/he wishes to apply for a pension sharing order. It is not information that lawyers will be able to evaluate. Clients will need to seek advice from financial advisors with expertise in advising clients on pension provision (see 1.5).

There are several pension arrangements where a CETV is not available. These include:

• Pensions administered outside the UK.
• Unfunded Unapproved Retirement Benefit Schemes (UURBS) (see 2.20).

There is no prescribed method for valuing pensions which fall into these categories.

5.3   The CETV

The CETV is the value of the member's interest which is available if the member's pension is to be transferred elsewhere. The calculation is based on each member's pensionable salary and will allow for revaluation through to retirement. It does not, however, make any allowance for salary increases that a scheme member would expect to receive if he stayed in service until retirement. Pension scheme members are entitled to receive a CETV quotation free of charge each year until the year before retirement.

In a money-purchase scheme, the value is effectively a surrender value (see Chapter 2, Table 2.1). In the early and middle years of scheme membership, it is likely to be much less than the value of the contributions that a scheme member has made because the pension providers take their profit and costs at the outset and on discontinuance.

Defined benefits, eg final-salary schemes, are more complicated to value, although they too are valued under the regulations by the CETV method. However, many benefits in a defined-benefits scheme are likely to be discretionary and subject to fluctuation if the underlying assets fluctuate in value. Additionally, what is being valued relies much more on actuarial assumptions of life expectancy and mortality than is the case in money-purchase schemes.

Example 5.1

Mr Gray is aged 50. He obtains a CETV quote for his accrued pension payable from age 65 from his occupational scheme of £12,000. He is told that no allowance has been made for discretionary increases to pension when in payment. These have historically been 5% per annum. In this case the CETV may undervalue his pension by 50%, ie the value allowing for pension increases would be £18,000.

5.4   Other ways of valuing pensions

- **Past Service Reserve**   The Past Service Reserve method of valuation takes account of reserves which are built in to cover the costs incurred for members who the scheme expects to stay with the employer and whose salary will therefore increase both in real terms (to keep pace with the increase in national average earnings) and because of career progression. The Past Service Reserve basis therefore gives a higher figure than the cash equivalent basis and is the basis usually considered necessary to buy year-for-year credits in a scheme into which a member transfers.

Example 5.2

Mr Gray's CETV might allow for 5% per annum increases over the 15-year period to retirement whereas the Past Service Reserve might allow for 8% per annum increases over the same period (the difference representing real increases in salary). On this basis, the Past Service Reserve would be 50% higher than the CETV.

Its value in divorce cases is difficult to assess. For example, if a pension is being valued in order to offset it to achieve a clean break (see Chapter 6), is it right to take account of future earning increases? That was not the approach adopted by Thorpe J in the case of *H v H* [1993] 2 FLR 335 (see 5.1), but may be appropriate in some cases. If a pension is being shared and the aim is to put the wife in the same position as her husband by sharing his pension equally, using the CETV as the basis of valuation and awarding her 50% would not provide her with half of the real value of the fund (see also 5.5).

- **Share of fund**   This is likely to be useful where the scheme is a small self-administered scheme (see 2.19) or a small occupational scheme (see 2.11). A share of fund valuation assesses a beneficiary's equitable interest in a proportionate share of the assets if, say, the fund were wound up. If the fund were in surplus, the member's share would be greater than the CETV. If it were in deficit, the reverse would apply. It may enable a decision to be taken as to whether a pension sharing order would be less valuable than a negotiated offset.

Example 5.3

If Mr Gray was a member of a small self-administered scheme with assets of £40,000 and the only other member was his twin brother who had identical benefits, it might be appropriate to take the value of his accrued benefits as £20,000, but his CETV might amount to merely £8,000 or £10,000.

5.5   The problem with CETVs

The CETV method, for the reasons stated above (see 5.3), values the member's interest in a pension scheme at the time the valuation takes place and on the basis that the interest is to be transferred to another pension scheme. Its advantages are:

- It is easily available.
- It is cheap, usually free.

Its disadvantages are:

- It may undervalue the member's interest in certain cases because not all discretionary benefits are taken into account, nor are future salary increases. Discretionary benefits can be extremely valuable. For example, early retirement is the norm in service schemes and fire brigade schemes, but the value of that discretionary benefit may not be included in the CETV. Penalties and charges applied when calculating the CETV may also reduce its value as against the value of the fund.
- As a tool in assessing how much a spouse needs in order to obtain the same level of pension as her spouse, it is defective. For example, a more useful indicator of loss in these cases is what it would cost to buy an equivalent benefit.

Quite apart from those considerations, there are other aspects of valuations which need to be borne in mind, in particular, the fact that the same sum of money will buy a smaller annuity for a woman than a man of the same age because of the woman's longer life expectancy.

5.6   The relevance of other valuations

5.6.1 Advising clients

In those cases where the CETV produces what may be an inappropriate valuation, a number of alternative approaches exist:

- Obtain another valuation using an expert and show this to the court or use it in negotiations to argue for a larger amount.
- Obtain a quotation to show what is needed to put the client in the position s/he wishes to achieve.

The court or the other party may be unwilling to accept a second valuation or quotation on the basis that the rules say that the CETV must be given (see 5.2 and Appendix I). The rules do provide that all pension interests must be disclosed and that, where available – ie in the vast majority of cases – the CETV must be provided. That is not the same as saying that *only* the CETV can be produced. There is no requirement that an asset can only be valued in one way in matrimonial proceedings, and the value of assets is frequently disputed. For example, it is not uncommon in disputed cases to have two valuations of property. Perhaps more pertinently there are several ways of valuing insurance policies, eg auction, actuarial or surrender values. There is nothing to say that only one type of valuation can be used. In the case of *T v T* [1998] 1 FLR 1072, Singer J not only permitted other valuations to be produced, but also said that the CETV would have been of no assistance in that case. Moreover, when the use of the CETV was first prescribed in matrimonial cases in 1996, the government produced a summary paper (reproduced at Appendix I.25) which makes it clear that the fact that the CETV must be produced does not debar the parties from providing additional information as to the future value of a pension (para 4). However, under the new ancillary relief procedure, the court has great control over the use of expert evidence and if another valuation is sought, the court's permission will usually be needed and the court will probably want to make an order for a single joint expert if possible. The position would seem to be slightly different where a party seeks to ask for a higher percentage of a shared pension on the basis of financial advice she has obtained when it would seem that a joint expert would not normally be the way to proceed, although this has not yet been tested.

However, the fact that a method of valuation has been prescribed is likely to make it harder to persuade others to accept an alternative. For this reason, it is important to ensure that any alternative valuation sets out clearly why the CETV does not produce a fair result. Again, the costs' implications must be considered carefully.

5.7   Conclusion

The position on different valuation methods at present remains uncertain and will remain so until judicial guidance is given on the use to be made of different types of valuation.

However, it should be remembered that the valuation is only one part of the exercise. At all times advisers need to look at their client's position after a settlement and calculate if what is proposed offers clients the appropriate level of financial provision. The valuation exercise alone will not do that. The following chapter looks at settlement issues in more detail.

Chapter Six

How the claim can be dealt with

6.1 Introduction

As mentioned (see Chapter 3), a large part of the problem with pensions was that the court could not make orders which attached to the pension itself even though that was often the largest asset. Nor was it easy to obtain deferred lump sum orders which effectively relied on pension assets which would become payable on retirement, because such orders could only be made if the money was to be payable in the foreseeable future (MCA 1973, s 25(2)(a)). Courts were thus left to try to offset claims for pension compensation against other assets, if these were available. Sometimes, where other assets were not available, the court could adjourn or defer claims. It could also hold up the divorce on the basis that the dissolution of the marriage would result in the respondent suffering grave financial or other hardship. This remains particularly relevant where pensions are concerned.

From 1 July 1996 the courts acquired another option, earmarking, and since 1 December 2000 have been able to make pension sharing orders in cases where a petition for divorce or nullity was issued after that date. The foreseeability test has also been removed in relation to pension benefits and they have been given a more central position in the s 25 exercise (see 6.2).

A pension sharing order creates two pensions from the pre-existing one. An earmarking order, on the other hand, leaves the pension intact but provides that the trustees of the pension scheme must pay a lump sum, periodical payments or death-in-service benefits as specified in the order direct to the party without pension rights. It does not create a separate pension.

Although the court has more options than hitherto, the problem is far from solved as the previous difficulties were not confined to the restricted powers of the court. Valuation (see Chapter 5) also caused and continues to cause problems; the law now provides that in most cases the method of valuation must be through the CETV (see 5.3). Although it may be that in some cases it will be possible and necessary to argue that a different method of looking at the future value of the pension is appropriate and in some – a very few – cases the CETV will not be available in any event (see Chapter 5), the CETV disclosure in the Form E may mislead the other party and the court as to the true value of the asset and its importance in the negotiation process.

Pensions will be an issue where there is an inequality of pension provision and divorce or separation results in the loss of pension benefits. Inequality of pension provision between spouses is common. This is usually because through the marriage the spouses have assumed their retirement would be provided for by one spouse's pension. In many cases, one spouse will have nothing or much less invested in a pension scheme. On divorce s/he loses the opportunity to enjoy a share of the spouse's pension when it is paid and often the security offered by a spouse's pension on the death of the scheme member. Since it is women who for the most part have no or less pension provision and it is they who live longer, the loss of a spouse's pension is a serious problem in many cases. Similarly, the loss of death-in-service benefits if the scheme member dies before retirement is a concern, although the latter can be made the subject of an earmarking order (see 6.4.4 and 6.6).

Offsetting (see 6.5) continues to remain attractive where there are other assets available because:

- It offers certainty. Once the offsetting compensation has been paid, the recipient spouse can never lose it. Apart from orders for the payment of death-in-service lump sums, earmarking orders fail if the party with pension rights dies before retirement age.
- It gives the recipient freedom to decide for herself how she wishes to make provision for her old age.
- It gives her additional capital when the order is made, which a share of her husband's pension under a pension sharing order does not (unless she is at retirement age and able to commute some of the pension share into a tax-free lump sum).
- It is likely to effect a clean break at least as far as capital is concerned, which is what most divorcing spouses want.
- It is unaffected by the other spouse's death.
- It is tax free; the majority of a pension bears tax.

The problem is that it can leave the party with pension rights with little available capital at a time when it is likely to be needed for rehousing. In these circumstances a pension sharing order may be the more attractive option.

Example 6.1
_____

Mr and Mrs Brown are in their early 40s. They have three young children aged ten, eight and six. They have a house worth £250,000. Mr Brown has been successful and the mortgage is now only £100,000.

He has a very good pension scheme. Mrs Brown has no pension. She did not work during the marriage and left work before she had accumulated any pension entitlement. The only cash available to the family to rehouse themselves is the £150,000 or so of equity in the matrimonial home. All of this will be required to provide modest accommodation with reasonable sized mortgages for the family in two homes.

Much as Mrs Brown would like a clean break from her husband, at least as far as any capital claims are concerned; there is insufficient money available to provide her with adequate security in her old age or to enable her to build up a pension of her own. She does not want to live in modest accommodation. She and the children have been used to a good standard of living in a reasonable house in a nice area. She would therefore like an order that gave her most if not all of the equity in the house. She could buy a house which could be sold for a smaller one when the children were grown up, thereby releasing additional capital. She prefers that to a pension sharing order, particularly as she has been told that she cannot obtain an earmarking order and a pension sharing order in respect of Mr Brown's pension. She wants an order earmarking Mr Brown's death-in-service benefits under his pension (they are four times his salary at the date of his death – the maximum allowed by the Inland Revenue to cover the maintenance payments Mr Brown is making for herself and the children. Mr Brown, however, wants a share of the equity in the home to at least put down a deposit on a new home for himself. He is willing to obtain life insurance cover for the maintenance payments and would agree to his wife having a share of his pension.

Although pension sharing, earmarking and offsetting are the three most widely considered options, they are not the only ones. In a limited number of cases, it may be possible to use the defence of grave hardship (see 6.11). In some cases, the most sensible solution is for the couple to stay married. In yet other circumstances a combination of solutions may be attractive.

6.2   The need to consider pensions and their role in the s 25 exercise

Until recently, there was little judicial guidance as to the way in which pensions should be dealt with within the discretionary scheme contained in MCA 1973, s 25. Many members of the public and journalists (and some lawyers too) believed that pensions were in some way different from other assets and that spouses acquired an entitlement to a share of the pension as they did not to other assets belonging to only one spouse.

Much of the confusion was removed by Singer J's clear judgment in the case of *T v T* [1998] 1 FLR 1072. The case concerned a childless marriage of 14 years. The husband and wife were both in their 40s. Mrs T sought compensation for the loss of pension benefits and earmarking orders. It was held:

- There was no requirement in s 25 to compensate for pension loss, nor an entitlement to part of a spouse's pension: '. . . if compensation were the norm . . . the provision to be made from pensions would be considered uniquely as a matter of right and entitlement, and thus take control of the conventional discretionary exercise.'
- Pension benefits were an asset to be taken into account like other assets as part of the s 25 exercise. Thus they had to be considered, but . . .
- . . . the court had first to consider whether an order for periodical payments, secured provision or a lump sum was appropriate, and second to consider how pension contributions should affect the terms of any such order. The answer to the second question might be not at all.

The decision is also important for the judge's views on pension valuations (see Chapter 5 and below) and earmarking orders (see 6.6).

Since the *T v T* judgment, the House of Lords ruled in *White v White* [2000] 3 WLR 1571. This seemed to argue for an approach to the s 25 factors which leans more towards equality between spouses. How this will affect judicial attitudes to pensions, particularly in the case of longer marriages, remains to be seen. In Scotland, where a different regime is in force, the spouses are usually awarded the value of half of the joint assets acquired or dealt with during the marriage. In the case of pensions, therefore, the value of the pension built up during the marriage is taken and put into the 'pot' which is then divided into two. It is not inconceivable that a similar approach, at least as far as capital is concerned, may become more common in England and Wales.

It is therefore not possible to lay down any standard set of criteria or a formula which will provide a solution applicable to every case as far as pensions are concerned. However, it is possible to make some general observations as to the probable importance of pensions and provision for retirement:

- The younger the spouses, the less likely the court is to be concerned with retirement provision and the smaller any award is likely to be. This might not be the case, however, if one spouse was unlikely to be able to work because she had the care of a handicapped child or was ill herself.
- Where the spouses are older and the marriage is a long one, the court will have the parties' retirement provisions very much in mind (see, for example, *K v K* [1997] 1 FLR 35).
- Where the couple are in their 40s say, and one spouse is or will be out of the employment market for some years because of child care commitments, it may be very difficult for her to rebuild her pension to an adequate level or a level approaching that of her husband. This is becoming a more acute problem as state provision for retirement diminishes. In this type of case, it may be that courts will incline more towards awarding the wife a half share of the pension built up during the marriage (see *T v T* [1998] 1 FLR 1072, *H v H* [1993] 2 FLR 335 and *White v White* [2000] 3 WLR 1571).
- The factors specific to each case, for example health, age disparity, earning capacity, must always be factored in and can dramatically affect the general observations made above.

It is very clear that pensions are an important factor when considering the financial position of spouses after a decree of divorce, judicial separation or nullity and, as Singer J said in *T v T*, they have to be considered in every case. The law and practice in this area has moved a long way in a relatively short space of time. Before 1 July 1996, pensions rated hardly a mention in the criteria contained in MCA 1973, s 25: they appeared only as an example of a benefit that might be lost in s 25(2)(h). That example was repealed by the amendments to s 25 introduced by PA 1995 and replaced with stronger provisions.

Now, pensions are included as one of the factors the court must take into account when considering the income, earning capacity, property and other financial resources which the parties to the marriage have or are likely to have under s 25(2)(a). Other resources are subject to the test that they must be likely to be received in the 'foreseeable future'. This does not apply to pensions (s 25B(1)). It means that a pension benefit can be taken into account even though it is not going to be paid in what the courts have decided is the foreseeable future. In *Milne v Milne* (1981) 2 FLR 286, CA, the court held that a benefit payable in more than ten years' time was not payable in the reasonably foreseeable future. However, this ceased to be good law for petitions filed after 1 July 1996.

Pensions are also one of the considerations to be taken into account when looking at the benefits a party to a marriage will lose on the grant of a decree of divorce or nullity (but not judicial separation) (ss 25(2)(h) and 25B(1)). In very many cases a spouse will lose the right to a widow or widower's pension on divorce, although it should be noted that today some pension schemes deprive a separated spouse of the right to survivors' benefits if he or she has been separated for more than a certain period of time, regardless of whether a decree of judicial separation has been made or a deed of separation entered into.

6.3 Ways of dealing with the claim

There are three major tools at the disposal of the courts and lawyers in relation to pensions – pension sharing, offsetting and earmarking/attachment. These are, however, not the only ways of tackling pensions.

Although the various approaches are examined individually below, a single method is not always the best solution and in some cases it is useful to employ more than one technique, as in example 6.4 below (see 6.5.2).

6.3.1 Pensions and public funding considerations

If public funding is made available for the conduct of a case and property is acquired or preserved as a result of the case then the Community Legal Service can recoup the client's legal costs paid by the Service subject to an exemption in matrimonial cases of the first £2,500 of property thus preserved or acquired.

When earmarking was introduced there was considerable discussion about the operation of the charge in relation to earmarking orders, some of which has now been resolved and some which remains in doubt.

Earmarked periodical payments orders are not subject to the charge.

Earmarked lump sums (that is, earmarked death in service orders and commution orders) may or may not be subject to the charge. This seems to depend on whether or not the pension is subject to a spendthrift clause, although the issue has not been altogether decided. If the charge does apply and the Service wish to recoup it against the pension order they will write to the pension provider stating that a sum to recoup the charge must be sent to the Service by the pension provider and that only the Service can give a good receipt for the money. However, many of these orders are still the subject of disputes between pension schemes and the Service. In every case, therefore, it is wise to check the position before an order is made. In any event, the award does not vest until it becomes payable, at which point the charge will be recouped, so no interest is payable.

Pension sharing orders present another problem so far unresolved: are they property acquired or preserved? They are regarded as such, but they are also a contingent asset which may never be paid at all. They will only be available as and when they become paid and then the charge, if levied, could only be levied against a lump sum (and not the regular pension in payment). However, this is very uncertain territory and the position should be clarified with the Service in every case.

Lump sum and property adjustment orders are subject to the charge in the normal way.

A note setting out the Community Legal Service's current thinking is reproduced at Appendix IX. It should be emphasised that this may change, however.

6.4 Pension sharing

6.4.1 Introduction

Pension sharing was introduced by WRAPA 1999 and is available in cases where the petition for divorce or nullity was filed after 1 December 2000;

it is not available for judicial separation. It is also available for applications made after 1 December 2000 under MFPA 1984, Pt III, which enables the English and Welsh courts to make ancillary relief orders after an overseas divorce.

Pension sharing deals with a long-standing problem faced by the courts, namely that whilst they had the power to adjust pension rights on divorce, this power was in practice unavailable. This is dealt with in more detail in Chapter 3. Earmarking or attachment orders became available after 1 July 1996, but these do not split pensions. They are orders requiring payments to be made directly from pension schemes to a member's former spouse (see 6.6). They do not create a separate pension for the former spouse.

Pension sharing enables the court to make orders (pension sharing orders) which transfer all or part of a pension or pensions from one spouse to the other. The person whose pension is reduced in this way is called the transferor and his/her pension suffers a pension debit. The recipient of the shared pension receives a pension credit and is called the transferee. Although a pension sharing order is intended to be final in relation to the pension shared in that marriage, it is not of itself a final order. Pensions can be made the subject of more than one sharing order if the orders are made in relation to different marriages, and a further pension sharing order could be sought in relation to the same marriage where the former spouse had a pension which was not the subject of a sharing order in relation to the marriage. A pension sharing order could be used as a means of capitalising ongoing periodical payments, for example as long as the divorce or nullity proceedings had been commenced after 1 December 2000 (see MCA 1973, s 31(7B)(ba) and WRAPA 1999, s 85(3)(b)).

Pension sharing can only be effected by means of a court order, although orders can be made by consent. An order can only be expressed as a percentage of the value of the pension, not as a figure.

6.4.2   General considerations

When considering whether or not to apply for or resist an application for a pension sharing order, consideration will need to be given to the following:

- A pension sharing order is one of a number of ways of dealing with pensions within the context of matrimonial proceedings. Pensions are not treated differently from other assets (see 6.2 above). Singer J's judgment in *T v T* [1998] 1 FLR 1072 therefore applies equally to pension sharing as it does to the rest of the s 25 exercise (see 6.2 and 6.4.3).
- The pension benefit(s) available for a pension sharing order. In particular, are any pension interests unavailable because they are already the subject of an earmarking order (see 6.4.4) or excluded from sharing altogether?
- What options are available to the transferee when she has obtained a pension credit? Will she be able to move her credit, must she leave it in the scheme or will she have to move it. How much will she have to pay? How will these options affect her choice (see 6.4.10 below)?
- What are the options for the transferor? Will he be able to rebuild his pension if it is shared (see 6.4.10 and 6.4.11 below)?
- Will the benefit to be gained by a pension sharing order be outweighed by the loss of the opportunity to obtain an earmarking order over, for

example, death-in-service benefits which may be useful to provide insurance for periodical payments (see 6.4.4)?

- Is the scheme underfunded and will that affect the value of the pension credit? If this is so and the underfunding affects the value of the payments made by the scheme, the pension scheme must tell the applicant for a pension sharing order (see 4.3.4);
- Does the CETV give a fair value (see Chapter 5)? If not, should the percentage sought be adjusted to take account of that?
- Should the pension share being sought be adjusted to take account of the different life expectancies of the parties? This may be an important factor.

Example 6.2

A pension sharing order provides that a pension with a CETV of £75,000 is shared, with each spouse receiving £37,500. Mr Smith is 65 years' old and his wife is 62. Mr Smith will receive a pension of about £250 per month. However, as Mrs Smith is younger and female she has a longer life expectancy, her pension will be about £200 a month on recent annuity rates. If the aim is to give both spouses the same pension provision, Mrs. Smith will need a greater share of the pension. If the pension had not been shared and Mr Smith had used his fund to buy an annuity, he would receive a pension of about £500 a month, thus illustrating the proposition that splitting a pension does not result in two portions which if added together make the same total as before. Mr Smith's pension scheme will not offer Mrs Smith the option of leaving her pension credit within the scheme. She must therefore find an alternative provider to take her credit and this may prove a difficult choice.

6.4.3　*What pensions can be shared*

The vast majority of pensions in the UK are able to be shared, although they will cease to be so if they are or have been made the subject of an earmarking order (see 6.4.4). The legislation provides that pension sharing is available in relation to '. . . a person's shareable pension rights under any pension arrangement other than an excepted public service scheme' (WRAPA 1999, s 27(1)). They include the second state pension but not the basic state pension.

Pension arrangements for which pension sharing is available are defined as:

- Occupational pension schemes.
- Personal pension schemes.
- Retirement annuity contracts.
- A pension that has already been shared.
- Additional state pension rights under the State Earnings Related Pension Scheme (SERPS) (WRAPA 1999, ss 46 and 47).

This means that almost all pensions administered in the UK can be made the subject of pension sharing orders, including those in payment. There are, however, restrictions, which are dealt with at 6.4.4, 6.4.5 and 6.4.10 below.

Excepted public service schemes have been defined by regulations to cover pensions payable to holders of what are termed the 'Great Offices of State', ie The Prime Minister, the Lord Chancellor and the Speaker of the House of Commons.

Some types of pension cannot be shared. They are:

- The basic state pension, although the second state pension SERPS can be shared (see 6.4.10 below).
- Graduated pension rights where these are the only rights held by the person concerned under a pension arrangement. The Graduated Pension Scheme was the State Earnings Related Scheme which began on 3 March 1961 and ended on 5 April 1975. Graduated rights which form part of other pension rights, eg SERPS, can be split.
- An annuity which has been purchased whether or not it is yet being paid.
- Survivors or dependants pensions (Pension Sharing (Valuation) Regulations 2000, SI 2000/1052, reg 2).

6.4.4   Pension sharing and earmarking

The ability to make a pension sharing order is lost in relation to a pension if it is already the subject of an earmarking order or it is proposed to make an earmarking order in relation to it. The result of the legislative provisions is that it is not possible to have an earmarking order and a pension sharing order in relation to the same pension even if one of the orders relates to a previous marriage (MCA 1973, s 24B(5), s 25B(7B) and s 25C(4)).

If a person has more than one pension, the legislation does not prevent a pension sharing order being made in respect of one pension and an earmarking order in relation to another.

This is an unfortunate situation as it means that in some cases people will have to choose between the two types of order, when ideally both are needed. This is likely to be of importance when a spouse needs a pension sharing order but would also like to earmark her former spouse's death-in-service benefit to 'insure' a periodical payments order, as the following example shows:

Example 6.3
***

Mr Blue works as a fireman. He and his wife are in their early 40s and have three children aged six, eight and ten. They have separated and both wish to buy new homes. They will need all their available capital to do so. Mrs Blue is to receive 75% of the available capital to enable her to rehouse herself and the children.

Mrs Blue stopped working just before the birth of the eldest child and has just started part-time work as a receptionist. She receives maintenance for herself and the children from Mr Blue. She and her husband have agreed that a pension sharing order would be appropriate as Mr Blue has a substantial pension and Mrs Blue has nothing by way of pension provision. They have agreed that she should receive a pension credit of 40% of the CETV value of his pension.

Mrs Blue is worried that there is no security for the maintenance payments if something were to happen to Mr Blue whilst she and/or the children are dependant on him. Mr Blue's pension scheme provides very generous death-in-service benefits, but these cannot be made the subject of an earmarking order because Mrs Blue wants a pension sharing order. Mr Blue has no other pension. He would take out life insurance even though he could not be ordered to do so, but this is prohibitively expensive given his occupation, the fact that he smokes and that his father died of a stroke at the age of 60. He has agreed to nominate Mrs Blue as the recipient of his death-in-service benefits, but Mrs Blue knows that he could change his mind later and also that the trustees of the pension scheme do not have to follow his wishes. Her solicitor tells her that if she opts for the shared pension and Mr Blue dies, she may have to fall back on a claim under the Inheritance Acts (IH(PFD)A 1975).

6.4.5 Sharing shared pensions

A pension sharing order may be made in relation to a pension that has already been the subject of a pension sharing order in proceedings relating to a different marriage (MCA 1973, s 24B(1)).

It is also possible to make a pension sharing order in relation to a pension credit obtained as a result of a pension sharing order made in proceedings relating to a previous marriage, including a shared SERPS pension (see 2.6).

However, it is not possible to apply for a second pension sharing order in relation to the same marriage in relation to the same pension. If there is a possibility of future applications, then it would be wise for a transferor to make future contributions into a pension which is already the subject of a sharing order in relation to that marriage.

6.4.6 Applying for a pension sharing order

The application must be made within the ancillary relief procedure and must be specifically applied for in the petition and on Form A or B (see Chapter 4). It is also available in proceedings brought under the MFPA 1984. If a pension sharing order is under consideration, the considerations set out in 6.4.2 above will need to be addressed at an early stage by the applicant and her advisors. It is likely that some specialist help will be required to enable her to evaluate the desirability of seeking a pension sharing order and gain some idea of what it is likely to produce and the charges that will be made for administering it. In most cases, the transferee will either have to or be able to take the pension credit to another scheme. S/he will need to have evaluated the desirability of that option and to do that will almost certainly need to seek advice from specialist financial advisers.

The procedure for applying for a pension sharing order and seeking information is set out in Chapter 4.

6.4.7 Drafting and form of pension sharing orders

Once a pension sharing order has been obtained, it must be drafted in a particular way as set out in FPR 1991. This applies equally to consent orders.

It is normally part of an order which makes other financial provision and the order will be drafted in the normal way, but will include a paragraph dealing with the sharing order (see Appendix III for a precedent of a pension sharing orders). The order must be in two parts: the order itself and an annex or annexes to it. The annex has been produced as a court form and is reprinted at Appendix III.

The order itself must state that there is a pension sharing order made in accordance with the annex or annexes attached to it. The annex must contain the following information:

- The name of the court making the order, the number and title of the proceedings.
- The fact that it is a pension sharing order made under WRAPA 1999, Pt IV.
- The names of the transferor and transferee.
- The transferor's National Insurance number.
- Enough information to identify the pension arrangement from which the pension credit is being taken.
- The percentage being transferred or the sum from which the percentage can be calculated.
- How the pension sharing charges are to be apportioned between the parties or alternatively that they are to be paid in full by the transferor.
- That the scheme has provided the information it is required to and that that information shows that the pension is one in relation to which a pension sharing order can be made. This is the information which the scheme must provide under the Pensions on Divorce etc (Provision of Information) Regulations 2000, SI 2000/1048, reg 4 (see 4.3.4).
- The date on which the order is to take effect.
- A statement that the person responsible for the pension arrangement must discharge his liability for the pension credit within four months of the order taking effect (see 6.4.8) or, if later, the first day on which the person responsible for the pension arrangement receives the order for ancillary relief, the decree of divorce or nullity and the information that must be provided before a pension sharing order can be implemented. That information is:
    - the names, and all names by which the transferee and transferor have been known, their addresses, National Insurance numbers and dates of birth;
    - the name of the pension arrangement to which the order relates and the transferor's membership or policy number;
    - if the transferee is a member of the scheme from which the credit is derived, her membership or policy number;
    - where the credit is being transferred to another scheme or provider (an external transfer), the name of the pension arrangement concerned, the address, the transferee's membership or policy number in that scheme and a contact name or title, address, telephone and fax numbers of someone who can be contacted in relation to the pension credit;
    - where a credit is being made from an underfunded scheme which is being wound up, whether the transferee has said whether s/he wants to transfer pension credit rights to another scheme; and
    - if requested by the pension scheme, information about the member's state of health (see 6.4.10) and any other information required before the sharing arrangement can be implemented. (FPR 1991, r 2.70)

6.4.8   *Implementation of pension sharing orders*

A pension sharing order is carried into effect by the person responsible for the scheme setting up a credit for the transferee, in the case of an internal transfer, or paying the credit to another pension provider in the case of an external transfer. The CETV must be recalculated and the order implemented according to the following procedures and time limits.

A pension sharing order must always be expressed as a percentage of the CETV on the valuation day, which will be chosen by the person responsible for the pension scheme but which must be within the implementation period, defined as four months beginning with the later of:

- the date on which the order takes effect; and
- the first date on which the person responsible for the pension arrangement is in receipt of the order, decree absolute or decree of nullity and annex, as set out above, containing all the information required.

Notwithstanding this, a pension sharing order may not take effect until after the pronouncement of decree absolute (MCA 1973, s 24B(2)). Nor can it take effect until seven days after the time allowed for filing any appeal and, if an appeal has been lodged, the order may not take effect until after the appeal has been heard (Divorce etc (Pensions) Regulations 2000, SI 2000/1123, reg 9). Pension schemes also consider they are unable to implement (and that time limits do not begin to run) until they are furnished with a full set of information (including the name, address and Inland Revenue approval details of the scheme or provider to which the transfer should be sent).

The implementation period is suspended if an application is made for leave to appeal out of time against the order. It remains suspended until the application and/or subsequent appeal has been disposed of and the result notified to the scheme (Pension Sharing (Implementation and Discharge of Liability) Regulations 2000, SI 2000/1053, reg 4).

When implementing the order, the person responsible for the scheme will obtain the CETV on the valuation date and calculate the value of the credit to be given to the transferee using the value obtained and the percentage ordered by the court. The value used will not therefore be the value that had to be provided on initial disclosure. In practice, it is unlikely to be very different however.

6.4.8.1 Death of the transferee before the liability for the pension credit has been discharged

If the recipient of a pension credit dies before reaching retirement age, the person responsible for the pension scheme must, within 21 days of being told of the death, notify those whom they feel should be notified (presumably the executors of the deceased person's estate and the surviving spouse, if any) as to how they propose to discharge their liability for the credit, and request a list of any further information they need in order to be able to do this and whether or not they intend to recover charges. If so, they must provide a schedule of charges.

The manner in which the liability will be discharged will depend on the scheme rules. In some cases it will be effected by payment of a lump sum, in others by payment of a pension or both a pension and a lump sum. Regulations also provide that schemes may discharge their liability by entering into an annuity contract and/or an insurance contract to provide benefits for survivors.

If the rules do not make provision for payments as set out above, the pension credit will be retained by the scheme from which it was derived (the Pensions on Divorce etc (Provision of Information) Regulations 2000,

SI 2000/1048, reg 6 and the Pension Sharing (Implementation and Discharge of Liability) Regulations 2000, SI 2000/1053, reg 6, both as amended by the Pension Sharing (Consequential and Miscellaneous Amendments) Regulations 2000, SI 2000/2691, see Appendix I).

6.4.9   What happens to a shared pension

A transferee in receipt of a pension sharing order may have a choice as to whether she leaves her pension credit in the scheme (an internal transfer) or takes it to another approved pension provider (an external transfer) or she may have to leave it in the scheme from which it is derived, eg her former husband's scheme. Which of these applies depends on the nature of, or the choices made by, the pension scheme. The options available should have been notified to applicants for a pension sharing order at an early stage, so as to give the applicant an opportunity to seek independent financial advice and reflect on whether or not she wishes to proceed with an application for an order (see 4.3).

External transfers are the subject of regulations which provide that to be effective they must:

- be made to qualified schemes, ie those which are approved by the Inland Revenue;
- be made to a scheme or arrangement which is willing to receive them; and
- be made with the consent of the transferee. The scheme may transfer credits as long as the two conditions set out above are met, without the consent of the transferee if s/he does not provide his/her consent in accordance with the regulations (see the Pension Sharing (Implementation and Discharge of Liability) Regulations 2000, SI 2000/1053, reg 7 as amended by the Pension Sharing (Consequential and Miscellaneous Amendments) Regulations 2000, SI 2000/2691, see Appendix I).

This means that where a transferee has the option of taking an external transfer and wishes to exercise that option (see below), s/he will need to find a scheme into which to put his/her credit which is willing to receive it and which is approved by the Revenue. This is his/her responsibility and in exercising it s/he will very likely need to seek independent financial advice. As can be seen from 6.4.7 above, if the pension credit is to be moved to another provider, this must be specified on the annex to the court order, so that the decision will need to be made and notified to the scheme before the credit can be transferred.

A pension credit is not subject to tax, and does not count against the transferee's own pension tax reliefs, but it cannot be transferred into the transferee's existing pension scheme or plan if s/he has one. It must therefore remain separate.

6.4.10   Options for the transferee

The different alternatives are:

- **Unfunded public sector schemes** Subject to one exception, the transferee must leave his/her pension credit in the scheme from which it came if the scheme is an unfunded public sector scheme. This covers a large number of employees, including members of the armed forces and the police, fire and health services (see 2.9). In these schemes, the transferee must leave his/her pension credit in the scheme from which it is taken – an internal transfer. However, it should not be thought that the transferee's pension will be linked to that of his/her former spouse. It will become a separate pension and s/he will be treated in much the same way as a deferred member of the scheme. The exception to this general rule occurs where the credit derives from a pension in a scheme which is closed to new members. Where this is the case, the transferee may be offered membership of an alternative public service scheme specified by regulations (WRAPA 1999, Sch 5, para 2(3) and(4)).

- **Other unfunded occupational pension schemes** Some occupational schemes may be unfunded and while some will be approved for tax purposes others, notably UURBS, will not (see 2.20). These can be made the subject of pension sharing orders. The pension scheme can decide whether to offer the transferee an internal transfer and if it does so, the transferee must accept it and leave the pension credit in the scheme as a separate pension from that of the former spouse. Alternatively, the scheme may offer the transferee the option of taking an external transfer. Where the scheme is an unapproved scheme, the employer who has established the scheme must also agree to an external transfer and agree to compensate the transferee for any tax liability which may arise as a result of the payment of the pension credit (WRAPA 1999, Sch 5, para 3 and the Pension Sharing (Implementation and Discharge of Liability) Regulations 2000, SI 2000/1053, reg 8). If an internal transfer is offered, the scheme can make this subject to a satisfactory medical examination by the transferee.

- **Funded occupational schemes and personal pensions** Most private occupational pension schemes are funded, ie they have enough funds set aside to meet the pension promises they have made. There is, moreover, a requirement now that they maintain minimum backing funds (the Minimum Funding Requirement, see 2.18.5). In a few cases the scheme may be underfunded and where a pension sharing order has been made, the value of the pension credit may be reduced (see 5.3).

  If the scheme is fully funded it will have the option of allowing the transferee to leave his/her credit within the scheme or insisting that she takes an external transfer. If an internal transfer is offered, the scheme can make this subject to a satisfactory medical examination by the transferee.

  Pension scheme trustees had to make this decision in the run up to the introduction of pension sharing on 1 December 2000. Although there are no published statistics, anecdotal evidence suggests that the majority of these schemes have decided against offering scheme membership to those in receipt of pension credits. In these circumstances, those in receipt of pension credits will be obliged to take an external transfer.

- **State scheme rights** The credit must remain within the state scheme and cannot be the subject of an external transfer.

- **Retirement annuity contracts and purchased annuities – pensions in payment** Particular provisions apply to Retirement Annuity Contracts and those pension arrangements where an annuity has already been bought to provide the pension. In these circumstances, the person responsible for the scheme may offer an external transfer or an internal transfer. If the latter is offered, the transferee must consent or accept an external transfer. However, the transferee may be forced into accepting an annuity provided by the pension arrangement where the pension is already in payment (WRAPA 1999, Sch 5, para 4 and the Pension Sharing (Implementation and Discharge of Liability) Regulations 2000, para 9).

6.4.11   Consequences for the transferor

Those whose pensions are made the subject of pension sharing orders will find that their pensions are subject to debits. Once their pension has been debited, what consequences follow? The legislation provides that where a pension suffers a debit each benefit which is included in the CETV is reduced (WRAPA 1999, s 31).

Where employers sponsoring occupational schemes have exercised their right to opt out of SERPS, they may have may have done so by making payments to a Contracted Out Money Purchase or Salary-Related Scheme (COMP or COSR) or to an appropriate personal pension (APP). Before 6 April 1997, COSR schemes had to pay a Guaranteed Minimum Pension (GMP) which was broadly equivalent to the SERPS benefit. Since then, such schemes do not have to pay a GMP but must meet other requirements, and any pension in payment which derives from employment after 6 April 1997 must increase by 5% per annum or in line with prices, whichever is the lower. Those in COMPs and APPs also have protected rights.

All these are affected by pension sharing as follows:

•   Protected rights in a COMP or APP which is subject to a pension sharing order are reduced by the percentage specified in the order.
•   A GMP is likewise reduced by the percentage specified in the order.
•   Any shortfall in the GMP or protected rights is made up by the payment of SERPS but is borne by the transferor (WRAPA 1999, s 32).

The DSS has produced a paper illustrating the various ways in which a pension may be affected by a pension debit including examples of the reductions applied as a result of these provisions. This is reproduced at Appendix I.34.

An issue that was debated at some length was whether or not it would be possible for transferors to rebuild their pension rights up to the maximum allowed by the Inland Revenue. The government agreed that members of occupational pension schemes may rebuild their pensions to the maximum allowed by the Inland Revenue if at the time the pension credit is implemented the transferor is earning less than a quarter of the earnings cap, currently (for the year 2000/2001) £91,800 pa, so that the transferor would have to earn less than £22,950 (see 2.19). The level of the earnings cap changes each year. The rebuilding provisions are subject to the rule that contributions in any one year must not exceed 15% of the employee's salary. The rebuilding provisions do not apply to personal pensions.

6.4.12   Variation of pension sharing orders

A pension sharing order is intended to be final in regard to the pension in respect of which it is made in the divorce to which it relates. There is therefore no provision for a pension sharing order to be varied after decree absolute has been made, although a pension sharing order can be varied before that (MCA 1973, s 31(2)(g)). If it is varied any variation can only come into effect after decree absolute has been pronounced (MCA 1973, s 31(4B)).

It follows that any application for variation of a pension sharing order can only be made before it has taken effect or would have taken effect but for the implementation of the order being stayed by virtue of the application to vary (MCA 1973, s 31(4A)(b)). Once an application for a variation of a pension sharing order has been made, the pension sharing order does not take effect until after the application has been determined.

6.4.13 Appeals

Since a pension sharing order cannot take effect until after the time for lodging an appeal has expired, or any appeal has been dealt with, it follows that appeals in relation to pension sharing orders will, in all but the most exceptional cases (see 6.6.4) take place before the pension sharing order has come into effect. If an appeal is lodged, the pension sharing order will not come into effect but will be stayed pending the outcome of the appeal (the Divorce etc (Pensions) Regulations 2000, SI 2000/1123, reg 9).

An appeal lodged out of time could be lodged after a pension sharing order had been implemented. Such an appeal could only be lodged with the leave of the court on the basis set out in *Barder v Caluori* [1987] 2 FLR 480, HL. A court hearing an appeal concerning or involving a pension sharing order that has been implemented cannot set the pension sharing order aside if the person responsible for the pension sharing scheme (or the Secretary of State in the case of shared state scheme rights) has acted to his detriment. This is not defined, but it is provided that when deciding whether or not a person has acted to his detriment, the court hearing the appeal can disregard any detriment it considers is insignificant (MCA 1973, s 40A). If an application for leave to appeal out of time is lodged before the pension sharing order is implemented, implementation will be suspended pending the outcome of that application (see 6.6.4).

On appeal, the court has the power to make further orders including pension sharing order(s) against other pensions (MCA 1973, s 40A) if it is unable to set the existing pension sharing order aside.

6.4.14 Pension sharing and bankruptcy

Pension sharing orders are treated in the same way as other financial orders in relation to a subsequent bankruptcy. The trustee in bankruptcy can apply to set aside any transaction made at an undervalue. The fact that the transaction is made under a court order does not affect this. The normal period within which the transaction is set aside is five years. Pension sharing orders are specifically brought within these provisions (WRAPA 1999, Sch 12, paras 70–72). The trustee will only be able to recover what are found to be excessive contributions, and then only when there are insufficient assets within the bankrupt's own scheme.

6.5 Offsetting

Offsetting involves compensating for loss of pension rights through the transfer of another asset or cash. It is usually effected by means of a property adjustment order or payment of a lump sum or by an undertaking to commute irrecoverably a lump sum or other benefits or maintain a life policy.

Offsetting is not entirely simple and, as with other forms of compensation, it can be difficult to put a value on a claim for compensation. For the reasons set out below, the CETV will not usually be the figure to be used as the final settlement figure. It will normally be adjusted to take account of various factors. Where offsetting is being considered, it is often a good idea to obtain a report from specialist pension advisors or actuaries which can give the adjusted figure and the arguments in support.

Offsetting will usually be used to provide for the loss of a spouse's pension or to enable the spouse to make her own adequate pension provision. The former is usually appropriate in cases where maintenance payments will continue indefinitely. The latter is likely to be more applicable to cases where the spouse without adequate pension rights wishes to have a lump sum to bring her up to an adequate pension level and then to make further provision for herself. It is important to remember that not everyone provides for retirement through pensions. Many high earners make provision in other ways, for example through other types of investments. When assessing pension provision it is important to look at what is reasonable and not simply compare what each spouse has. A financial advisor may be the best person to give that advice.

The amount needed to compensate for the loss of pension benefits is likely to be affected by the following factors:

• The pension when paid would, apart from a lump sum, bear tax at rates currently between 10% and 40%. A tax free lump sum of up to 25% of a money purchase scheme pension, or 1.5 of the member's final salary can also be taken, in which case the level of pension will be reduced. A lump sum payment on divorce is entirely free of tax. One element of the current debate is how much to discount for tax. Some lawyers and actuaries reduce the value of the payment as if no lump sum had been taken, on the basis that it may not be and that tax legislation may change and the lump sum become taxable. But this has been mooted for some time on the basis that tax free lump sums enjoy double tax relief. They attract tax relief when the pension contributions are made and are not taxed on payment. Also the evidence is that most people take the lump sum. Any legislation to change it is unlikely to be fully retrospective and at the very least would probably offer some transitional relief to those who are already members of pension schemes. It is also difficult to negotiate on the basis of future taxation changes.

• The adjustment is paid in cash rather than as a pension. There is no guidance as to the appropriate level for a discount for this factor. However, the fact that the cash is available now to invest seems to merit a discount. This factor does not apply in cases where the adjustment is being made through a property adjustment order and the property cannot be sold immediately. For example a wife is given a larger share in the matrimonial home to compensate her for lost pension entitlement but she cannot sell the house for some years. Although it has to be remembered that property values may rise too.

- The adjustment is paid now rather than in say five, 10 or 20 years time. Some actuaries argue that CETVs make allowances for early payment and some contingencies and should not be further discounted.
- The adjustment is certain rather than contingent. Many factors may intervene to prevent a pension being paid: the scheme member may die; the scheme may not be able to meet its obligations. Additionally, the recipient of the lump sum is freed from the risks associated with the possibility that the pension fund will perform poorly which will adversely affect the pension that the member will receive.
- Some final bonuses in money purchase schemes are not guaranteed. Some actuaries argue that as these bonuses have historically been highly volatile they should be excluded from the valuation.
- Age differences. If the spouse is much older than the scheme member the level of compensation should be reduced as her life expectancy is less. If the spouse is much younger then it will need to be increased.
- The sum may be reduced to take account of the fact that not all of the pension was built up during the period of cohabitation (see *H v H* [1993] 2 FLR 335 and *White v White* [2000] 3 WLR 1571.

6.5.1 Existing pension rights as setoffs

Quite often the spouse who is seeking compensation will have some pension entitlement herself, although it is much less than that of the other spouse. In these cases her pension value will need to be brought into account.

6.5.2 How to negotiate an offset

The factors outlined above have to be taken into account. There are really two ways of going about this:

- Legal advisers can put a value on the compensation figure taking account of the factors outlined above.
- Alternatively, they can seek actuarial advice.

These types of negotiations are an art rather than a science. Bearing this in mind a reasonable calculation might look like this:

Example 6.4

Actuarial value of member's pension rights accrued to the date of divorce	£300,000
Actuarial value of spouse's interest	£150,000
If the settlement is to be met out of other matrimonial assets, then deduct 40% to take account of tax that would be paid on any eventual pension	£60,000
Leaving	£90,000

Deduct 10% (say) to take account of early payment	£9,000
Leaving	£81,000
Deduct 10% (say) to take account of cash rather than periodical payments	£9,000
Leaving	£72,000
Deduct 10% (say) to take account of certainty as opposed to contingency	£9,000
Leaving	£63,000

Many lawyers now use actuaries to provide reports to help with offsetting negotiations. These reports will often produce very different results depending on whose behalf they are sought. This is because actuaries operate a range of different but perfectly acceptable assumptions.

6.6   Earmarking/attachment

Earmarking orders are available in cases where a decree of judicial separation, divorce or nullity is sought as long as the petition was filed after 1 July 1996 and for proceedings brought under MFPA 1984, Pt III, as long as the application was made after 1 December 2000, which enables the English and Welsh courts to make ancillary relief orders after a foreign divorce. Applications under MFPA 1984, Pt III   enable the court to make financial orders after a foreign decree.

6.6.1   *Orders that the court can make*

The court can make the following orders:

- An order that pension scheme trustees or managers pay all or part of the member's pension to his spouse as a periodical payments order. (MCA 1973, s 25B). Such an order will only come into effect when the party with pension rights takes his pension. So if the party with pension rights dies before the pension comes into payment, the order fails. It comes to an end when the pension scheme member dies because the pension ceases to be payable when the scheme member dies. Only survivors' and dependants' pensions (where available) will be paid after a scheme member dies after retirement and these cannot be made the subject of an earmarking order. It was made clear in the case of *T v T* [1998] 1 FLR 1072, and subsequently in *Burrow v Burrow* [1999] 1 FLR 508, that an order earmarking periodical payments is unlikely to be made unless the parties are at or near retirement.
- An order that the scheme member commutes (ie converts) his pension benefits to a lump sum up to the maximum allowed by the pension scheme (s 25B). Again, the order becomes effective only when the pension comes into payment so that if the party with pension rights dies before then, the order will not take effect. The court may also order that a scheme member does not exercise his right to commute any part of his pension to a lump

sum (MCA 1973, s 25(7A)). This is likely to be sought where an applicant for an earmarked periodical payments order wants to ensure that the pension level is kept as high as possible since normally the level of the pension paid is reduced if a commuted lump sum is taken.

- An order (where a pension scheme provides benefits if a member dies before retirement (see 2.15)) which requires the pension scheme to pay all or part of the death benefits to the other party (s 25C). Unfortunately, it is not possible to earmark a pension which is or has been the subject of a pension sharing order. Earmarking death-in-service benefits can provide a useful method of 'insuring' periodical payments as was done in *T v T* [1998] 1 FLR 1072 (and see 6.4.4 where this topic is considered in more detail).

Earmarking orders are all variants of periodical payments orders and lump sum orders (see ss 25B(2), (3), 25C(1)) and, unless otherwise provided, will have the same characteristics as these. Examples of earmarking orders are set out in Appendix III.

Unless there is power to do so in the trust deed, pension schemes cannot make any of these payments unless the court orders them to do so and will in any event only be obliged to make them under a court order. If the parties agree on the terms of an earmarking order, they will therefore need to have those made into a court order and to give notice to the pension scheme trustees before filing their application in court (see Chapter 4). Special provisions govern the making of consent orders where earmarking orders are sought (see 6.6.5).

Earmarking orders can only be effective where there are benefits available to meet them. They cannot be made so that the scheme has to pay more than is available for payment to the individual pension scheme member. Since 1 December 2000, it has only been possible to express an earmarking order as a percentage of the pension benefit attached by the order and not as a specified sum.

The scheme must also notify the beneficiary of an earmarking order of changes likely to result in a significant reduction of the pension benefits payable (see 6.6.6.1). An earmarking order may not meet the whole of a spouse's needs in retirement, especially if it is made some years before the husband's retirement. Additionally, it is highly unlikely that a court would make an earmarking order for periodical payments unless the pension scheme member was at or near retirement (see *T v T* [1998] 1 FLR 1072). When arguing for orders such as this, thought will have to be given as to whether or not the provision is adequate.

An important consideration is whether or not a spouse will be adequately provided for after her husband's death, should he predecease her.

Example 6.5

An order for periodical payments or a pension lump sum in favour of a wife does not survive her former husband's death. The possibility of the former husband dying before retirement might be safeguarded by life insurance taken out on his life and/or an order that all or part of his death-in-service benefits be paid to the former wife. If the husband dies after retirement, the position is more difficult. At that point, the former wife will be receiving maintenance under an earmarking order. This will cease on his death. Any spouse's pension payable will not be paid to the former wife. If the husband had remarried, his new wife will receive this. This example illustrates why pension sharing can be a preferred alternative in some cases.

6.6.2   Applying for an earmarking order

Earmarking orders can be made where the divorce, judicial separation or nullity petition was filed on or after 1 July 1996. The court cannot make an order of its own motion and an application must be made (FPR 1991, r 2.70). The petition should include a claim for the usual forms of ancillary relief, including orders for pension sharing and earmarking as is now provided in the standard forms of petition.

The application should be made on Form A or Form B. Examples of completed application forms are shown at Appendix III.

6.6.3   Service on the pension scheme

Since an earmarking order will involve the pension scheme trustees or managers making payments direct to the party without pension rights, it is obviously important that pension schemes have sufficient details to enable them to make the payments. Accordingly, the rules provide (see the FPR 1991, r 2.70(7)) that where an application for an earmarking order is sought, a copy of the Form A or B the draft of a consent order must be served on the person responsible for the pension arrangement together with the following information:

* An address to which any notice which the person responsible for the pension scheme trustees or managers is required to serve under the Divorce etc (Pensions) Regulations 2000, SI 2000/1123 is to be sent.
* An address to which any payment which the managers or trustees are required to pay the party without pension rights is to be sent.
* If that address is a bank or a building society or the Department of National Savings, sufficient details to enable payment to be made into the applicant's account (FPR 1991, r 2.70(7)).

6.6.4   The role of the pension scheme trustees and managers and their right to participate

Trustees or managers who are served with an application for an earmarking order can, within 21 days of being served, require the applicant to provide them with a copy of Section 2.16 of Form E, that is that part of the Form which deals with pensions. This must be provided to the pension scheme either at the time Form E has to be filed with the court or 21 days after being required to do so, whichever is the later. The latter requirement is applicable to those cases where it is not possible to make an application for an earmarking order before initial disclosure due to lack of information   (FPR 1991, r 2.70(8)) (see 4.3.1).

The person responsible for the scheme may, within 21 days of being supplied with section 2.16 of Form E, serve a statement on the parties and file it with the court. This will entitle the pension provider to attend the first appointment and the court must give him notice of that appointment within four days of the statement being filed (FPR 1991, r 2.70(8), (9) and (10)).

It is difficult to envisage circumstances where the trustees or managers of pension schemes would want to use these provisions to any great extent, except where the information provided by the applicant is incomplete or insufficient to enable them to comply with any order made, where they consider an order would for any reason be impracticable or where they want to make representations about the level of expenses they wish to recover. Indeed, since earmarking was introduced there have been virtually no cases where those responsible for pension schemes have made use of this provision.

6.6.5   Consent orders

The regulations provide that an earmarking order can be made by consent but the application must be made on Form A or B.

If the scheme was not served with the application at the outset (see Chapter 4) it must be before the order can be made and the scheme given 21 days to make any representations to the court or raise any objections. The scheme must also be served with a copy of the draft order and this must state that either the scheme has raised no objections to the order being made or that if it has the court has dealt with these (and note 6.6.6) (FPR 1991, r 2.70(11) and (12)). This is easy to forget during the course of negotiations but will hold up the making of the order if it is not done.

The regulations provide (see FPR 1991, r 2.61 in Appendix I) that two copies of the draft order must be lodged with the court, one of which must be endorsed with a statement signed by the respondent to the application signifying his agreement.

Additionally, a Statement of Information has to be lodged in the normal way. It must, in addition to the other matters prescribed, include where the order imposes a new requirement on the trustees or managers of a pension scheme by virtue of MCA 1973, ss 25B or 25C, a statement confirming that the trustees or managers have been served with notice of the application and that no objection to the making of such an order has been made by them within 14 days of being served.

6.6.6   The form of earmarking orders and the procedural requirements

When earmarking was first introduced pension schemes complained that the orders were often poorly drafted and impossible to implement. This problem was addressed in December 2000 when the Family Proceedings Rules were amended to impose tighter controls on the drafting of earmarking orders including those made by consent.

Now all earmarking orders must say on the face of the order that a pension attachment order is made in accordance with the annex or annexes attached to it. If there is more than one such order being made a separate annex should be completed for each order.

The rules now refer to earmarking orders as attachment orders.

The Court Service has produced the annex in a standard form for completion and this is reproduced as Appendix III.

The rules provide that the annex must contain the following information:

- The name of the court, the case number and the title of the proceedings;
- That the order is one made under the provisions of the MCA 1973, s 25(B)or (C);

- The names of the parties and the National Insurance number of the party with pension rights;
- Sufficient information to identify the pension scheme concerned and the rights or benefits to which the member is or may become entitled eg the policy or reference number;
- What the pension scheme must do, eg what percentage of the payment due should be made to the beneficiary under the order, who to make payments to etc;
- The address to which any notices required to be sent should be sent (see 6.6.4 and 6.6.6.1);
- The address and/or bank details to which payment should be made under the order;
- In the case of a consent order a statement that the pension scheme has made no objection to the order or that the court has considered any objection made (FPR 1991, r 2.70(15).

When the court makes, varies or discharges an earmarking order it must send a copy of the decree of divorce, judicial separation or nullity to the pension scheme, in the case of divorce or nullity a certificate stating that the decree has been made absolute and in every case a copy of the order and the annex to the order which affects that scheme (FPR 1991, r 2.70(16)) and trustees informed of changes of address or bank details (The Divorce, etc (Pensions) Regulations 1996, SI 1996/1676, reg 8(2)).

The regulations make it very clear that this obligation rests with the spouse who has obtained the order and practitioners will need to notify their client that this is so.

6.6.6.1   *After the order is made*

1. The obligations owed by the person in receipt of the order

Where:

- the details supplied earlier (see 6.6.6) have ceased to be accurate; or
- the order ceases to have effect because the spouse with the order has remarried or for another reason;

the spouse who has received the earmarking order must give notice of that to the trustees or managers of the pension scheme within 14 days of the event taking place.

Where it is not reasonably practicable for the pension scheme trustees to make the payments under the order because the details have not been given or kept up to date, the pension scheme must make the payment to the party with pension rights. The trustees are then discharged from their liability to make the payments under the order. The beneficiary will not be able to recover the payments from the scheme but will have to try and recover them from the scheme member. This is likely to be a difficult task.

If payments are made in error because the party without pension rights has failed to notify the pension scheme trustees or administrators of her remarriage, or other reason makes the order ineffective, the pension scheme is absolved from responsibility if it has made the payments in good faith and the pension scheme member will have to endeavor to apply for repayments of the sums paid in error from his former spouse.

2. The obligations of the pension scheme

COMPLETE TRANSFERS

If a pension scheme member transfers all his pension benefits to another scheme after an earmarking order has been made, the transferring scheme must tell the beneficiary under the order of the transfer and the receiving scheme (who must also be given a copy of the order, any variation of that order and other information to enable it to implement the order) within 21 days of the transfer.

The pension scheme must also give the new scheme a copy of the details provided by the applicant about payment (see 6.6.6) and any notification of changes in circumstances. The earmarking order will then become effective against the new scheme (MCA 1973, s 25D and the Divorce etc (Pensions) Regulations 2000, SI 2000/1123, reg 4).

The information which must be given to the beneficiary under the order consists of:

- Notification of the transfer.
- The date on which the transfer takes effect.
- The name and address of the trustees or managers of the new schemes(s).
- Notification that the earmarking order will have effect as if it had been made against the trustees or managers of the new scheme(s).

PARTIAL TRANSFERS AND OTHER EVENTS WHICH MUST BE NOTIFIED

If a scheme member transfers part of his pension benefits to a new scheme, the earmarking order remains effective against the original scheme. The scheme must tell the beneficiary of the partial transfer and give her the name and address of the trustees or managers of the new scheme(s) into which the pension benefits have been transferred. This is because the removal of part of the funds to another scheme may leave insufficient pension provision in the transferring fund to enable the order to be complied with in its entirety. The notification will enable a spouse to consider applying for a variation if necessary (Divorce etc (Pensions) Regulations 2000, reg 5D.

The scheme must also inform the beneficiary of an earmarking order of any event likely to result in a significant reduction in the benefits payable under the scheme and the likely extent of the reduction in the benefits payable. The regulations say that this obligation does not include a reduction in asset values caused by market conditions. Unfortunately, they do not specify what should be notified. One obvious example is where the value of the order is reduced because the scheme member has taken early retirement. It is possible to interpret the regulations to mean that the duty to notify arises if a scheme member reduces or stops contributing to the scheme. This could impose a heavy burden on pension schemes. At the time of writing, the precise scope and limits of this provision have still to be clarified.

Where a former spouse has to be notified of an event likely to lead to a reduction in the benefits payable this must be done within 14 days of the event taking place (Divorce etc (Pensions) Regulations 2000, reg 5).

3.   Variation and duration of orders

Orders for the payment of periodical payments or secured periodical payments from pension schemes are periodical payments orders and the normal rules which apply to those orders apply. They do not therefore survive the death or remarriage of the party receiving the benefit of the order.

If the party without pension rights remarries, an order for periodical payments will cease to have effect. An order for the payment of a lump sum will not, unless a specific provision has been inserted providing for the order to lapse on the occurrence of a specified event. Orders for the payment of lump sums cannot normally be varied unless they have been ordered to be paid by installments (MCA 1973, s 31(2)). However, specific provision is made in s 31(2)(dd) of the 1973 Act for the variation of lump sum orders made under ss 25B and 25C.

An order for the payment of death in service benefits will not lapse on remarriage unless expressed to do so but cannot be varied after the death of either of the parties (s 31(2)(dd) and s 31(2B)). Hence, it is important to consider whether such an order is necessary at the time of the divorce as it will be too late to apply for one after the scheme member dies. If the beneficiary of such an order dies before her former husband has retired, he will not at that stage be able to apply to vary the order and if he then dies before retirement the money due under the order will be paid into his former wife's estate.

6.6.6.2   *Tax and earmarking orders*

No tax is payable on a lump sum order. The scheme member receives the lump sum tax free and his former spouse is not taxed on any part of it paid as a lump sum. The same applies to death in service benefits.

The Inland Revenue have indicated that periodical payments will be treated as deferred maintenance and not taxable in the recipients' hands. The pension scheme member however will be liable to tax on his pension payments and this will need to be considered when drafting orders providing for payments of a percentage of the pension, as must now be done.

6.7   Staying married

There are occasions when this may be the best solution, especially for older couples who do not wish to remarry. It can offer the following advantages:

- When one spouse dies the survivor obtains the benefit of inheritance tax reliefs available to spouses.
- Inter vivos transfers between spouses domiciled in the UK are exempt from inheritance tax, even if at the time they are separated.

- The surviving spouse will usually be able to take the benefit of any survivor's pension or death-in-service benefits. In some cases it may not be possible for the loss of these benefits to be compensated. This should be checked in every case, as should the entitlement to benefits after separation, since today the entitlement sometimes ceases when the couple have separated.

These factors will need to be weighed up in each case before proceedings are issued. Even if no divorce proceedings are in contemplation, couples often wish to regularise arrangements. If agreed, these can be incorporated into a separation agreement. The following points, however, need to be borne in mind:

- The pension scheme member may need to make a nomination in relation to any death-in-service benefits which are not always paid automatically to a surviving spouse.
- The spouse's position after the scheme member's death needs to be considered to ensure that she is properly provided for. Otherwise, she may be forced into an Inheritance Act claim if her husband was domiciled in England and Wales. It should be remembered that pension scheme members may make elections on retirement which reduce the amount of a survivor's pension. For example, the pension will be reduced if the scheme member elects to take a larger lump sum or early retirement.

6.8 Building up a pension

Wives who have worked before having a family will sometimes have accumulated pension benefits. These are usually small because the wife's career has been interrupted. She may well want to rebuild her own pension but will be unable to do so without some financial assistance. Alternatively, she may have no pension but want to build one up now. If she intends to work, she will be able to make contributions to a pension from her earnings. A pension share may be used to give her a base upon which to build adequate pension provision. Additionally, if the client is working part-time or has low earnings, she may be reliant on ongoing maintenance from her former husband. When calculating her financial requirements, therefore, a sum should be put in for contributions to a pension (if she is working or some other form of investment if she is not) along with other items of routine expenditure. An example of how this might work in practice is set out below:

Example 6.6

Mrs Hill is 45 years old. She did not work for ten years while her children were young and for the last four years has only been able to work part time. She has a small pension from the job she had before the children were born. Meanwhile, her husband has been able to build up a large pension through his employment. Mrs Hill will need maintenance from her husband for some years before being self-supporting and is anxious to build up her own pension. A possible settlement here could include a pension sharing order to 'kick start' her pension. Her maintenance requirement should probably also include a sum to enable her to continue to make pension contributions into another pension during the period she receives maintenance from Mr Hill.

6.9　Rewriting pension schemes

It is sometimes possible to rewrite a pension scheme in order effectively to split the pension. The great advantage of rewriting a pension scheme is that it gives both spouses their own pension which is unaffected by the death of the other and not dependent on the contributions made or retirement of the other as is an earmarking order. It may be a possible solution where the pension is the only asset. It is unlikely to be of much practical use now that pension sharing is available.

Despite the fact that the process has been carried out by agreement, many spouses will wish to record the arrangement in a court order to evidence the fact that it has been carried out as part of a matrimonial settlement. There is no necessity to express such agreements as variations of settlements and indeed if the petition was filed after 1 December 2000 the court will not be able to make orders varying pensions as settlements (see below). They can be stated to be property adjustment orders or even payments for a lump sum.

This is a developing area of law and it is difficult to be precise but it seems that for this to be a possibility the following factors must be present:

- The parties must agree.
- The scheme trustees and the life assurers must also agree. If this route is being considered, write to the pension scheme at the earliest opportunity. A joint letter from both sets of solicitors will be helpful. One complaint that pension schemes make about family lawyers is that they always wait until the last minute to ask for information. Pension scheme trustees may need some time to consider whether or not to approve a suggested split and the earlier they are given notice of it the better.
- Third party rights must not be adversely affected. The trustees will be highly unlikely to agree to any arrangement that would adversely affect third party rights as it would almost certainly be in breach of their obligations as trustees. Although, as in *Pilkington v Pilkington* (1995) unreported, noted at [1995] Fam Law 264, the process can be carried out where there are more members, it is simpler in a single member scheme because there are no third party rights to be considered. Although third parties in this context are usually thought of as other scheme members, they may also include dependants other than spouses who may have contingent interests.
- The spouses will have to bear the administrative costs of carrying out the alterations to the scheme.
- The Inland Revenue must approve. They will not approve a scheme which provides benefits to anyone other than an employee, his widow, children, dependants or personal representatives (ICTA 1988, ss 590-591). An adviser such as an actuary should be employed to carry out the relevant negotiations with the Inland Revenue.
- The spouse who is to receive the benefit must have been capable of being a member of the scheme. This usually means where the scheme is an occupational scheme that she must have been employed by the company who set up the scheme. The spouse's benefits will be limited to those

permitted by the Revenue in relation to length of service and remuneration (see 2.19). If the spouse is not or has not been an employee then the benefits she can receive under such an arrangement will be limited to those of a dependant (see 2.16.3).

6.10 Variation of ante- and post-nuptial settlements

The court has the power to make an order varying an ante- or post- nuptial settlement for the benefit of the parties to the marriage and the children of the family (MCA 1973, s 24(1)(c); see Appendix I). This provision was used in the case of *Brooks v Brooks* [1996] AC 375 to provide an index-linked pension for Mrs Brooks from her husband's pension with the right to commute a part of that into a lump sum up to Inland Revenue limits and a contingent dependant's pension for her payable on her husband's death.

It is not possible for the court to make an order varying a pension as an ante or post nuptial settlement in cases where the petition was filed after 1 December 2000 (MCA 1973, s 24(1)(c) and (d)).However the court can make such orders after 1 December 2000 if the petition was filed before that date. For that reason some consideration is given to the procedure here.

6.10.1 Procedure

The power to vary a settlement is contained in MCA 1973, s 24(1)(c) and (d). The order is a species of property adjustment order and the petition will need to make a claim for such an order if the claim is being made by the petitioner.

The claim will need to be progressed by the filing of a Form A The application must be served on the settlor and the trustees of the settlement together with a copy of Form E (r 2.59(3)). Those who have been served can file an affidavit in reply within 14 days of service (r 2.59(5)).

The settlor in an application to vary a pension scheme will almost certainly be the applicant's spouse and the trustees will be the trustees of the pension scheme whose variation is sought. It is likely that the court will wish to join the trustees as parties to the application (see *T v T (joinder of third parties)* [1996] 2 FLR 357).

6.10.2 General points

Before embarking on this course of action the following points need to be borne in mind:

- It is not clear which schemes the court is likely to deem capable of being varied in this way.
- The scheme must have a nuptial element. What this means is still not entirely clear but it may mean that it must provide some spouse's and/or dependants' benefits. Does this have to be a post-nuptial settlement or can it be an ante-nuptial settlement? At the time of writing, the reported cases have only been concerned with pension schemes taken out after marriage, so they were clearly post- rather than ante-nuptial settlements but Nicholls LJ, in the case of *Brooks v Brooks* [1996] AC 375, clearly indicated that it could apply to both and there seems no obvious reason

why a pension scheme cannot be an ante-nuptial settlement. For example, if a man takes out a pension plan or joins a pension scheme when he is single and the scheme provides spousal and dependant benefits, that would seem to have the elements needed to constitute an ante nuptial settlement.

- The court is extremely unlikely to vary a pension if to do so would prejudice third party rights.
- The Inland Revenue must agree. An actuary should advise on this and undertake the negotiations with the Revenue. The amount, if any, that the Revenue will allow to be taken for a separate spouse's pension will depend on whether the spouse has an employment record which entitles her to a pension (see 6.9). If not, her pension may be limited to a dependant's pension which is also subject to Revenue limits (see 2.19).
- The trustees do not have to agree as the court can override their wishes.
- This route can be expensive and quite uncertain. It would be wise to see if there is another way.

6.11   Holding up the decree: grave hardship

It is possible for the court to refuse a decree of divorce and dismiss the petition if that would result in grave financial or other hardship to the Respondent (see MCA 1973, s 5).

This is subject to the following very important limitation:

- It is only open to the Respondent to a divorce petition based on the fact of five years' separation brought under MCA 1973, s 1(2)(e).

In the case of *Griffiths v Dawson & Co* [1993] 2 FLR 315 (see 1.5), Ewbank J found that Mrs Griffiths' solicitors had been negligent in not making use of the defence to force Mr Griffiths to compensate her for the loss of pension benefits that she would suffer on divorce.

The argument that grave hardship would result from a decree of divorce clearly applies to loss of pension benefits as in Mrs Griffiths' case. In various decisions, however, it has been made clear that a reasonable offer will constitute a good defence. In the case of *Parker v Parker* [1972] Fam 116 Cumming Bruce J said that the court's duty was to inquire whether a prima facie case of grave financial hardship has been raised by the respondent. If so the petition will be dismissed unless the petitioner puts forward a proposal 'which is acceptable to the court as reasonable in all the circumstances [and] which is sufficient to remove the element of grave financial hardship'. This view was subsequently approved in the case of *Le Marchant v Le Marchant* [1977] 3 All ER 610, CA.

In *K v K (financial relief: widow's pension)* [1997] 1 FLR 35, the husband petitioned for divorce on the basis of five years' separation. The wife resisted the granting of a decree on the basis that it would cause grave financial hardship because she would lose a substantial widow's pension of at least £5,800 index-linked. She was 50 and if she worked until 65 her own pension would only be £3,388 pa. The husband was able to retire from his employment as a police officer at 50 with an index-linked pension of £15,674, although he could carry on working until he was 55. The husband offered to commute the maximum allowed of his pension fund to a lump sum and pay half of that proportion of it which reflected the length of their matrimonial cohabitation in relation to his length of service in earning the pension. He also nominated the wife as the beneficiary of his £70,000 death in service insurance policy. He also offered to pay the wife one fifth of his pension when it was in payment and to take out a policy on the parties' joint lives for £15,000, although this cover would only last until he was 65. The judge considered the proposals to be inadequate to compensate the wife for the loss of the right to a substantial pension for the whole of her life in the event of her death.

The judge did not dismiss the petition but instead followed the advice given by Ormrod LJ in the case *Le Marchant v Le Marchant* [1977] 3 All ER 610, CA, and adjourned the case to a date to be fixed to enable the husband to make fresh proposals. It seems that during the adjournment suitable proposals were put forward and the decree pronounced. The proposals did not however form part of the law report.

This case illustrates the fact that earmarking orders will not necessarily be sufficient to compensate for the loss of a spouse's pension as they cease when the pension scheme member dies. The case also illustrates the potential use of pension sharing orders.

6.11.1 Staying decree absolute

The respondent to a petition founded on two or five years' separation can apply to the court for it to consider her financial position after divorce. This is conditional on the court having granted a decree on the basis of a finding that the parties were entitled to a divorce under either MCA 1973, s 1(2)(d) or s 1(2)(e) and having made no other findings as to the breakdown of the marriage.

When considering such an application the court must look at all the circumstances. These will include the age, health, conduct, earning capacity, financial resources and obligations of both spouses and the financial position of the respondent as it is likely to be after the death of the petitioner, if he dies first.

It should then only grant the decree absolute if satisfied:

- That the petitioner should not be required to make any financial provision for the respondent; or
- That the provision made is fair and reasonable or the best that can be made in the circumstances.

A decree absolute can be granted if these requirements are not met or if there are exceptional circumstances making the grant of a decree desirable without delay and the petitioner gives a satisfactory undertaking to the court that he will make such financial provision for the respondent as the court may approve. Courts will be more ready to adopt this route if the undertaking provides specific proposals for provision including term life cover until the substantive application for financial provision.

6.12 Adjourning the claim

The court can adjourn a claim for ancillary relief. This might be appropriate where lack of available resources means that no just solution can be reached at the time. In the case of *Roberts v Roberts* [1986] 2 All ER 483 it was said that adjournments of up to five years would be acceptable. The adjournment, however, does not have to be for a fixed period of time nor need it be made until a pension comes into payment. For example, the prospect of an inheritance may be sufficient to enable an adjournment to be granted (see *MT v MT* [1992] 1 FLR 362), or the expectation of an award of damages. The money thus acquired might then be utilised to make adequate pension provision for a spouse.

6.13   Continuing dependency

A former spouse who is receiving periodical payments from her former husband, at the time of his death may be entitled to a continuing pension as a dependant. The pension scheme benefits need to be checked in every case as benefits vary from scheme to scheme.

6.14   Inheritance Act claims

It should be the aim of every advisor to arrange their client's matrimonial affairs so as to avoid the likelihood or chance of a claim being made under IH(PFD)A 1975 after one of the spouses dies. In some cases, if adequate provision is not made for the spouse after the death of the pension scheme member the court may refuse a decree (see 6.11). It may be possible to provide for a spouse's support after the death of the other through insurance and this is discussed further in Chapter 7.

If a spouse is dependent on her former spouse at the time of his death she will, however, have a prima facie claim against his estate under the provisions of IH(PFD)A 1975 provided he was domiciled in England and Wales. This is likely to be so if an earmarking order has been made without any other provision to take account of that circumstance.

Chapter Seven

Insurance

7.1 Introduction

Insurance can have a useful part to play in the financial settlement on divorce. There are two main areas of concern:

*   First, the value of insurance policies held by the parties to a marriage; and
*   Secondly the use of insurance as a method of guaranteeing the pension rights payable at some time in the future.

There are some policy issues relating to insurance policies:

*   **Insurable interests** An insurance policy on one's own life is common practice; a policy on the life of another, particularly a spouse, and more particularly a former spouse, is open to the question of whether the policy is valid. An insurer will disclaim liability on an insurance policy if the person who pays the premiums or who expects to gain, does not have an 'insurable interest'. For more on this see paragraph 7.6 below.
*   **Medical condition** In addition, in practice, it is often difficult to arrange for a medical report on a person who may not be willing to be insured, or who is insured without his or her knowledge.
*   **Court powers** The court has no power either to order a party to take out an insurance policy, or that a party be medically examined.

7.2 Insurance policies as an asset

Insurance policies frequently have little or no value; assurance policies are more likely to be of value because:

*   Insurance pays out on the happening of a contingency which is uncertain, eg, death before a certain date. The value of this kind of policy is usually nominal.
*   Assurance operates as a form of investment policy which pays out when something definite happens, such as on a specified date, or death if earlier. These can be worth significant sums.

Life assurance policies are property and are within the jurisdiction of the court in matrimonial proceedings. A question that frequently arises in relation to them is how much they are worth. Their worth will diminish if the policy is surrendered before maturity for several reasons:

117

- **Tax** It may be that a policy enjoys tax relief (ie, the assets building up within the policy do not pay tax on investment income) which will be lost if the policy is surrendered before a specific date.
- **Administration costs** An insurer takes all or most of its selling and administration costs in the early years of the policy. If the policy is surrendered before its due term, the insurer may take all the profits which it expected to make over the life of the policy. The surrender value of many policies may be modest, and there have even been cases where the policies have a negative worth.

Often policies are a mixture of life insurance and savings, and it is not always easy to extrapolate the various elements. Many of the savings elements are complicated by showing returns based on an arbitrary bonus system ('with profits') or linked to the underlying value of the investments (unit-linked).

In simple terms policies can be valued in several ways:

- **By surrender value** What the policy would show if it is cashed in now. Often, especially where the policy has not run for many years, this value is very modest and in the case of a with-profits policy may even be an undervalue in its final year.
- **By fund value** The insurer may often show the value of the policy if it is not cashed in. For divorce purposes this shows the greatest value for the spouse; but it does not take account of the fact that it is only worth the amount stated if it is continued until maturity – and relatively few insurance policies are maintained for their full term.
- **By sale value** Sometimes life policies may be worth more on the open market than by surrender; a vigorous market in second-hand endowment policies (SHEPs) now exists (details are available in the financial services press, eg *Financial Advisor* or *Money Marketing*).

Dealing with the policies is usually straightforward; once it has been decided what they are worth:

- they can be sold or surrendered; or
- a payment made in lieu; or
- they can be transferred to the other party.

7.2.1 Transfers of policies

Transfers may be either:

- by way of assignment, which should be effected in a standard form to be effective (Law of Property Act 1925 (LPA 1925); Policies of Assurance Act 1867 (PAA 1867)), although there are equitable assignments; or
- by declaration of trust for the benefit of another. There are several ways of achieving this:
  - through the Married Women's Property Act 1882 (MWPA 1882);
  - through specific declaration of trust within the policy (although reference to a 'wife' unspecified will exclude a former spouse after divorce, unless the court makes an order under MCA 1973, s 24(1)(c)).

7.3 Insurance policies as security

Insurance policies can also be used to secure a pension benefit which is lost on divorce. There are several areas of protection required:

• Where a spouse's pension is lost on divorce, to insure the member's life to provide such a pension.
• Where there is an earmarking order that a member's pension or part of it be paid to a spouse, to insure a member's life until the death of the spouse.

In practice, it is now possible to arrange life insurance on the life of another without medical review.

The cost of those policies should normally be paid for by the spouse, with an allowance if necessary being made by an increase in any maintenance; the continuance of policies by the member may be difficult to police and enforce.

7.4 The structure of insurance policies

7.4.1 Protection or investment?

All insurance policies are designed primarily to provide some form of financial protection, or to provide a vehicle for investment, or to provide a combination of both protection and savings. No matter that there are numerous different generic types of policy, nor that hundreds of insurance companies attempt to differentiate their brand by incorporating certain frills or by clever marketing, a layman's attempt to identify the purpose and value of a life assurance policy should start from the identification of the mix between the protection and investment contents.

Section 7.5 below describes the main types of insurance policy the family lawyer is likely to encounter, but in line with the fundamental principle described above term assurance policies generally provide a high level of financial protection with no element of savings or investment (and therefore no intrinsic value). This contrasts with endowment policies which direct almost all of the policyholder's premium (after, of course, the insurance company's expenses) towards investment, building up value for the policyholder, and only a relatively minimal amount of protection.

7.4.2 Insurance policies as an asset

Where a policy includes some element of investment content an insurance company will always be willing and able to provide a *surrender value* (that is, the amount it would pay to the policyholder if the premiums were to be discontinued and the policy 'encashed') or a *paid up value* (where the premiums are discontinued but the policy allowed to remain in force until maturity), or a *current value* (which on the face of it may be expected to resemble the surrender value but in practice might be substantially higher as the initial charges levied by almost all insurance companies may be disregarded from this value either partially or entirely).

7.5　Investment methods within insurance policies

Where a policy includes some element of investment it is important to identify the way in which the value of that investment content accumulates throughout the term of the policy.

7.5.1　Non-profit policies

Under these policies the insurance company guarantees to pay a certain level of benefit either at maturity (that is, at the end of the term of years agreed at outset) or on earlier death. The policyholder is unconcerned about investment performance of the insurance company's funds.

Although there is absolute certainty of maturity and death benefit, there is no certainty of the surrender value of the policy which will have no obvious relationship with the premiums paid by the policyholder or the number of years over which those premiums have been paid.

With such policies the surrender value will almost invariably have most relevance to divorce settlements unless the maturity date is very close (within, say, the next three years) where the *known* maturity value is significantly higher than the surrender value even after allowing for a further three years' premiums and growth.

7.5.2　With-profit policies

Where a profit accumulates investment value through the with-profits method the policyholder is guaranteed a certain minimum level of benefit on maturity (for endowment policies) or on earlier death. This is known as the basic sum assured.

Each year the insurance company declares a rate of reversionary (annual) bonus which is usually expressed as a percentage either of the (initial) sum assured or as a percentage of the basic sum assured plus bonuses previously declared in respect of that policy. In any event, once the reversionary bonus is declared and attached to the policy it cannot subsequently be taken away from the policyholder. Thus, after the declaration of just one year's reversionary bonus the new guaranteed sum assured (being the minimum amount payable on maturity or earlier death) will be higher than the original basic sum assured. This process (of increasing value) continues throughout the term of the contract and so the value of the policy increases every year.

Importantly, however, whilst reversionary bonuses cannot be lost by the policyholder once they have been declared as regards claims on death or maturity, the value of the policy on early surrender bears no relationship either to the basic sum assured, or the attaching bonuses, or a combination of the two; the surrender value is actuarially calculated by the insurer with no reference to attaching reversionary bonuses. Thus the current value of the policy (the basic sum assured plus attaching bonuses) is not the correct value to be used in ancillary relief negotiations; it is far more appropriate to use the surrender value.

In addition to reversionary bonuses, the vast majority of insurance companies also declare a terminal (final) bonus which is typically only payable to the policyholder on death and maturity claims; usually no addition of terminal bonus is granted on early surrenders. The existence of terminal bonus payments is important as they can frequently add at least 50% to the payment which would otherwise have been made to the policyholder. The value of terminal bonuses for particular policies is very difficult to calculate, but the existence of the Second-Hand Endowment Policy (SHEP) market should make such deliberations needless.

7.5.3 Unit-linked policies

Most policies issued by insurance companies today are unit-linked. Premiums under these policies buy units in an investment fund, similar in concept to unit trusts, where the investments of many small savers are pooled within designated funds. The value of each unit within the fund is calculated at any given point in time as the value of the fund divided by the number of issued units.

The price of each unit depends on the investment performance of the fund's managers which is likely to be closely related to the performance of the underlying markets in which the fund is invested (eg, UK equities, Japan, Gilts, etc).

The value of a unit-linked policy is, therefore, the price of each unit multiplied by the number of units held. There is no element of terminal bonus and no SHEP market as the value of the policy is easily calculated. This value can, and will, fluctuate. It is therefore particularly crucial, with unit-linked policies, in ancillary relief negotiations to obtain an up-to-date valuation from the insurance company.

7.6   Who owns the policy?

It is crucial, during divorce settlements, to identify the owner of those insurance policies which have an investment content, and therefore a value. This is by no means always as simple as identifying the person on whose death the policy benefits become payable as those benefits will frequently be stipulated as being payable to someone other than the deceased's estate.

Moreover, even where policy benefits are noted as being payable to one or more individuals within the policy schedule, subsequently (or concurrently) the policy may be written under trust for the benefit of one or more third parties, or may be assigned.

Clearly, valuing a policy whose original policyholder is one of the spouses in the proceedings will be inappropriate where that policyholder has written the policy in trust for the benefit of others, or assigned it.

7.6.1 Definitions used by insurance companies

The *life assured* is the person or persons on whose death the policy benefits become payable (or on whose illness, where the policy provides benefits on illness rather than death). It is the state of health (amongst other factors) of this person or these people (as there may be more than one life assured) in whom the insurance company will take an interest when determining, whether to agree to the policy being effected and, if so, on what premium terms.

However, the life assured may not necessarily be the owner of the policy, even at the outset. The *assured* is the title given to the original owner of the policy, being the person to whom benefits will be payable on the occurrence of the contingency noted on the policy (eg, death of the life assured, illness of the life assured, etc). When the proposal form is first completed and submitted to the insurance company this person (or these people as, again, there may be more than one assured) is usually known as the *proposer*. When the policy comes into force, however, the proposer is redesignated the *assured*.

7.6.2 'Own life own benefit' policies

Here the assured and the life assured are one and the same person. Thus the policy owner is also the person on whose death benefits will be paid. Clearly, the policyholder will therefore never be able to personally benefit (as he will, as the life assured, be dead) and so the benefits will pass through his estate unless the policy has been written in trust (a sensible idea to avoid inheritance tax whilst retaining control of the identity of beneficiaries) or assigned (less flexible, of course, for the policyholder). Of course, endowment policies pay benefits either on death (to the assured's estate) or on maturity (to the assured directly).

7.6.3 'Life of another' policies

These policies have an assured (that is, a policyholder) different from the life assured. On the death of the life assured, or even on maturity (for endowment policies), benefits are payable to the assured.

Importantly, for one person to effect a life assurance on another person there is a legal requirement for *insurable interest* to exist between the life assured and the assured.

7.6.4 Insurable interest

Over two centuries ago a practice developed whereby anyone could effect life assurance on the death of anyone else, even if the assured and life assured had never met. Typical 'lives assured' included highwaymen, with proposers of insurance contracts being aware that if the life assured was ever caught they would be hung, and policy benefits would become payable.

This situation was determined to be undesirable and so legislation (Life Assurance Act 1774 (LAA 1774)) was introduced which requires proposers of life of another policies to be able to demonstrate they will lose financially on the death of the proposed life assured. Insurance can, even then, only be effected up to the level of the demonstrated financial loss. Typical assured/ life assured relationships include debtor/creditor and employer/key employee.

Importantly in the context of this book, an individual is presumed to have an unlimited level of insurable interest in his own life, and also the life of a spouse. Thus, whilst a couple remain married they can (as far as this requirement is concerned) insure each other for an unlimited level of death benefit but, after the divorce is completed a life of another policy could only be effected if one party can demonstrate they would lose financially on the death of the former spouse. This could, for example, occur where the proposer is a maintenance recipient and the proposed life assured is the maintenance payer.

7.6.5 'Joint life first death' policies

It is possible to have more than one life assured under a policy. Usually, joint life policies have two lives assured, and most commonly these are husband and wife. It is almost invariably the case that where a policy has two lives assured those people are also the policy owners (the '*assureds*').

Where a policy is designated as being *joint life first death* the death benefit is paid out on the death of either one of the lives assured. These policies are commonly used to provide financial support to a spouse, but are also commonplace where a policy is effected to provide death benefit to cover a mortgage loan.

7.6.6 'Joint life last survivor' policies

Where a policy is written in this way there are two lives assured – usually husband and wife – but the policy benefits are not paid until the death of both. Thus, neither life assured can benefit from the policy (unless it is an endowment policy, reaching maturity).

Almost invariably these policies are effected to fund a potential inheritance tax liability (which does not arise when a deceased's assets are passed to a spouse, but may arise on the death of both spouses).

All joint life policies provide problems on divorce particularly when they secure a mortgage or a matrimonial home which it is not proposed to sell.

7.7   Policies assigned or written in trust

Where a policy is effected under trust (that is, at the same time as it comes into force) or is subsequently transferred into trust, the policyholder gives up his title to the policy and any benefits payable under it. The trustees acquire legal title to the policy and the beneficiaries acquire beneficial or equitable title.

Accordingly, any intrinsic value within the policy should arguably not be deemed to be an asset of the spouse, but rather an asset of the beneficiaries.

7.7.1 Settlor as a beneficiary

The settlor – usually the original owner of the policy (the *assured*) would usually ideally seek to retain an interest in the policy, perhaps by effecting the trust so that he is a beneficiary or at the very least a potential beneficiary.

However, one of the main reasons for writing a policy in trust is to remove its value or potential value from the assured's estate for the reduction of inheritance tax (IHT) liability. Where the settlor is also a beneficiary or even a potential (future) beneficiary the Inland Revenue will usually 'see through' the existence of the trust and render the assured liable to IHT on the policy benefits as if the transfer into the trust had not taken place. Thus in most trusts there is a specific clause excluding the settlor from being a beneficiary either now or at any time in the future, thereby retaining the IHT benefits of effecting a life policy in trust.

Where, therefore, a life policy trust excludes the settlor as a beneficiary it would seem appropriate to disregard the value of the policy when assessing the value of the settlor's assets during divorce settlement negotiations. However, note should be taken of the settlor's powers as a trustee.

Where a life policy does not exclude the settlor from being a beneficiary, and in particular where the settlor is a trustee, the value of the policy should, at least arguably, be considered an asset of the settlor for the purposes of any divorce settlement, notwithstanding the existence of the trust.

7.7.2 Settlor as a trustee

Even where the settlor is excluded as a beneficiary (as discussed above), but especially where the settlor is not so excluded, the identity of the trustees should be investigated. Frequently a settlor will seek to retain at least some degree of control over the direction of the policy benefits, where it is written in trust, by appointing himself as one of the trustees (or even, indeed, the only trustee).

This appointment might also include special powers relating to the appointment of future trustees and changes in the identity of beneficiaries under the trust. Such wide powers could be argued, for the purposes of valuing a spouse's assets in divorce, as retaining the value of the asset for the settlor.

It is suggested that the facts of each case must be looked at individually, but always with the above considerations in mind.

7.7.3 Policies assigned

Title to the policy is transferred away from the original policyholder and so any value accruing to the policy cannot logically be held to be attributable to that original policy owner.

Frequently, however, endowment policies (usually low-cost endowment policies) are assigned to a lender as collateral security for a mortgage loan on a house, subject to reassignment when the loan is repaid. If, following a divorce settlement, such a loan is repaid or rescheduled, the endowment policy may be released and therefore available for consideration as an asset of either spouse individually, or both jointly (depending on the ownership of the policy). In any event, consideration should be particularly given to policies assigned in this way which are close to maturity as one might expect a surplus of maturity value to be paid to the policyholder even after the original mortgage loan has been repaid.

7.8   Types of life assurance policy

7.8.1 Term assurance

These policies pay a stipulated level of death benefit if the life assured (or either of the lives assured, in the case of joint life first death policies) dies within the specified policy term. Term assurance policies are designed to provide a high level of death benefit for a relatively low cost and include no element of investment for the policyholder. Thus, there is neither a maturity value nor a surrender value and cannot be valued as an asset of the policyholder during divorce settlements.

It has been argued, on the other hand, that (at least under divorce law in England and Wales) on the basis that we should be identifying the value of the benefits which have been lost by a spouse 'by reason of the dissolution or annulment of the marriage that party will have lost the chance of acquiring' (MCA 1973, s 25(2)(h)) rather than the value of assets which have accumulated, the loss by one spouse of potential death benefits on the other spouse should be considered. If successful, such a claim could result – in particular where the life assured under the policy is now uninsurable due to ill health – in the spouse having to be granted an interest in the policy benefits (preferably by assignment) or some other trade-off of assets.

7.8.2 Whole of life policies

These policies guarantee to pay a certain level of death benefit to the assured whenever death occurs. There is no finite term on the policy which, therefore, must in all cases sooner or later pay its death benefit (in the knowledge that everyone has to die someday) so long as the policy remains in force.

There is no maturity date for whole of life policies but they do (or can) acquire a surrender value which, nonetheless, will invariably be low as they are designed primarily to provide a relatively high level of death benefit (though not as high as for term assurance) throughout the life assured's life for a given level of premium, with little emphasis on investment content.

Whole of life policies may be either non-profit (guaranteed, and fixed, level of death benefit), with-profit (guaranteed minimum level of death benefit, increasing every year with the addition of bonuses), or unit-linked (with the level of death benefit being the greater of a guaranteed sum assured and the value of the units standing to the credit of the policy at the date of death).

7.8.3 Endowment policies

These policies pay a benefit at the end of a predetermined period of years, this date being known as the maturity date, or on the life assured's earlier death.

Endowment policies are designed primarily as a vehicle for savings and investments, and usually include only a minimal amount of death benefit. As such, a surrender value accumulates relatively quickly.

Endowment policies may be either non-profit (guaranteed and fixed, level of death *and* maturity benefit), with-profit (guaranteed minimum level of death and maturity benefit, increasing every year with the addition of bonuses), or unit-linked (with the level of death benefit being the greater of a basic sum assured and the value of the units standing to the credit of the policy at the date of death, and the maturity benefit being the value of the units at maturity).

7.8.4 Life assured in ill health

Whatever is agreed between the parties as to the value to be considered, or not, of a particular life assurance policy, the surrender of the policy (or 'lapse' as it might perhaps more accurately be described, as the policy has no value to surrender) should be avoided at all costs where the life assured has since the inception of the policy become uninsurable, usually due to progressive deterioration of health. If, for whatever reason, the policyholder allows this policy to lapse he could find replacement life assurance difficult or impossible

to acquire or, at the very least, much more expensive than for proposed lives
assured in better health.

Such a consideration is particularly important for *own life own benefit* policies
where the policyholder (the *assured*) is the same person as the *life assured*.

7.9   The second-hand policy market

Progressively becoming known as the Traded Endowment Policies (TEPs) or
Traded Insurance Policies (TIPs), a Second-Hand Endowment Policy (SHEP)
is a policy which is sold (assigned) from the original policyholder to a third
party for a consideration greater than the policy's surrender value (quoted by
the insurance company).

7.9.1   Why might a third party offer a higher value than the insurance
company which issued the policy?

First, such a situation only arises with the 'traditional' non-profit and (more
frequently) with-profit policies. Unit-linked policies are never the subject of
SHEP sales. Under those traditional policies the insurer guarantees the level,
or minimum level, or maturity and death benefit. For with-profits policies
once a reversionary bonus has been declared it cannot subsequently be
withdrawn if the policy is held to maturity. For both reasons the insurance
company carries at least some of the risk of future investment returns on its
fund falling short of projections and thus will usually adopt a conservative
approach to bonus declarations and surrender declarations – in the latter case
because generous surrender values could lead to a high level of early
surrenders which could decimate the fund to the extent that continuing
policyholders could be detrimentally affected.

This conservatism, though, has in many instances led to surrender values
falling well short of what might be calculated or estimated as being fair,
projecting the policy forward to its maturity value at which time terminal
bonuses will usually be added to significantly increase the eventual payout
to the policyholder. This is where an outside investor (in some cases
institutional investors) can identify a value higher than that offered by the
insurance company, yet still at a level which gives it a realistic expectation
of above average annual growth rates with (arguably) a low degree of risk
(that future bonus rates fall short of expectations).

Everyone wins. The insurance company wins because it suffers a lower
level of early surrenders. The policyholder wins by obtaining a value from
the SHEP market higher than he would have received on surrender. The
investor wins (he hopes) from an attractive rate of growth over a known
future term of years.

7.9.2   In the interests of which spouse?

Which spouse benefits from a SHEP quotation higher than the surrender
value? The spouse claiming against that value will clearly benefit as the
claim for value will be higher. In this respect, one might perceive the
policyholder spouse to be the loser but it is always open to that spouse to sell

the policy on the SHEP market for a higher amount than he would have received as a surrender value. Thus, arguably, both spouses can benefit unless the policyholder funds the spouse's claim from other resources and plans to maintain the premiums under the policy in question.

7.9.3 *Fixed price sale, or auction*

Most companies will offer a fixed price to the seller of a suitable life policy (usually a with-profits endowment policy) on receipt of certain details of the policy which may be telephoned, posted, or faxed to their office. The seller therefore knows in advance how much he will receive.

In far fewer instances the policyholder may instead send his policy details to be auctioned at frequent dedicated insurance policy auctions, usually stipulating a reserve price. Subject to that reserve (which should clearly be pitched at least as high as the surrender value from the insurance company) being exceeded, the policyholder cannot accurately predict in advance how much will be the consideration he will receive and may, accordingly, fare somewhat better or worse than a fixed price sale.

7.9.4 *Obtaining a quotation*

Free quotations are readily available from around 20 SHEP market makers (see 7.2). The divorce lawyer can then use the quotation in negotiations. Quotations can vary quite dramatically between market makers and so it is advisable to approach several market makers in each instance.

Should the policyholder subsequently decide to sell his policy through these channels, almost all market makers are prepared to pay a commission to an introducer of (usually) 3% of the sale proceeds. This could potentially be claimed by the introducing solicitor, or (see the next section) by a 'SHEP broker'.

7.9.5 *SHEP brokers*

There are a small, but increasing, number of intermediaries who specialise in broking a policy's details around all (or at least most) of the SHEP market makers to obtain the highest quotation for a sale. Very often their efforts result in a significantly higher value than could have been obtained by an approach to only one or two market makers.

7.10 Protecting maintenance payments

In this section the possible use of insurance policies to protect value of periodic maintenance payments is considered.

7.10.1 *The need*

Should the death of a maintenance payer occur prior to that of the recipient, those maintenance payments will usually cease. For this reason it could legitimately be argued that all maintenance recipients should seriously consider effecting a life assurance policy on the life of the maintenance payer for a sum assured sufficient to provide a continuation of the maintenance payments. Reluctance by such a recipient on the grounds of affordability of premiums should be set against the likely parlous state of finances on the maintenance-payer's untimely death. Perhaps agreement (with appropriate undertakings) for the maintenance payer to meet the cost of the premiums could be reached as an integral part of the divorce settlement. Insurance may also be a useful way of providing cover for children's maintenance and school fees. Frequently a decreasing term order may be most appropriate.

7.10.2 Inheritance Act 1975 (IHA 1975)

However, there may in some instances be sound reasons why the maintenance payer should be willing or even eager to effect such a policy and pay the premiums. Under the provisions of the Inheritance Act 1975 (IHA 1975), an individual may be able to claim against the estate of a former spouse if that individual is receiving maintenance payments from that former spouse at the time of his death. Where such a claim is successfully made, the executors of the deceased's estate would normally negotiate a lump sum settlement rather than one based on continuing maintenance payments. In any event, a payment from the value of the estate to a former spouse is almost certainly not what the deceased would have envisaged, especially where he or she has remarried – possibly with children by that marriage.

Where the possibility of a claim under the Act is recognised and there is a desire to protect the estate, then it is the practise of certain solicitors to seek an undertaking from the maintenance recipient, during ancillary relief deliberations and negotiations, to forego future rights to such a claim. Unless some additional benefit is given to that spouse to protect her future position, such an undertaking should not generally be given. However, where the maintenance payer undertakes to effect and maintain the premiums for a suitable life assurance policy with an appropriate sum assured (to continue maintenance payments after his death) against the maintenance recipient's undertaking to waive all rights to a claim under the Inheritance Act then a satisfactory conclusion may be identified; the maintenance recipient protects his or her income and the maintenance payer protects his or her estate.

7.10.3 Suitable policies

Suitable policies include term assurance policies where the term of the need is known, or whole of life policies (which, for the same level of death benefit, have higher premiums) where the term of the need is not known and may transpire to be of long duration. A policy with an increasing sum assured may be advisable in some circumstances.

7.10.4 How the policy should be written

A policy could be effected on an *own life own benefit* basis by the maintenance payer. For absolute security for the recipient this policy can then be assigned but this, of course, loses the flexibility for the life assured (that is, the maintenance payer) to subsequently amend the beneficial interest in the policy if, for example, the maintenance payments cease and there accordingly becomes no further need for protection of the spouse.

It is better, then, for the maintenance payer (but not for the recipient) to write this policy in trust for the spouse in the first instance, but with the maintenance payer as trustee with power to amend the beneficiary. Even more preferable for the maintenance payer is to effect an own life own benefit policy with the benefits falling to his estate or the beneficiaries of his estate (under his will). In this way, a sum assured is provided to his nominated beneficiaries which is designed to be sufficient to meet the likely cost of a successful claim under the Inheritance Act, noting that the payment under the policy would then be available to his beneficiaries personally as additional capital if a claim under that Act is not made, or is unsuccessful.

Alternatively, a *life of another policy* could be effected by the maintenance recipient on the life of the maintenance payer.

Whichever method is used, the policy can be effected at the time of the divorce (with the issue of premium payer being a part of the divorce settlement) or subsequently.

7.11 Life assurance and earmarked pension awards

Earmarking awards have been available for several years as an alternative to other solutions in respect of claims against the value of a spouse's pension rights, in divorce settlements.

The role of life assurance, alongside earmarking awards, should be appreciated.

7.11.1 Protecting an earmarked award – pension

Earmarked awards terminate on the death of either the pension scheme member (against whose rights the award has been made) or that member's spouse. It could therefore be considered prudent for the spouse, having successfully applied for such an award, to effect life assurance on the scheme member to a level that recompenses, on his death, the value of the lost ongoing rights to the earmarked award. Without this protection an apparently valuable earmarked award could prove worthless on the untimely death of the pension scheme member.

Suitable policies include term assurance (if the protection is only needed in the event of death during a limited time period) and whole of life policies (in recognition that pension benefits are payable throughout the member's lifetime, although the additional cost of this policy over term assurance may be prohibitive).

7.11.2 Protecting an earmarked award – lump sum death-in-service

If account has not or cannot be taken, in the ancillary relief settlement, of the value of the spouse's lost interest in lump sum death-in-service benefit (commonly a feature of occupational pension schemes) a life assurance policy as described above should have a sum assured sufficient not only to replace the lost earmarked pension award, but also the lost value of this lump sum payment.

Here, a term assurance policy is likely to be most appropriate as the benefit expires on the pension scheme member's retirement.

7.12 Summary

Life assurance policies seem destined to become an increasingly important aspect in divorce settlements, whether as an asset to be valued, a policy to protect future maintenance payments or a policy to insure against the death of a scheme member against whom an earmarked pension award has been granted.

Chapter Eight

After the divorce

8.1 Introduction

With the proliferation of both the varieties of pension rights and the three main remedies available to divorcing parties, the planning for members and their spouses after divorce has become a significant element in financial advising after divorce. In practice, many parties will be too financially stretched to think much about rebuilding pensions, or have other priorities.

One issue is that in some cases, at least so far as pensions are concerned, the best advice would be to stay married, even if living apart, since in most cases the survivor's benefits will be paid as of right to the widow/widower. However, some schemes now exclude separated spouses from being regarded as a survivor automatically entitled to rights, and in personal pension arrangements (and the former retirement annuity policies) a spouse's pension is an option, so may not be available in any event. And finally, as ever, any death-in-service benefits are payable at the discretion of the trustees. But remaining married, in a few cases, may be a viable option (and see 6.7).

Once the divorce has been completed, however, there is little going back, and the paragraphs below explore some of the practice to be carried out by the parties and some options available to them.

8.2 Dependency

Regardless of any arrangement on divorce, or even as a consequence of a divorce, a former spouse can be regarded as a dependent by trustees, and therefore deserving of a dependent's pensions, if any. This is payable at the discretion of trustees, but today it is not always essential to prove financial dependency. The member of the scheme has a number of options available following a divorce, depending on the nature of any order made against his pension rights. However, the payment of dependant's benefits cannot be guaranteed in any way, and the level of any pensions will always be uncertain. On the other hand, sometimes trustees can be sympathetic to hard-luck cases, but if no application is made, no benefit will be paid. An ex-spouse should always, therefore, make her position known to the trustees on the death of the member (see 6.13).

8.3 The use and abuse of insurance

Insurance, as explained in Chapter 7, can be a useful tool to ensure payment of benefits or in lieu of benefits where direct pension payments cannot be achieved. In practice, however, there are only a few areas where insurance after the divorce can make a material difference, especially where the former husband is older and where insurance premiums will be high. It is sometimes thought that life insurance can produce money out of thin air, and while it can do in some cases, it requires both the happening of an event (which may not happen) and the payment of a premium or series of premiums (which may not be affordable).

8.4   Moving overseas

Members can find that they need to move or even transfer their domicile overseas. Transferring pension rights overseas today is much easier than before, but it is not always clear that enforcement of an earmarking order can be made easily against an overseas scheme, even where registered in a local jurisdiction, since overseas scheme may have prohibitions (such as the UK once had) against court interference in pension rights.

Some scheme members may have transferred their rights overseas, especially where they enjoy the benefits of a funded unapproved retirement benefits scheme, so as to put them out of the earmarking or sharing jurisdiction of the UK courts. Such assets must of course nonetheless always be declared.

8.5   Joint membership

It is not that rare to find that both spouses are members of a particular pension scheme, especially an occupational scheme. Such arrangements should pose few difficulties in practice, although schemes may need to amend their administrative systems to ensure that Inland Revenue tax capping does not apply to a spouse with a pension credit in the usual way.

8.6   Enforcement

Enforcement is rarely an issue. Scheme managers and trustees if served with an order will invariably comply, provided it is a valid order and one which is within their powers to follow.

In other cases, a simple court application will ensure compliance, but it should be noted that enforcement overseas is all but impossible.

8.7   The use of the Inheritance (Provision for Family and Dependants) Act 1975

If with hindsight a pension arrangement turns out to be worth much more than was originally anticipated, it may be possible to seek an order for variation under the Inheritance (Provision for Family and Dependants) Act 1975 (IH(PFD)A 1975). Death-in-service benefits when paid will not normally be available under the Act, since they will not fall within the estate. It is normally employed only as a last resort, and depends on the spouse's reasonable needs at the time of death. It is also an uncertain remedy, depending on the assets available at death and the interests of competing claims (see 6.14).

8.8   Use of income drawdown and phased annuities

Particular issues apply where there is a sharing order applied to a personal pension, often a self-invested personal pension, where income drawdown applies. Income drawdown is an arrangement whereby a personal pension scheme member can decide how much of the fund value of a personal pension to withdraw before being compelled to buy an annuity at the age of 75. These payments are flexible, being broadly between 35% and 100% of what the annuity would have been. Any earmarking order will therefore need to be flexible enough to cope with the flexibility of such payments; recalcitrant husbands may need to be encouraged, perhaps by court orders, to disclose how much is being paid in any one year. The problem for a former spouse, of course, is that the member can decide not only when to start drawing but also how much to draw at any one time. It may also be useful to note that on death, if there is any money remaining in the fund, it is taxed at 35% before being paid to the personal representatives.

8.9   Rebuilding pension rights

8.9.1 Scheme member

Individuals who are members who have had some of their pension rights shared with a former spouse may find that the pension rights that remain are insufficient for their needs. If the divorced member earns below one-quarter of the earnings cap (which in 2000/01 is £91,800, ie £22,950) and is in a salary-related scheme, any pension debit can be ignored (if the employer agrees). How the missing pension is to be replaced is up to an agreement between the employer and employee, presumably by additional contributions in some way.

Other divorced members have other options open to them, depending on their particular situation. The position is deeply confusing:

- If he is not in an occupational scheme, they may simply make additional contributions to any personal pension they have, to make use of their existing limits as follows:
  Up to age 50   17.5%
  51–55   20.0%
  56–60   22.5%
  60–74   27.5%
- If he is in an occupational scheme approved under a new tax regime (ie one that has a limit on contributions that applies to personal pensions) and has not earned more than £30,000 pa in any of the five previous tax years, not including tax years before 2000/01, he can raise his contributions to the level permitted by the scheme, and make contributions in addition (if they do not exceed the limits above) to a separate stakeholder pension up to £3,600 pa. In the alternative, he may wish to make additional voluntary contributions up to the Revenue maxima.
- If he is in an occupational pension approved under the old regime, ie with different benefit restrictions, or a salary-related scheme, and he is not a controlling director and does not earn more than £30,000 as above, in addition, he may wish to make additional voluntary contributions as set out above. In this case there are, of course, no contribution caps as in the first bulleted point,

although there are other 'headroom checks' to ensure that excess benefits are not gained; these checks do not apply to stakeholder contributions.

The difficulty in most cases is that people earning under these limits do not normally have substantial disposable income from which to make such contributions.

8.9.2   *Former spouse*

The ex-spouse has a number of options open to her. If she has a sharing order, she may of course seek to have her pension credit stay with the former spouse's pension scheme, if they will permit it, or if the scheme is seriously underfunded. She may wish to have the transfer payment of the pension credit paid to another occupational scheme or to perhaps a personal pension or stakeholder pension. Such payments do not count towards her Revenue limits and she is free to use any tax breaks she may have in addition. If she does not give notice to the paying scheme in time, they may have a default insurance company to pay it to.

Where she has an earmarking order in her favour, she must be meticulous in informing the pension scheme managers or trustees as to her address or any change of address.

If she moves address and fails to inform the trustees, they may, if they cannot trace her, pay her former spouse instead. She must also tell them if she remarries, and her personal representatives must inform them of her death, so that they can stop paying any earmarked pension, although earmarked lump sums remain payable.

Former spouses now (from April 2001) have the right to make contributions to a stakeholder pension arrangement of up to £3,600 pa without the need to have net relevant or other earnings. Contributions to personal pensions and occupational schemes can only be made out of earnings. While there is clearly no immediate tax advantage in making such contributions, and the funds in a pension scheme are locked away until retirement, the investments within a stakeholder are by and large untaxed, and the opportunity will prove attractive to many former spouses.

8.10   Insolvency

In relation to personal insolvencies (bankruptcies) that took place after 29 May 2000, pension rights are generally not taken as part of the estate of the bankrupt (WRAPA 1999, ss11–16; Welfare Reform and Pensions Act 1999 (Commencement No 7) Order 2000, SI 2000/1382, art 2(a)). Bankruptcy orders should not therefore affect any earmarking orders to pay pensions or lump sums. In any event, such orders could not have affected a sharing order in the usual course of events.

However, this protection against bankruptcy does not apply to non-approved pension arrangements, such as funded unapproved pension schemes (FURBS) or unfunded unapproved pension schemes (UURBS). In practice it may be that potential bankrupts will remove such schemes to an offshore jurisdiction, where protective trusts may bite so that the trustee in bankruptcy cannot attack them, although they will of course have to be disclosed.

Accordingly, in most cases, subsequent bankruptcy of a member after an order for sharing or earmarking has been made should not now make any difference to an ex-spouse.

Rights which have not yet been acquired as a result of a pensions sharing order (ie pension credits) but are about to be are also categorically protected (WRAPA 1999, s 11(12) and the Insolvency Act 1986, s 342D–F).

Chapter Nine

Implications for pension scheme practice

9.1   Background

Pension fund design is based, due to Revenue constraints and inertia, on the social norms of many years ago. Pension schemes designed in the 1920s, when the present structure emerged, did not expect a significant number of divorces amongst their membership, and the Revenue rules under which pension schemes operate reflected that different society.

If ever those Revenue rules were appropriate, by 1990 they no longer remained so. Over the last quarter century, in particular, family structures changed substantially. First, the incidence of marriage was and is falling significantly. There were 436,000 marriages in 1974; in 1995 there were 322,000, a fall of around one-quarter. At the same time, the incidence of divorce was and is rising, equally significantly. There were 113,500 divorces in 1974 and 155,500 in 1995, an increase of over one-third. The implication for pension funds was clear; an increasing proportion of scheme members, deferred members and retired members are divorced, some more than once. So far as pensioners are concerned, only around 3% are presently divorced, but by 2025, the percentage is expected to have risen to about 13%. Pension funds are therefore likely to be paying fewer spouse's pensions, and complying with more court orders in respect of earmarking or sharing. What is not clear, however, is the volume of such orders; some expect substantial numbers of pensions sharing; others expect a modest growth. It is thought, for example, that there have been relatively few earmarking orders since their introduction in 1996 – perhaps fewer than 1,000 in a pension scheme membership of around ten million.

The areas where pension schemes are having some difficulty, however, are those involving cohabitation and same-sex relationships. Proposals have been published that such relationships should carry property rights equivalent to marriage; as yet, however, there are no firm indications of developments and this chapter does not deal with the issue.

The law has now, as explained in earlier chapters, been amended to reflect these societal changes. Pension schemes are now faced with coping with two major reforms in the last five years: they have to be able to recognise in their administrative structures the possibilities and consequences of a court order for earmarking or for sharing (or indeed multiple orders).

9.1.1 Earmarking and sharing in principle

There are conflicting views as to which of the new remedies are the easier for schemes to administer.

Some consider that earmarking is less troublesome. In 1996, PA 1995, s 166 gave the courts jurisdiction to make orders against pension scheme trustees for the first time, a power eventually known as earmarking. Under earmarking, the member's pension rights continue in the scheme, but part of the pension or commuted lump sum is earmarked for the former spouse – payable directly to the former spouse from the same date as the member's own benefits become payable. The administration system needs to cope with the need to endorse member's rights with the order, to implement the order when the time comes, to distinguish and calculate periodical payment and lump sum orders, and to endorse transfers with the order when they occur. It also needs to reflect the fact that Scottish court orders, which differ markedly (no earmarking can be made against the member's pension), need to be separately recorded. Orders may also be made in relation to any lump sum death benefit, in which case the sum due becomes payable on the death of the member or pensioner.

For divorcing couples, there were (and are) disadvantages with earmarking both in principle and in practice (see 6.4.4). This was the reason for the introduction of sharing, formerly known as splitting.

In sharing, the member's benefits are valued and shared out between him and the spouse at the time of divorce, so that two separate pension entitlements arise. Where the scheme rules permit, it is possible for both the member and the spouse to keep their rights within the scheme (the internal scheme option) – the (ex-)spouse is largely treated as a deferred pensioner. If the spouse transfers her rights to another pension scheme or arrangement outside the scheme (the external scheme option), the scheme is immune from further liability (WRAPA 1999, Pt IV, Schs 3, 6 and 9).

However, the way in which the operation of sharing is designed is intended broadly to try to protect schemes from excessive expense and disruption. The provisions are set out in regulations of quite extraordinary (and unnecessary) complexity. Sharing applies not only to direct rights under occupational schemes, but also to rights under a personal pension, SERPS and other pension arrangements (eg insurance contract or retirement annuity premium, stakeholder pensions). It does not apply to the basic state pension and only in a half-hearted way to public sector unfunded schemes. In particular:

- There is no retrospection; sharing orders can only be made against schemes by the court in proceedings on divorce and annulment (not judicial separation) provided they are issued after 1 December 2000.
- There is no compulsion on the parties to share (unless the court requires it); offsetting and earmarking remain as options, and will often be preferred.
- Unfunded public sector schemes are not subject to external transfers.
- Funded schemes have the choice of applying the internal or external option.
- There is no need for contracted-out schemes to have separate certification to hold 'safeguarded rights' (ie contracted-out rights which form part of a pension share).
- There is a much-criticised delay in the introduction of the sharing of state benefits.

A member who enters into an agreement to pension share, or in respect of whom a court has made a sharing order, is subject to a pension debit; the spouse receives an equivalent credit. The member's rights are calculated on a cash equivalent basis and spouses can argue for whatever percentage of cash equivalent they think right (up to 100%).

Discretionary benefits are not normally taken into account (unless the trustees decide otherwise). Money purchase schemes can make a 'once and for all' reduction.

Schemes may charge the reasonable costs of sharing to the individuals concerned, and a scale is being introduced.

9.2   Policy issues for pension funds

There are several practical concerns for scheme trustees and administrators.

First is the setting of policy guidelines. Trustees will need to set out principles indicating whether, for example, earmarking and sharing should apply to death-in-service benefits, and whether the cash equivalent method (or some other method) be used as the appropriate basis of valuation for these benefits. It is too early to indicate the way in which most trustees are moving, but the expectation is that most trustees will elect for the restrictive options, at least in the early stages.

Second is the issue of maintaining proper administration. It is crucial for schemes to ensure that the orders are both compliable and complied with. Third, there is the question of how much to charge for the service of supplying information and then implementing the order. Fourth, there is no doubt that demand will emerge from members for the right to rebuild their pension rights if they can afford to and if the employer will contribute. And finally, there is no doubt that, because of lack of experience in the courts, the advisers and the parties will create a demand for training and external advice.

In the meantime, there are unsettled issues. In particular, it is not clear whether pension schemes which decide not to offer an internal transfer option and instead specify a default option must comply with the requirements of FSA 1986. Almost all larger schemes have decided that they will not offer former spouses the right to remain within their schemes as a form of deferred member; in practice they will then normally offer to transfer the pension credit to a scheme of the ex-spouse's choice. If no such scheme is specified they will normally indicate that the credit will be transferred to a pensions provider nominated by the member's scheme. While there has been some extensive debate about whether scheme trustees have to comply with 'know your client' and 'best practice' requirements, in practice this is clearly impossible, and only pedants would consider there had been a breach of the compliance requirements. Some schemes are taking the view, which is reasonable, that they are not in breach of the requirement to transfer unless they have been informed of the destination required by the ex-spouse, but while this may be correct, and a safe-harbour, it does nothing to take the ex-spouse off the books of the scheme.

9.3   Documentation

In relation to earmarking, the duty of trustees is simply to comply with any order (and to object to the terms of such orders where they are inappropriate).

There are no documentation issues other than in subsequent revisions of scheme rules, where it might be sensible to insert legislative pointers.

Documentation becomes important, however, in relation to sharing. For the most part, in relation to sharing (unlike much other pensions legislation) WRAPA 1999 is not overriding, with just three exceptions:

- the establishment of pension debits (WRAPA 1999, s 31) which operate to diminish the rights of the member with pension rights;
- the priority in winding up for pension credits (WRAPA 1999, s 38); and
- the fiscal legislation (Finance Act 1999 (FA 1999), Sch 10; Retirement Benefits Schemes (Sharing of Pensions on Divorce or Annulment) Regulations 2000, SI 2000/1085).

Scheme documents may or will need to cope with the remaining provisions of sharing, although earmarking needs no such changes. Before making such changes, scheme trustees need to establish their policy, and only then reflect that policy in the rules.

In relation to sharing, trustees (or in the language of the legislation 'the person responsible for a pension arrangement') need to make decisions:

- on whether to allow former spouses to be given an 'internal scheme option', ie to make them members of the scheme, or merely to allow former spouses to take an external transfer. (Unfunded public sector schemes do not need to consider the question; they cannot provide the external option.) Most schemes do not need to offer an internal option, but they do need to make provision for a default option, ie if the former spouse makes no decision as to where to place the rights, the scheme must do so for her. Schemes, however, might wish to allow former spouses to be an internal member, perhaps where the scheme is underfunded and the former spouse does not give consent to a transfer, or where the former spouse dies before liability to pay the pensions credit is discharged and no instructions have been received by the trustees from the former spouse;
- where the internal option is offered to former spouses, on the extent of rights to be offered. In such cases, ex-spouses may need to be defined, perhaps as a special class. Defining such a member simply as a deferred pensioner, for example, will bring the former spouse into the member nominated trustee procedures. In addition, there may be employer's consents to any changes to be obtained, especially since the costs of changes ultimately fall upon the employer; and
- on details of the policy, including the way and amount of charging for costs. The benefits which will attach to the pension credit, documentation (including any rule changes, notices to members and disclosure) and changing and paying for changes to administrative systems.

9.4 Transfers

In deciding what to offer former spouses the options are:

- an external transfer (a compulsory option, ie former spouses must be offered this as an option); or
- an internal transfer (a true option, ie trustees do not need to offer this); or

- forcing an external transfer, ie where the former spouse does not consent to an external transfer and where internal transfer is not offered or not accepted where it is offered, and to insist on a default external transfer.

In deciding whether and how to force an external transfer, the trustees may need to consider a number of external issues. First, if the scheme is underfunded on the Minimum Funding Requirement basis (the minimum funding standard), then some observers suggest that the regulations indicate that the ex-spouse must be offered the option of keeping the pension credit in the scheme. It is therefore considered it might be wise (if this is the case) that pension scheme systems should make allowance for the possible future contingency of such underfunding.

The wisdom of the policy of not offering the internal transfer option has been explored above (see 9.2) and most scheme drafts are providing that in extreme circumstances an internal option will be available, to comply with the legislation. In practice, the routine of informing the ex-spouse with a sharing order that unless instructions are given to the contrary within a reasonable time the pension credit will be transferred to a default pensions provider seems a reasonable way of meeting both the needs of the pension scheme and the problems of an indolent or indecisive ex-spouse without breaching the compliance requirements of FSA 1986 and its successor.

For some time there has been concern about whether scheme trustees are subject to compliance with the regime imposed by FSA 1986 when choosing a receiving vehicle to transfer a pension sharing credit to for an ex-spouse who does not select her or her own recipient of the transfer payment or who may even wish that his or her rights remain in the scheme.

9.5 Authorisation

9.5.1 Trustees and authorisation

A person needs to be authorised under FSA 1986 in order to carry on investment business in the United Kingdom. An unauthorised person is guilty of a criminal offence and may be imprisoned or fined (or both).

Safeguarded rights (ie that part of the rights relating to the SERPS pension) can only be transferred to another contracted-out scheme with the ex-spouse's consent, or to an insurer without such consent if the trustees think it reasonable to do so. It is not clear whether trustees can make a general declaration as to reasonableness or must consider each case on its merits. Where the sums involved are small, it may not make sense to transfer to an insurer, where the expenses may be disproportionate or indeed where the insurer may decline to accept the transfer.

Where ex-spouses are offered (or if the argument above is accepted, must be offered) an internal transfer, it is not necessary to offer the same benefits as scheme members, provided the benefits that are offered do not breach Revenue limits and are equal to the pensions credit. Trustees may not think it appropriate, for example, to offer a cash option or dependent benefits, but may have to justify the exercise of their discretion at some future time.

Administrative costs are usually the driving force in making such decisions. It is not clear whether it will be more or less expensive to keep ex-spouses in the scheme or to ensure they are transferred elsewhere; costings are easier where administration is outsourced and separate pricing is available from the service provider. In practice, if sharing orders are as rare as earmarking orders proved to be, it may be that trustees could ask for individual decisions to be made rather than making a general policy or spending substantial sums on upgrading administrative systems. In particular, where an order is made in respect of a member already in receipt of a pension, it might be easier to continue paying the separate parts of the pension to both parties than to arrange an external transfer, particularly where both parties are scheme members.

9.5.2 Existing approved schemes: Revenue rules

There is nothing for schemes to do immediately to meet Revenue requirements. The rules of all retirement benefit schemes approved before 10 May 2000 and which continue to be so approved on or after 1 December 2000 are automatically modified so as to include the fiscal controls on sharing (FA 1999, Sch 10, para 18(5); Finance Act 1991, Schedule 10, Paragraph 18 First and Second Appointed Days) Order 2000, SI 2000/1093, art 2). The overriding legislation deems the scheme rules to contain provisions satisfying the conditions of new subsections of ICTA 1988 (ICTA 1988, s 590(3)(bb) and (da)), whether the schemes are approved under the mandatory or discretionary requirements. The general principles are set out in two Inland Revenue updates to the Practice Notes (Pension Schemes Office, Update No 60, 10 February 2000; Update No 62, 28 April 2000).

The legislation does not automatically allow the rebuilding of rights, since the standard scheme override 'may be too restrictive for certain scheme members so that the regulations have been amended so as to provide certain exceptions and modifications' (Sch 10 para, 18(10) and (11)). In simple English, these weasel words mean that the Inland Revenue will allow limited rebuilding of pensions rights for 'moderate earners', whom it defines as people earning under one-quarter of the pensions cap (in 2000/2001, the cap was £91,800). But scheme rules may need to be changed to reflect this relaxation.

The main tax legislation (ICTA 1988, s 590(3)(bb)) limits the maximum benefits payable to employee scheme members to those which he or she could have had under the retirement benefits scheme as if there had been no pensions debit. It therefore prevents a scheme member rebuilding their benefits following a pensions share over and above that allowed to any other scheme member. ICTA 1988 also limits the tax-free lump sum following a pensions share to 2.25 times the pension payable in the first year. The problem is that because of the proliferation of Revenue regimes (depending on the date on which a member joined the scheme), members who suffer from different caps will be differently affected.

9.5.3 Schemes not yet approved (ie seeking approval)

All pension schemes where an application for approval has been made but approval not yet granted and all pension schemes seeking approval on or after 10 May 2000 need to comply with the need to have rules which conform to the requirements of pensions sharing, in particular the limits in rebuilding of pensions.

FA 1999 changes in general took effect from 1 December 2000. To allow schemes to be ready for the introduction of pensions sharing there was a 'first appointed day' (10 May 2000). On or after the 10 May, any occupational pension scheme or personal pension scheme seeking approval had to include pension sharing provisions in its rules in anticipation of the changes coming into force. If the application for approval was made before the first appointed day but the scheme had not obtained approval by that day, the pension sharing provisions had to be included before it could be approved.

The Pension Schemes Office offers standard wording for scheme rule amendments to cover the provisions. (A draft of a further Update and model rules were included in a consultation document issued to the industry on 26 January 2000).

Where a scheme has already been submitted for approval, for example on interim documentation, practitioners may wish to submit full documentation before the first appointed day to enable the scheme to be approved.

9.6   Taxation and the Inland Revenue

9.6.1   Introduction

The Pension Schemes Office have been determined to ensure that pensions sharing in particular is not employed as a tax leakage device, rather as the school fees orders on divorce were employed in the early 1980s. Earmarking does not pose such a problem, since it merely involves an attachment order on a single member's rights. They have therefore imposed rigorous, if not draconian, limits on the way in which rights may be shared and in certain cases rebuilt, and required schemes to impose certain controls. In doing so they have accepted that:

- In England, Wales and Northern Ireland, pension sharing settlements are possible only by court order; in Scotland, the majority of settlements are by agreement, although a few are by court order.
- Pension sharing is not compulsory; it remains possible to offset or earmark/attach pension rights.
- In certain cases (cynically, where the member can in fact rarely afford to rebuild rights after sharing) the limits need not be imposed.

The PSO requires in due course that all schemes include pension sharing provisions in the governing documentation. Any scheme (whether occupational or personal) which sought approval after 10 May 2000 was and is required to include the pension sharing provisions in its rules in anticipation of the changes coming into force. Where application for approval was made before 10 May 2000 but the scheme had not obtained approval by that day, the pension sharing provisions had to be included before it could be approved.

9.6.2   Transitional

Where an occupational pension scheme or personal pension scheme approved before the 10 May 2000 was resubmitted for approval because of amendments to the rules in the period between 10 May 2000 and 1 December 2000, certain requirements were abrogated:

9.6.2.1   For occupational pension schemes

- ICTA 1988, s 590(3)(bb) which prevents rebuilding;
- ICTA 1988, s 590(3)(da) which limits the member's retirement lump sum.

9.6.2.2   For personal pension schemes

- ICTA 1988, s 636(3A) which limits the amount of annuity to a surviving spouse or dependant of the member.

  This was to protect such a scheme from having its approval withdrawn solely on grounds that the requirements (which were provisions that did not come into force until 1 December 2000) were not reflected in its rules. Schemes to which this paragraph applied were not required to incorporate the pension sharing provisions in their rules before 1 December 2000. Personal pension schemes approved before 10 May 2000 were permitted to amend their rules before 1 December 2000 to introduce provisions for pension sharing. In these cases they were required to include the limits.

For occupational pension schemes approved before 10 May 2000 and which continue to be approved on and after 1 December 2000, the new limits set out above are applied by statutory override (FA 1999, Sch 10, para 18(5)). The effect of the override is to deem such schemes to have those provisions in their rules.

Schemes are not expected to rely on overriding provisions indefinitely, and must incorporate the pension sharing requirements in their rules at the earliest convenient opportunity (normally, when the rules are amended for other purposes other than a trivial way).

In some cases the statutory override is too restrictive and regulations (Retirement Benefits Schemes (Sharing of Pensions on Divorce or Annulment) Regulations 2000, SI 2000/185; Retirement Benefits Schemes (Restriction on Discretion to Approve Excepted Provisions) Regulations 2000, SI 2000/1087 – 'disapplication regulations') were introduced to widen the limits. They:

- exclude from the rebuilding restriction in ICTA 1988, s 590(3)(bb) scheme members on modest earnings (ie under one-quarter of the earnings cap);
- exclude from both the rebuilding restriction in ICTA 1988, s 590(3)(bb) and the lump sum restriction in ICTA 1988, s 590(3)(da), Simplified Defined Contribution Schemes. This is because such schemes are controlled by limits on contributions, therefore the restrictions are inherent;
- modify the effect of ICTA 1988, s 590(3)(da) for members with 'pre 17 March 1987 continued rights' (see Glossary). For these members, the lump sum is calculated on a special basis (see IR Update No 62, para 74).
- exclude from the lump sum restriction in ICTA 1988, s 590(3)(da) those employees who are members of schemes which provide only a lump sum retirement benefit, which does not exceed $3/80$ of the employee's final remuneration for each year of service up to a maximum of 40;
- exclude from the lump sum restriction in ICTA 1988, s 590(3)(da) those employees who are members of schemes which provide for a pension and a separate lump sum rather than a commutable pension.

For occupational pension schemes approved on or after 10 May 2000, the appropriate exceptions and modifications are set out in the Inland Revenue Pension Scheme Office Practice Notes IR12 (1997). Standard wording for rules for occupational pension schemes is available to ease approval. There are model rules for personal pension schemes for both contracting-out and non-contracting-out schemes, and the model rules must be used to replace the existing versions.

9.6.3   *Changes to the legislative structure of pensions taxation*

Previous pensions tax law (ICTA 1988, Ch IV, Pt XIV) was constructed on the basis of providing benefits for an individual scheme member (employee in the case of an occupational pension scheme) with benefits for a surviving spouse or dependant after the death of the scheme member. The assignment or surrender of any pension or annuity was not generally allowed. Since a sharing order or agreement would otherwise have contravened the former ban on assignment or surrender, FA 1999 removed the ban. In particular, for personal pension schemes the ban was removed on benefits in the form of:

- income withdrawals (which are regarded separately from annuities); and
- a retirement lump sum (which is a separate form of benefit and not a part of the annuity).

No special tax reliefs are given for divorcing couples. A scheme member who wants to rebuild a shared pension can in theory do so within the general rules for benefits and contributions.

Both occupational pension schemes and personal pension schemes are able to provide benefits from shared pension rights for an ex-spouse. Where, in the case of an occupational pension scheme, the ex-spouse is also an employee member of the same scheme, the shared pension does not restrict the benefits given to him or her in respect of the employment (although the scheme has to treat the benefits as separate in its administration). This was done to help maintain fairness in the treatment of the ex-spouse's pension. With a personal pension scheme, the amount of the member's annuity is not, in any event, subject to a statutory limit.

For both occupational pension schemes and personal pension schemes, the changes also ensure that the shared pension given to the ex-spouse receives broadly the same treatment as the pension rights of a scheme member. So, for example, if the scheme member can receive a tax-free lump sum on retirement, the option is also available to the ex-spouse.

9.6.3.1   *Technical amendments*

There were consequential amendments to small self administered scheme regulations (SASSs), the AVC rules and the rule requiring scheme amendments to be filed within three years (the Retirement Benefits Schemes (Restriction on Discretion to Approve) (Small Self administered Schemes) Regulations 1991, SI 1991/1614; the Retirement Benefits Schemes (Restriction on Discretion to Approve) (Additional Voluntary Contributions) Regulations 1993, SI 1993/3016; and the Retirement Benefits Schemes (Restrictions on Discretion to Approve) (Excepted Provisions) Regulations 2000, SI 2000/1087).

9.6.3.2 Small self administered schemes

There are minor relaxations for SASSs; 'scheme member' in the regulations now includes any ex-spouse with pension credit rights (which makes him or her subject to that panoply of conditions and restrictions which apply to other members); the numerical limit of fewer than 12 scheme members does not include ex-spouses who qualify as scheme members because of rights arising from a pension sharing order (to prevent schemes ceasing to be SSAS's simply because pension sharing causes the scheme membership to increase to 12 or more).

9.6.3.3 Additional voluntary contributions

Where the ex-spouse is also a scheme member in respect of service as an employee, and is paying AVCs, then the ex-spouse pension credit rights can be ignored for the purposes of calculating the maximum benefits that can be paid (provided the scheme administers the benefits separately). But the transfer of pension rights to an ex-spouse (the 'pension credit') is added back for an employee when calculating maximum benefits (unless he is a 'modest earner').

9.6.3.4 Pension credits

Pension credit rights allocated to an ex-spouse following a pension share must be secured independently from those of the scheme member. If the scheme agrees, they may be retained in the member's occupational pension scheme (including a Free Standing Additional Voluntary Contributions Scheme) and benefits paid from that scheme in due course. The scheme trustees decide how, if at all, to give effect to those pension credit rights in the scheme.

Since few schemes have made arrangements to admit former spouses to membership, because the regulatory requirements are perceived as too onerous, in almost all cases they are in practice transferred to another pension arrangement. In any event, an ex-spouse who is initially given scheme membership may, subsequently, ask for a transfer of the pension credit rights if desired. This right may be exercised independently of any benefit rights arising as an employee. (In the case of a personal pension scheme, including a group personal pension scheme, the ex-spouse will not have a contract with the scheme; it is necessary, if the pension credit rights are to continue in the same scheme, for a new contract to be made and this will become an 'arrangement' as mentioned in the legislation with the ex-spouse as a new member.) Where the ex-spouse is already a member, it is possible to add the pension credit rights to the existing arrangements.

Pension credit rights arising from an approved pension scheme can be transferred only to another approved arrangement – and subsequent transfers of those rights may also be made only to an approved arrangement. Pension credit rights may be transferred to an overseas scheme (subject to the usual PSO rules). For personal pension schemes, the ex-spouse may transfer out to another scheme even though the scheme member has already passed the pension date and is receiving payments of income withdrawal.

Where an ex-spouse's pension credit rights are secured by an annuity contract, the contracts qualify for 'pension business' treatment (ICTA 1988, s 431B as amended).

9.6.3.5   *Date pension credit rights available*

The date at which the pension can begin to be paid (and lump sums taken) depends on the sort of pension arrangement under which they arise. They are generally payable as follows:

- Occupational pension scheme approved under ICTA 1988, s 590 (mandatory approval): payable between age 60 and 75.
- Occupational pension scheme approved under ICTA 1988, s 591 (discretionary approval): payable between age 50 and 75, or earlier on grounds of exceptional circumstances of serious ill health or on the grounds of incapacity where, in the case of the latter, the ex-spouse is simultaneously taking employee benefits on these grounds under the scheme in which the pension credits are held.
- Personal pension scheme: payable between age 50 and 75.
- Retirement annuity contract: payable between age 60 and 75 or earlier than the prescribed age ranges for personal pension schemes and retirement annuity contracts on the grounds of incapacity by reference to any occupation of the ex-spouse.
- Buy out contract: payable between age 50 and 75 except where the origin is an ICTA 1988, s 590 approved scheme.

Annuity purchase deferral and income drawdown arrangements (see PSO Updates No 8 for personal pension schemes and No 54 for occupational pension schemes) can apply to pension credit rights.

9.6.4   *Form of pension credit rights: general*

The ex-spouse may be given rights which broadly follow those available to the scheme member (subject to the special rules on safeguarded rights, see below, and WRAPA 1999, s 36). This maintains consistency with the normal tax rules for pensions.

Where, for example, a scheme member could exchange part of a pension for a lump sum at the time of retirement, the ex-spouse may be given a similar option.

But where, on the other hand, an ex-spouse's pension credit rights arise from an arrangement which does not allow for a tax-free retirement lump sum, for example a Free-Standing Additional Voluntary Contributions Scheme, the ex-spouse may receive benefits in pension form only. Similarly, if the scheme member has already taken a tax-free lump sum under the scheme before pension sharing took place, then the ex-spouse can receive benefits in pension form only.

Where the ex-spouse's pension credit rights are transferred in circumstances where those rights cannot be taken in lump sum form, a nil certificate (see Inland Revenue Practice Notes, para PN 10.35) must be provided to the receiving scheme by the transferring scheme.

9.6.5   *Form of pension credit rights: personal pension schemes and retirement annuity contracts*

9.6.5.1   *Personal pension schemes*

Pension credit rights are available and payable from the fund of the ex-spouse as segregated from the fund of the original member. The range of benefits is exhaustive:

- an annuity;
- income withdrawals;
- a tax-free lump sum of 25% of the fund; and
- where the ex-spouse dies before the pension credit rights come into payment, a tax-free lump sum in the form of a return of the fund or an annuity to a surviving spouse or dependant of the ex-spouse where the ex-spouse dies after the pension credit rights (paid as an annuity) come into payment an annuity to a surviving spouse or dependant of the ex-spouse. If the pension credit rights were being paid by income withdrawals, then the survivors of the ex-spouse may opt for income withdrawals, an annuity or a lump sum taxed at 35% (ICTA 1988, s 648B).

9.6.5.2   *Retirement annuity contracts*

As retirement annuity contracts are no longer available, any pension credit rights must be secured, as before, by a transfer either to a personal pension scheme or to an occupational pension scheme of which the ex-spouse is already a member. The benefits then payable follow normal requirements in accordance with the rules of the receiving scheme applicable to transfers.

9.6.6   *Form of pension credit rights: occupational pension schemes*

9.6.6.1   *Scheme approved under ICTA 1988, s 591*

The following benefits are available where pension credit rights arise under a scheme approved under ICTA 1988, s 591 which is not a Simplified Defined Contribution Scheme:

- A pension.
- A tax-free lump sum of 2.25 times the initial annual rate of pension before commutation to be paid (3 times the initial annual rate of the separate pension in a separate pension and lump sum scheme). If, however, the pension credit rights arise from an arrangement which does not allow for a tax-free lump sum, then none will be available. If a tax-free retirement lump sum has already been taken by the scheme member before pension sharing took place, then the ex-spouse may receive benefits in pension form only.
- Where the ex-spouse dies before the pension credit rights come into payment, a tax-free lump sum death benefit of 25% of what would have been the cash equivalent of the pension credit rights at the date of death. The balance of the cash equivalent may be used to provide non-commutable pensions for any widow, widower or dependants ('survivors') of the ex-spouse. If there are no survivors, the balance of the cash equivalent should be treated as surplus under normal rules.
- Where the ex-spouse dies after the pension sharing order, agreement or equivalent provision is made but before it is implemented by the scheme, death benefits may be paid on the basis of the immediately preceding bulleted point. This applies irrespective of whether the scheme member's benefits were in payment at the time of the pension sharing order, agreement or equivalent provision.
- A pension guarantee, together with non-commutable pensions payable for any widow, widower or dependants of the ex-spouse in the event of

the ex-spouse's death after the pension credit rights have come into payment.
- Full commutation of the pension credit rights on grounds of triviality or exceptional circumstances of serious ill health.

9.6.6.2   Simplified Defined Contribution Scheme

The following benefits are available where pension credit rights arise under a Simplified Defined Contribution Scheme:

- A pension.
- A tax-free lump sum of 25% of the fund value underpinning the ex-spouse's pension credit rights at the time of payment. If, however, a tax-free retirement lump sum has already been taken by the scheme member before pension sharing took place, then the ex-spouse may receive benefits in pension form only.
- Death benefits before the pension credit rights come into payment (see PN 22.25).
- Where the ex-spouse dies after the pension sharing order, agreement or equivalent provision is made but before it is implemented by the scheme, death benefits may be paid on the basis of the immediately preceding bulleted point. This applies irrespective of whether the scheme member's benefits were in payment at the time of the pension sharing order, agreement or equivalent provision; death benefits once the pension credit rights have come into payment (see PN 22.26–28).
- Full commutation of the pension credit rights on grounds of triviality or exceptional circumstances of serious ill health (see PN 22.22).

9.6.6.3   ICTA 1988, s 590 approved scheme

The Revenue permit the following benefits where pension credit rights arise under an ICTA 1988, s 590 approved scheme:

- A pension.
- A tax-free lump sum of 2.25 times the initial annual rate of pension before commutation to be paid. If, however, a tax-free retirement lump sum has already been taken by the scheme member before pension sharing took place, then the ex-spouse may receive benefits in pension form only.
- A non-commutable pension payable to the widow or widower of the ex-spouse in the event of the ex-spouse's death after the pension credit rights have come into payment.

9.6.6.4   Buy-out policy

Where a buy-out contract is subject to a pension sharing order, the ex-spouse's pension credit rights may be transferred to another pension arrangement in accordance with normal requirements. In circumstances where a new buy-out contract is effected to house the ex-spouse's pension credit rights arising from other than an ICTA 1988, s 590 approved scheme, it must satisfy Inland Revenue requirements (see PN 10.44–45) although no limit is required on pension.

9.6.6.5 *Limit on pension credit rights payable*

The following limits apply to benefits from pension credit rights for, or in respect of, an ex-spouse.

9.6.6.6 *Pension*

There is broadly no limit under the tax approval rules on the pension for an ex-spouse from pension credit rights. This applies irrespective of the type of pension scheme under which the pension credit rights arise.

9.6.6.7 *Lump sum 'retirement' benefits*

For occupational pension schemes and buy-out contracts, the amount of tax-free lump sum available depends upon the type of pension scheme under which the pension credit rights arise (see above). For personal pension schemes, the lump sum is up to 25% of the fund forming the pension credit rights.

9.6.6.8 *Death benefits before payment of pension credit rights*

Where an ex-spouse's pension credit rights arise from a personal pension scheme:

- the fund forming the pension credit rights may be paid as a lump sum under ICTA 1988, s 637A. This amount is free of income tax;
- or an annuity may be paid to a spouse or dependant of the ex-spouse; and
- the survivor's annuity must not exceed the amount of annuity payable to the ex-spouse as scheme member or the survivor may opt for income withdrawals.

Where pension credit rights arise under an ICTA 1988, s 591 approved occupational pension scheme (excluding a Simplified Defined Contribution Scheme). a lump sum death benefit of 25% of the cash equivalent of the pension credit rights at the date of death may be paid out.

Any pension payable to a widow, widower or dependant ('survivor') of the ex-spouse, must not exceed two-thirds of the pension, before commutation, that could have been provided for the ex-spouse on the date of death from the pension credit rights. Where the ex-spouse is below the age of 50 at the date of death, an age 50 annuity rate should be used to determine the pension that could have been provided to the ex-spouse. Where there is more than one survivor, separate pensions may be provided for each. No individual pension may exceed the two-thirds limit above, nor may the total of the pensions to be paid exceed that which could have been provided for the ex-spouse at the date of death. Such pensions may be fully commuted on grounds of triviality (see PN 8.10 14).

There are no limits imposed on death benefits where the pension credit rights arise from a Simplified Defined Contribution Scheme (see PN 22.15).

Where the pension credit rights arise from an ICTA 1988, s 590 approved occupational pension scheme, no death benefits are permissible if the ex-spouse dies before pension credit rights come into payment.

9.6.6.9   *Death benefits after pension credit rights have come into payment*

Where an ex-spouse's pension credit rights arise from a personal pension scheme, the benefits payable will depend on whether the pension credit rights were being paid as an annuity or by income withdrawals.

If by annuity

* then any benefit payable must be in the form of an annuity to a surviving spouse or dependant of the ex-spouse.

If by income withdrawals

* then the benefit may be paid as an annuity to a surviving spouse or dependant of the ex-spouse; or
* as income withdrawals as opted by the survivor; or
* as a lump sum taxed at 35% under ICTA 1988, s 648B.

Where pension credit rights arise under an ICTA 1988, s 591 approved occupational pension scheme, including a Simplified Defined Contribution Scheme, a lump sum death benefit may be paid out under a five-year guarantee (see PN 12.10 and 22.2–8). Such a lump sum must not exceed the total of the instalments failing due after the ex-spouse's death. Where the ex-spouse dies during the guarantee period and is drawing the pension credit rights under an income drawdown arrangement, the balance of instalments may be based on the amount of pension the ex-spouse would otherwise have been receiving if s/he had opted for 100% withdrawal. For these purposes, 100% is determined at the date of commencement of income drawdown, irrespective of any subsequent variations. Any undrawn amounts of pension (that is, the difference between 100% withdrawal and the amounts actually drawndown) for periods prior to the date of death may be paid in addition.

Where pension credit rights arise under an ICTA 1988, s 591 approved occupational pension scheme other than in a Simplified Defined Contribution scheme, any pension payable to a survivor of an ex-spouse, must not exceed two-thirds of the pension before commutation payable to the ex-spouse at the date the pension credit rights became payable, increased in proportion to the subsequent rise in the retail prices index. Where there is more than one survivor, separate pensions may be provided for each. No individual pension may exceed the $^2/_3$ limit above nor may the total of the pensions to be paid exceed that payable to the ex-spouse from commencement, increased by the retail prices index as above. Such pensions may be fully commuted on grounds of triviality (see PN 8.10–14).

There are no limits imposed on survivor's benefits in these circumstances where the pension credit rights arise from a Simplified Defined Contribution Scheme (see PN 22.15).

Where the pension credit rights arise from a ICTA 1988, s 590 approved occupational pension scheme, the only benefit payable in these circumstances is a pension for the widow or widower of the ex-spouse. Such a pension must not exceed two-thirds of the pension, before commutation, payable to the ex-spouse.

Where pension credit rights arise from a buy out policy, the benefits must be subject to the limits appropriate to the type of pension scheme under which they originated.

9.6.6.10 *Ex-spouse also an employee and entitled to benefits as an employee under an occupational pension scheme*

Ex-spouse pension credit rights, or any widow's or widower's benefits arising from those rights, are not taken into account in applying the tax approval limits to (FA 1999, Sch 10, para 2(8)):

- benefits for the ex-spouse as an employee scheme member; and
- benefits for the widow or widower of an ex-spouse which arise as a result of that ex-spouse's employee scheme membership.

This is, however, subject to the pension credit rights being treated in the occupational pension scheme in question as separate from those which arise as an employee or the widow/widower of an employee. This principle is extended in the case of occupational pension schemes approved under ICTA 1988, s 591 to cover dependants' pensions.

Unless the occupational pension scheme makes provision for separate treatment as above, the pension credit rights are taken into account in applying the tax approval limits to benefits for the ex-spouse as an employee scheme member or for the widow/widower (or dependants in the case of an ICTA 1988, s 591 approved occupational pension scheme) of the employee scheme member as appropriate.

An ex-spouse's pension credit rights maybe fully commuted on grounds of triviality. Where the ex-spouse's pension credit rights are provided from an occupational pension scheme under which the ex-spouse is also entitled to benefits as an employee, the benefits from the pension credit rights must be aggregated with those in respect of the employment for the purpose of the triviality limit in PN 8.10. In addition, an ex-spouse's pension credit rights may be fully commuted on grounds of exceptional circumstances of serious ill health. If the ex-spouse satisfies the criteria for full commutation of pension on these grounds (see PN 8.16), such commutation may take place immediately irrespective of the age of the ex-spouse.

For personal pension schemes, the ex-spouse may, if the scheme administrator agrees, continue to hold the pension credit rights in the same scheme as the original scheme member. The ex-spouse enters into a new contract (which may be divided into more than one personal pension arrangement) and becomes a member of the scheme. If the ex-spouse has net relevant earnings, contributions may be paid to the arrangements. Alternatively, the pension credit rights can be transferred to another personal pension scheme or to an occupational pension scheme of which the ex-spouse is already a member.

9.6.7   Taxation of pension credit rights

Normally, income tax is payable on pension payments. An ex-spouse's benefits that are payable in the same circumstances are also taxable (the intention of the legislation being to maintain consistency with the normal tax rules for pensions), so that:

- Pension annuity payments or income withdrawals to an ex-spouse or the widow, widower or dependants of an ex-spouse are chargeable to tax on the recipient under Schedule E.
- Lump sum retirement benefits paid to the ex-spouse are tax-free; lump sum death benefits paid under personal pension schemes
  - before the payment of pension credit rights, any lump sum is tax free
  - after the payment of pension credit rights, the only sum available is on death during payments of income withdrawals. This is taxed at 35% (ICTA 1988, s 648B).
- Lump sum death benefits paid under occupational pension schemes or buy-out contracts on the death of the ex-spouse, are, subject to a discretionary distribution power being exercised, tax free.
- There is no provision for full commutation of the pension credit rights under personal pension schemes on grounds of serious ill health, neither is commutation on trivial grounds available (although see IR76, para 9.32). This triviality test applies to the pension credit rights alone.
- If the ex-spouse's pension credit rights under an occupational pension scheme or buyout contract are fully commuted on grounds of triviality or exceptional circumstances of serious ill health, they are taxed under ICTA 1988, s 599. The amount of lump sum retirement benefit that would otherwise have been payable to the ex-spouse is deducted and ICTA 1988, s 599 tax charge applied to the balance.

  If the ex-spouse is also an employee and the scheme does not make provision for separate treatment of ex-spouse's pension credit rights, the pension credit rights will be treated for tax approval limits purposes as part of the employee benefits. Full commutation of both pension credit rights and the employee pension means that ICTA 1988, s 599 tax charge is applied to the lump sum commutation payment after deducting the largest lump sum which would have been payable in respect of service as an employee.
- Any payments, other than a pension, to or for the benefit of an ex-spouse which are not expressly authorised by the rules of the occupational pension scheme are taxed under ICTA 1988, s 600, and under ICTA 1988, s 647 for a personal pension scheme.

9.6.8   Pension debits for scheme members

Where the scheme member's pension rights are shared on divorce, there is a reduction in those rights known as a 'pension debit'. Where the member is not a 'modest earner' (see 'administrative easement' below) and it is therefore necessary to take the pension debit into account as an aggregable benefit, it is calculated as set out below.

9.6.8.1 ICTA 1988, ss 590 and 591 approved schemes (other than Simplified Defined Contribution Schemes)

The pension debit permanently reduces the maximum approvable benefits for the scheme member. The scheme member's benefits may, therefore, only be rebuilt up to the reduced maxima, unless he is regarded as having moderate earnings. Such individuals may ignore the pension debit and rebuild the shared pension within the normal benefit and contribution limits.

9.6.8.2 Simplified Defined Contribution Schemes (SDCSs)

For SDCS, which are rare in practice, the only limitation is on continuing contributions (see PN 22.9–11).

9.6.8.3 Personal pension schemes and retirement annuity contracts

There is no restriction on the amount of ongoing personal pension contributions or retirement annuity premiums payable following a pension share. These continue to be payable by reference to net relevant earnings. The level of benefits available depends as ever on the value of the fund after deducting the pension debit.

On the death of the scheme member, the amount of any annuity payable to a surviving spouse (not the ex-spouse from the pension share) or dependant, must not exceed the amount of annuity that could have been paid to the scheme member after deducting the pension debit (ICTA 1988, s 636(3A)).

9.6.8.4 Buy-out contracts

Any monetary limits on the member's lump sum retirement benefit or pension (see PN 10.45(c) and PN 10.46) is reduced to take account of the pension debit.

9.6.9 'Administrative easement' for 'moderate earners' (ie rebuilding)

Members of ICTA 1988, s 591 approved occupational pension schemes (other than Simplified Defined Contributions Schemes) can rebuild their pension rights except:

- controlling directors (Retirement Benefits Schemes (Sharing of Pensions on Divorce or Annulment) Regulations 2000, SI 2000/1085, reg 5(5)); and
- those whose earnings, exceed one-quarter of the permitted maximum determined at its level for the year of assessment in which the marriage was dissolved or annulled. For this purpose earnings mean:
  - those in respect of pensionable service to which the scheme relates; and
  - which were received during the year of assessment immediately preceding the year of assessment in which the dissolution or annulment occurred; and
  - from which tax was deducted under PAYE.

Where the easement applies, pension debits can be ignored in calculating the member's maximum permissible total benefits, both pension and lump sum, under the scheme. This is a once and for all test as at the date of divorce and if satisfied, the pension debit is permanently ignored, irrespective of subsequent employment changes.

9.6.10   *Calculation of pension debits*

9.6.10.1   Members of occupational pension schemes approved under ICTA 1988, s 590 or under s 591, other than Simplified Defined Contribution Schemes

Where the individual is prohibited from rebuilding, the pension debit must be calculated. It is brought into account as part of a member's aggregable benefits in determining the Inland Revenue maximum approvable benefits, both pension and lump sum, payable under the scheme.

The Inland Revenue provide examples of how this operates. The examples assume that the whole of the pension debit is subject to statutory revaluation although if the debit includes some GMP rights, then that part of the debit is subject to GMP revaluation in the normal way.

Example 9.1

Assuming . . .

- Defined benefit scheme.
- An active scheme member with 20 year's membership at the date of divorce.
- The member earns £30,000.
- Defined benefit scheme provides 1/60th of final salary for each year of service
- Under the pension sharing order, agreement or equivalent provision the member's pension rights are subject to a debit of 40% of the cash equivalent.

. . . then . . .

- Deferred pension at the date of divorce: 20/60 x £30,000 = £10,000.
- Cash equivalent for pension sharing calculated by scheme actuary: £100,000.
- Pension debit ordered by the court (40% of the cash equivalent): £40,000.

. . . and then when the member retires at age 60 after 30 years service with a final salary of (say) £48,000 . . .

- Full pension entitlement (ignoring the debit): 30/60 x £48,000 = £24,000.
- Using the statutory Revaluation Order in force at the date of retirement, the scheme actuary calculates that the deferred pension of £4,000 (40% of the deferred pension of £10,000) given up at the date of divorce is equivalent to a pension of £6,000 a year at retirement. This is known as the 'negative deferred pension'.
- The member's actual pension will be: £24,000 - £6,000 = £18,000.

Example 9.2

Assume . . .

* Money purchase scheme.

* A scheme member with 20 year's membership at the date of divorce. The member earns £30,000 a year at that date.

* Total funds accumulated for the member at the date of divorce amount to £100,000.

* Under the pension sharing order, agreement or equivalent provision the member's pension rights are subject to a debit of 40% of the cash equivalent.

. . . then . . .

* The £40,000 awarded to the former spouse at the date of divorce is increased between that date and the member's normal retirement date (or other relevant date as the case may be) at the rate of investment yield achieved by the member's remaining fund in that period. Where, for whatever reason, it is not possible to use such a actual investment yield, the fund is deemed to increase at 8.5% per annum (see PN 13.10(a)).

* The resulting capital fund is then turned into a pension equivalent by applying a suitable annuity rate appropriate to the member's normal retirement date (or other relevant date as the case may be). Where the pension debit in part or whole would have been subject to limited price indexation (LPI) increases, an LPI annuity rate should be used. Where no part of the pension debit would have been subject to LPI increases, a single level life annuity rate is used. In neither situation can a guarantee be reflected in the annuity rate.

9.6.11   Limits on scheme member's benefits

The imposition of pension debits affects a scheme member's maximum approvable benefits in different ways.

9.6.11.1   Aggregable benefits

Where it is necessary to bring the pension debit into account for the purposes of determining a member's maximum approvable benefits under occupational pension schemes approved under ICTA 1988, ss 590 or 591 the maximum approvable benefits are permanently reduced. For ICTA 1988, s 590 approved schemes:

* A pension of 1/60th of final remuneration for each year of service (up to a maximum of 40) reduced by the amount of pension debit; and
* a lump sum retirement benefit by commutation of pension of 2.25 times the initial annual rate of pension after reduction to take account of the pension debit.

For s 591 approved schemes, other than Simplified Defined Contribution Schemes:

* a pension not exceeding the relevant limits set out in Parts 7 or 10 of PN as appropriate to the scheme member's circumstances and the particular

tax regime to which he or she is subject, reduced by the amount of pension debit;

- for members with pre-17 March 1987 continued rights, a lump sum retirement benefit by commutation of pension not exceeding the greater of:
  - 2.25 times the initial annual rate of pension after reduction to take account of the pension debit; or
  - an amount determined in accordance with the scheme rules as if there had been no pension share, but then reduced by 2.25 times the amount of the negative deferred pension (see paragraph 70 above);
- for members with pre-17 March 1987 continued rights in schemes providing for a pension and a separate lump sum rather than a commutable pension, a lump sum retirement benefit not exceeding the greater of:
  - three times the initial annual rate of pension after reduction to take account of the pension debit; or
  - an amount determined in accordance with the scheme rules as if there had been no pension share but then reduced by 3 times the amount of the negative deferred pension (see paragraph 70 above);
- for members with pre-1 June 1989 continued rights or without continued rights, a lump sum retirement benefit by commutation of pension of 2.25 times the initial annual rate of pension after reduction to take account of the pension debit; and
- for members with pre-1 June 1989 continued rights or without continued rights in schemes providing for a pension and a separate lump sum rather than a commutable pension, a lump sum retirement benefit of 3 times the initial annual rate of pension after reduction to take account of the pension debit.

In ICTA 1988, s 591 approved schemes providing lump sum retirement benefits only, where lump sum accrual does not exceed $^3/_{80}$ of final remuneration for each year of service, an amount determined in accordance with the scheme rules reduced by the amount of the lump sum allocated to the ex-spouse is payable. For the purpose of this reduction, the amount of the lump sum allocated to the ex-spouse at the date of divorce should be increased between that date and the date that the member takes his or her lump sum retirement benefit. The increase in that period is in accordance with the statutory Revaluation Order in force at the date the member takes his or her lump sum retirement benefit.

9.6.11.2   *Effect of pension debit on relevant earnings for personal pension eligibility for controlling directors*

A controlling director cannot count earnings from an employment as relevant earnings (ICTA 1988, s 644(6A)–(6E)) if:

- the controlling director receives or has received benefits from an occupational pension scheme for the same employer; or
- the controlling director receives benefits from a personal pension scheme which has earlier received a transfer payment from an occupational pension scheme for the same employer.

'Employer' includes an employer which carries on the business formerly carried on by the employer, and for a period giving rise to benefits for the controlling director.

It is not possible to avoid this restriction by having a 100% pension debit with the intention of nullifying existing benefits; the pension debit is deemed to be continued to be received by the controlling director (ICTA 1988, s 644(6EA)). However, if the ex-spouse was also a controlling director subject to this rule, the receipt of a pension credit is a separate matter which does not affect the operation of this rule for any pension debit applicable to the same individual.

9.6.11.3 Transfers

Where:

- benefits against which a pension debit exists are transferred to an occupational pension scheme, other than a Simplified Defined Contribution Scheme
- which is a scheme of the same or associated employer or one where continuous service is given
- and the rebuilding permission does not apply

then details of the amount of pension debit to be applied to the member's transferred benefits must be passed on to the receiving scheme. This is to ensure that the necessary restrictions on the member's benefits are maintained in that scheme.

Where:

- benefits against which a pension debit exists are transferred to an occupational pension scheme, other than a Simplified Defined Contribution Scheme
- which is a scheme of a new unassociated employer or
- one where continuous service treatment is not applicable
- and the rebuilding of rights does not apply

details of the amount of pension debit to be applied to the member's transferred benefits, must again be passed on since those benefits may need to be treated as retained benefits for the purpose of the new scheme's limits rule (eg see PN, Parts 7, 8 and 10). Where it is necessary, to bring the retained benefits into account for the purposes of the new scheme's limits rule, the pension debit (both pension and where appropriate lump sum) must be included as part of the member's retained benefits.

Where benefits against which a pension debit exists are transferred to a personal pension scheme or a buy out policy and the pensions rebuilding easements do not apply, details of the amount of pension debit to be applied to the member's transferred benefits must be passed on to the provider in question.

9.6.11.4 Lump sum certificates

Where a lump sum certificate is required in respect of a transferring member (see PN 10.332 and 16.17), the amount certified must be appropriately reduced by the sum of 2.25 times the negative deferred pension at the relevant date.

9.6.11.5   Retained benefits: personal pension schemes and retirement annuity   contracts

For the purpose of valuing the pension debit derived from a personal pension scheme or retirement annuity contract, the method in Example 9.2 for money purchase schemes set out above is used.

9.6.11.6   Death benefits

Lump sum

Pension sharing has no effect on the amount of the lump sum that may be paid following the member's death in service. The limits set out in PN 11.23 continue to apply and no account need be taken of any lump sum death benefit payable on the death of the ex-spouse before the pension credit rights come into payment.

Pension

Where the right to rebuild pensions does not apply, pension sharing will, however, have the effect of reducing the maximum widows', widowers' or dependants' pension payable in the event of the member's death in service or death in retirement (see PN 11.78 and PN 12.23). This is because the member's maximum approvable benefits are effectively permanently reduced. For similar reasons, the maximum amount available under a guarantee (see PN 12.9–10) is reduced.

9.6.11.7   Full commutation of member's pension

Where a member whose pension has been affected by a pension sharing order or provision subsequently fully commutes the pension on grounds of triviality or exceptional circumstances of serious ill health, the tax charge under ICTA 1988, s 599 (see PN 17.27) is on the excess of the commutation payment over an amount calculated in accordance with PN 17.28(b).

9.6.12   Scheme rules

The PSO has produced standard wording for scheme rule amendments to cover its requirements. The standard wording for occupational pension schemes does not, however, cover contracting-out requirements and the PSO does not examine rules/amendments to cover such requirements. When submitting rules or amendments to the PSO, practitioners need to indicate which of them relate solely to contracting-out requirements.

9.7   Administration

There is little doubt that the length and complexity of the legislation is something that the pensions movement could do without. The quality of the drafting of the regulations is truly abysmal and it may well be that the substantial ambiguities that persist will cause some problems with, for example, the Pensions Ombudsman. However, in practice, the administration may cause few real problems or little preparatory work, especially if schemes adopt a relaxed attitude to charging.

In practice, many of the problems will emerge from the lack of anticipation by the legal profession and family mediators. The introduction of earmarking showed that pension funds had to cope with last minute requests for information from family lawyers, and requests have included demands for information which are inappropriate and which disclose a lack of understanding of what pension schemes offer and how they operate. And the wording of court orders (not always submitted in draft beforehand) have meant schemes incurring costs to explain what is and is not possible under the provisions both of the law and their own rules.

Similar difficulties can be anticipated with the introduction of sharing, though it may be in practice that, as with earmarking, there will be few demands for it as a remedy, unless the considerable publicity that its introduction has generated in itself creates demand. It also has the considerable advantage of being a 'cleaner break' than for example earmarking, for both pension funds and divorcing couples.

9.7.1   *Amending the terms of the scheme*

It is unlikely that many schemes will need to amend the rules of their scheme immediately to comply with the earmarking or sharing provisions. Two parts of the Act are expressly overriding: the creation of the pensions debit (s 31) and the priority of pension credits on winding up (s 38).

These provisions overcome any legal problems which would otherwise emerge when reducing a member's entitlement or security either under the rules or under law.

There are, however, areas where amendments to scheme rules may be advisable to protect the interests of the scheme, to reduce exposure to disputes and to ensure coverage of technical issues (eg the way in which safeguarded rights in contracted-out schemes are treated).

9.7.2   *Pension credits*

If an order is made to share a pension, the shared pension (the pension credit) carries certain rights, obligations and limitations. These include:

* Normal benefit age: the normal benefit age must be between 60 and 65 and is defined as the earliest age at which a person who has pension credit rights under the scheme is entitled to receive a pension by virtue of those rights, disregarding any scheme rule making special provisions as to early payment of pension on grounds of ill health or otherwise. A scheme must not provide for payment of pension credit in lump sum form before normal benefit age except in prescribed circumstances (Pension Sharing (Pension Credit Benefit) Regulations 2000, SI 2000/1054, regs 3 and 4). These include, for example, the forced commutation of trivial benefits or where there is a terminal illness (ie an expectation of death within one year).
* The pension credit must be paid from the scheme's resources or bought out or transferred (in certain circumstances without the member's consent) (PSA 1993 as amended by WRAPA 1999, s 37).

The scheme rules should, however, set out the details of pension credit rights where the scheme decides (or is required) to provide an internal transfer. Clarity, if possible, is essential, since the power of amendment of the scheme rules on pension credits once in place is limited by, for example, PA 1995, s 67. While in many areas the treatment of a spouses pension credits will reflect the way in which deferred pensions are treated generally, there are obvious differences related to the fact that the spouse will not have had a contract of employment with the employer.

It might be preferable, therefore, in many cases for the scheme rules to provide that the benefits for the ex-spouse should be in another, albeit equivalent, form. This could be money purchase, a fixed benefit or even based on notional service. Trustees also need to consider whether limited price indexation is to be given, available as an optional alternative to revaluation.

Rules should also deal with whether or not the pension credit member (a person not in contemplation when the scheme was established and who has not been employed by the employer) is to be considered in any distribution of any surplus, any general improvement of benefits, or benefit from any generous early retirement benefits.

Schemes can provide benefits which do not follow the requirements of conventional pension credit benefits in relation to amount, recipient and timing of payment where the member consent or the scheme wishes to buy out the pension credit benefit from an insurer, provided the trustees consider it reasonable to do so and at least 30 days notice has been given to the person entitled to the pension credit rights and there is no outstanding transfer notice given to that person. With the person's consent, the scheme can provide money purchase benefits instead of the pension credit benefits.

Funded schemes which choose the external transfer option will have to make few changes. There was doubt at one time as to whether compulsory internal membership was required where a spouse who had elected an external transfer died before the transfer was completed. The regulations make it clear that compulsory membership is not intended; and the share can presumably be paid to the estate of the deceased spouse.

9.7.3   Standard procedures

The standardisation of procedures is essential to allow the legislation to work without imposing excessive administrative burdens on schemes. Accordingly, the information required for implementation of pensions sharing and earmarking orders is made in a standard format, as is notice to the scheme.

9.7.4   Review of pension sharing order

One concern for pension schemes is whether they can be varied once orders have been made, since there are significant administrative costs in varying records. The Act incorporates a special channel of appeals for pension sharing, a system criticised by the Family Law Bar Association. While orders do not generally come into effect before the divorce is final, the courts do have the right to make, vary or discharge pension sharing orders (along with financial provision and property adjustment orders). However, the court is unable to set aside or vary the order if the trustees (or other persons responsible for the arrangement) have acted to their detriment following the taking effect of the order, eg by making a transfer payment to another scheme or arrangement.

9.8 Practice for scheme managers

Scheme trustees and managers of occupational schemes are the persons 'responsible for the pension arrangements'. Once these individuals have been served with a copy of the order, the decree of divorce and other relevant information, they have four months to implement the pension credit. Failure to discharge the liability within that period will mean the trustees having to notify OPRA. OPRA may impose civil penalties, but may also extend the implementation period.

9.8.1 *Duty to provide information*

Schemes must provide the information usually provided to members requesting information under the Disclosure Regulations (Pensions on Divorce etc (Provision of Information) Regulations 2000, SI 2000/1048; cf the Occupational Pension Schemes (Disclosure of Information) Regulations 1996, SI 1996/1655 and the Personal Pension Schemes (Disclosure of Information) Regulations 1987, SI 1987/1110 for personal pension arrangements).

The estimated CETV or 'value of the member's rights' (the difference is not explained, but presumably it allows other forms of valuation to be provided) must be provided as at a date chosen by the 'personal responsible for the pension arrangement' and must be within three months of the date of the request (Divorce etc (Pensions) Regulations 2000, SI 2000/1123, reg 4(4)). It must be calculated as at a date specified by the court in preliminary hearings. The information must also be given to the member within 10 working days after the valuation date (ibid reg 4(5)). The CETV is the same as that used for other transfer values, ie it normally does not include past service reserves, survivor's benefits or discretionary benefits.

9.8.1.1 *No requirement for special transfer valuations*

The original specifications for the regulations indicated that schemes also had to supply an estimate, in writing, of what proportion of the CETV or value of the member's rights is in its opinion attributable to any pension or other periodical payment under the arrangement to which a spouse of the member would or might become entitled to in the event of the member's death. This is not required under the implemented regulations, and the government took note of the fact that few computer systems were set up to provide this. However, where available it is a handy indication to the parties of the values they need to negotiate about.

Scheme trustees and managers of funded occupational schemes or a personal pension are required to deal with requests for transfers of pension credit benefit. The regulations set out how often the person entitled to the benefit may ask for information and the circumstances in which transfers may be made. Failure to comply makes managers and trustees subject to penalty by OPRA. A transfer notice cannot be withdrawn where the trustees or managers have already entered into an agreement with a third party, eg by buying an annuity from an insurer.

9.8.2   *Provision of information before a sharing order*

The regulations (Pensions on Divorce etc (Provision of Information) Regulations 2000, SI 2000/1048, reg 2) require schemes to provide the following information:

- The usual information (valuation, basis of valuation, benefits covered, whether internal option, default transfer arrangement and charges).
- The full name and address of the scheme to which the order should be sent.
- If the scheme is an occupational one, whether it is winding up and if so, the date on which the winding up began, the trustees' name and addresses, the reasons for the winding up, whether the CETV will be reduced because of any underfunding, and whether member's rights are subject to a pensions sharing order or agreement, an earmarking order, an earmarking order in Scotland, an earmarking order in Northern Ireland, a forfeiture order, a bankruptcy order (sequestration in Scotland), whether the scheme includes rights which are not shareable, whether charge are to be paid in full at the beginning of the implementation period, whether any additional charges are to be imposed during the sharing period, whether the member is a trustee of the scheme, whether the trustees can require information about the member's health and whether additional information is required. Information about health is a delicate area; the DSS consider it may be subject to the provisions of the Human Rights Act 1998 (HRA 1998), although this seems improbable.

9.8.3   *Provision of other information after a sharing order*

Schemes must provide, within 14 days after sharing orders have been made:

To both any new scheme provider and the (former) spouse
- every order made by the court made on the scheme
- any variation of the order
- all information supplied by the spouse
- any, notice given by the other party to the scheme
- any notices received by schemes transferring into the scheme

To the spouse or former spouse
- the fact that pension rights have been transferred
- the date on which the transfer takes affect
- the name and address of the personal responsible for the scheme
- the fact that the order made by the court is to have effect as if it had been made in respect of the person responsible for the new arrangement.

The spouse/former spouse is not entitled to the CETV, although they seem to be able to seek the basis on which the CETV is calculated, presumably including the extent to which discretionary benefits are included.

To the member and the new member
- where there has been an event (eg a wind up, a remarriage of one of the parties or one of the other particulars that has been given has changed) that significantly reduces the benefits, within 14 days of the event. In any event the ordinary disclosure rules apply to members, including a valuation of rights or accrued rights and the basis on which the valuation has been calculated and which benefits are included, whether there is an internal scheme option, what happens if there is no internal option and what the charges will be. The information must be provided within three months of the date the scheme receives the request, or six weeks before a court hearing, if earlier.

It is curious that the rules provide greater rights of information to divorcing members than to the spouses of ordinary members in respect of which no sharing order has been made.

The regulations deal with amendments to cash equivalents to cater for pensioners. They also allow schemes to ask for medical evidence where the pension is in payment.

A scheme which has not been given the latest mailing information by the (former) spouse, is not responsible for failure to pay the benefits due (reg 8(4)) but must pay the member instead (SI 2000/1048, reg 8(5)).

9.8.4   Court procedure

The scheme may, if it wishes, appeal against any earmarking or sharing order (reg 11). At present, schemes need comply only with a court order on earmarking and sharing.

9.8.5   Duty to establish administrative systems

Administrative systems need to:

- ensure that requests for information are met within the time limits and that they are bona fide;
- ensure that CETV calculations are provided within the time limits, and in the special form required;
- ensure that court orders are properly checked for compliability;
- ensure that courts orders are complied with and registered on the system;
- ensure that requests for extension of time are made properly, or requests for extra time lodged with OPRA; and
- ensure that notification is made of any changes to the arrangements.

9.8.5.1   Time for implementation

The sharing order or arrangement for a pension credit must be implemented within four months of the day on which the order takes effect (the later of the decree absolute or the relevant period for appealing against the pension sharing order plus seven days) or the date on which the scheme receives the relevant documentation. OPRA can give an extension of time on request, provided the request is made before the time runs out and amongst other things the scheme is being wound up or is ceasing to be contracted out or the interests of members will be prejudiced (usually because the scheme is underfunded) or there is a dispute or insufficient information. There are sanctions for failure to meet time limits of £1,000 per individual trustee or manager and £10,000 for any other person.

9.8.5.2   *Duty to choose default qualifying arrangement*

Schemes probably have a duty to choose a default qualifying arrangement, especially where they do not offer an internal option, ie to make the former spouse a member of the scheme.

The issues involved in selecting a default option are explored in 9.3.1.

Occupational pension schemes in particular are covered by the Act under s 191. This provides broadly that managing the assets of an occupational pension scheme does come within the ambit of FSA 1986 (and therefore requires authorisation) unless all decisions, or all day to day decisions, are delegated in a permitted manner. This section is intended to cover the management of assets, in other words the investment of assets (see FSA 1986, Sch 1 para 14).

In relation to sharing, the question is whether a decision by the trustees of an occupational scheme to transfer the pension credit of a spouse, in default of any action by the spouse, to a permitted receiving vehicle constitutes the carrying on of investment business under FSA 1986.

There are two main concerns:

*   whether the receiving vehicle is an 'investment' under FSA 1986, Sch 1 Part I and, if so,
*   whether the decision to transfer the spouse to such a vehicle is 'investment business', which it will be if (and only if) it falls within any of the activities specified under FSA 1986, Sch 1, Part II.

Is the receiving arrangement an investment?   Potential receiving vehicles may well come within the definition of 'investments', such as a personal pension whether insurance based, unit-trust based or self-invested. Certain personal pensions may not fall within the definition, for example a deposit-based personal pension. Nor are trust-based occupational schemes, which are expressly exempt from the definition of 'investments' (FSA 1986, Sch 1, para 11, note 1).

The only option under the pension sharing legislation for a non-consenting ex-spouse may be therefore a deferred annuity contract. A deferred annuity contract comes within the list of FSA 1986 'investments', as it is technically a long-term insurance policy.

Buying the annuity

For FSA 1986 purposes it makes a difference whether a person is acting as either principal or agent in relation to the 'transaction'. Since the end result of the trustees' actions is that the spouse will hold an investment (such as a long-term insurance policy or, perhaps, a personal pension) the trustees could appear to arranging for the spouse to acquire an investment. However, in circumstances where the arrangement may be being made contrary to the wishes of the spouse, it is hard to identify the trustees as the agent of the spouse.

Equally, as the trustees are giving and receiving consideration – the payment of a sum in exchange for the discharge of their liability to the spouse – it seems possible to argue that the trustees are in fact acting in some sense as principal; in some ways it can also be argued that although the annuity is in the name of the spouse it is an asset of the scheme. Alternatively it may be said that it is the trustees' purchase of an asset to be transferred to the former spouse. Most observers indicate that trustees act as principal in entering into such a transaction.

Whether the purchase is investment business Assuming the annuity or personal pension is an 'investment', the trustees need to ensure that their activities do not constitute (1) dealing in, (2) arranging deals in, (3) management of, or (4) giving investment advice in relation to, investments (see below).

The Financial Services Authority issues general guidance (see SIB Guidance Release 2/88, Pensions Advice and Management) on trustees' compliance requirements in these areas, indicating that:

- Where trustees purchase policies in order to match scheme liabilities in the case of a particular member in the name of the member and the member has decided the choice of policy, this is regarded as dealing. In practice however there is an exemption (FSA 1986, Sch 1, para 17) for dealings by persons as principals and even if they are not exempt are usually regarded as not being engaged in the business of dealing.
- Where trustees act on a member's instructions on the investment of his AVCs it is not 'management'. However, if the trustees exercise a discretion not to follow the member's instructions but to select other assets, this is regarded as day-to-day investment management. The FSA 1986 view in this area seems excessive and is probably not correct.
- In deciding whether trustees are carrying on business, generally where deals are arranged and there is no commercial benefit derived directly or indirectly by the trustees this suggests, in the absence of contrary indications, that the activity is not being engaged in as a business. Some suggest that trustees have a commercial interest, namely the discharge of their own liability to the spouse, although such a suggestion seems very thin.

There are four areas therefore where trustees might be exposed; if they deal in investments, if they arrange deals in investments, if they manage investments or if they give investment advice.

'Buying, selling, subscribing for or underwriting investments or offering or agreeing to do so, either as principal or as an agent.' In practice trustees are clearly buying investments as principal avoiding the need for trustees to be authorised under FSA 1986 due to the nature of the exemptions in relation to principals dealing for themselves.

'Making, or offering or agreeing to make (a) arrangements with a view to another person buying, selling, subscribing for or underwriting a particular investment; or (b) arrangements with a view to a person who participates in the arrangements buying, selling, subscribing for or underwriting investments.' If, as seems clear, trustees are not arranging a deal in investments (because they are acting as principal) no other person (ie the spouse) is 'buying' an investment.

'Managing, or offering or agreeing to manage, assets belonging to another person if – (a) those assets consist of or include investments; or (b) the arrangements for their management are such that those assets may consist of or include investments at the discretion of the person managing or offering or agreeing to manage them and either they have at any time since the date of the coming into force of section 3 of this Act done so or the arrangements have at any time (whether before or after that date) been held out as arrangements under which they would do so.' When a pension credit right is initially created, the assets relating to the pension credit are at that time assets of the scheme managed by the trustees and are subject to the FSA 1986, s 191.

Some might argue that it is an act of 'day-to-day investment management' if the trustees agree to acquiesce in a request by the spouse to provide internal membership where the trustees have not offered that option, or where the spouse asks the trustees not to invoke the default external option whilst she takes independent financial advice (where the time limit is about to expire). This position, where the ex-spouse has no rights to membership, is very different however to that of trustees who disregard a member's instructions on investing his own AVCs; in the sharing case, they are not using a discretion to override a member's (or spouse's) directions, since the spouse is not entitled to give such directions. It does not matter whether the spouse asks them to provide internal membership or not to do anything for a further period while the spouse's own appropriate arrangements are made, as a spouse has no such right under the legislation (although trustees may be prepared to grant such an extension in certain circumstances with appropriate protection, and a failure to do so might arguably expose them to a claim using the internal dispute resolution option in the scheme).

The decision (whether on an individual basis or a general policy basis) to transfer spouses to a particular investment is clearly not a day-to-day investment decision, since it reflects a strategic decision, and lacks any element of investment management.

Nonetheless, trustees need to carefully document the decision to provide external transfers as the default option. The decision should be expressed as a strategic decision, and include reference to the advice of an authorised investment consultant as to the appropriate vehicle for such transfers (both as a matter of general prudence and to cover any implications which the sections of PA 1995 dealing with trustees' decisions regarding investments may have here), preferably in advance of any individual case coming before the trustees in question.

'Giving, or offering or agreeing to give, to persons in their capacity as investors or potential investors advice on the merits of their purchasing, selling, subscribing for or underwriting an investment, or exercising any right conferred by an investment to acquire, dispose of, underwrite or convert an investment.' Advising on the sort of transaction envisaged under the external default transfer route might be considered to be giving investment advice.

However, trustees will need to ensure that they, as the administrators of their scheme, are aware that they cannot and must not give advice to members or spouses as to whether they should accept the default option or make their own arrangements.

Whilst FSA 1986 does permit unauthorised persons to give 'generic' advice, such as comparing the features and benefits of, for example, an occupational scheme with a personal pension arrangement, it is important to ensure that the advice does not involve a consideration of the merits of a particular product. Scheme members and their former spouse's should be encouraged to seek independent financial advice.

Pensions Act 1995 – Winding-up

The purchase of annuities for ex-spouses reflects the way trustees who exercise their powers under the Pensions Act 1995, s 74 to buy-out members' benefits where a scheme is winding-up. This may be done without the consent of any individual concerned, and there is a statutory discharge for trustees who comply with the Act, which however may not give full protection against a (criminal) breach of FSA 1986, however improbable that seems. It has never been suggested that in these circumstances trustees might be carrying on investment business under FSA 1986.

Conclusion

It seems generally agreed by practitioners that there are no compliance issues for trustees arising in relation to the pension sharing legislation and in particular any default clause for the ex-spouse's transfer values. It is reassuring that while PA 1995, s 74 involves the same or similar issues, no concern has ever been expressed by the pensions industry or regulators.

Trustees who are nonetheless uncomfortable with their position may prefer to grant internal default transfer or, where available, to seek products which are clearly outside the need for compliance, such as deposit-based personal pensions.

9.8.5.3 *Internal option provision*

While many of the government's consultative documents indicate that a deferred spouse who takes an internal option instead of an external transfer could be treated as a 'deferred pension', in practice this is somewhat misleading. Deferred pensioners once had some form of contact with the employer; a person with an internal option will, however, not necessarily participate in surplus distribution or survivor's benefits, or even have the right to vote for a member nominated trustee.

Many schemes will designate people with internal option rights as a separate group, rather than a deferred pensioner, to avoid confusion and the granting of rights it does not wish to grant. Such a group may also specifically have designated rights, the basis on which the credit is given and the power available to amend schemes. Most rules will arrange for trustees to be discharged by reference to statutory compliance and contracted-out schemes will need to refer to the provisions on safeguarded rights (ie shared elements of SERPS).

Schemes which decide to offer only external rights may wish to consider granting special protection for trustees who comply with the regulations.

9.8.5.4   Trustee protection

Duties have a battery of compliance requirements: providing information; providing CETVs; meeting time limits; charging costs within limits; and complying with orders or agreements. Regulations (Pension Sharing (Implementation and Discharge of Liability) Regulations, SI 2000/1053; WRAPA 1999, Sch 5) protect trustees, provided they are compliant. Most trustees will discharge their obligations by transferring credits to an appropriate scheme (eg another occupational scheme or personal pension scheme).

9.8.5.5   Unfunded schemes

Transfers from unfunded schemes must be with the member's consent and with compensation for any tax liability for the former spouse, so such transfers are highly unlikely. Internal transfers are therefore normally recommended for private sector unfunded schemes.

9.8.5.6   Recovery schemes

Managers of personal pension schemes which receive a transfer payment are regulated by the provisions of The Personal Pension Scheme (Transfer Payments) Regulations 2001, SI 2001/119, reg 13.

9.9   Contracted-out schemes

9.9.1   Background

There was much debate about whether sharing, in particular, should apply to the second tier of state pensions; the first tier was never in debate, it being an element of social security rather than a financial asset. The 1999 legislation concluded that while earmarking should not apply to SERPS benefits or their equivalents (GMPs and requisite benefits), sharing should. Not only does sharing now apply to SERPS benefits, but also to the forthcoming stakeholder pensions and the state second pension (S2P), which also possess the characteristics of social security rather than private assets. The basic State Retirement Pension (and survivors' pensions) remain unshareable.

9.9.2   Safeguarded rights

Rights of a scheme member derived from membership of a contracted-out occupational or appropriate personal pension (APP) scheme (ie a personal pension scheme which provides contracted-out benefits) which are transferred to the former spouse as a result of a pension sharing order or agreement become 'safeguarded rights'. This is in distinction from the contracted-out rights built up by a *member* of a contracted-out occupational or APP scheme.

Scheme rules can specify whether all of the accrued rights that are subject to a pension share become safeguarded rights; safeguarded rights may therefore include some non-contracted-out rights and indeed safeguarded rights from a previous divorce.

The requirements for safeguarded rights broadly reflect those for contracted-out rights. The policy intention is to ensure that safeguarded rights (which are wholly or in part financed by rebates of National Insurance contributions and, in the case of appropriate personal pension schemes, tax relief on the employee's share of the rebate) are securely protected and used for the purpose for which they are intended – to provide an income in retirement.

The 'safeguarded' rights are ringfenced and are subject to broadly the same conditions that apply to post-1997 salary-related contracted-out rights or protected rights. Schemes are not required to provide survivors' benefits from safeguarded rights and they are not tracked by the Inland Revenue National Insurance Contributions Office's (IRNICO) Contracted-Out Employments Group (COEG).

A pension in respect of safeguarded rights must start to be paid between the ages of 60 and 65, unless early payment is appropriate, for example because of ill-health.

Since safeguarded rights are not tracked or monitored by COEG, schemes must themselves maintain accurate records when a former spouse's rights are preserved in the scheme, transferred or bought out through an insurance policy. Schemes also need to keep details of the pension sharing order, in order to record the percentage of the share on the member's pension account.

Safeguarded rights are broadly the rights which attach to *shared* SERPS benefits or their equivalents; *earmarking* cannot apply to such benefits. All contracted-out rights attributed to a former spouse following a pensions share are normally referred to by the term; where the scheme rules do not identify contracted-out and non-contracted-out rights separately, all the pension credits are safeguarded.

The rules for safeguarded rights are broadly in line with the regime for contracted-out rights (the one in place since 6 April 1997). For example, where the safeguarded rights are to provide money purchase benefits, the safeguarded rights requirements are similar to those for post 6 April 1997 protected rights with some exceptions, for example, schemes are not compelled to provide survivor's benefits from safeguarded rights (see Pension Sharing (Safeguarded Rights) Regulations 2000, SI 2000/1055 and DSS, Consultation Document, Chapter 6, December 1999).

Schemes need to reflect whether they wish to hold safeguarded rights and whether they meet the safeguarded requirements.

9.9.3 *Calculation services*

Since occupational pension and appropriate personal pensions schemes are required to provide a valuation of accrued pension rights to enable the courts to decide on the fairest overall settlement of assets, COEG uses existing calculation services currently to allow schemes to request a Guaranteed Minimum Pension (GMP)/Contracted-out Deduction (COD) calculation at any time during the pension sharing procedures. As with the existing Individual Calculation Service, calculations for pension sharing cases are free.

9.9.4   Pension sharing on divorce notification

Where pension rights have been shared, the courts formally notify the scheme which in turn must notify COEG. Schemes have four months in which to implement the pension sharing order. A form, 'Pension Sharing on Divorce Notification' CA2202 (available on the web for downloading (www.inlandrevenue.gov.uk)), must be completed by scheme administrators and providers to notify COEG of the pension share.

COEG then updates the National Insurance accounts of both the member and the former spouse to show that a 'Pension Share' has occurred. Details from the form are held on a database, which can be interrogated to answer any specific inquiries about the pension share itself.

9.9.5   Contracted-out deduction

When a member's pension rights are shared with a former spouse, a full COD is deducted from the member's Additional Pension under SERPS. The COD is not reduced to take account of any GMP or protected rights that are subject to a pension sharing order or agreement.

9.9.5.1   Statements of GMP liability

The calculation of contracted-out pension rights does not take account of any pension rights shared on divorce. The full GMP amount therefore continues to be notified. Statements which show a GMP amount (except for those issued by magnetic media) include the notation 'The amount quoted does not take account of any pension rights shared on divorce' whether or not a pension share has taken place.

9.9.6   Supervision of safeguarded rights

Schemes that opt to hold safeguarded rights after having elected to contract out are not required to advise COEG that they intend to start holding safeguarded rights. However, schemes that hold a contracting-out certificate must indicate at triennial re-assurance whether or not they hold safeguarded rights. In such cases, schemes need to confirm that they hold safeguarded rights and meet the prescribed requirements.

9.9.7   Cessation of contracting-out

Scheme that cease to be contracted-out have two years in which to make arrangements to secure all safeguarded rights held within the scheme.

9.9.7.1   Securing safeguarded rights – salary-related schemes

Safeguarded rights may be secured by:

- Transfer to a Contracted-out Money Purchase (COMP) scheme or the active COMP part of a Contracted-out Mixed Benefit (COMB) scheme.
- Transfer to a Contracted-out Salary-Related (COSR) scheme or the active COSR part of a COMB scheme.
- Transfer to an appropriate personal pension (APP) scheme.
- Purchase of an annuity.
- Preservation within the scheme.

9.9.7.2   Securing safeguarded rights – money purchase schemes

Safeguarded rights may be secured by:

- Transfer to a Contracted-out Money Purchase (COMP) scheme or the active COMP part of a Contracted-out Mixed Benefit (COMB) scheme.
- Transfer to a Contracted-out Salary-Related (COSR) scheme or the active COSR part of a COMB scheme.
- Transfer to an appropriate personal pension (APP) scheme.
- Purchase of an annuity.
- Preservation within the scheme.
- Provision of a pension.
- Appropriate policy of insurance.

Since safeguarded rights are not tracked or monitored by the Inland Revenue, COEG does not issue calculations or membership lists to the life office or administrator. Schemes should advise COEG as soon as all the safeguarded rights held by the scheme have been secured, although details of the individual arrangements are not required. Approval is confirmed by the issue of a letter to the scheme.

9.9.7.3   Restoration of state scheme rights (deemed buyback)

Safeguarded rights cannot be restored in the state scheme; they must be secured by some other approved means.

Where scheme trustees intend to secure members' contracted-out rights in the state scheme, COEG need to be able to calculate the correct Technical Amount for the restoration of their rights in SERPS. Occupational pension schemes must therefore inform COEG of any members whose contracted-out rights have been shared with a former spouse as part of the divorce settlement.

9.10   Costs and charges

The costs to the parties of bills rendered by pension scheme implementing earmarking came as something of an unwelcome surprise. But pension schemes had to pay for additional actuarial, legal and administrative costs, some of them quite substantial.

In an attempt to learn from this, pension schemes are encouraged to adopt standardised practices, so that court orders will be in a standard form, and fees charged by schemes will be underpinned by a standard scale of charges. The general principles underlying charges (whether for earmarking or sharing or any combination) include WRAPA 1999, ss 23, 24, 41; and the Pensions on Divorceetc (Charging) Regulations 2000, SI 2000/1049:

- that it is the divorcing couple, not scheme members generally, or the employer or trustees, who bear the administrative costs associated with a pension share;
- that where there is no agreement is made by the couple about costs or if there is no court order on the point costs are carried by the member; and
- that after the scheme has offered from the outset the parties a chance to pay charges, the scheme is able to deduct charges direct from the member. This avoids the prospect of a member resisting the divorce delaying divorce proceedings simply by refusing to pay the scheme's charges. Contracted-out schemes do not have to obtain separate certificates in relation to 'safeguarded' rights, to reduce administration costs.

9.10.1   The regulations

The underlying principle is that the parties, rather than the scheme, pay the costs of sharing. The government considered, however, that there was a need to balance the ability of pension arrangements to recover charges with the need of the couple to know what those charges are before a pensions sharing order or agreement is made. If, therefore, the Schedule of charges is not supplied at the time the basic information about the scheme is supplied, the scheme may not recover charges.

There are no specific limits on the charges, since it was concerned that any upper limit would come to be treated as a standard charge. However all charges must be:

- reasonable; and
- linked to the costs associated with each individual case. This might mean that it is not possible to spread or average the costs, and expensive cases should be charged more.

To control charges, the Dispute Regulations (Occupational Pension Schemes (Internal Dispute Resolution Procedures) Regulations 1996, SI 1996/1270 and the Personal and Occupational Pension Scheme (Pensions Ombudsman) Regulations 1996, SI 1996/2475) enable former spouses who qualify for a pension credit to obtain clarification about the pensions arrangement's charges and to dispute unreasonable charges. The NAPF has issued guidance to members on appropriate charges (NAPF *Guidance to Members* 2000, reproduced in Appendix VIII).

9.10.2   Recovering costs

The rules on recovering costs are set out in the Pensions on Divorce etc (Charging) Regulations 2000, SI 2000/1049. In order to be in a position to recover charges, schemes must:

- make clear the intention to charge (reg 2) when the parties make an inquiry in connection with pensions in relation to divorce, nullity or judicial separation proceedings;
- supply a schedule of charges at the time the enquiry is made. The schedule can be amended at any time and there is separate provision for late appeals (reg 2(7));
- set out in the schedule whether they intend to recover certain specific charges. For example, pension arrangements who want to offer internal membership to former spouses entitled to a pension credit can only make a charge in relation to the ongoing administration of the pension credit member's rights if such charges are clearly set out in the schedule of charges (reg 2(4)); and
- not charge for certain information (reg 3(2)), in particular
  - costs of compliance with a court order for valuation under the Pensions on Divorce etc (Provision of Information) Regulations 2000, SI 2000/1048;
  - where there has been no request for a valuation for over 12 months costs of information which should normally be supplied under the Provision of Information Regulations 2000; and
  - costs of information which should normally be supplied under the Occupational Pension Schemes (Disclosure of Information) Regulations 1996, SI 1996/1655 and the Personal Pension Schemes (Disclosure of Information) Regulations 1987, SI 1987/1110

which should normally be provided free under the regulations, the only charge being for those items specifically itemised in the schedule of charges.

In summary, charge can therefore only normally be made:

- for information not normally made available;
- valuations not normally made available; and
- additional administration costs as a consequence of any order.

It is therefore critical, if charging is to be made, to express the invoice carefully.

9.10.3 How to charge

A pension scheme can insist on payment up front before providing any information for which a charge can be made (reg 4(1)) but not where there is a court order for a member to obtain information or it is statutorily required information as above.

In particular, it can charge for 'pension sharing activity' or provision of information after receipt of an earmarking order. Such charges can only be reasonable and those which are incurred in relation to an individual case (presumably rather than standard charges, which makes it difficult to set out a schedule of charges!). It also limits costs to those costs incurred by a person responsible for a pension arrangement which are not directly related to the costs which arise in relation to an individual case. A 'not' may well have been accidentally inserted here; whatever the proper reading, it seems incomprehensible, but the provision presumably is intended to allow for additional valuation costs. How anyone will be able to determine which is what is not explained.

These additional costs include (reg 6(1)):

- implementing a pensions sharing order; and
- interest on unpaid costs, not exceeding 5%.

In any event, an invoice or statement must be issued in writing setting out the costs, the interest charged on costs and final costs. Costs can only be increased by the RPI up to a maximum of 5%. This provision is presumably a reference to ongoing administrative costs.

If the charges are not paid on time, the scheme can delay implementation; and if steps are to be taken to recover unpaid charges, the scheme must make it clear to the parties (before any order or agreement is made) that it will not implement until charges are paid. The scheme can make such a notification at any time before the making of the order (reg 7).

A payment in respect of one of the parties to the sharing order or agreement (eg the former spouse) on behalf of the other party (eg the member whose pension is to be shared) is recoverable from the other party as a debt and presumably can be set off against the pension rights.

There are explicit procedures (regs 9 and 10) for recovery of all charges from the person named or, if there is no-one named, from the accrued rights of the member whose pension is to be shared or earmarked. Schemes can recover outstanding charges at any time during the period beginning 21 days after the charges have been requested and ending 21 days after liability for the pension credit has been discharged. The time limits do not apply to periodical post-order charges.

9.10.4   *The recommended charges*

Scheme members have a right to appeal against non-standard charges through the Pensions Ombudsman. Whether the scale reflects the actual costs to a scheme is not yet known, and there will be little in the structure to reflect the costs of checking whether the court order is acceptable, or appearing before the court or responding to additional requests for information by the parties or their lawyers. There are no charges imposed by IRNICO in respect of SERPS rights.

9.11   Rebuilding shared pension rights

Members whose rights are debited following a pension share are mostly prevented by Inland Revenue rules from rebuilding them. This is because the debit is included as part of the member's pension rights in calculating whether or not the member exceeds Revenue maxima. Even non-contributory members who could pay up to 15% of pay towards rebuilding can find themselves unable to reach the permitted maximum.

There is a paradox in that a couple that marries and then divorces is worse off than those who cohabit without marrying (who are treated as separate individuals with separate tax and pension allowances). It also militates against second families managing to build up retirement income and, in particular, the position of women in retirement.

In March 1999, the Inland Revenue introduced a superficial relaxation (letter to NAPF, 22 March 1999). It indicated that while they did not wish to give special tax reliefs to people whose pensions have been shared, they agreed to grant a limited casement. This involved treating the shared pension (ie the pension rights awarded to the ex-spouse) for tax limit purposes in broadly the same way as pension benefits from earlier employments. The relaxation is now set out in the otherwise impenetrable Retirement Benefits Schemes (Sharing of Pensions on Divorce or Annulment) Regulations 2000, SI 2000/1085 amending FA 1999, Sch 10).

The normal tax approval rule is that the maximum pension on retirement from all employments is two-thirds of final pay. But there are exceptions for schemes which provide pensions of $1/60$ or less pa or where the scheme members have moderate earnings. This approach is extended to pension shares, with the result that for most scheme members on moderate earnings, ie annual remuneration not exceeding one-quarter of the 'earnings cap' (£22,950 for 2000/2001) at the time of divorce (other than controlling directors), pension debits are ignored in arriving at the tax approval benefit limits under occupational pension schemes. This allows, said the Revenue, almost all occupational pension scheme members on moderate incomes who pension share to pay extra contributions within the annual 15% limit on employee contributions. To avoid special tax reliefs for divorced couples, the 15% member contribution limit on earnings continues to apply, as do the contribution limits for personal pensions. If in future the earnings threshold for the casement on retained benefits is increased, the Revenue intend that the same threshold will be extended to the casement for pension sharers.

The improvement is largely cosmetic (even though a wedge in the hitherto impregnable Revenue limits fortress). Few members earning 25% or less of the cap are exempted, and those that are will usually find it hard, especially after a divorce, to afford to pay additional contributions.

Details are set out above at 8.9.

9.12 Advice and training

One of the burdens on pension schemes in the past has been the continuous stream of inappropriate orders (not always draft) coming across their desks, and the requests for information and advice which family law practitioners are unable, through lack of training and experience, to understand.

The latest sharing provisions have prompted an understanding within the Judicial Studies Board and the Law Society of the need for training, not only to benefit lawyers and the courts and their clients, but also reduce the call for resources on pension funds. That training will take some time to have an impact, but will clearly make life easier for scheme managers over the next few years.

Appendices

Appendix I

Legislation and other sources

The majority of the amendments to the Matrimonial Causes Act are made by the Pensions Act 1995 and the Welfare Reform and Pensions Act 1999. For reasons of space, provisions applicable to proceedings issued before 1 December 2000 are not included, except where temporarily relevant.

This compilation contains the relevant parts (as amended) of the legislation and other sources listed below. (Amendments introduced by the Pension Sharing (Consequential and Miscellaneous Amendments) Regulations 2000, SI 2000/ 2691 are incorporated in the amended provisions but not separately reproduced.)

Separate legislation applies in Scotland; the relevant statutory instruments are reproduced as mentioned. Parallel Northern Ireland legislation is not reproduced, although see The Pensions on Divorce etc (Provision of Information) Regulations (Northern Ireland) 2000, SR 2000/142; The Pensions on Divorce etc (Charging) regulations (Northern Ireland) 2000 SR 2000/143; The Pension Sharing (Valuation) Regulations (Northern Ireland) 2000 SR 2000/144; The Pension Sharing (Implementation and Discharge of Liability) Regulations (Northern Ireland) Regulations 2000, SR 2000/145; The Pension Sharing (Pension Credit Benefit) Regulations (Northern Ireland) 2000, SR 2000/146; The Pension Sharing (Safeguarded Rights) Regulations (Northern Ireland) 2000, SR 2000/147.

Contents

Matrimonial Causes Act 1973

21A Pension sharing orders

(1) For the purposes of this Act, a pension sharing order is an order which—

    (a) provides that one party's—

        (i) shareable rights under a specified pension arrangement, or

        (ii) shareable state scheme rights

            be subject to pension sharing for the benefit of the other party, and

    (b) specifies the percentage value to be transferred.

(2) In subsection (1) above—

    (a) the reference to shareable rights under a pension arrangement is to rights in relation to which pension sharing is available under Chapter I of Part IV of the Welfare Reform and Pensions Act 1999, or under corresponding Northern Ireland legislation,

    (b) the reference to shareable state scheme rights is to rights in relation to which pension sharing

    (c) 'party' means a party to a marriage. . . .

24B Pension sharing orders in connection with divorce proceedings

(1) On granting a decree of divorce or a decree of nullity of marriage or at any time thereafter (whether before or after the decree is made absolute), the court may, on an application made under this section, make one or more pension sharing orders in relation to the marriage.

(2) A pension sharing order under this section is not to take effect unless the decree on or after which it is made has been made absolute.

(3) A pension sharing order under this section may not be made in relation to a pension arrangement which—

    (a) is the subject of a pension sharing order in relation to the marriage, or

    (b) has been the subject of pension sharing between the parties to the marriage.

(4) A pension sharing order under this section may not be made in relation to shareable state scheme rights if—

    (a) such rights are the subject of a pension sharing order in relation to the marriage, or

    (b) such rights have been the subject of pension sharing between the parties to the marriage.

(5) A pension sharing order under this section may not be made in relation to the rights of a person under a pension arrangement if there is in force a requirement imposed by virtue of section 25B or 25C below which relates to benefits or future benefits to which he is entitled under the pension arrangement.

24C   Pension sharing orders: duty to stay

(1) No pension sharing order may be made so as to take effect before the end of such period after the making of the order as may be prescribed by regulations made by the Lord Chancellor.

(2) The power to make regulations under this section shall be exercisable by statutory instrument which shall be subject to annulment in pursuance of a resolution of either House of Parliament.

24D   Pension sharing orders: apportionment of charges

If a pension sharing order relates to rights under a pension arrangement, the court may include in the order provision about the apportionment between the parties of any charge under section 41 of the Welfare Reform and Pensions Act 1999 (charges in respect of pension sharing costs), or under corresponding Northern Ireland legislation.

25   Matters to which the court is to have regard in deciding how to exercise its powers under ss 23, 24 and 24A

(1) It shall be the duty of the court in deciding whether to exercise its powers under section 23, 24, 24A or 24B above and, if so, in what manner, to have regard to all the circumstances of the case, first consideration being given to the welfare while a minor of any child of the family who has not attained the age of eighteen.

(2) As regards the exercise of the powers of the court under section 23(1)(a), (b) or (c), 24, 24A or 24B above in relation to a party to the marriage, the court shall in particular have regard to the following matters—

(a) the income, earning capacity, property and other financial resources which each of the parties to the marriage has or is likely to have in the foreseeable future, including in the case of earning capacity any increase in that capacity which it would in the opinion of the court be reasonable to expect a party to the marriage to take steps to acquire;

(b) the financial needs, obligations and responsibilities which each of the parties to the marriage has or is likely to have in the foreseeable future;

(c) the standard of living enjoyed by the family before the breakdown of the marriage;

(d) the age of each party to the marriage and the duration of the marriage;

(e) any physical or mental disability of either of the parties to the marriage;

(f) the contributions which each of the parties has made or is likely in the foreseeable future to make to the welfare of the family, including any contribution by looking after the home or caring for the family;

(g) the conduct of each of the parties, if that conduct is such that it would in the opinion of the court be inequitable to disregard it;

(h) in the case of proceedings for divorce or nullity of marriage, the value to each of the parties to the marriage of any benefit which, by reason of the dissolution or annulment of the marriage, that party will lose the chance of acquiring.

(3) As regards the exercise of the powers of the court under section 23(1)(d), (e) or (f), (2) or (4), 24 or 24A above in relation to a child of the family, the court shall in particular have regard to the following matters—

(a) the financial needs of the child;

(b) the income, earning capacity (if any), property and other financial resources of the child;

(c) any physical or mental disability of the child;

(d) the manner in which he was being and in which the parties to the marriage expected him to be educated or trained;

(e) the considerations mentioned in relation to the parties to the marriage in paragraphs (a), (b), (c) and (e) of subsection (2) above;

(4) As regards the exercise of the powers of the court under section 23(1)(d), (e) or (f), (2) or (4), 24 or 24A above against a party to a marriage in favour of a child of the family who is not a child of that party, the court shall also have regard—

(a) to whether that party assumed any responsibility for the child's maintenance, and, if so, to the extent to which, and the basis upon which, that party assumed such responsibility and to the length of time for which that party discharged such responsibility;

(b) to whether in assuming and discharging such responsibility that party did so knowing that the child was not his her own;

(c) to the liability of any other person to maintain the child.

25A Exercise of court's powers in favour of party to marriage on decree of divorce or nullity of marriage

(1) Where on or after the grant of a decree or nullity of marriage the court decides to exercise its powers under section 23(1)(a), (b) or (c), 24, 24A or 24B above in favour of a party to the marriage, it shall be the duty of the court to consider whether it would be appropriate so to exercise those powers that the financial obligations of each party towards the other will be terminated as soon after the grant of the decree as the court considers just and reasonable.

(2) Whether the court decides in such a case to make a periodical payments or secured periodical payments order in favour of a party to the marriage, the court shall in particular consider whether it would be appropriate to require those payments to be made or secured only for such a term as would in the opinion of the court be sufficient to enable the party in whose favour the order is made to adjust without undue hardship to the termination of his or her financial dependence on the other party.

(3) Where on or after the grant of a decree of divorce or nullity of marriage an application is made by a party to the marriage for a periodical payments or secured periodical payments order in his or her favour, then, if the court considers that no continuing obligation should be imposed on either party to make or secure periodical payments in favour of the other, the court may dismiss the application with a direction that the applicant shall not be entitled to make any further application in relation to that marriage for an order under section 23(1)(a) or (b) above.

25B Pensions

(1) The matters to which the court is to have regard under section 25(2) above include—

(a) in the case of paragraph (a), any benefits under a pension arrangement which a party to the marriage has or is likely to have, and

(b) in the case of paragraph (h), any benefits under a pension arrangement which, by reason of the dissolution or annulment of the marriage, a party to the marriage will lose the chance of acquiring,

and, accordingly, in relation to benefits under a pension arrangement, section 25(2)(a) above shall have effect as if 'in the foreseeable future' were omitted.

(2) [*Repealed by Welfare Reform and Pensions Act 1999 Schedule 4, Para 1(2), Schedule 10, Part II.*]

(3) The following provisions apply where, having regard to any benefits under a pension arrangement, the court determines to make an order under section 23 above.

(4) To the extent to which the order is made having regard to any benefits under a pension arrangement, the order may require the person responsible for the pension arrangement in question, if at any time any payment in respect of any benefits under the arrangement becomes due to the party with pension rights, to make a payment for the benefit of the other party.

(5) The order must express the amount of any percentage required to be made by virtue of subsection (4) above as a percentage of the payment which becomes due to the party with pension rights.

(6) Any such payment by the person responsible for the arrangement—

(a) shall discharge so much of his liability to the party with pension rights as corresponds to the amount of the payment, and

(b) shall be treated for all purposes as a payment made by the party with pension rights in or towards the discharge of his liability under the order.

(7) Where the party with pension rights has a right of commutation under the arrangement, the order may require him to exercise it to any extent and this section applies to any payment due in consequence of commutation in pursuance of the order as it applies to other payments in respect of benefits under the arrangement.

(7A) The power conferred by subsection (7) above may not be exercised for the purpose of commuting a benefit payable to the party with pension rights to a benefit payable to the other party.

(7B) The power conferred by subsection (4) or (7) above may not be exercised in relation to a pension arrangement which—

(a) is the subject of a pension sharing order in relation to the marriage, or

(b) has been the subject of pension sharing between the parties to the marriage.

(7C) In subsection (1) above, references to benefits under a pension arrangement include any benefits by way of pension, whether under a pension arrangement or not.

25C   Pensions: lump sums

(1) The power of the court under section 23 above to order a party to a marriage to pay a lump sum to the other party includes, where the benefits which the party with pension rights has or is likely to have under a pension arrangement include any lump sum payable in respect of his death, power to make any of the following provision by the order.

(2) The court may—

(a) if the person responsible for the pension arrangement in question has power to determine the person to whom the sum, or any part of it, is to be paid, require him to pay the whole or part of that sum, when it becomes due, to the other party,

(b) if the party with pension rights has power to nominate the person to whom the sum, or any part of it, is to be paid, require the party with pension rights to nominate the other party in respect of the whole or part of that sum,

(c) in any other case, require the person responsible for the arrangement in question to pay the whole or part of that sum, when it becomes due, for the benefit of the other party instead of to the person to whom, apart from the order, it would be paid.

(3) Any payment by the person responsible for the arrangement under an order made under section 23 above by virtue of this section shall discharge so much of his liability in respect of the party with pension rights as corresponds to the amount of the payment.

(4) The powers conferred by this section may not be exercised in relation to a pension arrangement which—

  (a) is the subject of a pension sharing order in relation to the marriage, or

  (b) has been the subject of pension sharing between the parties to the marriage.

25D Pensions: supplementary

(1) Where—

  (a) an order made under section 22A or 23 above by virtue of section 25B or 25C above imposes any requirement on the person responsible for a pension arrangement ('**the first arrangement**') and the party with pension rights acquires rights under another pension arrangement ('**the second arrangement**') which are derived (directly or indirectly) from the whole of his rights under the first arrangement, and

  (b) the person responsible for the new arrangement has been given notice in accordance with regulations made by the Lord Chancellor,

the order shall have effect as if it has been made instead in respect of the person responsible for the new arrangement.

(2) The Lord Chancellor may by regulations—

  (a) in relation to any provision of sections 25B or 25C above which authorises the court making an order under section 23 above to require the person responsible for a pension arrangement to make a payment for the benefit of the other party, make provision as to the person to whom, and the terms on which, the payment is to be made,

  (ab) make, in relation to a payment under a mistaken belief as to the continuation in force of a provision included by virtue of section 25B or 25C above in an order under section 22A or 23 above, provision about the rights or liabilities of the payer, the payee or the person to whom the payment was due,

  (b) require notices to be given in respect of changes of circumstances relevant to such orders which include provision made by virtue of section 25B and 25C above,

  (ba) make provision for the person responsible for a pension arrangement to be discharged in prescribed circumstances from a requirement imposed by virtue of section 25B or 25C above,

  (c) [*Repealed by Welfare Reform and Pensions Act 1999 Schedule 4 para 3(e); Schedule 10 Part II.*]

  (d) [*Repealed by Welfare Reform and Pensions Act 1999 Schedule 4 para 3(e).*]

  (e) make provision about calculation and verification in relation to the valuation of—

    (i)   benefits under a pension arrangement

    (ii) shareable state scheme rights,

    for the purposes of the court's functions in connection with the exercise of its powers under any of sections 22A to 24D above.

(2A) Regulations under subsection (2)(e) above may include provision by reference to regulations under section 22 or 41(4) of the Welfare Reform and Pensions Act 1999.

(2B) Regulations under subsection (2) may make different provision for different cases.

(2C) The Secretary of State may by regulations—

  (a) impose on the person responsible for a pension arrangement, or the Secretary of State, requirements with respect to the supply of information relevant to the exercise of the court's powers under any of sections 22A to 24G above, 25B and 25C above,

(b) make provision about calculation and verification in relation to the valuation of—

    (i)   benefits under a pension arrangement, or

    (ii) shareable state scheme rights,

    for the purposes of regulations under paragraph (a) above,

(c) make provision for the purpose of enabling the person responsible for a pension arrangement to recover prescribed charges in respect of—

    (i)   complying with an order under section 22A or 23 above, so far as it includes provision made by virtue of section 25B or 25C above, or

    (ii) providing information in accordance with regulations under paragraph (a) above.

(2D) Regulations under subsection (2)(e) or (2C)(b) above may include provision for calculation or verification in accordance with guidance from time to time prepared by a person prescribed by the regulations.

(2E) Subsections (3) to (6) of section 68 of the Welfare Reform and Pensions Act 1999 (Regulations) shall have effect in relation to power to make regulations under subsection (2C) above as they have effect in relation to power to make regulations under that Act.

(2F) Power to make regulations under this section shall be exercisable by statutory instrument which shall be subject to annulment in pursuance of a resolution of either House of Parliament.'

(3) In this section and sections 25B and 25C above—

    '**occupational pension scheme**' has the same meaning as in the Pension Schemes Act 1993;

    '**the party with pension rights**' means the party to the marriage who has or is likely to have benefits under a pension arrangement and 'the other party' means the other party to the marriage;

    '**pension arrangement**' means—

(a) an occupational pension scheme,

(b) a personal pension scheme,

(c) a retirement annuity contract,

(d) an annuity or insurance policy purchased, or transferred, for the purpose of giving effect to rights under an occupational pension scheme or a personal pension scheme, and

(e) an annuity purchased, or entered into, for the purpose of discharging liability in respect of a pension credit under section 21(1)(b) of the Welfare Reform and Pensions Act 1999 or under corresponding Northern Ireland legislation;

    '**personal pension scheme**' has the same meaning as in the Pension Schemes Act 1993;

    '**prescribed**' means prescribed by regulations;

    '**retirement annuity contract**' means a contract or scheme approved under Chapter III of Part XIV of the Income and Corporation Taxes Act 1988;

    '**shareable state scheme rights**' has the same meaning as in section 21(2A) above; and

    '**trustees or managers**', in relation to an occupational pension scheme or a personal pension scheme, means—

(a) in the case of a scheme established under a trust, the trustees of the scheme, and

(b) in any other case, the managers of the scheme.

(4) In this section and sections 25B and 25C above, references to the person responsible for a pension arrangement are—

(a) in the case of an occupational pension scheme or a personal pension scheme, to the trustees or managers of the scheme,

(b) in the case of a retirement annuity contract or an annuity falling within paragraph (d) or (e) of the definition of 'pension arrangement' above, the provider of the annuity, and

(c) in the case of an insurance policy falling within paragraph (d) of the definition of that expression, the insurer.

31   Variation, discharge etc. of certain orders for financial relief

(1) Where the court has made an order to which this section applies, then, subject to the provisions of this section and of section 28(1A) above, the court shall have power to vary or discharge the order or to suspend any provision thereof temporarily and to revive the operation of any provision so suspended.

(2) This section applies to the following orders [*under this Part of this Act*], that is to say—

(a) any [*order for maintenance pending suit and any*] interim order for maintenance;

(b) any periodical payments order;

(c) any secured periodical payments order;

(d) any order made by virtue of section 23(3)(c) or 27(7)(b) above (provision for payment of a lump sum by instalments);

(dd) any deferred order made by virtue of section 21(1)(c) (lump sums) which includes provision made by virtue of—

(i)   section 25B(4), or

(ii) section 25(C),

(provision of pension rights)

(de) any other order for the payment of a lump sum, if it is made at a time when no divorce order has been made, and no separation order is in force, in relation to the marriage;

(e) any order under section 23A of a kind referred to in section 21(2)(b), (c) or (d) which is made on or after the making of a separation order;

(ea) any order under section 23A which is made at a time when no divorce order has been made, and no separation order is in force, in relation to the marriage;

(f) any order made under section 24A(1) above for the sale of property.

(g) a pension sharing order under section 24B above which is made at a time before the decree has been made absolute.

(2A) Where the court has made an order referred to in subsection 2(a), (b) or (c) above, then subject to the provisions of this section, the court shall have power to remit the payment of any arrears due under the order or of any part thereof.

(2B) Where the court has made an order referred to in subsection 2(dd)(ii) above, this section shall cease to apply to the order on the death of either of the parties to the marriage.

(3) The powers exercisable by the court under this section in relation to an order shall be exercisable also in relation to any instrument executed in pursuance of the order.

(4) The court shall not exercise the powers conferred by this section in relation to an order for a settlement under section 24(1)(b) or for a variation of settlement under section 24(1)(c) or (d) above except on an application made in proceedings—

    (a) for the rescission of the decree of judicial separation by reference to which the order was made, or

    (b) for the dissolution of the marriage in question.

(4A) In relation to an order which falls within paragraph (g) of subsection (2) above (**'the subsection (2) order'**)—

    (a) the powers conferred by this section may be exercised—

        (i) only on an application made before the subsection (2) order has or, but for paragraph (b) below, would have taken effect; and

        (ii) only if, at the time when the application is made, the decree has not been made absolute; and

    (b) an application made in accordance with paragraph (a) above prevents the subsection (2) order from taking effect before the application has been dealt with.

(4B) No variation of a pension sharing order shall be made so as to take effect before the decree is made absolute.

(4C) The variation of a pension sharing order prevents the order taking effect before the end of such period after the making of the variation as may be prescribed by regulations made by the Lord Chancellor.

(4D) The variation of a pension sharing order prevents the order taking effect before the end of such period after the making of the variation as may be prescribed by rules made by the Lord Chancellor.

(5) Subject to subsections (7A) to (7G) below and without prejudice to any power exercisable by virtue of subsection (2)(d), (e) or (g) above or otherwise than by virtue of this section no property adjustment order or pension sharing order shall be made on an application for the variation of a periodical payments or secured periodical payments order made (whether in favour of a party to a marriage or in favour of a child of the family) under section 22A or 23 above, and no order for the payment of a lump sum shall be made on an application for the variation of a periodical payments or secured periodical payments order in favour of a party to a marriage (whether made under section 22A, 23 or under section 27 above).

(6) Where the person liable to make payments under a secured periodical payments order has died, an application under this section relating to that order (and to any order made under section 24A(1) above which requires the proceeds of sale of property to be used for securing those payments) may be made by the person entitled to payments under the periodical payments order or by the personal representatives of the deceased person, but no such application shall, except with the permission of the court, be made after the end of the period of six months from the date on which representation in regard to the estate of that person is first taken out.

(7) In exercising the powers conferred by this section the court shall have regard to all the circumstances of the case, first consideration being given to the welfare while a minor of any child of the family who has not attained the age of eighteen, and the circumstances of the case shall include any change in any of the matters to which the court was required to have regard when making the order to which the application relates, and—

    (a) in the case of a periodical payments or secured periodical payments order made in favour of a party to the marriage the court shall, if the marriage has been dissolved or annulled consider whether in all the circumstances and after having regard to any such change it would be appropriate to vary the order so that payments under the order are required to be made or secured only for such further period as will in the opinion of the court be sufficient in the light of any proposed exercise by the court, where the marriage has been dissolved, of its powers under subsection (7B) below, to enable the party in whose favour the order was made to adjust without undue hardship to the termination of those payments;

(b) in a case where the party against whom the order was made has died, the circumstances of the case shall also include the changed circumstances resulting from his or her death.

(7A) . . .

(7B) . . .

(7C) . . .

(7D) . . .

(7E). . .

(7F). . .

(7G)   Subsections (3) to (5) of section 24B above apply in relation to a pension sharing order under subsection (7B) above as they apply in relation to a pension sharing order under that section.

(7H)   Section 24C(5) to (7) above apply in relation to a pension sharing order under subsection (7B) above as they apply in relation to such an order under section 24B above. . .

(8) The personal representatives of a deceased person against whom a secured periodical payments order was made shall not be liable for having distributed any part of the estate of the deceased after the expiration of the period of six months referred to in subsection (6) above on the ground that they ought to have taken into account the possibility that the court might permit an application under this section to be made after that period by the person entitled to payments under the order; but this subsection shall not prejudice any power to recover any part of the estate so distributed arising by virtue of the making of an order in pursuance of this section.

(9) In considering for the purposes of subsection (6) above the question when representation was first taken out, a grant limited to settled land or to trust property shall be left out of account and a grant limited to real estate or to personal estate shall be left out of account unless a grant limited to the remainder of the estate has previously been made or is made at the same time.

(10) Where the court, in exercise of its powers under this section, decides to vary or discharge a periodical payments or a secured periodical payments order, then, subject to section 28(1) and (2) above, the court shall have power to direct that the variation or discharge shall not take effect until the expiration of such period as may be specified in the order. . .

(11). . .

(12). . .

(13). . .

(14). . .

(15) The power to make regulations under subsection (4C) above shall be exercisable by statutory instrument which shall be subject to annulment in pursuance of a resolution of either House of Parliament.

31A Variation etc following reconciliations

(1)–(7). . .

31B Discharge of pension sharing orders on making of separation orders

Where, after the making of a pension sharing order under section 24B above in relation to a marriage, a separation order is made in relation to the marriage, the pension sharing order is discharged.

. . .

40A   Appeals relating to pension sharing orders which have taken effect

(1) Subsections (2) and (3) below apply where an appeal against a pension sharing order is begun on or after the day on which the order takes effect.

(2) If the pension sharing order relates to a person's rights under a pension arrangement, the appeal court may not set aside or vary the order if the person responsible for the pension arrangement has acted to his detriment in reliance on the taking effect of the order.

(3) If the pension sharing order relates to a person's shareable state scheme rights, the appeal court may not set aside or vary the order if the Secretary of State has acted to his detriment in reliance on the taking effect of the order.

(4) In determining for the purposes of subsection (2) or (3) above whether a person has acted to his detriment in reliance on the taking effect of the order, the appeal court may disregard any detriment which in its opinion is insignificant.

(5) Where subsection (2) or (3) above applies, the appeal court may make such further orders (including one or more pension sharing orders) as it thinks fit for the purpose of putting the parties in the position it considers appropriate.

(6) Section 24C above only applies to a pension sharing order under this section if the decision of the appeal court can itself be the subject of an appeal.

(6) In subsection (2) above, the reference to the person responsible for the pension arrangement is to be read in accordance with section 25D(4) above.

Social Security Contributions and Benefits Act 1992

45B   Reduction of additional pension in Category A retirement pension: pension sharing

(1) The weekly rate of the additional pension in a Category A retirement pension shall be reduced as follows in any case where-

    (a) the pensioner has become subject to a state scheme pension debit, and

    (b) the debit is to any extent referable to the additional pension.

(2) If the pensioner became subject to the debit in or after the final relevant year, the weekly rate of the additional pension shall be reduced by the appropriate weekly amount.

(3) If the pensioner became subject to the debit before the final relevant year, the weekly rate of the additional pension shall be reduced by the appropriate weekly amount multiplied by the relevant revaluation percentage.

(4) The appropriate weekly amount for the purposes of subsections (2) and (3) above is the weekly rate, expressed in terms of the valuation day, at which the cash equivalent, on that day, of the pension mentioned in subsection (5) below is equal to so much of the debit as is referable to the additional pension.

(5) The pension referred to above is a notional pension for the pensioner by virtue of section 44(3)(b) above which becomes payable on the later of-

    (a) his attaining pensionable age, and

    (b) the valuation day.

(6) For the purposes of subsection (3) above, the relevant revaluation percentage is the percentage specified, in relation to earnings factors for the tax year in which the pensioner became subject to the debit, by the last order under section 148 of the Administration Act to come into force before the final relevant year.

(7) Cash equivalents for the purposes of this section shall be calculated in accordance with regulations.

(8) In this section-

    '**final relevant year**' means the tax year immediately preceding that in which the pensioner attains pensionable age;

    '**state scheme pension debit**' means a debit under section 41(1)(a) of the Welfare Reform and Pensions Act 1999 (debit for the purposes of this Part of this Act);

    '**valuation day**' means the day on which the pensioner became subject to the state scheme pension debit.

55A   Shared additional pension

(1) A person shall be entitled to a shared additional pension if he is-

    (a) over pensionable age, and

    (b) entitled to a state scheme pension credit.

(2) A person's entitlement to a shared additional pension shall continue throughout his life.

(3) The weekly rate of a shared additional pension shall be the appropriate weekly amount, unless the pensioner's entitlement to the state scheme pension credit arose before the final relevant year, in which case it shall be that amount multiplied by the relevant revaluation percentage.

(4) The appropriate weekly amount for the purposes of subsection (3) above is the weekly rate, expressed in terms of the valuation day, at which the cash equivalent, on that day, of the pensioner's entitlement, or prospective entitlement, to the shared additional pension is equal to the state scheme pension credit.

(5) The relevant revaluation percentage for the purposes of that subsection is the percentage specified, in relation to earnings factors for the tax year in which the entitlement to the state scheme pension credit arose, by the last order under section 148 of the Administration Act to come into force before the final relevant year.

(6) Cash equivalents for the purposes of this section shall be calculated in accordance with regulations.

(7) In this section—

'final relevant year' means the tax year immediately preceding that in which the pensioner attains pensionable age;

'state scheme pension credit' means a credit under section 41(1)(b) of the Welfare Reform and Pensions Act 1999 (credit for the purposes of this Part of this Act);

'valuation day' means the day on which the pensioner becomes entitled to the state scheme pension credit.

55B   Reduction of shared additional pension: pension sharing

(1) The weekly rate of a shared additional pension shall be reduced as follows in any case where—

(a) the pensioner has become subject to a state scheme pension debit, and

(b) the debit is to any extent referable to the pension.

(2) If the pensioner became subject to the debit in or after the final relevant year, the weekly rate of the pension shall be reduced by the appropriate weekly amount.

(3) If the pensioner became subject to the debit before the final relevant year, the weekly rate of the additional pension shall be reduced by the appropriate weekly amount multiplied by the relevant revaluation percentage.

(4) The appropriate weekly amount for the purposes of subsections (2) and (3) above is the weekly rate, expressed in terms of the valuation day, at which the cash equivalent, on that day, of the pension mentioned in subsection (5) below is equal to so much of the debit as is referable to the shared additional pension.

(5) The pension referred to above is a notional pension for the pensioner by virtue of section 55A above which becomes payable on the later of-

(a) his attaining pensionable age, and

(b) the valuation day.

(6) For the purposes of subsection (3) above, the relevant revaluation percentage is the percentage specified, in relation to earnings factors for the tax year in which the pensioner became subject to the debit, by the last order under section 148 of the Administration Act to come into force before the final relevant year.

(7) Cash equivalents for the purposes of this section shall be calculated in accordance with regulations.

(8) In this section—

'final relevant year' means the tax year immediately preceding that in which the pensioner attains pensionable age;

'**state scheme pension debit**', means a debit under section 41(1)(a) of the Welfare Reform and Pensions Act 1999 (debit for the purposes of this Part of this Act);

'**valuation day**' means the day on which the pensioner became subject to the state scheme pension debit.

55C Increase of shared additional pension where entitlement is deferred

(1) For the purposes of this section, a person's entitlement to a shared additional pension is deferred—

(a) where he would be entitled to a Category A or Category B retirement pension but for the fact that his entitlement to such a pension is deferred, if and so long as his entitlement to such a pension is deferred, and

(b) otherwise, if and so long as he does not become entitled to the shared additional pension by reason only of not satisfying the conditions of section 1 of the Administration Act (entitlement to benefit dependent on claim),

and, in relation to a shared additional pension, 'period of deferment' shall be construed accordingly.

(2) Where a person's entitlement to a shared additional pension is deferred, the rate of his shared additional pension shall be increased by an amount equal to the aggregate of the increments to which he is entitled under subsection (3) below, but only if that amount is enough to increase the rate of the pension by at least 1 per cent.

(3) A person is entitled to an increment under this subsection for each complete incremental period in his period of enhancement.

(4) The amount of the increment for an incremental period shall be $^1/_7$th per cent of the weekly rate of the shared additional pension to which the person would have been entitled for the period if his entitlement had not been deferred.

(5) Amounts under subsection (4) above shall be rounded to the nearest penny, taking any $^1/_2$p as nearest to the next whole penny.

(6) Where an amount under subsection (4) above would, apart from this subsection, be a sum less than $^1/_2$p, the amount shall be taken to be zero, notwithstanding any other provision of this Act, the Pensions Act 1995 or the Administration Act.

(7) Where one or more orders have come into force under section 150 of the Administration Act during the period of enhancement, the rate for any incremental period shall be determined as if the order or orders had come into force before the beginning of the period of enhancement.

(8) The sums which are the increases in the rates of shared additional pensions under this section are subject to alteration by order made by the Secretary of State under section 150 of the Administration Act.

(9) In this section—

'**incremental period**' means any period of six days which are treated by regulations as days of increment for the purposes of this section in relation to the person and pension in question; and

'**period of enhancement**', in relation to that person and that pension, means the period which—

(a) begins on the same day as the period of deferment in question, and

(b) ends on the same day as that period or, if earlier, on the day before the 5th anniversary of the beginning of that period.

Pension Schemes Act 1993

PART IIIA

SAFEGUARDED RIGHTS

68A   Safeguarded rights

(1) Subject to subsection (2), the safeguarded rights of a member of an occupational pension scheme or a personal pension scheme are such of his rights to future benefits under the scheme as are attributable (directly or indirectly) to a pension credit in respect of which the reference rights are, or include, contracted-out rights or safeguarded rights.

(2) If the rules of an occupational pension scheme or a personal pension scheme so provide, a member's safeguarded rights are such of his rights falling within subsection (1) as—

    (a) in the case of rights directly attributable to a pension credit, represent the safeguarded percentage of the rights acquired by virtue of the credit, and

    (b) in the case of rights directly attributable to a transfer payment, represent the safeguarded percentage of the rights acquired by virtue of the payment.

(3) For the purposes of subsection (2)(a), the safeguarded percentage is the percentage of the rights by reference to which the amount of the credit is determined which are contracted-out rights or safeguarded rights.

(4) For the purposes of subsection (2)(b), the safeguarded percentage is the percentage of the rights in respect of which the transfer payment is made which are contracted-out rights or safeguarded rights.

(5) In this section—

    '**contracted-out rights**' means such rights under, or derived from—

    (a) an occupational pension scheme contracted-out by virtue of section 9(2) or (3), or

    (b) an appropriate personal pension scheme,

    as may be prescribed;

    '**reference rights**', in relation to a pension credit, means the rights by reference to which the amount of the credit is determined.

68B   Requirements relating to safeguarded rights

Regulations may prescribe requirements to be met in relation to safeguarded rights by an occupational pension scheme or a personal pension scheme.

68C   Reserve powers in relation to non-complying schemes

(1) This section applies to—

    (a) any occupational pension scheme, other than a public service pension scheme, and

    (b) any personal pension scheme.

(2) If any scheme to which this section applies does not comply with a requirement prescribed under section 68B and there are any persons who—

    (a) have safeguarded rights under the scheme, or

    (b) are entitled to any benefit giving effect to such rights under the scheme,

the Inland Revenue may direct the trustees or managers of the scheme to take or refrain from taking such steps as they may specify in writing for the purpose of safeguarding the rights of persons falling within paragraph (a) or (b).

(3) A direction under subsection (2) shall be final and binding on the trustees or managers to whom the direction is given and any person claiming under them.

(4) An appeal on a point of law shall lie to the High Court or, in Scotland, the Court of Session from a direction under subsection (2) at the instance of the trustees or managers, or any person claiming under them.

(5) A direction under subsection (2) shall be enforceable—

    (a) in England and Wales, in a county court, as if it were an order of that court, and

    (b) in Scotland, by the sheriff, as if it were an order of the sheriff and whether or not the sheriff could himself have given such an order.

68D   Power to control transfer or discharge of liability

Regulations may prohibit or restrict the transfer or discharge of any liability under an occupational pension scheme or a personal pension scheme in respect of safeguarded rights except in prescribed circumstances or on prescribed conditions. . . .

PART IVA

REQUIREMENTS RELATING TO PENSION CREDIT BENEFIT

CHAPTER I

PENSION CREDIT BENEFIT UNDER OCCUPATIONAL SCHEMES

101A   Scope of Chapter I

(1) This Chapter applies to any occupational pension scheme whose resources are derived in whole or part from—

    (a) payments to which subsection (2) applies made or to be made by one or more employers of earners to whom the scheme applies, or

    (b) such other payments by the earner or his employer, or both, as may be prescribed for different categories of scheme.

(2) This subsection applies to payments—

    (a) under an actual or contingent legal obligation, or

    (b) in the exercise of a power conferred, or the discharge of a duty imposed, on a Minister of the Crown, government department or any other person, being a power or duty which extends to the disbursement or allocation of public money.

101B   Interpretation

In this Chapter—

    '**scheme**' means an occupational pension scheme to which this Chapter applies;

'**pension credit rights**' means rights to future benefits under a scheme which are attributable (directly or indirectly) to a pension credit;

'**pension credit benefit**', in relation to a scheme, means the benefits payable under the scheme to or in respect of a person by virtue of rights under the scheme attributable (directly or indirectly) to a pension credit;

'**normal benefit age**', in relation to a scheme, means the earliest age at which a person who has pension credit rights under the scheme is entitled to receive a pension by virtue of those rights (disregarding any scheme rule making special provision as to early payment of pension on grounds of ill-health or otherwise).

101C   Basic principle as to pension credit benefit

(1) Normal benefit age under a scheme must be between 60 and 65.

(2) A scheme must not provide for payment of pension credit benefit in the form of a lump sum at any time before normal benefit age, except in such circumstances as may be prescribed.

101D   Form of pension credit benefit and its alternatives

(1) Subject to subsection (2) and section 101E, a person's pension credit benefit under a scheme must be—

   (a) payable directly out of the resources of the scheme, or

   (b) assured to him by such means as may be prescribed.

(2) Subject to subsections (3) and (4), a scheme may, instead of providing a person's pension credit benefit, provide—

   (a) for his pension credit rights under the scheme to be transferred to another occupational pension scheme or a personal pension scheme with a view to acquiring rights for him under the rules of the scheme, or

   (b) for such alternatives to pension credit benefit as may be prescribed.

(3) The option conferred by subsection (2)(a) is additional to any obligation imposed by Chapter II of this Part.

(4) The alternatives specified in subsection (2)(a) and (b) may only be by way of complete or partial substitute for pension credit benefit—

   (a) if the person entitled to the benefit consents, or

   (b) in such other cases as may be prescribed.

101E   Discharge of liability where pension credit or alternative benefits secured by insurance policies or annuity contracts

(1) A transaction to which section 19 applies discharges the trustees or managers of a scheme from their liability to provide pension credit benefit or any alternative to pension credit benefit for or in respect of a member of the scheme if and to the extent that-

   (a) it results in pension credit benefit, or any alternative to pension credit benefit, for or in respect of the member being appropriately secured (within the meaning of that section),

   (b) the transaction is entered into with the consent of the member or, if the member has died, of the member's widow or widower, and

   (c) such requirements as may be prescribed are met.

(2) Regulations may provide that subsection (1)(b) shall not apply in prescribed circumstances.

CHAPTER II
TRANSFER VALUES

101F   Power to give transfer notice

(1) An eligible member of a qualifying scheme may by notice in writing require the trustees or managers of the scheme to use an amount equal to the cash equivalent of his pension credit benefit for such one or more of the authorised purposes as he may specify in the notice.

(2) In the case of a member of an occupational pension scheme, the authorised purposes are—

   (a) to acquire rights allowed under the rules of an occupational pension scheme, or personal pension scheme, which is an eligible scheme;

   (b) to purchase from one or more insurance companies such as are mentioned in section 19(4)(a), chosen by the member and willing to accept payment on account of the member from the trustees or managers, one or more annuities which satisfy the prescribed requirements; and

   (c) in such circumstances as may be prescribed, to subscribe to other pension arrangements which satisfy prescribed requirements.

(3) In the case of a member of a personal pension scheme, the authorised purposes are-

   (a) to acquire rights allowed under the rules of an occupational pension scheme, or personal pension scheme, which is an eligible scheme; and

   (b) in such circumstances as may be prescribed, to subscribe to other pension arrangements which satisfy prescribed requirements.

(4) The cash equivalent for the purposes of subsection (1) shall—

   (a) in the case of a salary related occupational pension scheme, be taken to be the amount shown in the relevant statement under section 101H, and

   (b) in any other case, be determined by reference to the date the notice under that subsection is given.

(5) The requirements which may be prescribed under subsection (2) or (3) include, in particular, requirements of the Inland Revenue.

(6) In subsections (2) and (3), references to an eligible scheme are to a scheme-

   (a) the trustees or managers of which are able and willing to accept payment in respect of the member's pension credit rights, and

   (b) which satisfies the prescribed requirements.

(7) In this Chapter, '**transfer notice**' means a notice under subsection (1).

101G   Restrictions on power to give transfer notice

(1) In the case of a salary related occupational pension scheme, the power to give a transfer notice may only be exercised if—

   (a) the member has been provided with a statement under section 101H, and

   (b) not more than 3 months have passed since the date by reference to which the amount shown in the statement is determined.

(2) The power to give a transfer notice may not be exercised in the case of an occupational pension scheme if—

   (a) there is less than a year to go until the member reaches normal benefit age, or

   (b) the pension to which the member is entitled by virtue of his pension credit rights, or benefit in lieu of that pension, or any part of it has become payable.

(3) Where an eligible member of a qualifying scheme—

(a) is entitled to make an application under section 95 to the trustees or managers of the scheme, or

(b) would be entitled to do so, but for the fact that he has not received a statement under section 93A in respect of which the guarantee date is sufficiently recent,

he may not, if the scheme so provides, exercise the power to give them a transfer notice unless he also makes an application to them under section 95.

(4) The power to give a transfer notice may not be exercised if a previous transfer notice given by the member to the trustees or managers of the scheme is outstanding.

101H   Salary related schemes: statements of entitlement

(1) The trustees or managers of a qualifying scheme which is a salary related occupational pension scheme shall, on the application of an eligible member, provide him with a written statement of the amount of the cash equivalent of his pension credit benefit under the scheme.

(2) For the purposes of subsection (1), the amount of the cash equivalent shall be determined by reference to a date falling within-

(a) the prescribed period beginning with the date of the application, and

(b) the prescribed period ending with the date on which the statement under that subsection is provided to the applicant.

(3) Regulations may make provision in relation to applications under subsection (1) and may, in particular, restrict the making of successive applications.

(4) If trustees or managers to whom subsection (1) applies fail to perform an obligation under that subsection, section 10 of the Pensions Act 1995 (power of the Regulatory Authority to impose civil penalties) shall apply to any trustee or manager who has failed to take all such steps as are reasonable to secure that the obligation was performed.

101I   Calculation of cash equivalents

Cash equivalents for the purposes of this Chapter shall be calculated and verified in the prescribed manner.

101J   Time for compliance with transfer notice

(1) Trustees or managers of a qualifying scheme who receive a transfer notice shall comply with the notice-

(a) in the case of an occupational pension scheme, within 6 months of the valuation date or, if earlier, by the date on which the member to whom the notice relates reaches normal benefit age, and

(b) in the case of a personal pension scheme, within 6 months of the date on which they receive the notice.

(2) The Regulatory Authority may, in prescribed circumstances, extend the period for complying with the notice.

(3) If the Regulatory Authority are satisfied—

(a) that there has been a relevant change of circumstances since they granted an extension under subsection (2), or

(b) that they granted an extension under that subsection in ignorance of a material fact or on the basis of a mistake as to a material fact,

they may revoke or reduce the extension.

(4) Where the trustees or managers of an occupational pension scheme have failed to comply with a transfer notice before the end of the period for compliance—

    (a) they shall, except in prescribed cases, notify the Regulatory Authority of that fact within the prescribed period, and

    (b) section 10 of the Pensions Act 1995 (power of the Regulatory Authority to impose civil penalties) shall apply to any trustee or manager who has failed to take all such steps as are reasonable to ensure that the notice was complied with before the end of the period for compliance.

(5) If trustees or managers to whom subsection (4)(a) applies fail to perform the obligation imposed by that provision, section 10 of the Pensions Act 1995 shall apply to any trustee or manager who has failed to take all such steps as are reasonable to ensure that the obligation was performed.

(6) Regulations may—

    (a) make provision in relation to applications under subsection (2), and

    (b) provide that subsection (4) shall not apply in prescribed circumstances.

(7) In this section, '**valuation date**', in relation to a transfer notice given to the trustees or managers of an occupational pension scheme, means—

    (a) in the case of a salary related scheme, the date by reference to which the amount shown in the relevant statement under section 101H is determined, and

    (b) in the case of any other scheme, the date the notice is given.

101K   Withdrawal of transfer notice

(1) Subject to subsections (2) and (3), a person who has given a transfer notice may withdraw it by giving the trustees or managers to whom it was given notice in writing that he no longer requires them to comply with it.

(2) A transfer notice may not be withdrawn if the trustees or managers have already entered into an agreement with a third party to use the whole or part of the amount they are required to use in accordance with the notice.

(3) If the giving of a transfer notice depended on the making of an application under section 95, the notice may only be withdrawn if the application is also withdrawn.

101L   Variation of the amount required to be used

(1) Regulations may make provision for the amount required to be used under section 101F(1) to be increased or reduced in prescribed circumstances.

(2) Without prejudice to the generality of subsection (1), the circumstances which may be prescribed include—

    (a) failure by the trustees or managers of a qualifying scheme to comply with a notice under section 101F(1) within 6 months of the date by reference to which the amount of the cash equivalent falls to be determined, and

    (b) the state of funding of a qualifying scheme.

(3) Regulations under subsection (1) may have the effect of extinguishing an obligation under section 101F(1).

101M   Effect of transfer on trustees' duties

Compliance with a transfer notice shall have effect to discharge the trustees or managers of a qualifying scheme from any obligation to provide the pension credit benefit of the eligible member who gave the notice.

101N   Matters to be disregarded in calculations

In making any calculation for the purposes of this Chapter—

    (a) any charge or lien on, and

    (b) any set-off against,

the whole or part of a pension shall be disregarded.

101O   Service of notices

A notice under section 101F(1) or 101K(1) shall be taken to have been given if it is delivered to the trustees or managers personally or sent by post in a registered letter or by recorded delivery service.

101P   Interpretation of Chapter II

(1) In this Chapter—

'**eligible member**', in relation to a qualifying scheme, means a member who has pension credit rights under the scheme;

'**normal benefit age**', in relation to an eligible member of a qualifying scheme, means the earliest age at which the member is entitled to receive a pension by virtue of his pension credit rights under the scheme (disregarding any scheme rule making special provision as to early payment of pension on grounds of ill-health or otherwise);

'**pension credit benefit**', in relation to an eligible member of a qualifying scheme, means the benefits payable under the scheme to or in respect of the member by virtue of rights under the scheme attributable (directly or indirectly) to a pension credit;

'**pension credit rights**', in relation to a qualifying scheme, means rights to future benefits under the scheme which are attributable (directly or indirectly) to a pension credit;

'**qualifying scheme**' means a funded occupational pension scheme and a personal pension scheme;

'**Regulatory Authority**' means the Occupational Pensions Regulatory Authority;

'**transfer notice**' has the meaning given by section 101F(7).

(2) For the purposes of this Chapter, an occupational pension scheme is salary related if—

    (a) it is not a money purchase scheme, and

    (b) it does not fall within a prescribed class.

(3) In this Chapter, references to the relevant statement under section 101H, in relation to a transfer notice given to the trustees or managers of a salary related occupational pension scheme, are to the statement under that section on which the giving of the notice depended.

(4) For the purposes of this section, an occupational pension scheme is funded if it meets its liabilities out of a fund accumulated for the purpose during the life of the scheme.

101Q   Power to modify Chapter II in relation to hybrid schemes

Regulations may apply this Chapter with prescribed modifications to occupational pension schemes—

    (a) which are not money purchase schemes, but

    (b) where some of the benefits that may be provided are money purchase benefits.

Pensions Act 1995

166   Pensions on divorce etc

(1) *[Inserts ss 25B–D Matrimonial Causes Act 1973 as above.]*

(2) *[Amends s 25 Matrimonial Causes Act 1973 as above.]*

(3) *[Amends s 31 Matrimonial Causes Act 1973 as above.]*

(4) Nothing in the provisions mentioned in subsection (5) applies to a court exercising its powers under section 23 of the Matrimonial Causes Act 1973 (financial provision in connection with divorce proceedings, etc.) in respect of any benefits under a pension scheme (within the meaning of section 25B(1) of the Matrimonial Causes Act 1973) which a party to the marriage has or is likely to have.

(5) The provisions referred to in subsection (4) are—

  (a) Section 203(1) and (2) of the Army Act 1955, 203(1) and of the Air Force Act 1955, 128G(1) and (2) of the Naval Discipline Act 1957 or 159(4) and (4A) of the Pension Schemes Act 1993 (which prevent assignment, or orders being made restraining a person from receiving anything which he is prevented from assigning),

  (b) section 91 of this Act,

  (c) any provision of any enactment (whether passed or made before or after this Act is passed) corresponding to any of the enactments mentioned in paragraphs (a) and (b), and

  (d) any provision of the scheme in question corresponding to any of those enactments.

(6) Subsections (3) to (7) of section 25B, and section 25C of the Matrimonial Causes Act 1973, as inserted by this section, do not affect the powers of the court under section 31 of that Act (variation, discharge, etc.) in relation to any order made before the commencement of this section.

Welfare Reform and Pensions Act 1999

PART III PENSIONS ON DIVORCE ETC

15   Orders in England and Wales

Schedule 3 (which amends the Matrimonial Causes Act 1973 for the purposes of enabling the court to make pension sharing orders in connection with proceedings in England and Wales for divorce or nullity of marriage, and for supplementary purposes) shall have effect.

16   Orders in Scotland

[Not reproduced.]

Sections 25B to 25D of the Matrimonial Causes Act 1973
17   Amendments

Schedule 4 (which amends the sections about pensions inserted in the Matrimonial Causes Act 1973 by section 166 of the Pensions Act 1995) shall have effect.

18   Extension to overseas divorces etc

[Amends Matrimonial and Family Proceedings Act 1984 (financial relief in England and Wales after overseas divorce etc); adds s 18(3A), 18(7); inserts s 21(1)(be) and 21(1)(bf) and adds s 21(2)-(6).]

PART IV PENSION SHARING

CHAPTER I
SHARING OF RIGHTS UNDER PENSION ARRANGEMENTS

Pension sharing mechanism
19   Scope of mechanism

(1) Pension sharing is available under this Chapter in relation to a person's shareable rights under any pension arrangement other than an excepted public service pension scheme.

(2) For the purposes of this Chapter, a person's shareable rights under a pension arrangement are any rights of his under the arrangement, other than rights of a description specified by regulations made by the Secretary of State.

(3) For the purposes of subsection (1), a public service pension scheme is excepted if it is specified by order made by such minister of the Crown or government department as may be designated by the Treasury as having responsibility for the scheme.

20   Activation of pension sharing

(1)   Section 21 applies on the taking effect of any of the following relating to a person's shareable rights under a pension arrangement—

(a)   a pension sharing order under the Matrimonial Causes Act 1973,

(b)   provision which corresponds to the provision which may be made by such an order and which—

(i)   is contained in a qualifying agreement between the parties to a marriage, and

(ii)   takes effect on the dissolution of the marriage under the Family Law Act 1996,

(c)   provision which corresponds to the provision which may be made by such an order and which—

(i)   is contained in a qualifying agreement between the parties to a marriage or former marriage, and

(ii)   takes affect after the dissolution of the marriage under the Family Law Act 1996,

(d)   an order under Part III of the Matrimonial and Family Proceedings Act 1984 (financial relief in England and Wales in relation to overseas divorce etc.) corresponding to such an order as is mentioned in paragraph (a),

(e)   a pension sharing order under the Family Law (Scotland) Act 1985,

(f)   provision which corresponds to the provision which may be made by such an order and which—

(i)   is contained in a qualifying agreement between the parties to a marriage,

(ii)   is in such form as the Secretary of State may prescribe by regulations, and

(iii)   takes effect on the grant, in relation to the marriage, of decree of divorce under the Divorce (Scotland) Act 1976 or of declarator of nullity,

(g)   an order under Part IV of the Matrimonial and Family Proceedings Act 1984 (financial relief in Scotland in relation to overseas divorce etc.) corresponding to such an order as is mentioned in paragraph (e),

(h)   a pension sharing order under Northern Ireland legislation,

(i)   an order under Part IV of the Matrimonial and Family Proceedings (Northern Ireland) Order 1989 (financial relief in Northern Ireland in relation to overseas divorce etc.) corresponding to such an order as is mentioned in paragraph (h).

(2)   For the purposes of subsection (1)(b) and (c), a qualifying agreement is one which—

(a)   has been entered into in such circumstances as the Lord Chancellor may prescribe by regulations, and

(b)   satisfies such requirements as the Lord Chancellor may so prescribe.

(3)   For the purposes of subsection (1)(f) a qualifying agreement is one which—

(a)   has been entered into in such circumstances as the Secretary of State may prescribe by regulations, and

(b)   is registered in the Books of Council and Session.

(4)   Subsection (1)(b) does not apply if—

(a)   the pension arrangement to which the provision relates is the subject of a pension sharing order under the Matrimonial Causes Act 1973 in relation to the marriage, or

(b)   there is in force a requirement imposed by virtue of section 25B or 25C of that Act (powers to include in financial provision orders requirements relating to benefits under pension arrangements) which relates to benefits or future benefits to which the person to whose rights the provision relates is entitled under the pension arrangement to which it relates.

(5) Subsection (1)(c) does not apply if—

   (a) the marriage was dissolved by an order under section 3 of the Family Law Act 1996 (divorce not preceded by separation) and the satisfaction of the requirements of section 9(2) of that Act (settlement of future financial arrangements) was a precondition to the making of the order,

   (b) the pension arrangement to which the provision relates—

      (i) is the subject of a pension sharing order under the Matrimonial Causes Act 1973 in relation to the marriage, or

      (ii) has already been the subject of pension sharing between the parties, or

   (c) there is in force a requirement imposed by virtue of section 25B or 25C of that Act which relates to benefits or future benefits to which the person to whose rights the provision relates is entitled under the pension arrangement to which it relates.

(6) Subsection (1)(f) does not apply if there is in force an order under section 12A(2) or (3) of the Family Law (Scotland) Act 1985 relating to the pension arrangement to which the provision relates.

(7) For the purposes of this section, an order or provision falling within subsection (1)(e), (f) or (g) shall be deemed never to have taken effect if the person responsible for the arrangement to which the order or provision relates does not receive before the end of the period of 2 months beginning with the relevant date—

   (a) copies of the relevant matrimonial documents, and

   (b) such information relating to the parties to the marriage as the Secretary of State may prescribe by regulations.

(8) The relevant date for the purposes of subsection (7) is—

   (a) in the case of an order or provision falling within subsection (1)(e) or (f), the date of the extract of the decree or declarator responsible for the divorce or annulment to which the order or provision relates, and

   (b) in the case of an order falling within subsection (1)(g), the date of disposal of the application under section 28 of the Matrimonial and Family Proceedings Act 1984.

(9) The reference in subsection (7)(a) to the relevant matrimonial documents is—

   (a) in the case of an order falling within subsection (1)(e) or (g), to copies of the order and the order, decree or declarator responsible for the divorce or annulment to which it relates, and

   (b) in the case of provision falling within subsection (1)(f), to—

      (i) copies of the provision and the order, decree or declarator responsible for the divorce or annulment to which it relates, and

      (ii) documentary evidence that the agreement containing the provision is one to which subsection (3)(a) applies.

(10) The sheriff may, on the application of any person having an interest, make an order—

   (a) extending the period of 2 months referred to in subsection (7), and

   (b) if that period has already expired, providing that, if the person responsible for the arrangement receives the documents and information concerned before the end of the period specified in the order, subsection (7) is to be treated as never having applied.

21   Creation of pension debits and credits

(1)   On the application of this section—

(a)   the transferor's shareable rights under the relevant arrangement become subject to a debit of the appropriate amount, and

(b)   the transferee becomes entitled to a credit of that amount as against the person responsible for that arrangement.

(2)   Where the relevant order or provision specifies a percentage value to be transferred, the appropriate amount for the purposes of subsection (1) is the specified percentage of the cash equivalent of the relevant benefits on the valuation day.

(3)   Where the relevant order or provision specifies an amount to be transferred, the appropriate amount for the purposes of subsection (1) is the lesser of—

(a)   the specified amount, and

(b)   the cash equivalent of the relevant benefits on the valuation day.

(4)   Where the relevant arrangement is an occupational pension scheme and the transferor is in pensionable service under the scheme on the transfer day, the relevant benefits for the purposes of subsections (2) and (3) are the benefits or future benefits to which he would be entitled under the scheme by virtue of his shareable rights under it had his pensionable service terminated immediately before that day.

(5)   Otherwise, the relevant benefits for the purposes of subsections (2) and (3) are the benefits or future benefits to which, immediately before the transfer day, the transferor is entitled under the terms of the relevant arrangement by virtue of his shareable rights under it.

(6)   The Secretary of State may by regulations provide for any description of benefit to be disregarded for the purposes of subsection (4) or (5).

(7)   For the purposes of this section, the valuation day is such day within the implementation period for the credit under subsection (1)(b) as the person responsible for the relevant arrangement may specify by notice in writing to the transferor and transferee.

(8)   In this section—

'**relevant arrangement**' means the arrangement to which the relevant order or provision relates;

'**relevant order or provision**' means the order or provision by virtue of which this section applies;

'**transfer day**' means the day on which the relevant order or provision takes effect;

'**transferor**' means the person to whose rights the relevant order or provision relates;

'**transferee**' means the person for whose benefit the relevant order or provision is made.

22   Cash equivalents

(1)   The Secretary of State may by regulations make provision about the calculation and verification of cash equivalents for the purposes of section 21.

(2)   The power conferred by subsection (1) includes power to provide for calculation or verification—

(a)   in such manner as may, in the particular case, be approved by a person prescribed by the regulations, or

(b)   in accordance with guidance from time to time prepared by a person so prescribed.

Pension debits

23 Reduction of benefit

(1) Subject to subsection (2), where a person's shareable rights under a pension arrangement are subject to a pension debit, each benefit or future benefit—

  (a) to which he is entitled under the arrangement by virtue of those rights, and

  (b) which is a qualifying benefit,

is reduced by the appropriate percentage.

(2) Where a pension debit relates to the shareable rights under an occupational pension scheme of a person who is in pensionable service under the scheme on the transfer day, each benefit or future benefit—

  (a) to which the person is entitled under the scheme by virtue of those rights, and

  (b) which corresponds to a qualifying benefit,

is reduced by an amount equal to the appropriate percentage of the corresponding qualifying benefit.

(3) A benefit is a qualifying benefit for the purposes of subsections (1) and (2) if the cash equivalent by reference to which the amount of the pension debit is determined includes an amount in respect of it.

(4) The provisions of this section override any provision of a pension arrangement to which they apply to the extent that the provision conflicts with them.

(5) In this section—

  '**appropriate percentage**', in relation to a pension debit, means—

  (a) if the relevant order or provision specifies the percentage value to be transferred, that percentage;

  (b) if the relevant order or provision specifies an amount to be transferred, the percentage which the appropriate amount for the purposes of subsection (1) of section 21 represents of the amount mentioned in subsection (3)(b) of that section;

  '**relevant order or provision**', in relation to a pension debit, means the pension sharing order or provision on which the debit depends;

  '**transfer day**', in relation to a pension debit, means the day on which the relevant order or provision takes effect.

24 Effect on contracted-out rights

(1) The Pension Schemes Act 1993 shall be amended as follows.

(2) *[Amends Pension Schemes Act 1993 s 10 (protected rights).]*

(3) *[Amends Pension Schemes Act 1993 s 15 by inserting s15A (Reduction of guaranteed minimum in consequence of pension debit).]*

(4) *[Amends Pension Schemes Act 1993 s 47 (entitlement to guaranteed minimum pensions for the purposes of the relationship with social security benefits.)]*

(5) *[Amends Pension Schemes Act 1993 s 181(1) by adding definition of 'pension debit'.]*

Pension credits

25 Time for discharge of liability

(1) A person subject to liability in respect of a pension credit shall discharge his liability before the end of the implementation period for the credit.

(2) Where the trustees or managers of an occupational pension scheme have not done what is required to discharge their liability in respect of a pension credit before the end of the implementation period for the credit—

    (a) they shall, except in such cases as the Secretary of State may prescribe by regulations, notify the Regulatory Authority of that fact within such period as the Secretary of State may so prescribe, and

    (b) section 10 of the Pensions Act 1995 (power of the Regulatory Authority to impose civil penalties) shall apply to any trustee or manager who has failed to take all such steps as are reasonable to ensure that liability in respect of the credit was discharged before the end of the implementation period for it.

(3) If trustees or managers to whom subsection (2)(a) applies fail to perform the obligation imposed by that provision, section 10 of the Pensions Act 1995 shall apply to any trustee or manager who has failed to take all reasonable steps to ensure that the obligation was performed.

(4) On the application of the trustees or managers of an occupational pension scheme who are subject to liability in respect of a pension credit, the Regulatory Authority may extend the implementation period for the credit for the purposes of this section if it is satisfied that the application is made in such circumstances as the Secretary of State may prescribe by regulations.

(5) In this section 'the Regulatory Authority' means the Occupational Pensions Regulatory Authority.

26 'Implementation period'

(1) For the purposes of this Chapter, the implementation period for a pension credit is the period of 4 months beginning with the later of—

    (a) the day on which the relevant order or provision takes effect, and

    (b) the first day on which the person responsible for the pension arrangement to which the relevant order or provision relates is in receipt of—

        (i) the relevant matrimonial documents, and

        (ii) such information relating to the transferor and transferee as the Secretary of State may prescribe by regulations.

(2) The reference in subsection (1)(b)(i) to the relevant matrimonial documents is to copies of—

    (a) the relevant order or provision, and

    (b) the order, decree or declarator responsible for the divorce or annulment to which it relates,

and, if the pension credit depends on provision falling within subsection (1)(f) of section 20, to documentary evidence that the agreement containing the provision is one to which subsection (3)(a) of that section applies.

(3) Subsection (1) is subject to any provision made by regulations under section 33(2)(a).

(4) The Secretary of State may by regulations—

    (a) make provision requiring a person subject to liability in respect of a pension credit to notify the transferor and transferee of the day on which the implementation period for the credit begins;

    (b) provide for this section to have effect with modifications where the pension arrangement to which the relevant order or provision relates is being wound up;

    (c) provide for this section to have effect with modifications where the pension credit depends on a pension sharing order and the order is the subject of an application for leave to appeal out of time.

(5) In this section-

'**relevant order or provision**', in relation to a pension credit, means the pension sharing order or provision on which the pension credit depends;

'**transferor**' means the person to whose rights the relevant order or provision relates;

'**transferee**' means the person for whose benefit the relevant order or provision is made.

27   Mode of discharge of liability

(1) Schedule 5 (which makes provision about how liability in respect of a pension credit may be discharged) shall have effect.

(2) Where the person entitled to a pension credit dies before liability in respect of the credit has been discharged—

(a) Schedule 5 shall cease to have effect in relation to the discharge of liability in respect of the credit, and

(b) liability in respect of the credit shall be discharged in accordance with regulations made by the Secretary of State.

Treatment of pension credit rights under schemes
28   Safeguarded rights

[Amends Pension Schemes Act 1993 s 68.]

29   Requirements relating to pension credit benefit

[Amends Pension Schemes Act 1993 s 101.]

30   Treatment in winding up

(1) *[Amends Pensions Act 1995 s73 (treatment of rights on winding up of an occupational pension scheme to which section 56 of that Act (minimum funding requirement) applies).]*

(2) In the case of an occupational pension scheme which is not a scheme to which section 56 of the Pensions Act 1995 applies, rights attributable (directly or indirectly) to a pension credit are to be accorded in a winding up the same treatment—

(a) if they have come into payment, as the rights of a pensioner member, and

(b) if they have not come into payment, as the rights of a deferred member.

(3) Subsection (2) overrides the provisions of a scheme to the extent that it conflicts with them, and the scheme has effect with such modifications as may be required in consequence.

(4) In subsection (2)—

(a) '**deferred member**' and '**pensioner member**' have the same meanings as in Part I of the Pensions Act 1995,

(b) '**pension credit**' includes a credit under Northern Ireland legislation corresponding to section 21(1)(b), and

(c) references to rights attributable to a pension credit having come into payment are to the person to whom the rights belong having become entitled by virtue of the rights to the present payment of pension or other benefits.

Indexation

31   Public service pension schemes

(1) The Pensions (Increase) Act 1971 shall be amended as follows.

(2)–(5) *[Amends Pensions (Increase) Act 1971.]*

32   Other pension schemes

(1) The Secretary of State may by regulations make provision for a pension to which subsection (2) applies to be increased, as a minimum, by reference to increases in the retail prices index, so far as not exceeding 5% per annum.

(2) This subsection applies to—

   (a) a pension provided to give effect to eligible pension credit rights of a member under a qualifying occupational pension scheme, and

   (b) a pension provided to give effect to safeguarded rights of a member under a personal pension scheme.

(3) In this section—

   'eligible', in relation to pension credit rights, means of a description prescribed by regulations made by the Secretary of State;

   'pension credit rights', in relation to an occupational pension scheme, means rights to future benefits under the scheme which are attributable (directly or indirectly) to a credit under section 21(1)(b) or under corresponding Northern Ireland legislation.

   'qualifying occupational pension scheme' means an occupational pension scheme which is not a public service pension scheme;

   'safeguarded rights' has the meaning given in section 68A of the Pension Schemes Act 1993.

Charges by pension arrangements

33   Charges in respect of pension sharing costs

(1) The Secretary of State may by regulations make provision for the purpose of enabling the person responsible for a pension arrangement involved in pension sharing to recover from the parties to pension sharing prescribed charges in respect of prescribed descriptions of pension sharing activity.

(2) Regulations under subsection (1) may include—

   (a) provision for the start of the implementation period for a pension credit to be postponed in prescribed circumstances;

   (b) provision, in relation to payments in respect of charges recoverable under the regulations, for reimbursement as between the parties to pension sharing;

   (c) provision, in relation to the recovery of charges by deduction from a pension credit, for the modification of Schedule 5;

   (d) provision for the recovery in prescribed circumstances of such additional amounts as may be determined in accordance with the regulations.

(3) For the purposes of regulations under subsection (1), the question of how much of a charge recoverable under the regulations is attributable to a party to pension sharing is to be determined as follows—

> (a) where the relevant order or provision includes provision about the apportionment of charges under this section, there is attributable to the party so much of the charge as is apportioned to him by that provision;
>
> (b) where the relevant order or provision does not include such provision, the charge is attributable to the transferor.

(4) For the purposes of subsection (1), a pension arrangement is involved in pension sharing if section 21 applies by virtue of an order or provision which relates to the arrangement.

(5) In that subsection, the reference to pension sharing activity is to activity attributable (directly or indirectly) to the involvement in pension sharing.

(6) In subsection (3)—

> (a) the reference to the relevant order or provision is to the order or provision which gives rise to the pension sharing, and
>
> (b) the reference to the transferor is to the person to whose rights that order of provision relates.

(7) In this section '**prescribed**' means prescribed in regulations under subsection (1).

Adaptation of statutory schemes

34   Extension of scheme-making powers

(1) Power under an Act to establish a pension scheme shall include power to make provision for the provision, by reference to pension credits which derive from rights under—

> (a) the scheme, or
>
> (b) a scheme in relation to which the scheme is specified as an alternative for the purposes of paragraph 2 of Schedule 5,

of benefits to or in respect of those entitled to the credits.

(2) Subsection (1) is without prejudice to any other power.

(3) Subsection (1) shall apply in relation to Acts whenever passed.

(4) No obligation to consult shall apply in relation to the making, in exercise of a power under an Act to establish a pension scheme, of provision of a kind authorised by subsection (1).

(5) In this section—

> '**pension credit**' includes a credit under Northern Ireland legislation corresponding to section 21(1)(b);
>
> '**pension scheme**' means a scheme or arrangement providing benefits, in the form of pensions or otherwise, payable on termination of service, or on death or retirement, to or in respect of persons to whom the scheme or arrangement applies.

35   Power to extend judicial pension schemes

(1) The appropriate minister may by regulations amend the Sheriffs' Pensions (Scotland) Act 1961, the Judicial Pensions Act 1981 or the Judicial Pensions and Retirement Act 1993 for the purpose of—

> (a) extending a pension scheme under the Act to include the provision, by reference to pension credits which derive from rights under—

(i)   the scheme, or

(ii) a scheme in relation to which the scheme is specified as an alternative for the purposes of paragraph 2 of Schedule 5,

of benefits to or in respect of those entitled to the credits, or

(b) restricting the power of the appropriate minister to accept payments into a pension scheme under the Act, where the payments represent the cash equivalent of rights under another pension scheme which are attributable (directly or indirectly) to a pension credit.

(2) Regulations under subsection (1)—

(a) may make benefits provided by virtue of paragraph (a) of that subsection a charge on, and payable out of, the Consolidated Fund;

(b) may confer power to make subordinate legislation.

(3) The appropriate minister for the purposes of subsection (1) is—

(a) in relation to a pension scheme whose ordinary members are limited to those who hold judicial office whose jurisdiction is exercised exclusively in relation to Scotland, the Secretary of State, and

(b) in relation to any other pension scheme, the Lord Chancellor.

(4) In this section—

'**pension credit**' includes a credit under Northern Ireland legislation corresponding to section 21(1)(b);

'**pension scheme**' means a scheme or arrangement providing benefits, in the form of pensions or otherwise, payable on termination of service, or on death or retirement, to or in respect of persons to whom the scheme or arrangement applies.

Supplementary

36   Disapplication of restrictions on alienation

(1) Nothing in any of the following provisions (restrictions on alienation of pension rights) applies in relation to any order or provision falling within section 20(1)—

(a) section 203(1) and (2) of the Army Act 1955, section 203(1) and (2) of the Air Force Act 1955, section 128G(1) and (2) of the Naval Discipline Act 1957 and section 159(4) and (4A) of the Pension Schemes Act 1993,

(b) section 91 of the Pensions Act 1995,

(c) any provision of any enactment (whether passed or made before or after this Act is passed) corresponding to any of the enactments mentioned in paragraphs (a) and (b), and

(d) any provision of a pension arrangement corresponding to any of those enactments.

(2) In this section, '**enactment**' includes an enactment comprised in subordinate legislation (within the meaning of the Interpretation Act 1978).

37   Information

(1) The Secretary of State may by regulations require the person responsible for a pension arrangement involved in pension sharing to supply to such persons as he may specify in the regulations such information relating to anything which follows from the application of section 21 as he may so specify.

(2) Section 168 of the Pension Schemes Act 1993 (breach of regulations) shall apply as if this section were contained in that Act (otherwise than in Chapter II of Part VII).

(3) For the purposes of this section, a pension arrangement is involved in pension sharing if section 21 applies by virtue of an order or provision which relates to the arrangement.

38   Interpretation of Chapter I

(1) In this Chapter—

'**implementation period**', in relation to a pension credit, has the meaning given by section 26;

'**occupational pension scheme**' has the meaning given by section 1 of the Pension Schemes Act 1993;

'**pension arrangement**' means—

(a) an occupational pension scheme,

(b) a personal pension scheme,

(c) a retirement annuity contract,

(d) an annuity or insurance policy purchased, or transferred, for the purpose of giving effect to rights under an occupational pension scheme or a personal pension scheme, and

(e) an annuity purchased, or entered into, for the purpose of discharging liability in respect of a credit under section 21(1)(b) or under corresponding Northern Ireland legislation;

'**pension credit**' means a credit under section 21(1)(b);

'**pension debit**' means a debit under section 21(1)(a);

'**pensionable service**', in relation to a member of an occupational pension scheme, means service in any description or category of employment to which the scheme relates which qualifies the member (on the assumption that it continues for the appropriate period) for pension or other benefits under the scheme;

'**personal pension scheme**' has the meaning given by section 1 of the Pension Schemes Act 1993;

'**retirement annuity contract**' means a contract or scheme approved under Chapter III of Part XIV of the Income and Corporation Taxes Act 1988;

'**shareable rights**' has the meaning given by section 19(2);

'**trustees or managers**', in relation to an occupational pension scheme or a personal pension scheme means—

(a) in the case of a scheme established under a trust, the trustees of the scheme, and

(b) in any other case, the managers of the scheme.

(2) In this Chapter, references to the person responsible for a pension arrangement are—

(a) in the case of an occupational pension scheme or a personal pension scheme, to the trustees or managers of the scheme,

(b) in the case of a retirement annuity contract or an annuity falling within paragraph (d) or (e) of the definition of '**pension arrangement**' in subsection (1), to the provider of the annuity, and

(c) in the case of an insurance policy falling within paragraph (d) of the definition of that expression, to the insurer.

(3) In determining what is '**pensionable service**' for the purposes of this Chapter-

(a) service notionally attributable for any purpose of the scheme is to be disregarded, and

(b) no account is to be taken of any rules of the scheme by which a period of service can be treated for any purpose as being longer or shorter than it actually is.

CHAPTER II

SHARING OF STATE SCHEME RIGHTS

39 Shareable state scheme rights

(1) Pension sharing is available under this Chapter in relation to a person's shareable state scheme rights.

(2) For the purposes of this Chapter, a person's shareable state scheme rights are—

(a) his entitlement, or prospective entitlement to a Category A retirement pension by virtue of section 44(3)(b) of the Contributions and Benefits Act (earnings-related additional pension), and

(b) his entitlement, or prospective entitlement, to a pension under section 55A of that Act (shared additional pension).

40 Activation of benefit sharing

(1) Section 41 applies on the taking effect of any of the following relating to a person's shareable state scheme rights—

(a) a pension sharing order under the Matrimonial Causes Act 1973,

(b) provision which corresponds to the provision which may be made by such an order and which—

(i) is contained in a qualifying agreement between the parties to a marriage, and

(ii) takes effect on the dissolution of the marriage under the Family Law Act 1996,

(c) provision which corresponds to the provision which may be made by such an order and which—

(i) is contained in a qualifying agreement between the parties to a marriage or former marriage, and

(ii) takes effect after the dissolution of the marriage under the Family Law Act 1996,

(d) an order under Part III of the Matrimonial and Family Proceedings Act 1984 (financial relief in England and Wales in relation to overseas divorce etc.) corresponding to such an order as is mentioned in paragraph (a),

(e) a pension sharing order under the Family Law (Scotland) Act 1985,

(f) provision which corresponds to the provision which may be made by such an order and which—

(i) is contained in a qualifying agreement between the parties to a marriage,

(ii) is in such form as the Secretary of State may prescribe by regulations, and

(iii) takes effect on the grant, in relation to the marriage, of decree of divorce under the Divorce (Scotland) Act 1976 or of declarator of nullity,

(g) an order under Part IV of the Matrimonial and Family Proceedings Act 1984 (financial relief in Scotland in relation to overseas divorce etc.) corresponding to such an order as is mentioned in paragraph (e),

(h) a pension sharing order under Northern Ireland legislation,

(i) an order under Part IV of the Matrimonial and Family Proceedings (Northern Ireland) Order 1989 (financial relief in Northern Ireland in relation to overseas divorce etc.) corresponding to such an order as is mentioned in paragraph (h).

(2) For the purposes of subsection (1)(b) and (c), a qualifying agreement is one which—

    (a) has been entered into in such circumstances as the Lord Chancellor may prescribe by regulations, and

    (b) satisfies such requirements as the Lord Chancellor may so prescribe.

(3) For the purposes of subsection (1)(f), a qualifying agreement is one which—

    (a) has been entered into in such circumstances as the Secretary of State may prescribe by regulations, and

    (b) is registered in the Books of Council and Session.

(4) Subsection (1)(b) does not apply if the provision relates to rights which are the subject of a pension sharing order under the Matrimonial Causes Act 1973 in relation to the marriage.

(5) Subsection (1)(c) does not apply if—

    (a) the marriage was dissolved by an order under section 3 of the Family Law Act 1996 (divorce not preceded by separation) and the satisfaction of the requirements of section 9(2) of that Act (settlement of future financial arrangements) was a precondition to the making of the order,

    (b) the provision relates to rights which are the subject of a pension sharing order under the Matrimonial Causes Act 1973 in relation to the marriage, or

    (c) shareable state scheme rights have already been the subject of pension sharing between the parties.

(6) Subsection (1)(f) does not apply if there is in force an order under section 12A(2) or (3) of the Family Law (Scotland) Act 1985 relating to the pension arrangement to which the provision relates.

(7) For the purposes of this section, an order or provision falling within subsection (1)(e), (f) or (g) shall be deemed never to have taken effect if the Secretary of State does not receive before the end of the period of 2 months beginning with the relevant date—

    (a) copies of the relevant matrimonial documents, and

    (b) such information relating to the parties to the marriage as the Secretary of State may prescribe by regulations.

(8) The relevant date for the purposes of subsection (7) is—

    (a) in the case of an order or provision falling within subsection (1)(e) or (f), the date of the extract of the decree or declarator responsible for the divorce or annulment to which the order or provision relates, and

    (b) in the case of an order falling within subsection (1)(g), the date of disposal of the application under section 28 of the Matrimonial and Family Proceedings Act 1984.

(9) The reference in subsection (7)(a) to the relevant matrimonial documents is—

    (a) in the case of an order falling within subsection (1)(e) or (g), to copies of the order and the order, decree or declarator responsible for the divorce or annulment to which it relates, and

    (b) in the case of provision falling within subsection (1)(f), to—

        (i) copies of the provision and the order, decree or declarator responsible for the divorce or annulment to which it relates, and

        (ii) documentary evidence that the agreement containing the provision is one to which subsection (3)(a) applies.

(10) The sheriff may, on the application of any person having an interest, make an order—

    (a) extending the period of 2 months referred to in subsection (7), and

(b) if that period has already expired, providing that, if the Secretary of State receives the documents and information concerned before the end of the period specified in the order, subsection (7) is to be treated as never having applied.

41   Creation of state scheme pension debits and credits

(1) On the application of this section—

    (a) the transferor becomes subject, for the purposes of Part II of the Contributions and Benefits Act (contributory benefits), to a debit of the appropriate amount, and

    (b) the transferee becomes entitled, for those purposes, to a credit of that amount.

(2) Where the relevant order or provision specifies a percentage value to be transferred, the appropriate amount for the purposes of subsection (1) is the specified percentage of the cash equivalent on the transfer day of the transferor's shareable state scheme rights immediately before that day.

(3) Where the relevant order or provision specifies an amount to be transferred, the appropriate amount for the purposes of subsection (1) is the lesser of—

    (a) the specified amount, and

    (b) the cash equivalent on the transfer day of the transferor's relevant state scheme rights immediately before that day.

(4) Cash equivalents for the purposes of this section shall be calculated in accordance with regulations made by the Secretary of State.

(5) In determining prospective entitlement to a Category A retirement pension for the purposes of this section, only tax years before that in which the transfer day falls shall be taken into account.

(6) In this section—

    '**relevant order or provision**' means the order or provision by virtue of which this section applies;

    '**transfer day**' means the day on which the relevant order or provision takes effect;

    '**transferor**' means the person to whose rights the relevant order or provision relates;

    '**transferee**' means the person for whose benefit the relevant order or provision is made.

42   Effect of state scheme pension debits and credits

(1)-(2) *[Amends Contributions and Benefits Act to give effect to debits and credits under SERPS.]*

43   Interpretation of Chapter II

In this Chapter—

    '**shareable state scheme rights**' has the meaning given by section 39(2); and

    '**tax year**' has the meaning given by section 122(1) of the Contributions and Benefits Act.

SCHEDULE 3
PENSION SHARING ORDERS: ENGLAND AND WALES

1   The Matrimonial Causes Act 1973 is amended as follows.

2   *[Amends Matrimonial Causes Act 1973 s21.]*

3   *[Amends Matrimonial Causes Act 1973 by inserting s24B-24G after s 24A.]*

4   *[Amends Matrimonial Causes Act 1973 s25.]*

5   *[Amends Matrimonial Causes Act 1973 s25A.]*

6   *[Amends Matrimonial Causes Act 1973 s31.]*

(1)   Section 31 (variation, discharge etc. of certain orders for financial relief) is amended as follows.

(2)   *[Inserts s31(2)(g).]*

(3)   *[Amends s31(4A).]*

(4)   *[Inserts s31(4C) and (4D).]*

(5)   *[Amends s31(5).]*

(6)   In subsection (7B), after paragraph (b) there is inserted—

'(ba) one or more pension sharing orders;'

(7)   *[Inserts s31(7G) and 7(H).]*

(8)   *[Inserts s31(15).]*

7   *[Inserts s31(B).]*

8   In section 33A (consent orders), in subsection (3), in the definition of 'order for financial relief', after 'property adjustment order,' there is inserted 'any pension sharing order,'.

9   *[Amends Matrimonial Causes Act 1973, by adding s40A after section 40.]*

SCHEDULE 4

AMENDMENTS OF SECTIONS 25B TO 25D OF THE MATRIMONIAL CAUSES ACT 1973

1   *[Amends Matrimonial Causes Act 1973 s25B.]*

2   *[Amends Matrimonial Causes Act 1973 s25C.]*

3   *[Amends Matrimonial Causes Act 1973 s25D.]*

SCHEDULE 5

PENSION CREDITS: MODE OF DISCHARGE

1   Funded pension schemes

(1)   This paragraph applies to a pension credit which derives from—

    (a)   a funded occupational pension scheme, or

    (b)   a personal pension scheme.

(2)   The trustees or managers of the scheme from which a pension credit to which this paragraph applies derives may discharge their liability in respect of the credit by conferring appropriate rights under that scheme on the person entitled to the credit—

    (a)   with his consent, or

    (b)   in accordance with regulations made by the Secretary of State.

(3)   The trustees or managers of the scheme from which a pension credit to which this paragraph applies derives may discharge their liability in respect of the credit by paying the amount of the credit to the person responsible for a qualifying arrangement with a view to acquiring rights under that arrangement for the person entitled to the credit if—

    (a)   the qualifying arrangement is not disqualified as a destination for the credit,

(b) the person responsible for that arrangement is able and willing to accept payment in respect of the credit, and

(c) payment is made with the consent of the person entitled to the credit, or in accordance with regulations made by the Secretary of State.

(4) For the purposes of sub-paragraph (2), no account is to be taken of consent of the person entitled to the pension credit unless—

(a) it is given after receipt of notice in writing of an offer to discharge liability in respect of the credit by making a payment under sub-paragraph (3), or

(b) it is not withdrawn within 7 days of receipt of such notice.

2 Unfunded public service pension schemes

(1) This paragraph applies to a pension credit which derives from an occupational pension scheme which is—

(a) not funded, and

(b) a public service pension scheme.

(2) The trustees or managers of the scheme from which a pension credit to which this paragraph applies derives may discharge their liability in respect of the credit by conferring appropriate rights under that scheme on the person entitled to the credit.

(3) If such a scheme as is mentioned in sub-paragraph (1) is closed to new members, the appropriate authority in relation to that scheme may by regulations specify another public service pension scheme as an alternative to it for the purposes of this paragraph.

(4) Where the trustees or managers of a scheme in relation to which an alternative is specified under sub-paragraph (3) are subject to liability in respect of a pension credit, they may—

(a) discharge their liability in respect of the credit by securing that appropriate rights are conferred on the person entitled to the credit by the trustees or managers of the alternative scheme, and

(b) for the purpose of so discharging their liability, require the trustees or managers of the alternative scheme to take such steps as may be required.

(5) In sub-paragraph (3), 'the appropriate authority', in relation to a public service pension scheme, means such Minister of the Crown or government department as may be designated by the Treasury as having responsibility for the scheme.

3 Other unfunded occupational pension schemes

(1) This paragraph applies to a pension credit which derives from an occupational pension scheme which is—

(a) not funded, and

(b) not a public service pension scheme.

(2) The trustees or managers of the scheme from which a pension credit to which this paragraph applies derives may discharge their liability in respect of the credit by conferring appropriate rights under that scheme on the person entitled to the credit.

(3) The trustees or managers of the scheme from which a pension credit to which this paragraph applies derives may discharge their liability in respect of the credit by paying the amount of the credit to the person responsible for a qualifying arrangement with a view to acquiring rights under that arrangement for the person entitled to the credit if—

(a) the qualifying arrangement is not disqualified as a destination for the credit,

(b) the person responsible for that arrangement is able and willing to accept payment in respect of the credit, and

(c) payment is made with the consent of the person entitled to the credit, or in accordance with regulations made by the Secretary of State.

4   Other pension arrangements

(1) This paragraph applies to a pension credit which derives from—

(a) a retirement annuity contract,

(b) an annuity or insurance policy purchased or transferred for the purpose of giving effect to rights under an occupational pension scheme or a personal pension scheme, or

(c) an annuity purchased, or entered into, for the purpose of discharging liability in respect of a pension credit.

(2) The person responsible for the pension arrangement from which a pension credit to which this paragraph applies derives may discharge his liability in respect of the credit by paying the amount of the credit to the person responsible for a qualifying arrangement with a view to acquiring rights under that arrangement for the person entitled to the credit if—

(a) the qualifying arrangement is not disqualified as a destination for the credit,

(b) the person responsible for that arrangement is able and willing to accept payment in respect of the credit, and

(c) payment is made with the consent of the person entitled to the credit, or in accordance with regulations made by the Secretary of State.

(3) The person responsible for the pension arrangement from which a pension credit to which this paragraph applies derives may discharge his liability in respect of the credit by entering into an annuity contract with the person entitled to the credit if the contract is not disqualified as a destination for the credit.

(4) The person responsible for the pension arrangement from which a pension credit to which this paragraph applies derives may, in such circumstances as the Secretary of State may prescribe by regulations, discharge his liability in respect of the credit by assuming an obligation to provide an annuity for the person entitled to the credit.

(5) In sub-paragraph (1)(c), '**pension credit**' includes a credit under Northern Ireland legislation corresponding to section 21(1)(b).

5   Appropriate rights

For the purposes of this Schedule, rights conferred on the person entitled to a pension credit are appropriate if—

(a) they are conferred with effect from, and including, the day on which the order, or provision, under which the credit arises takes effect, and

(b) their value, when calculated in accordance with regulations made by the Secretary of State, equals the amount of the credit.

6   Qualifying arrangements

(1) The following are qualifying arrangements for the purposes of this Schedule—

(a) an occupational pension scheme,

(b) a personal pension scheme,

(c) an appropriate annuity contract,

(d) an appropriate policy of insurance, and

(e) an overseas arrangement within the meaning of the Contracting-out (Transfer and Transfer Payment) Regulations 1996.

(2) An annuity contract or policy of insurance is appropriate for the purposes of sub-paragraph (1) if, at the time it is entered into or taken out, the insurance company with which it is entered into or taken out—

(a) is carrying on ordinary long-term insurance business in the United Kingdom or any other member State, and

(b) satisfies such requirements as the Secretary of State may prescribe by regulations.

(3) In this paragraph, '**ordinary long-term insurance business**' has the same meaning as in the Insurance Companies Act 1982.

7 Disqualification as destination for pension credit

(1) If a pension credit derives from a pension arrangement which is approved for the purposes of Part XIV of the Income and Corporation Taxes Act 1988, an arrangement is disqualified as a destination for the credit unless—

(a) it is also approved for those purposes, or

(b) it satisfies such requirements as the Secretary of State may prescribe by regulations.

(2) If the rights by reference to which the amount of a pension credit is determined are or include contracted-out rights or safeguarded rights, an arrangement is disqualified as a destination for the credit unless—

(a) it is of a description prescribed by the Secretary of State by regulations, and

(b) it satisfies such requirements as he may so prescribe.

(3) An occupational pension scheme is disqualified as a destination for a pension credit unless the rights to be acquired under the arrangement by the person entitled to the credit are rights whose value, when calculated in accordance with regulations made by the Secretary of State, equals the credit.

(4) An annuity contract or insurance policy is disqualified as a destination for a pension credit in such circumstances as the Secretary of State may prescribe by regulations.

(5) The requirements which may be prescribed under sub-paragraph (1)(b) include, in particular, requirements of the Inland Revenue.

(6) In sub-paragraph (2)—

'**contracted-out rights**' means such rights under, or derived from-

(a) an occupational pension scheme contracted-out by virtue of section 9(2) or (3) of the Pension Schemes Act 1993, or

(b) a personal pension scheme which is an appropriate scheme for the purposes of that Act,

as the Secretary of State may prescribe by regulations;

'**safeguarded rights**' has the meaning given by section 68A of the Pension Schemes Act 1993.

8 Adjustments to amount of pension credit

(1) If—

(a) a pension credit derives from an occupational pension scheme,

(b) the scheme is one to which section 56 of the Pensions Act 1995 (minimum funding requirement for funded salary related schemes) applies,

(c) the scheme is underfunded on the valuation day, and

(d) such circumstances as the Secretary of State may prescribe by regulations apply,

paragraph 1(3) shall have effect in relation to the credit as if the reference to the amount of the credit were to such lesser amount as may be determined in accordance with regulations made by the Secretary of State.

(2) Whether a scheme is underfunded for the purposes of sub-paragraph (1)(c) shall be determined in accordance with regulations made by the Secretary of State.

(3) For the purposes of that provision, the valuation day is the day by reference to which the cash equivalent on which the amount of the pension credit depends falls to be calculated.

9 If—

(a) a person's shareable rights under a pension arrangement have become subject to a pension debit, and

(b) the person responsible for the arrangement makes a payment which is referable to those rights without knowing of the pension debit,

this Schedule shall have effect as if the amount of the corresponding pension credit were such lesser amount as may be determined in accordance with regulations made by the Secretary of State.

10 The Secretary of State may by regulations make provision for paragraph 1(3), 3(3) or 4(2) to have effect, where payment is made after the end of the implementation period for the pension credit, as if the reference to the amount of the credit were to such larger amount as may be determined in accordance with the regulations.

General

11 Liability in respect of a pension credit shall be treated as discharged if the effect of paragraph 8(1) or 9 is to reduce it to zero.

12 Liability in respect of a pension credit may not be discharged otherwise than in accordance with this Schedule.

13 Regulations under paragraph 5(b) or 7(3) may provide for calculation of the value of rights in accordance with guidance from time to time prepared by a person specified in the regulations.

14 In this Schedule—

'**funded**', in relation to an occupational pension scheme, means that the scheme meets its liabilities out of a fund accumulated for the purpose during the life of the scheme;

'**public service pension scheme**' has the same meaning as in the Pension Schemes Act 1993.

SCHEDULE 6

EFFECT OF STATE SCHEME PENSION DEBITS AND CREDITS

1 The Contributions and Benefits Act is amended as follows.

2 *[Amends Contributions and Benefits Act 1992 by adding ss45B after s45A.]*

Finance Act 1999

Pensions and insurance etc

79 Sharing of pensions on divorce etc

Schedule 10 to this Act (which for purposes connected with the sharing of pensions between ex-spouses, makes provision with respect to pensions and annuities) shall have effect.

SCHEDULE 10
SHARING OF PENSIONS ETC ON DIVORCE OR ANNULMENT

1 Definition of 'pension business'

(1) Section 431B of the Taxes Act 1988 (meaning of 'pension business') shall be amended as follows.

(2) In subsection (2)—

    (a) in paragraph (e) (contracts in substitution of contracts under paragraph (d)), after '(d) above' there shall be inserted 'or this paragraph'; and

    (b) after that paragraph there shall be inserted the following paragraph—

        '(ea) any contract which is entered into, for purposes connected with giving effect to any pension sharing order or provision made in relation to a contract falling within paragraph (d) or (e) above or this paragraph and by means of which relevant benefits (see subsections (3) and (4) below), and no other benefits, are secured;'.

(3) After that subsection there shall be inserted the following subsection—

    '(2A) For the purposes of subsection (2)(d) above the members of and contributors to a scheme or fund shall be deemed to include any person who by virtue of any pension sharing order or provision (within the meaning of Part XIV) has become entitled to any credit as against the persons having the management of the scheme or fund.'

(4) In subsection (3) (meaning of 'relevant benefits')—

    (a) for 'subsection (2)(d) and (e)' there shall be substituted 'subsection (2)(d) to (ea)'; and

    (b) after the words 'subsection (2)(e)', wherever they occur, there shall be inserted 'or (ea)'.

2 Approval of retirement benefit schemes

(1) In subsection (2) of section 590 of the Taxes Act 1988 (conditions for approval of scheme), for paragraph (a) there shall be substituted—

    '(a) that the scheme is bona fide established for the sole purpose (subject to any enactment or Northern Ireland legislation requiring or allowing provision for the value of any rights to be transferred between schemes or between members of the same scheme) of providing relevant benefits in respect of service as an employee;'.

(2) After that paragraph there shall be inserted the following paragraph—

   '(aa)   that those benefits do not include any benefits payable to a person other than—

      (i)   the employee or a scheme member's ex-spouse,

      (ii) a widow, widower, child, or dependant of the employee or of a scheme member's ex-spouse, or

      (iii) the personal representatives of the employee or of a scheme member's ex-spouse;'.

(3) In subsection (3) of that section (conditions for automatic approval), for paragraph (c) there shall be substituted the following paragraphs—

   '(ba) that any benefit for an ex-spouse, or for the widow or widower of an ex-spouse, is a benefit in relation to which the scheme satisfies the conditions set out in subsection (3A) below;

   (bb) that the scheme does not allow any rights debited to a scheme member as a consequence of a pension sharing order or provision to be replaced with any rights which that scheme member would not have been able to acquire (in addition to the debited rights) had the order or provision not been made;

   (c) that no benefits are payable under the scheme other than those mentioned in paragraphs (a), (b) and (ba) above;'.

(4) In paragraph (d) of that subsection (restriction on surrender, commutation and assignment)—

   (a) for 'except' there shall be substituted 'except—

      (i)   for the purpose of giving effect to a pension sharing order or provision, or

      (ii) in so far as the commutation of a benefit for an ex-spouse is allowed by virtue of subsection (3A) below, or

      (iii) ';

   and

   (b) for 'his pension' there shall be substituted 'a pension provided for him'.

(5) After that paragraph there shall be inserted the following paragraph—

   '(da) that, in a case in which—

      (i)   a lump sum may be obtained by the commutation of a part of a pension provided for an employee, and

      (ii) the amount of that pension is affected by the making of a pension sharing order or provision,

    the lump sum does not exceed the sum produced by multiplying by 2.25 the amount which (after effect has been given to the pension sharing order or provision) is the amount of that pension for the first year in which it is payable;'.

(6) After subsection (3) of that section there shall be inserted the following subsection—

   '(3A) The conditions mentioned in subsection (3)(ba) above are—

      (a) that any benefit for an ex-spouse takes the form of a pension (with or without an entitlement to commute a part of that pension);

      (b) that any benefit for an ex-spouse is a pension payable only on the attainment by the ex-spouse of a specified age of not less than 60 and not more than 75;

      (c) that any entitlement to commute a part of the pension is exercisable only on its becoming payable;

(d) that any benefit for the widow or widower of an ex-spouse is confined to a non-commutable pension payable on the death of the ex-spouse at a time when the ex-spouse is already entitled to receive a pension under the scheme;

(e) that any pension provided for the widow or widower of an ex-spouse is of an amount not exceeding two-thirds of the pension payable to the ex-spouse;

(f) that, in a case in which a lump sum may be obtained by the commutation of a part of a pension provided for an ex-spouse, the lump sum does not exceed the sum produced by multiplying the amount of the pension for the first year in which it is payable by 2.25.'

(7) In subsection (4) of that section (conditions that are referred to as 'the prescribed conditions'), for 'subsections (2) and (3)' there shall be substituted 'subsections (2) to (3A)'.

(8) After subsection (4A) of that section there shall be inserted the following subsections—

'(4B) For the purposes of this section a benefit provided under any scheme is provided for an ex-spouse or the widow or widower of an ex-spouse, and shall be treated as not provided for an employee or the widow or widower of an employee, to the extent (and to the extent only) that—

(a) it is provided for a person who is, or is the widow or widower of, either—

(i) an employee who is an ex-spouse; or

(ii) a scheme member's ex-spouse;

and

(b) it is as an ex-spouse, or as the widow or widower of an ex-spouse, that that person is the person for whom the benefit is provided.

(4C) For the purposes of this section a benefit provided for any person under any scheme is provided for that person as an ex-spouse, or as the widow or widower of an ex-spouse, to the extent (and to the extent only) that—

(a) the benefit is provided in respect of rights of an ex-spouse that are or represent rights conferred on the ex-spouse as a consequence of a pension sharing order or provision; and

(b) the scheme makes provision for the benefit to be treated as provided separately from any benefits which are provided under the scheme for the same person as an employee or as the widow or widower of an employee.

(4D) In this section 'scheme member', in relation to a scheme, means—

(a) an employee; or

(b) a person entitled to any relevant benefits under the scheme as a consequence of a pension sharing order or provision.

(4E) The following rules shall apply in calculating for the purposes of subsection (3)(da) or (3A)(f) above the amount of a person's pension for the first year in which it is payable—

(a) if the pension payable for the year changes, the initial pension payable shall be taken;

(b) it shall be assumed that that person will survive for the year; and

(c) the effect of commutation shall be ignored.

(4F) A pension provided for an ex-spouse who is an employee, or for the widow or widower of such an ex-spouse, shall be disregarded in any determination of whether the conditions set out in subsection (3)(e) to (h) above are satisfied or continue to be satisfied in the case of that employee.'

3 Discretionary approval of retirement benefit schemes

In section 591(2) of the Taxes Act 1988—

(a) in paragraph (b) (discretion to approve schemes providing benefits for widows on the death in service of an employee), after 'widows' there shall be inserted 'and widowers'; and

(b) after that paragraph there shall be inserted the following paragraph—

'(ba) which provides pensions for the widows and widowers of ex-spouses dying before the age at which their pensions become payable and for the children or dependants of ex-spouses; or'.

4 Non-approved retirement benefit schemes

In subsection (5) of section 595 of the Taxes Act 1988 (charge to tax in respect of certain sums paid by employer etc.), after 'wife' there shall be inserted 'or husband,' and after 'widow' there shall be inserted 'or widower or'.

5   In section 596 of the Taxes Act 1988, after subsection (3) (relief where a taxed contribution does not result in the payment of benefits) there shall be inserted the following subsection—

'(4) Relief shall not be given under subsection (3) above in respect of tax on any sum if—

(a) the reason for there having been no payment in respect of, or in substitution for, the benefits, or part of the benefits, in question, or

(b) the event by reason of which there will be no such payment,

is a reduction or cancellation, as a consequence of any pension sharing order or provision, of the employee's rights in respect of the benefits.'

6   In section 596A(8)(c) (lump sums provided under non-approved schemes), after the word 'employee,', in the first place where it occurs, there shall be inserted 'an ex-spouse of the employee,'.

7 Charge on pensions commuted in special circumstances

(1) In section 599 of the Taxes Act 1988 (charge to tax where pension commuted in special circumstances), the words 'Subject to subsection (1A) below,' shall be inserted at the beginning of subsection (1); and the following subsections shall be inserted after that subsection—

'(1A) Subsection (1) above shall have effect in relation to the commutation of the whole or any part of a pension the amount of which has been affected by the making of any pension sharing order or rovision as if paragraph (a) and the words after paragraph (b) were omitted.

(1B)   Where—

(a) a scheme to which this section applies contains a rule allowing, in special circumstances, a payment in commutation of the entire pension provided under the scheme for an ex-spouse, and

(b) any pension is commuted, whether wholly or not, under the rule,

tax shall be charged on the amount by which the sum receivable exceeds the largest sum which would have been receivable in commutation of any part of the pension under any rule of the scheme authorising the commutation of a part (but not the whole) of the pension.

(1C) A pension provided for an ex-spouse shall be disregarded when applying subsection (1) above in relation to the commutation of any pension provided for an employee.

(1D) A pension provided for an employee shall be disregarded when applying subsection (1B) above in relation to the commutation of any pension provided for an ex-spouse.

(1E) Subsections (4B) and (4C) of section 590 apply for the purposes of subsections (1C) and (1D) above as they apply for the purposes of that section.'

(2) In subsection (6) of that section, after 'subsection (1) above' there shall be inserted ', or in applying subsection (1B) above'.

8 Charge on unauthorised payments

(1) In subsection (1) of section 600 of the Taxes Act 1988 (charge on unauthorised payments to employees), after 'an employee' there shall be inserted 'or an ex-spouse'.

(2) In subsection (2) of that section (person charged), for the words from 'the employee' to 'shall' there shall be substituted 'the employee or, as the case may be, the ex-spouse shall (whether or not he is the recipient of the payment)'.

9 Definition of 'retirement benefits scheme'

(1) In subsections (3) and (4)(b) of section 611 of the Taxes Act 1988 (definition of 'retirement benefits scheme'), for the words 'employees' and 'employee', wherever occurring, there shall be substituted, respectively, the words 'scheme members' and 'scheme member'.

(2) After subsection (5) of that section there shall be inserted the following subsection—

'(6) In this section 'scheme member', in relation to a scheme means—

(a) an employee; or

(b) a person whose rights under the scheme derive from a pension sharing order or provision.'

10 Interpretation of Chapter I

(1) In subsection (1) of section 612 of the Taxes Act 1988 (interpretation of Chapter I of Part XIV), in the definition of 'relevant benefits', after the word 'death', in the first place where it occurs, there shall be inserted ', or by virtue of a pension sharing order or provision'.

(2) In subsection (2) of that section (references to the provision of relevant benefits to include the provision of benefits under contracts with third parties)—

(a) after 'Chapter' there shall be inserted ', in relation to a scheme,';

(b) for 'of an employer' there shall be substituted 'or ex-spouses'; and

(c) after 'or the employee' there shall be inserted 'or ex-spouse'.

(3) After that subsection there shall be inserted the following subsection—

'(2A) In subsection (2) above the reference to the employer is a reference to the person who is the employer in relation to the scheme.'

11   Overseas pensions

In section 615(6)(b) of the Taxes Act 1988 (funds annuities from which are paid without deduction of tax to non-UK residents), after 'purpose' there shall be inserted '(subject to any enactment or Northern Ireland legislation requiring or allowing provision for the value of any rights to be transferred between schemes or between members of the same scheme)'.

12   Rules prohibiting surrender or assignment of annuities etc.

(1) In section 634(6) of the Taxes Act 1988 (restriction on assignment or surrender of annuities), for 'except that' there shall be substituted 'except that—

    (a) an annuity may be assigned or surrendered for the purpose of giving effect to a pension sharing order or provision; and

    (b) '.

(2) In section 634A(6) of that Act (restriction on assignment or surrender of right to income withdrawals), after 'surrender' there shall be inserted ', except for the purpose of giving effect to a pension sharing order or provision'.

(3) In section 635(5) of that Act (restriction on assignment or surrender of right to payment of lump sum), after 'surrender' there shall be inserted ', except for the purpose of giving effect to a pension sharing order or provision'.

13   Annuity payable on the death of a member

(1) In section 636 of the Taxes Act 1988 (annuity payable after death of member to spouse or dependants), after subsection (3) there shall be inserted the following subsection—

    '(3A)   The references in subsection (3) above—

        (a) to the annual amount or highest annual amount of an annuity of which the member was in receipt before his death, and

        (b) to the highest annual amount of an annuity that would have been payable if it had been purchased on the day before the member's death,

    shall each be construed in a case where payments of that annuity were or would have been affected by the making of any pension sharing order or provision as if the only payments of that annuity to be taken into account were those that have been or would have been so affected.'

(2) In subsection (10) of that section (restriction on assignment or surrender of annuities payable after death of member), for 'except that' there shall be substituted 'except that—

    (a) an annuity may be assigned or surrendered for the purpose of giving effect to a pension sharing order or provision; and

    (b) '.

14   Rule in section 636A prohibiting assignment or surrender

In section 636A(7) of the Taxes Act 1988 (restriction on assignment or surrender of right to income withdrawals after death of member), after 'surrender' there shall be inserted ', except for the purpose of giving effect to a pension sharing order or provision'.

15   Meaning of 'relevant earnings'

(1) In section 644 of the Taxes Act 1988 (which for the purposes of references to relevant earnings contains provisions in subsections (6A) to (6F) for excluding the income of controlling directors), after subsection (6E) there shall be inserted the following subsection—

'(6EA)   Where—

> (a)   there is a time at which a person would be in receipt of any benefits under a scheme but for any debit to which any of his rights under that scheme became subject by virtue of any pension sharing order or provision, and

> (b)   the benefits he would be in receipt of are benefits payable in respect of past service with a company,

> that person shall be deemed for the purposes of subsections (6A) to (6E) above to be in receipt at that time of benefits under that scheme and the benefits which he is deemed to be in receipt of shall be deemed to be benefits in respect of past service with that company.'

(2) In subsection (6F) of that section (construction of subsections (6A) to (6E))—

> (a)   in the words before paragraph (a), for '(6E)' there shall be substituted '(6EA)';

> (b)   in paragraph (c) (benefits in respect of past service), after 'the company' there shall be inserted 'but do not include references to benefits which (within the meaning of section 590) are provided for him as an ex-spouse'; and

> (c)   in paragraph (d) (transfer payment in respect of past service), at the end there shall be inserted 'but do not include references to any transfer payment made for the purpose of giving effect to a pension sharing order or provision.'

16   Purchased life annuities

In section 657(2) of the Taxes Act 1988 (annuities not treated as purchased life annuities within section 656), after paragraph (e) there shall be inserted '; or

> (f)   to any annuity purchased, for purposes connected with giving effect to any pension sharing order or provision, for consideration which derives from—

>> (i)   a retirement benefits scheme (within the meaning of Chapter I of this Part) of a description mentioned in section 596(1);

>> (ii)   sums satisfying the conditions for relief under section 619;

>> (iii)   any such scheme or arrangements as are mentioned in paragraph (d) or (e) above; or

>> (iv)   the surrender, in whole or in part, of an annuity falling within paragraph (da) above or this paragraph, or of a contract for such an annuity.'

17   Interpretation of Part XIV

In Chapter VI of Part XIV of the Taxes Act 1988 (interpretation of Part XIV), the following section shall be inserted after section 659C—

'659D   Interpretation of provisions about pension sharing.

(1) In this Part 'ex-spouse' means a party to a marriage that has been dissolved or annulled and, in relation to any person, means the other party to a marriage with that person that has been dissolved or annulled.

(2) References in this Part to a pension sharing order or provision are references to any such order or provision as is mentioned in section 24(1) of the Welfare Reform and Pensions Act 1999 (rights under pension sharing arrangements).'

18 Commencement etc

(1) In this paragraph—

'the first appointed day' means such day as the Treasury may by order appoint as the first appointed day for the purposes of this paragraph;

'the second appointed day' means such day falling after the first appointed day as the Treasury may by order appoint as the second appointed day for the purposes of this paragraph.

(2) The power of the Treasury to appoint a day as the second appointed day for the purposes of this paragraph shall include power so to appoint different days for different purposes.

(3) Subject to sub-paragraph (4) below, paragraphs 2 and 3(b) above apply for the purposes of the grant or withdrawal at any time on or after the first appointed day of any approval of a retirement benefits scheme (whenever made or approved).

(4) Section 590(3)(bb) and (da) of the Taxes Act 1988 shall be disregarded for the purposes of determining whether any retirement benefits scheme approved before the first appointed day satisfies the prescribed conditions at any time before the second appointed day.

(5) Every retirement benefits scheme which—

(a) has, before the first appointed day, been approved by the Board for the purposes of Chapter I of Part XIV of the Taxes Act 1988, and

(b) by virtue of having been approved before that day continues to be so approved on or after the second appointed day,

shall have effect, so long as it continues to be approved on and after the second appointed day and notwithstanding anything in the rules of the scheme, as if (so far as it does not already do so) it contained provision satisfying the conditions set out in section 590(3)(bb) and (da) of the Taxes Act 1988.

(6) Paragraph 6 above applies to any lump sum provided on or after the second appointed day.

(7) Paragraph 8 above applies to any payment on or after the second appointed day.

(8) Subject to sub-paragraph (9) below, paragraphs 12 to 14 above apply for the purposes of—

(a) the grant at any time on or after the first appointed day of any approval of a personal pension scheme (whenever made);

(b) the withdrawal at any time on or after that day of approval of any personal pension scheme or personal pension arrangements (whenever approved).

(9) Section 636(3A) of the Taxes Act 1988 shall be disregarded for the purposes of determining whether any personal pension scheme approved before the first appointed day, or any of the arrangements made by an individual in accordance with such a scheme, satisfies the prescribed conditions at any time before the second appointed day.

(10) The Board may by regulations provide that, in such circumstances as may be prescribed by the regulations, this Schedule shall apply in the case of retirement benefits schemes approved before the first appointed day with such exceptions, exclusions and modifications as may be so prescribed.

(11) Regulations under sub-paragraph (10) above may include such incidental, supplemental, consequential and transitional provision as the Board think appropriate.

Family Proceedings Rules 1991

SI 1991/1247

ANCILLARY RELIEF

[2.51A   Application of ancillary relief rules]

[(1) The procedures set out in rules 2.51B to 2.70 ("the ancillary relief rules") apply to any ancillary relief application and to any application under section 10(2) of the Act of 1973.

(2)   In the ancillary relief rules, unless the context otherwise requires:

"applicant" means the party applying for ancillary relief;

"respondent" means the respondent to the application for ancillary relief;

"FDR appointment" means a Financial Dispute Resolution appointment in accordance with rule 2.61E.]

[2.51B   The overriding objective]

[(1) The ancillary relief rules are a procedural code with the overriding objective of enabling the court to deal with cases justly.

(2)   Dealing with a case justly includes, so far as is practicable—

    (a)   ensuring that the parties are on an equal footing;

    (b)   saving expense;

    (c)   dealing with the case in ways which are proportionate—

        (i)   to the amount of money involved;

        (ii) to the importance of the case;

        (iii) to the complexity of the issues; and

        (iv) to the financial position of each party;

    (d)   ensuring that it is dealt with expeditiously and fairly; and

    (e)   allotting to it an appropriate share of the court's resources, while taking into account the need to allot resources to other cases.

(3)   The court must seek to give effect to the overriding objective when it—

    (a)   exercises any power given to it by the ancillary relief rules; or

    (b)   interprets any rule.

(4)   The parties are required to help the court to further the overriding objective.

(5)   The court must further the overriding objective by actively managing cases.

(6)   Active case management includes—

    (a)   encouraging the parties to co-operate with each other in the conduct of the proceedings;

    (b)   encouraging the parties to settle their disputes through mediation, where appropriate;

    (c)   identifying the issues at an early date;

    (d)   regulating the extent of disclosure of documents and expert evidence so that they are proportionate to the issues in question;

(e) helping the parties to settle the whole or part of the case;

(f) fixing timetables or otherwise controlling the progress of the case;

(g) making use of technology; and

(h) giving directions to ensure that the trial of a case proceeds quickly and efficiently.]

[2.52   Right to be heard on ancillary questions]

A respondent may be heard on any question of ancillary relief without filing an answer and whether or not he has returned to the court office an acknowledgment of service stating his wish to be heard on that question.

[2.53   Application by petitioner or respondent for ancillary relief]

(1) Any application by a petitioner, or by a respondent who files an answer claiming relief, for—

(a) an order for maintenance pending suit,

(b) a financial provision order,

(c) a property adjustment order,

[(d) a pension sharing order,]

shall be made in the petition or answer, as the case may be.

(2) Notwithstanding anything in paragraph (1), an application for ancillary relief which should have been made in the petition or answer may be made subsequently—

(a) by leave of the court, either by notice in Form A or at the trial, or

(b) where the parties are agreed upon the terms of the proposed order, without leave by notice in Form A.

(3) An application by a petitioner or respondent for ancillary relief, not being an application which is required to be made in the petition or answer, shall be made by notice in [Form A].

[2.54   Application by parent, guardian etc for ancillary relief in respect of children]

(1) Any of the following persons, namely—

(a) a parent or guardian of any child of the family,

(b) any person in whose favour a residence order has been made with respect to a child of the family, and any applicant for such an order,

(c) any other person who is entitled to apply for a residence order with respect to a child,

(d) a local authority, where an order has been made under section 30(1)(a) of the Act of 1989 placing a child in its care,

(e) the Official Solicitor, if appointed the guardian ad litem of a child of the family under rule 9.5, and

(f) a child of the family who has been given leave to intervene in the cause for the purpose of applying for ancillary relief,

may apply for an order for ancillary relief as respects that child by notice in [Form A].

(2) In this rule 'residence' order has the meaning assigned to it by section 8(1) of the Act of 1989.

2.55 . . .

2.56 . . .

[2.57   Children to be separately represented on certain applications]

(1) Where an application is made to the High Court or a divorce county court for an order for a variation of settlement, the court shall, unless it is satisfied that the proposed variation does not adversely affect the rights or interests of any children concerned, direct that the children be separately represented on the application, either by a solicitor or by a solicitor and counsel, and may appoint the Official Solicitor or other fit person to be guardian ad litem of the children for the purpose of the application.

(2) On any other application for ancillary relief the court may give such a direction or make such appointment as it is empowered to give or make by paragraph (1).

(3) Before a person other than the Official Solicitor is appointed guardian ad litem under this rule there shall be filed a certificate by the solicitor acting for the children that the person proposed as guardian has no interest in the matter adverse to that of the children and that he is a proper person to be such guardian.

2.58 . . .

[2.59   Evidence on application for property adjustment or avoidance of disposition order]

(1) . . .

(2) Where an application for a property adjustment order or an avoidance of disposition order relates to land, the notice in [Form A] shall identify the land and—

  (a) state whether the title to the land is registered or unregistered and, if registered, the Land Registry title number; and

  (b) give particulars, so far as known to the applicant, of any mortgage of the land or any interest therein.

(3) [Copies of Form A and of Form E completed by the applicant], shall be served on the following persons as well as on the respondent to the application, that is to say—

  (a) in the case of an application for an order for a variation of settlement . . . , the trustees of the settlement and the settlor if living;

  (b) in the case of an application for an avoidance of disposition order, the person in whose favour the disposition is alleged to have been made;

and such other persons, if any, as the district judge may direct.

(4) In the case of an application to which paragraph [(2)] refers, a copy of [Form A], shall be served on any mortgagee of whom particulars are given pursuant to that paragraph; any person so served may apply to the court in writing, within 14 days after service, for a copy of the applicant's [Form E].

(5) Any person who—

  (a) is served with [copies of Forms A and E] pursuant to paragraph (3), or

  (b) receives [a copy of Form E] following an application made in accordance with paragraph (4), may, within 14 days after service or receipt, as the case may be, [file a statement] in answer.

[(6) A statement filed under paragraph (5) shall be sworn to be true.]

[2.60   Service of statement in answer]

[(1) Where a form or other document filed with the court contains an allegation of adultery or of an improper association with a named person ("the named person"), the court may direct that the party who filed the relevant form or document serve a copy of all or part of that form or document on the named person, together with Form F.

(2) If the court makes a direction under paragraph (1), the named person may file a statement in answer to the allegations.

(3) A statement under paragraph (2) shall be sworn to be true.

(4) Rule 2.37(3) shall apply to a person served under paragraph (1) as it applies to a co-respondent.]

[2.61   Information on application for consent order for financial relief]

(1) Subject to paragraphs (2) and (3), there shall be lodged with every application for a consent order under any of sections 23, 24 or 24A of the Act of 1973 two copies of a draft of the order in the terms sought, one of which shall be indorsed with a statement signed by the respondent to the application signifying his agreement, and a statement of information (which may be made in more than one document) which shall include—

    (a)   the duration of the marriage, the age of each party and of any minor or dependent child of the family;

    (b)   an estimate in summary form of the approximate amount or value of the capital resources and net income of each party and of any minor child of the family;

    (c)   what arrangements are intended for the accommodation of each of the parties and any minor child of the family;

    (d)   whether either party has remarried or has any present intention to marry or to cohabit with another person;

    [(dd) where the order *imposes any requirement on the trustees or managers of a pension scheme by virtue of section* [includes provision to be made under section 24B,] 25B or 25C of the Act of 1973, a statement confirming that *those trustees or managers have been served with notice of the application* [the person responsible for the pension arrangement in question has been served with the documents required by rule 2.70(11)] and that no objection to such an order has been made by *them* [that person] within 14 days from such service;]

    (e)   where the terms of the order provide for a transfer of property, a statement confirming that any mortgagee of that property has been served with notice of the application and that no objection to such a transfer has been made by the mortgagee within 14 days from such service; and

    (f)   any other especially significant matters.

(2) Where an application is made for a consent order varying an order for periodical payments paragraph (1) shall be sufficiently complied with if the statement of information required to be lodged with the application includes only the information in respect of net income mentioned in paragraph (1)(b) [(and, where appropriate, a statement under paragraph (1)(dd))], and an application for a consent order for interim periodical payments pending the determination of an application for ancillary relief may be made in like manner.

(3) Where all or any of the parties attend the hearing of an application for financial relief the court may dispense with the lodging of a statement of information in accordance with paragraph (1) and give directions for the information which would otherwise be required to be given in such a statement to be given in such a manner as it sees fit.

[2.61A Application for ancillary relief]

[(1) A notice of intention to proceed with an application for ancillary relief made in the petition or answer or an application for ancillary relief must be made by notice in Form A.

(2) The notice must be filed:

(a) if the case is pending in a divorce county court, in that court; or

(b) if the case is pending in the High Court, in the registry in which it is proceeding.

(3) Where the applicant requests an order for ancillary relief that includes provision to be made by virtue of section [24B,] 25B or 25C of the Act of 1973 the terms of the order requested must be specified in the notice in Form A.

(4) Upon the filing of Form A the court must:

(a) fix a first appointment not less than 12 weeks and not more than 16 weeks after the date of the filing of the notice and give notice of that date;

(b) serve a copy on the respondent within 4 days of the date of the filing of the notice.

(5) The date fixed under paragraph (4) for the first appointment, or for any subsequent appointment, must not be cancelled except with the court's permission and, if cancelled, the court must immediately fix a new date.]

[2.61B Procedure before the first appointment]

[(1) Both parties must, at the same time, exchange with each other, and each file with the court, a statement in Form E, which—

(a) is signed by the party who made the statement;

(b) is sworn to be true, and

(c) contains the information and has attached to it the documents required by that Form.

(2) Form E must be exchanged and filed not less than 35 days before the date of the first appointment.

(3) Form E must have attached to it:

(a) any documents required by Form E; *and*

(b) any other documents necessary to explain or clarify any of the information contained in Form E[; and

(c) any documents furnished to the party producing the form by a person responsible for a pension arrangement, either following a request under rule 2.70(2) or as part of a "relevant valuation" as defined in rule 2.70(4)].

(4) Form E must have no documents attached to it other than the documents referred to in paragraph (3).

(5) Where a party was unavoidably prevented from sending any document required by Form E, that party must at the earliest opportunity:

(a) serve copies of that document on the other party; and

(b) file a copy of that document with the court, together with a statement explaining the failure to send it with Form E.

(6) No disclosure or inspection of documents may be requested or given between the filing of the application for ancillary relief and the first appointment, except—

    (a) copies sent with Form E, or in accordance with paragraph (5); or

    (b) in accordance with paragraph (7).

(7) At least 14 days before the hearing of the first appointment, each party must file with the court and serve on the other party—

    (a) a concise statement of the issues between the parties;

    (b) a chronology;

    (c) a questionnaire setting out by reference to the concise statement of issues any further information and documents requested from the other party or a statement that no information and documents are required;

    (d) a notice in Form G stating whether that party will be in a position at the first appointment to proceed on that occasion to a FDR appointment.

(8) Where an order for ancillary relief is requested that includes provision to be made under section 25B or 25C of the Act of 1973, the applicant must file with the court and serve on the respondent at least 14 days before the hearing of the first appointment, confirmation that rule 2.70(4) has been complied with.

(9) At least 14 days before the hearing of the first appointment, the applicant must file with the court and serve on the respondent, confirmation of the names of all persons served in accordance with rule 2.59(3) and (4), and that there are no other persons who must be served in accordance with those paragraphs.]

[2.61C   Expert evidence]

[CPR rules 35.1 to 35.14 relating to expert evidence (with appropriate modifications), except CPR rules 35.5(2) and 35.8(4)(b) apply to all ancillary relief proceedings.]

[2.61D   The first appointment]

[(1) The first appointment must be conducted with the objective of defining the issues and saving costs.

(2) At the first appointment the district judge—

    (a) must determine—

        (i)   the extent to which any questions seeking information under rule 2.61B must be answered; and

        (ii) what documents requested under rule 2.61B must be produced,

and give directions for the production of such further documents as may be necessary;

    (b) must give directions about—

        (i)   the valuation of assets (including, where appropriate, the joint instruction of joint experts);

        (ii) obtaining and exchanging expert evidence, if required; and

        (iii) evidence to be adduced by each party and, where appropriate, about further chronologies or schedules to be filed by each party;

    (c) must, unless he decides that a referral is not appropriate in the circumstances, direct that the case be referred to a FDR appointment;

    (d) must, where he decides that a referral to a FDR appointment is not appropriate, direct one of the following:

  (i) that a further directions appointment be fixed;

  (ii) that an appointment be fixed for the making of an interim order;

  (iii) that the case be fixed for final hearing and, where that direction is given, the district judge must determine the judicial level at which the case should be heard; or

  (iv) that the case be adjourned for out-of-court mediation or private negotiation or, in exceptional circumstances, generally;

 (e) must consider whether, having regard to all the circumstances (including the extent to which each party has complied with this Part, and in particular the requirement to send documents with Form E), to make an order about the costs of the hearing; and

 (f) may—

  (i) make an interim order where an application for it has been made in accordance with rule 2.69F returnable at the first appointment;

  (ii) having regard to the contents of Form G filed by the parties, treat the appointment (or part of it) as a FDR appointment to which rule 2.61E applies;

  (iii) in a case where an order for ancillary relief is requested that includes provision to be made under section 25B or 25C of the Act of 1973, require any party to request a valuation under regulation 4 of the Divorce etc (Pensions) Regulations 1996 from the trustees or managers of any pension scheme under which the party has, or is likely to have, any benefits.

(3) After the first appointment, a party is not entitled to production of any further documents except in accordance with directions given under paragraph (2)(a) above or with the permission of the court.

(4) At any stage:

 (a) a party may apply for further directions or a FDR appointment;

 (b) the court may give further directions or direct that the parties attend a FDR appointment.

(5) Both parties must personally attend the first appointment unless the court orders otherwise.]

[2.61E The FDR appointment]

[(1) The FDR appointment must be treated as a meeting held for the purposes of discussion and negotiation and paragraphs (2) to (9) apply.

(2) The district judge or judge hearing the FDR appointment must have no further involvement with the application, other than to conduct any further FDR appointment or to make a consent order or a further directions order.

(3) Not later than 7 days before the FDR appointment, the applicant must file with the court details of all offers and proposals, and responses to them.

(4) Paragraph (3) includes any offers, proposals or responses made wholly or partly without prejudice, but paragraph (3) does not make any material admissible as evidence if, but for that paragraph, it would not be admissible.

(5) At the conclusion of the FDR appointment, any documents filed under paragraph (3), and any filed documents referring to them, must, at the request of the party who filed them, be returned to him and not retained on the court file.

(6) Parties attending the FDR appointment must use their best endeavours to reach agreement on the matters in issue between them.

(7) The FDR appointment may be adjourned from time to time.

(8) At the conclusion of the FDR appointment, the court may make an appropriate consent order, but otherwise must give directions for the future course of the proceedings, including, where appropriate, the filing of evidence and fixing a final hearing date.

(9) Both parties must personally attend the FDR appointment unless the court orders otherwise.]

[2.61F   Costs]

[(1) At every court hearing or appointment each party must produce to the court an estimate in Form H of the costs incurred by him up to the date of that hearing or appointment.

(2) The parties' obligation under paragraph (1) is without prejudice to their obligations under paragraphs 4.1 to 4.11 of the Practice Direction relating to CPR Part 44.]

[2.62   Investigation by district judge of application for ancillary relief]

(1) . . .

(2) An application for an avoidance of disposition order shall, if practicable, be heard at the same time as any related application for financial relief.

(3) . . .

(4) At the hearing of an application for ancillary relief the district judge shall, subject to rules 2.64, 2.65 and 10.10 investigate the allegations made in support of and in answer to the application, and may take evidence orally and may at any stage of the proceedings, whether before or during the hearing, order the attendance of any person for the purpose of being examined or cross-examined and order the [disclosure and inspection] of any document or require further [statements].

[(4A) A statement filed under paragraph (4) shall be sworn to be true.]

(5) . . .

(6) . . .

(7) Any party may apply to the court for an order that any person do attend an appointment [(an "inspection appointment")] before the court and produce any documents to be specified or described in the order, the [inspection] of which appears to the court to be necessary for disposing fairly of the application for ancillary relief or for saving costs.

(8) No person shall be compelled by an order under paragraph (7) to produce any document at [an inspection] appointment which he could not be compelled to produce at the hearing of the application for ancillary relief.

(9) The court shall permit any person attending [an inspection] appointment pursuant to an order under paragraph (7) above to be represented at the appointment.

2.63 . . .

. . .

[2.64   Order on application for ancillary relief]

(1) Subject to rule 2.65 the district judge shall, after completing his investigation under rule 2.62, make such order as he thinks just.

(2) Pending the final determination of the application, [and subject to rule 2.69F,] the district judge may make an interim order upon such terms as he thinks just.

(3) RSC Order 31, rule 1 (power to order sale of land) shall apply to applications for ancillary relief as it applies to causes and matters in the Chancery Division.

[2.65   Reference of application to judge]

The district judge may at any time refer an application for ancillary relief, or any question arising thereon, to a judge for his decision.

[2.66   Arrangements for hearing of application etc by judge]

(1) Where an application for ancillary relief or any question arising thereon has been referred or adjourned to a judge, the proper officer shall fix a date, time and place for the hearing of the application or the consideration of the question and give notice thereof to all parties.

(2) The hearing or consideration shall, unless the court otherwise directs, take place in chambers.

(3) Where the application is proceeding in a divorce county court which is not a court of trial or is pending in the High Court and proceeding in a district registry which is not in a divorce town, the hearing or consideration shall take place at such court of trial or divorce town as in the opinion of the district judge is the nearest or most convenient.

For the purposes of this paragraph the Royal Courts of Justice shall be treated as a divorce town.

(4) In respect of any application referred to him under this rule, a judge shall have the same powers [to make directions as a district judge has under these rules].

[2.67   Request for periodical payments order at same rate as order for maintenance pending suit]

(1) Where at or after the date of a decree nisi of divorce or nullity of marriage an order for maintenance pending suit is in force, the party in whose favour the order was made may, if he has made an application for an order for periodical payments for himself in his petition or answer, as the case may be, request the district judge in writing to make such an order (in this rule referred to as a 'corresponding order') providing for payments at the same rate as those provided for by the order for maintenance pending suit.

(2) Where such a request is made, the proper officer shall serve on the other spouse a notice in [Form I] requiring him, if he objects to the making of a corresponding order, to give notice to that effect to the court and to the applicant within 14 days after service of the notice on [Form I].

(3) If the other spouse does not give notice of objection within the time aforesaid, the district judge may make a corresponding order without further notice to that spouse and without requiring the attendance of the applicant or his solicitor, and shall in that case serve a copy of the order on the applicant as well as on the other spouse.

[2.68   Application for order under section 37(2)(a) of Act of 1973]

(1) An application under section 37(2)(a) of the Act of 1973 for an order restraining any person from attempting to defeat a claim for financial provision or otherwise for protecting the claim may be made to the district judge.

(2) Rules 2.65 and 2.66 shall apply, with the necessary modifications, to the application as if it were an application for ancillary relief.

[2.69   Offers to settle]

[(1) Either party to the application may at any time make a written offer to the other party which is expressed to be "without prejudice except as to costs" and which relates to any issue in the proceedings relating to the application.

(2) Where an offer is made under paragraph (1), the fact that such an offer has been made shall not be communicated to the court, except in accordance with rule 2.61E(3), until the question of costs falls to be decided.]

[2.69A   Interpretation of rules 2.69B to 2.69D]

[2.69B   Judgment or order more advantageous than an offer made by the other party]

[(1) This rule applies where the judgment or order in favour of the applicant or respondent is more advantageous to him than an offer made under rule 2.69(1) by the other party.

(2) The court must, unless it considers it unjust to do so, order that other party to pay any costs incurred after the date beginning 28 days after the offer was made.]

[2.69C   Judgment or order more advantageous than offers made by both parties]

[[(1) This rule applies where

(a) both the applicant and the respondent have made offers under rule 2.69(1); and

(b) the judgment or order in favour of the applicant or the respondent, as the case may be, is more advantageous to him than both of the offers referred to in paragraph (a).

(2) The court may, where it considers it just, order interest in accordance with paragraph (3) on the whole or part of any sum of money (excluding interest and periodical payments) to be awarded to the applicant or respondent, as the case may be.

(3) Interest under paragraph (2) may be at a rate not exceeding 10 per cent above base rate for some or all of the period beginning 28 days after the offer was made.

(4) The court may also order that the applicant or respondent, as the case may be, is entitled to:

(a) his costs on the indemnity basis beginning 28 days after the offer was made; and

(b) interest on those costs at a rate not exceeding 10 per cent above base rate.]

(5) The court's powers under this rule are in addition to its powers under rule 2.69B.]

[2.69D   Factors for court's consideration under rules 2.69B and 2.69C]

[(1) In considering whether it would be unjust, or whether it would be just, to make the orders referred to in rules 2.69B and 2.69C, the court must take into account all the circumstances of the case, including—

(a) the terms of any offers made under rule 2.69(1);

(b) the stage in the proceedings when any offer was made;

(c) the information available to the parties at the time when the offer was made;

(d) the conduct of the parties with regard to the giving or refusing to give information for the purposes of enabling the offer to be made or evaluated; and

(e) the respective means of the parties.

(2) The power of the court to award interest under rule 2.69C(2) and (4)(b) is in addition to any other power it may have to award interest.]

[2.69E   Open proposals]

[(1) Not less than 14 days before the date fixed for the final hearing of an application for ancillary relief, the applicant must (unless the court directs otherwise) file with the court and serve on the respondent an open statement which sets out concise details, including the amounts involved, of the orders which he proposes to ask the court to make.

(2) Not more than 7 days after service of a statement under paragraph (1), the respondent must file with the court and serve on the applicant an open statement which sets out concise details, including the amounts involved, of the orders which he proposes to ask the court to make.]

[2.69F   Application for interim orders]

[(1) A party may apply at any stage of the proceedings for an order for maintenance pending suit, interim periodical payments or an interim variation order.

(2) An application for such an order must be made by notice of application and the date fixed for the hearing of the application must be not less than 14 days after the date the notice of application is issued.

(3) The applicant shall forthwith serve the respondent with a copy of the notice of application.

(4) Where an application is made before a party has filed Form E, that party must file with the application and serve on the other party, a draft of the order requested and a short sworn statement explaining why the order is necessary and giving the necessary information about his means.

(5) Not less than 7 days before the date fixed for the hearing, the respondent must file with the court and serve on the other party, a short sworn statement about his means, unless he has already filed Form E.

(6) A party may apply for any other form of interim order at any stage of the proceedings with or without notice.

(7) Where an application referred to in paragraph (6) is made with notice, the provisions of paragraphs (1) to (5) apply to it.

(8) Where an application referred to in paragraph (6) is made without notice, the provisions of paragraph (1) apply to it.]

[2.70   Pensions]

[*(1)* . . .

(2) Where by virtue of rule 2.62(4) the district judge has power to order [disclosure] of any document, he shall also have power to require either party to request a valuation under regulation 4 from the trustees or managers of any pension scheme under which that party has or is likely to have any benefits.

(3) No order including provision made by virtue of section 25B or 25C of the Act of 1973 shall be made unless such provision has been sought by way of—

    [*(a) Form A in accordance with rule 2.61A; or*]

    (b) ...

    (c) a draft order lodged in accordance with rule 2.61.

(4) Where an application is made for an order which by virtue of section 25B or 25C of the Act of 1973 imposes any requirement on the trustees or managers of a pension scheme, a copy of [Form A], shall be served on those trustees or managers together with the following:

    (a) an address to which any notice which the trustees or managers are required to serve under the Divorce etc (Pensions) Regulations 1996 is to be sent;

    (b) an address to which any payment which the trustees or managers are required to make to the applicant is to be sent; and

    (c) where the address in sub-paragraph (b) is that of a bank, a building society or the Department of National Savings, sufficient details to enable payment to be made into the account of the applicant.

(5) Trustees or managers of a pension scheme on whom a copy of such a notice is served may, within 14 days after service, require the applicant to provide them with a copy of the affidavit supporting his application.

(6) Trustees or managers of a pension scheme who receive a copy of an affidavit as required pursuant to paragraph (5) may within 14 days after receipt file an affidavit in answer.

(7) Trustees or managers of a pension scheme who file an affidavit pursuant to paragraph (6) may file therewith a notice to the court requiring an appointment to be fixed; and where such a notice is filed

    (a) the proper officer shall fix an appointment for the hearing or further hearing of the application and give not less than 14 days' notice of that appointment to the petitioner, the respondent and the trustees or managers of the pension scheme; and

    (b) the trustees or managers of the pension scheme shall be entitled to be represented at any such hearing.

(8) Where the petitioner and the respondent have agreed on the terms of an order which by virtue of section 25B or 25C of the Act of 1973 imposes any requirement on the trustees or managers of a pension scheme, then unless service has already been effected under paragraph (4), they shall serve on the trustees or managers notice of the application together with the particulars set out in sub-paragraphs (a), (b) and (c) of paragraph (4), and no such order shall be made unless either

    (a) the trustees or managers have not made any objection within 14 days after the service on them of such notice; or

    (b) the court has considered the objection made by the trustees or managers

    and for the purpose of considering any such objection the court may make such direction as it sees fit for the trustees or managers to attend before it or to furnish written details of their objection.

(9) Upon the making, amendment or revocation of an order which by virtue of section 25B or 25C of the Act of 1973 imposes any requirement on the trustees or managers of a pension scheme, the party in whose favour the order is or was made shall serve a copy of that order, or as the case may be of the order amending or revoking that order, upon the trustees or managers.

(10) In this rule—

    (a) every reference to a regulation by number alone means the regulation so numbered in the Divorce etc (Pensions) Regulations 1996;

(b) all words and phrases defined in section 25D(3) and (4) of the Act of 1973 have the meanings assigned by those subsections.]

[(1) This rule applies where an application for ancillary relief has been made, or notice of intention to proceed with the application has been given, in Form A, or an application has been made in Form B, and the applicant or respondent has or is likely to have any benefits under a pension arrangement.

(2) When the court fixes a first appointment as required by rule 2.61A(4)(a), the party with pension rights shall, within seven days after receiving notification of the date of that appointment, request the person responsible for each pension arrangement under which he has or is likely to have benefits to furnish the information referred to in regulation 2(2) and (3)(b) to (f) of the Pensions on Divorce etc (Provision of Information) Regulations 2000.

(3) Within seven days of receiving information under paragraph (2) the party with pension rights shall send a copy of it to the other party, together with the name and address of the person responsible for each pension arrangement.

(4) A request under paragraph (2) above need not be made where the party with pension rights is in possession of, or has requested, a relevant valuation of the pension rights or benefits accrued under the pension arrangement in question.

(5) In this rule, a relevant valuation means a valuation of pension rights or benefits as at a date not more than twelve months earlier than the date fixed for the first appointment which has been furnished or requested pursuant to any of the following provisions:—

(a) the Pensions on Divorce etc (Provision of Information) Regulations 2000;

(b) regulation 5 of and Schedule 2 to the Occupational Pension Schemes (Disclosure of Information) Regulations 1996 and regulation 11 of and Schedule 1 to the Occupational Pension Schemes (Transfer Value) Regulations 1996;

(c) section 93A or 94(1)(a) or (aa) of the Pension Schemes Act 1993;

(d) section 94(1)(b) of the Pension Schemes Act 1993 or paragraph 2(a) (or, where applicable, 2(b)) of Schedule 2 to the Personal Pension Schemes (Disclosure of Information) Regulations 1987.

(6) Upon making or giving notice of intention to proceed with an application for ancillary relief including provision to be made under section 24B (pension sharing) of the Act of 1973, or upon adding a request for such provision to an existing application for ancillary relief, the applicant shall send to the person responsible for the pension arrangement concerned a copy of Form A.

(7) Upon making or giving notice of intention to proceed with an application for ancillary relief including provision to be made under section 25B or 25C (pension attachment) of the Act of 1973, or upon adding a request for such provision to an existing application for ancillary relief, the applicant shall send to the person responsible for the pension arrangement concerned—

(a) a copy of Form A;

(b) an address to which any notice which the person responsible is required to serve on the applicant under the Divorce etc (Pensions) Regulations 2000 is to be sent;

(c) an address to which any payment which the person responsible is required to make to the applicant is to be sent; and

(d) where the address in sub-paragraph (c) is that of a bank, a building society or the Department of National Savings, sufficient details to enable payment to be made into the account of the applicant.

(8) A person responsible for a pension arrangement on whom a copy of a notice under paragraph (7) is served may, within 21 days after service, require the applicant to provide

him with a copy of section 2.16 of the statement in Form E supporting his application; and the applicant must then provide that person with the copy of that section of the statement within the time limited for filing it by rule 2.61B(2), or 21 days after being required to do so, whichever is the later.

(9) A person responsible for a pension arrangement who receives a copy of section 2.16 of Form E as required pursuant to paragraph (8) may within 21 days after receipt send to the court, the applicant and the respondent a statement in answer.

(10) A person responsible for a pension arrangement who files a statement in answer pursuant to paragraph (9) shall be entitled to be represented at the first appointment, and the court must within 4 days of the date of filing of the statement in answer give the person notice of the date of the first appointment.

(11) Where the parties have agreed on the terms of an order including provision under section 25B or 25C (pension attachment) of the Act of 1973, then unless service has already been effected under paragraph (7), they shall serve on the person responsible for the pension arrangement concerned—

    (a) the notice of application for a consent order under rule 2.61(1);

    (b) a draft of the proposed order under rule 2.61(1), complying with paragraph (13) below; and

    (c) the particulars set out in sub-paragraphs (b), (c) and (d) of paragraph (7) above.

(12) No consent order under paragraph (11) shall be made unless either—

    (a) the person responsible has not made any objection within 21 days after the service on him of such notice; or

    (b) the court has considered any such objection

and for the purpose of considering any objection the court may make such direction as it sees fit for the person responsible to attend before it or to furnish written details of his objection.

(13) An order for ancillary relief, whether by consent or not, including provision under section 24B (pension sharing), 25B or 25C (pension attachment) of the Act of 1973, shall—

    (a) in the body of the order, state that there is to be provision by way of pension sharing or pension attachment in accordance with the annex or annexes to the order; and

    (b) be accompanied by an annex containing the information set out in paragraph (14) or paragraph (15) as the case may require; and if provision is made in relation to more than one pension arrangement there shall be one annex for each pension arrangement.

(14) Where provision is made under section 24B (pension sharing) of the Act of 1973, the annex shall state—

    (a) the name of the court making the order, together with the case number and the title of the proceedings;

    (b) that it is a pension sharing order made under Part IV of the Welfare Reform and Pensions Act 1999;

    (c) the names of the transferor and the transferee;

    (d) the national insurance number of the transferor;

    (e) sufficient details to identify the pension arrangement concerned and the transferor's rights or benefits from it (for example a policy reference number);

    (f) the specified percentage, or where appropriate the specified amount, required in order to calculate the appropriate amount for the purposes of section 29(1) of the Welfare Reform and Pensions Act 1999 (creation of pension debits and credits);

(g) how the pension sharing charges are to be apportioned between the parties or alternatively that they are to be paid in full by the transferor;

(h) that the person responsible for the pension arrangement has furnished the information required by regulation 4 of the Pensions on Divorce etc (Provision of Information) Regulations 2000 and that it appears from that information that there is power to make an order including provision under section 24B (pension sharing) of the Act of 1973;

(i) the day on which the order or provision takes effect; and

(j) that the person responsible for the pension arrangement concerned must discharge his liability in respect of the pension credit within a period of 4 months beginning with the day on which the order or provision takes effect or, if later, with the first day on which the person responsible for the pension arrangement concerned is in receipt of—

   (i) the order for ancillary relief, including the annex;

   (ii) the decree of divorce or nullity of marriage; and

   (iii) the information prescribed by regulation 5 of the Pensions on Divorce etc (Provision of Information) Regulations 2000;

provided that if the court knows that the implementation period is different from that stated in sub-paragraph (j) by reason of regulations under section 34(4) or 41(2)(a) of the Welfare Reform and Pensions Act 1999, the annex shall contain details of the implementation period as determined by those regulations instead of the statement in sub-paragraph (j).

(15) Where provision is made under section 25B or 25C (pension attachment) of the Act of 1973, the annex shall state—

(a) the name of the court making the order, together with the case number and the title of the proceedings;

(b) that it is an order making provision under section 25B or 25C, as the case may be, of the Act of 1973;

(c) the names of the party with pension rights and the other party;

(d) the national insurance number of the party with pension rights;

(e) sufficient details to identify the pension arrangement concerned and the rights or benefits from it to which the party with pension rights is or may become entitled (for example a policy reference number);

(f) in the case of an order including provision under section 25B(4) of the Act of 1973, what percentage of any payment due to the party with pension rights is to be paid for the benefit of the other party;

(g) in the case of an order including any other provision under section 25B or 25C of the Act of 1973, what the person responsible for the pension arrangement is required to do;

(h) the address to which any notice which the person responsible for the pension arrangement is required to serve on the other party under the Divorce etc (Pensions) Regulations 2000 is to be sent, if not notified under paragraph (7)(b);

(i) an address to which any payment which the person responsible for the pension arrangement is required to make to the other party is to be sent, if not notified under paragraph (7)(c);

(j) where the address in sub-paragraph (i) is that of a bank, a building society or the Department of National Savings, sufficient details to enable payment to be made into the account of the other party, if not notified under paragraph (7)(d); and

(k) where the order is made by consent, that no objection has been made by the person responsible for the pension arrangement, or that an objection has been received and considered by the court, as the case may be.

(16) A court which makes, varies or discharges an order including provision under section 24B (pension sharing), 25B or 25C (pension attachment) of the Act of 1973, shall send to the person responsible for the pension arrangement concerned—

(a) a copy of the decree of divorce, nullity of marriage or judicial separation;

(b) in the case of divorce or nullity of marriage, a copy of the certificate under rule 2.51 that the decree has been made absolute; and

(c) a copy of that order, or as the case may be of the order varying or discharging that order, including any annex to that order relating to that pension arrangement but no other annex to that order.

(17) The documents referred to in paragraph (16) shall be sent within 7 days after the making of the relevant order, or within 7 days after the decree absolute of divorce or nullity or decree of judicial separation, whichever is the later.

(18) In this rule—

(a) all words and phrases defined in sections 25D(3) and (4) of the Act of 1973 have the meanings assigned by those subsections;

(b) all words and phrases defined in section 46 of the Welfare Reform and Pensions Act 1999 have the meanings assigned by that section.]

Pensions Act 1995 (Commencement) (No 5) Order 1996

SI 1996/1675

Made 26 June 1996

The Lord Chancellor, in exercise of the powers conferred on him by sections 174(2) and (3) and 180(3) and (4) of the Pensions Act 1995, hereby makes the following Order:

1 [Citation]

This Order may be cited as the Pensions Act 1995 (Commencement) (No 5) Order 1996.

2 [References]

In this Order—

    (a) every reference to a section by number alone means the section so numbered in the Matrimonial Causes Act 1973;

    (b) all words and phrases defined in section 25D(3) and (4) have the meanings assigned by that section.

3 [Commencement]

Subject to the following articles of this Order, section 166 of the Pensions Act 1995 shall come into force on the following dates:

    (a) in relation to the amendment to the Matrimonial Causes Act 1973 consisting of the insertion of section 25D(2), (3) and (4), the day following the day on which this Order was made;

    (b) for all other purposes, 1st August 1996.

4 [Applicability]

(1) Subject to paragraph (2), sections 25B and 25C shall have effect in relation to applications for an order under section 23—

    (a) which are made on or after 1st August 1996, or

    (b) which are made before that date and amended on or after that date pursuant to rule 3 of the Family Proceedings (Amendment) (No 2) Rules 1996 so as to include provision under section 25B or 25C.

(2) Where a petition for divorce, nullity of marriage or judicial separation was presented before 1st July 1996 the Matrimonial Causes Act 1973 shall have effect in relation to those proceedings, including any answer or cross petition filed in those proceedings, as if section 166 of the Pensions Act 1995 had not come into force.

5   Limits

No order under section 23 shall be made requiring the trustees or managers of a pension scheme to make periodical payments to the party without pension rights with effect from a date earlier than 6th April 1997.

Explanatory note

(This note is not part of the Order)

This Order brings into force section 166 of the Pensions Act 1995 on 1 August 1996, with the following exceptions:

(a)   the inserted section 25D(2) to (4) of the Matrimonial Causes Act 1973, empowering the Lord Chancellor to make regulations, comes into force on the day after the making of the Order;

(b)   periodical payments made by a pension fund to a spouse without pension rights may not be ordered so as to commence before 6 April 1997;

(c)   the inserted sections 25B and 25C of the Matrimonial Causes Act 1973 do not apply to proceedings commenced by petition before 1 July 1996.

I.9

Pensions on Divorce etc (Provision of Information) Regulations 2000

SI 2000/1048

Made 13 April 2000
Laid before Parliament 19 April 2000
Coming into force 1 December 2000

The Secretary of State for Social Security, in exercise of the powers conferred upon him by sections 168(1) and (4), 181(1)[1] and 182(2) and (3) of the Pension Schemes Act 1993[2] and sections 23(1)(a), (b)(i), (c)(i) and (2), 34(1)(b)(ii), 45(1) and 83(4) and (6) of the Welfare Reform and Pensions Act 1999 and of all other powers enabling him in that behalf, after consulting such persons as he considered appropriate,[3] hereby makes the following Regulations:

1 Citation, commencement and interpretation

(1) These Regulations may be cited as the Pensions on Divorce etc. (Provision of Information) Regulations 2000 and shall come into force on 1st December 2000.

(2) In these Regulations—

'**the 1993 Act**' means the Pension Schemes Act 1993;

'**the 1995 Act**' means the Pensions Act 1995;

'**the 1999 Act**' means the Welfare Reform and Pensions Act 1999;

'**the Charging Regulations**' means the Pensions on Divorce etc. (Charging) Regulations 2000;[4]

'**the Implementation and Discharge of Liability Regulations**' means the Pension Sharing (Implementation and Discharge of Liability) Regulations 2000;[5]

'**the Valuation Regulations**' means the Pension Sharing (Valuation) Regulations 2000;[6]

'**active member**' has the meaning given by section 124(1) of the 1995 Act;[7]

'**day**' means any day other than—

(a) Christmas Day or Good Friday; or

(b) a bank holiday, that is to say, a day which is, or is to be observed as, a bank holiday or a holiday under Schedule 1 to the Banking and Financial Dealings Act 1971;[8]

'**deferred member**' has the meaning given by section 124(1) of the 1995 Act;

'**implementation period**' has the meaning given by section 34(1) of the 1999 Act;

'**member**' means a person who has rights to future benefits, or has rights to benefits payable, under a pension arrangement;

'**money purchase benefits**' has the meaning given by section 181(1) of the 1993 Act;[9]

'**normal benefit age**' has the meaning given by section 101B of the 1993 Act;[10]

247

'**notice of discharge of liability**' means a notice issued to the member and his former spouse by the person responsible for a pension arrangement when that person has discharged his liability in respect of a pension credit in accordance with Schedule 5 to the 1999 Act;

'**notice of implementation**' means a notice issued by the person responsible for a pension arrangement to the member and his former spouse at the beginning of the implementation period notifying them of the day on which the implementation period for the pension credit begins;

'**occupational pension scheme**' has the meaning given by section 1 of the 1993 Act;

'**the party with pension rights**' and '**the other party**' have the meanings given by section 25D(3) of the Matrimonial Causes Act 1997;[11]

'**pension arrangement**' has the meaning given in section 46(1) of the 1999 Act;

'**pension credit**' means a credit under section 29(1)(b) of the 1999 Act;

'**pension credit benefit**' means the benefits payable under a pension arrangement or a qualifying arrangement to or in respect of a person by virtue of rights under the arrangement in question which are attributable (directly or indirectly) to a pension credit;

'**pension credit rights**' means rights to future benefits under a pension arrangement or a qualifying arrangement which are attributable (directly or indirectly) to a pension credit;

'**pension sharing order or provision**' means an order or provision which is mentioned in section 28(1) of the 1999 Act;

'**pensionable service**' has the meaning given by section 124(1) of the 1995 Act;

'**person responsible for a pension arrangement**' has the meaning given by section 46(2) of the 1999 Act;

'**personal pension scheme**' has the meaning given by section 1 of the 1993 Act;[12]

'**qualifying arrangement**' has the meaning given by paragraph 6 of Schedule 5 to the 1999 Act;

'**retirement annuity contract**' means a contract or scheme approved under Chapter III of Part XIV of the Income and Corporation Taxes Act 1988;[14]

'**salary related occupational pension scheme**' has the meaning given by regulation 1A of the Occupational Pension Schemes (Transfer Values) Regulations 1996;[15]

'**the Regulatory Authority**' means the Occupational Pensions Regulatory Authority;

'**transfer day**' has the meaning given by section 29(8) of the 1999 Act;

'**transferee**' has the meaning given by section 29(8) of the 1999 Act;

'**transferor**' has the meaning given by section 29(8) of the 1999 Act;

'**trustees or managers**' has the meaning given by section 46(1) of the 1999 Act.

2   Basic information about pensions and divorce

(1) The requirements imposed on a person responsible for a pension arrangement for the purposes of section 23(1)(a) of the 1999 Act (supply of pension information in connection with divorce etc.) are that he shall furnish—

(a) on request from a member, the information referred to in paragraphs (2) and (3)(b) to (f);

(b) on request from the spouse of a member, the information referred to in paragraph (3); or

(c) pursuant to an order of the court, the information referred to in paragraph (2), (3) or (4),

to the member, the spouse of the member, or, as the case may be, to the court.

(2) The information in this paragraph is a valuation of pension rights or benefits accrued under that member's pension arrangement.

(3) The information in this paragraph is—

(a) a statement that on request from the member, or pursuant to an order of the court, a valuation of pension rights or benefits accrued under that member's pension arrangement, will be provided to the member, or, as the case may be, to the court;

(b) a statement summarising the way in which the valuation referred to in paragraph (2) and sub-paragraph (a) is calculated;

(c) the pension benefits which are included in a valuation referred to in paragraph (2) and sub-paragraph (a);

(d) whether the person responsible for the pension arrangement offers membership to a person entitled to a pension credit, and if so, the types of benefits available to pension credit members under that arrangement;

(e) whether the person responsible for the pension arrangements intends to discharge his liability for a pension credit other than by offering membership to a person entitled to a pension credit; and

(f) the schedule of charges which the person responsible for the pension arrangement will levy in accordance with regulation 2(2) of the Charging Regulations (general requirements as to charges).

(4) The information in this paragraph is any other information relevant to any power with respect to the matters specified in section 23(1)(a) of the 1999 Act and which is not specified in Schedule 1 or 2 to the Occupational Pension Schemes (Disclosure of Information) Regulations 1996[16] (basic information about the scheme and information to be made available to individuals), or in Schedule 1 or 2 to the Personal Pension Schemes (Disclosure of Information) Regulations 1987[17] (basic information about the scheme and information to be made available to individuals), in a case where either of those Regulations applies.

(5) Where the member's request for, or the court order for the provision of, information includes a request for, or an order for the provision of, a valuation under paragraph (2), the person responsible for the pension arrangement shall furnish all the information requested, or ordered, to the member—

(a) within 3 months beginning with the date the person responsible for the pension arrangement receives that request or order for the provision of the information;

(b) within 6 weeks beginning with the date the person responsible for the pension arrangement receives the request, or order, for the provision of the information, if the member has notified that person on the date of the request or order that the information is needed in connection with proceedings commenced under any of the provisions referred to in section 23(1)(a) of the 1999 Act; or

(c) within such shorter period specified by the court in an order requiring the person responsible for the pension arrangement to provide a valuation in accordance with paragraph (2).

(6) Where—

(a) the member's request for, or the court order for the provision of, information does not include a request or an order for a valuation under paragraph (2); or

(b) the member's spouse requests the information specified in paragraph (3), the person responsible for the pension arrangement shall furnish that information to the member, his spouse, or the court, as the case may be, within one month beginning with the date that person responsible for the pension arrangement receives the request for, or the court order for the provision of, the information.

(7) At the same time as furnishing the information referred to in paragraph (1), the person responsible for a pension arrangement may furnish the information specified in regulation 4(2) (provision of information in response to a notification that a pension sharing order or provision may be made).

3   Information about pensions and divorce: valuation of pension benefits

(1) Where an application for financial relief under any of the provisions referred to in section 23(1)(a)(i) or (iii) of the 1999 Act (supply of pension information in connection with domestic and overseas divorce etc. in England and Wales and corresponding Northern Ireland powers) has been made or is in contemplation, the valuation of benefits under a pension arrangement shall be calculated and verified for the purposes of regulation 2 of these Regulations in accordance with—

  (a) paragraph (3), if the person with pension rights is a deferred member of an occupational pension scheme;

  (b) paragraph (4), if the person with pension rights is an active member of an occupational pension scheme;

  (c) paragraphs (5) and (6), if—

   (i) the person with pension rights is a member of a personal pension scheme; or

   (ii) those pension rights are contained in a retirement annuity contract; or

  (d) paragraphs (7) to (9), if—

   (i) the pension of the person with pension rights is in payment;

   (ii) the rights of the person with pension rights are contained in an annuity contract other than a retirement annuity contract; or

   (iii) the rights of the person with pension rights are contained in a deferred annuity contract other than a retirement annuity contract.

(2) Where an application for financial provision under any of the provisions referred to in section 23(1)(a)(ii) of the 1999 Act (corresponding Scottish powers) has been made, or is in contemplation, the valuation of benefits under a pension arrangement shall be calculated and verified for the purposes of regulation 2 of these Regulations in accordance with regulation 3 of the Divorce etc. (Pensions) (Scotland) Regulations 2000[18] (valuation).

(3) Where the person with pension rights is a deferred member of an occupational pension scheme, the value of the benefits which he has under that scheme shall be taken to be—

  (a) in the case of an occupational pension scheme other than a salary related scheme, the cash equivalent to which he acquired a right under section 94(1)(a) of the 1993 Act[19] (right to cash equivalent) on the termination of his pensionable service, calculated on the assumption that he has made an application under section 95 of that Act[20] (ways of taking right to cash equivalent) on the date on which the request for the valuation was received; or

  (b) in the case of a salary related occupational pension scheme, the guaranteed cash equivalent to which he would have acquired a right under section 94(1)(aa) of the 1993 Act[21] if he had made an application under section 95(1) of that Act, calculated on the assumption that he has made such an application on the date on which the request for the valuation was received.

(4) Where the person with pension rights is an active member of an occupational pension scheme, the valuation of the benefits which he has accrued under that scheme shall be calculated and verified—

    (a) on the assumption that the member had made a request for an estimate of the cash equivalent that would be available to him were his pensionable service to terminate on the date on which the request for the valuation was received; and

    (b) in accordance with regulation 11 of and Schedule 1 to the Occupational Pension Schemes (Transfer Values) Regulations 1996[22] (disclosure).

(5) Where the person with pension rights is a member of a personal pension scheme, or those rights are contained in a retirement annuity contract, the value of the benefits which he has under that scheme or contract shall be taken to be the cash equivalent to which he would have acquired a right under section 94(1)(b) of the 1993 Act, if he had made an application under section 95(1) of that Act on the date on which the request for the valuation was received.

(6) In relation to a personal pension scheme which is comprised in a retirement annuity contract made before 4th January 1988, paragraph (5) shall apply as if such a scheme were not excluded from the scope of Chapter IV of Part IV of the 1993 Act by section 93(1)(b) of that Act (scope of Chapter IV).

(7) Except in a case to which, or to the extent to which, paragraph (9) applies, the cash equivalent of benefits in respect of a person referred to in paragraph (1)(d) shall be calculated and verified in such manner as may be approved in a particular case by—

    (a) a Fellow of the Institute of Actuaries;

    (b) a Fellow of the Faculty of Actuaries;[23] or

    (c) a person with other actuarial qualifications who is approved by the Secretary of State, at the request of the person responsible for the pension arrangement in question, as being a proper person to act for the purposes of this regulation in connection with that arrangement.

(8) Except in a case to which paragraph (9) applies, cash equivalents are to be calculated and verified by adopting methods and making assumptions which—

    (a) if not determined by the person responsible for the pension arrangement in question, are notified to him by an actuary referred to in paragraph (7); and

    (b) are certified by the actuary to the person responsible for the pension arrangement in question as being consistent with 'Retirement Benefit Schemes—Transfer Values (GN11)' published by the Institute of Actuaries and the Faculty of Actuaries and current at the date on which the request for the valuation is received.[24]

(9) Where the cash equivalent, or any portion of it represents rights to money purchase benefits under the pension arrangement in question of the person with pension rights, and those rights do not fall, either wholly or in part, to be valued in a manner which involves making estimates of the value of benefits, then that cash equivalent, or that portion of it, shall be calculated and verified in such manner as may be approved in a particular case by the person responsible for the pension arrangement in question, and by adopting methods consistent with the requirements of Chapter IV of Part IV of the 1993 Act (protection for early leavers—transfer values).

(10) Where paragraph (3), (4) or (9) has effect by reference to provisions of Chapter IV of Part IV of the 1993 Act, section 93(1)(a)(i) of that Act[25] (scope of Chapter IV) shall apply to those provisions as if the words 'at least one year' had been omitted from section 93(1)(a)(i).

4   Provision of information in response to a notification that a pension sharing order or provision may be made

(1) A person responsible for a pension arrangement shall furnish the information specified in paragraph (2) to the member or to the court, as the case may be—

    (a) within 21 days beginning with the date that the person responsible for the pension arrangement received the notification that a pension sharing order or provision may be made; or

    (b) if the court has specified a date which is outside the 21 days referred to in sub-paragraph (a), by that date.

(2) The information referred to in paragraph (1) is—

    (a) the full name of the pension arrangement and address to which any order or provision referred to in section 28(1) of the 1999 Act (activation of pension sharing) should be sent;

    (b) in the case of an occupational pension scheme, whether the scheme is winding up, and, if so,—

       (i)   the date on which the winding up commenced; and

       (ii) the name and address of the trustees who are dealing with the winding up;

    (c) in the case of an occupational pension scheme, whether a cash equivalent of the member's pension rights, if calculated on the date the notification referred to in paragraph (1)(a) was received by the trustees or managers of that scheme, would be reduced in accordance with the provisions of regulation 8(4), (6) or (12) of the Occupational Pension Schemes (Transfer Values) Regulations 1996[26] (further provisions as to reductions of cash equivalents);

    (d) whether the person responsible for the pension arrangement is aware that the member's rights under the pension arrangement are subject to any, and if so, to specify which, of the following—

       (i)   any order or provision specified in section 28(1) of the 1999 Act;

       (ii) an order under section 23 of the Matrimonial Causes Act 1973[27] (financial provision orders in connection with divorce etc.), so far as it includes provision made by virtue of section 25B or 25C of that Act[28] (powers to include provisions about pensions);

       (iii) an order under section 12A(2) or (3) of the Family Law (Scotland) Act 1985[29] (powers in relation to pensions lump sums when making a capital sum order) which relates to benefits or future benefits to which the member is entitled under the pension arrangement;

       (iv) an order under Article 25 of the Matrimonial Causes (Northern Ireland) Order 1978,[30] so far as it includes provision made by virtue of Article 27B or 27C of that Order (Northern Ireland powers corresponding to those mentioned in paragraph (2)(d)(ii));

       (v)   a forfeiture order;

       (vi) a bankruptcy order;

       (vii) an award of sequestration on a member's estate or the making of the appointment on his estate of a judicial factor under section 41 of the Solicitors (Scotland) Act 1980[31] (appointment of judicial factor);

    (e) whether the member's rights under the pension arrangement include rights specified in regulation 2 of the Valuation Regulations (rights under a pension arrangement which are not shareable);

    (f) if the person responsible for the pension arrangement has not at an earlier stage provided the following information, whether that person requires the charges specified in regulation 3 (charges recoverable in respect of the provision of basic information), 5 (charges in respect of pension sharing activity), or 6 (additional amounts recoverable in respect of pension sharing activity) of the Charging Regulations to be paid before the commencement of the implementation period, and if so,—

    (i)   whether that person requires those charges to be paid in full; or

    (ii) the proportion of those charges which he requires to be paid;

(g)   whether the person responsible for the pension arrangement may levy additional charges specified in regulation 6 of the Charging Regulations, and if so, the scale of the additional charges which are likely to be made;

(h)   whether the member is a trustee of the pension arrangement;

(i)   whether the person responsible for the pension arrangement may request information about the member's state of health from the member if a pension sharing order or provision were to be made;

(j)   [*deleted*]

(k)   whether the person responsible for the pension arrangement requires information additional to that specified in regulation 5 (information required by the person responsible for the pension arrangement before the implementation period may begin) in order to implement the pension sharing order or provision.

5   Information required by the person responsible for the pension arrangement before the implementation period may begin

The information prescribed for the purposes of section 34(1)(b) of the 1999 Act (information relating to the transferor and the transferee which the person responsible for the pension arrangement must receive) is—

(a)   in relation to the transferor—

    (i)   all names by which the transferor has been known;

    (ii) date of birth;

    (iii) address;

    (iv) National Insurance number;

    (v) the name of the pension arrangement to which the pension sharing order or provision relates; and

    (vi) the transferor's membership or policy number in that pension arrangement;

(b)   in relation to the transferee—

    (i)   all names by which the transferee has been known;

    (ii) date of birth;

    (iii) address;

    (iv) National Insurance number; and

    (v) if the transferee is a member of the pension arrangement from which the pension credit is derived, his membership or policy number in that pension arrangement;

(c)   where the transferee has given his consent in accordance with paragraph 1(3)(c), 3(3)(c) or 4(2)(c) of Schedule 5 to the 1999 Act (mode of discharge of liability for a pension credit) to the payment of the pension credit to the person responsible for a qualifying arrangement—

    (i)   the full name of that qualifying arrangement;

    (ii) its address;

    (iii) if known, the transferee's membership number or policy number in that arrangement; and

(iv) the name or title, business address, business telephone number, and, where available, the business facsimile number and electronic mail address of a person who may be contacted in respect of the discharge of liability for the pension credit;

(d) where the rights from which the pension credit is derived are held in an occupational pension scheme which is being wound up, whether the transferee has given an indication whether he wishes to transfer his pension credit rights which may have been reduced in accordance with the provisions of regulation 16(1) of the Implementation and Discharge of Liability Regulations (adjustments to the amount of the pension credit—occupational pension schemes which are underfunded on the valuation day) to a qualifying arrangement; and

(e) any information requested by the person responsible for the pension arrangement in accordance with regulation 4(2)(i) or (k).

6   Provision of information after the death of the person entitled to the pension credit before liability in respect of the pension credit has been discharged

(1) Where the person entitled to the pension credit dies before the person responsible for the pension arrangement has discharged his liability in respect of the pension credit, the person responsible for the pension arrangement shall, within 21 days of the date of receipt of the notification of the death of the person entitled to the pension credit, notify in writing any person whom the person responsible for the pension arrangement considers should be notified of the matters specified in paragraph (2).

(2) The matters specified in this paragraph are—

(a) how the person responsible for the pension arrangement intends to discharge his liability in respect of the pension credit;

(b) whether the person responsible for the pension arrangement intends to recover charges from the person nominated to receive pension credit benefits, in accordance with regulations 2 to 9 of the Charging Regulations, and if so, a copy of the schedule of charges issued to the parties to pension sharing in accordance with regulation 2(2)(b) of the Charging Regulations (general requirements as to charges); and

(c) a list of any further information which the person responsible for the pension arrangement requires in order to discharge his liability in respect of the pension credit.

7   Provision of information after receiving a pension sharing order or provision

(1) A person responsible for a pension arrangement who is in receipt of a pension sharing order or provision relating to that arrangement shall provide in writing to the transferor and transferee, or, where regulation 6(1) applies, to the person other than the person entitled to the pension credit referred to in regulation 6 of the Implementation and Discharge of Liability Regulations (discharge of liability in respect of a pension credit following the death of the person entitled to the pension credit), as the case may be,—

(a) a notice in accordance with the provisions of regulation 7(1) of the Charging Regulations (charges in respect of pension sharing activity—postponement of implementation period);

(b) a list of information relating to the transferor or the transferee, or, where regulation 6(1) applies, the person other than the person entitled to the pension credit referred to in regulation 6 of the Implementation and Discharge of Liability Regulations, as the case may be, which—

(i) has been requested in accordance with regulation 4(2)(i) and (k), or, where appropriate, 6(2)(c), or should have been provided in accordance with regulation 5;

(ii) the person responsible for the pension arrangement considers he needs in order to begin to implement the pension sharing order or provision; and

(iii) remains outstanding;

(c) a notice of implementation; or

(d) a statement by the person responsible for the pension arrangement explaining why he is unable to implement the pension sharing order or agreement.

(2) The information specified in paragraph (1) shall be furnished in accordance with that paragraph within 21 days beginning with—

(a) in the case of sub-paragraph (a), (b) or (d) of that paragraph, the day on which the person responsible for the pension arrangement receives the pension sharing order or provision; or

(b) in the case of sub-paragraph (c) of that paragraph, the later of the days specified in section 34(1)(a) and (b) of the 1999 Act (implementation period).

8 Provision of information after the implementation of a pension sharing order or provision

(1) The person responsible for the pension arrangement shall issue a notice of discharge of liability to the transferor and the transferee, or, as the case may be, the person entitled to the pension credit by virtue of regulation 6 of the Implementation and Discharge of Liability Regulations no later than the end of the period of 21 days beginning with the day on which the discharge of liability in respect of the pension credit is completed.

(2) In the case of a transferor whose pension is not in payment, the notice of discharge of liability shall include the following details—

(a) the value of the transferor's accrued rights as determined by reference to the cash equivalent value of those rights calculated and verified in accordance with regulation 3 of the Valuation Regulations (calculation and verification of cash equivalents for the purposes of the creation of pension debits and credits);

(b) the value of the pension debit;

(c) any amount deducted from the value of the pension rights in accordance with regulation 9(2)(c) of the Charging Regulations (charges in respect of pension sharing activity—method of recovery);

(d) the value of the transferor's rights after the amounts referred to in sub-paragraphs (b) and (c) have been deducted; and

(e) the transfer day.

(3) In the case of a transferor whose pension is in payment, the notice of discharge of liability shall include the following details—

(a) the value of the transferor's benefits under the pension arrangement as determined by reference to the cash equivalent value of those rights calculated and verified in accordance with regulation 3 of the Valuation Regulations;

(b) the value of the pension debit;

(c) the amount of the pension which was in payment before liability in respect of the pension credit was discharged;

(d) the amount of pension which is payable following the deduction of the pension debit from the transferor's pension benefits;

(e) the transfer day;

(f) if the person responsible for the pension arrangement intends to recover charges, the amount of any unpaid charges—

    (i) not prohibited by regulation 2 of the Charging Regulations (general requirements as to charges); and

    (ii) specified in regulations 3 and 6 of those Regulations;

(g) how the person responsible for the pension arrangement will recover the charges referred to in sub-paragraph (f), including—

    (i) whether the method of recovery specified in regulation 9(2)(d) of the Charging Regulations will be used;

    (ii) the date when payment of those charges in whole or in part is required; and

    (iii) the sum which will be payable by the transferor, or which will be deducted from his pension benefits, on that date.

(4) In the case of a transferee—

(a) whose pension is not in payment; and

(b) who will become a member of the pension arrangement from which the pension credit rights were derived,

the notice of discharge of liability to the transferee shall include the following details

    (i) the value of the pension credit;

    (ii) any amount deducted from the value of the pension credit in accordance with regulation 9(2)(b) of the Charging Regulations;

    (iii) the value of the pension credit after the amount referred to in sub-paragraph (b)(ii) has been deducted;

    (iv) the transfer day;

    (v) any periodical charges the person responsible for the pension arrangement intends to make, including how and when those charges will be recovered from the transferee; and

    (vi) information concerning membership of the pension arrangement which is relevant to the transferee as a pension credit member.

(5) In the case of a transferee who is transferring his pension credit rights out of the pension arrangement from which those rights were derived, the notice of discharge of liability to the transferee shall include the following details—

(a) the value of the pension credit;

(b) any amount deducted from the value of the pension credit in accordance with regulation 9(2)(b) of the Charging Regulations;

(c) the value of the pension credit after the amount referred to in sub-paragraph (b) has been deducted;

(d) the transfer day; and

(e) details of the pension arrangement, including its name, address, reference number, telephone number, and, where available, the business facsimile number and electronic mail address, to which the pension credit has been transferred.

(6) In the case of a transferee, who has reached normal benefit age on the transfer day, and in respect of whose pension credit liability has been discharged in accordance with paragraph 1(2), 2(2), 3(2) or 4(4) of Schedule 5 to the 1999 Act (pension credits: mode of discharge—funded pension schemes, unfunded public service pension schemes, other unfunded pension schemes, or other pension

Pensions on Divorce etc (Provision of Information) Regulations 2000

arrangements), the notice of discharge of liability to the transferee shall include the following details—

    (a) the amount of pension credit benefit which is to be paid to the transferee;

    (b) the date when the pension credit benefit is to be paid to the transferee;

    (c) the transfer day;

    (d) if the person responsible for the pension arrangement intends to recover charges, the amount of any unpaid charges—

        (i) not prohibited by regulation 2 of the Charging Regulations; and

        (ii) specified in regulations 3 and 6 of those Regulations; and

    (e) how the person responsible for the pension arrangement will recover the charges referred to in sub-paragraph (d), including—

        (i) whether the method of recovery specified in regulation 9(2)(e) of the Charging Regulations will be used;

        (ii) the date when payment of those charges in whole or in part is required; and

        (iii) the sum which will be payable by the transferee, or which will be deducted from his pension credit benefits, on that date.

(7) In the case of a person entitled to the pension credit by virtue of regulation 6 of the Implementation and Discharge of Liability Regulations, the notice of discharge of liability shall include the following details—

    (a) the value of the pension credit rights as determined in accordance with regulation 10 of the Implementation and Discharge of Liability Regulations (calculation of the value of appropriate rights);

    (b) any amount deducted from the value of the pension credit in accordance with regulation 9(2)(b) of the Charging Regulations;

    (c) the value of the pension credit;

    (d) the transfer day; and

    (e) any periodical charges the person responsible for the pension arrangement intends to make, including how and when those charges will be recovered from the payments made to the person entitled to the pension credit by virtue of regulation 6 of the Implementation and Discharge of Liability Regulations.

9 Penalties

Where any trustee or manager of an occupational pension scheme fails, without reasonable excuse, to comply with any requirement imposed under regulation 6, 7 or 8, the Regulatory Authority may require that trustee or manager to pay within 28 days from the date of its imposition, a penalty which shall not exceed—

    (a) £200 in the case of an individual, and

    (b) £1,000 in any other case.

10 Provision of information after receipt of an earmarking order

(1) The person responsible for the pension arrangement shall, within 21 days beginning with the day that he receives—

    (a) an order under section 23 of the Matrimonial Causes Act 1973, so far as it includes provision made by virtue of section 25B or 25C of that Act (powers to include provision about pensions);

    (b) an order under section 12A(2) or (3) of the Family Law (Scotland) Act 1985; or

(c)   an order under Article 25 of the Matrimonial Causes (Northern Ireland) Order 1978, so far as it includes provision made by virtue of Article 27B or 27C of that Order (Northern Ireland powers corresponding to those mentioned in sub-paragraph (a)),

issue to the party with pension rights and the other party a notice which includes the information specified in paragraphs (2) and (5), or (3), (4) and (5), as the case may be.

(2)   Where an order referred to in paragraph (1)(a), (b) or (c) is made in respect of the pension rights or benefits of a party with pension rights whose pension is not in payment, the notice issued by the person responsible for a pension arrangement to the party with pension rights and the other party shall include a list of the circumstances in respect of any changes of which the party with pension rights or the other party must notify the person responsible for the pension arrangement.

(3)   Where an order referred to in paragraph (1)(a) or (c) is made in respect of the pension rights or benefits of a party with pension rights whose pension is in payment, the notice issued by the person responsible for a pension arrangement to the party with pension rights and the other party shall include—

(a)   the value of the pension rights or benefits of the party with pension rights;

(b)   the amount of the pension of the party with pension rights after the order has been implemented;

(c)   the first date when a payment pursuant to the order is to be made; and

(d)   a list of the circumstances, in respect of any changes of which the party with pension rights or the other party must notify the person responsible for the pension arrangement.

(4)   Where an order referred to in paragraph (1)(a) or (c) is made in respect of the pension rights of a party with pension rights whose pension is in payment, the notice issued by the person responsible for a pension arrangement to the party with pension rights shall, in addition to the items specified in paragraph (3), include—

(a)   the amount of the pension of the party with pension rights which is currently in payment; and

(b)   the amount of pension which will be payable to the party with pension rights after the order has been implemented.

(5)   Where an order referred to in paragraph (1)(a), (b) or (c) is made the notice issued by the person responsible for a pension arrangement to the party with pension rights and the other party shall include—

(a)   the amount of any charges which remain unpaid by—

(i)   the party with pension rights; or

(ii)   the other party,

in respect of the provision by the person responsible for the pension arrangement of information about pensions and divorce pursuant to regulation 3 of the Charging Regulations, and in respect of complying with an order referred to in paragraph (1)(a), (b) or (c); and

(b)   information as to the manner in which the person responsible for the pension arrangement will recover the charges referred to in sub-paragraph (a), including—

(i)   the date when payment of those charges in whole or in part is required;

(ii)   the sum which will be payable by the party with pension rights or the other party, as the case may be; and

(iii)   whether the sum will be deducted from payments of pension to the party with pension rights, or, as the case may be, from payments to be made to the other party pursuant to an order referred to in paragraph (1)(a), (b) or (c).

Signed by authority of the Secretary of State for Social Security

Jeff Rooker

Minister of State, Department of Social Security

13th April 2000

Explanatory note

(This note is not part of the Regulations)

These Regulations set out the requirements imposed on a person responsible for a pension arrangement with respect to the supply of information to members and their spouses (or former spouses) in relation to pensions on divorce, separation or nullity.

Regulation 1 provides for citation, commencement and interpretation.

Regulation 2 sets out what basic information persons responsible for a pension arrangement must provide to a member, his spouse or the court in relation to pensions on divorce, separation or nullity.

Regulation 3 provides for how valuations of pension benefits are to be calculated and verified for the purposes of the provision of information in respect of pensions on divorce, separation or nullity.

Regulation 4 specifies the information which a person responsible for a pension arrangement must provide to a member and his spouse in response to a notification that a pension sharing order or provision may be made, and the circumstances in which that information must be provided.

Regulation 5 sets out the information which will be required by the person responsible for the pension arrangement from the member and his former spouse before the implementation period may begin.

Regulation 6 specifies the information a person responsible for a pension arrangement must provide to the former spouse's representative, and the person who has been nominated by the former spouse to receive the pension credit benefit if the former spouse dies before liability in respect of the pension credit is discharged (the nominee).

Regulation 7 specifies the information a person responsible for a pension arrangement must provide to a member and his former spouse, or the nominee, as the case may be, when a pension sharing order or provision has been received.

Regulation 8 sets out the information which a person responsible for a pension arrangement must provide to a member and his former spouse, or the nominee, as the case may be, once a pension sharing order or provision has been implemented.

Regulation 9 sets out the maximum penalties which the Occupational Pensions Regulatory Authority may impose if the trustees or managers of an occupational pension scheme fail to comply with the requirements to furnish the information specified in regulation 6, 7 or 8 within the prescribed time limits.

Regulation 10 sets out the information which a person responsible for a pension arrangement must furnish to the party to the marriage with pension rights and the other party to the marriage after receiving an earmarking order.

An assessment of the cost to business of the provisions of the Welfare Reform and Pensions Act 1999, including these Regulations, is detailed in the Regulatory Impact Assessment for that Act. A copy of this Assessment has been placed in the libraries of both Houses of Parliament. Copies can be obtained by post from the Department of Social Security, Pensions on Divorce, 3rd Floor, The Adelphi, 1–11 John Adam Street, London WC2N 6HT.

Notes

[1] Section 181(1) is cited because of the meaning there given to 'prescribed' and 'regulations'.

[2] 1993 c. 48. A new section 168 was substituted by section 155(1) of the Pensions Act 1995 (c. 26). Section 168 applies to these Regulations by virtue of section 45(2) of the Welfare Reform and Pensions Act 1999 (c. 30).

[3] *See* section 83(11) of the Welfare Reform and Pensions Act 1999.

[4] SI 2000/1049.

[5] SI 2000/1053.

[6] SI 2000/1052.

[7] Section 124(1) is amended by the Welfare Reform and Pensions Act 1999.

[8] 1971 c. 80.

[9] Section 181 was amended by the Pensions Act 1995, the Industrial Tribunals Act 1996 (c. 17), and is amended by the Welfare Reform and Pensions Act 1999.

[10] Section 101B is inserted by section 37 of the Welfare Reform and Pensions Act 1999.

[11] 1973 c. 18. Section 250 was inserted by section 166 of the Pensions Act 1995 and is amended by paragraph 3 of Schedule 4 to the Welfare Reform and Pensions Act 1999.

[12] The definition of 'personal pension scheme' was amended by paragraph 3(1)(a) of Schedule 2 to the Welfare Reform and Pensions Act 1999.

[13] 1985 c. 37. Section 10 was amended by section 167(2) of the Pensions Act 1995 and is amended by paragraph 8 of Schedule 12 to the Welfare Reform and Pensions Act 1999.

[14] 1988 c. 1.

[15] SI 1996/1847. Regulation 1A was inserted by paragraph 12(3) of Schedule 1 to SI 1997/786.

[16] SI 1996/1655. Paragraph 12A was added to Schedule 1 and paragraph 6A was added to Schedule 2 by paragraph 10(7) and (8) respectively of Schedule 1 to SI 1997/786.

[17] SI 1987/1110; relevant amending instruments are SI 1988/474, 1992/1531, 1993/519, 1994/1062, 1996/776, 1996/1435 and 1997/786.

[18] S.SI 2000/112.

[19] Section 94(1)(a) was amended by section 154 of the Pensions Act 1995.

[20] Section 95 was amended by paragraph 3 of Schedule 6 to the Pensions Act 1995.

[21] Section 94(1)(aa) was inserted by section 154(2) of the Pensions Act 1995.

[22] SI 1996/1847.

[23] The Institute of Actuaries is at Staple Inn Hall, High Holborn, London WC1V 7QJ. The Faculty of Actuaries is at Maclaurin House, 18 Dublin Street, Edinburgh EH1 3PP.

[24] The publication 'Retirement Benefit Schemes—Transfer Values (GN11)' may be obtained from the Institute of Actuaries, Staple Inn Hall, High Holborn, London WC1V 7QJ, and from the Faculty of Actuaries, Maclaurin House, 18 Dublin Street, Edinburgh EH1 3PP. The publication is also available on the following internet web-site: http://www.actuaries.org.uk.

[25] Section 93(1)(a) was substituted by section 152(2) of the Pensions Act 1995.

[26] SI 1996/1847.

[27] 1973 c. 18.

[28] Sections 25B and 25C were inserted by section 166 of the Pensions Act 1995, and are amended by paragraphs 1 and 2 respectively of Schedule 4 to the Welfare Reform and Pensions Act 1999.

[29] Section 12A is amended by paragraph 9 of Schedule 12 to the Welfare Reform and Pensions Act 1999.

[30] SI 1978/1045 (N.I. 15). Articles 27B and 27C were inserted by article 162 of SI 1995/3213 (N.I. 22), and were amended by paragraphs 1 and 2 of Schedule 4 to SI 1999/3147 (N.I. 11).

[31] 1980 c. 46.

The Pensions on Divorce etc (Charging) Regulations 2000

SI 2000/1049

Made 13 April 2000
Laid before Parliament19 April 2000
Coming into force 1 December 2000

The Secretary of State for Social Security, in exercise of the powers conferred upon him by sections 23(1)(d) and (3), 24, 41(1) and (2) and 83(4) and (6) of the Welfare Reform and Pensions Act 1999[1] and of all other powers enabling him in that behalf, after consulting such persons as he considered appropriate,[2] hereby makes the following Regulations:

1 Citation, commencement and interpretation

(1) These Regulations may be cited as the Pensions on Divorce etc. (Charging) Regulations 2000 and shall come into force on 1st December 2000.

(2) In these Regulations, unless the context otherwise requires—

'**the 1999 Act**' means the Welfare Reform and Pensions Act 1999;

'**the Provision of Information Regulations**' means the Pensions on Divorce etc. (Provision of Information) Regulations 2000;[3]

'**day**' means any day other than—

(a) Christmas Day or Good Friday; or

(b) a bank holiday, that is to say, a day which is, or is to be observed as, a bank holiday or a holiday under Schedule 1 to the Banking and Financial Dealings Act 1971;[4]

'**implementation period**' has the meaning given by section 34(1) of the 1999 Act;

'**normal pension age**' has the meaning given by section 180 of the Pension Schemes Act 1993;

'**notice of implementation**' has the meaning given by regulation 1(2) of the Provision of Information Regulations;

'**pension arrangement**' has the meaning given to that expression in section 46(1) of the 1999 Act;

'**pension credit**' means a credit under section 29(1)(b) of the 1999 Act;

'**pension credit benefit**' has the meaning given by section 101B of the Pensions Schemes Act 1993;[5]

'**pension credit rights**' has the meaning given by section 101B of the Pension Schemes Act 1993;

'**pension sharing activity**' has the meaning given by section 41(5) of the 1999 Act;

'**pension sharing order or provision**' means an order or provision which is mentioned in section 28(1) of the 1999 Act;

'**person responsible for a pension arrangement**' has the meaning given to that expression in section 46(2) of the 1999 Act;

'**the Regulatory Authority**' means the Occupational Pensions Regulatory Authority;

'**the relevant date**' has the meaning given by section 10(3) of the Family Law (Scotland) Act 1985;[6]

'**trustees or managers**' has the meaning given by section 46(1) of the 1999 Act.

2 General requirements as to charges

(1) Subject to paragraph (8), a person responsible for a pension arrangement shall not recover any charges incurred in connection with—

   (a) the provision of information under—

      (i) regulation 2 of the Provision of Information Regulations (basic information about pensions and divorce);

      (ii) regulation 4 of those Regulations (provision of information in response to a notification that a pension sharing order or provision may be made); or

      (iii) regulation 10 of those Regulations (provision of information after receipt of an earmarking order);

   (b) complying with any order specified in section 24 of the 1999 Act (charges by pension arrangements in relation to earmarking orders); or

   (c) any description of pension sharing activity specified in regulation 5 of these Regulations, unless he has complied with the requirements of paragraphs (2) to (5).

(2) The requirements mentioned in paragraph (1) are that the person responsible for a pension arrangement shall, before a pension sharing order or provision is made—

   (a) inform the member or his spouse, as the case may be, in writing of his intention to recover costs incurred in connection with any of the matters specified in sub-paragraph (a), (b) or (c) of paragraph (1); and

   (b) provide the member or his spouse, as the case may be, with a written schedule of charges in accordance with paragraphs (3) and (4) in respect of those matters specified in sub-paragraph (a) or (c) of paragraph (1) for which a charge may be recoverable.

(3) No charge shall be recoverable in respect of any of the items mentioned in paragraph (4) unless the person responsible for a pension arrangement has specified in the written schedule of charges mentioned in paragraph (2)(b) that a charge may be recoverable in respect of that item.

(4) The items referred to in paragraph (3) are—

   (a) the provision of a cash equivalent other than one which is provided in accordance with the provisions of—

      (i) section 93A or 94 of the 1993 Act[7] (salary related schemes: right to statement of entitlement, and right to cash equivalent);

      (ii) regulation 11(1) of the Occupational Pension Schemes (Transfer Values) Regulations 1996[8] (disclosure); or

      (iii) regulation 5 (information to be made available to individuals) of, and paragraph 2(b) of Schedule 2 (provision of cash equivalent) to the Personal Pension Schemes (Disclosure of Information) Regulations 1987;[9]

   (b) subject to regulation 3(2)(b) or (c), as the case may be, the provision of a valuation in accordance with regulation 2(2) of the Provision of Information Regulations;

   (c) whether a person responsible for a pension arrangement intends to recover the cost of providing membership of the pension arrangement to the person entitled to a pension credit, before or after the pension sharing order is implemented;

(d) whether the person responsible for a pension arrangement intends to recover additional charges in the circumstances prescribed in regulation 6 of these Regulations in respect of pension sharing activity described in regulation 5 of these Regulations;

(e) whether the charges are inclusive or exclusive of value added tax, where the person responsible for a pension arrangement is required to charge value added tax in accordance with the provisions of the Value Added Tax Act 1994;[10]

(f) periodical charges in respect of pension sharing activity which the person responsible for a pension arrangement may make when a person entitled to a pension credit becomes a member of the pension arrangement from which the pension credit is derived;

(g) whether the person responsible for a pension arrangement intends to recover charges specified in regulation 10 of these Regulations.

(5) In the case of the cost referred to in paragraph (4)(c) or the charges to be imposed in respect of pension sharing activity described in regulation 5 of these Regulations, the person responsible for a pension arrangement shall provide—

(a) a single estimate of the overall cost of the pension sharing activity;

(b) a range of estimates of the overall cost of the pension sharing activity which is dependent upon the complexity of an individual case; or

(c) a breakdown of the cost of each element of pension sharing activity for which a charge shall be made.

(6) Subject to regulation 9(3) and (4), a person responsible for a pension arrangement shall recover only those sums which represent the reasonable administrative expenses which he has incurred or is likely to incur in connection with any of the activities mentioned in paragraph (1), or in relation to a pension sharing order having been made the subject of an application for leave to appeal out of time.

(7) The requirements of paragraph (2) do not apply in connection with the recovery by a person responsible for a pension arrangement of costs incurred in relation to a pension sharing order having been made the subject of an application for leave to appeal out of time.

(8) The information specified in regulation 2(2) and (3) of the Provision of Information Regulations shall be provided to the member or his spouse without charge unless

(a) the person responsible for the pension arrangement has furnished the information to the member, his spouse or the court within a period of 12 months immediately prior to the date of the request or the court order for the provision of that information;

(b) the member has reached normal retirement age on or before the date of the request or the court order for the provision of information;

(c) the request or the court order for the provision of the information is made within 12 months prior to the member reaching normal pension age; or

(d) the circumstances referred to in regulation 3(2)(b)(i) apply.

3   Charges recoverable in respect of the provision of basic information

(1) Subject to paragraph (2), the charges prescribed for the purposes of section 23(1)(d) of the 1999 Act (charges which a person responsible for a pension arrangement may recover in respect of supplying pension information in connection with divorce etc.) are any charges incurred by the person responsible for the pension arrangement in connection with the provision of any of the information set out in—

(a) regulation 2 of the Provision of Information Regulations which may be recovered in accordance with regulation 2(8) of these Regulations;

(b) regulation 4 of those Regulations; or

(c) regulation 10 of those Regulations.

(2) The charges mentioned in paragraph (1) shall not include any costs incurred by a person responsible for a pension arrangement in respect of the matters specified in sub-paragraphs (a) to (f)—

    (a) any costs incurred by the person responsible for a pension arrangement which are directly related to the fulfilment of his obligations under regulation 2(3) of the Provision of Information Regulations, other than charges which may be recovered in the circumstances described in regulation 2(8) of these Regulations;

    (b) any costs incurred by the person responsible for the pension arrangement as a result of complying with a request for, or an order of the court requiring, a valuation under regulation 2(2) of the Provision of Information Regulations, unless—

        (i) he is required by a member or a court to provide that valuation in less than 3 months beginning with the date the person responsible for the pension arrangement receives that request or order for the valuation;

        (ii) the valuation is requested by a member who is not entitled to a cash equivalent under any of the provisions referred to in regulation 2(4)(a);

        (iii) a member has requested a cash equivalent in accordance with any of those provisions within 12 months immediately prior to the date of the request for a valuation under regulation 2(2) of the Provision of Information Regulations;

    (c) any costs incurred by the person responsible for the pension arrangement as a result of providing a valuation of benefits calculated and verified in accordance with regulation 3 of the Divorce etc. (Pensions) (Scotland) Regulations 2000[11] (valuation), unless—

        (i) he is required by the court to provide that valuation in less than 3 months beginning with the date the person responsible for the pension arrangement receives that order;

        (ii) the valuation is requested by a member who is not entitled to a cash equivalent under any of the provisions referred to in regulation 2(4)(a);

        (iii) a member has requested a cash equivalent in accordance with any of those provisions within 12 months immediately prior to the date of the request for a valuation under regulation 2(2) of the Provision of Information Regulations; or

        (iv) the relevant date is more than 12 months immediately prior to the date the person responsible for the pension arrangement receives the request for the valuation;

    (d) any costs incurred by the trustees or managers of—

        (i) an occupational pension scheme in connection with the provision of information under regulation 4 of the Occupational Pension Schemes (Disclosure of Information) Regulations 1996[12] (basic information about the scheme); or

        (ii) a personal pension scheme in connection with the provision of information under regulation 4 of the Personal Pension Schemes (Disclosure of Information) Regulations 1987[13] (basic information about the scheme), which the trustees or managers shall provide to the member free of charge under those Regulations;

(e) any costs incurred by the trustees or managers of an occupational pension scheme, or a personal pension scheme, as the case may be, in connection with the provision of a transfer value in accordance with the provisions of—

   (i)   section 93A or 94 of the 1993 Act;

   (ii) regulation 11(1) of the Occupational Pension Schemes (Transfer Values) Regulations 1996; or

   (iii) regulation 5 of, and paragraph 2(b) of Schedule 2 to, the Personal Pension Schemes (Disclosure of Information) Regulations 1987; or

(f) any costs not specified by the person responsible for a pension arrangement in the information on charges provided to the member pursuant to regulation 2 of the Provision of Information Regulations with the exception of any additional amounts under regulation 6(1)(a) of these Regulations.

4   Charges in respect of the provision of information—method of recovery

(1) A person responsible for a pension arrangement may recover the charges specified in regulation 3(1) by using either of the methods described in sub-paragraph (a) or (b)—

(a) requiring payment of charges at any specified time between the request for basic information and the completion of the implementation of a pension sharing order or provision, or the compliance with an order specified in section 24 of the 1999 Act, as the case may be; or

(b) subject to paragraph (2), requiring as a condition of providing information in accordance with—

   (i)   regulation 2 of the Provision of Information Regulations; or

   (ii) regulation 10 of those Regulations, that payment of the charges to which regulation 3(1) refers shall be made in full by the member before the person responsible for the pension arrangement becomes obliged to provide the information.

(2) Paragraph (1)(b) shall not apply—

(a) where a court has ordered a member to obtain the information specified in regulation 2 of the Provision of Information Regulations;

(b) where, in accordance with regulation 2(8) of these Regulations, the person responsible for the pension arrangement shall provide that information without charge; or

(c) where the person responsible for the pension arrangement is required to supply that information by virtue of regulation 4 of the Provision of Information Regulations.

5   Charges in respect of pension sharing activity

(1) The charges prescribed in respect of prescribed descriptions of pension sharing activity for the purposes of section 41(1) of the 1999 Act (charges in respect of pension sharing costs) are any costs reasonably incurred by the person responsible for the pension arrrangement in connection with pension sharing activity other than those costs specified in paragraph (3).

(2) The descriptions of pension sharing activity prescribed for the purposes of section 41(1) of the 1999 Act are any type of activity which fulfils the requirements of section 41(5) of the 1999 Act.

(3) The costs specified in this paragraph are any costs which are not directly related to the costs which arise in relation to an individual case.

6   Additional amounts recoverable in respect of pension sharing activity

(1) The circumstances in which a person responsible for a pension arrangement may recover additional amounts are—

(a) where a period of more than 12 months has elapsed between the person responsible for the pension arrangement supplying information in accordance with regulation 2 of the Provision of Information Regulations and the taking effect of an order or provision specified in subsection (1) of section 28 of the 1999 Act (activation of pension sharing); or

(b) in the case of an occupational pension scheme, where the trustees or managers of that scheme undertake activity from time to time associated with pension credit rights or pension credit benefit in that scheme which belong to a member.

(2) For the purposes of section 41(2)(d) of the 1999 Act, the additional amounts are

(a) in the circumstances described in paragraph (1)(a), interest calculated at a rate not exceeding increases in the retail prices index on the amounts of any charges not yet due, or of any charges requested but yet to be recovered, which are specified in the schedule of charges issued to the member in accordance with regulation 2(2)(b) of these Regulations; and

(b) in the circumstances described in paragraph (1)(b), an amount not exceeding an increase calculated by reference to increases in the retail prices index on the amounts which relate to the costs referred to in regulation 2(4)(d) and which are specified in the schedule of charges provided to the member and his spouse in accordance with regulation 2(2)(b).

(3) Where a person responsible for a pension arrangement intends to recover an additional amount specified in paragraph (2)(a) in the circumstances described in paragraph (1)(a), he shall set out this intention, the rate of interest to be used, and the total costs recoverable in the notice of implementation and final costs issued in accordance with regulation 7 of the Provision of Information Regulations (provision of information after receiving a pension sharing order or provision).

(4) Where the trustees or managers of an occupational pension scheme intend to recover an additional amount specified in paragraph (2)(b) in the circumstances described in paragraph (1)(b), they shall inform the parties involved in pension sharing in writing of this intention in the schedule of charges issued in accordance with regulation 2(2)(b) of these Regulations.

7   Charges in respect of pension sharing activity—postponement of implementation period

(1) The circumstances when the start of the implementation period may be postponed are when a person responsible for a pension arrangement—

(a) issues a notice to the member and the person entitled to the pension credit no later than 21 days after the day on which the person responsible for the pension arrangement receives the pension sharing order or provision; and

(b) in that notice, requires the charges specified in regulation 3, 5 or 6 to be paid before the implementation of the pension sharing order or provision is commenced.

(2) Paragraph (1) shall apply only if the person responsible for the pension arrangement has specified at a stage no later than in his response to the notification that a pension sharing order or provision may be made, issued in accordance with regulation 4 of the Provision of Information Regulations—

(a) that he requires the charges mentioned in paragraph (1) to be paid before the implementation period is commenced; and either

(b) whether he requires those charges to be paid in full; or

(c) the proportion of those charges which he requires to be paid as full settlement of those charges.

(3) Once payment of the charges mentioned in paragraph (1) has been made in accordance with the requirements of the person responsible for the pension arrangement—

(a) that person shall—

(i) issue the notice of implementation in accordance with regulation 7(1)(c) of the Provision of Information Regulations, and

(ii) begin the implementation period for the pension credit, within 21 days from the date the charges are paid, provided that the person responsible for the pension arrangement would otherwise be able to begin to implement the pension sharing order or provision, and

(b) subject to paragraph (4), that person shall not be entitled to recover any further charges in respect of the pension sharing order or provision in question.

(4) Paragraph (3)(b) shall not apply—

(a) in relation to the recovery of charges referred to in regulations 2(4)(d) and 6(2)(b); or

(b) where the pension credit depends on a pension sharing order and the order is the subject of an application for leave to appeal out of time.

8 Charges in respect of pension sharing activitiy—reimbursement as between the parties to pension sharing

A payment in respect of charges recoverable under regulation 3, 5 or 6 made by one party to pension sharing on behalf of the other party to pension sharing, shall be recoverable by the party who made the payment from that other party as a debt.

9 Charges in respect of pension sharing activity—method of recovery

(1) Subject to paragraphs (7) and (8), a person responsible for a pension arrangement may recover the charges specified in regulations 3, 5 and 6 by using any of the methods described in paragraph (2).

(2) The methods of recovery described in this paragraph are—

(a) subject to regulation 7 requiring the charges referred to in paragraph (1) to be paid before the implementation period for the pension sharing order or provision is commenced;

(b) deduction from a pension credit;

(c) deduction from the accrued rights of the member;

(d) where a pension sharing order or provision is made in respect of a pension which is in payment, deduction from the member's pension benefits;

(e) where liability in respect of a pension credit is discharged by the person responsible for the pension arrangement in accordance with paragraph 1(2), 2(2), or 3(2) of Schedule 5 to the 1999 Act (mode of discharge of liability for pension credits), deduction from payments of pension credit benefit; or

(f) deduction from the amount of a transfer value which is calculated in accordance with—

(i) regulation 7 of the Occupational Pension Schemes (Transfer Values) Regulations 1996[14] (manner of calculation and verification of cash equivalents); or

(ii) regulation 3 of the Personal Pension Schemes (Transfer Values) Regulations 1987[15] (manner of calculation and verification of cash equivalents).

(3) A person responsible for a pension arrangement shall not recover charges referred to in paragraph (1) by using any of the methods described in paragraph (2)(b), (c), (d), (e) or (f) unless—

(a) a pension sharing order or provision corresponding to any order or provision specified in subsection (1) of section 28 of the 1999 Act has been made;

(b) the implementation period has commenced;

(c) where a pension sharing order has been made, the person responsible for a pension arrangement is not aware of an appeal against the order having begun on or after the day on which the order takes effect;

(d) there are charges which are unpaid and for which the party, to whom paragraph (2)(b), (c), (d), (e) or (f) applies, is liable;

(e) the person responsible for the pension arrangement has issued a notice of implementation in accordance with regulation 7 of the Provision of Information Regulations;

(f) the person responsible for a pension arrangement specifies in the notice of implementation that recovery of the charges may be made by using any of those methods; and

(g) 21 days have elapsed since the notice of implentation was issued to the parties to pension sharing in accordance with the requirements of regulation 7 of the Provision of Information Regulations.

(4) If a pension sharing order or provision includes provision about the apportionment between the parties to pension sharing of any charge under section 41 of the 1999 Act or under corresponding Northern Ireland legislation, by virtue of section 24D of the Matrimonial Causes Act 1973[16] (pension sharing orders: apportionment of charges) or section 8A of the Family Law (Scotland) Act 1985[17] (pension sharing orders: apportionment of charges), the recovery of charges using any of the methods described in paragraph (2) by the person responsible for the pension arrangement shall comply with the terms of the order or provision.

(5) A person responsible for a pension arrangement shall not recover charges referred to in paragraph (1) by using any of the methods described in paragraph (2), from a party to pension sharing, if that party has paid in full the proportion of the charges for which he is liable.

(6) A person responsible for a pension arrangement may recover charges by using any of the methods described in paragraph (2)(b), (c) or (d)—

(a) at any time within the implementation period prescribed by section 34 of the 1999 Act ('implementation period');

(b) following an application by the trustees or managers of an occupational pension scheme, such longer period as the Regulatory Authority may allow in accordance with section 33(4) of the 1999 Act (extension of time for discharge of liability); or

(c) within 21 days after the end of the period referred to in sub-paragraph (a) or (b).

(7) Where the commencement of the implementation period is postponed, or its operation ceases in accordance with regulation 4 of the Pension Sharing (Implementation and Discharge of Liability) Regulations 2000[18] (postponement or cessation of implementation period where an application is made for leave to appeal out of time) a person responsible for a pension arrangement may require any outstanding charges referred to in paragraph (1) to be paid immediately, in respect of—

(a) all costs which have been incurred prior to the date of postponement or cessation; or

(b) any reasonable costs related to—

(i)   the application for leave to appeal out of time; or

(ii) the appeal out of time itself.

(8) Paragraph (7) applies even if, prior to receiving the notification of the application for leave to appeal out of time, a person responsible for a pension arrangement has indicated to the parties to pension sharing that he will not be using the method of recovery specified in paragraph (2)(a).

10   Charges in relation to earmarking orders

The prescribed charges which a person responsible for a pension arrangement may recover in respect of complying with an order specified in section 24 of the 1999 Act are those charges which represent the reasonable administrative expenses which he has incurred or is likely to incur by reason of the order.

Signed by authority of the Secretary of State for Social Security.

Jeff Rooker Minister of State, Department of Social Security

13th April 2000

Explanatory note *(This note is not part of the Regulations)*

These Regulations set out the circumstances in which a person responsible for a pension arrangement may recover charges in respect of the provision of information in connection with pensions on divorce, separation or nullity, complying with an earmarking or attachment order, or in connection with pension sharing activity.

Regulation 1 provides for citation, commencement and interpretation of the Regulations.

Regulation 2 specifies the requirements which must be met by persons responsible for pension arrangements before they may recover charges.

Regulation 3 specifies what charges a person responsible for a pension arrangement may recover as a result of providing information in accordance with the Pensions on Divorce etc. (Provision of Information) Regulations 2000.

Regulation 4 sets out how a person responsible for a pension arrangement may recover charges in respect of the provision of information.

Regulation 5 specifies the charges which are recoverable in respect of pension sharing activity.

Regulation 6 provides that additional amounts such as interest may be recovered by a person responsible for a pension arrangement in respect of pension sharing activity even though these amounts may not have been included in the schedule of charges issued to the member.

Regulation 7 provides that a person responsible for a pension arrangement may postpone the commencement of the implementation period pending the payment in full or in part of outstanding charges in respect of pension sharing activity.

Regulation 8 provides that if one party to pension sharing pays the other party's proportion of the charges, he may recover from the other party the amount paid as a debt.

Regulation 9 sets out how a person responsible for a pension arrangement may recover charges in respect of pension sharing activity.

Regulation 10 specifies the prescribed charges which are recoverable by a person responsible for a pension arrangement in relation to complying with an earmarking order.

An assessment of the cost to business of the provisions of the Welfare Reform and Pensions Act 1999, including these Regulations, is detailed in the Regulatory Impact Assessment for that Act. A copy of this Assessment has been placed in the libraries of both Houses of Parliament. Copies can be obtained by post from the Department of Social Security, Pensions on Divorce, 3rd Floor, The Adelphi, 1–11 John Adam Street, London WC2N 6HT.

Notes

[1]   1999 c. 30.

[2]   *See* section 83(11) of the Welfare Reform and Pensions Act 1999.

[3]   SI 2000/1048.

[4]   1971 c. 80.

[5]   1993 c. 48. Section 101B is inserted by section 37 of the Welfare Reform and Pensions Act 1999.

[6]   1985 c. 37. Section 10 was amended by section 167(2) of the Pensions Act 1995 (c. 26), and is amended by paragraph 8 of Schedule 12 to the Welfare Reform and Pensions Act 1999.

[7]   Section 93A was inserted by section 153 of the Pensions Act 1995. Section 94 was amended by section 154 of the Pensions Act 1995.

[8]   SI 1996/1847 to which there are amendments not relevant to these Regulations.

[9]   SI 1987/1110; relevant amending instruments are SI 1988/474, 1992/1531, 1994/1062, 1996/776, 1996/1435 and 1997/786.

[10]   1994 c 23.

[11]   S.SI 2000/112.

[12]   SI 1996/1655. Regulation 4 was amended by regulation 6(2) of SI 1997/3038.

[13]   Regulation 4 was amended by regulation 6(a) and (b) of SI 1988/474 and regulation 19 of SI 1992/1531.

[14]   SI 1996/1847. Regulation 7 was amended by regulation 12(4) of SI 1997/786.

[15]   SI 1987/1112. Regulation 3 was amended by paragraph 17(5) of Schedule 2 to SI 1994/1062.

[16]   1973 c 18. Section 24D is inserted by paragraph 4 of Schedule 3 to the Welfare Reform and Pensions Act 1999.

[17]   Section 8A is inserted by paragraph 7 of Schedule 12 to the Welfare Reform and Pensions Act 1999.

[18]   SI 2000/1053.

Divorce etc (Notification and Treatment of Pensions) (Scotland) Regulations 2000

SI 2000/1050

Made 13 April 2000
Laid before Parliament 19 April 2000
Coming into force 1 December 2000

The Secretary of State for Social Security, in exercise of the powers conferred upon him by section 23(1)(a)(ii) of the Welfare Reform and Pensions Act 1999[1] and sections 10(8) and (10) and 12A(8) of the Family Law (Scotland) Act 1985,[2] and of all other powers enabling him in that behalf hereby makes the following Regulations.

1 Citation, commencement and interpretation

(1) These Regulations may be cited as the Divorce etc. (Notification and Treatment of Pensions) (Scotland) Regulations 2000 and shall come into force on 1st December 2000.

(2) These Regulations shall not affect any action for divorce commenced before 1st December 2000 or any action for declarator of nullity of marriage commenced before that date.

(3) In these Regulations:

'**the 1985 Act**' means the Family Law (Scotland) Act 1985;

'**the 1999 Act**' means the Welfare Reform and Pensions Act 1999;

'**the other party**' means the other party to a marriage;

'**pension arrangement**' has the meaning given by section 46(1) of the 1999 Act, and any expression used in these Regulations to which a meaning is assigned in section 12A of the 1985 Act shall have the same meaning in these Regulations as in that section.

2 Notices under section 12A of the 1985 Act[3]

(1) This regulation applies in the circumstances set out in section 12A(6)(a) of the 1985 Act.

(2) Where this regulation applies, the person responsible for the first pension arrangement shall, within 21 days after the date of the transfer, give notice in accordance with the following paragraphs of this regulation to:

(a) the person responsible for the new pension arrangement; and

(b) the other party.

(3) The notice to the person responsible for the new pension arrangement shall consist of a copy of the following documents:

(a) every order made under section 12A(2) or (3) of the 1985 Act imposing any requirement upon the person responsible for the first pension arrangement;

(b) any order under section 12A(7) of the 1985 Act varying such an order;

(c) any notice given by any other party to the person responsible for the first pension arrangement under regulation 5 of these Regulations; and

(d) where the rights of the liable party under the first pension arrangement were derived in whole or in part from a transfer from a previous pension arrangement, any notice under paragraph (2)(a) of this regulation given on the occasion of that transfer.

(4) The notice to the other party shall contain the following particulars—

(a) the fact that all the accrued rights of the liable party under the first pension arrangement have been transferred to the new pension arrangement;

(b) the date on which the transfer takes effect;

(c) the name and address of the person responsible for the new pension arrangement; and (d) the fact that the order made under section 12A(2) or (3) of the 1985 Act is to have effect as if it had been made instead of respect of the person responsible for the new pension arrangement.

3 [Notices]

(1) This regulation applies where—

(a) section 12A(6) of the 1985 Act has already applied; and

(b) the liable party has transferred all his accrued rights for the second or any subsequent time to another new pension arrangement.

(2) Where this regulation applies, the person responsible for the pension arrangement from which the transfer is made to the other new pension arrangement shall, within 21 days after the date of the transfer, give notice to the other party of—

(a) the fact that all the accrued rights of the liable party have been transferred to the other new pension arrangement;

(b) the date on which the transfer takes effect;

(c) the name and address of the person responsible for the other new pension arrangement; and (d) the fact that the court may, on an application by any person having interest, vary any order under section 12A(2) or (3) of the 1985 Act.

4 [Notices]

(1) This regulation applies where—

(a) an order under section 12A(2) or (3) of the 1985 Act has been made imposing any requirement on the person responsible for the pension arrangement; and

(b) some but not all of the accrued rights of the liable party have been transferred from the pension arrangement.

(2) Where this regulation applies, the person responsible for the pension arrangement from which the transfer is made shall, within 21 days after the date of the transfer, give notice to the other party of—

(a) the likely extent of the reduction in the benefits payable under the arrangement as a result of the transfer;

(b) the name and address of the person responsible for the pension arrangement under which the liable party has acquired transfer of credits as a result of the transfer;

(c) the date on which the transfer takes effect; and (d) the fact that the court may, on an application by any person having an interest, vary an order under section 12A(2) or (3) of the 1985 Act.

5   [Change of address]

(1) This regulation applies where—

  (a) an order under section 12A(2) or (3) of the 1985 Act has been made imposing any requirements on the person responsible for the pension arrangement; and

  (b) there has been a change in the name or address of the other party.

(2) Where this regulation applies, the other party shall, within 21 days of the occurrence of the change mentioned in paragraph (1)(b) of this regulation, give notice of that change to the person responsible for the pension arrangement.

6   [Transfers]

(1) This regulation applies where—

  (a) a transfer of accrued rights has taken place in the circumstances set out in section 12A(6)(a) of the 1985 Act;

  (b) notice has been given in accordance with regulation 2(2)(a) and (b) of these Regulations; and

  (c) there has been a change in the name or address of the other party but the other party has not, before receiving notice under regulation 2(2)(b), given notice of that change to the person responsible for the first pension arrangement under regulation 5(2) of these Regulations.

(2) Where this regulation applies, the reference in regulation 5(2) to the person responsible for the pension arrangement shall be construed as a reference to the person responsible for the new pension arrangement and not the person responsible for the first pension arrangement.

(3) Subject to paragraph (4), where this regulation applies and the other party, within one year from the transfer, gives to the person responsible for the first pension arrangement notice of that change in purported compliance with regulation 5(2), the person responsible for the first pension arrangement shall—

  (a) send that notice to the person responsible for the new pension arrangement; and

  (b) give the other party a second notice under regulation 2(2)(b), and the other party shall thereupon be deemed to have given notice under regulation 5(2) to the person responsible for the new pension arrangement.

(4) Upon complying with paragraph (3) above, the person responsible for the first pension arrangement shall be discharged from any further obligation under that paragraph, whether in relation to the change in question or any further change in the name or address of the other party which may be notified to them by the other party.

7   [Delivery of notice]

A notice under these Regulations may be sent by ordinary first class post to the last known address of the intended recipient and shall be deemed to have been received on the seventh day following the date of posting.

8   Revocations

(1) Subject to paragraph (2), there are hereby revoked:—

  (a) regulations 4 to 10 of the Divorce etc (Pensions) (Scotland) Regulations 1996,[4] and regulations 1 and 2 thereof insofar as they relate to regulations 4 to 10; and

(b) regulations 5 to 8 of the Divorce etc (Pensions) (Scotland) Amendment Regulations 1997,[5] and regulations 1, 2 and 3 thereof insofar as they relate to regulations 5 to 8.

(2) Notwithstanding paragraph (1), the regulations specified in paragraph (1) shall continue to apply to any action for divorce commenced before 1st December 2000 and any action for declarator of marriage commenced before that date.

Signed by authority of the Secretary of State for Social Security.

Jeff Rooker Minister of State, Department of Social Security

13th April 2000

Explanatory note   *(This note is not part of the Regulations)*

These Regulations make provision with respect to the supply of information under section 12A of the Family Law (Scotland) Act 1985 about court orders for payment of pension lump sums where parties divorce or their marriage is declared to be null. They also revoke earlier Regulations of 1996 which had previously made comparable provision.

Regulations 2 to 7 make provision for notices to be given by persons responsible for pension arrangements in respect of the various changes of circumstances which are relevant to orders made under section 12A(2) or (3) of the 1985 Act.

Regulation 8 revokes regulations 1 and 2 (partially) and 4 to 10 of the Divorce etc (Pensions) (Scotland) Regulations 1996 and regulations 1, 2 and 3 (partially) and 5 to 8 of the Divorce etc (Pensions) (Scotland) (Amendment) Regulations 1997.

The assessment of the cost to business of the provisions of the Welfare Reform and Pensions Act 1999, including these Regulations, is detailed in the Regulatory Impact Assessment for that Act.

A copy of this Assessment has been placed in the libraries of both Houses of Parliament. Copies can be obtained by post from the Department of Social Security, Pensions on Divorce, Third Floor, The Adelphi, 1–11 John Adam Street, London WC2N 6HT.

Notes

[1]   1999 c. 30.

[2]   1985 c. 37. Sections 10(8) and (10) and 12A(8) were inserted by section 167(2)(b) and (3) of the Pensions Act 1995 c. 26. Section 10(10) contains a definition of 'prescribed' relevant to the exercise of the statutory powers under which these Regulations are made.

[3]   Section 12A was amended by paragraph 9 of Schedule 12 to the Welfare Reform and Pensions Act 1999.

[4]   SI 1996/1901. Regulations 2, 4, 5, 8 and 9 were amended, and regulation 8A was inserted, by SI 1997/745.

[5]   SI 1997/745.

The Pensions on Divorce etc (Pension Sharing) (Scotland) Regulations 2000

SI 2000/1051 (S.5)

Made 13 April 2000
Laid before Parliament 19 April 2000
Coming into force 1 December 2000

The Secretary of State for Social Security, in exercise of the powers conferred upon him by sections 28(1)(f)(ii) and (3)(a) and 48(1)(f)(ii) and (3)(a) of the Welfare Reform and Pensions Act 1999[1] and of all other powers enabling him in that behalf, after consulting such persons as he considered appropriate,[2] hereby makes the following Regulations:

1 Citation, commencement and interpretation

(1) These Regulations may be cited as the Pensions on Divorce etc. (Pension Sharing) (Scotland) Regulations 2000 and shall come into force on 1st December 2000.

(2) In these Regulations—

'**the 1985 Act**' means the Family Law (Scotland) Act 1985;[3]

'**the 1999 Act**' means the Welfare Reform and Pensions Act 1999;

'**pension arrangement**' has the meaning given by section 46(1) of the 1999 Act;

'**qualifying arrangement**' has the meaning given by paragraph 6 of Schedule 5 to the 1999 Act;

'**transferee**' and '**transferor**' have, in regulations 2 and 3, the meaning given by section 29(8), and, in regulations 4 and 5, the meaning given by section 49(6), of the 1999 Act.

2 Sharing of rights under pension arrangements

Prescribed form of provision corresponding to provision in a pension sharing order under the 1985 Act

For the purposes of section 28(1)(f)(ii) of the 1999 Act, the provision which corresponds to the provision which may be made by a pension sharing order under the 1985 Act shall be in a form which contains in an annex to, and which is separable from, the qualifying agreement referred to in section 28(1)(f)(i) of the 1999 Act, the following information—

(a) in relation to the party who is the transferor—

(i) all names by which the transferor has been known;

(ii) date of birth;

(iii) address;

(iv) national insurance number;

(v) the name and address of the pension arrangement to which the pension sharing provision relates, and

276

    (vi) the transferor's membership number or policy number in that pension arrangement;

(b) in relation to the party who is the transferee—

    (i) all names by which the transferee has been known;

    (ii) date of birth;

    (iii) address;

    (iv) national insurance number, and

    (v) if the transferee is a member of the pension arrangement from which a pension credit is derived, his membership number in that pension arrangement;

(c) details of—

    (i) the amount to be transferred to the transferee, or

    (ii) the specified percentage of the cash equivalent of the relevant benefits on the valuation day to be transferred to the transferee;

(d) where the transferee has given his consent, in accordance with paragraph 1(3)(c), 3(3)(c) or 4(2)(c) of Schedule 5 to the 1999 Act (mode of discharge of liability for a pension credit), to the payment of a pension credit to the person responsible for a qualifying arrangement—

    (i) the full name of that qualifying arrangement;

    (ii) its address;

    (iii) if known, the transferee's membership number or policy number in that arrangement, and

    (iv) the name or title, business address, business telephone number and, where available, the business facsimile number and electronic mail address of a person who may be contacted in respect of the discharge of liability for the pension credit;

(e) details of the provision about the apportionment (if any) made by the transferor and the transferee of liability for any charges levied by the person responsible for the pension arrangement in relation to pension sharing under Chapter I of Part IV of the 1999 Act, and

(f) confirmation by the transferor that he has intimated to the pension arrangement his intention with respect to pension sharing and that the pension arrangement has acknowledged receipt of the intimation.

3   Circumstances in which an agreement is to be entered into, in order to be considered a 'qualifying agreement' under section 28(1)(f) of the 1999 Act

A qualifying agreement is, for the purposes of section 28(1)(f) of the 1999 Act, one which the transferor and transferee have entered into in order to determine the financial settlement on divorce and in respect of which the transferor has intimated to the person responsible for a pension arrangement prior to the making of the agreement the intention to have the transferor's pension rights under the pension arrangement shared with the transferee.

4   Sharing of State Scheme Rights Prescribed form of provision corresponding to provision in a pension sharing order under the 1985 Act

For the purposes of section 48(1)(f)(ii) of the 1999 Act, the provision which corresponds to the provision which may be made by a pension sharing order under the 1985 Act shall be in a form which contains in an annex to, and which is separable from, the qualifying agreement referred to in section 48(1)(f)(i) of the 1999 Act, the following information—

(a) in relation to the party who is the transferor—

(i)   full name;

(ii) date of birth;

(iii) address;

(iv) national insurance number, and

(v) details of the specified amount or, as appropriate, the specified percentage of the cash equivalent on the transfer day of the transferor's relevant state scheme rights immediately before that day;

(b) in relation to the party who is the transferee—

(i)   full name by which the transferee is or will be known;

(ii) date of birth;

(iii) address, and

(iv) national insurance number, and

(c) a statement by the transferor and the transferee that they have received confirmation from the Secretary of State that shareable state scheme rights are held in the name of the transferor and that on the grant of decree of divorce or declarator of nullity of marriage a pension-sharing agreement will be implemented.

5   Circumstances in which an agreement is to be entered into, in order to be considered a 'qualifying agreement' under section 48(1)(f) of the 1999 Act

A qualifying agreement is, for the purposes of section 48(1)(f) of the 1999 Act, one which the transferor and transferee have entered into in order to determine the financial settlement on divorce and in respect of which they have received confirmation from the Secretary of State that shareable state scheme rights are held in the name of the transferor.

Signed by authority of the Secretary of State for Social Security.

Jeff Rooker Minister of State, Department of Social Security

13th April 2000

Explanatory note   *(This note is not part of the Regulations)*

These Regulations make provision with respect to pension-sharing in Scotland, under the Welfare Reform and Pensions Act 1999, where parties divorce or their marriage is declared to be null.

Regulations 2 and 3 relate to the sharing of rights under pension arrangements.

Regulations 4 and 5 relate to the sharing of state scheme rights. Section 29 of the 1999 Act provides for the creation of a right of one party to a marriage in the other party's shareable rights under a pension arrangement and for the creation of a corresponding liability of that other party. Section 28 of the 1999 Act provides that the provisions of section 29 apply when a pension-sharing arrangement is activated. Section 28 specifies various forms of pension-sharing. In particular, it specifies a provision for pension-sharing which corresponds to the provision which may be made in a pension sharing order under the Family Law (Scotland) Act 1985 and which is in such form as the Secretary of State may prescribe.

Regulation 2 prescribes the form of that provision. Section 28 also provides that the provision corresponding to the pension-sharing order under the 1985 Act is to be contained in a qualifying agreement between the parties to a marriage and that a qualifying agreement is one which has been entered into in such circumstances as the Secretary of State may prescribe.

Regulation 3 prescribes those circumstances. Section 49 of the 1999 Act provides for the creation of a right of one party to a marriage in the other party's shareable state scheme rights and for the creation of the corresponding liability of that other party ('benefit sharing'). Section 48 of the 1999 Act provides that the provisions of section 49 apply when benefit sharing is activated. Section 48 specifies various forms of benefit sharing. In particular, it specifies a provision for benefit sharing which corresponds to the provision which may be made in a pension sharing order under the Family Law (Scotland) Act 1985 and which is in such form as the Secretary of State may prescribe.

Regulation 4 prescribes the form of that provision. Section 48 also provides that the provision corresponding to the pension sharing order under the 1985 Act is to be contained in a qualifying agreement between the parties to the marriage and that a qualifying agreement is one which has been entered into in such circumstances as the Secretary of State may prescribe.

Regulation 5 prescribes those circumstances.

An assessment of the cost to business of the provisions of the Welfare Reform and Pensions Act 1999, including these Regulations, is detailed in the Regulatory Impact Assessment for that Act. A copy of this Assessment has been placed in the libraries of both Houses of Parliament. Copies can be obtained by post from the Department of Social Security, Pensions on Divorce, 3rd Floor, The Adelphi, 1–11 John Adam Street, London WC2N 6HT.

Notes

[1] 1999 c. 30.

[2] *See* section 83(11) of the Welfare Reform and Pensions Act 1999.

[3] 1985 c. 37.

Pension Sharing (Valuation) Regulations 2000

SI 2000/1052

Made 13 April 2000
Laid before Parliament 19 April 2000
Coming into force 1 December 2000

The Secretary of State for Social Security, in exercise of the powers conferred upon him by sections 27(2), 30(1) and (2) and 83(4) and (6) of the Welfare Reform and Pensions Act 1999,[1] and of all other powers enabling him in that behalf, after consulting such persons as he considered appropriate,[2] hereby makes the following Regulations:

1 Citation, commencement and interpretation

(1) These Regulations may be cited as the Pension Sharing (Valuation) Regulations 2000 and shall come into force on 1st December 2000.

(2) In these Regulations—

'**the 1993 Act**' means the Pension Schemes Act 1993;[3]

'**the 1995 Act**' means the Pensions Act 1995;[4]

'**the 1999 Act**' means the Welfare Reform and Pensions Act 1999;

'**employer**' has the meaning given by section 181(1) of the 1993 Act;

'**occupational pension scheme**' has the meaning given by section 1 of the 1993 Act;

'**pension arrangement**' has the meaning given by section 46(1) of the 1999 Act;

'**relevant arrangement**' has the meaning given by section 29(8) of the 1999 Act;

'**relevant benefits**' has the meaning given by section 612 of the Income and Corporation Taxes Act 1988;[5]

'**scheme**' means an occupational pension scheme;

'**scheme actuary**', in relation to a scheme to which section 47(1)(b) of the 1995 Act applies, means the actuary mentioned in section 47(1)(b) of that Act;

'**transfer credits**' has the meaning given by section 181(1) of the 1993 Act;

'**transfer day**' has the meaning given by section 29(8) of the 1999 Act;

'**transferor**' has the meaning given by section 29(8) of the 1999 Act;

'**trustees or managers**' has the meaning given by section 46(1) of the 1999 Act;

'**valuation day**' has the meaning given by section 29(7) of the 1999 Act.

2 Rights under a pension arrangement which are not shareable

(1) Rights under a pension arrangement which are not shareable are—

    (a) subject to paragraph (2), any rights accrued between 1961 and 1975 which relate to contracted-out equivalent pension benefit within the meaning of section 57 of the National Insurance Act 1965[6] (equivalent pension benefits, etc.);

    (b) any rights in respect of which a person is in receipt of—

    (i) a pension;

    (ii) an annuity;

    (iii) payments under an interim arrangement within the meaning of section 28(1A) of the 1993 Act[2] (ways of giving effect to protected rights); or

    (iv) income withdrawal within the meaning of section 630(1) of the Income and Corporation Taxes Act 1988[8] (interpretation), by virtue of being the widow, widower or other dependant of a deceased person with pension rights under a pension arrangement; and

  (c) any rights which do not result in the payment of relevant benefits.

(2) Paragraph (1)(a) applies only when those rights are the only rights held by a person under a pension arrangement.

3 Calculation and verification of cash equivalents for the purposes of the creation of pension debits and credits

For the purposes of section 29 of the 1999 Act (creation of pension debits and credits), cash equivalents may be calculated and verified—

  (a) where the relevant arrangement is an occupational pension scheme in accordance with regulations 4 and 5; or

  (b) in any other case, in accordance with regulations 6 and 7.

4 Occupational pension schemes: manner of calculation and verification of cash equivalents

(1) In a case to which, or to the extent to which, paragraph (2) or (5) does not apply, cash equivalents are to be calculated and verified in such manner as may be approved in a particular case by the scheme actuary or, in relation to a scheme to which section 47(1)(b) of the 1995 Act (professional advisers) does not apply, by—

  (a) a Fellow of the Institute of Actuaries;

  (b) a Fellow of the Faculty of Actuaries;[9] or

  (c) a person with other actuarial qualifications who is approved by the Secretary of State, at the request of the trustees or managers of the scheme in question, as being a proper person to act for the purposes of these Regulations in connection with that scheme

and, subject to paragraph (2), in the following paragraphs of this regulation and in regulation 5 'actuary' means the scheme actuary or, in relation to a scheme to which section 47(1)(b) of the 1995 Act does not apply, the actuary referred to in sub-paragraph (a), (b) or (c) of this paragraph.

(2) Where the transferor in respect of whose rights a cash equivalent is to be calculated and verified, is a member of a scheme having particulars from time to time set out in regulations made under section 7 of the Superannuation Act 1972[10] (superannuation of persons employed in local government service, etc.), that cash equivalent shall be calculated and verified in such manner as may be approved by the Government Actuary or by an actuary authorised by the Government Actuary to act on his behalf for that purpose and in such a case 'actuary' in this regulation and in regulation 5 means the Government Actuary or the actuary so authorised.

(2A) Where the person with pension rights is a deferred member of an occupational pension scheme on the transfer day, the value of the benefits which he has accrued under that scheme shall be taken to be—

  (a) in the case of an occupational pension scheme other than a salary related scheme, the cash equivalent to which he acquired a right under section

94(1)(a) of the 1993 Act (right to cash equivalent) on the termination of his pensionable service, calculated on the assumption that he has made an application under section 95(1) of that Act (ways of taking right to cash equivalent); or

(b) in the case of a salary related occupational pension scheme, the guaranteed cash equivalent to which he would have acquired a right under section 94(1)(aa) of the 1993 Act if he had made an application under section 95(1) of that Act.

(2B) Where the person with pension rights is an active member of an occupational pension scheme on the transfer day, the value of the benefits which he has accrued under that scheme shall be calculated and verified—

(a) on the assumption that the member had made a request for an estimate of the cash equivalent that would be available to him were his pensionable service to terminate on the transfer day; and

(b) in accordance with regulation 11 of, and Schedule 1 to, the Occupational Pension Schemes (Transfer Values) Regulations 1996 (disclosure).

(3) Except in a case to which paragraph (5) applies, cash equivalents are to be calculated and verified by adopting methods and making assumptions which—

(a) if not determined by the trustees or managers of the scheme in question, are notified to them by the actuary; and

(b) are certified by the actuary to the trustees or managers of the scheme—

(i) as being consistent with 'Retirement Benefit Schemes—Transfer Values (GN11)' published by the Institute of Actuaries and the Faculty of Actuaries and current on the valuation day;[11]

(ii) as being consistent with the methods adopted and assumptions made, at the time when the certificate is issued, in calculating the benefits to which entitlement arises under the rules of the scheme in question for a person who is acquiring transfer credits under those rules; and

(iii) in the case of a scheme to which section 56 of the 1995 Act (minimum funding requirement) applies as providing as a minimum an amount, consistent with the methods adopted and assumptions made in calculating, for the purposes of section 57 of that Act (valuation and certification of assets and liabilities), the liabilities mentioned in section 73(3)(a), (aa), (b), (c)(i) and (d) of that Act[12] (preferential liabilities on winding up), subject, in any case where the cash equivalent calculation is made on an individual and not a collective basis, to any adjustments which are appropriate to take account of that fact.

(4) If, by virtue of Schedule 5 to the Occupational Pension Schemes (Minimum Funding Requirement and Actuarial Valuations) Regulations 1996[13] (modifications), section 56 of the 1995 Act applies to a section of a scheme as if that section were a separate scheme, paragraph (3)(b)(iii) shall apply as if that section were a separate scheme and if the reference therein to a scheme were accordingly a reference to that section.

(5) Where a cash equivalent or any portion of a cash equivalent relates to money purchase benefits which do not fall to be valued in a manner which involves making estimates of the value of benefits, then that cash equivalent or that portion shall be calculated and verified in such manner as may be approved in particular cases by the trustees or managers of the scheme; and by adopting methods consistent with the requirements of Chapter IV of Part IV of the 1993 At (protection for early leavers—transfer values).

5 Occupational pension schemes: further provisions as to the calculation of cash equivalents and increases and reductions of cash equivalents

(1) Where it is the established custom for additional benefits to be awarded from the scheme at the discretion of the trustees or managers or the employer, the cash equivalent shall, unless the trustees or managers have given a direction that cash equivalents shall not take account of such benefits, take account of any such additional benefits as will accrue to the transferor if the custom continues unaltered.

(2) The trustees or managers shall not make a direction such as is mentioned in paragraph (1) unless, within 3 months before making the direction, they have consulted the actuary and have obtained the actuary's written report on the implications for the state of funding of the scheme of making such a direction, including the actuary's advice as to whether or not in the actuary's opinion there would be any adverse implications for the funding of the scheme should the trustees or managers not make such a direction.

(3) Subject to paragraph (6), in the case of a scheme to which section 56 of the 1995 Act applies, each respective part of the cash equivalent which relates to liabilities referred to in section 73(3)(a), (aa), (b), (c)(i) or (d) of the 1995 Act may be reduced by the percentage which is the difference between—

    (a) 100 per cent; and

    (b) the percentage of the liabilities mentioned in the relevant paragraph of section 73(3) which the actuarial valuation shows the scheme assets as being sufficient to satisfy where the actuarial valuation is the latest actuarial valuation obtained in accordance with section 57 of the 1995 Act before the valuation day.

(4) If, by virtue of Schedule 5 to the Occupational Pension Schemes (Minimum Funding Requirement and Actuarial Valuations) Regulations 1996, section 56 of the 1995 Act applies to a section of a scheme as if that section were a separate scheme, paragraph (3) shall apply as if that section were a separate scheme, and as if the reference therein to a scheme were accordingly a reference to that section.

(5) The reduction referred to in paragraph (3) shall not apply to a case where liability in respect of a pension credit is to be discharged in accordance with—

    (a) paragraph 1(2) of Schedule 5 to the 1999 Act (pension credits: mode of discharge—funded pension schemes); or

    (b) paragraph 1(3) of that Schedule, in a case where regulation 7(2) of the Pension Sharing (Implementation and Discharge of Liability) Regulations 2000 applies.

(6) Where a scheme has begun to be wound up, a cash equivalent may be reduced to the extent necessary for the scheme to comply with sections 73 and 74 of the 1995 Act[14] (discharge of liabilities by insurance, etc.), and the Occupational Pension Schemes (Winding Up) Regulations 1996.[15]

(7) If, by virtue of the Occupational Pension Schemes (Winding Up) Regulations 1996, section 73 of the 1995 Act applies to a section of a scheme as if that section were a separate scheme, paragraph (6) shall apply as if that section were a separate scheme and as if the references therein to a scheme were accordingly references to that section.

(8) Where all or any of the benefits to which a cash equivalent relates have been surrendered, commuted or forfeited before the date on which the trustees or managers discharge their liability in respect of the pension credit in accordance with the provisions of Schedule 5 to the 1999 Act, the cash equivalent of the benefits so surrendered, commuted or forfeited shall be reduced to nil.

(9) In a case where two or more of the paragraphs of this regulation fall to be applied to a calculation, they shall be applied in the order in which they occur in this regulation.

6 Other relevant arrangements: manner of calculation and verification of cash equivalents

(1) Except in a case to which paragraph (3) applies, cash equivalents are to be calculated and verified in such manner as may be approved in a particular case by—

    (a) a Fellow of the Institute of Actuaries;

    (b) a Fellow of the Faculty of Actuaries; or

    (c) a person with other actuarial qualifications who is approved by the Secretary of State, at the request of the person responsible for the relevant arrangement, as being a proper person to act for the purposes of this regulation and regulation 7 in connection with that arrangement, and in paragraph (2) 'actuary' means any person such as is referred to in sub-paragraph (a), (b) or (c) of this paragraph.

(1A) Where the person with pension rights is a member of a personal pension scheme, or those rights are contained in a retirement annuity contract, the value of the benefits which he has accrued under that scheme or contract on the transfer day shall be taken to be the cash equivalent to which he would have acquired a right under section 94(1)(b) of the 1993 Act, if he had made an application under section 95(1) of that Act on the date on which the request for the valuation was received.

(1B) In relation to a personal pension scheme which is comprised in a retirement annuity contract made before 4th January 1988, paragraph (2) shall apply as if such a scheme were not excluded from the scope of Chapter IV of Part IV of the 1993 Act by section 93(1)(b) of that Act (scope of Chapter IV).

(2) Except in a case to which paragraph (3) applies, cash equivalents are to be calculated and verified by adopting methods and making assumptions which—

    (a) if not determined by the person responsible for the relevant arrangement, are notified to them by an actuary; and

    (b) are certified by an actuary to the person responsible for the relevant arrangement as being consistent with 'Retirement Benefit Schemes—Transfer Values (GN11)', published by the Institute of Actuaries and the Faculty of Actuaries and current on the valuation day.

(3) Where a transferor's cash equivalent, or any portion of it—

    (a) represents his rights to money purchase benefits under the relevant arrangement; and

    (b) those rights do not fall, either wholly or in part, to be valued in a manner which involves making estimates of the value of benefits, then that cash equivalent, or that portion of it, shall be calculated and verified in such manner as may be approved in a particular case by the person responsible for the relevant arrangement, and by adopting methods consistent wit the requirements of Chapter IV of Part I of the 1993 Act.

(4) This regulation and regulation 7 apply to a relevant arrangement other than an occupational pension scheme.

7 Other relevant arrangements: reduction of cash equivalents

Where all or any of the benefits to which a cash equivalent relates have been surrendered, commuted or forfeited before the date on which the person responsible for the relevant arrangement discharges his liability for the pension credit in accordance with the provisions of Schedule 5 to the 1999 Act, the cash equivalent of the benefits so surrendered, commuted or forfeited shall be reduced in proportion to the reduction in the total value of the benefits.

Signed by authority of the Secretary of State for Social Security.

Jeff Rooker Minister of State, Department of Social Security

13th April 2000

Explanatory note *(This note is not part of the Regulations)*

These Regulations specify the types of pension rights which are not subject to pension sharing, and make provision for the calculation and verification of cash equivalents for the purpose of creating pension debits and credits. Regulation 1 provides for citation, commencement and interpretation.

Regulation 2 specifies rights under a pension arrangement which are not subject to pension sharing.

Regulation 3 specifies that the calculation and verification of cash equivalents for the purposes of creating pension debits and credits may be made by reference to these Regulations.

Regulations 4 and 5 specify how cash equivalents in respect of rights in occupational pension schemes may be calculated and verified.

Regulations 6 and 7 specify how cash equivalents in respect of rights in pension arrangements other than occupational pension schemes may be calculated and verified.

An assessment of the cost to business of the provisions of the Welfare Reform and Pensions Act 1999, including these Regulations, is detailed in the Regulatory Impact Assessment for that Act. A copy of this Assessment has been placed in the libraries of both Houses of Parliament. Copies can be obtained by post from the Department of Social Security, Pensions on Divorce, 3rd Floor, The Adelphi, 1-11 John Adam Street, London WC2N 6HT.

Notes

[1] 1999 c. 30.

[2] *See* section 83(11) of the Welfare Reform and Pensions Act 1999.

[3] 1993 c. 48.

[4] 1995 c. 26.

[5] 1988 c. 1. Section 612 was amended by sections 103(2) and 258 of, and paragraph 12 of Part V of Schedule 26 to, the Finance Act 1994 (c. 9).

[6] 1965 c. 51. Section 57 is continued in force by virtue of regulation 3 of SI 1974/2057.

[7] Section 28(1A) is amended by paragraph 5(3) of Schedule 2 to the Welfare Reform and Pensions Act 1999.

[8] The definition of 'income withdrawal' was inserted by paragraph 1 of Schedule 11 to the Finance Act 1995 (c. 4).

[9] The Institute of Actuaries is at Staple Inn Hall, High Holborn, London WC1V 7QJ. The Faculty of Actuaries is at Maclaurin House, 18 Dublin Street, Edinburgh EH1 3PP.

[10] 1972 c. 11.

[11] The publication 'Retirement Benefit Schemes—Transfer Values (GN11)' may be obtained from the Institute of Actuaries, Staple Inn Hall, High Holborn, London WC1V 7QJ and from the Faculty of Actuaries, Maclaurin House, 18 Dublin Street, Edinburgh EH1 3PP. The publication is also available on the following internet web-site: http://www.actuaries.org.uk.

[12] Section 73 was modified by regulation 3 of SI 1996/3126 and is amended by section 38(1) of, and paragraph 55 of Schedule 12 to, the Welfare Reform and Pensions Act 1999.

[13] SI 1996/1536. Schedule 5 was amended by SI 1997/786 and 1997/3038.

[14] Section 74 is amended by paragraph 56 of Schedule 12 to the Welfare Reform and Pensions Act 1999.

[15] SI 1996/3126, amended by SI 1997/786, and SI 1999/3198.

Pension Sharing (Implementation and Discharge of Liability) Regulations 2000

SI 2000/1053

Made 13 April 2000
Laid before Parliament 19 April 2000
Coming into force 1 December 2000

The Secretary of State for Social Security, in exercise of the powers conferred upon him by sections 10(2)(b), 124(1)[1] and 174(2) and (3) of the Pensions Act 1995,[2] sections 33(2)(a) and (4), 34(4)(c), 35(2)(b) and 83(4) and (6) of, and paragraphs 1(2)(b), (3)(c), 3(3)(c), 4(2)(c), (4), 5(b), 6(2)(b), 7(1)(b), (2)(a), (2)(b), (3), (4), (6), 8(1), (2), 9, 10, and 13 of Schedule 5 to, the Welfare Reform and Pensions Act 1999,[3] and of all other powers enabling him in that behalf, after consulting such persons as he considered appropriate,[4] hereby makes the following Regulations:

PART I
GENERAL

1 Citation, commencement and interpretation

(1) These Regulations may be cited as the Pension Sharing (Implementation and Discharge of Liability) Regulations 2000 and shall come into force on 1 December 2000.

(2) In these Regulations—

'**the 1993 Act**' means the Pension Schemes Act 1993;[5]

'**the 1995 Act**' means the Pensions Act 1995;

'**the 1999 Act**' means the Welfare Reform and Pensions Act 1999;

'**base rate**' means the base rate for the time being quoted by the reference banks or, where there is for the time being more than one such base rate, the base rate which, when the base rate quoted by each bank is ranked in a descending sequence of seven, is fourth in the sequence;

'**the implementation period**' has the meaning given by section 34 of the 1999 Act;

'**The Inland Revenue**' means the Commissioners of Inland Revenue;

'**normal benefit age**' has the meaning given by section 101B of the 1993 Act;[7]
'**occupational pension scheme**' has the meaning given by section 1 of the 1993 Act; 'pension arrangement' has the meaning given by section 46(1) of the 1999 Act;

'**pension credit**' means a credit under section 29(1)(b) of the 1999 Act;

'**pension sharing order or provision**' means an order which is mentioned in section 28(1) of the 1999 Act;

'**personal pension scheme**' has the meaning given by section 1 of the 1993 Act;[8]

'**person responsible for a pension arrangement**' has the meaning given to that expression in section 46(2) of the 1999 Act;

'**the reference banks**' means the seven largest institutions for the time being which—

(a) are authorised by the Financial Services Authority under the Banking Act 1987;[10]

(b) are incorporated in and carrying on within the United Kingdom a deposit-taking business (as defined in section 6, but subject to any order under section 7 of that Act);[11] and

(c) quote a base rate in sterling; and for the purpose of this definition the size of an institution at any time is to be determined by reference to the gross assets denominated in sterling of that institution, together with any subsidiary (as defined in section 736 of the Companies Act 1985),[12] as shown in the audited end of year accounts last published before that time;

'**the Regulatory Authority**' means the Occupational Pensions Regulatory Authority;[13]

'**safeguarded rights**' has the meaning given in section 68A(1) of the 1993 Act;[14]

'**scheme actuary**', in relation to a scheme to which section 47(1)(b) of the 1995 Act applies, means the actuary mentioned in section 47(1)(b) of that Act;

'**section 9(2B) rights**' has the meaning given in regulation 1(2) of the Occupational Pension Schemes (Contracting-out) Regulations 1996;[15]

'**transferee**' has the meaning given by section 34 (5) of the 1999 Act;

'**transferor**' has the meaning given by section 34 (5) of the 1999 Act;

'**trustees or managers**', in relation to an occupational pension scheme or a personal pension scheme means—

(a) in the case of a scheme established under a trust, the trustees of the scheme, and

(b) in any other case, the managers of the scheme;

'**the valuation day**' has the meaning given in section 29(7) of the 1999 Act.

PART II

EXTENSION, POSTPONEMENT OR CESSATION OF IMPLEMENTATION PERIOD

2   Time period for notification to the Regulatory Authority of failure by the trustees or managers of an occupational pension scheme to discharge their liability in respect of a pension credit

The period prescribed for the purposes of section 33(2)(a) of the 1999 Act (period within which notice must be given of non-discharge of pension credit liability) is the period of 21 days beginning with the day immediately following the end of the implementation period.

3   Circumstances in which an application for an extension of the implementation period may be made

The circumstances in which an application may be made for the purposes of section 33(4) of the 1999 Act (application for extension of period within which pension credit liability is to be discharged) are that the application is made to the Regulatory Authority before the end of the implementation period; and—

  (a) the Regulatory Authority is satisfied that—

    (i) the scheme is being wound up or is about to be wound up;

    (ii) the scheme is ceasing to be a contracted-out scheme;

    (iii) the financial interests of the members of the scheme generally will be prejudiced if the trustees or managers do what is needed to discharge their liability for the pension credit within that period;

    (iv) the transferor or the transferee has not taken such steps as the trustees or managers can reasonably expect in order to satisfy them of any matter which falls to be established before they can properly discharge their liability for the pension credit;

    (v) the trustees or managers have not been provided with such information as they reasonably require properly to discharge their liability for the pension credit within the implementation period;

    (vi) the transferor or the transferee has disputed the amount of the cash equivalent calculated and verified for the purposes of section 29 of the 1999 Act (creation of pension debits and credits);

  (b) the provisions of section 53 of the 1993 Act[16] (supervision: former contracted-out schemes) apply; or

  (c) the application has been made on one or more of the grounds specified in paragraph (a) or (b), and the Regulatory Authority's consideration of the application cannot be completed before the end of the implementation period.

4 Postponement or cessation of implementation period when an application is made for leave to appeal out of time

(1) The modifications to the operation of section 34 of the 1999 Act ('implementation period') where the pension credit depends on a pension sharing order and the order is the subject of an application for leave to appeal out of time are—

  (a) where the implementation period has not commenced, its commencement shall be postponed; or

  (b) where the implementation period has commenced, its operation shall cease and it shall not commence afresh until the person responsible for the pension arrangement has received the documents referred to in paragraph (2).

(2) The postponement or cessation referred to in paragraph (1)(a) or (b) shall continue until the person responsible for the pension arrangement is in receipt of—

  (a) confirmation from the court that the order which was the subject of the application for leave to appeal out of time has not been varied or discharged; or

  (b) a copy of the varied pension sharing order.

(3) Where the person responsible for the pension arrangement has discharged his liability in respect of the pension credit which depends on a pension sharing order and that person subsequently receives notification of an application for leave to appeal out of time in respect of that order, he shall inform the court within 21 days from the date on which he received the notification that liability in respect of that pension credit has been discharged.

5 Civil penalties

For the purpose of section 33(2)(b) or (3) of the 1999 Act, the maximum amount of the penalty which may be imposed by the Regulatory Authority under section 10(2)(b) of the 1995 Act is—

(a) £1,000 in the case of an individual, and

(b) £10,000 in any other case.

PART III
DEATH OF PERSON ENTITLED TO A PENSION CREDIT BEFORE LIABILITY IN RESPECT OF THE PENSION CREDIT IS DISCHARGED

6   Discharge of liability in respect of a pension credit following the death of the person entitled to the pension credit

(1) The person responsible for the pension arrangement shall following the death of the person entitled to the pension credit discharge his liability in respect of a pension credit in accordance with this regulation.

(2) Where the rules or provisions of a pension arrangement so provide and provided that any requirements of the Inland Revenue under Part XIV of the Income and Corporation Taxes Act 1988 are satisfied, the person responsible for the pension arrangement shall discharge his liability in respect of a pension credit by undertaking to—

(a) make—

(i)   a payment of a lump sum; or

(ii) payments of a pension; or

(iii) payments of both a lump sum and a pension, to one or more persons; or

(b) enter into an annuity contract or take out a policy of insurance with an insurance company for the benefit of one or more persons; or

(c) make a payment or, as the case may be, payments under sub-paragraph (a) and enter into an annuity contract or take out an insurance policy under sub-paragraph (b).

(3) Where paragraph (2)(b) or (c) applies, the annuity contract entered into or insurance policy taken out must satisfy the requirements of paragraph 6(2) of Schedule 5 to the 1999 Act (qualifying arrangements) and regulation 11 of these Regulations.

(4) Where the provisions of paragraph (2) do not apply, liability in respect of a pension credit shall be discharged by retaining the value of the pension credit in the pension arrangement from which that pension credit was derived.

(5) Where—

(a) liability in respect of a pension credit has been discharged in accordance with paragraph (2); and

(b) the value of the payment or payments made, the annuity contract entered into or the insurance policy taken out, as the case may be, is less than the value of the pension credit, the value of an amount equal to the difference between the value of the pension credit and the value of that payment or those payments, that contract or policy, as the case may be, shall be retained in the pension arrangement from which that pension credit was derived.

PART IV
DISCHARGE OF LIABILITY IN RESPECT OF A PENSION CREDIT

7   Funded pension schemes

(1) The circumstances in which the trustees or managers of a scheme, to which paragraph 1 of Schedule 5 to the 1999 Act applies, may discharge their liability in respect of a pension credit in accordance with sub-paragraph (2)(b) of that paragraph are where—

    (a) the person entitled to the credit has failed to provide his consent in accordance with paragraph 1(2)(a) and (4) of that Schedule; and

    (b) the circumstances set out in paragraph 1(3) of that Schedule do not apply.

(2) The circumstances in which the trustees or managers of a scheme, to which paragraph 1 of Schedule 5 to the 1999 Act applies, may discharge their liability in respect of a pension credit in accordance with sub-paragraph (3)(c) of that paragraph are where—

    (a) the person entitled to the credit has failed to provide his consent in accordance with paragraph 1(3)(c) of that Schedule; and

    (b) either—

        (i) the person entitled to the pension credit has failed to provide his consent in accordance with paragraph 1(2)(a) and (4) of that Schedule; or

        (ii) the trustees or managers of the scheme have not discharged their liability in accordance with paragraph (1) above.

8 Unfunded occupational pension schemes other than public service pension schemes

(1) The circumstances in which the trustees or managers of a scheme, to which paragraph 3 of Schedule 5 to the 1999 Act applies, may discharge their liability in respect of a pension credit in accordance with sub-paragraph (3)(c) of that paragraph are those specified in—

    (a) sub-paragraphs (a) and (b) of paragraph (2), in the case of an approved scheme; and

    (b) sub-paragraphs (a), (b) and (c) of paragraph (2), in the case of an unapproved scheme.

(2) The circumstances specified in this paragraph are—

    (a) the liability of the trustees or managers has not been discharged in accordance with the provisions of paragraph 3(2) of that Schedule;

    (b) the person entitled to the pension credit has not consented to the discharge of liability in accordance with paragraph 3(3) of that Schedule; and

    (c) the employer who is associated with the scheme from which the pension credit derives—

        (i) consents to the trustees or managers discharging their liability for the credit in accordance with paragraph 3(3) of that Schedule; and

        (ii) agrees to compensate the person entitled to the credit fully for any tax liability which he may incur as a result of the trustees or managers of the scheme discharging their liability for the credit in accordance with paragraph 3(3) of that Schedule.

(3) In this regulation 'approved scheme' means an occupational pension scheme which is approved for the purposes of Part XIV of the Income and Corporation Taxes Act 1988[17] and an 'unapproved scheme' means an occupational pension scheme which is not approved for those purposes.

9 Other pension arrangements

(1) The circumstances in which the person responsible for a pension arrangement, to which paragraph 4 of Schedule 5 to the 1999 Act applies, may discharge his liability in respect of a pension credit in accordance with sub-paragraph (2)(c) of that paragraph are where his liability has not been discharged in accordance with the provisions of paragraph 4(3) or (4) of that Schedule.

(2) The circumstances in which the person responsible for the pension arrangement may discharge his liability in respect of the pension credit under paragraph 4(4) of Schedule 5 to the 1999 Act are where the person responsible for the pension arrangement has not discharged his liability in accordance with the provisions of—

(a) paragraph (1) above;

(b) paragraph 4(2) of that Schedule; or

(c) paragraph 4(3) of that Schedule.

10   Calculation of the value of appropriate rights

(1) Except in a case to which paragraph (4) applies, the value of the rights conferred on a person entitled to a pension credit shall be calculated by adopting methods and making assumptions which the scheme actuary or, in relation to a scheme to which section 47(1)(b) of the 1995 Act (professional advisers) does not apply, by a person referred to in paragraph (2), has certified to the person responsible for the pension arrangement as being consistent with—

(a) the methods adopted and assumptions made when transfers of other pension rights are received by the person responsible for the pension arrangement; and

(b) the Guidance Note 11 'Retirement Benefit Schemes—Transfer Values' published by the Institute of Actuaries and the Faculty of Actuaries[18] and which is current on the valuation day.

(2) A person referred to in this paragraph is—

(a) a Fellow of the Institute of Actuaries;

(b) a Fellow of the Faculty of Actuaries; or

(c) a person with other actuarial qualifications who is approved by the Secretary of State, at the request of the person responsible for the pension arrangement in question, as being a proper person to act for the purposes of these Regulations in connection with that scheme.

(3) Where the person entitled to a pension credit in respect of whom a cash equivalent is to be calculated and verified is a member of a scheme having particulars from time to time set out in regulations made under section 7 of the Superannuation Act 1972[19] (superannuation of persons employed in local government service, etc.), that cash equivalent shall be calculated and verified in such manner as may be approved by the Government Actuary or by an actuary authorised by the Government Actuary to act on his behalf for that purpose.

(4) Where the rights conferred on a person entitled to a pension credit are derived from money purchase rights in whole or in part, the value of those rights shall be calculated by the person responsible for the pension arrangement in a manner consistent with the methods adopted and assumptions made when transfers of other pension rights are received by the person responsible for the pension arrangement, and by adopting methods consistent with the requirements of Chapter IV of Part IV of the 1993 Act (protection for early leavers—transfer values).

11   Qualifying arrangements

(1) The requirements referred to in paragraph 6(2)(b) of Schedule 5 to the 1999 Act (requirements applying to annuity contracts or policies of insurance for the purpose of sub-paragraph (1) of that paragraph) are that the annuity contract is entered into or the insurance policy is taken out with an insurance company which is—

(a) authorised under section 3 or 4 of the Insurance Companies Act 1982[20] (authorisation of insurance business) to carry on long term business (within the meaning of section 1 of that Act[21] (classification));

(b) in the case of a friendly society authorised under section 32 of the Friendly Societies Act 1992[22] (grant of authorisation by Commission: general) to carry out long term business under any of the Classes specified in Head A of Schedule 2 to that Act (the activities of a friendly society: long term business); or

(c) an EC company as defined in section 2 of the Insurance Companies Act 1982[23] (restriction on carrying on insurance business), and which falls within paragraph (2).

(2) An EC company falls within this paragraph if it—

(a) carries on ordinary long-term insurance business (within the meaning of section 96(1) of the Insurance Companies Act 1982[24]) in the United Kingdom through a branch in respect of which such of the requirements of Part I of Schedule 2F to that Act[25] (recognition in the United Kingdom of EC and EFTA companies: EC companies carrying on business etc. in the United Kingdom) as are applicable have been complied with; or

(b) provides ordinary long term insurance in the United Kingdom and such of the requirements of Part I of Schedule 2F to that Act as are applicable have been complied with in respect of insurance.

12 Disqualification as a destination for pension credit—general

The requirements referred to in paragraph 7(1)(b) of Schedule 5 to the 1999 Act (requirements to be satisfied to qualify pension arrangements as destinations for pension credits) are that the pension arrangement—

(a) is an arrangement which carries on pension business as defined by section 431B of the Income and Corporation Taxes Act 1988[26] (meaning of 'pension business');

(b) is an overseas arrangement within the meaning given by regulation 1(2) of the Contracting-out (Transfer and Transfer Payment) Regulations 1996[27] (citation, commencement and interpretation); or

(c) is an overseas scheme within the meaning given by regulation 1(2)[28] of the Contracting-out (Transfer and Transfer Payment) Regulations 1996.

13 Disqualification as a destination for pension credit—contracted-out or safeguarded rights

(1) The descriptions of pension arrangements referred to in paragraph 7(2)(a) of Schedule 5 to the 1999 Act (pension arrangements which qualify as destinations for pension credits, where the rights by reference to which the amount of the credits are determined are or include contracted-out rights or safeguarded rights) are—

(a) a contracted-out salary related occupational pension scheme which satisfies the requirements of section 9(2)[29] of the 1993 Act (requirements for certification of occupational salary related schemes);

(b) a contracted-out money purchase occupational pension scheme which satisfies the requirements of section 9(3)[30] of the 1993 Act (requirements for certification of occupational money purchase schemes);

(bb) a contracted-out occupational pension scheme to which section 149 of the 1995 Act (hybrid occupational pension schemes) applies;

(c) an appropriate personal pension scheme within the meaning of section 7(4)[31] of the 1993 Act (issue of appropriate scheme certificates);

(d) an annuity contract or an insurance policy which satisfies the requirements of paragraph 6 of Schedule 5 to the 1999 Act (qualifying arrangements);

(e) an overseas arrangement within the meaning given by regulation 1(2) of the Contracting-out (Transfer and Transfer Payment) Regulations 1996; or (f) an overseas scheme within the meaning given by regulation 1(2) of the Contracting-out (Transfer and Transfer Payment) Regulations 1996.

(2) The requirements referred to in paragraph 7(2)(b) of Schedule 5 to the 1999 Act (requirements to be satisfied by a pension arrangement which qualifies as a destination for a pension credit, where the rights by reference to which the amount of the credit are determined are or include contracted-out rights or safeguarded rights) are—

    (a) in relation to the descriptions of pension arrangement referred to in paragraph (1)(a) to (d), the requirements specified in the Pension Sharing (Safeguarded Rights) Regulations 2000[32] to be met by an occupational pension scheme or a personal pension scheme;

    (b) in relation to the descriptions of pension arrangement referred to in paragraph (1)(e), the requirements specified in regulation 15 (disqualification as a destination for pension credit—annuity contracts and insurance policies) and regulation 7(3) and (4) of the Pension Sharing (Safeguarded Rights) Regulations 2000[33] (the pension and annuity requirements—money purchase schemes);

    (c) in relation to the descriptions of pension arrangement referred to in paragraph (1)(f) and (g), the requirements specified in regulation 11 of the Contracting-out (Transfer and Transfer Payment) Regulations 1996 (transfer payments to overseas schemes or arrangements in respect of section 9(2B) rights), as if the references in that regulation to—

        (i) 'earner' were to 'the person entitled to a pension credit'; and

        (ii) 'accrued section 9(2B) rights' were to 'safeguarded rights'.

(3) The rights for the purposes of paragraph 7(6) of Schedule 5 to the 1999 Act (meaning of 'contracted-out' rights under or derived from an occupational pension scheme or a personal pension scheme) are those which fall within the categories specified in regulation 2 of the Pension Sharing (Safeguarded Rights) Regulations 2000 (definition of contracted-out rights).

14   Disqualification as a destination for pension credit—occupational pension schemes

The calculation of the value of the rights of the person entitled to the pension credit for the purposes of paragraph 7(3) of Schedule 5 to the 1999 Act shall be made in accordance with the methods adopted and assumptions made by the scheme which are consistent with the methods adopted and assumptions made by that scheme when transfers of other pension rights are received by the scheme.

15   Disqualification as a destination for pension credit—annuity contracts and insurance policies

(1) The circumstances referred to in paragraph 7(4) of Schedule 5 to the 1999 Act (circumstances in which an annuity contract or insurance policy is disqualified as a destination for a pension credit) are where the requirements specified in paragraphs (2) to (7) are not satisfied.

(2) The annuity contract or insurance policy must provide that that contract or policy, as the case may be, may not be assigned or surrendered unless—

    (a) the person entitled to the pension credit; or

    (b) if the person entitled to the pension credit has died, his widow or widower, has consented to the assignment or surrender.

(3) The benefits previously secured by the annuity contract or insurance policy become secured, or are replaced by benefits which are secured by another qualifying arrangement.

(4) The annuity contract or insurance policy, as the case may be, must provide that the benefits secured by that contract or policy may be commuted if either—

(a) the conditions set out in paragraph (5) are satisfied; or

(b) the conditions set out in paragraph (6) are satisfied.

(5) The conditions referred to in paragraph (4)(a) are—

(a) the benefits secured by the annuity contract or insurance policy have become payable, and the aggregate of those benefits does not exceed £260 per annum;

(b) an actuary certifies that the methods and assumptions to be used to calculate any benefit in a lump sum form will result in the benefit being broadly equivalent to the annual amount of benefits which would have been payable in pension benefits; and

(c) all of the interest of the person entitled to the pension credit under the annuity contract or insurance policy is discharged upon payment of a lump sum.

(6) The conditions referred to in paragraph (4)(b) are—

(a) the benefits secured by the annuity contract or insurance policy have become payable and the person entitled to the pension credit requests or consents to the commutation; (b) the person entitled to the pension credit is suffering from serious ill health prior to normal benefit age; and

(b) the insurance company with which the annuity contract is entered into, or with which the insurance policy is taken out, assumes an obligation to pay the benefits secured by the annuity contract or insurance policy to—

(i) the person entitled to the pension credit;

(ii) the trustees of a trust for the benefit of the person entitled to the pension credit; or

(iii) the trustees of a trust for the benefit of the dependants of the person entitled to the pension credit.

(7) The annuity contract or insurance policy must contain, or be endorsed with, terms so as to provide for any increase in accordance with regulation 32 of the Pension Sharing (Pension Credit Benefit) Regulations 2000[34] (increase of relevant pension) which would have been applied to the benefits which have become secured or been replaced by the annuity contract or insurance policy had the discharge of liability not taken place.

(8) In this regulation— 'serious ill health' means ill health which is such as to give rise to a life expectancy of less than one year from the date on which commutation of the benefits secured by the annuity contract or insurance policy is applied for.

16 Adjustments to the amount of the pension credit—occupational pension schemes which are underfunded on the valuation day

(1) The circumstances referred to in paragraph 8(1)(d) of Schedule 5 to the 1999 Act (adjustments to amount of pension credit) are—

(a) the discharge of liability in respect of the pension credit in accordance with paragraph 1(3) of Schedule 5 to the 1999 Act is at the request, or with the consent, of the person entitled to the pension credit;

(b) the person entitled to the pension credit has refused an offer by the trustees or managers of the occupational pension scheme from which the pension credit is derived to discharge their liability in respect of the pension credit, without any reduction in the amount of the credit, in accordance with the provisions of paragraph 1(2) of Schedule 5 to the 1999 Act (conferring appropriate rights in that scheme on the person entitled to the pension credit); and

(c) prior to making his request or giving his consent in accordance with sub-paragraph (a) the person entitled to the pension credit has received from the trustees or managers of the occupational pension scheme from which the pension credit is derived, a written statement which provides the following information—

(i)   the reasons why the amount of the pension credit has been reduced;

(ii) the amount by which the pension credit has been reduced; and

(iii) where possible, an estimate of the date by which it will be possible to pay the full, unadjusted amount of the pension credit.

(2) The lesser amount referred to in paragraph 8(1) of Schedule 5 to the 1999 Act may be determined for the purposes of that paragraph by reducing the amount of the pension credit which relates to liabilities referred to in section 73(3)(a), (aa), (b), (c)(i) or (d) of the 1995 Act[35] (preferential liabilities on winding-up) by the percentage which is the difference between—

(a) 100 per cent.; and

(b) the percentage of the pension credit which the actuarial valuation shows the scheme assets as being sufficient to satisfy, where the actuarial valuation is the latest actuarial valuation obtained in accordance with section 57 of the 1995 Act (valuation and certification of assets and liabilities) before the valuation day.

(3) If, by virtue of Schedule 5 to the Occupational Pension Schemes (Minimum Funding Requirement and Actuarial Valuations) Regulations 1996,[36] section 56 of the 1995 Act (minimum funding requirement) applies to a section of a scheme as if that section were a separate scheme, paragraph (2) shall apply as if that section were a separate scheme, and as if the reference therein to a scheme were accordingly a reference to that section.

17   Adjustments to the amount of the pension credit—payments made without knowledge of the pension debit

For the purposes of paragraph 9 of Schedule 5 to the 1999 Act (adjustments to amount of pension credit), where the cash equivalent of the member's shareable rights after deduction of the payment referred to in sub-paragraph (b) of that paragraph, is less than the amount of the pension debit, the pension credit shall be reduced to that lesser amount.

18   Adjustments to the amount of the pension credit—increasing the amount of the pension credit

(1) For the purposes of paragraph 10 of Schedule 5 to the 1999 Act (adjustments to amount of pension credit) the trustees or managers of an occupational pension scheme to which paragraph 1(3) or 3(3) of Schedule 5 to the 1999 Act applies shall increase the amount of the pension credit by—

(a) the amount, if any, by which the amount of that pension credit falls short of what it would have been if the valuation day had been the day on which the trustees or managers make the payment; or

(b) if it is greater, interest on the amount of that pension credit calculated on a daily basis over the period from the valuation day to the day on which the trustees or managers make the payment, at an annual rate of one per cent. above the base rate.

(2) For the purposes of paragraph 10 of Schedule 5 to the 1999 Act the trustees or managers of a personal pension scheme to which paragraph 1(3) of Schedule 5 to the 1999 Act applies, or a person responsible for a pension arrangement to which paragraph 4(2) of Schedule 5 to the 1999 Act applies, shall increase the amount of the pension credit by—

    (a) the interest on the amount of that pension credit, calculated on daily basis over the period from the valuation day to the day on which the trustees or managers or the person responsible for the pension arrangement make the payment, at the same rate as that payable for the time being on judgment debts by virtue of section 17 of the Judgments Act 1838;[37] or

    (b) if it is greater, the amount, if any, by which the amount of that pension credit falls short of what it would have been if the valuation day had been the day on which the trustees or managers or the person responsible for the pension arrangement make the payment.

Signed by authority of the Secretary of State for Social Security

Jeff Rooker Minister of State, Department of Social Security

13th April 2000

Explanatory note   *(This note is not part of the Regulations)*

These Regulations provide for the circumstances in which the implementation period may be extended, postponed or in which it may cease, and how a person responsible for a pension arrangement may discharge his liability in respect of a pension credit.

Part I and regulation 1 provide for citation, commencement and interpretation.

Part II and regulations 2 to 5 deal with the extension, postponement or cessation of the implementation period.

Regulation 2 specifies the period within which the trustees or managers of an occupational pension scheme are to notify the Occupational Pensions Regulatory Authority (OPRA) should they fail to discharge their liability in respect of a pension credit within the implementation period.

Regulation 3 sets out the circumstances in which OPRA may grant an extension of the implementation period.

Regulation 4 provides for the postponement or cessation of the implementation period for a pension credit when an application is made for leave to appeal out of time.

Regulation 5 sets out the maximum penalties which OPRA may impose in any case where OPRA is satisfied that a trustee or manager has not taken all reasonable steps to ensure that their liability for the pension credit was discharged within the implementation period, or to ensure that OPRA was notified of the failure to discharge that liability within the period prescribed by regulation 2.

Part III and regulation 6 provide for how liability in respect of a pension credit may be discharged in the event of the death of the person entitled to a pension credit.

Part IV and regulations 7 to 18 provide for how liability in respect of a pension credit may be discharged. Regulations 7 and 8 set out the circumstances in which the trustees or managers of a funded pension scheme and an unfunded pension scheme other than a public service scheme may discharge their liability in respect of a pension credit.

Regulation 9 sets out the circumstances in which a person responsible for an annuity contract or an insurance policy may discharge his liability in respect of a pension credit.

Regulation 10 provides for how the value of appropriate rights is to be calculated.

Regulation 11 specifies the requirements to be met by annuity contracts or policies of insurance in order for them to be qualifying arrangements.

Regulations 12 to 15 specify the requirements to be met by a pension arrangement in order for it not to be disqualified as a destination for a pension credit.

Regulations 16 to 18 specify the circumstances in which the amount of a pension credit may be reduced or increased.

An assessment of the cost to business of the provisions of the Welfare Reform and Pensions Act 1999, including these Regulations, is detailed in the Regulatory Impact Assessment for that Act. A copy of this Assessment has been placed in the libraries of both Houses of Parliament. Copies can be obtained by post from the Department of Social Security, Pensions on Divorce, 3rd Floor, The Adelphi, 1–11 John Adam Street, London WC2N 6HT.

Notes

[1] Section 124(1) is cited because of the meaning there given to 'prescribed' and 'regulations'.

[2] 1995 c. 26.

[3] 1999 c. 30.

[4] See sections 120(1) of the Pensions Act 1995 and 83(11) of the Welfare Reform and Pensions Act 1999.

[5] 1993 c. 48.

[6] Section 8(2) was amended by paragraph 23(a) of Schedule 5 to the Pensions Act 1995.

[7] Section 101B is inserted by section 37 of the Welfare Reform and Pensions Act 1999.

[8] The definition of 'personal pension scheme' is amended by paragraph 3(1)(a) of Schedule 2 to the Welfare Reform and Pensions Act 1999.

[9] Section 10 was amended by paragraph 25 of Schedule 5 to the Pensions Act 1995, and by paragraph 36 of Schedule 1 to the Social Security Contributions (Transfer of Functions, etc.) Act 1999 (c. 2).

[10] 1987 c. 22.

[11] Section 7 was amended by section 23(1) of, and paragraphs 1 and 4 of Schedule 5 to, the Bank of England Act 1998 (c. 11).

[12] 1985 c. 6. Section 736 was substituted by section 144(1) of the Companies Act 1989 (c. 40).

[13] The Occupational Pensions Regulatory Authority is established under section 1 of the Pensions Act 1995.

[14] Section 68A is inserted by section 36 of the Welfare Reform and Pensions Act 1999.

[15] SI 1996/1172. This definition was substituted by paragraph 4(2) of Schedule 1 to SI 1997/786.

[16] Section 53 was amended by paragraph 48 of Schedule 5 to the Pensions Act 1995 and by paragraphs 52 and 53 of Schedule 1 to the Social Security Contributions (Transfer of Functions, etc.) Act 1999.

[17] 1988 c. 1.

[18] The publication 'Retirement Benefit Schemes—Transfer Values (GN11)' may be obtained from the Institute of Actuaries', Staple Inn Hall, High Holborn, London WC1V 7QJ, and from the Faculty of Actuaries, Maclaurin House, 18 Dublin Street, Edinburgh EH1 3PP. The publication is also available on the following internet web-site: http://www.actuaries.org.uk.

[19] 1972 c. 11.

[20] 1982 c. 50, as amended by the European Economic Area Act 1993 (c. 51).

[21] Section 1 was amended by SI 1990/1159.

[22] 1992 c. 40. Section 32 was amended by SI 1994/1984.

[23] Section 2 was amended by regulation 4(2) of SI 1994/1696 and 1994/3132.

[24] There are amendments to section 96(1) which are not relevant to these Regulations.

[25] Schedule 2F was inserted by SI 1994/1696.

[26] Section 431B was inserted by paragraph 2 of Schedule 8 to the Finance Act 1995 (c. 4).

[27] SI 1996/1462.

[28] The definition of 'overseas scheme' was amended by paragraph 7(2) of Schedule 1 to SI 1997/786.

[29] Section 9(2) was substituted by section 136(3) of the Pensions Act 1995.

[30] Section 9(3) was amended by section 136(4) of, and paragraph 24 of Schedule 5, Part III of Schedule 7 to, the Pensions Act 1995, and by paragraph 35(3) of Schedule 1 to the Social Security Contributions (Transfer of Functions, etc.) Act 1999.

[31] Section 7(4) was amended by paragraph 22(b) of Schedule 5, and by Part III of Schedule 7 to the Pensions Act 1995.

[32] SI 2000/1055.

[33] SI 2000/1055.

[34] SI 2000/1054.

[35] Section 73(3) was modified by regulation 3 of SI 1996/3126 and is amended by section 38(1) of the Welfare Reform and Pensions Act 1999.

[36] SI 1996/1536. Schedule 5 was amended by SI 1997/786 and SI 1997/3038.

[37] 1 & 2 Vic. c. 110; the rate of interest was amended by SI 1993/564.

Pension Sharing (Pension Credit Benefit) Regulations 2000

SI 2000/1054

Made 13 April 2000
Laid before Parliament 19 April 2000
Coming into force 1 December 2000

ARRANGEMENT OF REGULATIONS

PART IV

Indexation

The Secretary of State for Social Security, in exercise of the powers conferred upon him by sections 68D, 101C(2), 101D(1)(b), (2)(b) and (4)(b), 101E(2), 101F(2)(b), (c), (3)(b), and (6)(b), 101H(2)(a) and (b), and (3), 101I, 101J(2), 101L(1), (2)(a) and (b), and (3), 101P(2)(b), 101Q, 181(1)[1] and 182(2) and (3) of the Pension Schemes Act 1993],[2] sections 10(2)(b), 124(1)[3] and 174(2) and (3) of the Pensions Act 1995,[4] and sections 40(1) and (3) and 83(4) and (6) of the Welfare Reform and Pensions Act 1999[5] and of all other powers enabling him in that behalf, after consulting such persons as he considered appropriate,[6] hereby makes the following Regulations:

PART I

GENERAL

1   Citation, commencement and interpretation

These Regulations may be cited as the Pension Sharing (Pension Credit Benefit) Regulations 2000 and shall come into force on 1st December 2000.

(2)   In these Regulations—

    '**the 1993 Act**' means the Pension Schemes Act 1993;

    '**the 1995 Act**' means the Pensions Act 1995;

    '**the 1999 Act**' means the Welfare Reform and Pensions Act 1999;

    '**the Taxes Act**' means the Income and Corporation Taxes Act 1988;[7]

    '**active member**', in relation to an occupational pension scheme, means a person who is in pensionable service under the scheme;

'**appropriate scheme**' shall be construed in accordance with section 9(5) of the 1993 Act;

'**base rate**' means the base rate for the time being quoted by the reference banks or, where there is for the time being more than one such base rate, the base rate which, when the base rate quoted by each bank is ranked in a descending sequence of seven, is fourth in the sequence;

'**contracted-out rights**' has the meaning given by section 68A(5) of the 1993 Act;[8]

'**eligible member**' has the meaning given by section 101P(1) of the 1993 Act;[9]

'**employer**' has the meaning given by section 181(1) of the 1993 Act;

'**incapacity**' means physical or mental deterioration which is sufficiently serious to prevent a person from following his normal employment or which seriously impairs his earning capacity;

'**the Inland Revenue**' means the Commissioners of Inland Revenue;

'**member**' means a member of an occupational pension scheme or a personal pension scheme and includes an eligible member;

'**money purchase benefits**' has the meaning given by section 181(1) of the 1993 Act;[10]

'**money purchase contracted-out scheme**' has the meaning given by section 8(1)(a)(ii) of the 1993 Act;

'**money purchase scheme**' has the meaning given by section 181(1) of the 1993 Act;

'**normal benefit age**' has the meaning given by section 101B of the 1993 Act;[11]

'**occupational pension scheme**' has the meaning given by section 1 of the 1993 Act;

'**overseas arrangement**' has the meaning given by regulation 1(2) of the Contracting-out (Transfer and Transfer Payment) Regulations 1996;[12]

'**overseas scheme**' has the meaning given by regulation 1(2) of the Contracting-out (Transfer and Transfer Payment) Regulations 1996;[13]

'**pension credit benefit**' has the meaning given by—

(a)   section 101B of the 1993 Act insofar as that expression is used in Part II of these Regulations; and

(b)   section 101P of the 1993 Act insofar as that expression is used in Part III of these Regulations;

'**pension credit rights**' has the meaning given by—

(a)   section 101B of the 1993 Act insofar as that expression is used in Part II of these Regulations; and

(b)   section 101P of the 1993 Act insofar as that expression is used in Part III of these Regulations;

'**pensionable service**' has the meaning given by section 124(1) of the Pensions Act 1995;[14]

'**personal pension scheme**' has the meaning given by section 1 of the 1993 Act;[15]

'**principal appointed day**' has the meaning given by section 7(2B) of the 1993 Act;[16]

'**qualifying occupational pension scheme**' has the meaning given by section 40(3) of the 1999 Act;

'**qualifying scheme**' has the meaning given by section 101P(1) of the 1993 Act;

'**the reference banks**' means the seven largest institutions for the time being which—

(a) are authorised by the Financial Services Authority under the Banking Act 1987;[17]

(b) are incorporated in and carrying on within the United Kingdom a deposit-taking business (as defined in section 6, but subject to any order under section 7 of that Act;[18] and

(c) quote a base rate in sterling;

and for the purpose of this definition the size of an institution at any time is to be determined by reference to the gross assets denominated in sterling of that institution, together with any subsidiary (as defined in section 736 of the Companies Act 1985[19]), as shown in the audited end of year accounts last published before that time;

'**Regulatory Authority**' means the Occupational Pensions Regulatory Authority;

'**relevant pension**' means a pension to which section 40(2) of the 1999 Act applies;

'**safeguarded rights**' has the meaning given by section 68A of the 1993 Act;[20]

'**salary related contracted-out scheme**' has the meaning given by section 8(1)(a)(i) of the 1993 Act;[21]

'**scheme**' has the meaning given by section 101B of the 1993 Act;[22]

'**statement of entitlement**' means the statement of the amount of the cash equivalent of an eligible member's pension credit benefit under a qualifying scheme referred to in section 101H(1) of the 1993 Act;

'**transfer credits**' means rights allowed to a person under the rules of an occupational or personal pension scheme by reference to a transfer to that scheme of his accrued rights from another scheme (including any transfer credits allowed by that scheme);

'**transfer notice**' has the meaning given by section 101F(7) of the 1993 Act;

'**trustees or managers**' has the meaning given by section 46(1) of the 1999 Act;

'**valuation date**' has the meaning given by section 101J(7) of the 1993 Act.

2 Salary related schemes

For the purposes of Chapter II of Part IVA of the 1993 Act[23] (requirements relating to pension credit benefit—transfer values) and these Regulations, an occupational pension scheme is salary related if it is not a money purchase scheme and it is not a scheme—

(a) the only benefit provided by which (other than money purchase benefits) are death benefits; and

(b) under the provisions of which no member has accrued rights (other than rights to money purchase benefits).

PART II
PENSION CREDIT BENEFIT UNDER OCCUPATIONAL PENSION SCHEMES

3 Commutation of the whole of pension credit benefit

(1) Subject to paragraphs (3) and (4) and regulation 9 of the Pension Sharing (Safeguarded Rights) Regulations 2000[24] (ways of giving effect to safeguarded rights—salary related schemes), the circumstances in which the whole of the pension credit benefit may be commuted for the purposes of section 101C(2) of the 1993 Act (payment of pension credit benefit in the form of a lump sum before normal benefit age) are those described in paragraph (2).

(2) The circumstances described in this paragraph are that—

    (a) the person entitled to the pension credit benefit is suffering from serious ill health prior to normal benefit age; or

    (b) the aggregate of total benefits payable to the person under an occupational pension scheme, including any pension credit benefit, does not exceed £260 per annum.

(3) This regulation does not apply to an occupational pension scheme which is approved under section 590 of the Taxes Act[25] (mandatory approval).

(4) In this regulation, 'serious ill health' means ill health which is such as to give rise to a life expectancy of less than one year from the date on which commutation of the pension credit benefit is applied for.

4   Commutation of part of pension credit benefit

(1) Subject to paragraphs (2) and (3) and regulation 9 of the Pension Sharing (Safeguarded Rights) Regulations 2000, the circumstances in which part of the pension credit benefit may be commuted for the purposes of section 101C(2) of the 1993 Act (payment of pension credit benefit in the form of a lump sum before normal benefit age) are—

    (a) that the person entitled to the pension credit benefit—

        (i) subject to paragraph (2), is suffering from an incapacity prior to normal benefit age; or

        (ii) has reached the age of 50; and

    (b) that the commutation would not prevent approval or continuing approval of the scheme under section 591 of the Taxes Act[26] (discretionary approval).

(2) Paragraph (1)(a)(i) applies where the person entitled to the pension credit benefit

    (a) is an active member of the occupational pension scheme in which his pension credit rights are held; and

    (b) has become entitled to the early payment of benefits derived from his accrued rights, other than his pension credit rights, in that scheme as a result of his incapacity prior to normal benefit age.

(3) Safeguarded rights which are held in a money purchase contracted-out scheme shall not be commuted where the circumstances specified in paragraph (1)(a) apply.

(4) This regulation does not apply to an occupational pension scheme which is approved under section 590 of the Taxes Act.

5   Means of assuring pension credit benefit

(1) The prescribed means by which a person's pension credit benefit under a scheme must be assured for the purposes of section 101D(1)(b) of the 1993 Act (form of pension credit benefit and its alternatives) is by means of a transaction to which section 19 of the 1993 Act (discharge of liability where guaranteed minimum pensions are secured by insurance policies or annuity contracts) applies.

(2) A transaction referred to in paragraph (1) must satisfy the requirements of regulation 12, 13 or 14 (discharge of liability where pension credit benefit or alternative benefits are secured by insurance policies or annuity contracts, conditions on which insurance policies and annuity contracts may be commuted, or other requirements applying to insurance policies and annuity contracts).

(3) Where a transaction referred to in paragraph (1) applies, the insurance policy must be taken out, or the annuity contract must be entered into, with an insurance company which is—

(a) authorised under section 3 or 4 of the Insurance Companies Act 1982[27] (authorisation of insurance business) to carry on long term business (within the meaning of section 1 of that Act[28] (classification));

(b) in the case of a friendly society, authorised under section 32 of the Friendly Societies Act 1992[29] (grant of authorisation by Commission: general) to carry out long term business under any of the Classes specified in Head A of Schedule 2 to that Act (the activities of a friendly society: long term business); or

(c) an EC company as defined in section 2(6) of the Insurance Companies Act 1982[30] (restriction on carrying on insurance business), and which falls within paragraph (4).

(4) An EC company falls within this paragraph if it—

(a) carries on ordinary long-term insurance business (within the meaning of section 96(1) of the Insurance Companies Act 1982[31]) in the United Kingdom through a branch in respect of which such of the requirements of Part I of Schedule 2F to that Act[32] (recognition in the United Kingdom of EC and EFTA companies: EC companies carrying on business etc. in the United Kingdom) as are applicable have been complied with; or

(b) provides ordinary long term insurance in the United Kingdom and such of the requirements of Part I of Schedule 2F to that Act as are applicable have been complied with in respect of insurance.

6 Alternatives to pension credit benefit

(1) The prescribed alternatives to pension credit benefit which a scheme may provide for the purposes of section 101D(2) of the 1993 Act are described in regulations 7 to 9.

(2) For the purposes of section 101D(4)(b) of the 1993 Act, the cases in which the alternatives described in regulations 7 to 9 may be provided without the consent of the person entitled to the benefit are described in regulations 7(4) and 8(4).

7 Early retirement or deferred retirement

(1) Subject to paragraph (2), the scheme may provide benefits which are different from those required to constitute pension credit benefit in respect of the—

(a) amount;

(b) recipient; and

(c) time at which the benefits are payable.

(2) The benefits referred to in paragraph (1) must include a benefit that is payable to the person entitled to the pension credit benefit.

(3) The benefit of the person entitled to the benefit must not be payable before normal benefit age except in the circumstances referred to in regulation 3 or 4 (commutation of the whole of pension credit benefit, or commutation of part of pension credit benefit).

(4) Benefits consisting of, or including, a benefit that becomes payable to the person entitled to the benefit before normal benefit age may be provided without that person's consent where—

(a) that person's earning capacity is destroyed or seriously impaired by incapacity or serious ill heath; and

(b) in the opinion of the trustees or managers of the scheme, the person entitled to the benefit is incapable of deciding whether it is in his interests to consent.

(5) Any scheme rule that allows the alternative described in this regulation must require the trustees or managers of the scheme to be reasonably satisfied that, when the benefit of the person entitled to the benefit becomes payable, the total value of the benefits to be provided under this regulation is at least equal to the amount described in regulation 11 (value of alternatives to pension credit benefit).

(6) In this regulation, 'serious ill health' means ill health which is such as to give rise to a life expectancy of less than one year from the date on which the benefit of the person entitled to the pension credit becomes payable.

8   Bought out benefits

(1) The scheme may provide for benefits different from those required to constitute pension credit benefit to be appropriately secured by a transaction to which section 19 of the 1993 Act applies (discharge of liability where guaranteed minimum pensions are secured by insurance policies or annuity contracts).

(2) Any scheme rule that allows the alternative described in this regulation must require the trustees or managers of the scheme to be reasonably satisfied that, except where paragraph (3) applies, the payment made to the insurance company is at least equal to the amount described in regulation 11.

(3) The exception to paragraph (2) is where the person entitled to the benefit is requiring the trustees or managers to provide the alternative by exercising his right to give a transfer notice under section 101F of the 1993 Act (power to give transfer notice).

(4) A scheme may allow the alternative described in this regulation to be provided without the consent of the person entitled to the pension credit where—

  (a)   the person entitled to the pension credit will be able to assign or surrender the insurance policy or annuity contract on the conditions set out in regulation 3 of the Occupational Pension Schemes (Discharge of Liability) Regulations 1997[33] (conditions on which policies of insurance and annuity contracts may be assigned or surrendered); and

  (b) the requirements of paragraph (5) are satisfied.

(5) The requirements of this paragraph are that—

  (a) the scheme is being wound up; or

  (b) the trustees or managers of the scheme consider that, in the circumstances, it is reasonable for the scheme to provide the alternative without the consent of the person entitled to the benefit and the requirements of paragraph (6) are satisfied.

(6) The requirements of this paragraph are that all the conditions set out in sub-paragraphs (a) and (b) are satisfied, namely—

  (a) the trustees or managers of the scheme give the person entitled to the benefit at least 30 days' written notice of their intention to take out the insurance policy or enter into the annuity contract unless the person entitled to the benefit exercises a right to give a transfer notice under section 101F of the 1993 Act (the first mentioned notice being sent to that person at his last known address or delivered to that person personally); and

  (b) when the trustees or managers of the scheme agree with the insurance company to take out the insurance policy or enter into the annuity contract, there is no outstanding transfer notice by the person entitled to the benefit under section 101F of the 1993 Act.

(7) For the purposes of this regulation 'appropriately secured' means secured by an insurance policy or annuity contract to which regulation 5 applies.

9   Money purchase benefits

(1) The scheme may, with the consent of the person entitled to the benefit, provide money purchase benefits instead of all or any of the benefits that constitute pension credit benefit.

(2) Any scheme rule which allows this alternative must require the trustees or managers of the scheme to be reasonably satisfied that the amount allocated to provide money purchase benefits in respect of the person entitled to the benefit is at least equal to the amount described in regulation 11.

10   Transfer of a person's pension credit rights without consent

(1) For the purposes of section 101D(4) of the 1993 Act (form of pension credit benefit and its alternatives), the trustees or managers of an occupational pension scheme may provide for a person's pension credit rights under that scheme to be transferred to another occupational pension scheme without that person's consent where the conditions set out in paragraphs (2) and either (3) or (7), as the case may be, are satisfied.

(2) The condition set out in this paragraph is that the trustees or managers of the transferring scheme consider that, in the circumstances, it is reasonable for the transfer to be made without the person's consent and the requirements of paragraph (5) are satisfied.

(3) The condition set out in this paragraph is that, subject to paragraph (6), a relevant actuary certifies to the trustees or managers of the transferring scheme that—

    (a) the transfer credits to be acquired for each person with pension credit rights under the receiving scheme are, broadly, no less favourable than the rights to be transferred; and

    (b) where it is the established custom for discretionary benefits or increases in benefits to be awarded under the transferring scheme, there is good cause to believe that the award of discretionary benefits or increases in benefits under the receiving scheme will (making allowance for any amount by which transfer credits under the receiving scheme are more favourable than the rights to be transferred) be broadly no less favourable.

(4) For the purpose of paragraph (3)(b), the relevant actuary shall, in considering whether there is good cause, have regard to all the circumstances of the case and in particular—

    (a) to any established custom of the receiving scheme with regard to the provision of discretionary benefits or increases in benefits; and

    (b) to any announcements made with regard to the provision of such benefits under the receiving scheme.

(5) The requirements of this paragraph are that all the conditions set out in sub-paragraphs (a) and (b) are satisfied, namely—

    (a) the trustees or managers of the scheme give the person with pension credit rights at least 30 days' written notice of their intention to transfer those rights to another occupational pension scheme unless the person with those rights exercises a right to give a transfer notice under section 101F of the 1993 Act (the first mentioned notice being sent to that person at his last known address or delivered to that person personally); and

    (b) when the trustees or managers of the scheme agree with the trustees or managers of the receiving scheme to transfer those rights, there is no outstanding transfer notice by the person with pension credit rights under section 101F of the 1993 Act.

(6) Paragraph (3) does not apply where the whole of the pension credit rights to be transferred are derived from rights accrued in a money purchase scheme.

(7) The condition set out in this paragraph is that any scheme rule which allows the transfer of a person's pension credit rights derived from rights accrued in a money purchase scheme without the consent of the person with those rights must require the trustees or managers of the scheme to be reasonably satisfied that the amount transferred is at least equal to the amount described in regulation 11.

(8) In this regulation—

'relevant actuary' means—

(a) where the transferring scheme is a scheme for which an actuary is required under section 47 of the 1995 Act (professional advisers) to be appointed, the individual for the time being appointed in accordance with subsection (1) of that section as actuary for that scheme;

(b) in any other case, a Fellow of the Institute of Actuaries, a Fellow of the Faculty of Actuaries,[34] or a person with other actuarial qualifications who is approved by the Secretary of State, at the request of the trustees or managers of the scheme, as being a proper person to act for the purposes of this regulation in connection with the scheme.

(9) Where the pension credit rights which are to be transferred in accordance with this regulation are or include safeguarded rights, the pension credit rights must be transferred to either a salary related contracted-out scheme or a money purchase contracted-out scheme.

11   Value of alternatives to pension credit benefit

The amount referred to in regulations 7, 8 and 9 is an amount equal to the value of the benefits (or, where the alternative is provided by way of partial substitute for pension credit benefit, the relevant part of the benefits) that have accured to or in respect of the person entitled to the benefit.

12   Discharge of liability where pension credit benefit or alternative benefits are secured by insurance policies or annuity contracts

The requirements which must be met for the purposes of section 101E(1)(c) of the 1993 Act (discharge of liability where pension credit or alternative benefits are secured by insurance policies or annuity contracts) are those described in regulations 13 and 14.

13   Conditions on which pension credit benefit secured by insurance policies and annuity contracts may be commuted

Pension credit benefit secured by an insurance policy or an annuity contract may be commuted if it satisfies the requirements of regulation 3 or 4 (commutation of the whole of pension credit benefit, or commutation of part of pension credit benefit).

14   Other requirements applying to insurance policies and annuity contracts

The requirements described in this regulation are—

(a) that the insurance company with which the insurance policy is taken out or the annuity contract is entered into assumes an obligation to the person entitled to the benefit or to the trustees of a trust for the benefit of the person entitled to the benefit and, if appropriate, dependants of his, to pay the benefits secured by that policy or contract to him or, as the case may be, to dependants of his, or to the trustees of such a trust; and

(b) that the insurance policy or annuity contract contains, or is endorsed with, terms so as to provide for any increase, which would have been applicable as a consequence of section 40 of the 1999 Act (indexation: other pension schemes) had the discharge of liability of the pension credit benefit, or its alternative, not taken place, to apply to the benefits which have become secured or been replaced by that policy or contract.

15   Further conditions on which liability may be discharged

(1) Subsection (1)(b) of section 101E of the 1993 Act (transactions with the consent of the person entitled to the benefit which discharge liability where pension credit or alternative benefits secured by insurance policies or annuity contracts) shall not apply in the circumstances described in paragraph (2), (3), (4) or (5).

(2) The circumstances described in this paragraph are that—

(a) the person entitled to the benefit is dead and the benefit is payable to a person other than his widow or widower; and

(b) the arrangement for securing the pension credit benefit or its alternative was made at the request of the person entitled to it.

(3) The circumstances described in this paragraph are that the benefit is provided as an alternative to pension credit benefit by virtue of regulation 8(4) (bought out benefits without consent).

(4) The circumstances described in this paragraph are that—

(a) the scheme is being wound up;

(b) sections 73 and 74 of the 1995 Act[35] (preferential liabilities on winding up, and discharge of liabilities by insurance, etc.) and the Occupational Pension Schemes (Winding Up) Regulations 1996[36] do not apply;

(c) the person entitled to the benefit is able to assign or surrender the insurance policy or the annuity contract; and

(1) the condition set out in section 101E(1)(a) of the 1993 Act is satisfied.

(5) The circumstances described in this paragraph are that—

(a) the trustees or managers of the scheme consider that, in the circumstances, it is reasonable for the scheme to provide the alternative without the consent of the person entitled to the benefit;

(b) the trustees or managers of the scheme give the person entitled to the benefit at least 30 days' written notice of their intention to take out the insurance policy or enter into the annuity contract, unless the person entitled to the benefit exercises a right to give a transfer notice under section 101F of the 1993 Act (power to give transfer notice) (the first mentioned notice being sent to that person at his last known address or delivered to that person personally); and

(c) when the trustees or managers of the scheme agree with the insurance company to take out the insurance policy or enter into the annuity contract, there is no outstanding transfer notice given by the person entitled to the benefit under section 101F of the 1993 Act.

(6) The payment made to the insurance company in the circumstances described in paragraph (5) must be at least an amount equal to the value of the pension credit benefit which has accrued to the person entitled to the benefit at the date the payment is made.

PART III

TRANSFER VALUES

16 Transfer payments in respect of safeguarded rights—general

(1) A transfer of liability from—

  (a) a salary related contracted-out scheme (or a scheme which has ceased to be a salary related contracted-out scheme); or

  (b) a money purchase contracted-out scheme or an appropriate scheme (or a scheme which has ceased to be a money purchase contracted-out scheme or an appropriate scheme),

may give effect to the safeguarded rights of a person entitled to a pension credit by the making of a transfer payment to a scheme referred to in paragraph (2).

(2) A transfer payment in respect of safeguarded rights may be made to—

  (a) an appropriate scheme;

  (b) a money purchase contracted-out scheme;

  (c) a salary related contracted-out scheme;

  (d) a personal pension scheme which has ceased to be an appropriate scheme; or

  (e) an occupational pension scheme which has ceased to be contracted-out,

in accordance with regulations 17 to 19 and no such transfer may be made otherwise.

(3) In this regulation and in regulations 17 to 19 a 'transfer payment' means a transfer payment such as is described in this regulation.

17 Transfer payments to money purchase contracted-out schemes and appropriate schemes

A transfer of any liability in respect of safeguarded rights may be made to a money purchase contracted-out scheme or an appropriate scheme if—

  (a) the person with pension credit rights consents;

  (b) the transfer payment (or, if it forms part of a larger payment giving effect to both safeguarded and other rights, that part of it which gives effect to safeguarded rights) is of an amount at least equal to the cash equivalent of the safeguarded rights to which effect is being given, as calculated and verified in a manner consistent with regulations 3 to 7 of the Pension Sharing (Valuation) Regulations 2000[37] (calculation, verification and reduction of cash equivalents);

  (c) in the case of a transfer payment to a money purchase contracted-out scheme, the person with pension credit rights is employed by an employer who is a contributor to the receiving scheme; and

  (d) the transfer payment is applied so as to provide money purchase benefits under the receiving scheme for or in respect of the person with pension credit rights in respect of safeguarded rights.

18 Transfer payments to salary related contracted-out schemes

A transfer of any liability in respect of safeguarded rights may be made to a salary related contracted-out scheme if—

  (a) the person with pension credit rights consents;

  (b) the transfer payment (or, if it forms part of a larger payment giving effect to both safeguarded and other rights, that part of it which gives effect to safeguarded rights) is of an amount at least equal to the cash equivalent of the safeguarded rights to which effect is being given, as calculated and verified in a manner consistent with regulations 3 to 7 of the Pension Sharing (Valuation) Regulations 2000;

(c) the person with pension credit rights is employed by an employer who is a contributor to the receiving scheme; and

(d) the transfer payment is applied to provide rights for the person with pension credit rights which, had they accrued in the receiving scheme, would be provided in accordance with the rules of the receiving scheme relating to earners who are in employment which is contracted-out in relation to the receiving scheme or have been in employment which was so contracted-out on or after the principal appointed day.

19 Transfer payments to overseas schemes or overseas arrangements

A transfer of any liability in respect of safeguarded rights may be made to an overseas scheme or an overseas arrangement if—

(a) the person with pension credit rights consents;

(b) the trustees or managers of the transferring scheme have taken reasonable steps to satisfy themselves that the person with pension credit rights has emigrated on a permanent basis and, where the receiving scheme is an occupational pension scheme, that he has entered employment to which the receiving scheme applies;

(c) the transfer payment (or, if it forms part of a larger payment giving effect to both safeguarded and other rights, that part which gives effect to safeguarded rights) is of an amount at least equal to the cash equivalent of the safeguarded rights to which effect is being given, as calculated and verified in a manner consistent with regulations 3 to 7 of the Pension Sharing (Valuation) Regulations 2000;

(d) the person with pension credit rights has acknowledged that he accepts that the scheme or arrangement to which the transfer payment is to be made may not be regulated in any way by the law of the United Kingdom and that as a consequence there may be no obligation under that law on the receiving scheme or arrangement or its trustees or managers to provide any particular value or benefit in return for the transfer payment; and

(e) the trustees or managers of the transferring scheme have taken reasonable steps to satisfy themselves that the person with pension credit rights has received a statement from the receiving scheme or arrangement showing the benefits to be awarded in respect of the transfer payment and the conditions (if any) on which these could be forfeited or withheld.

20 Requirements to be met by annuities

Subject to regulation 19, the prescribed requirements referred to in section 101F(2)(b) of the 1993 Act (cash equivalent to be used for purchasing annuities) are those specified in regulation 15(2) to (7) of the Pension Sharing (Implementation and Discharge of Liability) Regulations 2000[38] (disqualification as a destination for pension credit—annuity contracts and insurance policies).

21 Requirements of other pension arrangements

(1) The prescribed requirements referred to in section 101F(2)(c) and (3)(b) of the 1993 Act (cash equivalent of pension credit benefit to be used to subscribe to other

pension arrangements which satisfy prescribed requirements) are that the pension arrangement to which it is proposed to subscribe—

 (a) is an overseas arrangement;

 (b) if it is an overseas arrangement and the cash equivalent is or includes the cash equivalent of safeguarded rights, the arrangement is one to which a transfer payment in respect of such rights may be made in accordance with regulation 6 or 9 of the Pension Sharing (Safeguarded Rights) Regulations 2000 (ways of giving effect to safeguarded rights—money purchase schemes, and ways of giving effect to safeguarded rights—salary related schemes); or

 (c) if the scheme from which rights are transferred is of a kind described in any of sub-paragraphs (a) to (e) of paragraph (2), satisfies the requirements of the Inland Revenue.

(2) The kinds of scheme mentioned in paragraph (1)(c) are—

 (a) purposes of Chapter I of Part XIV of the Taxes Act (pension schemes, social security benefits, life annuities etc: retirement benefit schemes);

 (b) a scheme which is being considered for approval by the Inland Revenue for the purposes of Chapter I of Part XIV of the Taxes Act;

 (c) a relevant statutory scheme as defined in section 611A(1)[39] (definition of relevant statutory scheme) of the Taxes Act;

 (d) of the Taxes Act (superannuation funds approved before 6th April 1980) applies; and

 (e) a scheme which is approved by the Inland Revenue under Chapter IV of Part XIV of the Taxes Act.

(3) The prescribed circumstances referred to in section 101F(2)(c) and (3)(b) of the 1993 Act are those referred to in paragraph (1)(b) and (c).

22 Requirements to be met by an eligible scheme

(1) The prescribed requirements referred to in section 101F(6)(b) of the 1993 Act (references to an eligible scheme which satisfies the prescribed requirements) are that—

 (a) if the eligible member's cash equivalent (or any portion of it to be used under section 101F(2) or (3) of the 1993 Act) is or includes the cash equivalent of safeguarded rights, then the eligible scheme under whose rules rights are acquired is one—

  (i) to which those safeguarded rights may be transferred; or

  (ii) to which a transfer payment in respect of those safeguarded rights may be made,

 in accordance with regulations 16 to 19 of these Regulations (transfers of safeguarded rights) and regulation 9(5)(c) of the Pension Sharing (Safeguarded Rights) Regulations 2000;[40] and

 (b) if the scheme from which pension credit rights are transferred or from which a transfer payment of such rights is made is of a kind described in any of sub-paragraphs (a) to (e) of paragraph (2) of regulation 21, the eligible scheme to which pension credit rights are transferred or to which a transfer payment in respect of those rights is made is of a kind described in paragraph (2)(a), (c) or (e) of regulation 21.

(2) In this regulation 'eligible scheme' means a scheme described in section 101F(6) of the 1993 Act.

23   Statements of entitlement

(1) Subject to paragraph (2), for the purposes of subsection (2)(a) of section 101H of the 1993 Act (salary related schemes: statements of entitlement), the prescribed period beginning with the date of the eligible member's application under that section for a statement of entitlement is a period of 3 months.

(2) Where the trustees or managers of the scheme are for reasons beyond their control unable within the period referred to in paragraph (1) to obtain the information required to calculate the cash equivalent, the prescribed period is such longer period as they may reasonably require as a result of that inability, provided that such longer period does not exceed 6 months beginning with the date of the eligible member's application.

(3) For the purposes of subsection (2)(b) of section 101H of the 1993 Act, the prescribed period is the period of 10 days (excluding Saturdays, Sundays, Christmas Day, New Year's Day and Good Friday) ending with the date on which the statement of entitlement is provided to the eligible member.

(4) For the purposes of subsection (3) of section 101H of the 1993 Act, an eligible member who has made an application under section 101H(1) of the 1993 Act for a statement of entitlement may not, within a period of 12 months beginning on the date of that application, make any further such application unless the rules of the scheme provide otherwise or the trustees or managers allow him to do so.

24   Manner of calculation and verification of cash equivalents

(1) Except in a case to which, or to the extent to which, paragraph (2) or (5) applies, cash equivalents are to be calculated and verified in such manner as may be approved in particular cases by the scheme actuary or, in relation to a scheme to which section 47(1)(b) of the 1995 Act does not apply, by—

 (a) a Fellow of the Institute of Actuaries;

 (b) a Fellow of the Faculty of Actuaries; or

 (c) a person with other actuarial qualifications who is approved by the Secretary of State, at the request of the trustees or managers of the scheme in question, as being a proper person to act for the purposes of these Regulations in connection with that scheme,

and, subject to paragraph (2), in this regulation, 'actuary' means the scheme actuary or, in relation to a scheme to which section 47(1)(b) of the 1995 Act does not apply, the actuary referred to in sub-paragraph (a), (b) or (c) of this paragraph.

(2) Where the eligible member in respect of whom a cash equivalent is to be calculated and verified is an eligible member of an occupational pension scheme having particulars from time to time set out in regulations made under section 7 of the Superannuation Act 1972[41] (superannuation of persons employed in local government service, etc.), that cash equivalent shall be calculated and verified in such manner as may be approved by the Government Actuary or by an actuary authorised by the Government Actuary to act on his behalf for that purpose and in such a case 'actuary' in this regulation means the Government Actuary or the actuary so authorised.

(3) Except in a case to which paragraph (5) applies, cash equivalents are to be calculated and verified by adopting methods and making assumptions which—

 (a) if not determined by the trustees or managers of the scheme in question, are notified to them by the actuary; and

 (b) are certified by the actuary to the trustees or managers of the scheme—

  (i) as being consistent with the requirements of Chapter II of Part IVA of the 1993 Act;

(ii) as being consistent with 'Retirement Benefit Schemes—Transfer Values (GN11)' published by the Institute of Actuaries and the Faculty of Actuaries[42] and current on the valuation date;

(iii) as being consistent with the methods adopted and assumptions made, on the valuation date, in calculating the benefits to which entitlement arises under the rules of the scheme in question for a person who is acquiring transfer credits including transfer credits in respect of pension credit rights under those rules; and

(iv) in the case of a scheme to which section 56 of the 1995 Act (minimum funding requirement) applies, as providing as a minimum an amount consistent with the methods and assumptions adopted in calculating, for the purposes of section 57 of that Act (valuation and certification of assets and liabilities), the liabilities mentioned in paragraphs (a), (c)(i) and (d) of section 73(3) of that Act, subject, in any case where the cash equivalent calculation is made on an individual and not a collective basis, to any adjustments which are appropriate to take account of that fact.

(4) If, by virtue of Schedule 5 of the Occupational Pension Schemes (Minimum Funding Requirement and Actuarial Valuations) Regulations 1996[43] (modifications), section 56 of the 1995 Act applies to a section of a scheme as if that section were a separate scheme, paragraph (3)(b)(iv) shall apply as if that section were a separate scheme and as if the reference therein to a scheme were accordingly a reference to that section.

(5) Where a cash equivalent or any portion of a cash equivalent relates to money purchase benefits which do not fall to be valued in a manner which involves making estimates of the value of benefits, then that cash equivalent or that portion shall be calculated and verified in such manner as may be approved in a particular case by the trustees or managers of the scheme and in accordance with methods consistent with the requirements of Chapter IV of Part IV of the 1993 Act (protection for early leavers—transfer values) and Chapter II of Part IVA of the 1993 Act.

25   Time period for notification to the Regulatory Authority of failure by the trustees or managers of an occupational pension scheme to comply with a transfer notice

The period prescribed for the purpose of section 101J(4)(a) of the 1993 Act (time for compliance with transfer notice) is the period of 21 days beginning with the day immediately following the end of the period for compliance specified in section 101J(1) of that Act.

26   Extension of time limits for payment of cash equivalents

The Regulatory Authority may grant an extension of the period mentioned in section 101J(1)(a) of the 1993 Act to the trustees or managers of an occupational pension scheme if the trustees or managers have within that period applied to the Regulatory Authority for an extension and—

(a) the Regulatory Authority is satisfied that—

(i) the scheme is being wound up or is about to be wound up;

(ii) the scheme is ceasing to be a contracted-out scheme;

(iii) the interests of the members of the scheme generally will be prejudiced if the trustees or managers do what is needed to carry out what is required within that period;

(iv) the eligible member has not taken all such steps as the trustees or managers can reasonably expect in order to satisfy them of any matter which falls to be established before they can properly carry out what the eligible member requires;

(v) the trustees or managers have not been provided with such information as they reasonably require properly to carry out what the eligible member requires; or

(vi) the eligible member's statement of entitlement has been reduced or increased under regulation 27 or 28 or the eligible member has disputed the amount of the cash equivalent;

(b) the provisions of section 53 of the 1993 Act[44] (supervision: former contracted-out schemes) apply; or

(2) an application has been made for an extension on one or more of the grounds specified in paragraph (a) or (b) and the Regulatory Authority's consideration of the application cannot be completed before the end of the period mentioned in section 101J(1)(a) of the 1993 Act.

27 Increases and reductions of cash equivalents before a statement of entitlement has been sent to the eligible member

(1) A cash equivalent referred to in section 101H of the 1993 Act shall not be reduced under this regulation once a statement of the value of that cash equivalent has been sent to the eligible member and a direction referred to in paragraph (2) shall not affect such a cash equivalent unless that direction is made before that cash equivalent.

(2) Where it is the established custom for additional benefits to be awarded from the scheme at the discretion of the trustees or managers or the employer, the cash equivalent shall, unless the trustees or managers have given a direction that cash equivalents shall not take account of such benefits, take account of any such additional benefits as will accrue to the eligible member in question if the custom continues unaltered.

(3) The trustees or managers shall not make a direction such as is mentioned in paragraph (2) unless, within 3 months before making the direction, they have consulted the actuary and have obtained the actuary's written report on the implications for the state of funding of the scheme of making such a direction, including the actuary's advice as to whether or not in the actuary's opinion there would be any adverse implications for the funding of the scheme should the trustees or managers not make such a direction.

(4) In the case of a scheme to which section 56 of the 1995 Act applies, each respective part of the cash equivalent which relates to liabilities referred to in paragraph (a), (c)(i) or (d) of section 73(3) of the 1995 Act may be reduced by the percentage which is the difference between—

(a) 100 per cent; and

(b) the percentage of the liabilities mentioned in the relevant paragraph of section 73(3) which the actuarial valuation shows the scheme assets as being sufficient to satisfy,

where the actuarial valuation is the latest actuarial valuation obtained in accordance with section 57 of the 1995 Act prior to the date by reference to which the cash equivalent is determined under section 101F(4) of the 1993 Act (power to give transfer notice).

(5) If, by virtue of Schedule 5 to the Occupational Pension Schemes (Minimum Funding Requirement and Actuarial Valuations) Regulations 1996, section 56 of the 1995 Act applies to a section of a scheme as if that section were a separate

scheme, paragraph (4) shall apply as if that section were a separate scheme and as if the reference therein to a scheme were accordingly a reference to that section.

(6)   Where an eligible member's cash equivalent is to be used for acquiring transfer credits under the rules of another scheme or for acquiring rights under the rules of a personal pension scheme and the receiving scheme has undertaken to provide benefits at least equal in value to the benefits represented by that cash equivalent on payment of a lesser sum, including nil, then that cash equivalent shall be reduced to that lesser sum.

(7)   Where all or any of an eligible member's benefits have been appropriately secured by a transaction to which section 19 of the 1993 Act (discharge of liability of guaranteed minimum pensions secured by insurance policies or annuity contracts) applies, the cash equivalent in respect of those benefits shall be reduced to nil.

(8)   For the purposes of paragraph (7), 'appropriately secured' means the same as in section 19 of the 1993 Act except that an insurance policy or annuity contract which is taken out or entered into with an authorised friendly society (referred to in regulation 5(3)(b) of these Regulations), but which otherwise satisfies the conditions for being appropriate for the purposes of section 19, is to be treated as if it were appropriate for the purposes of that section provided the terms of such policy or contract are not capable of being amended, revoked or rescinded.

(9)   Where a scheme has (in the case of a cash equivalent mentioned in section 101H of the 1993 Act, before the valuation date) begun to be wound up, a cash equivalent may be reduced to the extent necessary for the scheme to comply with section 73 of the 1995 Act and the Occupational Pension Schemes (Winding Up) Regulations 1996.[45]

(10)   If, by virtue of regulations made under section 73 of the 1995 Act, section 73 of that Act applies to a section of a scheme as if that section were a separate scheme, paragraph (9) shall apply as if that section were a separate scheme and as if the references therein to a scheme were accordingly references to that section.

(11)   Where all or any of the benefits to which a cash equivalent relates have been surrendered, commuted or forfeited before the date on which the trustees or managers do what is needed to carry out what the eligible member requires, the cash equivalent of the benefits so surrendered, commuted or forfeited shall be reduced to nil.

(12)   In a case where two or more of the paragraphs of this regulation fall to be applied to a calculation, they shall be applied in the order in which they occur in this regulation.

(13)   In this regulation 'actuary' has the meaning given by regulation 24.

28   Increases and reductions of cash equivalents once the statement of entitlement has been sent to the eligible member

(1)   This regulation applies to a cash equivalent when a statement of entitlement has been sent to an eligible member of a salary related scheme by the trustees or managers of that scheme.

(2)   Where all or any of the benefits to which the cash equivalent relates have been surrendered, commuted or forfeited before the date on which the trustees or managers do what is needed to carry out what the eligible member requires, that part of the cash equivalent which relates to the benefits so surrendered, commuted or forfeited shall be reduced to nil.

(3)   Where a scheme has on or after the valuation date begun to be wound up, a cash equivalent may be reduced to the extent necessary for the scheme to comply with sections 73 and 74 of the 1995 Act and the Occupational Pension Schemes (Winding Up) Regulations 1996.

(4)   If, by virtue of the Occupational Pension Schemes (Winding Up) Regulations 1996, section 73 of the 1995 Act applies to a section of a scheme as if that section were

a separate scheme, paragraph (3) shall apply as if that section were a separate scheme and as if the references therein to a scheme were accordingly references to that section.

(5) If an eligible member's cash equivalent falls short of or exceeds the amount which it would have been had it been calculated in accordance with Chapter II of Part IVA of the 1993 Act and these Regulations it shall be increased or reduced to that amount.

(6) In a case where two or more of the paragraphs of this regulation fall to be applied to a calculation, they shall be applied in the order in which they occur in this regulation except that where paragraph (5) falls to be applied it shall be applied as at the date on which it is established that the cash equivalent falls short of or exceeds the proper amount.

29 Increases of cash equivalents on late payment

(1) Subject to paragraph (2), if the trustees or managers of a scheme, having received an application under section 101F(1) of the 1993 Act (power to give transfer notice), fail to comply with the transfer notice within 6 months of the valuation date, the eligible member's cash equivalent, as calculated in accordance with regulations 24, 27 and 28, shall be increased by the amount, if any, by which that cash equivalent falls short of what it would have been if the valuation date had been the date on which the trustees or managers carry out what the eligible member requires.

(2) If the trustees or managers of a scheme, having received an application under section 101H of the 1993 Act, fail without reasonable excuse to do what is needed to carry out what the eligible member requires within 6 months of the valuation date, the eligible member's cash equivalent, as calculated in accordance with regulations 24, 27 and 28, shall be increased by—

(a) the interest on that cash equivalent calculated on a daily basis over the period from the valuation date to the date on which the trustees or managers carry out what the eligible member requires, at an annual rate of one per cent. above base rate; or, if it is greater,

(b) the amount, if any, by which that cash equivalent falls short of what it would have been if the valuation date had been the date on which the trustees or managers carry out what the eligible member requires.

30 Personal pension schemes: increases and reductions of cash equivalents

(1) If the whole or any part of the cash equivalent of the pension credit benefit under section 101F of the 1993 Act has been surrendered, commuted or forfeited before the date on which the trustees or managers comply with the transfer notice, the cash equivalent shall be reduced in proportion to the reduction in the total value of the benefits.

(2) If the trustees or managers of a personal pension scheme, having received a transfer notice under section 101F(1) of the 1993 Act, fail without reasonable excuse to comply with the transfer notice within 6 months of the valuation date, the eligible member's cash equivalent shall be increased by—

(a) the interest on that cash equivalent, calculated on a daily basis over the period from the date the notice is given until the date on which the trustees or managers carry out what the eligible member requires, at the same rate as that payable for the time being on judgment debts by virtue of section 17 of the Judgments Act 1838;[46] or, if it is greater,

(b) the amount, if any, by which that cash equivalent falls short of what it would have been if the date on which the transfer notice is given had been the date on which the trustees or managers comply with it.

31   Civil Penalties

Where section 10 of the 1995 Act[47] (civil penalties) applies by virtue of section 101H(4) or section 101J(4)(b) of the 1993 Act, the maximum amount for the purposes of section 10(1) of the 1995 Act shall be £1,000 in the case of an individual, and £10,000 in any other case.

PART IV
INDEXATION

32   Increase of relevant pension

(1) Subject to regulations 33 and 34, a relevant pension shall be increased each year by whichever is the lesser of—

   (a) either—

      (i)   the appropriate percentage; or

      (ii) where the rules of an occupational pension scheme require the relevant pension to be increased at intervals of not more than 12 months, the relevant percentage; or

   (b) 5 per cent.

(2) In this regulation—

   'appropriate percentage' means the revaluation percentage for the latest revaluation period specified in the order under paragraph 2 of Schedule 3 to the 1993 Act (revaluation of accrued pension benefits) which is in force at the time of the increase (expressions used in this definition having the same meaning as in that paragraph);

   'relevant percentage' means the lesser of—

   (a) the percentage increase in the retail prices index for the reference period, being a period determined, in relation to each periodic increase, under the rules of the scheme; or

   (b) the percentage for that period which corresponds to 5 per cent. per annum.

33   Annual increase in rate of pension: qualifying occupational and personal pension schemes

(1) The first increase required by regulation 32 in the rate of a relevant pension must take effect not later than the first anniversary of the date on which the pension is first paid; and subsequent increases must take effect at intervals of not more than 12 months.

(2) Where the first such increase takes effect on a date when the pension has been in payment for a period of less than 12 months, the increase must be of an amount at least equal to one twelfth of the amount of the increase so required (apart from this paragraph) for each complete month in that period.

34   Effect of increase above the statutory requirement: qualifying occupational pension schemes

(1) Where in any tax year the trustees or managers of a qualifying occupational pension scheme make an increase in a member's pension which is a relevant pension, not being an increase required by regulation 32, they may deduct the amount of the increase from any increase which but for this paragraph, they would be required to make under that regulation in the next tax year.

(2)   Where in any tax year the trustees or managers of such a scheme make an increase in a member's pension which is a relevant pension, and part of the increase is not required by regulation 32, they may deduct that part of the increase from any increase which, but for this paragraph, they would be required to make under that regulation in the next tax year.

(3)   Where by virtue of paragraph (1) or (2) any such pension is not required to be increased in pursuance of regulation 32, or not by the full amount that it otherwise would be, its amount shall be calculated for any purposes as if it had been increased in pursuance of regulation 32 or, as the case may be, by that full amount.

35   Definition of eligible pension credit rights

For the purposes of section 40(3) of the 1999 Act, pension credit rights are eligible if they fall within the descriptions in paragraph (a) or (b)—

  (a)   rights which are derived from—

    (i)   rights attributable to pensionable service on or after 6th April 1997 (excluding rights derived from additional voluntary contributions); or

    (ii)   in the case of money purchase benefits, rights attributable to payments in respect of employment on or after 6th April 1997 (excluding rights derived from additional voluntary contributions),

    of the member whose pension rights were the subject of a pension sharing order or provision; or

  (b)   safeguarded rights.

Signed by authority of the Secretary of State for Social Security.

Jeff Rooker

Minister of State, Department of Social Security

13th April 2000

Explanatory note

(This note is not part of the Regulations)

These Regulations provide for the requirements relating to, and the indexation of, pension credit benefit.

Part I and regulation 1 provide for citation, commencement and interpretation of the Regulations.

Regulation 2 specifies the classes of occupational pension scheme which are not salary related.

Part II sets out requirements relating to pension credit benefit under occupational pension schemes.

Regulations 3 and 4 specify the circumstances in which pension credit benefit may be commuted.

Regulation 5 sets out how pension credit benefit may be secured.

Regulations 6 to 9 set out the alternatives to pension credit benefit which a scheme may provide.

Regulation 10 provides for the circumstances in which a person's pension credit rights may be transferred from one occupational pension scheme to another without that person's consent.

Regulation 11 specifies what the value of the alternatives to pension credit benefit must be.

Regulations 12 to 14 set out the requirements to be met where pension credit benefit or alternatives to pension credit benefit are secured by insurance policies or annuity contracts.

Regulation 15 describes further conditions on which liability for pension credit benefit or alternatives to pension credit benefit may be discharged.

Part III contains regulations 16 to 31 which deal with transfer values in respect of pension credit benefit.

Regulations 16 to 19 specify the circumstances in which transfer payments may be made in respect of safeguarded rights.

Regulations 20 to 22 describe requirements to be met by annuities, other pension arrangements, and eligible schemes in respect of transfer values.

Regulation 23 sets out the provisions relating to statements of entitlement.

Regulations 24 and 27 to 30 provide how cash equivalents are to be calculated and the circumstances in which they can be increased or reduced.

Regulation 25 specifies the period within which the trustees or managers of an occupational pension scheme are to notify the Occupational Pensions Regulatory Authority (OPRA) should they fail to comply with a transfer notice within the period prescribed by section 101J(1) of the Pension Schemes Act 1993.

Regulation 26 provides for OPRA to extend the statutory time limits for payment of cash equivalents on the application of the trustees or managers of an occupational pension scheme.

Regulation 31 specifies the maximum penalties which OPRA may impose in any case where OPRA is satisfied that a trustee or manager has not taken all reasonable steps to ensure that the obligation to provide the member with a statement of entitlement, or where OPRA is informed that the trustees or managers have failed to comply with a transfer notice within the period specified in section 101J(1) of the Pension Schemes Act 1993, is fulfilled.

Part IV contains regulations 32 to 35. Regulations 32 to 34 provide for how a pension, to which section 40(2) of the Welfare Reform and Pensions Act 1999 applies, is to be increased. Regulation 35 defines eligible pension credit rights.

An assessment of the cost to business of the provisions of the Welfare Reform and Pensions Act 1999, including these Regulations, is detailed in the Regulatory Impact Assessment for that Act. A copy of this Assessment has been placed in the libraries of both Houses of Parliament. Copies can be obtained by post from the Department of Social Security, Pensions on Divorce, 3rd Floor, The Adelphi, 1–11 John Adam Street, London WC2N 6HT.

Notes

[1] Section 181(1) is cited because of the meaning there given to 'prescribed' and 'regulations'.

[2] 1993 c. 48. Sections 101C, 101D, 101E, 101F, 101H, 101I, 101J, 101L, 101P and 101Q are inserted by section 37 of the Welfare Reform and Pensions Act 1999 (c. 30).

[3] Section 124(1) is cited because of the meaning there given to 'prescribed' and 'regulations'.

[4] 1995 c. 26.

[5] 1999 c. 30.

[6] See section 120(1) of the Pensions Act 1995 and section 83(11) of the Welfare Reform and Pensions Act 1999.

[7] 1988 c. 1.

[8] Section 68A is inserted by section 36 of the Welfare Reform and Pensions Act 1999.

[9]   Section 101P is inserted by section 37 of the Welfare Reform and Pensions Act 1999.

[10] Section 181 was amended by the 1995 Act, the Industrial Tribunals Act 1996 (c.17) and is amended by the Welfare Reform and Pensions Act 1999.

[11]   Section 101B is inserted by section 37 of the Welfare Reform and Pensions Act 1999.

[12]   SI 1996/1462 as amended by SI 1997/786.

[13]   The definition of 'overseas scheme' was amended by SI 1997/786.

[14]   Section 124 is amended by paragraph 61 of Schedule 12 to the Welfare Reform and Pensions Act 1999.

[15]   The definition of 'personal pension scheme' is amended by paragraph 3(1)(a) of Schedule 2 to the Welfare Reform and Pensions Act 1999.

[16]   Section 7(2B) was inserted by section 136(1) of the Pensions Act 1995.

[17]   1987 c. 22.

[18]   Section 7 was amended by section 23(1) of, and paragraphs 1 and 4 of Schedule 5 to, the Bank of England Act 1998.

[19]   1985 c. 6. Section 736 was substituted by section 144(1) of the Companies Act 1989 (c. 40).

[20]   Section 68A is inserted by section 36 of the Welfare Reform and Pensions Act 1999.

[21]   Section 8(1)(a)(i) was substituted by section 136(2) of the Pensions Act 1995.

[22]   Section 101B is inserted by section 37 of the Welfare Reform and Pensions Act 1999.

[23]   Part IVA is inserted by section 37 of the Welfare Reform and Pensions Act 1999.

[24]   SI 2000/1055.

[25]   Section 590 was amended by section 35 of, and paragraphs 1, and 18(1), (2) of Part I of Schedule 3 to, the Finance Act 1988 (c. 39), sections 75 and 187(1) of, and paragraphs 1, 3(1) to (4), and 18(2) and (3) of Part I of Schedule 6, and Part IV of Schedule 17 to, the Finance Act 1989 (c. 26), and by sections 34, 36(2), (3), and 123 of, and Part V of Schedule 19 to, the Finance Act 1991 (c. 31).

[26]   Section 591 was amended by section 146 and paragraphs 1 and 6 of Part I of Schedule 13 to, the Finance Act 1988, sections 107 and 258 of, and paragraph 12 of Part V of Schedule 26 to, the Finance Act 1994 (c. 9), and sections 59(1), (2), and 60(1) of the Finance Act 1995 (c. 4).

[27]   1982 c. 50, as amended by the European Economic Area Act 1993 (c. 51).

[28]   Section 1 was amended by SI 1990/1159.

[29]   1992 c. 40. Section 32 was amended by SI 1994/1984.

[30]   Section 2 was amended by regulation 2(a) of SI 1987/2130, section 300(2) of, and paragraph 31 of Schedule 2 to, the Trade Union and Labour Relations (Consolidation) Act 1992 (c. 52), regulation 4(2) of SI 1994/1696 and regulation 3(1) of SI 1994/3132.

[31]   There are amendments to section 96(1) which are not relevant to these Regulations.

[32]   Schedule 2F was inserted by SI 1996/1696.

[33]   SI 1997/784.

[34]   The Institute of Actuaries is at Staple Inn Hall, High Holborn, London WC1V 7QJ. The Faculty of Actuaries is at Maclaurin House, 18 Dublin Street, Edinburgh EH1 3PP.

[35]   Section 73 was modified by regulation 3 of SI 1996/3126, as amended by SI 1999/3198. Section 73 is amended by section 38(1) of, and paragraph 55 of Schedule 12 to, the Welfare Reform and Pensions Act 1999. Section 74 is amended by paragraph 56 of Schedule 12 to that Act.

[36]   SI 1996/3126, amended by SI 1997/786, and SI 1999/3198.

[37]   SI 2000/1052.

[38]   SI 2000/1053.

[39]   Section 611A(1) was inserted by section 75 of, and paragraphs 1, 15 and 18(1) of Part I of Schedule 6 to, the Finance Act 1989.

[40]   SI 2000/1055.

[41]   1972 c. 11.

[42]   The publication 'Retirement Benefit Schemes—Transfer Values (GN11)' may be obtained from the Institute of Actuaries, Staple Inn Hall, High Holborn, London WC1V 7QJ and from the Faculty of Actuaries, Maclaurin House, 18 Dublin Street, Edinburgh EH1 3PP. The publication is also available on the following internet website: http://www.actuaries.org.uk.

[43]   SI 1996/1536. Schedule 5 was amended by SI 1997/786 and SI 1997/3038.

[44]   Section 53 was amended by paragraph 48 of Schedule 5 to the Pensions Act 1995 and by paragraphs 52 and 53 of Schedule 1 to the Social Security Contributions (Transfer of Functions, etc.) Act 1999.

[45]   SI 1996/3126, amended by SI 1997/786, and SI 1999/3198.

[46]   1 & 2 Vic. c. 110; the rate of interest was amended by SI 1993/564.

[47]   Section 10 is amended by paragraph 11 of Schedule 2 to the Welfare Reform and Pensions Act 1999.

The Pension Sharing (Safeguarded Rights) Regulations 2000

SI 2000/1055

Made 13 April 2000
Laid before Parliament 19 April 2000
Coming into force 1 December 2000

The Secretary of State for Social Security, in exercise of the powers conferred upon him by sections 68A(5), 68B, 68D, 181(1)[1] and 182(2) and (3) of the Pension Schemes Act 1993[2] and of all other powers enabling him in that behalf, after consulting such persons as he considered appropriate,[3] hereby makes the following Regulations:

1 Citation, commencement and interpretation

(1) These Regulations may be cited as the Pension Sharing (Safeguarded Rights) Regulations 2000 and shall come into force on 1st December 2000.

(2) In these Regulations—

'**the 1993 Act**' means the Pension Schemes Act 1993;

'**the 1999 Act**' means the Welfare Reform and Pensions Act 1999;

'**the Pension Credit Benefit Regulations**' means the Pension Sharing (Pension Credit Benefit) Regulations 2000;[4]

'**appropriate scheme**' and '**appropriate personal pension scheme**' shall be construed in accordance with section 9(5) of the 1993 Act;[5]

'**guaranteed minimum pension**' has the meaning given by section 8(2) of the 1993 Act;[6]

'**the Inland Revenue**' means the Commissioners of Inland Revenue;

'**interim arrangement**' means an interim arrangement which complies with section 28A of the 1993 Act,[7] and satisfies the conditions specified in regulation 6 of the Personal and Occupational Pension Schemes (Protected Rights) Regulations 1996;[8]

'**member**' means member of an occupational pension scheme or a personal pension scheme;

'**money purchase contracted-out scheme**' has the meaning given by section 8(1)(a)(ii) of the 1993 Act;

'**normal benefit age**' has the meaning given by section 101B of the 1993 Act;[9]

'**occupational pension scheme**' has the meaning given by section 1 of the 1993 Act;

'**personal pension scheme**' has the meaning given by section 1 of the 1993 Act;[10]

'**pension credit**' means a credit under section 29(1)(b) of the 1999 Act;

'**pension credit benefit**' has the meaning given by section 101P(1) of the 1993 Act;[11]

'**protected rights**' has the meaning given by section 10 of the 1993 Act;[12]

'**salary related contracted-out scheme**' has the meaning given by section 8(1)(a)(i) of the 1993 Act;[13]

'**section 9(2B) rights**' has the same meaning as in regulation 1(2) of the Occupational Pension Schemes (Contracting-out) Regulations 1996[14];

'**trustees or managers**' has the meaning given by section 46(1) of the 1999 Act.

2   Definition of contracted-out rights

For the purposes of section 68A(5) of the 1993 Act (safeguarded rights) 'contracted-out rights' are such rights, under or derived from an occupational pension scheme, or an appropriate personal pension scheme, as fall within the following categories—

(a)   entitlement to payment of, or accrued rights to, guaranteed minimum pensions;

(b)   protected rights;

(c)   section 9(2B) rights; or

(d)   any of the rights in sub-paragraph (a), (b) or (c) above which themselves derive from any of those rights which have been the subject of a transfer payment.

3   Requirements for schemes holding safeguarded rights

(1)   The trustees or managers of a money purchase contracted-out scheme, a salary related contracted-out scheme, or an appropriate scheme may hold safeguarded rights under the scheme, if the scheme has satisfied the requirements—

(a)   in these Regulations for the preservation of safeguarded rights under the scheme; or

(b)   in regulations 16 to 19 of the Pension Credit Benefit Regulations (transfers of safeguarded rights), for the transfer of safeguarded rights under the scheme.

(2)   The trustees or managers of an occupational pension scheme which has ceased to contract out or a personal pension scheme which has ceased to be an appropriate scheme may hold safeguarded rights under the scheme if the Inland Revenue has approved the arrangements made, or to be made, in relation to the scheme, or for the scheme's purposes, for the preservation or transfer of safeguarded rights under the scheme.

(3)   The arrangements referred to in paragraph (2) in respect of an occupational pension scheme shall not be approved by the Inland Revenue unless the conditions specified in paragraph (4) or (5) are satisfied.

(4)   To the extent that the arrangements concern the transfer or discharge of safeguarded rights, the Inland Revenue must be satisfied that such arrangements will be completed within 2 years of the date of cessation or such later date as the Inland Revenue may specify in relation to a particular case or class of case.

(5)   To the extent that the arrangements concern the preservation of safeguarded rights within the scheme, the scheme must comply with the requirements of sub-paragraph (a) or (b), as the case may be—

(a)   in the case of a salary related contracted-out scheme, the scheme must continue to satisfy the requirements of section 9(2) of the 1993 Act and any regulations which would apply to that scheme by reason of it being a scheme to which section 9(2) of that Act relates, other than section 9(2B)(a) of that Act (requirement to comply with section 12A of that Act) and any regulations which relate to compliance with that section, and the scheme must contain a protection rule within the meaning given to that expression in regulation 45(3A) of the Occupational Pension Schemes (Contracting-out) Regulations 1996[15] (approval of arrangements for schemes ceasing to be contracted-out);

    (b) in the case of a money purchase contracted-out scheme, the scheme must continue to satisfy the requirements of section 9(3) of that Act and any regulations which apply to the scheme by reason of it being a scheme to which section 9(3) of that Act relates.

4   Identification of safeguarded rights

Where the rules of an occupational pension scheme or appropriate scheme make such provision as is mentioned in section 68A(2) of the 1993 Act (safeguarded rights), the rules must require the trustees or managers to make provision for the identification of safeguarded rights.

5   Valuation of safeguarded rights in money purchase schemes

Where the rules of a money purchase contracted-out scheme, an appropriate scheme or a scheme which has ceased to be a contracted-out scheme or an appropriate scheme make such provision as is mentioned in section 68A(2) of the 1993 Act, the value of the safeguarded rights must be calculated in a manner no less favourable than that in which the value of—

    (a) any other rights which the member with safeguarded rights has under that scheme or, as the case may be, has accrued under that scheme up to the date that the scheme ceased to be a contracted-out scheme or an appropriate scheme; and

    (b) any protected rights under the scheme from which the member's safeguarded rights are derived are calculated.

6   Ways of giving effect to safeguarded rights—money purchase schemes

(1) The rules of a scheme must provide for effect to be given to the safeguarded rights of a member either—

    (a) by the provision of a pension or the purchase of an annuity which satisfies the requirements specified in—

        (i) paragraph (4) or (5), as the case may be; and

        (ii) regulation 7 (the pension and annuity requirements—money purchase schemes); or

    (b) in any other case, in such of the ways provided for by the following paragraphs as the rules may specify.

(2) Where the scheme provides for the member to elect to receive payments in accordance with this paragraph, and the member so elects, effect shall be given to his safeguarded rights during the interim period by the making of payments under an interim arrangement which—

    (a) complies with the requirements of section 28A(1), (3), (4) and (5) and 28B of the 1993 Act (requirements for interim arrangements and information about interim arrangements),[16] except insofar as those provisions concern payments to be made to the member's widow or widower; and

    (b) satisfies the conditions prescribed in regulations 6 and 7 of the Personal and Occupational Pension Schemes (Protected Rights) Regulations 1996[17] (interim arrangements and payments made under interim arrangements), except insofar as those provisions concern payments to be made to the member's widow, widower, a person in accordance with directions given by the member, or to the member's estate, in the event of the death of the member, as if references in those provisions to protected rights were to safeguarded rights.

(3) Where paragraph (2) applies, paragraphs (4) to (7), and regulations 7 and 8 (the pension and annuity requirements—money purchase schemes, and insurance companies that may provide safeguarded rights by way of annuities) apply in order to give effect to the member's safeguarded rights from the end of the period referred to in paragraph (2).

(4) Effect may be given to safeguarded rights by the provision by the scheme of a pension, or, subject to paragraph (5), an annuity, which complies with the requirements of regulations 7 and 8 of these Regulations and regulations 32 and 33 of the Pension Credit Benefit Regulations (increase of relevant pension and annual increase in rate of pension: qualifying occupational and personal pension schemes), provided that—

   (a) the pension or annuity gives effect to all the safeguarded rights of the member, and the terms on which the pension is provided, or the terms of the purchase of the annuity—

       (i)   satisfy the requirements of sub-paragraphs (b) to (d);

       (ii) make no provision other than such as is necessary to establish what the initial rate and the method of payment of the pension or annuity are to be, and that it shall continue to be paid throughout the lifetime of the member; and

       (iii) make no provision other than such as is necessary to satisfy the requirements of sub-paragraphs (b) to (d);

   (b) the rate of the pension or annuity is determined without regard to the sex of the member;

   (c) except with the consent of the member, the pension or annuity, if paid in arrears, is paid no less frequently than by monthly instalments; and

   (d) the pension or annuity is paid no less frequently than by annual instalments.

(5) Where paragraph (4) applies, an annuity may be provided if—

   (a) the rules of the scheme do not provide for a pension; or

   (b) the member so elects.

(6) Effect may be given to safeguarded rights by the making of a transfer payment in such circumstances and subject to such conditions as are prescribed in regulations 16 to 19 and regulation 24 of the Pension Credit Benefit Regulations (manner of calculation and verification of cash equivalents) in the case of a money purchase contracted-out scheme, an appropriate scheme, or a scheme which has ceased to be a contracted-out scheme or an appropriate scheme—

   (a) to another money purchase contracted-out scheme or to a salary related contracted-out scheme, if the person with safeguarded rights is an active member of such a scheme; or

   (b) to an appropriate scheme,

where the scheme to which the payment is made satisfies the requirements prescribed in regulation 22 of the Pension Credit Benefit Regulations (requirements to be met by an eligible scheme).

(7) Effect may be given to safeguarded rights by the provision of a lump sum in accordance with the provisions of regulation 3 or 4 of the Pension Credit Benefit Regulations (commutation of the whole or part of pension credit benefit).

(8) If the member has died—

   (a) after having elected to receive payments in accordance with paragraph (2); or

   (b) without effect being given to safeguarded rights under paragraph (3), (4), (5), (6) or (7), effect may be given to those rights by the payment, as soon as practicable, of a lump sum or a pension or annuity, or both a lump sum and a pension or annuity in accordance with the provisions of regulation 6 of the Pension Sharing (Implementation and Discharge of Liability) Regulations 2000 (discharge of liability in respect of a pension credit following the death of the person entitled to the pension credit).

(9) The rules of a scheme may provide for effect to be given to the safeguarded rights of a member by making payments to—

(a) the widow or widower of the member;

(b) another person in accordance with a direction given by the member; or

(c) in any other case, to the member's estate,

if the member dies after he has become entitled to the payment of benefit derived from his safeguarded rights.

(10) In this regulation—

'**the interim period**' means the period beginning with the starting date in relation to the member in question and ending with the termination date;

'**scheme**' means a money purchase contracted-out scheme or an appropriate scheme;

'**the starting date**' means the date, which must not be earlier than the member's 60th birthday, by reference to which the member elects to begin to receive payments under the interim arrangement;

'**the termination date**' means the date by reference to which the member elects to terminate the interim arrangement, and that date must not be later than the member's 75th birthday.

7   The pension and annuity requirements—money purchase schemes

(1) For the purposes of regulation 6(4) (ways of giving effect to safeguarded rights—money purchase schemes) the pension requirements are those specified in paragraph (2), and the annuity requirements are those specified in paragraphs (3) and (5).

(2) A pension complies with the pension requirements if in the case of a money purchase contracted-out scheme or an appropriate scheme it commences on a date not earlier than the member's 60th birthday, and not later than his 65th birthday, or on such later date as has been agreed by him, and continues until the date of his death.

(3) An annuity complies with the annuity requirements if—

(a) it commences on a date not earlier than the member's 60th birthday, and not later than his 65th birthday, or on such later date as has been agreed by him, and continues until the date of his death; and

(b) it is provided by an insurance company which—

(i) satisfies the conditions specified in regulation 8 (insurance companies that may provide safeguarded rights by way of annuities); and

(ii) subject to paragraphs (5) and (6), has been chosen by the member.

(4) Where the member has elected under regulation 6(2) to receive payments under an interim arrangement—

(a) in the case of a money purchase contracted-out scheme, a pension or annuity; or

(b) in the case of an appropriate scheme, an annuity,

must commence on the termination date and must continue until the date of the member's death.

(5) A member is only to be taken to have chosen an insurance company if he gives notice of his choice to the trustees or managers of the scheme—

(a) within a period of 5 months (or such longer period as the rules of the scheme may allow) beginning on the date which is 6 months earlier than that on which he will attain the age referred to in the following provisions of this sub-paragraph, as the case may be, where the trustees or managers of the scheme know of no reason to suppose that the pension or annuity will not commence on the date on which the member will attain—

  (i) in the case of a money purchase contracted-out scheme the normal benefit age if that age is not less than 60 years; or

  (ii) in the case of an appropriate scheme, the agreed age at which he is entitled to receive benefits under the scheme if that age is not less than 60 years; and

(b) in any other case—

  (i) if the date of the agreement in respect of when the pension or annuity is to commence ('the date of agreement') is more than one month before the agreed date for commencement of payment ('the agreed date'), within a period beginning on the date of agreement and ending one month before the agreed date; and

  (ii) on the date of agreement if that date is not more than one month before the agreed date,

or such longer period as the rules of the scheme may allow.

(6) If a member fails to give notice of his choice of insurance company in accordance with paragraph (5), the trustees or managers of the scheme may choose the insurance company instead.

(7) In this regulation **'the termination date'** has the meaning given by regulation 6(10).

8   Insurance companies that may provide safeguarded rights by way of annuities

(1) A money purchase contracted-out scheme or an appropriate scheme may only discharge its liability in respect of safeguarded rights in accordance with regulation 6(4) above if the annuity is provided by an insurance company which satisfies the conditions set out in paragraphs (2) to (4) below.

(2) The insurance company must be—

(a) authorised under section 3 or 4 of the Insurance Companies Act 1982[18] (authorisation of insurance business) to carry on long term business (within the meaning of section 1 of that Act[19] (classification)); or

(b) in the case of a friendly society, authorised under section 32 of the Friendly Societies Act 1992[20] (grant of authorisation by Commission: general) to carry out long term business under any of the Classes specified in Head A of Schedule 2 to that Act (the activities of a friendly society: long term business); or

(c) an EC company as defined in section 2(6) of the Insurance Companies Act 1982[21] (restriction on carrying on insurance business), and which falls within this sub-paragraph if it—

  (i) carries on ordinary long-term insurance business (within the meaning of section 96(1) of that Act[22]) in the United Kingdom through a branch in respect of which such of the requirements of Part I of Schedule 2F to that Ac[23] (recognition in the United Kingdom of EC and EFTA companies: EC companies carrying on business etc. in the United Kingdom) as are applicable have been complied with; or

  (ii) provides ordinary long term insurance in the United Kingdom and such of the requirements of Part I of Schedule 2F to that Act as are applicable have been complied with in respect of insurance.

(3) The insurance company must offer annuities with a view to purchase of those annuities by money purchase contracted-out schemes or appropriate schemes in order to give effect to the safeguarded rights of their members, without having regard to the sex of the members either in making the offers or in determining the rates at which the annuities are paid.

(4) Where the annuities are issued by a friendly society as described in paragraph (2)(b), the insurance company must provide that the terms of the annuities are not capable of being amended, revoked or rescinded.

9   Ways of giving effect to safeguarded rights—salary related schemes

(1) The rules of a salary related contracted-out scheme which satisfy the requirements of section 9(2B) of the 1993 Act[24] must provide for effect to be given to the safeguarded rights of a member by the provision of a pension for life except where the circumstances specified in paragraph (2), (3) or (4) apply.

(2) The circumstances specified in this paragraph are that the member consents to a transaction by which the trustees or managers of the scheme are to discharge their liability in respect of safeguarded rights and the transaction to discharge the liability satisfies all the conditions specified in paragraphs (6) and (7).

(3) The circumstances specified in this paragraph are that a transfer payment may be made in such circumstances and subject to such conditions as are prescribed in regulations 16 to 19 and regulation 24 of the Pension Credit Benefit Regulations in the case of a salary related contracted-out scheme—

(a) to another salary related contracted-out scheme or to a money purchase contracted-out scheme, if the person with safeguarded rights is an active member of such a scheme; or

(b) to an appropriate scheme,

where the scheme to which the payment is made satisfies the requirements prescribed in regulation 22 of the Pension Credit Benefit Regulations.

(4) The circumstances specified in this paragraph are that effect may be given to safeguarded rights by the provision of—

(a) a lump sum in accordance with the provisions of regulation 3 or 4 of the Pension Credit Benefit Regulations; or

(b) a lump sum or a pension or annuity, or both a lump sum and a pension or annuity, in accordance with the provisions of regulation 6 of the Pension Sharing (Implementation and Discharge of Liability) Regulations 2000.

(5) For the purposes of paragraph (2) 'transaction' means—

(a) the taking out of an insurance policy or a number of such policies;

(b) the entry into an annuity contract or a number of such contracts; or

(c) the transfer of pensions and accrued rights to such a policy or policies or such a contract or contracts.

(6) The insurance policy or annuity contract must be taken out or entered into with an insurance company such as is described in regulation 8(2).

(7) The insurance policy or annuity contract must contain provision to the effect, or must be endorsed so as to provide that—

(a) the benefits secured under the policy or contract shall become payable with the beneficiary's consent, and the beneficiary—

(i) has reached normal benefit age; or

(ii) is suffering from an incapacity or serious ill health prior to normal benefit age;

(b) any rights of a beneficiary to a payment under the policy or contract which derive from a pension or accrued rights under the salary related contracted-out scheme shall be treated as if this regulation were applicable to them; and

(c) any increase in accordance with regulation 32 of the Pension Credit Benefit Regulations (increase of relevant pension) which would have been applied to the benefits derived from safeguarded rights which have become secured or been replaced by the annuity contract or insurance policy, is applied to them.

(8) The rules of a salary related contracted-out scheme may provide for effect to be given to the safeguarded rights of a member by making payments to—

(a) the widow or widower of the member;

(b) another person in accordance with a direction given by the member; or

(c) in any other case, to the member's estate,

if the member dies after he has become entitled to the payment of benefit derived from his safeguarded rights.

(9) For the purposes of paragraph (7)—

'beneficiary' means a member of a salary related contracted-out scheme, in respect of whose safeguarded rights the trustees or managers of that scheme have discharged their liability by entering into an insurance policy or an annuity contract;

'incapacity' means physical or mental deterioration which is sufficiently serious to prevent a person from following his normal employment or which seriously impairs his earning capacity;

'serious ill health' has the same meaning as in regulation 3(4) of the Pension Credit Benefit Regulations.

10   Payable age in salary related contracted-out schemes

In respect of pension credit benefit arising out of safeguarded rights, schemes must provide for pension credit benefit to be paid by reference to an age which is equal for men and women and which—

(a) in the case of a scheme which is exempt approved within the meaning of section 592(1) of the Income and Corporation Taxes Act 1988[26] (tax reliefs: exempt approved schemes) or a scheme which has applied for such approval which has not yet been determined, is permitted under the rules of that scheme in accordance with that approval; or

(b) in the case of a relevant statutory scheme within the meaning of section 611A of the Income and Corporation Taxes Act 1988[27] (definition of relevant statutory scheme), is permitted under the regulations or rules governing the scheme as a relevant statutory scheme.

11   Investment and resources of safeguarded rights

All payments made in respect of safeguarded rights which are paid to a money purchase contracted-out scheme in respect of one of its members must be applied so as to provide money purchase benefits for or in respect of that member except so far as they are used—

(a) to defray the administrative expenses of the scheme, including the administration costs incurred by the scheme in respect of which the scheme may levy a charge in accordance with the Pensions on Divorce etc. (Charging)

Regulations 2000,[28] insofar as those costs relate to pension sharing in that member's case; or

(b) to pay commission.

12 Suspension and forfeiture of safeguarded rights

(1) Except in the circumstances referred to in paragraphs (2) and (3), the rules of an occupational or personal pension scheme must not permit the suspension or forfeiture of a member's safeguarded rights or of payments giving effect to them.

(2) The circumstances in which the rules of an occupational or personal pension scheme may provide for payments giving effect to a member's safeguarded rights to be suspended are those described in paragraph (1) of regulation 9 of the Personal and Occupational Pension Schemes (Protected Rights) Regulations 1996 (suspension of payments giving effect to protected rights), as if in that regulation—

(a) the reference to section 32 of the 1993 Act (suspension or forfeiture) was to this regulation; and

(b) the references to protected rights were to safeguarded rights.

(3) The circumstances in which the rules of an occupational or personal pension scheme may provide for payments giving effect to a member's safeguarded rights to be forfeited are those described in paragraph (2) of regulation 9 of the Personal and Occupational Pension Schemes (Protected Rights) Regulations 1996 (forfeiture of payments giving effect to protected rights), as if in that regulation—

(a) the reference to section 32 of the 1993 Act was to this regulation; and

(b) the references to protected rights were to safeguarded rights.

Signed by authority of the Secretary of State for Social Security.

Jeff Rooker

Minister of State, Department of Social Security

13th April 2000

Explanatory note

(This note is not part of the Regulations)

These Regulations provide for the treatment of safeguarded rights by pension arrangements once a pension has been shared.

Regulation 1 provides for citation, commencement and interpretation of the Regulations.

Regulation 2 defines contracted-out rights.

Regulation 3 describes the requirements to be satisfied by schemes holding safeguarded rights.

Regulation 4 provides for the identification of safeguarded rights.

Regulation 5 sets out how safeguarded rights in money purchase schemes are to be valued.

Regulation 6 describes the ways of giving effect to safeguarded rights in money purchase schemes.

Regulation 7 describes the requirements which pensions and annuities provided by money purchase schemes must meet in order for them to be used to give effect to safeguarded rights.

Regulation 8 sets out the conditions which an insurance company must satisfy if it is to provide an annuity in order to give effect to safeguarded rights.

Regulation 9 describes the ways of giving effect to safeguarded rights in salary related schemes.

Regulation 10 sets out the payable age in respect of safeguarded rights in salary related contracted-out schemes.

Regulation 11 sets out how payments made in respect of safeguarded rights should be invested and used.

Regulation 12 specifies the circumstances in which payments in respect of safeguarded rights may be suspended or forfeited.

An assessment of the cost to business of the provisions of the Welfare Reform and Pensions Act 1999, including these Regulations, is detailed in the Regulatory Impact Assessment for that Act. A copy of this Assessment has been placed in the libraries of both Houses of Parliament. Copies can be obtained by post from the Department of Social Security, Pensions on Divorce, 3rd Floor, The Adelphi, 1-11 John Adam Street, London WC2N 6HT.

Notes

[1] Section 181(1) is cited because of the meaning there given to 'prescribed' and 'regulations'.

[2] 1993 c. 48. Sections 68A, 68B and 68D are inserted by section 36 of the Welfare Reform and Pensions Act 1999 (c. 30).

[3] See section 83(11) of the Welfare Reform and Pensions Act 1999.

[4] SI 2000/1054.

[5] Section 9 was amended by section 136 of, and paragraph 24 of Schedule 5 and Part III of Schedule 7 to, the Pensions Act 1995, and paragraph 35 of Schedule 1 to the Social Security Contributions (Transfer of Functions, etc.) Act 1999 (c. 2).

[6] Section 8 was amended by section 136(2) of, and paragraph 23 of Schedule 5 to, the Pensions Act 1995 and paragraph 126 of Schedule 7 to the Social Security Act 1998 (c. 14). See also regulations 6 and 7 of SI 1996/1461 and regulation 12 of SI 1996/1462.

[7] Section 28A is inserted by section 143 of the Pensions Act 1995.

[8] SI 1996/1537, amended by SI 1997/786 and SI 1999/3198.

[9] Section 101B is inserted by section 37 of the Welfare Reform and Pensions Act 1999.

[10] The definition of 'personal pension scheme' is amended by paragraph 3(1)(a) of Schedule 2 to the Welfare Reform and Pensions Act 1999.

[11] Section 101P is inserted by section 37 of the Welfare Reform and Pensions Act 1999.

[12] Section 10 was amended by paragraph 25 of Schedule 5 to the Pensions Act 1995, and by paragraph 36 of Schedule 1 to the Social Security Contributions (Transfer of Functions, etc.) Act 1999.

[13] Section 8(1)(a)(i) was substituted by section 136(2) of the Pensions Act 1995.

[14] SI 1996/1172. The relevant amending instrument is SI 1997/786.

[15] SI 1996/1172. Regulation 45 was amended by and paragraph (3A) inserted by regulation 3(b) of SI 1997/819.

[16] Sections 28A and 28B were inserted by section 143 of the Pensions Act 1995. Section 28B was amended by paragraph 41 of Schedule 1 to the Social Security Contributions (Transfer of Functions, etc.) Act 1999.

[17] SI 1996/1537 as amended by SI 1997/786.

[18] 1982 c. 50, as amended by the European Economic Area Act 1993 (c. 51).

[19] Section 1 was amended by SI 1990/1159.

[20] 1992 c. 40. Section 32 was amended by SI 1994/1984.

[21] Section 2 was amended by regulation 2(a) of SI 1987/2130, section 300(2) of, and paragraph 31 of Schedule 2 to the Trade Union and Labour Relations (Consolidation) Act 1992 (c. 52), regulation 4(2) of SI 1994/1696 and regulation 3(1) of SI1994/3132.

[22] There are amendments to section 96(1) which are not relevant to these Regulations.

[23] Schedule 2F was inserted by SI 1996/1696.

[24] Section 9(2B) was inserted by section 136(3) of the Pensions Act 1995, and was amended by paragraph 35(2)(a) and (b) of Schedule 1 to the Social Security Contributions (Transfer of Functions, etc.) Act 1999.

[25] SI 2000/1053.

[26] 1988 c. 1.

[27] Section 611A(1) was inserted by section 75 of, and paragraphs 1, 15 and 18(1) of Part I of Schedule 6 to, the Finance Act 1989 (c. 26).

[28] SI 2000/1049.

The Retirement Benefits Schemes (Sharing of Pensions on Divorce or Annulment) Regulations 2000

SI 2000/1085

Made 14 April 2000
Laid before the House of Commons 19 April 2000
Coming into force 10 May 2000

The Commissioners of Inland Revenue, in exercise of the powers conferred on them by paragraph 18(10) and (11) of Schedule 10 to the Finance Act 1999,[1] hereby make the following Regulations:

1 Citation, commencement and effect

(1) These Regulations may be cited as the Retirement Benefits Schemes (Sharing of Pensions on Divorce or Annulment) Regulations 2000 and shall come into force on 10th May 2000.

(2) Regulations 3 to 8 have effect in relation to schemes which have been approved by the Board under section 591 of the Taxes Act 1988[2] before 10th May 2000.

2 Interpretation

(1) In these Regulations:

'**the Board**' means the Commissioners of Inland Revenue;

'**director**' has the meaning given by section 612(1) of the Taxes Act 1988;

'**ex-spouse**' has the meaning given by section 659D(1) of the Taxes Act 1988;

'**moderate earner**' has the meaning given by regulation 5(4) to (6);

'**pension sharing order or provision**' means any such order or provision as is mentioned in section 28(1) of the Welfare Reform and Pensions Act 1999 or Article 25(1) of the Welfare Reform and Pensions (Northern Ireland) Order 1999;

'**the permitted maximum**' has the meaning given by section 590C of the Taxes Act 1988;

'**Schedule 10**' means Schedule 10 to the Finance Act 1999;

'**scheme**' means a retirement benefits scheme;

'**simplified defined contribution scheme**' has the meaning given by regulation 2(1) of the Retirement Benefits Schemes (Restriction on Discretion to Approve) (Additional Voluntary Contributions) Regulations 1993;

'**the Taxes Act 1988**' means the Income and Corporation Taxes Act 1988.

3 Prescribed modifications of Schedule 10 in prescribed circumstances

Regulations 4 to 8 prescribe circumstances in which Schedule 10 shall apply with the modifications prescribed by those regulations in the case of schemes approved by the Board before 10th May 2000.

4 Modification of Schedule 10 in relation to simplified defined contribution schemes

(1) In the circumstances prescribed by paragraph (2), Schedule 10 shall apply to a scheme with the modification prescribed by paragraph (3).

(2) The circumstances prescribed by this paragraph are circumstances where a scheme is a simplified defined contribution scheme.

(3) The modification prescribed by this paragraph is that paragraph 18(5) of Schedule 10 shall be omitted.

5 Modifications of Schedule 10 as regards members of schemes who are moderate earners

(1) In the circumstances prescribed by paragraph (2), Schedule 10 shall apply to a scheme as regards an employee within that paragraph with the modification prescribed by paragraph (3).

(2) The circumstances prescribed by this paragraph are circumstances where the employee:

    (a) is a member of a scheme which is not a simplified defined contribution scheme;

    (b) is an ex-spouse whose rights under the scheme have been debited as a consequence of a pension sharing order or provision; and

    (c) is a moderate earner.

(3) The modification prescribed by this paragraph is that paragraph 18(5) of Schedule 10 shall be omitted.

(4) In this regulation, and in regulations 6 to 8, 'moderate earner' means an employee:

    (a) who is not a controlling director of a company which is his employer, and

    (b) whose earnings at the date at which his marriage was dissolved or annulled were not more than 25 per cent. of the permitted maximum for the year of assessment in which the dissolution or annulment occurred.

(5) For the purposes of paragraph (4)(a), an employee is a controlling director of a company which is his employer if he is a director of the company to whom section 417(5)(b) of the Taxes Act 1988 applies either:

    (a) at the date on which the marriage was dissolved or annulled, or

    (b) at any time within the period of ten years before that date.

(6) For the purposes of paragraph (4)(b), an ex-spouse's earnings shall be taken to be the total amounts of emoluments:

    (a) which were paid to the ex-spouse in consequence of pensionable service to which the scheme relates during the year of assessment before the year of assessment in which the marriage was dissolved or annulled, and

    (b) from which tax was deducted in accordance with the Income Tax (Employment) Regulations 1993.

6 Modifications of Schedule 10 as regards members who are not moderate earners – schemes providing lump sum retirement benefits only

(1) In the circumstances prescribed by paragraph (2), Schedule 10 shall apply to a scheme as regards an employee within that paragraph with the modification prescribed by paragraph (3).

(2) The circumstances prescribed by this paragraph are circumstances where the employee:

    (a) is a member of a scheme which:

    (i)   is not a simplified defined contribution scheme; and

    (ii) provides him with lump sum retirement benefits only which do not exceed three eightieths of his final remuneration for each year of service up to a maximum of 40;

  (b) is an ex-spouse whose rights under the scheme have been debited as a consequence of a pension sharing order or provision; and

  (c) is not a moderate earner.

(3) The modification prescribed by this paragraph is that in paragraph 18(5) of Schedule 10 the words 'and (da)' shall be omitted.

7   Modifications of Schedule 10 as regards members who are not moderate earners – schemes providing lump sums otherwise than by the commutation of a part of a pension

(1) In the circumstances prescribed by paragraph (2), Schedule 10 shall apply to a scheme as regards an employee within that paragraph with the modification prescribed by paragraph (3).

(2) The circumstances prescribed by this paragraph are circumstances where the employee—

  (a) is a member of a scheme which:

    (i)   is not a simplified defined contribution scheme; and

    (ii) provides him with a lump sum otherwise than by the commutation of a part of a pension;

  (b) is an ex-spouse whose rights under the scheme have been debited as a consequence of a pension sharing order or provision;

  (c) is not a moderate earner; and

  (d) is not an employee within regulation 8(2)(b).

(3) The modifications prescribed by this paragraph are that:

  (a) in paragraph 18(5) of Schedule 10:

    (i)   the words 'and (da)' shall be omitted; and

    (ii) at the end after the words 'the Taxes Act 1988' there shall be added the words 'and provision of the description set out in subparagraph (5A) below'; and

  (b) After paragraph 18(5) of Schedule 10 there shall be inserted the following subparagraph:

    '(5A) The description of provision referred to in sub-paragraph (5) above is provision providing that in a case in which:

      (a) a lump sum may be obtained otherwise than by the commutation of a part of a pension provided for an employee, and

      (b) the amount of that pension is affected by the making of a pension sharing order or provision,

    the lump sum does not exceed the sum produced by multiplying by 3 the amount which (after effect has been given to the pension sharing order or provision) is the amount of the pension for the first year in which it is payable calculated in accordance with section 590(4E)(') of the Taxes Act 1988.'

8   Modifications of Schedule 10 as regards members of schemes who are not moderate earners and to whom paragraphs 2, 3, 4 and 6 of Schedule 23 to the Taxes Acts 1988 do not apply

(1) In the circumstances prescribed by paragraph (2), Schedule 10 shall apply to a scheme as regards an employee within that paragraph with the modifications prescribed by paragraph (3).

(2) The circumstances prescribed by this paragraph are circumstances where

   (a) the employee is a member of a scheme which:

      (i) is not a simplified defined contribution scheme; and

      (ii) provides for a lump sum either by the commutation of a part of a pension or otherwise; and

   (b) the employee:

      (i) in the case of a scheme approved by the Board before 23rd July 1987, was a member of the scheme before 17th March 1987; or

      (ii) is an employee as regards whom the provisions contained in paragraphs 2, 3, 4 and 6 of Schedule 23 to the Taxes Act 1988 are disapplied either by regulation 3 or 4ZA of the Occupational Pension Schemes (Transitional Provisions) Regulations 1988 or by virtue of a direction of the Board made under regulation 11 of those Regulations; or

      (iii) is an employee who:

         (a) was a member of a scheme before 17th March 1987, and

         (b) on or after 17th March 1987 becomes a member of another scheme to which Schedule 23 to the Taxes Act 1988 does not apply,

      and whom the Board, in exercising their discretion under section 591 of the Taxes Act 1988, allow to be treated as having been a member of that other scheme before 17th March 1987; and

   (c) the employee:

      (i) is an ex-spouse whose rights under the scheme have been debited as a consequence of a pension sharing order or provision; and

      (ii) is not a moderate earner.

(3) The modifications prescribed by this paragraph are that:

   (a) in paragraph 18(5) of Schedule 10:

      (i) the words 'and (da)' shall be omitted; and

      (ii) at the end after the words 'the Taxes Act 1988' there shall be added the words 'and provision of the description set out in subparagraph (5AA) below'; and

   (b) after paragraph 18(5) of Schedule 10 there shall be inserted the following sub-paragraphs:

   '(5AA) The description of provision referred to in sub-paragraph (5) above is provision providing that in a case in which:

      (a) a lump sum may be obtained either by the commutation of a part of a pension provided for an employee or otherwise, and

      (b) the amount of the pension is affected by the making of a pension sharing order or provision,

   the lump sum shall not exceed the greater of either A or B.

   (5B) In sub-paragraph (5AA) above, A is the sum produced by multiplying by either:

      (a) 2.25, in the case of a scheme which provides for a lump sum by the commutation of a part of a pension, or

      (b) 3, in the case of a scheme which provides for a lump sum otherwise than by the commutation of a part of a pension,

   the amount which (after effect has been given to the pension sharing order or provision) is the amount of the pension for the first year in which it is payable calculated in accordance with section 590(4E) of the Taxes Act 1988.

(5C) In sub-paragraph (5AA) above, B is the sum produced by the following formula:

C—D

Where:

C   is the amount of the lump sum determined in accordance with the rules of the scheme as if no pension sharing order or provision had been made, and

D   is the sum produced by multiplying by either:

(a)   2.25, in the case of a scheme which provides for a lump sum by the commutation of a part of a pension, or

(b)   3, in the case of a scheme which provides for a lump sum otherwise than by the commutation of a part of a pension,

the amount by which the employee's benefits or future benefits under the scheme are reduced under section 31 of the Welfare Reform and Pensions Act 1999 or Article 28 of the Welfare Reform and Pensions (Northern Ireland) Order 1999.'

Nick Montagu

Tim Flesher

Two of the Commissioners of Inland Revenue

14th April 2000

Explanatory note (This note is not part of the Regulations)

These Regulations provide for the modification of provisions contained in Schedule 10 to the Finance Act 1999 (sharing of pensions etc. on divorce or annulment) ('Schedule IV) in prescribed circumstances. The modifications relate to the application of the Schedule in the case of retirement benefits schemes approved by the Board of Inland Revenue under section 591 of the Income and Corporation Taxes Act 1988 ('the Taxes Act 1988') before 10th May 2000.

The modifications are of paragraph 18(5) of Schedule 10 which provides that a scheme which has been approved before the day appointed by the Treasury as the first appointed day for the purposes of paragraph 18 of Schedule 10 shall have effect as long as it continues to be approved on or after the day to be appointed by the Treasury as the second appointed day for the purposes of that paragraph as if it contained provision satisfying the conditions set out in section 590(3)(bb) and (da) of the Taxes Act 1988 (conditions for automatic approval).

Regulation 1 provides for commencement, citation and effect, and regulation 2 for interpretation.

Regulations 3 introduces regulations 4 to 8 which prescribe both the circumstances in which Schedule 10 applies with modifications and the modifications themselves.

Regulation 4 disapplies paragraph 18(5) of Schedule 10 as regards simplified defined contribution schemes.

Regulations 5 to 8 prescribe modifications of Schedule 10 in relation to schemes which are not simplified defined contribution schemes. The circumstances prescribed by regulation 5 concern members of schemes who are not controlling directors of a company which is their employer and whose earnings at the date of their divorce are moderate ('moderate earners'). The circumstances prescribed by regulations 6 to 8 concern members of schemes who are not moderate earners.

Regulation 5 disapplies paragraph 18(5) of Schedule 10 where the member is a moderate earner.

Regulation 6 modifies paragraph 18(5) of Schedule 10 in circumstances where a scheme provides an employee who is not a moderate earner with lump sum retirement benefits only which do not exceed three eightieths of his final remuneration for each year of service.

Regulation 7 modifies paragraph 18(5) of Schedule 10 in circumstances where a scheme provides an employee who is not a moderate earner with a lump sum otherwise than by the commutation of a part of a pension.

Regulation 8 modifies paragraph 18(5) of Schedule 10 as regards certain scheme members who are not moderate earners and who continue to accrue benefits on the basis that they would have done before 17th March 1987.

Notes

[1] 1999 c16.

[2] 1988 c.1. Section 591 was amended by paragraph 6 of Schedule 13 to the Finance Act 1988 (c.39), section 107 of, and Part V(12) of Schedule 26 to, the Finance Act 1994 (c.9), section 59(2) of the Finance Act 1995 (c.4), and paragraph 3 of Schedule 10 to the Finance Act 1999.

The Retirement Benefits Schemes (Restriction on Discretion to Approve) (Small Self-administered Schemes) (Amendment) Regulations 2000

SI 2000/1086

Made 14 April 2000
Laid before the House of Commons 19 April 2000
Coming into force 10 May 2000

The Commissioners of Inland Revenue, in exercise of the powers conferred on them by section 591(6) of the Income and Corporation Taxes Act 1988,[1] hereby make the following Regulations:

1   Citation and commencement

These Regulations may be cited as the Retirement Benefits Schemes (Restriction on Discretion to Approve) (Small Self-administered Schemes) (Amendment) Regulations 2000 and shall come into force on 10 May 2000.

2   Amendments to regulation 2(1) of the Retirement Benefits Schemes (Restriction on Discretion to Approve) (Small Self-administered Schemes) Regulations 1991

(1) Regulation 2(1) of the Retirement Benefits Schemes (Restriction on Discretion to Approve) (Small Self-administered Schemes) Regulations 1991(b) shall be amended as follows.

(2) After the definition of 'employer' there shall be inserted the following definition:

'**ex-spouse**' has the meaning given by section 659D(1)[2] of the Act;'.

(3) After the definition of 'pensioneer trustee' there shall be inserted the following definition:

'**pension sharing order or provision**' means any such order or provision as is mentioned in section 28(1) of the Welfare Reform and Pensions Act 1999(b) or Article 25(1) of the Welfare Reform and Pensions (Northern Ireland) Order 1999(c).'

(4) For the definition of 'scheme member' there shall be substituted the following definition:

'**scheme member**' in relation to a scheme means:

(a) a member of the scheme to whom benefit is currently accruing as a result of service as an employee, or

(b) a person who is an ex-spouse of a member of the scheme and whose rights under the scheme derive from a pension sharing order or provision;'.

(5) In the definition of 'small self-administered scheme' in sub-paragraph (c) after the words 'scheme members' there shall be added the words 'to whom benefits are currently accruing as a result of service as employees'.

Nick Montague
Tim Flesher
Two of the Commissioners of Inland Revenue
14th April 2000

Explanatory note (This note is not part of the Regulations)

These Regulations make amendments to the Retirement Benefits Schemes (Restriction on Discretion to Approve) (Small Self-administered Schemes) Regulations 1991 (SI 1991/1614) ('the principal Regulations') which impose restrictions on the Board of Inland Revenue's discretion to approve under section 591 of the Income and Corporation Taxes Act 1988 (c.1) retirement benefits schemes that are small self-administered schemes.

Regulation 1 provides for citation and commencement.

Regulation 2 amends regulation 2(1) of the principal Regulations. The main purpose of the amendments is to ensure that the definition of 'scheme member' includes members' ex-spouses whose rights derive from a pension sharing order or provision under the Welfare Reform and Pensions Act 1999 (c.30) or the Welfare Reform and Pensions (Northern Ireland) Order 1999 (SI 1999/3147 (NI 11)). Amendments are made also so as to ensure that schemes do not fall outside the definition of 'small self-administered scheme' as a consequence of the widening of the definition of 'scheme member'.

Notes

[1] 1988 c.1. Section 591(6) was amended by paragraph 6 of Schedule 13 to the Finance Act 1988 (c. 39).

[2] SI 1991/1614 relevantly amended by SI 1998/728.

The Retirement Benefits Schemes (Restriction on Discretion to Approve) (Excepted Provisions) Regulations 2000

SI 2000/1087

Made 14 April 2000
Laid before the House of Commons 19 April 2000
Coming into force 10 May 2000

The Commissioners of Inland Revenue, in exercise of the powers conferred on them by section 591A(2) of the Income and Corporation Taxes Act 1988,[1] hereby make the following Regulations:

1 Citation and commencement

These Regulations may be cited as the Retirement Benefits Schemes (Restriction on Discretion to Approve) (Excepted Provisions) Regulations 2000 and shall come into force on 10th May 2000 immediately after the coming into force of the 2000 Regulations and the second 2000 Regulations.

2 Interpretation

In these Regulations:

'**the 1991 Regulations**' means the Retirement Benefits Schemes (Restriction on Discretion to Approve) (Small Self-administered Schemes) Regulations 1991[2]

'**the 1993 Regulations**' means the Retirement Benefits Schemes (Restriction on Discretion to Approve) (Additional Voluntary Contributions) Regulations 1993;[3]

'**the 2000 Regulations**' means the Retirement Benefits Schemes (Restriction on Discretion to Approve) (Small Self-administered Schemes) (Amendment) Regulations 2000);[4]

'**the second 2000 Regulations**' means the Retirement Benefits Schemes (Restriction on Discretion to Approve) (Additional Voluntary Contributions) (Amendment) Regulations 2000.[5]

3 Description of provisions

Regulations 4 and 5 specify descriptions of provisions for the purposes of subsection (2) of section 591 A of the Income and Corporation Taxes Act 1988, each provision so specified being a provision of a required description within the meaning of subsection (5)(b) of that section.

4 The description of provision specified in this regulation consists of the provisions specified in regulations 4 to 9 of the 1991 Regulations, read together with paragraph (1) of regulation 2 of the 1991 Regulations as that paragraph is amended by regulation 2 of the 2000 Regulations.

5 The description of provision specified in this regulation consists of:

(a) the provisions specified in regulation 5 of the 1993 Regulations as amended by regulation 3 of the second 2000 Regulations; and

(b) the provisions specified in regulations 4 and 5 of the 1993 Regulations, read together with regulation 6 of the 1993 Regulations as that regulation is amended by regulation 4 of the second 2000 Regulations.

Nick Montagu

Tim Flesher

Two of the Commissioners of Inland Revenue

14th April 2000

Explanatory note (This note is not part of the Regulations)

The Retirement Benefits Schemes (Restriction on Discretion to Approve) (Small Self-administered Schemes) Regulations 1991 ('the 1991 Regulations') and the Retirement Benefits Schemes (Restriction on Discretion to Approve) (Additional Voluntary Contributions) Regulations 1993 ('the 1993 Regulations') restrict the Board of Inland Revenue's discretion to approve retirement benefits schemes under section 591 of the Income and Corporation Taxes Act 1988 ('the Taxes Act').

The 1991 Regulations are amended by the Retirement Benefits Schemes (Restriction on Discretion to Approve) (Small Self-administered Schemes) (Amendment) Regulations 2000 ('the 2000 Regulations') (SI 2000/1086) and the 1993 Regulations are amended by the Retirement Benefits Schemes (Restriction on Discretion to Approve) (Additional Voluntary Contributions) (Amendment) Regulations 2000 ('the second 2000 Regulations') (SI 2000/1088).

By virtue of section 591A of the Taxes Act ('section 591A') the 1991 Regulations and the 1993 Regulations also apply to retirement benefits schemes approved by the Board before the coming into force of those Regulations or any amendments to those Regulations ('existing approved schemes') except to the extent that any provisions in the 1991 Regulations or the 1993 Regulations are disapplied by separate Regulations made under section 591A.

These Regulations disapply in relation to existing approved schemes the provisions in regulations 4 to 9 of the 1991 Regulations, read together with regulation 2(1) of the 1991 Regulations as amended by the 2000 Regulations. They also disapply in relation to existing approved schemes the provisions in regulation 5 of the 1993 Regulations as amended by regulation 3 of the second 2000 Regulations, and the provisions in regulations 4 and 5 of the 1993 Regulations, read together with regulation 6 of the 1993 Regulations as amended by regulation 4 of the second 2000 Regulations.

Notes

[1] 1988 c.1. Section 591A was inserted by section 35 of the Finance Act 1991 (c.31).

[2] SI 1991/1614 amended by SI 1998/728 and SI 1998/1315.

[3] SI 1993/3016.

[4] SI 2000/1086.

[5] SI 2000/1088.

I.20

The Retirement Benefits Schemes (Restriction on Discretion to Approve) (Additional Voluntary Contributions) (Amendment) Regulations 2000

SI 2000/1088

Made 14 April 2000
Laid before the House of Commons 19 April 2000
Coming into force 10 May 2000

The Commissioners of Inland Revenue, in exercise of the powers conferred on them by section 591(6) of the Income and Corporation Taxes Act 1988,[1] hereby make the following Regulations:

1 Citation and commencement

These Regulations may be cited as the Retirement Benefits Schemes (Restriction on Discretion to Approve) (Additional Voluntary Contributions) (Amendment) Regulations 2000 and shall come into force on 10th May 2000.

2 Interpretation

In these Regulations, 'the principal Regulations' means the Retirement Benefits Schemes (Restriction on Discretion to Approve) (Additional Voluntary Contributions) Regulations 1993[2] and 'regulation' means a regulation of the principal Regulations.

3 Amendment of regulation 5 of the principal Regulations

In regulation 5(5):

    (a) in sub-paragraph (a) before the word 'pension' there shall be inserted the words 'subject to regulation 5A,';

    (b) in sub-paragraph (b) before the words 'pension equivalent' there shall be inserted the words 'subject to regulation 5A,'.

4 Insertion of new regulation 5A in the principal Regulations

After regulation 5 there shall be inserted the following regulation:

'5A Special rules for determining pension and pension equivalent

(1) This regulation shall apply in determining whether—

    (a) any amount is payable for the purposes of the meaning of 'pension' given by regulation 5(5)(a), or

    (b) any additional amount is payable for the purposes of the meaning of 'pension equivalent' given by regulation 5(5)(b).

(2) Where the rules of a scheme established by a relevant employer, or to which a relevant employer is a contributor, provide for any benefit payable to any person as the result of a credit under a pension sharing order or provision to be treated as provided separately from any benefits which are provided under the scheme for that person as an employee, any pension sharing order or provision in favour of an employee who is an ex-spouse which affects the amount or additional amount payable shall not be taken into account in relation to that employee.

(3) Subject to paragraph (4), where any pension sharing order or provision made against an employee who is an ex-spouse affects the amount or additional amount payable, the order or provision shall not be taken into account in relation to that employee and accordingly:

(a) any amount payable shall be treated as increased by an amount equal to the relevant reduction;

(b) any additional amount payable shall be treated as increased by the amount produced by multiplying the relevant reduction by 2.25.

(4) Paragraph (3) shall not apply where the employee is a moderate earner.

(5) In this regulation—

(a) '**ex-spouse**' has the meaning given by section 659D(1)[3] of the Taxes Act;

(b) '**moderate earner**' means an employee:

(i) who is not a controlling director of a company which is his employer, and

(ii) whose earnings at the date at which his marriage was dissolved or annulled were not more than 25 per cent of the permitted maximum for the year of assessment in which the dissolution or annulment occurred;

(c) '**pension sharing order or provision**' means any such order or provision as is mentioned in section 28(1) of the Welfare Reform and Pensions Act 1999[4] or Article 25(1) of the Welfare Reform and Pensions (Northern Ireland) Order 1999;[5]

(d) '**the permitted maximum**' has the meaning given by section 590C of the Taxes Act 1988;

(e) '**the relevant date**' has the meaning given by regulation 5(5)(c);

(f) '**the relevant reduction**' means the total amount by which the employee's benefits or future benefits under the scheme are reduced under section 31 of the Welfare Reform and Pensions Act 1999, or Article 28 of the Welfare Reform and Pensions (Northern Ireland) Order 1999, on the relevant date.

(6) For the purposes of paragraph (5)(b)(1), an employee is a controlling director of a company which is his employer if he is a director of the company to whom section 417(5)(b) of the Taxes Act 1988 applies either—

(a) at the date on which the marriage was dissolved or annulled, or

(b) at any time within the period of ten years before that date.

(7) For the purposes of paragraph (5)(b)(ii), an ex-spouse's earnings shall be taken to be the total amounts of emoluments:

(a) which were paid to the ex-spouse in consequence of pensionable service to which the scheme relates during the year of assessment before the year of assessment in which the marriage was dissolved or annulled, and

(b) from which tax was deducted in accordance with the Income Tax (Employment) Regulations 1993.[6]

5   Amendment of regulation 6 of the principal Regulations

In regulation 6(7) for the word 'respectively' there shall be substituted the words 'respectively, read together with regulation 5A,'.

Nick Montagu
Tim Flesher
Two of the Commissioners of Inland Revenue
14th April 2000

Explanatory note (This note is not part of the Regulations)

These Regulations make amendments to the Retirement Benefits Schemes (Restriction on Discretion to Approve) (Additional Voluntary Contributions) Regulations 1993 (S.I. 1993/3016) ('the principal Regulations'). The principal Regulations impose restrictions relating to the repayment to an employee of surplus funds arising from the provision of benefits under schemes to which the employee pays additional voluntary contributions and also restrict the Board of Inland Revenue's discretion to approve such schemes under section 591 of the Income and Corporation Taxes Act 1988 (c.1).

Regulation 4 of the principal Regulations restricts the Board's discretion in relation to schemes which are freestanding additional voluntary contributions schemes where the rules of the scheme do not require the administrator to comply with the requirements of the regulation and, so far as they concern such schemes, of regulation 6 of the principal Regulations (calculation of surplus funds). Regulation 5 of the principal Regulations makes similar provision in relation to schemes which are not freestanding additional voluntary contributions schemes.

The purpose of the amendments made by these Regulations is to ensure that, in general, the operation of the principal Regulations is not affected where a pension sharing order or provision is made in favour of an ex-spouse under the Welfare Reform and Pensions Act 1999 (c.30) or the Welfare Reform and Pensions (Northern Ireland) Order 1999 (S.I. 1999/3147 (N.I. 11)). There is an exception in relation to an employee against whom such order or provision is made who would be a moderate earner if the order or provision were taken into account.

Regulation 1 provides for citation and commencement, and regulation 2 for interpretation.

Regulation 3 amends regulation 5(5) of the principal Regulations in consequence of the amendments made by regulation 4 of these Regulations.

Regulation 4 inserts a new regulation 5A in the principal Regulations providing for special rules for determining the meaning of 'pension' and 'pension equivalent' given by regulation 5(5) of the principal Regulations where a pension sharing order or provision has been made.

Regulation 5 amends regulation 6(7) of the principal Regulations in consequence of the amendments made by regulation 3 of these Regulations.

Notes

[1] 1988 C.1. Section 591 was amended by paragraph 6 of Schedule 13 to the Finance Act 1988 (c.39), section 107 of, and Part V(12) of Schedule 26 to, the Finance Act 1994 (c.9), and section 59(2) of the Finance Act 1995 (c.4).

[2] SI 1993/3016.

[3] Section 659D was inserted by paragraph 17 of Schedule 10 to the Finance Act 1999 (c16).

[4] 1999 c 30.

[5] SI 1999/3147 (NI 11).

[6] SI 1993/744 amended by SI 1993/2276, 1994/775 and 1212, 1995/216, 447, 853,1223 and 1284, 1996/804, 980, 1312, 2381, 2554 and 2631, 1997/214, 1998/2484 and 1999/70, 824 and 2155.

The Finance Act 1999, Schedule 10, Paragraph 18, (First and Second Appointed Days) Order 2000

SI 2000/1093

Made 18 April 2000

The Treasury, in exercise of the powers conferred on them by paragraph 18(1) of Schedule 10 to the Finance Act 1999,[1] hereby make the following Order:

1 This Order may be cited as the Finance Act 1999, Schedule 10, Paragraph 18, (First and Second Appointed Days) Order 2000.

2 For the purposes of paragraph 18 of Schedule 10 to the Finance Act 1999

(a) the day appointed as 'the first appointed day' is 10th May 2000;

(b) the day appointed as 'the second appointed day' is 1st December 2000.

Bob Ainsworth

Clive Betts

18th April 2000   Two of the Lords Commissioners of Her Majesty's Treasury

---

Explanatory note (This note is not part of the Order)

Schedule 10 to, the Finance Act 1999 (c. 16) ('Schedule 1 V) makes changes to the taxation of pension schemes where pension rights are shared on divorce or annulment.

The changes complement the provisions of the Welfare Reform and Pensions Act 1999 (c.30) and the Welfare Reform and Pensions (Northern Ireland) Order 1999 (S.I. 1999/3147 (N.I. 11)).

Paragraph 18 of Schedule 10 provides for certain of the provisions of Schedule 10 to have effect by reference to 'the first appointed day' or 'the second appointed day'. The Treasury may by order appoint these days under paragraph 18(1) of Schedule 10.

This Order appoints 10th May 2000 as 'the first appointed day', and 1st December 2000 as 'the second appointed day', for the purposes of paragraph 18 of Schedule 10.

Note

[1] 1999 c.16

The Divorce etc (Pensions) Regulations 2000

SI 2000/1123

Made 14 April 2000
Laid before Parliament 19 April 2000
Coming into force 1 December 2000

The Lord Chancellor, in exercise of the powers conferred on him by sections 24C, 25D(1)(b), (2) and (3) and 31(4C) of the Matrimonial Causes Act 1973[1] and section 21(4) of the Matrimonial and Family Proceedings Act 1984,[2] makes the following Regulations:

1 Citation, commencement and transitional provisions

(1) These Regulations may be cited as the Divorce etc. (Pensions) Regulations 2000 and shall come into force on 1st December 2000.

(2) These Regulations shall apply to any proceedings for divorce, judicial separation or nullity of marriage commenced on or after 1st December 2000, and any such proceedings commenced before that date shall be treated as if these Regulations had not come into force.

2 Interpretation

In these Regulations:

    (a) a reference to a section by number alone means the section so numbered in the Matrimonial Causes Act 1973;

    (b) 'the 1984 Act' means the Matrimonial and Family Proceedings Act 1984;

    (c) expressions defined in sections 21A[3] and 25D(3) have the meanings assigned by those sections;

    (d) every reference to a rule by number alone means the rule so numbered in the Family Proceedings Rules 1991.[4]

3 Valuation

(1) For the purposes of the court's functions in connection with the exercise of any of its powers under Part II of the Matrimonial Causes Act 1973, benefits under a pension arrangement shall be calculated and verified in the manner set out in regulation 3 of the Pensions on Divorce etc. (Provision of Information) Regulations 2000,[5] and—

    (a) the benefits shall be valued as at a date to be specified by the court (being not earlier than one year before the date of the petition and not later than the date on which the court is exercising its power);

    (b) in determining that value the court may have regard to information furnished by the person responsible for the pension arrangement pursuant to any of the provisions set out in paragraph (2); and

(c) in specifying a date under sub-paragraph (a) above the court may have regard to the date specified in any information furnished as mentioned in sub-paragraph (b) above.

(2) The relevant provisions for the purposes of paragraph (1)(b) above are:

(a) the Pensions on Divorce etc. (Provision of Information) Regulations 2000;

(b) regulation 5 of and Schedule 2 to the Occupational Pension Schemes (Disclosure of Information) Regulations 1996[6] and regulation 11 of and Schedule 1 to the Occupational Pension Schemes (Transfer Value) Regulations 1996;[7]

(c) section 93A or 94(1)(a) or (aa) of the Pension Schemes Act 1993;[8]

(d) section 94(1)(b) of the Pension Schemes Act 1993 or paragraph 2(a) (or, where applicable, 2(b)) of Schedule 2 to the Personal Pension Schemes (Disclosure of Information) Regulations 1987][9].

4 Pension attachment: notices

(1) This regulation applies in the circumstances set out in section 25D(1)(a) (transfers of pension rights).

(2) Where this regulation applies, the person responsible for the first arrangement shall give notice in accordance with the following paragraphs of this regulation to

(a) the person responsible for the new arrangement, and

(b) the other party.

(3) The notice to the person responsible for the new arrangement shall include copies of the following documents:

(a) every order made under section 23 imposing any requirement on the person responsible for the first arrangement in relation to the rights transferred;

(b) any order varying such an order;

(c) all information or particulars which the other party has been required to supply under any provision of rule 2.70 for the purpose of enabling the person responsible for the first arrangement:—

(i) to provide information, documents or representations to the court to enable it to decide what if any requirement should be imposed on that person; or

(ii) to comply with any order imposing such a requirement;

(d) any notice given by the other party to the person responsible for the first arrangement under regulation 6;

(e) where the pension rights under the first arrangement were derived wholly or partly from rights held under a previous pension arrangement, any notice given to the person responsible for the previous arrangement under paragraph (2) of this regulation on the occasion of that acquisition of rights.

(4) The notice to the other party shall contain the following particulars:

(a) the fact that the pension rights have been transferred;

(b) the date on which the transfer takes effect;

(c) the name and address of the person responsible for the new arrangement;

(d) the fact that the order made under section 23 is to have effect as if it had been made in respect of the person responsible for the new arrangement.

(5) Both notices shall be given:

(a) within the period provided by section 99 of the Pension Schemes Act 1993 for the person responsible for the first arrangement to carry out what the member requires; and

    (b) before the expiry of 21 days after the person responsible for the first arrangement has made all required payments to the person responsible for the new arrangement.

5   Pension attachment: reduction in benefits

(1) This regulation applies where:

    (a) an order under section 23 or under section 17[10] of the 1984 Act has been made by virtue of section 25B or 25C imposing any requirement on the person responsible for a pension arrangement;

    (b) an event has occurred which is likely to result in a significant reduction in the benefits payable under the arrangement, other than:

        (i) the transfer from the arrangement of all the rights of the party with pension rights in the circumstances set out in section 25D(1)(a), or

        (ii) a reduction in the value of assets held for the purposes of the arrangement by reason of a change in interest rates or other market conditions.

(2) Where this regulation applies, the person responsible for the arrangement shall, within 14 days of the occurrence of the event mentioned in paragraph (1)(b), give notice to the other party of:

    (a) that event;

    (b) the likely extent of the reduction in the benefits payable under the arrangement.

(3) Where the event mentioned in paragraph (1)(b) consists of a transfer of some but not all of the rights of the party with pension rights from the arrangement, the person responsible for the first arrangement shall, within 14 days of the transfer, give notice to the other party of the name and address of the person responsible for any pension arrangement under which the party with pension rights has acquired rights as a result of that event.

6   Pension attachment: change of circumstances

(1) This regulation applies where:

    (a) an order under section 23 or under section 17 of the 1984 Act has been made by virtue of section 25B or 25C imposing any requirement on the person responsible for a pension arrangement; and

    (b) any of the events set out in paragraph (2) has occurred.

(2) Those events are:

    (a) any of the particulars supplied by the other party under rule 2.70 for any purpose mentioned in regulation 4(3)(c) has ceased to be accurate; or

    (b) by reason of the remarriage of the other party or otherwise, the order has ceased to have effect.

(3) Where this regulation applies, the other party shall, within 14 days of the event, give notice of it to the person responsible for the pension arrangement.

(4) Where, because of the inaccuracy of the particulars supplied by the other party under rule 2.70 or because the other party has failed to give notice of their having ceased to be accurate, it is not reasonably practicable for the person responsible for the pension arrangement to make a payment to the other party as required by the order:

    (a) it may instead make that payment to the party with pension rights, and

    (b) it shall then be discharged of liability to the other party to the extent of that payment.

(5)   Where an event set out in paragraph (2)(b) has occurred and, because the other party has failed to give notice in accordance with paragraph (3), the person responsible for the pension arrangement makes a payment to the other party as required by the order:

(a)   its liability to the party with pension rights shall be discharged to the extent of that payment, and

(b)   the other party shall, within 14 days of the payment being made, make a payment to the party with pension rights to the extent of that payment.

7   Pension attachment: transfer of rights

(1)   This regulation applies where:

(a)   a transfer of rights has taken place in the circumstances set out in section 25D(1)(a);

(b)   notice has been given in accordance with regulation 4(2)(a) and (b);

(c)   any of the events set out in regulation 6(2) has occurred; and

(d)   the other party has not, before receiving notice under regulation 4(2)(b), given notice of that event to the person responsible for the first arrangement under regulation 6(3).

(2)   Where this regulation applies, the other party shall, within 14 days of the event, give notice of it to the person responsible for the new arrangement.

(3)   Where, because of the inaccuracy of the particulars supplied by the other party under rule 2.70 for any purpose mentioned in regulation 4(3)(c) or because the other party has failed to give notice of their having ceased to be accurate, it is not reasonably practicable for the person responsible for the new arrangement to make a payment to the other party as required by the order:

(a)   it may instead make that payment to the party with pension rights, and

(b)   it shall then be discharged of liability to the other party to the extent of that payment.

(4)   Subject to paragraph (5), where this regulation applies and the other party, within one year from the transfer, gives to the person responsible for the first arrangement notice of the event set out in regulation 6(2) in purported compliance with regulation 7(2), the person responsible for the first arrangement shall:

(a)   send that notice to the person responsible for the new arrangement, and

(b)   give the other party a second notice under regulation 4(2)(b); and the other party shall be deemed to have given notice under regulation 7(2) to the person responsible for the new arrangement.

(5)   Upon complying with paragraph (4) above, the person responsible for the first arrangement shall be discharged from any further obligation under regulation 4 or 7(4), whether in relation to the event in question or any further event set out in regulation 6(2) which may be notified to it by the other party.

8   Service

A notice under regulation 4, 5, 6 or 7 may be sent by fax or by ordinary first class post to the last known address of the intended recipient and shall be deemed to have been received on the seventh day after the day on which it was sent.

9   Pension sharing order not to take effect pending appeal

(1)   No pension sharing order under section 24B or variation of a pension sharing order under section 31[11] shall take effect earlier than 7 days after the end of the period for filing notice of appeal against the order.

(2) The filing of a notice of appeal within the time allowed for doing so prevents the order taking effect before the appeal has been dealt with.

10   Revocation

The Divorce etc. (Pensions) Regulations 1996[12] and the Divorce etc. (Pensions) (Amendment) Regulations 1997[13] are revoked.

Signed by authority of the Lord Chancellor

Jane Kennedy Parliamentary Secretary, Lord Chancellor's Department

Date 14 April 2000

Explanatory note   *(This note is not part of the Regulations)*

These Regulations make provision pursuant to orders, including those made after proceedings overseas, for ancillary relief in proceedings for divorce, judicial separation or nullity which relate to the pension rights of a party to the marriage. In particular, they provide for:

(a)   the valuation of pension rights by the court;

(b)   notices of change of circumstances to be provided by the person responsible for the pension arrangement to the party without pension rights, or by that party to the person responsible to the pension arrangement; and

(c)   the stay period during which pension sharing orders cannot take effect.

Notes

[1] 1973 c. 18; section 24C was inserted by paragraph 4 of Schedule 3 to the Welfare Reform and Pensions Act 1999 (c. 30). Sections 25B, 25C and 25D were inserted by section 166(1) of the Pensions Act 1995 (c. 26) and amended by Schedule 4 to the Welfare Reform and Pensions Act 1999. Section 31(4C) was inserted by paragraph 7 of Schedule 3 to the Welfare Reform and Pensions Act 1999.

[2] 1984 c. 42; section 21(4) was inserted by section 22(5) of the Welfare Reform and Pensions Act 1999.

[3] Section 21A was inserted by paragraph 2 of Schedule 3 to the Welfare Reform and Pensions Act 1999.

[4] 1991/1247, as amended by SI 1992/2067, 1996/1674, 1778 and 1997/637.

[5] SI 2000/1048.

[6] SI 1996/1655, as amended by S.I. 1997/786 and 3038.

[7] SI 1996/1847.

[8] 1993 c. 48; section 93A was inserted by section 153 of the Pensions Act 1995 (c. 26).

[9] SI 1987/1110.

[10] Section 17 was amended by paragraph 3 of Schedule 12 to the Welfare Reform and Pensions Act 1999.

[11] Section 24B was inserted by paragraph 4, and section 31 was amended by paragraph 7, of Schedule 3 to the Welfare Reform and Pensions Act 1999.

[12] SI 1996/1676.

[13] SI 1997/636.

I.23

The Sharing of State Scheme Rights (Provision of Information and Valuation) (No 2) Regulations 2000

SI 2000/2914

Made 28 September 2000
Laid before Parliament 4 October 2000
Coming into force 1 December 2000

The Secretary of State for Social Security, in exercise of the powers conferred upon him by sections 45B(7),[1] 55A(6),[2] 55B(7),[3] 122(1)[4] and 175(3) and (4)[5] of the Social Security Contributions and Benefits Act 1992[6] and sections 23(1)(a), (b)(ii) and (c)(i) and (2), 49(4)[7] and 83(4) and (6) of the Welfare Reform and Pensions Act 1999 and of all other powers enabling him in that behalf, after agreement by the Social Security Advisory Committee that proposals to make regulation 4 of these Regulations should not be referred to it[8] and after consulting such persons as he considered appropriate,[9] hereby makes the following Regulations:

1 Citation, commencement and interpretation

(1) These Regulations may be cited as the Sharing of State Scheme Rights (Provision of Information and Valuation) Regulations 2000 and shall come into force on 1st December 2000.

(2) In these Regulations— 'the 1992 Act' means the Social Security Contributions and Benefits Act 1992; 'the 1999 Act' means the Welfare Reform and Pensions Act 1999; 'shareable state scheme rights' has the meaning given by section 47(2) of the 1999 Act.

2 Basic information about the sharing of state scheme rights and divorce

(1) The requirements imposed on the Secretary of State for the purposes of section 23(1)(a) of the 1999 Act (supply of pension information in connection with divorce etc.) are that he shall furnish—

(a) the information specified in paragraphs (2) and (3)—

(i) to a person who has shareable state scheme rights on request from that person; or

(ii) to the court, pursuant to an order of the court; or

(b) the information specified in paragraph (3) to the spouse of a person who has shareable state scheme rights, on request from that spouse.

(2) The information specified in this paragraph is a valuation of the person's shareable state scheme rights.

(3) The information in this paragraph is an explanation of—

(a) the state scheme rights which are shareable;

(b) how a pension sharing order or provision will affect a person's shareable state scheme rights; and

353

(c) how a pension sharing order or provision in respect of a person's shareable state scheme rights will result in the spouse of the person who has shareable state scheme rights becoming entitled to a shared additional pension.

(4) The Secretary of State shall furnish the information specified in paragraphs (2) and (3) to the court or, as the case may be, to the person who has shareable state scheme rights within—

(a) 3 months beginning with the date the Secretary of State receives the request or, as the case may be, the order for the provision of that information;

(b) 6 weeks beginning with the date the Secretary of State receives the request or, as the case may be, the order for the provision of the information, if the person who has shareable state scheme rights has notified the Secretary of State on the date of the request or order that the information is needed in connection with proceedings commenced under any of the provisions referred to in section 23(1)(a) of the 1999 Act; or

(c) such shorter period specified by the court in an order requiring the Secretary of State to provide a valuation in accordance with paragraph (2).

(5) Where—

(a) the request made by the person with shareable state scheme rights for, or the court order requiring, the provision of information does not include a request or, as the case may be, an order for a valuation under paragraph (2); or

(b) the spouse of the person with shareable state scheme rights requests the information specified in paragraph (3), the Secretary of State shall furnish that information to the person who has shareable state scheme rights, his spouse, or the court, as the case may be, within one month beginning with the date the Secretary of State receives the request or the court order for the provision of that information.

3   Information about the sharing of state scheme rights and divorce: valuation of shareable state scheme rights

Where an application for financial relief or financial provision under any of the provisions referred to in section 23(1)(a) of the 1999 Act has been made or is in contemplation, the valuation of shareable state scheme rights shall be calculated and verified for the purposes of regulation 2(2) of these Regulations in such manner as may be approved by or on behalf of the Government Actuary.

4   Calculation and verification of cash equivalents for the purposes of the creation of state scheme pension debits and credits

For the purposes of—

(a) section 49 of the 1999 Act (creation of state scheme pension debits and credits);

(b) section 45B of the 1992 Act (reduction of additional pension in Category A retirement pension: pension sharing);

(c) section 55A of the 1992 Act (shared additional pension); and (d) section 55B of the 1992 Act (reduction of shared additional pension: pension sharing),

cash equivalents shall be calculated and verified in such manner as may be approved by or on behalf of the Government Actuary.

Signed by authority of the Secretary of State for Social Security

Jeff Rooker

Minister of State, Department of Social Security

26th October 2000

Explanatory note *(This note is not part of the Regulations)*

These Regulations make provision in connection with the sharing, on divorce or nullity of marriage, of rights to the additional pension component of a state retirement pension.

Regulation 1 provides for citation, commencement and interpretation.

Regulation 2 specifies the information which the Secretary of State must supply to the parties to a marriage or the court in relation to the sharing of state scheme rights. This regulation also specifies the time limits within which that information must be furnished.

Regulation 3 sets out how the value of the state scheme rights must be calculated and verified when a valuation of those rights is requested in connection with the sharing of those rights.

Regulation 4 provides for how cash equivalents shall be calculated and verified for the purposes of the creation of state scheme pension debits and credits, the reduction of the additional pension, the creation of the shared additional pension and the reduction of the shared additional pension, as a result of pension sharing.

These Regulations do not impose any costs on business.

Notes

[1]   Section 45B is inserted by paragraph 2 of Schedule 6 to the Welfare Reform and Pensions Act 1999 (c. 30) and amended by section 41(2) of the Child Support, Pensions and Social Security Act 2000 (c. 19).

[2]   Section 55A is inserted by paragraph 3 of Schedule 6 to the Welfare Reform and Pensions Act 1999 and amended by section 41(3) of the Child Support, Pensions and Social Security Act 2000.

[3]   Section 55B is inserted by paragraph 3 of Schedule 6 to the Welfare Reform and Pensions Act 1999 and amended by section 41(4) of the Child Support, Pensions and Social Security Act 2000.

[4]   Section 122(1) is cited because of the meaning there given to 'prescribe'.

[5]   Section 175(4) was amended by paragraph 29(4) of Schedule 3 to the Social Security Contributions (Transfer of Functions etc.) Act 1999 (c. 2).

[6]   1992 c. 4.

[7]   Section 49 is amended by section 41(1) of the Child Support, Pensions and Social Security Act 2000.

[8]   See section 173(1)(b) of the Social Security Administration Act 1992 (c. 5).

[9]   See section 83(11) of the Welfare Reform and Pensions Act 1999.

The Pension Sharing (Excepted Schemes) Order 2000

SI 2000/3088

Made 20 November 2000
Laid before Parliament 20 November 2000
Coming into force 1 December 2000

The President of the Council, having been designated by the Treasury as having responsibility for the public service pension schemes referred to in article 2, in exercise of the powers conferred by section 27(3) of the Welfare Reform and Pensions Act 1999[1] hereby makes the following Order:

1 Title and commencement

This Order may cited as the Pension Sharing (Excepted Schemes) Order 2000.

2 Exception of public service pension schemes

The public service pension schemes relating to the following offices are excepted:

Prime Minister and First Lord of the Treasury;

Lord Chancellor; and

Speaker of the House of Commons.

Rt. Hon Margaret Beckett MP
President of the Council
20 November 2000

Explanatory Note *(This note is not part of the Order)*

This Order excepts the public service pension schemes relating to the offices of the Prime Minister and First Lord of the Treasury, Lord Chancellor and Speaker of the House of Commons for the purposes of section 27(1) of the Welfare Reform and Pensions Act 1999. Section 27(1) makes provision for pension sharing other than in relation to an excepted public service pension scheme.

Notes

[1] 1999 c. 30.

The Personal Pension Schemes (Transfer Payments) Regulations 2001

SI 2001/119

Made 23 January 2001

Laid before Parliament 24 January 2001

Coming into force In accordance with regulation 1

The Commissioners of Inland Revenue, in exercise of the powers conferred on them by section 638(2) and (7A) of the Income and Corporation Taxes Act 1988,[1] hereby make the following Regulations:

1. Citation, commencement and effect

(1) These Regulations may be cited as the Personal Pension Schemes (Transfer Payments) Regulations 2001 and shall come into force for the purposes of –

    (a) regulations 13 and 14, and

    (b) regulation 3 so far as it relates to regulation 13,

on 14th February 2001, and for all other purposes on 6th April 2001.

(2) Regulation 10 shall have effect in accordance with regulation 15(1)

. . .

13. Obligations where there is a pension sharing order or provision

(1) Where –

    (a) a transfer payment has been accepted by a personal pension scheme in the circumstances described in regulation 5(3) (omitting sub-paragraph (b)(ii) and the word 'either' preceding sub-paragraph (b)(i)), and

    (b) a pension sharing order or provision is subsequently made against the individual in respect of whom the payment was made,

the administrator of the receiving scheme shall recalculate the amount shown on the certificate referred to in regulation 5(2) or (3)(b), according to any debit to which the individual's rights under the scheme become subject by virtue of that order or provision, and shall prepare and sign a replacement certificate in respect of the individual's rights remaining after the reduction referred to in section 29 of the 1999 Act[2] or Article 26 of the 1999 Order[3] has taken place.

(2) where –

    (a) a transfer payment has been accepted by a personal pension scheme in the circumstances described in regulation 5(3) (omitting sub-paragraph (b)(i) and the word 'either' which precedes it), and

    (b) a pension sharing order or provision is subsequently made against the individual in respect of whom the payment was made,

the administrator of the receiving scheme shall prepare and sign a certificate in respect of the pension credit to which the transferee becomes entitled, showing that no amount may be paid out of the original payment by way of lump sum to the transferee.

(3) Where, after the date which is a member's pension date in relation to the arrangements in question, a pension sharing order or provision is made against that member, the administrator of the scheme shall prepare and sign a certificate in respect of the pension credit to which the transferee becomes entitled, showing that no amount may be paid out of the pension credit by way of lump sum to the transferee.

(4) The reference in paragraph (1) to a certificate referred to in regulation 5(2) or (3)(b) includes a reference to a certificate given under regulation 4 of the Personal Pension Schemes (Transfer Payments) Regulations 1988.[4]

PART V

EXCEPTIONS TO SECTION 638(7A) OF
THE TAXES ACT AND SUPPLEMENTAL

14. Exceptions to section 638(7A) of the Taxes Act

(1) Paragraphs (2) and (3) prescribe situations which fall within the exception in section 638(7A) of the Taxes Act[5] with regard to the making of transfer payments.

(2) The first situation is where –

   (a) the transfer payment is from the personal pension scheme ('the paying scheme') to another personal pension scheme ('the receiving scheme');

   (b) income withdrawals are being made by the member from the paying scheme with respect to which the conditions in section 634A[6] of the Taxes Act are satisfied, and the period of deferral of the purchase of an annuity has not ended;

   (c) the transfer payment comprises the whole of the funds held under any arrangement which is the subject of the transfer payment;

   (d) where any of the funds referred to in sub-paragraph (c) was the subject of, or represents the proceeds of, an earlier transfer payment made in accordance with this paragraph ('the earlier transfer payment'), the period between the earlier transfer payment and the transfer payment referred to in sub-paragraph (a) is not less than one year;

   (e) the arrangements made in accordance with the receiving scheme ('the new arrangements') were set up by the member for the purpose of accepting the transfer payment, or a previous or contemporaneous transfer payment which fell or falls within this first situation, and prohibit the acceptance of –

      (i) contributions, or

      (ii) further transfer payments which do not all within this first situation'

   (f) under the new arrangements the member elects to defer the purchase of such an annuity as is mentioned in section 634 of the Taxes Act,[7] and to make income withdrawals as mentioned in sub-paragraph (b), and that election takes effect simultaneously with the transfer payment; and

   (g) no benefit referred to in section 633(1)(b) or (d) of the Taxes Act[8] is payable under the new arrangements.

(3) The second situation is where –

   (a) the transfer payment is from the paying scheme to another personal pension scheme ('the receiving scheme');

   (b) the member referred to in section 634 of the Taxes Act ('the original member') has died;

   (c) a surviving spouse or dependant referred to in section 636 of the Taxes Act is making income withdrawals from the paying scheme with respect to which the conditions in section 636A of the Taxes Act[9] are satisfied, and the period of deferral of the purchase of an annuity has not ended;

(d) the arrangements made in accordance with the receiving scheme by the surviving spouse or dependant ('the substitute member') were set up for the purpose of accepting the transfer payment, or a previous or contemporaneous transfer payment which fell or falls within this second situation, and prohibit the acceptance of –

(i) contributions, or

(ii) further transfer payments which do not fall within this second situation;

(e) under the arrangements referred to in sub-paragraph (d) ('the new arrangements') the substitute member elects to defer the purchase of an annuity and to make income withdrawals with respect to which the conditions in section 634A of the Taxes Act are satisfied;

(f) the income withdrawals referred to in sub-paragraph (e) cannot be made after the original member would have attained the age of 75 or, if earlier, after the substitute member attains that age;

(g) the election referred to in sub-paragraph (e) takes effect simultaneously with the transfer payment

(h) any benefit under the new arrangements corresponds to a benefit which would have been payable to the same person under the paying scheme (and 'the same person' means the same individual, without having regard to the way in which that or any other individual is defined in the new arrangements); and

(i) the conditions in paragraph (2)(c), (d) and (g) are satisfied (construing the references in paragraph (2)(d) to 'this paragraph' and 'sub-paragraph (a)' as if they were references to the present paragraph and sub-paragraph (a) of this paragraph).

Explanatory Note *(This note is not part of the Regulations)*

Regulation 13 imposes obligations relating to the preparation of lump sum certificates where a pension sharing order or provision has been made.

Regulation 14 prescribes exceptions to section 638(7A) of the Taxes Act, allowing the transfer of funds which are subject to income drawdown in the circumstances specified.

Notes

[1] 1988 c. 1; subsection (7A) was inserted by paragraph 9 of Schedule 11 to the Finance Act 1995 (c.4).

[2] 1999 c.30.

[3] S.I. 1999/3147 (N.I. 11).

[4] S.I. 1988/1014; regulation 4 was amended by S.I. 1989/115.

[5] Section 638(7A) was inserted by paragraph 9 of Schedule 11 to the Finance Act 1995.

[6] Section 634A was inserted by paragraph 4 of Schedule 11 to the Finance Act 1995.

[7] Section 634 was amended by paragraph 12 of Schedule 10 to the Finance Act 1999 (c. 16).

[8] Section 633(1) was amended by paragraph 3 of Schedule 11 to the Finance Act 1995 and section 172 of the Finance Act 1996 (c. 8).

[9] Section 636A was inserted by paragraph 7 of Schedule 11 to the Finance Act 1995, and amended by paragraph 14 of Schedule 10 to the Finance Act 1999 and paragraph 12 of Schedule 13 to the Finance Act 2000 (c. 17).

Lord Chancellor's Department's Summary Paper

The provisions of the regulations under section 166 of the Pensions Act 1995

Issued by Family Policy Division, Lord Chancellor's Department, Rm 5.16, Selborne House, 54-60 Victoria Street, London SW1E 6QW, June 1996

Valuation of pensions

1   Power is taken in section 166(1) of the Pensions Act 1995 for the Lord Chancellor to make Regulations prescribing the method of valuing pension rights for the purposes of orders for financial provision upon divorce under the Matrimonial Causes Act 1973. Under the Matrimonial Causes Act 1973 currently and as amended by the Pensions Act 1995, when considering financial provision on divorce, the Court has to have regard to benefits under a pension which a spouse 'has or is likely to have' in the future.

2   With regard to the rights under the pension that the scheme member currently has, the prescribed method of valuation is to be a calculation of the Cash Equivalent Transfer Value (CETV) provided by the pension scheme(s) of which the party with the pension rights is a member. Schemes will be obliged to provide a CETV calculation where they are subject to the CETV legislation and the Court will be obliged to consider the CETV calculation.

3   The prescribed method will apply to active and deferred scheme members. It will be calculated by the scheme in accordance with existing legislation and, where applicable, with existing guidance produced by the Institute and Faculty of Actuaries. Unfunded schemes subject to the CETV legislation are included in the prescribed method of valuation and are obliged to provide calculations of CETVs.

4   The Regulations will remain silent as to the provision of information as to the future expectations of a pension. This will mean that the scheme member is only required to provide a CETV calculation for the purposes of valuation of his or her current rights under the scheme. It will also mean that the parties will not be barred from providing additional information as to the future expectation of the pension. The Court may, but will not be obliged, to take this into account in deciding the quantum of the Court order to reflect the loss of the future benefit of the pension to the party without pension rights. It will also mean that the scheme(s) will not be required to provide anything other than a calculation of the CETV to the scheme member.

5   The basic state pension and State Earnings Related Pension Scheme (SERPS) will be excluded from the prescribed method of valuation as it is not appropriate to them. The substitution rules relating to the basic state pension, whereby a former spouse's National Insurance record may be substituted for a person's own, will mean that a former spouse will normally qualify for a basic state pension in his/her own right The Department of Social Security Benefits Agency offers a pensions forecasting service from which a quotation of the notional capital value of the accrued net SERPS entitlement will be available on request. The loss of the benefit of both the basic state pension and SERPS by the party without pension rights would still be taken into account by the Court

6   Schemes will be required (upon written request when the CETV calculation is requested) to identify, in a 'broad brush' manner, the proportion of the total CETV attributable to the value of the spouse's pension payable on death before or after retirement

Date at which CETV should be calculated

7   The trustees or managers of the scheme will be required to calculate the CETV as soon as practicable, but within 3 months of its request, and provide it to the member within 10 working days of calculation in accordance with DSS Regulations.

8   The Regulations will specify the date on which the pensionable service is assumed to have terminated to enable the calculation of the CETV. For active scheme members this will be the date on which the scheme actually calculates the transfer value and for deferred members it is to be the actual date of termination of pensionable service.

Adjustments to the CETV

Death in service benefits

9   There will not be a prescribed method of valuing such benefits. The scheme information to which members are entitled under DSS Regulations will provide information as to their nature.

De minimis

10   Although it will not be possible to exclude any pension rights from consideration by the Court, the prescribed method of valuation is not to apply to pensions which have not vested for the purpose of preservation under scheme rules.

Non-availability of CETV

Pensions in payment

11   The prescribed method of valuation is to be the amount of the pension payments being paid by the scheme to the scheme member.

12   Where a pension is within one year of payment, the party without pension rights is not usually entitled to a CETV. It has, therefore, been decided that, where the scheme has information available as to the amount of the regular payments to be made under the pension in payment, that will be the prescribed method. Where that amount is not available from the scheme, the scheme will be required to produce a CETV.

Personal pensions & retirement annuity contracts

13   Personal Pension Arrangements entered into after 1 July 1988 may be ascribed a transfer value. The transfer value provided by the personal pension arrangement providers is to be the prescribed method of valuation for divorce purposes. Retirement Annuity Contracts entered into prior to 1 July 1988 do not allow members to transfer rights to another scheme. The internal transfer value provided by the contract providers will, therefore, be the prescribed method of valuation.

Use of other methods of valuation

14   In so far as pension rights accrued up to the time when the Court considers financial provision on divorce are concerned, the divorcing parties will not be permitted to use any method of valuation other than the prescribed methods. It would, however, be open to them to dispute whether the prescribed method had been correctly applied.

15   The Regulations will not prevent the parties providing further information as to the future expectation of the pension, and will not prevent the Court from taking account of that information in circumstances where it deems the Cash Equivalent Transfer Value method of valuation provides an inappropriate or inadequate indication.

16   The prescribed method cannot be used for discretionary benefits not included in the CETV or pensions administered outside England and Wales. Regulations cannot, therefore, bar other methods of valuing such pension benefits.

Provision of information to the scheme member

17   DSS Regulations currently allow for a CETV to be provided to scheme members once every 12 months. It is intended that the scheme member will be able to make one extra request every twelve months for a CETV calculation for the purposes of divorce proceedings, even if they have already received such a calculation within the last 12 months under DSS Regulations. It is intended that the Court will be able to order provision of a further CETV if there are exceptional circumstances requiring a further valuation.

18   It is intended that the next 12 months is to run from the date of the last CETV calculation under DSS Regulations, as pension schemes often have an annual date for generation of CETV information for members. Schemes will be able to charge for the provision of calculation of the CETV over and above what they are required to provide under DSS Regulations.

19   If the scheme member refuses to provide a valuation, the Court may request a valuation directly from the scheme and/or require the trustees or managers of the scheme to attend Court. If this were to be the case, and such instances are likely to be rare, the scheme could ask the Court to order the scheme member to pay the scheme's costs of attending Court, as the scheme member's non compliance with the order would have necessitated the scheme's attendance.

Other circumstances

20   Regulations will allow the Court to require the scheme member to provide information on any pension or accrued rights not subject to the prescribed method of valuation.

Route of application

21   Where a party intends to make application in respect of a pension, they must give notice of the application to the scheme and the scheme member. The party without pension rights will also be required to provide the scheme with a contact address and the name, address and account details of an account (bank or building society) into which payments under an attachment order may be made. This may be the address of a third party, such as a solicitor. Failure to provide this may be grounds for the scheme to object to the making of an attachment order.

22   Within 14 days of service of the application on the pension scheme, the scheme may request a copy of the party without pension right's affidavit supporting their application. Within 14 days of receipt of the affidavit, the scheme may file an affidavit in reply or apply to make representations to the Court or to be joined as a party to the proceedings. Where the Court makes an attachment order, a copy of the order is to be served on the scheme by the party without pension rights.

Notices from the party without pension rights

23 It is intended that once the Court has made an attachment order, the party without pension rights will be required to inform the scheme in writing of any change of his or her name, address or account details as soon as they have occurred.

24 An attachment order ceases upon remarriage of the party without pension rights as under current law. The party without pension rights is, therefore, to inform the scheme of their remarriage. The party without pension rights will also be required to comply with reasonable requests for information to facilitate payment under an order and as to their continued eligibility to receive payments from the scheme.

25 In the event of any over-payment to the party without pension rights as a result of a failure to comply with the requirement to inform the scheme of their remarriage or with a request from the scheme for information as to continuing eligibility, any application by the party with pension rights to recover such over-payment is to be made against the party without pension rights, not the pension scheme.

26 Where the scheme is unable to make payment to the party without pension rights through the party's failure to provide information for payment purposes, the scheme is to pay sums due to the party with pension rights. Any application to the Court to recover payments which the party without pension rights had not received, would be made against the scheme member.

Notices in respect of the party with pension rights

Complete transfer of pension rights

27 Where there is a transfer of all pension rights in respect of which an attachment order has been made, the order automatically affects the new scheme providing appropriate notices are given. The original scheme will be required to notify the new scheme of the order. The original scheme will send the new scheme a copy of the Court order and details of the name and contact address of the party without pension rights and their account details. As with all transfers currently, the new scheme cannot be compelled to accept a transfer. This will remain the case where there is an attachment order in force in respect of a pension.

28 The original scheme will also be required to notify the party without pension rights of the transfer, to their last recorded address, indicating a complete transfer of rights has taken place, giving details of the new scheme and stating that the order remains in force. The order will lapse on a deemed buyback into the State scheme.

Partial transfer of pension rights

29 In the case of a partial transfer, the original scheme could only comply with the order to the extent that it was able in the light of the reduced benefits. The party without pension rights would receive part payment from the scheme and then seek the remainder from the scheme member. The order does not transfer to the new scheme on partial transfer. The original scheme will be required to notify the party without pension rights of the partial transfer and that such transfer may affect the terms of the attachment order. The party without pension rights would then be able to decide whether to make application to Court or variation of the attachment order.

30 An order requiring the scheme member to nominate the party without pension rights as beneficiary of a lump sum payable on death would take effect to the extent that, if there were not sufficient funds to make a full payment in compliance with the terms of the order, the original scheme would be obliged to make a part payment.

Other circumstances

31   It is intended that a duty be placed on the trustees and managers of the pension scheme to notify the party without pension rights of any action by the party with pension rights or the scheme which will result in a reduction to the benefits payable under the attachment order. This is intended to ensure that the party without pension rights is aware of any changes to the pension which could reduce the eventual amount of payments made from it, so that he or she can consider whether to apply to the Court for variation of the Court order. It is also intended to ensure as far as possible that scheme members cannot avoid liability under an order by transferring pension assets. It should be noted, however, that such a requirement would not necessitate schemes providing notification to the party without pension rights of reductions to the value of the pension resulting from minor market fluctuations.

Route of payment under an attachment order

32   Payments under an attachment order will be made direct to the party without pension rights. The Court does not have power to order a party without pension rights to open a bank or building society account or other suitable account into which payments could be made. Regulations will, therefore, refer to payments being made direct to the account of the party without pension rights by any method by which a specific amount may be paid from the scheme's account to the account of the party without pension rights, for example, by standing order.

33   The party without pension rights will be required to ensure that the scheme has up to date information as to his or her personal details. There will be no obligation on the scheme to check whether these details have changed. The obligation to inform rests on the party without pension rights.

34   The President of the Family Division has agreed to make a Practice Direction encouraging the making of orders directly affecting pension schemes only where the payee has an account into which payment could be made via the BACS system.

Recovery of administrative expenses by schemes

35   Schemes will be able to recover their reasonable administrative expenses of:

- providing information on the value of any benefits under the scheme, in so far as its provision exceeds the requirements of DSS Regulations. Such costs are to be recouped by charging a fee to the scheme member. This fee may be recouped from the Legal Aid Fund if the party with pension rights is legally aided.

- complying with attachment orders. Schemes will be able to recoup their 'reasonable' costs of creating records, providing notices of change of circumstances and making payments under orders from the scheme member.

36   The Court will need to take account of the likely quantum of those costs and when and from whom they will be recoverable when making an attachment order.

Commencement

37   The new provisions will apply to the Court's consideration of financial provision where the petition for divorce, judicial separation or nullity has been presented to the Court on or after 1 July 1996 and where the prescribed notice of application has been filed with the Court on or after 1 August 1996. In addition, where the petition has been presented to the Court on or after 1 July 1996 and where the prescribed notice of application has been filed with the Court before 1 August 1996, the Regulations will

allow an amended application to be filed on or after 1 August to allow the provisions of section 166 of the 1995 Act to apply.

38 Provisions which directly affect schemes, will not affect them to the extent of having to make a payment under an order under section 166 of the 1995 Act until 6 April 1997 with one exception. Orders requiring schemes to make a one off lump sum payment to the party without pension rights are to be capable of taking effect from 1 July 1996, even if the order involves schemes making payment prior to 6 April 1997. Only orders containing a direction for the scheme to pay periodical payments direct to the party without pension rights, therefore, will not take effect until 6 April 1997.

Inland Revenue: Draft model rules for pension sharing on divorce: personal pension schemes

RULES

1 Introduction

This Scheme is a personal pension scheme designed for approval from the Inland Revenue under Chapter IV, Part XIV Income and Corporation Taxes Act 1988 and whose sole purpose is the provision of annuities, income withdrawals or lump sums under Arrangements made between the Provider and the Members in accordance with the Scheme. The Scheme is not a personal pension scheme for which an Appropriate Scheme Certificate will be sought from the Occupational Pensions Board under the Social Security Act 1986.

2 Interpretation and definitions

2.1 References to any Act of Parliament or regulations shall include any amendment or enactment thereof and, where the context so admits, words importing the singular shall include the plural and vice versa.

2.2 The following expressions shall have the following meanings:

'**Act**' Income and Corporation Taxes Act 1988.

'**Annuitant**' A person other than a Member who, under a Member's Arrangement, has an entitlement to an annuity from the Scheme.

'**Annuitant's Fund**' The value from time to time of those funds deriving from a Member's Fund which have been set aside for the purchase of an annuity for a particular Annuitant.

'**Appropriate Scheme Certificate**' A certificate issued by the Occupational Pensions Board in accordance with Part 1 of the Social Security Act 1986 and any regulations made thereunder.

'**Approved Scheme**' A personal pension scheme approved under the provisions of Chapter IV of Part XIV of the Income and Corporation Taxes Act 1988.

'**Arrangement**' An arrangement made by a Member with the Scheme for the provision of benefits in accordance with these Rules.

'**Dependant**' An individual who is or who immediately before a Member's death or retirement was financially dependant on the Member, or a child or adopted child of the Member who has not attained the age of 18 or has not ceased to receive fulltime educational or vocational training.

'**Employer**' A current employer of the Member.

'**Insurer**' An insurance company, EC company or friendly society as described in Section 659B of the Act.

'**Manager**' As defined in Rule 16.2.

'**Member**' An individual who has made an Arrangement with the Scheme, and may include an ex-spouse who has pension credit rights following the issue of a Pension Sharing Order.

'**Member's Fund**' The aggregate, under an Arrangement, of the accumulated values of the contributions paid to the Scheme by or in respect of the Member and any transfer payment accepted by the Scheme in respect of the Member it may also include any pension credit rights arising from a Pension Sharing Order, but excluding:

(a) the value of any contract or part of a contract to which contributions have been applied under the provisions of Rule 7.4 or Rule 7.7, and

(b) any administrative expenses of the Scheme and any payments of commission,

(c) any Pension Debit arising as a result of a Pension Sharing Order.

'**Net Relevant Earnings**' As defined in Section 646 of the Act.

'**Pension Credit Rights**' means rights to benefits arising under Section 29, Welfare Reform and Pensions Act 1999.

'**Pension Date**' The date determined under Rule 8.

'**Pension Debit**' means a debit under Section 29(1)(a) Welfare Reform and Pensions Act 1999.

'**Pension Sharing Order**' means a split of pension rights, arising after divorce under the provisions of Welfare Reform and Pensions Act 1999.

'**Provider**' The person who established the Scheme.

'**Rules**' The rules of the Scheme as amended from time to time.

'**Schedule**' The schedule accompanying these Rules.

'**Scheme**' This personal pension scheme.

'**Scheme Administrator**' The person appointed for the time being under Rule 4.1 and who is identified in the Schedule.

'**Special Commissioners**' The persons defined in Section 4 of the Taxes Management Act 1970.

'**Tax Year**' A period beginning on 6 April and ending on the next following 5 April.

3   The Provider

3.1   The Provider is identified in the Schedule and is a person described in Section 632(1) of the Act or in any regulations made thereunder and, where applicable, is authorised to carry on investment business as described in Section 632(2) of the Act.

3.2   If the Provider ceases to be a person described in Section 632(1) or in any regulations made under the Act or, if applicable, ceases to be authorised to carry on investment business-as described in Section 632(2), notice of such cessation shall be given immediately by the Scheme Administrator to the Inland Revenue.

4   Scheme Administrator

4.1   The Provider shall appoint a person resident in the United Kingdom to be the Scheme Administrator. The Scheme Administrator shall be responsible for the management of the Scheme and for the discharge of the duties imposed upon the Scheme Administrator by these Rules and by the Act and any regulations made thereunder.

4.2   The Provider may at any time by notice remove the Scheme Administrator and appoint another person resident in the United Kingdom as Scheme Administrator. If another Person is not appointed, the Provider, if resident in the United Kingdom, shall be the Scheme Administrator.

5   Amendments to rules and arrangements

5.1   No amendments shall be made to these Rules or to the Schedule accompanying the Rules without the prior approval of the Inland Revenue.

5.2   No alterations shall be made to a Member's Arrangement if those alterations would prejudice the approval of the Scheme under Chapter IV, Part XIV of the Act.

5.3   Subject to Rules 5.1 and 5.2 the Provider may amend at any time any of the Rules or the Schedule or, with the agreement of the Member, the terms of the Member's Arrangement.

5.4   The agreement of the Member to an amendment to the Arrangement shall not be required in respect of any change in terms which is made in accordance with a condition contained in the Arrangement made with the Member.

6   Membership

6.1   Membership of the Scheme is open to any individual who has not attained the age of 75. An individual who wishes to become a Member of the Scheme or who, already being a Member, wished to make a further Arrangement shall complete an application form in a form prescribed by the Scheme Administrator in which the individual agrees to be bound by the Rules and the Scheme Administrator, on behalf of the Provider, agrees to administer the Scheme in accordance with the Rules and the Arrangement. If a Member makes more than one Arrangement at the same time, and if the application form so provides, only one application need be made for those Arrangements. If the Scheme Administrator agrees, an ex-spouse who has Pension Credit Rights from a Pension Sharing Order may become a member of the Scheme.

6.2   Membership of the Scheme shall, subject to Rule 6.1, be at the absolute discretion of the Scheme Administrator.

7   Contributions and application of contributions

7.1   **General**   The Scheme shall not accept contributions other than those paid by a Member or by an Employer in respect of the Member. Nor shall the Scheme accept, in relation to any one of a Member's Arrangements, contributions paid after the Pension Date under that Arrangement.

7.2   **Member's contributions**   A Member may only pay contributions in a Tax Year for which the Member has Net Relevant Earnings. The only exception to the Rule is when Section 641 of the Act allows 'carry back' of contributions.

7.3   **Application of contributions for benefits**   The accumulated value of the contributions to the Scheme shall be used to provide benefits in accordance with the Rules, except so far as they are used to meet the administrative costs of the Scheme and to pay commission.

7.4   **Application of contributions for benefits**   A Member may, if allowed to do so under the Scheme, elect in writing to the Scheme Administrator that the whole or part of the contributions paid by or in respect of the Member under the Scheme shall be applied as premiums under a life insurance contract with an Insurer to provide a lump sum on the death of the Member before a specified age which must be before the attainment of age 75. This lump sum, which shall be a separate lump sum from that described in Rule 11.13, shall be payable in accordance with Rule 11. 17. Provided that rights to benefits under such a life insurance contract may not be assigned and Rule 11. 17c shall not apply unless this proviso is expressly deleted in the contract documentation in respect of specific Arrangements or part of Arrangements.

7.5   The total contributions applied by all Approved Schemes in the way described in Rule 7.4 when aggregated with any similar contributions paid under a contract approved under Chapter III, Part XIV of the Act shall not exceed the amount upon which tax relief is available in accordance with Sections 640(3) and 642 of the Act.

7.6   A transfer payment accepted by the Scheme under Rule 13.1 is not a contribution for the purpose of Section 639(1) of the Act and shall not be applied in the way described in Rule 7.4.

7.7   Waiver of contributions A Member may, if allowed to do so under the Scheme, elect in writing to the Scheme Administrator that not more than 25% of the contributions paid to the Scheme by or on respect of the Member be applied as a premium under a contract of insurance which provides for:

   a.   the Member's contributions and, if he or she wishes, those of an Employer to be waived for any period during which, by reason of incapacity, the Member is not able to follow his or her occupation and for the Member's Fund to be increased in relation to that period as though those contributions had been paid and, where appropriate, for any contract of insurance as described in Rule 7.4 to remain in force notwithstanding the fact that the premium has not been paid; and/or

   b.   the annuity payable to an incapacitated Member whose Pension Date has been determined under Rule 8.2 to be enhanced in a way and to an extent acceptable to the Inland Revenue.

7.8   Limit of contributions The aggregate amount of the contributions paid in a Tax Year by a Member and by an Employer in respect of the Member to all Approved Schemes and to all contracts and schemes approved under Chapter III, Part XIV of the Act shall not exceed the limits set by the Act.

7.9   Repayment of excess contributions A Member who pays a contribution to the Scheme may, if entitled to do so, deduct from the contribution when paid, and may retain, an amount equal to income tax at the basic rate on the contribution. If a Member has made such a deduction from all the contributions paid to the Scheme in a Tax Year, the Scheme Administrator must, at the end of that year and in respect of that Member, be satisfied that the limits described in Rule 7.8 have not been exceeded. If these limits have been exceeded (or if in any case the Inland Revenue tell the Scheme Administrator that they have been exceeded) the Scheme Administrator shall arrange for the excess to be repaid from the Scheme unless the Member proves to the satisfaction of the Scheme Administrator that it has been repaid by another Approved Scheme. If the contributions paid by the Member were paid after deduction of tax at the basic rate, the amount repayable will be the gross contribution before deduction of tax from which the Scheme Administrator will deduct tax at the same rate as was deducted from the contribution when paid or deemed to be paid for contributions carried back under Section 641 of the Act. The Scheme Administrator may adjust a repayment of contributions to take account of expenses and interest.

7.10   If an excess of contributions is to be paid by this Scheme, the Scheme Administrator shall ensure that any contributions made by the Member's Employers are not repaid until the excess is first deducted by the extent of the level of the Member's own contributions to all Approved Schemes in that Tax Year.

7.11   Investment of contributions A Member may, if allowed to do so under the Scheme, choose how the contributions and any transfer payment accepted by the Scheme in respect of the Member should be invested as between:

   a.   stocks and shares quoted on the UK Stock Exchange including securities traded on the Unlisted Securities Market,

   b.   stocks and shares traded on an overseas stock exchange being one recognised by the Inland Revenue,

   c.   unit trusts and investment trusts,

   d.   managed funds and unit-linked funds of an Insurer,

e.   deposit accounts, and

f.   commercial property.

8   Pension date

8.1   General A Member's Pension Date is the date on which the Member's Fund shall be applied to provide benefits for the Member and, subject to Rules 8.2 and 8.3, shall be a date no later than the day before that on which age 75 is attained or earlier ,than the date on which age 50 is attained as shall be notified to the Scheme Administrator in writing.

8.2   Incapacitated Member The Pension Date of a Member who becomes permanently incapacitated may be a date earlier than that on which age 50 is attained. A Member will be treated as permanently incapacitated if the Scheme Administrator has considered suitable medical evidence and is satisfied that the Member is incapable through infirmity of body or mind of carrying on his or her own occupation or any occupation of similar nature for which he or she is trained or fitted. The Scheme Administrator shall produce the medical evidence to the Inland Revenue if required.

8.3   Recognised occupation If a Member is on a recognised occupation the Pension Date for an Arrangement made in respect of that occupation may be a date earlier than that on which age 50 is attained. The Scheme Administrator shall not treat a Member as being in such an occupation unless the Inland Revenue have agreed that the Member's occupation is a recognised one; that is, one in which persons customarily retire before attaining the age of 50. This paragraph shall not apply to Pension Credit Rights of an ex-spouse from a Pension Sharing Order following a divorce.

8.4   On the admission to the Scheme of a Member who is in a recognised occupation the Scheme Administrator shall, in respect of the Arrangement which relates to that occupation, ensure that

a.   contributions to that Arrangement paid by the Member and, where appropriate, the Member's Employer are limited by reference to the Net Relevant Earnings from that occupation and from no other;

b.   the Pension Date chosen is not earlier than the date on which the Member attains the age agreed by the Inland Revenue as being the age at which the individuals in that particular occupation customarily retire; and

c.   all contributions to that Arrangement will cease if the Member ceases to carry on that occupation before the Pension Date.

8.5   If a Member who has been treated as being in recognised occupation ceases to carry on that occupation before the Pension Date he or she must immediately advise the Scheme Administrator.

9   Benefits

9.1   Annuities Subject to Rule 9. 10, at a Member's Pension Date the Member's Fund shall be applied to provide an annuity for the Member, any annuities under the provisions of Rule 12 and, if he or she has so elected in writing to the Scheme Administrator, the lump sum specified in Rule 10. The Scheme Administrator may only buy an annuity from an Insurer and must be satisfied that any person who is or may be entitled to payment of that annuity may enforce that entitlement.

9.2   The Member may choose from which Insurer the annuity is to be secured and shall give the Scheme Administrator written details of the choice no later than a date prescribed by the Scheme Administrator. If the Member fails to provide such details by that date the Scheme Administrator will select the Insurer from which the annuity is to be secured.

9.3   An annuity payable to the Member shall be payable for life and may be guaranteed for a period of up to 10 years notwithstanding the Member's death within that period.

9.4   The Member's annuity:

a. may be a level annuity, a variable annuity, or an annuity which increases in payment by a fixed percentage or on some other basis as arranged with the Insurer, and

b. must be paid in instalments not less frequently than annually an may be paid in advance or arrear.

9.5 If the Member's annuity is payable for a guaranteed period notwithstanding the Member's death within that period the Member may elect in writing to the Scheme Administrator and before its commencement that the annuity shall cease after his or her death but before the expiry of the guaranteed period on the happening of any of the following:-

a. the marriage of the Annuitant;

b. the Annuitant attaining age 18 or ceasing to be in full-time educational or vocational training if later.

9.6 The Member's annuity shall not be capable of surrender or, except as stated in Rule 9.7, of assignment. But the ban on surrender and assignment will not apply where the Scheme Administrator is complying with a Pension Sharing Order.

9.7 A Member's annuity payable for a guaranteed period notwithstanding the Member's death with that period may be assigned by will or by the Member's legal personal representatives in the distribution of the estate so as to give effect to a testamentary disposition, or to the rights of those entitled on an intestacy, or to an appropriation of it to a legacy or to a share or interest in the estate.

9.8 If the Scheme is to take the form of individual irrevocable trusts for each Member, the benefits for each Member under the Scheme will be held under a trust to be established by the Scheme Administrator for the benefit of that Member in a form approved by the Inland Revenue. If the Scheme is to take that form, or if it is established under a single irrevocable trust and the Arrangements are not to take the form of insurance contracts, the Member must also enter into a binding agreement by deed with the Scheme Administrator as trustee in a form approved by the Inland Revenue not to require withdrawal of the trust funds, or income from those trust funds to be paid to the Member, otherwise than for the payment of benefits under the Scheme at the time provided by the Rules.

9.9 The Scheme Administrator may only buy an annuity from an Insurer with a Member's Fund if the Scheme Administrator is satisfied that any person who is or may be entitled to payment of that annuity may enforce that entitlement:

a. under a trust;

b. under a deed poll; or

c. under Scottish law.

9.10 Annuity deferral The Member may choose to defer the purchase of the annuity specified in Rule 9.1 (even if the lump sum specified in Rule 10 is taken at Pension Date) and shall so notify the Scheme Administrator in writing no later than the date referred to in Rule 9.2. The Member shall also notify the Scheme Administrator in writing when he or she wished the deferral to end, providing at least one month's notice. The annuity must be purchased before the Member's 75th birthday.

9.11 Income Withdrawals Whilst the Member's annuity is deferred under Rule 9.10, the Member shall make income withdrawals from the Member's Fund (excluding any lump sum paid under Rule 10) in accordance with Rules 9.12 and 9.13. No income withdrawals shall be made after the Member attains the age of 75.

9.12 The aggregate amount of income withdrawals in each of the three successive periods of twelve months beginning with the Member's Pension Date shall not exceed the amount of the annuity purchasable on Pension Date calculated by reference to the amount of the Member's Fund (excluding any lump sum paid under Rule 10) and the current published tables of annuity rates prepared for this purpose by the Government Actuary. Such income withdrawals shall not be less than 35% of the annuity so calculated. This minimum limit shall not apply for the twelve month period during which the annuity is purchased or the Member dies.

9.13   The maximum and minimum annual income withdrawals for each period of three years succeeding the first, shall be calculated by reference to the amount of the Member's Fund remaining on the first day of each period and the Government Actuary's annuity rate tables current at that date.

10   Lump sum to member

10.1   A Member may opt no later than a date prescribed by the Scheme Administrator but which shall not be later than the Pension Date to receive a lump sum. The lump sum shall be payable when the Member's annuity under Rule 9.1 is first payable (or would have been payable but for an election to defer under Rule 9.10) and the following conditions shall apply:

    a.   if the Arrangement was made before 27 July 1989 the lump sum shall not exceed 25% of the amount at the time the lump sum is paid of the Member's Fund being used to provide the Member's annuity, ie the amount shall not include any part of the Member's Fund being used to provide annuities under Rule 12.1.

    b.   if the Arrangement was made on or after 27 July 1989 the lump sum shall not exceed 25% of the value at the time the lump sum is paid of the Member's Fund.

    c.   for the purposes of Rule 10.1a. and Rule 10.1b. there shall be excluded from the Member's Fund the accumulated value of any transfer payment accepted in respect of a Member and which had its origins in a source described in Rule 13.3b., d., e. and f. unless no certificate as described in Rule 10.1d. is relevant in respect of that part of any such transfer payment.

    d.   the Member may also receive as a lump sum the accumulated value of so much of any transfer payment accepted in respect of him or her from a source described in Rule 13.3b, d., e. and f. as has been certified as payable in that form. In no circumstances, however, may the lump sum paid under this Rule 10 exceed the limit set under Section 635 of the Act.

10.2   The right to payment of a lump sum is not capable of surrender or assignment. But the ban on surrender or assignment will not apply where the Scheme Administrator is complying with a Pension Sharing Order.

11   Death of a member before pension date

11.1   General In the event of the death of a Member before the Pension Date the Member's Fund shall be applied to provide the benefits described in Rule 11.

11.2   Annuities Subject to Rule 11. 18, if the Member elected in writing to the Scheme Administrator at such time before the Pension Date as the Scheme Administrator prescribed, and the Scheme Administrator agreed, an annuity shall be paid to the Member's surviving spouse and/or Dependant. The annuity shall be secured by the application of the Member's Fund (excluding any amount which is to be paid as a lump sum under the provisions of Rule 11.14b) as a premium under an annuity contract issued by an Insurer previously chosen by the Member or Annuitant in a A.A form prescribed by the Scheme Administrator.

11.3   Annuities may be paid to one or more Dependants and may be paid whether or not any annuity is being paid to a surviving spouse.

11.4 The aggregate annual amount (or, if that amount varies, the aggregate of the initial annual amounts) of all annuities payable under Rules 11.2, 11.3 and 11.14 and which are payable under the same Arrangement shall not exceed the highest annual amount of the annuity that would have been payable under that Arrangement to the Member (ignoring any entitlement to commute part of it for a lump sum) had the Pension Date under that Arrangement been the day before the date of death. Any part of the Member's Fund that cannot be used to secure an annuity under Rule 11.2 will be used by the Scheme Administrator to meet general administration expenses of the Scheme. Where a Member has a Pension Debit arising from a Pension Sharing Order, the annuities payable under this Rule must not exceed the amount of annuity that could have been paid to the Member after deducting the Pension Debit.

11.5 An annuity payable under Rule 11.2 shall be payable for life (except as stated in Rules 11.7 and 11.8) and may be guaranteed for a period of up to 10 years notwithstanding the death of the Annuitant within that period.

11.6 An annuity payable under Rule 11.2:

    a.   may be a level annuity, a variable annuity or an annuity which increases in payment by a fixed percentage or on some other basis as arranged with the Insurer, and

    b.   must be paid in instalments not less frequently than annually and may be paid in advance or arrear.

11.7 An annuity payable under Rule 11.2 may cease on the marriage of the Annuitant but where an annuity is payable to a Dependant solely by virtue of that Dependant being under the age of 18 at the date of death of the Member; that annuity shall cease to be payable on the date on which the Annuitant attains age 18 or ceases to be in full-time educational or vocational training if that is later.

11.8 If an annuity payable under Rule 11.2 is payable for a guaranteed period notwithstanding the death of the Annuitant within that period the original may elect in writing to the Scheme Administrator and before its commencement that the annuity shall cease after his or her death but before the expiry of the guaranteed period on the happening of any of the following:

    a.   the marriage of a later Annuitant to whom it is payable;

    b.   the later Annuitant to whom it is payable attaining the age of 18 or ceasing to be in full-time educational or vocational training if that is later.

11.9 An annuity paid under Rule 11.2 shall not be capable of surrender or, except as stated in Rule 11.10, of assignment. But the ban on surrender and assignment will not apply where the Scheme Administrator is complying with a Pension Sharing Order.

11.10 Any annuity paid under Rule 11.2 and payable for a guaranteed period notwithstanding the death of the Annuitant within that period may be assigned by will or by the Annuitant's legal personal representatives in the distribution of the estate so as to give effect to a testamentary disposition, or to the rights of those entitled on an intestacy, or to an appropriation of it to a legacy or to a share or interest in the estate.

11.11 The payment of an annuity to a surviving spouse shall commence as soon a practicable after the death of the Member but the surviving spouse may with the consent of the Insurer elect that payment of the annuity shall commence at:

    a.   the expiry of any guaranteed period during which the Member's annuity is payable; or

    b.   any time up to the date the surviving spouse attains age 60, if later.

11.12 The payment of an annuity to a Dependant shall commence as soon as practicable after the death of the Member.

11.13 Lump sum In the event of there being no annuities payable under Rule 11.2 the Member's Fund, excluding any amount which is required by virtue of Rule 11.14

to be applied for the purpose of securing an annuity or annuities, shall be paid as a lump sum in accordance with Rule 11.17.

11.14   Application of a transfer on the death of a Member   A Member in respect of whom the Scheme has accepted a transfer payment consisting of or including funds which have at any time been held for the provision of benefits for the Member by a scheme or schemes of the kind described in Rule 13.3b., d., e. or f. may elect in writing to the Scheme Administrator that on death before the Member's Pension Date the Scheme Administrator shall:

    a.   apply the whole of the accumulated value of the transfer payment to secure an annuity payable to the Member's surviving spouse or a Dependant; or

    b.   subject to Rule 11.16, pay a lump sum of up to 25% of the accumulated value to the transfer payment in accordance with Rule 11.17 and apply the balance to secure an annuity payable to the Member's surviving spouse or a Dependant.

11.15   Any annuities payable under Rule 11.14 shall be subject to the conditions in Rules 11.3 to 11.12.

11.16   Where the Scheme Administrator is satisfied that there is no surviving spouse and no annuity is to be paid to a Dependant, the Member's Fund shall be paid as a lump sum in accordance with Rule 11.17.

11.17   Payment of lump sum   Any lump sum payable under this Rule shall be paid by the Scheme Administrator as soon as practicable. The lump sum shall be paid:

    a.   in accordance with any specific provision regarding payment of such sums under the contract or contracts applying to the Arrangements in question; or

    b.   if a. is not applicable and at the time of the Member's death the Scheme Administrator is satisfied that the contract is subject to a valid trust under which no beneficial interest in a benefit can be payable to the Member, the Member's estate, or the Member's legal personal representatives, to the trustees from time to time of the trust; or

    c.   subject to the proviso in Rule 7.4, if a., and b. are not applicable and the benefit arises under Rule 7.4 and at the time of the Member's death, the contract is vested in an assignee, to the assignee; or

    d.   if a., b. and c. are not applicable, at the discretion of the Scheme Administrator to or for the benefit of any one or more of the following in such proportions as it decides:

        i.   any persons (including trustees) whose names the Member has notified to the Scheme Administrator in writing prior to the date of the Member's death;

        ii.   the Member's spouse, children and remoter issue;

        iii.   the Member's Dependants;

        iv.   the individuals entitled under the Member's will to any interest in the estate;

        v.   the Member's legal personal representatives.

    For this purpose a relationship acquired by legal adoption is as valid as a blood relationship.

If by the second anniversary of the Member's death the Scheme Administrator has been unable to pay the whole of the lump sum in accordance with this Rule, the unpaid amount will be transferred to a separate account outside the scheme until it can be repaid.

11.18   Annuity deferral   The purchase of any annuity payable under Rule 11.2 may be deferred at the written option of the Annuitant unless he or she has attained the age of 75 or has made an election under Rule 11.11 (b). Subject to Rule 11.7, the Annuitant shall notify the Scheme Administrator in writing when he or she wishes the deferral to end, providing at least one month's notice. The annuity must be purchased before the earlier of the Member's 75th birthday and the Annuitant's 75th birthday.

11.19 Income withdrawals Whilst any annuity is deferred under Rule 11.18, the Annuitant shall make income withdrawals from the Annuitant's Fund in accordance with Rules 11.20 and 11.21. No income withdrawals shall be made after the date on which the Member would have attained the age of 75 or if earlier, the day before the date on which the Annuitant attains that age. Nor shall the Annuitant make any income withdrawals after ceasing to be entitled to an annuity under Rule 11.7 (any Annuitant's Fund remaining at the date of such cessation will be used to meet general administrative expenses of the Scheme).

11.20 The aggregate amount of income withdrawals in each of the three successive periods of twelve months beginning with the date of the Member's death shall not exceed the amount of the annuity purchasable on that date calculated by reference to the amount of the Annuitant's Fund and the current published tables of annuity rates prepared for this purpose by the Government Actuary. Such income withdrawals shall not be less than 35% of the annuity so calculated. This minimum limit shall not apply for the twelve month period during which the annuity is purchased or the Annuitant dies or ceases to be entitled to an annuity under Rule 11.7.

11.21 The maximum and minimum annual income withdrawals for each period of three years succeeding the first shall be calculated by reference to the amount of the Annuitant's Fund remaining on the first day of each such period and the Government Actuary's annuity rate tables current at that date.

11.22 If an Annuitant dies after electing to defer his or her annuity under Rule 11.18 but before the annuity is purchased, the Annuitant's Fund shall be paid as a lump sum in accordance with Rule 11.17. For the purposes of this Rule, the word 'Member' in Rule 11.17 shall be read as 'Annuitant'.

12   Death of member on or after pension date

12.1 If the Member elected in writing to the Scheme Administrator at such time before the Pension Date as the Scheme Administrator prescribed, and the Scheme Administrator agreed, an annuity shall be paid to the Member's surviving spouse and/ or a Dependant and shall be secured at his or her Pension Date under a contract issued by an Insurer. For the purpose of this Rule 12.1 the Member or the Annuitant may choose the Insurer and written details of the choice shall be given to the Scheme Administrator no later than a date prescribed by the Scheme Administrator. If such details are not supplied by that date the Scheme Administrator will select the Insurer from which the annuity is to be secured.

12.2 The annuity or annuities payable under Rule 12.1 shall be subject to the conditions in Rules 11.3 and 11.12 except that the aggregate annual amount (or, if that amount varies, the aggregate amount of the initial. annual amounts) of all annuities to which Rule 12.1 applies and which are payable under the same Arrangement shall not exceed the annual amount (or if the annual amount varies, the highest annual amount) of the annuity payable to the Member at the date of death. Any part of the Member's Fund that cannot be used to secure an annuity under Rule 12.2 will be used by the Scheme Administrator for the purpose of the Scheme. Where the Member has a Pension Debit arising under a Pension Sharing Order, the annuities paid under this Rule must not exceed the amount of the annuity payable to the Member after deducting the Pension Debit.

12.3   Death of Member During Annuity Deferral Period If the Member dies after electing to defer his or her annuity under Rule 9.10 but before the annuity is purchased, the Member's Fund may be applied to or for the benefit of the Member's surviving spouse and/or Dependant(s). Each such Annuitant may choose, in writing, to receive his or her Annuitant's Fund in one of the following ways:

a.   purchase of an annuity, either immediately, or following a period of deferral during which income withdrawals shall be made in accordance with Rules 11.20 and 11.21, or

b.   payment of the Annuitant's Fund as a lump sum.

The option under a. to defer annuity purchase and take income withdrawals shall not be available to any Annuitant who makes an election under Rule 11.11(b), or who has already attained the age of 75. The annuity must be purchased before the earlier of the Member's 75th birthday and the Annuitant's 75th birthday.

Any Annuitant making income withdrawals under option a. may nevertheless choose option b. at any time within the two years following the death of the Member.

No Annuitant shall make any income withdrawals after ceasing to be entitled to an annuity under Rule 11.7. Subject to the preceding paragraph, any Annuitant's Fund remaining at the date of such cessation will be used to meet general administrative expenses of the Scheme.

Where the Member's Fund is not to be applied to or for the benefit of a surviving spouse and/or Dependant, it shall be applied in accordance with Rule 11.17.

12.4 Death of Annuitant During Annuity Deferral Period If an Annuitant who has chosen under Rule 12.3(a) to receive an annuity after a period of deferral, dies before the annuity is purchased, the Annuitant's Fund shall be paid as a lump sum in accordance with Rule 11.17. For the purposes of this Rule, the word 'Member' in Rule 11.17 shall be read as 'Annuitant'.

12.5 Taxation of Lump Sum Paid During Annuity Deferral Period Payment of a lump sum under Rule 12.3(b) or 12.4 shall be made after deduction of tax at the rate specified in Section 64813(2) of the Act.

13   Transfers to the scheme

13.1   The Scheme Administrator may accept, on a written request being made by a Member and subject to the conditions of Rules 13.2, 13.3, 13.4, 13.5, 15.1 and Rule 15.2, a transfer payment from any of the schemes described in Rule 13.3 representing the interests of the Member and the interests, if any, of the Member's spouse or Dependants in those schemes.

13.2   The Scheme Administrator shall, when accepting and applying a transfer payment comply with the requirements of the Act and any regulations made thereunder and generally with all Inland Revenue requirements.

13.3   The schemes from which the Scheme Administrator may accept a transfer payment are:

a.   an Approved Scheme;

b.   a retirement benefits scheme approved or being considered for approval under Chapter 1 or Part XIV of the Act;

c.   a retirement annuity contract or trust scheme approved under Chapter III or Part XIV of the Act;

d.   a relevant statutory scheme as described in S611A ICTA 1988;

e.   a deferred annuity contract securing benefits by virtue of previous membership of:

i.   a scheme under b. above; or

ii.   a scheme under d. above;

f.   such other source as may be permitted by the Inland Revenue.

13.4   If the source of a transfer payment is an Approved Scheme, the Scheme Administrator shall ascertain from the administrator of the transferring scheme the proportion of the transfer payment which consists of funds which have at any time been held for the provision of benefits for the Member by a scheme or schemes of the kind described in Rule 13.3b, d., e. or f.

13.5 A transfer payment is not a contribution for the purposes of Section 639(1) of the Act and must not be applied for the purpose of Rule 7.4.

14 Transfers out of the scheme

14.1 The Scheme Administrator shall, on a written request made by a Member in a form prescribed by the Scheme Administrator, transfer the Member's Fund in respect of that Member to the scheme administrator or trustee of a scheme of which the Member has become a Member, or which is able and willing to accept the transfer payment, and which is:

a. an Approved Scheme;

b. a retirement benefits scheme approved under Chapter 1 of Part XIV of the Act and to which the employer of the individual contributes or has contributed;

c. a relevant statutory scheme as described in S61 1A ICTA 1988; or

d. a scheme approved for the purposes of this Rule 14.1 by the Inland Revenue.

14.2 A Member may withdraw the application for a transfer payment by notice in writing to the Scheme Administrator at any time up to the point when the Scheme Administrator is committed to a third party in carrying out the Member's request. A Member who has withdrawn an application may make another.

14.3 If a transfer payment is made to an Approved Scheme the Scheme Administrator shall, within 30 days' after the date on which the transfer is made, provide the administrator of the receiving scheme with information regarding the proportion of the transfer payment which consists of funds which have at any time been held for the provision of benefits for the Member by a scheme or schemes of the kind described in Rule 13.3b, d, e or f and any other information which the administrator may reasonably require.

14.4 The Scheme Administrator shall, when making a transfer payment, comply generally with all Inland Revenue requirements, with the requirements of the Act and any regulations made thereunder and with the requirements of the Pensions Schemes Act 1993 and any regulations made thereunder. Whereas transfers may not normally be made after Pension Date, a Member with pension credit rights may transfer out in accordance with Rule 14. This will apply where the pension credit rights were acquired after the Pension Date of the Member with the pension debit and who was receiving income withdrawals.

14.4 A Member may choose that different parts of the Members Fund be transferred as described in Rule 14.1 to different schemes, but he or she must choose that the whole of the Member's Fund be transferred.

15 Conditions for all transfers

15.1 All transfer payments to be accepted under Rule 13 or made under Rule 14 shall, subject to Rule 15.2, be effected by a direct payment between the Scheme Administrator and the administrator or trustee of the other scheme or through a financial intermediary acceptable to both parties and must be completed before the Member's Pension Date.

15.2 All transfer payments accepted from a deferred annuity contract securing benefits by virtue of previous membership of a retirement benefit scheme approved or being considered for approval under Chapter 1 of Part XIV of the Act shall be effected by a direct payment between the insurance company which issued that contract and the Scheme Administrator, or through a financial intermediary acceptable to both parties.

16 Investments and deposits

16.1 The rights under the Scheme of a Member or any beneficiary are solely to those rights given to them by these Rules and any Arrangements made thereunder.

16.2 The provisions of Rules 16.3 to 16.6 shall, subject to Rule 16.7 have effect from 1 November 1989 and for the purposes of those rules the Manager shall mean the person who holds the investments or deposits for the purpose of the Scheme.

16.3 Loans The Manager shall not use directly or indirectly any of the investments or deposits held for the purpose of the scheme to lend money to a Member or any person connected with a Member. The Manager shall also ensure that no loan from any source made to a Member shall in any way affect the return on the investments representing that Member's interest in the Scheme.

16.4 Other investments The Manager shall not, subject to Rule 16.5, enter into any investment transactions with a Member or any person connected with a Member. Investment transactions shall include the acquisitions by the Manager of a Member's commercial property or stocks or shares and the subsequent acquisition by the Member of any of the investments or deposits held for the purpose of the Scheme. All transactions in quoted United Kingdom or overseas securities shall take place through a recognised stock exchange.

16.5 The Manager shall not hold directly as an investment residential property or land connected with such a property, or personal chattels capable in any way of private use. This proviso shall not, subject to Rule16.4, apply to commercial land and property. The Manager may lease any commercial property to any business or partnership carried on by a person connected with a Member but the Manager shall then ensure that the lease, including the rent payable, is on commercial terms as determined by a professional valuation.

16.6 Connected transactions For the purposes of Rules 16.3, 16.4 and 16.5, a person is connected with a Member if that person falls within the definition of 'connected persons' in Section 839 of the Act. The Scheme Administrator shall ensure that any transaction falling within the provisions of these Rules is not one with a connected person, save where permitted by Rule 16.5. Also, a transaction need not be regarded as being with a Member or a connected person if it relates wholly to pooled funds. For this purpose pooled funds which are genuinely open to any member of the public, which are clearly described in the Provider's literature and disclosure documents as being standard funds open to all, where the investment management is undertaken by the Provider with no direction or influence by Members and where a common value is applied across the membership with no segregation or linking of particular assets to particular Members.

16.7 Transactions completed before 1 November 1989 The provisions of Rules 16.3 to 16.6 shall not apply to any transactions which fall within those provisions but which were completed before 1 November 1989.

17 Scheme rules and arrangements

The provisions of these Rules shall override those of any other documents constituting the Scheme which conflict with or have the effect of changing the meaning of any of the provisions in the Rules or which prejudice the sole purpose as stated in Rule 1.

18 Withdrawal of approval of scheme

If the Inland Revenue withdraw approval of the Scheme under the Act, the Scheme Administrator shall inform the Members of the withdrawal within 3 months of the later of the date on which the notice of withdrawal issued by the Inland Revenue is received and the date on which the notice is received that the Special Commissioners have dismissed any appeal against the decision of the Inland Revenue or have ruled that the decision is to have effect from a different date. The Scheme Administrator shall thereupon discontinue the Scheme as described in Rule 21.

19 Withdrawal of approval of an arrangement made by a member

If the Inland Revenue withdraw approval under the Act in relation to a Member's Arrangement, the Scheme Administrator shall inform the Member of such withdrawal within 3 months of the later of the date on which the Scheme Administrator receives the notice of withdrawal issued by the Inland Revenue and the date on which the notice is received that the Special Commissioners have dismissed any appeal against the decision of the Inland Revenue or have ruled that the decision is to have effect from a different date.

20 Powers to operate scheme as closed scheme

The Provider may at any time close the membership of the Scheme and may:

    a.   continue to accept contributions from or in respect of existing Members who shall continue to participate in the Scheme in accordance with the Rules and any Arrangements made under the Scheme; or

    b.   decline to accept further contributions but otherwise continue to operate the Scheme in accordance with the Rules.

21 Discontinuance of scheme

The Provider may at any time wind up the Scheme by giving notice to the Scheme Administrator. In that event the Scheme Administrator will notify each Member of his or her rights and options including the right to a transfer payment under Rule 14. When a Member does not make a choice under Rule 14, the Scheme Administrator will transfer the Member's Fund to an Approved Scheme of the Scheme Administrator's choice. The Member's consent will not be required for such a transfer.

22 Miscellaneous provisions

22.1 The Scheme Administrator may require any Member or any other person to whom an annuity or lump sum is payable under the Scheme to produce such evidence and information from time to time as is reasonably required for the purposes of the Scheme and if such evidence or information is not produced the Scheme Administrator may withhold payment of any annuity or lump sum in relation to which the evidence or information was required until such time as it is produced.

22.2 If in the opinion of the Scheme Administrator, any person to whom a benefit is payable under the Scheme is unable to manage his or her affairs for any reason, the Scheme Administrator may pay the benefit in whole or in part for the maintenance of that person and/or any of his or her Dependants. The receipt of the payee shall be a complete discharge to the Scheme Administrator for the benefit or part thereof so paid.

22.3 The Scheme Administrator may decide that any person who is entitled to a payment under the Scheme shall cease to have any claim to such payment if at least six years have passed from the date the payment became due and the address of the person is not known to the Scheme Administrator who shall have taken all reasonable steps to ascertain the address.

SUMMARY

Please see the attached model rules for approved personal pension schemes which include amendments for the administration of pension sharing on divorce. The use of the model rules once agreed and in force for the implementation of pension sharing will enable quicker approval under Chapter IV Part XIV ICTA 1988.

This version of the model rules is for personal pension schemes which are not to be used for contracting out of SERPs.

Schemes which are intended to be used for contracting out should use a separate version known as the integrated model rules. That version covers both tax approval requirements of the Inland Revenue and the requirements of Department of Social Security (DSS) legislation for appropriate personal pension schemes. It will be made available by the DSS.

There will be no model rules for use with retirement annuity contracts (RACs) approved under Chapter III Part XIV ICTA 1988. These contracts are in the form of insurance contracts between an individual and an insurance company or friendly society and there is no scheme structure. No new contracts have been sold since personal pensions were introduced on 1 July 1988 and any pension sharing arrangement involving RACs will usually be handled by a transfer of annuity rights to another type of pension scheme.

These draft rules enable an ex member of the personal pension scheme of the spouse with the pension debit. This will depend on the agreement of the scheme administrator. Alternatively, the ex-spouse may transfer to another pension scheme. This right to transfer extends to the situation where the other spouse's pension is already in payment by income withdrawals.

Once accepted as a member of the scheme, the ex-spouse is subject to the same conditions as apply to other members. But the ex-spouse will only be able to contribute if he or she has net relevant earnings.

Inland Revenue: Draft model rules for pension sharing on divorce: occupational schemes

Definitions

Ex-Spouse means an individual to whom Pension Credit Rights have been allocated following a pension sharing order, agreement or equivalent provisions.

[Ex-Spouse Participant is an individual who participates in the scheme.]

Insurance Company is as defined in Section 659 (B) of the Act.

Negative Deferred Pension means the amount of the deferred pension awarded to the Ex-Spouse under the court order, agreement or equivalent provisions, at the date of the divorce, revalued under the statutory Revaluation Order in force at Relevant Date. **Where a Pension Debit Member triggered the Relevant Date by leaving Pensionable Service, the amount of the Negative Deferred Pension must be increased to the same proportionate extent as any increase in the amount of his/her pension under the scheme and any Associated Scheme at the date on which the pension begins to be payable, compared with the amount of the maximum permissible pension under the scheme and any Associated Scheme at the Relevant Date.**

[Pension Credit means a credit under section 29(1)(b) of the Welfare Reform and Pensions Act 1999 or under corresponding Northern Ireland legislation.]

[Pension Credit Rights means rights to future benefits under a scheme which are attributable (directly or indirectly) to a Pension Credit.]

Pension Debit means a debit under section 29(1)(a) of the Welfare Reform and Pensions Act 1999 or under corresponding Northern Ireland legislation.

Pension Debit Member means a Member whose benefits have been permanently reduced by a Pension Debit. Such a Member will either be;

   (i) a Member who is a controlling director of a company which is his/her employer if he/she is a director of the company to whom paragraph (b) of section 417(5) of the Taxes Act 1988 applies either at the date on which the marriage was dissolved or annulled, or at any time within the period of 10 years before that date or,

  (ii) a Member whose earnings (which for these purposes were paid in consequence of Service during each of the three years of assessment before the year of assessment in which the marriage was dissolved or annulled, and from which tax was deducted in accordance with the Income Tax (Employment) Regulations 1993) exceed 1/4 of the Permitted Maximum in the year in which the date of divorce occurs.

   • [**Scheme Member** means a Member of the scheme to whom benefit is currently accruing as a result of service as an employee, or an Ex-Spouse participant whose rights under the scheme derive from a pension sharing order, agreement or equivalent provisions.]

2 Assignment

Rule [xx] is amended to permit the assignment of part or all of the Member's retirement benefits under the scheme to his/her Ex-Spouse [, or the assignment of part or all of the Ex-Spouse Participant's benefits under the scheme to his/her Ex-Spouse].

3

The following options will be available to the Ex-Spouse Participant, where the funds underpinning the Pension Credit Rights are segregated from any funds accrued in respect of Service.

   (i) A pensioner can be paid at any time between attaining age 50 and 75 at the request of the Ex-Spouse Participant. The Ex-Spouse Participant cannot defer commencement of the pension beyond his/her 75th birthday. If he/she is aged 75 or over at the date the pension sharing order is implemented, the pension must come into payment immediately. There is no limit on the amount of the pension. Such a pension should not be commuted, surrendered or assigned except in accordance with the rules. Such a pension must be payable for life.

  (ii) Where the Member who was formerly married to the Ex-Spouse Participant has already received a pension benefit, or Pension Credit Fights were transferred into the scheme with a lump sum nil certificate, no lump sum may be paid to the Ex-Spouse Participant. Otherwise, the Ex-Spouse Participant may choose to take a lump sum in commutation for part of the pension. The lump sum is limited to a maximum of 2.25 x the initial annual rate of pension at the time the pension first becomes payable.

 (iii) Where the Ex-Spouse Participant dies before benefits come into payment a lump sum death benefit can be paid to any person at the discretion of the trustees. The lump sum is limited to 25% of the fund underlying the Pension Credit Rights. The balance of the underlying fund may be used to provide a non-commutable pension to a widow, widower or dependants. The amount of pension payable to a widow, widower or dependant is limited to a maximum of $^{2}/_{3}$ of the amount of the pension that could have been paid to the Ex-Spouse Participant at the date of death if the whole fund underlying the Pension Credit Rights had been used to purchase an annuity at the best available market rate. Where more than one pension is to be paid the total of all the pensions cannot exceed the amount of the pension that could have been paid to the Ex-Spouse Participant. Such pensions must be payable for life, except that pensions paid to children must cease on the attainment of age 18 or. if later, on the cessation of full time education.

(iv) £ Where the Ex-Spouse Participant dies after pension has come into payment, a non-commutable pension may be payable to a widow, widower or dependant of the Ex-Spouse Participant.

The amount of pension payable to a widow, widower or dependant is limited to a maximum of $^2/_3$ of the initial annual pension which was paid to the Ex-Spouse Participant as increased by any rise in the Index since the commencement of the. Ex-Spouse Participant's pension.

Where more than one pension is to be paid the total of all the pensions cannot exceed the amount of the initial annual pension which was payable to the Ex-Spouse Participant, as increased by any rise in the Index since the commencement of the Ex-Spouse Participant's pension.

Such pensions must be payable for life, except that pensions paid to children must cease on the attainment of age 18 or, if later, on the cessation of full time education.

Where the Ex-Spouse Participant selected a 5 year guarantee and the guarantee period has not expired, the remaining balance of the pension instalments can be paid as a lump sum. Where the Ex-Spouse Participant selected a guarantee exceeding 5 years and the guarantee period has not expired, the remaining balance of the pension instalments must be paid in pension form to an individual or individuals at the discretion of the Trustees.

(v) [On the date the pension becomes payable (but not where the pension is paid in the form of income withdrawal), part of this may be surrendered for the purpose of securing under the scheme, on the death of the Ex-Spouse Participant, a pension payable to a widow, widower or dependants nominated by the Ex-Spouse Participant when exercising this option. The amount surrendered should not exceed the reduced pension that the Ex-Spouse Participant retains.]

(vi) Full commutation of the Pension Credit Rights on the grounds of triviality or exceptional circumstances of serious ill-health. Where the Ex-Spouse Participant is also entitled to benefits under the scheme as a Member, for the purposes of determining the aggregate value of the total benefits payable to the member under triviality rule [XX], benefits from Pension Credit Rights must be included.

(vii)The Ex-Spouse Participant may request that the Trustees arrange a transfer of his/her Pension Credit Rights to another scheme approved under Chapter 1 Part XIV of the Act or a scheme approved under Chapter IV Part XIV of the Act or any other arrangement approved for the purposes of this rule by the Board of Inland Revenue. The Trustees may, if they wish, confirm to the receiving scheme or arrangement, that the transfer value consists purely of funds for the benefit of an Ex-Spouse Participant.

(viii)At the point the pension becomes payable, the Ex-Spouse Participant may request that the Trustees arrange for the purchase of an annuity from an Insurance Company of his/her choice.

(ix) The rights to a Pension Credit Benefit under the scheme shall not be absolute, but shall be forfeited upon the bankruptcy of the Ex-Spouse Participant. Such benefits may then be paid to any individuals or individual as specified by the Trustees, in their absolute discretion.

4 Notwithstanding any other provisions of the rules, the benefits for a Pension Debit Member are additionally subject to the following limits:

(i) The pension shall not exceed the Aggregate Retirement Benefit in rule # less the Negative Deferred Pension in this scheme and the Negative Deferred Pension in any Associated scheme

(ii) The lump sum from this and any Associated Scheme shall not exceed:

    (a) for Pension Debit Members who are Class A Members or Class B Members, an amount determined by 2.25 x the initial annual rate of pension payable as calculated in sub-paragraph (i) above

    (b) for Pension Debit Members who are Class C Members, an amount of the greater of:

        (I) 2.25 x the initial annual rate of pension payable as calculated in sub-paragraph (i) above or,

        (II) an amount determined in accordance with rule [XX] as if there had been no Pension Debit, less 2.25 x the Negative Deferred Pension.

(iii) On the death of the Pension Debit Member, any pension for a widow, widower or dependant shall not exceed $^2/_3$ x (an amount determined in accordance with rule [XX] as if there had been no Pension Debit, less the Negative Deferred Pension).

5 The Trustees must give full details of the Pension Debit and a lump sum certificate specifying the maximum permissible lump sum, to the receiving scheme/arrangement where the fund underlying the benefits for a Pension Debit Member is transferred to another scheme approved under Chapter 1 Part XIV of the Act or a scheme approved under Chapter IV Part XIV of the Act or any other arrangement approved for the purposes of this rule by the Board of Inland Revenue.

6 Where the Trustees accept a transfer payment and are informed by the transferor that the transfer value consists purely of funds for an individual with the status of an ex-spouse participant in the former scheme or arrangement, then the Trustees may, if they wish, segregate the transfer payment from other funds held for the benefit of the Member. Such segregated benefits will not count towards any limit on benefits for that Member.

7 Where the Trustees accept a transfer payment and are informed by the transferor of the details of the current value of a Pension Debit relating to the transfer payment, the Trustees must include the then current value of the Pension Debit in the calculation of any limit on benefits for that Member.

NOTE

All text in square brackets is optional.

    • For Small Self-Administered Schemes the new definition of 'scheme member' replaces the current definition, where Ex-Spouses are permitted to join the scheme.

    • If the rules do not already contain a definition of 'Relevant Date', the definition below should be inserted:

    'Relevant Date shall mean the date of retirement, leaving Pensionable Service or death as the case may be.'

    Alternatively if the rules already define the circumstances covered by 'Relevant Date', but another defined term is used, that term should be substituted for 'Relevant Date' in the definition of Negative Deferred Pension.

    • If the rules do not already contain a definition of 'Index', the definition below should be inserted :

'Index shall mean the Government's Index of Retail Prices.'

Alternatively if the rules already cover indexation, but another defined term is used, that term should be substituted for 'Index' in Rule 3(iv).

The references to Rule [XX] in the above refers to the existing scheme rules and the appropriate rule number should be shown when drafting scheme specific rules.

SUMMARY

Please see other attachment with our draft rules to cover pension sharing on divorce. When we issued rules for consultation on the flexibility package outlined in Update 54, we explained how we envisaged the rules fitted into existing scheme documentation.

The model rules are only for use with schemes that are approved under section 591 ICTA 1988; they are not intended for use by schemes approved under section 590 ICTA 1988.

The model rules are intended to bolt onto existing scheme documentation and will be used in connection with our Standard Documentation certification procedures. Powers of alteration clauses will vary from scheme to scheme. It is therefore the responsibility of the drafters of scheme documentation to ensure that the model rules are brought into effect so that they fit into the existing scheme documentation.

Please note additionally the model rules are not intended for use without amendment with the following types of scheme:

(i)   Simplified Defined Contribution Schemes

(ii) Free Standing AVC Schemes

(iii) Pure Lump Sum Benefit Schemes

(iv) Schemes that provide a lump sum scheme by separate allocation rather than by commutation

We do not envisage that rules for Death in Service Schemes will need to be amended. Such schemes will not usually have any assets to share on the member's divorce.

The detailed operation of the draft rules

Please note that where a term is in capital letters it has either been defined in the bolt on rules or it is assumed to be one that is defined in the existing rules.

For the avoidance of doubt Class A, Class B and Class C Members have the following meanings:

Class A Member shall be any Member who is not a Class B or Class C Member

Class B Member shall mean any Member:

(a)   who, on or after 17 March 1987 and before 1 June 1989, joined the Scheme being a scheme which commenced before 14 March 1989, or

(b)   who the Board of Inland Revenue have agreed in writing to be a Class B Member by virtue of previous membership of a Relevant Scheme

and in either case, has not opted to become a Class A Member.

Class C Member shall mean any Member who joined the Scheme before 17th March 1987 or who joined subsequently and the Board of Inland Revenue have agreed in writing to be a Class C Member by virtue of previous membership of a Relevant Scheme and, in either case, has not opted to become a Class A Member.

The current definition of 'negative deferred pension' is applicable only to defined benefit schemes. It will need to be extended to cover money purchase schemes, once a decision is made on the method of valuing the pension.

Please note that rule 3 and certain definitions have been shown in square brackets because they are optional and will only need to be adopted by schemes offering membership to ex-spouses. Where this is the case, the scheme eligibility rule will need widening to permit the ex-spouse to join. We have not attempted to draft an amended eligibility rule as such rules will vary widely from scheme to scheme. We have drafted the bolt on rules to distinguish between a member of a scheme by virtue of service with an employer ('member') and someone being offered scheme membership by virtue of a pension sharing order ('ex-spouse'). Drafters of scheme documentation using the bolt on will therefore need to ensure when they draft the extension to the eligibility clause, that they do not inadvertently classify ex-spouses as 'members'.

For SSASs which allow ex-spouses to join the scheme, a new definition of 'scheme member' must be adopted. In SSASs the definition of 'scheme member' is used to trigger the specific additional restrictions required by the SSAS Regulations : there will usually be a separate definition of 'member' for the purpose of scheme eligibility. Any SSAS which includes a definition of 'SSAS' in its scheme documentation must ensure that a suitable amendment is made to comply with the requirement stated in the second bullet point of paragraph 21 of the Update.

Please note that Rule 3 (v) is also optional, as all schemes do not permit members to allocate part of their pension benefits.

Pension Schemes Office Update No 60

10 February 2000

INTRODUCTION OF PENSION SHARING ON DIVORCE

Schemes affected

1   All pension schemes where an application for approval has been made but approval not yet granted.

2   All pension schemes seeking approval on or after the first appointed day.

Timetable

3   The legislation introducing pension sharing on divorce was contained in the Welfare Reform and Pensions Act and the 1999 Finance Act.

4   The Finance Act changes will, in general, take effect from the date that the provisions of the Welfare Reform and Pensions Act begin. This will be known as the 'second appointed day' and is expected to be around the end of the year 2000.

5   So that schemes can be ready for the introduction of pensions sharing there will also be a 'first appointed day' which will be set by Treasury Order. It is expected that this will be triggered 21 days after the laying of Inland Revenue and Department of Social Security Regulations. Those regulations are expected to be laid in early April 2000.

6   On or after the 'first appointed day' any occupational pension scheme or personal pension scheme seeking approval must include pension sharing provisions in its rules in anticipation of the changes coming into force. **So if the application for approval was made before the first appointed day, but the scheme had not obtained approval by that day the pension sharing provisions must be included before it can be approved.**

7   The full provisions will be set out in a further Update which is to follow. Pension Schemes Office will be offering standard wording for scheme rule amendments to cover the provisions. A draft of the further Update and model rules were included in a consultation document issued to the industry on 26 January 2000. It is anticipated that the finalised Update and model rules for both occupational pension schemes and personal pension scheme will be available from April 2000.

8   The first appointed day will be announced in an Inland Revenue Press Release when the Treasury Order is made. This will provide 21 days notice.

Action

9   Where a scheme has already been submitted for approval, for example on interim documentation, practitioners may wish to submit full documentation before the first appointed day to enable the scheme to be approved.

10   There will be schemes which have not yet been submitted for approval. If practitioners wish to obtain approval before the first appointed day, they should be submitted to the PSO as soon as possible in a fully approvable state.

Pension Schemes Office Update No 62

28 April 2000

Please pass a copy of this Update to everyone in your organisation who needs to see it.

The category of schemes covered by this Update is shown below.

Category: Occupational Pension Schemes, Personal Pension Schemes, Buy-out Contracts and Retirement Annuity Contracts

Action: All tax approved pension schemes must take the necessary steps to enable them to comply with pension sharing orders. Similarly, buyout contracts and retirement annuity contracts will require policy endorsements, so that pension sharing can take place.

Summary: This Update explains the changes to tax law and Inland Revenue practice to allow pension sharing in tax approved pension schemes.

It should be read by all practitioners, scheme administrators etc of tax approved pension schemes (both occupational and personal), where pension sharing might take place.

Enquiries:

Occupational Pension Schemes and Buy-out Contracts:

Jan Speyers 0115 974 1759, or

Trevor Smeath 0115 974 1643

Personal Pension Schemes and Retirement Annuity Contracts:

Alan Bateman 0115 974 1760, or

Mark Surry 0115 974 1765

PENSION SHARING ON DIVORCE OR NULLITY

Introduction

At present there are, broadly, two ways in which tax approved pension rights can be taken into account as part of a financial settlement on divorce or nullity of marriage. They can be either:

- offset against another assets in the financial settlement, or
- subject to an earmarking/attachment order

Pension sharing provisions in Schedule 10 to the Finance Act 1999 and changes to the Inland Revenue discretionary approval practice have been made to complement the introduction of social security and family law that is intended to provide a clean break between the parties to a divorce settlement in relation to pension sharing matters.

Contents of this Update

Paragraphs

How pension sharing works

1   When a couple divorce and there is a financial settlement, the pension rights of either spouse can be split between the parties at that date. Such a split takes place where a pension sharing order, agreement or equivalent provision in accordance with the Welfare Reform and Pensions Act which received Royal Assent on 11 November 1999, is made by the courts. In England, Wales and Northern Ireland, pension sharing settlements will be possible only by court order. In Scotland the majority of settlements will be by agreement although a few will be by court order.

2   Pension sharing is not compulsory. It will still be possible, as at present, to offset or earmark/attach pension rights.

3   Pension sharing works as follows:-

Spouses A and B were a married couple who subsequently divorced. Spouse A is a member of an occupational pension scheme or a personal pension scheme or has a retirement annuity contract or buy-out contract. Under pension sharing there will be a reduction in spouse A's pension rights. This reduction is known as the 'pension debit'. There will be a corresponding allocation of rights to spouse B. This is known as the 'pension credit'.

4   Pension credits may be retained in spouse A's pension scheme to provide an independent pension for spouse B or they may be transferred to another pension arrangement. More details are in paragraphs 24 to 26.

5   Pension debits reduce spouse A's pension rights. Instructions on the calculation of pension debits are in paragraph 70.

Pension debits can be ignored in calculating maximum permissible benefits in certain circumstances, see paragraphs 67 and 68.

6   Although pension sharing is not compulsory for divorcing couples, all schemes must include the pension sharing provisions in their governing documentation.

Commencement of changes

7 Measures described in this Update are contained in section 79 and Schedule 10, Finance Act 1999. The Act received Royal Assent on 27 July 1999. These changes complement the changes to Social Security, Matrimonial and Family Law contained in the Welfare Reform and Pensions Act.

8 The Finance Act changes will, in general, take effect from the date that the provisions of the Welfare Reform and Pensions Act begin. This will be known as the 'Second Appointed Day' and will be 1 December 2000. Once the changes are in force, divorcing couples will be able to share pension rights without affecting the tax approved status of the pension scheme.

9 On or after the 'First Appointed Day', any occupational pension scheme or personal pension scheme seeking approval must include the pension sharing provisions in its rules in anticipation of the changes coming into force. So if the application for approval was made before the First Appointed Day, but the scheme had not obtained approval by that day, the pension sharing provisions must be included before it can be approved. The First Appointed Day will be 10 May 2000.

10 Where an occupational pension scheme or personal pension scheme approved before the First Appointed Day is being reconsidered because of amendments to its rules in the period between that day and the date that the provisions of the Welfare Reform and Pensions Act begin - see paragraph 8 above, the following provisions are disapplied:

For occupational pension schemes

- subsection 590(3)(bb) Income and Corporation Taxes Act 1988 ('ICTA') which prevents rebuilding (see paragraph 60)
- subsection 590(3)(da) ICTA which limits the member's retirement lump sum (see paragraphs 73 to 75).

For personal pension schemes

- subsection 636(3A) ICTA which limits the amount of annuity to a surviving spouse or dependant of the member (see paragraph 65).

This is to protect such a scheme from having its approval withdrawn solely on grounds that these requirements (which are provisions that do not come into force until 1 December 2000) are not reflected in its rules. Schemes to which this paragraph applies, are not required to incorporate the pension sharing provisions in their rules before the Second Appointed Day.

11 For occupational pension schemes approved before the First Appointed Day and which continue to be approved on and after the date that the pension sharing provisions come into force (the Second Appointed Day), the provisions referred to in paragraph 10 will be applied by statutory override. This is contained in paragraph 18(5) of Schedule 10, Finance Act 1999. The effect of this override is to deem such schemes to have those provisions in their rules.

Personal pension schemes approved before the 'First Appointed Day' may wish to amend their rules before the 'Second Appointed Day' to introduce provisions for pension sharing. If they do, they should include the change mentioned in paragraph 66 despite the statutory disapplication mentioned in paragraph 10. However, the inclusion of that change will not be a factor in considering the approval status in the period before the 'Second Appointed Day'.

12 Schemes are not expected to rely on overriding provisions indefinitely. They should aim to incorporate the pension sharing requirements in their rules at the earliest convenient opportunity. Where, therefore, rules are being amended on or after the Second Appointed Day in other than a trivial way, the PSO will expect schemes to incorporate the pension sharing provisions in those amendments.

13   In some instances the overriding provisions in paragraph 11 above will be too restrictive for certain scheme members and so exceptions or modifications will be needed. These will be made by regulation. See paragraph 23 for more details.

14   For occupational pension schemes approved on or after the First Appointed Day, the appropriate exceptions and modifications will be reflected in changes to Practice Notes IR12 (1997)(PN). Standard wording for rules for occupational pension schemes will be made available to facilitate approval (see paragraph 86). For personal pension schemes approval on or after the First Appointed Day the legislation changes should be included in the rules. Model rules for personal pension schemes will become available for both contracting out and non-contracting out schemes, and these model rules should be used to replace the existing versions.

Legislation

Primary legislation

15   The measures contained in the Finance Act 1999 change the pension scheme tax rules for both occupational and personal pension schemes. The changes are, in the main, to section 590 ICTA for mandatory approval of occupational pension schemes and to certain sections of Chapter IV, Part XIV of ICTA for approval of personal pension schemes.

The following paragraphs provide a very broad outline of the changes.

16   Current pensions law in ICTA is constructed on the basis of providing benefits for an individual scheme member (employee in the case of an occupational pension scheme) with benefits for a surviving spouse or dependant after the death of the scheme member. The assignment or surrender of any pension or annuity is not generally allowed. As a transfer of pension rights in the manner described in paragraph 3 above would otherwise contravene the ban on assignment or surrender, Finance Act 1999 removes that ban where a pension sharing order, agreement or equivalent provision in accordance with the Welfare Reform and Pensions Act is made by the courts. For personal pension schemes the ban is additionally removed on benefits:

- in the form of income withdrawals (which are regarded separately from annuities)

- on a retirement lump sum (which is a separate form of benefit and not a part of the annuity).

17   No special tax reliefs are given for divorcing couples. A scheme member who wants to rebuild a shared pension can do so within the rules for benefits and contributions. More details can be found in paragraphs 59 onwards dealing with pension debits for scheme members.

18   Both occupational pension schemes and personal pension schemes are able to provide benefits from shared pension rights for an ex-spouse. Where, in the case of an occupational pension scheme, the ex-spouse is also an employee member of the same scheme, the shared pension does not restrict the benefits given to him or her in respect of the employment, subject always to paragraph 52. This is to help maintain fairness in the treatment of the ex-spouse's pension. With a personal pension scheme, the amount of the member's annuity would not, in any event, be subject to a statutory limit.

19   For both occupational pension schemes and personal pension schemes, the changes also ensure that the shared pension given to the ex-spouse receives broadly the same treatment as the pension rights of a scheme member. So for example, if the scheme member could receive a tax-free lump sum on retirement, this option will also be available to the ex-spouse. More details can be found in paragraphs 25 onwards dealing with pension credits for the ex-spouse.

Regulatory changes

20   Changes have been made to existing retirement benefits schemes regulations to reflect the pension sharing provisions. The regulations which have been amended are:

- The Retirement Benefits Schemes (Restriction on Discretion to Approve) (Small Self-administered Schemes) Regulations 1991 (SI 1991/1614)– **'SSAS regulations'**
- The Retirement Benefits Schemes (Restriction on Discretion to Approve) (Additional Voluntary Contributions) Regulations 1993 (S1 1993/3016)– **'AVC regulations'**

Brief details of the changes are given in paragraphs 22 and 23 below.

A further set of regulations - The Retirement Benefits Schemes (Restrictions on Discretion to Approve)(Excepted Provisions) Regulations 2000 (SI 2000/1087), ensure that these amending regulations do not trigger the three year deadline for scheme rule amendments (in section 5911A(2) ICTA).

21   The SSAS regulations have been amended by:

- extending the definition of 'scheme member' to include an ex-spouse with pension credit rights. This will ensure that where an ex-spouse is offered membership of a SSAS, the same conditions, restrictions etc will apply to him or her as apply to other members;
- making clear that the numerical limit of less than 12 scheme members does not include ex-spouses who qualify as scheme members because of rights arising from a pension sharing order. This is to prevent schemes ceasing to be SSAS's simply because pension sharing causes the scheme membership to increase to 12 or more.

22   The AVC regulations have been amended by:

- making clear that where the ex-spouse is also a scheme member in respect of service as an employee, and is paying AVCs, then the ex-spouse pension credit rights can be ignored for the purposes of calculating the maximum benefits that can be paid, subject always to paragraph 52;
- ensuring that the transfer of pension rights to an ex-spouse (the 'pension credit') will be added back for an employee when calculating maximum benefits other than for those within the easement described in paragraphs 67 and 68.

23   As mentioned in paragraph 13, regulations have been made to except/modify the effect of the override. These disapplication regulations:

- exclude from the rebuilding restriction in section 590(3)(bb) ICTA, those employees to whom the easement described in paragraphs 67 and 68 relates;
- exclude from both the rebuilding restriction in section 590(3)(bb) ICTA and the lump sum restriction in section 590(3)(da) ICTA, Simplified Defined Contribution Schemes. This is because such schemes are controlled by limits on contributions, therefore the restrictions are inherent;
- modify the effect of section 590(3)(da) ICTA for members with pre 17 March 1987 continued rights (see Glossary to PN). For these members the lump sum will be on the basis described in paragraph 74;
- exclude from the lump sum restriction in section 590(3)(da) ICTA, those employees who are members of schemes which provide only a lump sum retirement benefit, which does not exceed three eightieths of the employee's final remuneration for each year of service up to a maximum of 40;

- exclude from the lump sum restriction in section 590(3)(da) ICTA, those employees who are members of schemes which provide for a pension and a separate lump sum rather than a commutable pension.

Pension credits

24 Pension credit rights allocated to an ex-spouse following a pension share will be secured independently from those of the scheme member. They may be retained in the member's occupational pension scheme (including a Free-Standing Additional Voluntary Contributions Scheme) and benefits paid from that scheme in due course. Subject to Department of Social Security (DSS) requirements, it is for the scheme trustees to decide how to give effect to those pension credit rights in the scheme. Alternatively, they may be transferred to another pension arrangement. An ex-spouse who is initially given scheme membership may, subsequently, ask for a transfer of the pension credit rights if desired. This right may be exercised independently of any benefit rights arising as an employee. In the case of a personal pension scheme, the ex-spouse will not have a contract with the scheme. It will be necessary, if the pension credit rights are to continue in the same scheme, for a new contract to be made and this will become an 'arrangement' as mentioned in the legislation with the ex-spouse as a new member. If the ex-spouse is already a member, it may be possible to add the pension credit rights to the existing arrangements.

25 Subject to the penultimate sentence of this paragraph, pension credit rights arising from a tax approved pension scheme can be transferred only to another tax approved arrangement. Subsequent transfers of those rights may also be made only to a tax approved arrangement. Pension credit rights may be transferred to an overseas scheme provided the procedures and conditions set out in PN 10.39 and PN Appendix VI are met. For personal pension schemes, the ex-spouse may transfer out to another scheme even though the scheme member has already passed the pension date and is receiving payments of income withdrawal.

26 Where an ex-spouse's pension credit rights are to be secured by an annuity contract, amendments to section 431B ICTA ensure that the contract will qualify for 'pension business' treatment.

Date pension credit rights available

27 The payment date depends on the sort of pension arrangement under which they arise. They are, subject to DSS requirements, generally payable as follows:

- Occupational pension scheme approved under section 590 ICTA (mandatory approval): payable between age 60 and 75;
- Occupational pension scheme approved under section 591 ICTA (discretionary approval): payable between age 50 and 75, or earlier on grounds of exceptional circumstances of serious ill-health or, on the grounds of incapacity where, in the case of the latter, the ex-spouse is simultaneously taking employee benefits on these grounds under the scheme in which the pension credits are held;
- Personal pension scheme: payable between age 50 and 75;
- Retirement annuity contract: payable between age 60 and 75 or earlier than the prescribed age ranges for personal pension schemes and retirement annuity contracts on the grounds of incapacity by reference to any occupation of the ex-spouse;
- Buy-out contract: payable between age 50 and 75 except where the origin is a section 590 ICTA approved scheme.

28   The annuity purchase deferral and income drawdown arrangements set out in PSO Updates No 8 for personal pension schemes and 54 for occupational pension schemes may be applied to pension credit rights when they become payable.

Form of pension credit rights – general

29   Subject to any additional DSS requirements in relation to safeguarded rights (which are defined in section 36 of the Welfare Reform and Pensions Act), the ex-spouse may be given rights which broadly follow those available to the scheme member. This maintains consistency with the normal tax rules for pensions.

30   Where, for example, a scheme member could exchange part of a pension for a lump sum at the time of retirement, the ex-spouse may be given a similar option.

31   But where, on the other hand, an ex-spouse's pension credit rights arise from an arrangement which does not allow for a tax-free retirement lump sum, for example, a Free Standing Additional Voluntary Contributions Scheme, the ex-spouse may receive benefits in pension form only. Similarly, if the scheme member has already taken a tax-free lump sum under the scheme before pension sharing took place, then the ex-spouse may receive benefits in pension form only.

32   Where the ex-spouse's pension credit rights are transferred (see paragraph 24 above) in circumstances where those rights cannot be taken in lump sum form, a NIL certificate (see PN 10.35) must be provided to the receiving scheme by the transferring scheme.

Form of pension credit rights – personal pension schemes and retirement annuity contracts

Personal pension schemes

33   Pension credit rights are available and payable from the fund of the ex-spouse as segregated from the fund of the original member. The range of benefits are:

- an annuity;
- income withdrawals;
- a tax-free lump sum of 25% of the fund;
- where the ex-spouse dies before the pension credit rights come into payment, a ta-free lump sum in the form of a return of the fund or an annuity to a surviving spouse or dependant of the ex-spouse;
- where the ex-spouse dies after the pension credit rights (paid as an annuity) come into payment, an annuity to a surviving spouse or dependant of the ex-spouse. If the pension credit rights were being paid by income withdrawals, then the survivors of the ex-spouse may opt for income withdrawals, an annuity or a lump sum taxed at 35% under section 648B ICTA.

Retirement annuity contracts

34   As no new retirement annuity contracts can be created, the pension credit rights will be secured by a transfer either to a personal pension scheme, or to an occupational pension scheme of which the ex-spouse is already a member. The benefits then payable will follow normal requirements in accordance with the rules of the receiving scheme applicable to transfers.

Form of pension credit rights – occupational pension schemes

Scheme approved under s 591 ICTA 1988

35 Subject to DSS requirements, the following benefits are available where pension credit rights arise under a scheme approved under s 591 ICTA which is not a Simplified Defined Contribution Scheme:

- a pension;
- a tax-free lump sum of 2.25 x the initial annual rate of pension before commutation to be paid (3 times the initial annual rate of the separate pension in a separate pension and lump sum scheme). If, however, the pension credit rights arise from an arrangement which does not allow for a tax-free lump sum, then none will be available. If a tax-free retirement lump sum has already been taken by the scheme member before pension sharing took place then the ex-spouse may receive benefits in pension form only;
- where the ex-spouse dies before the pension credit rights come into payment, a tax-free lump sum death benefit of 25% of what would have been the cash equivalent of the pension credit rights at the date of death. The balance of the cash equivalent may be used to provide non-commutable pensions for any widow, widower or dependants ('survivors') of the ex-spouse. If there are no survivors, the balance of the cash equivalent should be treated as surplus under normal rules;
- where the ex-spouse dies after the pension sharing order, agreement or equivalent provision is made but before it is implemented by the scheme, death benefits may be paid on the basis of the immediately preceding bullet point. This applies irrespective of whether the scheme member's benefits were in payment at the time of the pension sharing order, agreement or equivalent provision;
- a pension guarantee together with non-commutable pensions payable for any widow, widower or dependants of the ex-spouse in the event of the ex-spouse's death after the pension credit rights have come into payment;
- full commutation of the pension credit rights on grounds of triviality or exceptional circumstances of serious ill-health.

Simplified Defined Contribution Scheme

36 Subject to DSS requirements, the following benefits are available where pension credit rights arise under a Simplified Defined Contribution Scheme:

- a pension;
- a tax-free lump sum of 25% of the fund value underpinning the ex-spouse's pension credit rights at the time of payment. If, however, a tax-free retirement lump sum has already been taken by the scheme member before pension sharing took place then the ex-spouse may receive benefits in pension form only;
- death benefits before the pension credit rights come into payment in accordance with PN 22.25;
- where the ex-spouse dies after the pension sharing order, agreement or equivalent provision is made but before it is implemented by the scheme, death benefits may be paid on the basis of the immediately preceding bullet point. This applies irrespective of whether the scheme member's benefits were in payment at the time of the pension sharing order, agreement or equivalent provision;
- death benefits once the pension credit rights have come into payment in accordance with PN 22.26–28;

- full commutation of the pension credit rights on grounds of triviality or exceptional circumstances of serious ill-health in accordance with PN 22.22.

Section 590 ICTA Approved Scheme

37 Subject to DSS requirements, the following benefits are available where pension credit rights arise under a section 590 ICTA approved scheme:

- a pension;
- a tax-free lump sum of 2.25 x the initial annual rate of pension before commutation to be paid. If however a tax-free retirement lump sum has already been taken by the scheme member before pension sharing took place then the ex-spouse may receive benefits in pension form only;
- a non-commutable pension payable to the widow or widower of the ex-spouse in the event of the ex-spouse's death after the pension credit rights have come into payment.

Buy-out Policy

38 Where a buy-out contract is subject to a pension sharing order, the ex-spouse's pension credit rights may be transferred to another pension arrangement in accordance with normal requirements. In circumstances where a new buy-out contract is effected to house the ex-spouse's pension credit rights arising from other than a section 590 ICTA approved scheme, it must satisfy Inland Revenue requirements set out in PN 10.44–45 although no limit is required on pension (see paragraph 40). Where exceptionally, the pension credit rights arise from a section 590 ICTA approved scheme, the buy-out contract to house those rights must comply with paragraph 37 above.

Limit on pension credit rights payable

39 The following limits apply to benefits from pension credit rights for or in respect of an ex-spouse.

Pension

40 Subject always to paragraph 52, there is no limit under the tax approval rules on the pension for an ex-spouse from pension credit rights. This applies irrespective of the type of pension scheme under which the pension credit rights arise.

Lump Sum 'retirement' benefits

41 For occupational pension schemes and buy-out contracts the amount of tax-free lump sum available depends upon the type of pension scheme under which the pension credit rights arise. See paragraphs 35 to 38 above. For personal pension schemes, the lump sum will be up to 25% of the fund forming the pension credit rights.

Death benefits before payment of pension credit rights

42 Where an ex-spouse's pension credit rights arise from a personal pension scheme:

- the fund forming the pension credit rights may be paid as a lump sum under section 637A ICTA. This amount is free of income tax;
- or an annuity may be paid to a spouse or dependant of the ex-spouse. This annuity must not exceed the amount of annuity payable to the ex-spouse as scheme member;
- or the survivor may opt for income withdrawals.

43   Where pension credit rights arise under a section 591 ICTA approved occupational pension scheme (excluding a Simplified Defined Contribution Scheme), a lump sum death benefit of 25% of the cash equivalent of the pension credit rights at the date of death may be paid out.

Any pension payable to a widow, widower or dependant ('survivor') of the ex-spouse, must not exceed $^2/_3$ of the pension, before commutation, that could have been provided for the ex-spouse on the date of death from the pension credit rights. Where the ex-spouse is below age 50 at the date of death, an age 50 annuity rate should be used to determine the pension that could have been provided to the ex-spouse. Where there is more than one survivor, separate pensions may be provided for each. No individual pension may exceed the $^2/_3$ limit above nor may the total of the pensions to be paid exceed that which could have been provided for the ex-spouse at the date of death. Such pensions may be fully commuted on grounds of triviality (see PN 8.10–14).

44   There are no limits imposed on death benefits where the pension credit rights arise from a Simplified Defined Contribution Scheme (see PN 22.15).

45   Where the pension credit rights arise from a section 590 ICTA approved occupational pension scheme, no death benefits are permissible if the ex-spouse dies before pension credit rights come into payment.

Death benefits after pension credit rights have come into payment

46   Where an ex-spouse's pension credit rights arise from a personal pension scheme the benefits payable will depend on whether the pension credit rights were being paid as an annuity or by income withdrawals.

If by annuity

- then any benefit payable must be in the form of an annuity to a surviving spouse or dependant of the ex-spouse.

If by income withdrawals

- then the benefit may be paid as an annuity to a surviving spouse or dependant of the ex-spouse;
- or as income withdrawals as opted by the survivor;
- or as a lump sum taxed at 35% under section 648B ICTA.

47   Where pension credit rights arise under a section 591 ICTA approved occupational pension scheme, including a Simplified Defined Contribution Scheme, a lump sum death benefit may be paid out under a 5 year guarantee (see PN 12.10 and 22.28). Such a lump sum must not exceed the total of the instalments falling due after the ex-spouse's death. Where the ex-spouse dies during the guarantee period and is drawing the pension credit rights under an income drawdown arrangement, the balance of instalments may be based on the amount of pension the ex-spouse would otherwise have been receiving if he/she had opted for 100% withdrawal. For these purposes, 100% is determined at the date of commencement of income drawdown irrespective of any subsequent variations. Any undrawn amounts of pension (that is, the difference between 100% withdrawal and the amounts actually drawndown) for periods prior to the date of death may be paid in addition.

48 Where pension credit rights arise under a section 591 ICTA approved occupational pension scheme other than in a Simplified Defined Contribution scheme, any pension payable to a survivor of an ex-spouse, must not exceed $^2/_3$ of the pension before commutation payable to the ex-spouse at the date the pension credit rights became payable, increased in proportion to the subsequent rise in the retail prices index. Where there is more than one survivor, separate pensions may be provided for each. No individual pension may exceed the $^2/_3$ limit above nor may the total of the pensions to be paid exceed that payable to the ex-spouse from commencement, increased by the retail prices index as above. Such pensions may be fully commuted on grounds of triviality (see PN 8.10 - 14).

49 There are no limits imposed on survivor's benefits in these circumstances where the pension credit rights arise from a Simplified Defined Contribution Scheme (see PN 22.15).

50 Where the pension credit rights arise from a section 590 ICTA approved occupational pension scheme, the only benefit payable in these circumstances is a pension for the widow or widower of the ex-spouse. Such a pension must not exceed $^2/_3$ of the pension, before commutation, payable to the ex-spouse.

51 Where pension credit rights arise from a buy-out policy, the benefits must be subject to the limits appropriate to the type of pension scheme under which they originated (see paragraph 38).

Ex-spouse also an employee and entitled to benefits as an employee under an occupational pension scheme

52 Sub-paragraph 2(8), Schedule 10, Finance Act 1999 ensures that the ex-spouse's pension credit rights or any widow's or widower's benefits arising from those rights, are not taken into account in applying the tax approval limits to:

- benefits for the ex-spouse as an employee scheme member;
- benefits for the widow or widower of an ex-spouse which arise as a result of that ex-spouse's employee scheme membership.

This is, however, subject to the pension credit rights being treated in the occupational pension scheme in question as separate from those which arise as an employee or the widow/widower of an employee.

53 The principle explained in paragraph 52, is extended in the case of occupational pension schemes approved under section 591 ICTA, to cover dependants' pensions.

54 Unless the occupational pension scheme makes provision for separate treatment as above, the pension credit rights will be taken into account in applying the tax approval limits to benefits for the ex-spouse as an employee scheme member or for the widow/widower (or dependants in the case of a section 591 ICTA approved occupational pension scheme) of the employee scheme member as appropriate.

55 As explained in paragraphs 35 and 36 above, an ex-spouse's pension credit rights may be fully commuted on grounds of triviality. Where the ex-spouse's pension credit rights are provided from an occupational pension scheme under which the ex-spouse is also entitled to benefits as an employee, the benefits from the pension credit rights must be aggregated with those in respect of the employment for the purpose of the triviality limit in PN 8.10.

56 As also explained in paragraphs 35 and 36 above, an ex-spouse's pension credit rights may be fully commuted on grounds of exceptional circumstances of serious ill-health. If the ex-spouse satisfies the criteria for full commutation of pension on these grounds (see PN 8.16), such commutation may take place immediately irrespective of the age of the ex-spouse.

57   For personal pension schemes, the ex-spouse may, if the scheme administrator agrees, continue to hold the pension credit rights in the same scheme as the original scheme member. The ex-spouse will enter into a new contract (which may be divided into more than one personal pension arrangement) and will become a member of the scheme. If the ex-spouse has net relevant earnings, contributions may be paid to the arrangements. Alternatively, the pension credit rights may be transferred to another personal pension scheme or to an occupational pension scheme of which the ex-spouse is already a member.

Taxation of pension credit rights

58   Where a tax charge would arise on the benefits of a scheme member, an ex-spouse's benefits that are payable in the same circumstances will be taxable. This maintains consistency with the normal tax rules for pensions. The position will be as follows:

- pension annuity payments or income withdrawals to an ex-spouse or the widow, widower or dependants of an ex-spouse, will be chargeable to tax on the recipient under Schedule E;

- lump sum retirement benefits paid to the ex-spouse within the limits set out in this Update, will be tax-free; lump sum death benefits paid under personal pension schemes

  - before the payment of pension credit rights, any lump sum will be tax-free;

  - after the payment of pension credit rights, the only sum available will be on death during payments of income withdrawals. This will be taxed at 35% under section 648B ICTA;

- lump sum death benefits paid in accordance with this Update under occupational pension schemes or buy-out contracts on the death of the ex-spouse, will, subject to a discretionary distribution power being exercised, be tax-free;

- as happens normally, there will be no provision for full commutation of the pension credit rights under personal pension schemes on grounds of serious ill-health. Neither is commutation on triviality grounds available except as provided under IR76 paragraph 9.32. This triviality test will apply to the pension credit rights alone;

- if the ex-spouse's pension credit rights under an occupational pension scheme or buyout contract are fully commuted on grounds of triviality or exceptional circumstances of serious ill-health, they will be taxed under section 599 ICTA. The amount of lump sum retirement benefit that would otherwise have been payable to the ex-spouse will be deducted and the section 599 ICTA tax charge applied to the balance.

  If the ex-spouse is also an employee and the scheme does not make provision for separate treatment of ex-spouse's pension credit rights, the pension credit rights will be treated for tax approval limits purposes, as part of the employee benefits. Full commutation of both pension credit rights and the employee pension will mean that the section 599 ICTA tax charge will be applied to the lump sum commutation payment after deducting the largest lump sum which would have been payable in respect of service as an employee;

- any payments, other than a pension, to or for the benefit of an ex-spouse, which are not expressly authorised by the rules of the occupational pension scheme, will be taxed under section 600 ICTA, and under section 647 ICTA for a personal pension scheme.

Pension debits for scheme members

59   Where the scheme member's pension rights are shared on divorce, there is a reduction in those rights known as a 'pension debit'. Where the member does not fall within the easement described in paragraphs 67 and 68 below and it is therefore necessary to take the pension debit into account as an aggregable benefit, it should be calculated as set out in paragraph 70 below.

Section 590 and 591 ICTA approved schemes (other than Simplified Defined Contribution Schemes)

60   The pension debit permanently reduces the maximum approvable benefits for the scheme member (see paragraphs 72 to 75 for more detail). The scheme member's benefits may, therefore, only be rebuilt up to the reduced maxima.

61   There is, however, an administrative easement for members of section 591 ICTA approved schemes with moderate earnings. They will be able to ignore the pension debit and rebuild the shared pension within the normal benefit and contribution limits. The easement is explained in paragraphs 67 and 68 below.

Simplified Defined Contribution Schemes

62   The only limitation is on continuing contributions. These must be restricted in accordance with PN 22.9–11.

Personal pension schemes and retirement annuity contracts

63   There will be no restriction on the amount of ongoing personal pension contributions or retirement annuity premiums payable following a pension share. These will continue to be payable by reference to net relevant earnings.

64   The amount of benefits payable will be by reference to the fund after deducting the pension debit.

65   On the death of the scheme member, the amount of any annuity payable to a surviving spouse (not the ex-spouse from the pension share) or dependant, must not exceed the amount of annuity that could have been paid to the scheme member after deducting the pension debit (Section 636(3A) ICTA).

Buy-out contracts

66   Any monetary limits on the member's lump sum retirement benefit or pension (see PN 10.45(c) and PN 10.46) should be reduced appropriately to take account of the pension debit.

Administrative easement

67   This applies to members of section 591 ICTA approved occupational pension schemes other than Simplified Defined Contributions Schemes except:

- controlling directors – see regulation 5(5) of the disapplication regulations referred to in paragraph 23 above;
- those whose earnings, exceed $1/4$ of the permitted maximum (see PN Glossary), determined at its level for the year of assessment in which the marriage was dissolved or annulled. For this purpose earnings mean:

-   those in respect of pensionable service to which the scheme relates, and
-   which were received during the year of assessment immediately preceding the year of assessment in which the dissolution or annulment occurred, and
-   from which tax was deducted under PAYE.

68   Where the easement applies, pension debits can be ignored in calculating the member's maximum permissible total benefits, both pension and lump sum, under the scheme. This is a once and for all test as at the date of divorce and if satisfied, the pension debit may be permanently ignored. This is irrespective of subsequent employment changes.

Calculation of pension debits

Members of occupational pension schemes approved under s 590 or under s 591 ICTA, other than Simplified Defined Contribution Schemes

69   In cases where the administrative easement described in paragraphs 67 and 68 does not apply, the pension debit must be calculated. It must be brought into account as part of a member's aggregable benefits in determining the Inland Revenue maximum approvable benefits, both pension and lump sum, payable under the scheme.

70   The following examples show how the process is intended to work in practice. For simplicity, the example assumes that the whole of the pension debit will be subject to statutory revaluation although if the debit includes some GMP rights, then that part of the debit will be subject to GMP revaluation in the normal way. The way in which this works is a feature of the Welfare Reform and Pensions Act rather than the tax rules.

Example 1

The facts are:

-   Defined benefit scheme.
-   An active scheme member with 20 year's membership at the date of divorce.
-   The member earns £30,000 a year at that date.
-   Defined benefit scheme provides $1/60$ of final salary for each year of service.
-   Under the pension sharing order, agreement or equivalent provision the member's pension rights are subject to a debit of 40% of the cash equivalent.

Results

-   Deferred pension at the date of divorce: $20/60$ x £30,000 = £10,000.
-   Cash equivalent for pension sharing calculated by scheme actuary: £100,000.
-   Pension debit ordered by the court (40% of the cash equivalent): £40,000.
-   The member retires at age 60 after 30 years service with a final salary of: £48,000.
-   Full pension entitlement (ignoring the debit): $30/60$ x £48,000 = £24,000.
-   Using the statutory Revaluation Order in force at the date of retirement, the scheme actuary calculates that the deferred pension of £4,000 (40% of the deferred pension of £10,000) given up at the date of divorce is equivalent to a pension of £6,000 a year at retirement. This is known as the 'negative deferred pension'.
-   The member's actual pension will be: £24,000 - £6,000 = £18,000.

Example 2

The facts are:

- Money purchase scheme:
- A scheme member with 20 year's membership at the date of divorce.
- The member earns £30,000 a year at that date.
- Total funds accumulated for the member at the date of divorce amount to £100,000.
- Under the pension sharing order, agreement or equivalent provision the member's pension rights are subject to a debit of 40% of the cash equivalent.

Results

The £40,000 awarded to the former spouse at the date of divorce will be increased between that date and the member's NIRD (or other relevant date as the case may be), at the rate of investment yield achieved by the member's remaining fund in that period. Where, for whatever reason, it is not possible to use such an investment yield, the fund should be increased in the above period at the rate of 8.5% per annum (in accordance with PN 13.10(a)).

The resulting capital fund is then turned into a pension equivalent by applying a suitable annuity rate appropriate to the member's NRID (or other relevant date as the case may be). Where the pension debit in part or whole would have been subject to LPI increases, an LPI annuity rate should be used. Where no part of the pension debit would have been subject to LPI increases, a single level life annuity rate should be used. In neither situation may a guarantee be reflected in the annuity rate.

Limits on scheme members benefits

71   The following paragraphs explain the effect of pension debits on a scheme member's maximum approvable benefits.

Aggregable benefits

72   Where it is necessary to bring the pension debit into account for the purposes of determining a member's maximum approvable benefits under occupational pension schemes approved under section 590 or section 591 ICTA the maximum approvable benefits are permanently reduced. The position is as follows.

73   Section 590 ICTA approved schemes:

- a pension of $^1/_{60}$ of final remuneration for each year of service (up to a maximum of 40) reduced by the amount of pension debit calculated in accordance with this Update;
- a lump sum retirement benefit by commutation of pension of 2.25 x the initial annual rate of pension after reduction to take account of the pension debit;

74   Section 591 approved schemes, other than Simplified Defined Contribution Schemes:

- a pension not exceeding the relevant limits set out in Parts 7 or 10 of PN as appropriate to the scheme member's circumstances and the particular tax regime to which he or she is subject, reduced by the amount of pension debit calculated in accordance with this Update;
- for members with pre 17 March 1987 continued rights, a lump sum retirement benefit by commutation of pension not exceeding the greater of:

- – 2.25 x the initial annual rate of pension after reduction to take account of the pension debit; or
- – an amount determined in accordance with the scheme rules as if there had been no pension share, but then reduced by 2.25 x the amount of the negative deferred pension – see paragraph 70 above.

- for members with pre 17 March 1987 continued rights in schemes providing for a pension and a separate lump sum rather than a commutable pension, a lump sum retirement benefit not exceeding the greater of:
  - – 3 x the initial annual rate of pension after reduction to take account of the pension debit; or
  - – an amount determined in accordance with the scheme rules as if there had been no pension share but then reduced by 3 x the amount of the negative deferred pension -see paragraph 70 above.

- for members with pre 1 June 1989 continued rights or without continued rights, a lump sum retirement benefit by commutation of pension of 2.25 x the initial annual rate of pension after reduction to take account of the pension debit;

- for members with pre 1 June 1989 continued rights or without continued rights in schemes providing for a pension and a separate lump sum rather than a commutable pension, a lump sum retirement benefit of 3 x the initial annual rate of pension after reduction to take account of the pension debit.

75   In section 591 ICTA approved schemes providing lump sum retirement benefits only, where lump sum accrual does not exceed $^3/_{80}$ of final remuneration for each year of service, an amount determined in accordance with the scheme rules reduced by the amount of the lump sum allocated to the ex-spouse. For the purpose of this reduction, the amount of the lump sum allocated to the ex-spouse at the date of divorce should be increased between that date and the date that the member takes his or her lump sum retirement benefit. The increase in that period should be in accordance with the statutory Revaluation Order in force at the date the member takes his or her lump sum retirement benefit.

Effect of pension debit on relevant earnings for personal pension eligibility for controlling directors

76   Under present rules (Section 644(6A) to (6E) ICTA), a controlling director cannot count earnings from an employment as relevant earnings if:

- the controlling director receives or has received benefits from an occupational pension scheme for the same employer; or

- the controlling director receives benefits from a personal pension scheme which has earlier received a transfer payment from an occupational pension scheme for the same employer.

For this purpose, 'employer' includes an employer which carries on the business formerly carried on by the employer mentioned above and for a period giving rise to benefits for the controlling director.

It will not be possible to avoid this restriction by having a 100% pension debit with the intention of nullifying existing benefits. Section 644(6EA) ICTA provides for the pension debit to be deemed to be continued to be received by the controlling director.

77   But if the ex-spouse was also a controlling director subject to this rule, the receipt of a pension credit is a separate matter which does not affect the operation of this rule for any pension debit applicable to the same individual.

Transfers

78 Where—

- benefits against which a pension debit exists are transferred to an occupational pension scheme, other than a Simplified Defined Contribution Scheme;

- which is a scheme of the same or associated employer; or

- one where continuous service is given;

- and the administrative easement described in paragraphs 67 and 68 does not apply;

then details of the amount of pension debit to be applied to the member's transferred benefits must be passed on to the receiving scheme. This is to ensure that the necessary restrictions on the member's benefits are maintained in that scheme.

79 Where—

- benefits against which a pension debit exists are transferred to an occupational pension scheme, other than a Simplified Defined Contribution Scheme;

- which is a scheme of a new unassociated employer; or

- one where continuous service treatment is not applicable;

- and the administrative easement described in paragraphs 67 and 68 does not apply;

details of the amount of pension debit to be applied to the member's transferred benefits, must again be passed on as in paragraph 78 above, since those benefits may need to be treated as retained benefits for the purpose of the new scheme's limits rule (eg see PN Parts 7, 8 and 10). Where it is necessary to bring the retained benefits into account for the purposes of the new scheme's limits rule, the pension debit (both pension and where appropriate lump sum) must be included as part of the member's retained benefits.

80 Where benefits against which a pension debit exists are transferred to a personal pension scheme or a buy-out policy and the administrative easement described in paragraph 67 and 68 does not apply, details of the amount of pension debit to be applied to the member's transferred benefits must be passed on to the provider in question.

Lump Sum Certificates

81 Where a lump sum certificate is required in respect of a transferring member (see PN 10.32 and 16.17), the amount certified must be appropriately reduced by the sum of 2.25 x the negative deferred pension at the relevant date calculated in accordance with paragraph 69.

Retained Benefits: Personal Pension Schemes and Retirement Annuity Contracts

82 For the purpose of valuing the pension debit derived from a personal pension scheme or retirement annuity contract, the methodology in Example 2 for money purchase schemes set out in paragraph 70 should be used.

Death benefits

83 Lump sum

Pension sharing has no effect on the amount of the lump sum that may be paid following the member's death in service. The limits set out in PN 11.2-3 continue to apply and no account need be taken of any lump sum death benefit payable on the death of the ex-spouse before the pension credit rights come into payment.

84   Pension

Where the administrative easement in paragraphs 67 and 68 does not apply, pension sharing will, however, have the effect of reducing the maximum widows', widowers' or dependants' pension payable in the event of the member's death in service or death in retirement (see PN 11.7-8 and PN 12.2-3). This is because the member's maximum approvable benefits will effectively be permanently reduced. For similar reasons, the maximum amount available under a guarantee (see PN 12.9-10) will be reduced.

Full commutation of member's pension

85   Where a member whose pension has been affected by a pension sharing order or provision, subsequently fully commutes the pension on grounds of triviality or exceptional circumstances of serious ill health, the tax charge under section 599 (see PN 17.27) will be on the excess of the commutation payment over an amount calculated in accordance with PN 17.28(b).

Scheme rules

86   The PSO will be offering standard wording for scheme rule amendments to cover the above in due course. Standard wording for occupational pension schemes will not cover contracting-out requirements and the PSO will not examine rules/amendments to cover such requirements. When submitting rules/amendments to PSO, practitioners should indicate which rules/amendments relate solely to contracting-out requirements.

Pension Schemes Office Update No 76

20 November 2000

Please pass a copy of this Update to everyone in your organisation who needs to see it.

The category of schemes covered by this Update is shown below. Italicised terms are explained in the glossary at the end.

Category: Occupational Pension Schemes, Personal Pension Schemes, Buy-out Contracts and Retirement Annuity Contracts

Action: Note the documentation and approval arrangements for occupational schemes relying on standard documentation which do not provide for pension sharing on divorce or nullity.

Summary: This Update explains the simple procedures that may be used for obtaining tax approval where occupational schemes rely on standard documentation which does not contain the new pension sharing on divorce provisions.

Enquiries: Barrie Raggett (Customer Service Manager): 0115 974 1692

E-mail: Barrie.Raggett@ir/gis/gov.uk

PENSION SHARING ON DIVORCE OR NULLITY

1 Since 10 May 2000 both occupational and personal pension schemes have been unable to be approved unless their documentation contains the new pension sharing on divorce provisions that will come into effect on 1 December 2000. Full details of the new approval requirements were set out in PSO Updates Nos. 60 and 62.

2 Examiners of occupational pension schemes have noticed that some practitioners are confused about the arrangements that they can use to make their standard documents confirm with the new pension sharing on divorce provisions. We believe that this is due to the wording of the form PS 3CS, which has now been amended.

3 Where approval is sought using existing standard documentation that does not contain the new provisions, it will be sufficient to simply bolt-on the model rules that were issued with Mrs. Nesbitt's (Deputy Director's) letter of 28th April 2000 (this letter was sent only to practitioner that have standards agreed with this office). If you wish to receive a copy of the model bolt-on rules please telephone our helpdesk on 0115 974 1600. Where this bolt-on method is used, practitioners should submit the standard Documentation certificate (PS 176, PS 5 or PS 6 as appropriate). In the case of the PS 176 the following wording should be added under box E on the form, for PS 5 the wording should be added under item b. on the form and under item a. on the PS 6 form:

"Pension Sharing on Divorce model rules dated 4.2000 adopted, ex spouses not permitted to join scheme" or "Pension Sharing on Divorce model rules dated 4/2000 adopted, ex-spouses permitted to join scheme".

4 Where this procedure is followed the PSO needs neither a copy of the model rules that have been adopted nor the rules that have been so amended.

5 Information on the use of the model bolt-on rules is set out in the final part of them, which is headed "Usage and limitation of model rules".

I.31

Pension Schemes Office Update No 84

22 January 2001

Please pass a copy of this Update to everyone in your organisation who needs to see it. The category of schemes covered by this Update is shown below. Italicised terms are explained in the glossary at the end.

Category: Occupational Pension Schemes, Buy-out Contracts, Personal Pension Schemes and Retirement Annuity Contacts.

Action: Note the changes and clarifications relating to pension sharing on divorce and take appropriate action.

Current Position: PSO Update No 62 (Pension Sharing on Divorce or Nullity) sets out the changes to tax law and Inland Revenue practice to allow pension sharing in tax approved pension schemes.

Summary: This Update:

- modifies the calculation of the Pension Debit in money purchase schemes, and
- clarifies some other areas of practice relating to pension sharing on divorce.

It should be read by all practitioners, scheme administrators etc of tax approved pension schemes (both occupational and personal), where pension sharing might take place.

Enquiries: Occupational Pension Schemes and Buy-out Contracts:

Trevor Smeath – 0115 974 1607, or

Jan Speyers – 0115 974 1759

Personal Pension Schemes and Retirement Annuity Contracts:

Alan Bateman – 0115 974 1760, or

Mark Surry – 0115 974 1765

PENSION SHARING ON DIVORCE OR NULLITY – CALCULATION OF THE PENSION DEBIT IN MONEY PURCHASE SCHEMES AND OTHER MISCELLANEOUS POINTS

Introduction

1. Tax law and Inland Revenue practice has fundamentally changed to allow tax approved schemes to accommodate the new pension sharing on divorce provisions that came into force on 1 December 2000. Details of these changes are contained in PSO Update No 62, issued on 28 April 2000.

2. Since the issue of PSO Update No 62, a number of issues have been raised concerning certain aspects of the application of the new Inland Revenue practice relating to pension sharing, in particular the calculation of the pension debit in money purchase schemes.

Calculation of pension debits – money purchase occupational pension schemes

3. Example 2 in paragraph 70 of PSO Update No 62 showed how the pension debit should be calculated in practice for money purchase schemes. In a letter dated 13 October 2000, the main representatives of the pensions industry were informed that a revised approach to the calculation of pension debits in money purchase schemes was being considered and that meantime, Example 2 in the Update should be disregarded.

4. The principle behind the calculation of the pension debit in Example 2 was to take the amount of fund awarded to the former spouse at the date of divorce and increase it by the investment return achieved by the member's remaining fund between the date of divorce and the member's *NRD* (or other *relevant date* as the case may be). The resulting, notional, fund would then be converted into a pension equivalent at the member's *NRD* (or other *relevant date*) for the purpose of establishing the Inland Revenue maximum approvable benefit for the member.

5. After publication of PSO Update No 62, we received representations about Example 2 in paragraph 70 of the Update. It was pointed out that using the approach in Example 2 might result in a member's entitlement to benefit being completely extinguished. This could happen if the member's fund made exceptional investment returns. The pension debit, determined by the same rate of return, could then be equal to or more than the appropriate Inland Revenue maximum approvable benefit for the member. This is an extreme possibility but it highlighted that the method of calculation in Example 2 in PSO Update No 62 might lead to unintended and undesirable results.

6. Following further consideration of the matter in consultation with the Government Actuary's Department (GAD), we have now developed a revised approach. Under the revised approach the pension debit will be calculated on the basis of an immediate conversion into a notional pension equivalent of the fund awarded to the former spouse at the date of divorce. The pension equivalent established at the date of divorce will then be revalued between the date of divorce and the member's *relevant date*. The rate of revaluation is the same statutory revaluation for non-GMPs that applies for defined benefit schemes. The pension debit will be determined in this way for both Inland Revenue maximum benefit checks and the maximum permissible funding rates for money purchase earmarked contracts and small self-administered schemes that are described in Appendices VIII and IX of *PN*. The funding guidelines will be updated to reflect this in due course.

7. GAD has provided tables of factors that will be used solely to determine the pension equivalent of the pension debit at the date of divorce. The factors establish, at a present day value, the amount of the notional equivalent deferred pension at the member's *NRD*. They have been prepared on the following assumptions:

- a post-retirement net return of 3% pa (the same as for Factors[1] and [3] in the funding guidelines at Appendices VIII and IX of *PN*)
- a pre-retirement net return of 4% pa (implying 4.33% pa increases)
- no allowance for any spouse's pension after retirement.

The tables of factors are called "Factor 5" to complement the existing "Factors 1 to 4" used in Appendices VIII and IX of *PN*. The assumptions underlying the factors will be reviewed periodically in conjunction with reviews for funding (see paragraphs 10 and 11 in Appendices VIII and IX of *PN*). Copies of the tables including Factor [5] are attached to this Update. Only Factor [5] is new.

8. The following illustrative example shows how the pension debit will be brought into account as part of a member's aggregable Inland Revenue maximum approvable benefit, both pension and lump sum, that can be paid from money purchase occupational pension schemes approved under section 590 or section 591 of the *Taxes Act*. The pension debit can be ignored for members of section 591 approved schemes who fall within the administrative easement described in paragraphs 67 and 68 of PSO Update No 62 or for members of simplified defined contributions schemes.

Example

The facts are:

- money purchase scheme
- active member – male, age 40
- 10 years service at date of divorce
- member earns £90,000 a year at date of divorce
- no *retained benefits*
- total funds accumulated for the member at the date of divorce amount to £250,000
- under the pension sharing order, agreement or equivalent provision the member's pension rights are subject to a debit of 50% of the fund accumulated for the member at the date of divorce.

Results

at date of divorce:

- debit at date of divorce - £125,000

  (50% of member's fund at date of divorce)

- notional equivalent deferred pension - £19,516

  (£125,000/6.405 – the factor of 6.405 taken from the "Factor 5" table for a male age 40).

Results

at member's *NRD* – age 60:

- member's *final remuneration* - £200,000 a year
- member's service to *NRD* – 30 years
- member's "gross" pension at *NRD* (ignoring debit) – £133,333 (2/3x£200,000)
- notional equivalent deferred pension, revalued to the member's *NRD* = £38,833 (the notional pension equivalent of the debit established at the date of divorce, £19,516, is revalued between the date of divorce and the member's *NRD* by the rate of statutory revaluation that applies for a deferred, non-GMP, defined benefit – for the purpose of this example only, the rate is 3.5% a year compound)
- maximum Inland Revenue approvable pension before commutation = £94,500 (£133,333-£38,833).

9. The methodology described above may be adapted as necessary and used for the purpose of valuing benefits from *personal pension schemes* and *retirement annuity contracts*. Such a valuation may be needed when calculating retained benefits, and paragraph 82 of PSO Update No 62 should be amended accordingly.

10. It is proposed to include as an Appendix to *PN*, examples of how to calculate pension debits in both defined benefit and money purchase schemes at various *relevant dates*. The worked Example in paragraph 8 above will be extended to show the effects of the debit at the various *relevant dates*. The examples will correspond to the examples provided by the Department of Social Security with assistance from both GAD and the Inland Revenue (and which also appear on the DSS website).

MISCELLANEOUS POINTS MADE SINCE THE ISSUE OF PSO UPDATE NO 62

Occupational Pension Schemes

Pension Sharing Order made on a Pension in Payment - Administrative Easement

11. The administrative easement that allows for the pension debit to be ignored when a member's maximum permissible total benefits are calculated is described in paragraphs 67 and 68 of PSO Update No 62. Basically, for the easement to apply, the member

- must not be a *controlling director*, and
- have earnings as described in paragraph 67 of PSO Update No 62 not exceeding ¼ of the *permitted maximum* at the time of the divorce.

12. The administrative easement will not generally be capable of being applied where the divorced member has already retired and is in receipt of benefits. In these circumstances, for the purposes of determining the member's maximum approvable benefits in accordance with *PN* 9.1, the pension debit must always be brought into account.

Re-profiling Compulsory Purchase Annuities in Payment

13. A pension sharing order might require an already purchased annuity to be shared following divorce where the terms of that annuity were such that on the pensioner member's (first named annuitant's) death, a pension is be paid to the widow(er) of the deceased pensioner member (second named annuitant). Following the pension sharing order, the pensioner member's ex-spouse and the second named annuitant might be the same person. In such cases the pensioner member's re-profiled ongoing annuity payments can be based on the pensioner member's life only. This is provided the ongoing amount does not exceed the maximum permissible amount that can be paid to the pensioner member, taking into account the pension debit (see paragraph 12).

14. Alternatively, the annuity could be re-drawn on the basis of an annuity continuing to be paid on the death of the member to some other individual or individuals who qualify as a *dependant* of the member but were not originally nominated for such a benefit. This would be subject to the rules allowing for a reallocation of benefits.

15. Basing the ongoing annuity payments on a single life basis would not be acceptable if the scheme to which the annuity relates pays a widow's(er's) pension to whoever is the member's spouse at the time of the member's death. Pension Credit Benefits – Serious Ill-health Commutation below Age 50

16. The pension credit benefits for an ex-spouse held in an occupational pension scheme approved under section 591 of the *Taxes Act* (including a simplified defined contribution scheme) can be fully commuted on the grounds of the ex-spouse being in exceptional circumstances of serious ill-health (see paragraphs 35 and 36 of PSO Update No 62).

17. If the ex-spouse is under age 50 at the time of full commutation on the grounds of exceptional circumstances of serious ill-health, an appropriate age 50 annuity rate can be used to determine.the amount of pension that could have been provided for the ex-spouse from the pension credit benefits. The deductible lump sum for the purpose of the tax charge under section 599 of the *Taxes Act* can be calculated by reference to the amount of pension that would have been payable using the appropriate age 50 annuity rate.

Personal Pension Schemes and Retirement Annuity Contracts

Annuity in Payment

18. In a similar situation to that described above in paragraph 13, a pension sharing order may require an annuity originating from a *personal pension scheme* or *retirement annuity contract* to be split to provide separate annuities for the member and the ex-spouse. Generally the form of the original member's annuity should continue on the same basis after the pension sharing order has been implemented. But if the member had a joint life annuity prior to that time, there would be no objection to the annuity then being recalculated on a single life basis. The form of the annuity for the ex-spouse would be expected, in any event, to be on a single life basis.

Income Withdrawals in Payment

19. The fund of a member of a *personal pension scheme* who is taking income withdrawal payments may be split in order to provide an ex-spouse with pension credit rights. In these circumstances the ex-spouse would have the option of either continuing with income withdrawal payments (based on the age of the ex-spouse) or of purchasing an annuity. No further lump sum could be taken from the pension credit rights.

20. The implementation of a pension share is not an event which changes the annual limits (35%/100%) of income withdrawal. Such limits will continue to be applied to the original member's fund despite the fund's reduction by the pension debit. But the limits will be revised following the next triennial review.

Glossary

Controlling director: a director of a company who directly or indirectly controls 20% or more of the ordinary share capital in that company – see Glossary to *PN* for full definition.

Dependant: a person financially dependent on a scheme member – see Glossary to *PN* for full definition.

Final remuneration: see Glossary to *PN* for full definition.

NRD: normal retirement date.

Permitted maximum: defined in section 590C of the *Taxes Act* – see Glossary to *PN* for more details.

Personal pension scheme: a scheme approved under Chapter IV, Part XIV of the *Taxes Act* – for more details see Glossary to *PN* and IR 76 (2000) – Personal Pension Schemes Guidance Notes. **PN**: IR12 (1997) – Practice Notes on Approval of Occupational Pension Schemes.

Relevant date: the member's date of retirement, leaving pensionable service or death as the case may be.

Retained benefits: retirement benefits from earlier employments – see Glossary to *PN* for full definition.

Retirement annuity contract: a contract approved under Chapter III, Part XIV of the *Taxes Act* – see Glossary to *PN* for more details.. **Taxes Act**: Income and Corporation Taxes Act 1988, as amended.

APPENDIX

Factors used in Appendices VIII & IX of *PN* - note only "Factor [5]" is new

Male 60 – married

Age	Factor [1]	Factor [2]	Factor [3]	Factor [4]	Factor [5]
25	10.4265	26.3833	6.2395	21.2472	3.5564
26	10.5829	25.8046	6.4267	20.8958	3.6986
27	10.7417	25.2173	6.6195	20.5339	3.8466
28	10.9028	24.6211	6.8180	20.1611	4.0005
29	11.0663	24.0160	7.0226	19.7771	4.1605
30	11.2323	23.4018	7.2333	19.3815	4.3269
31	11.4008	22.7784	7.4503	18.9742	4.5000
32	11.5718	22.1456	7.6738	18.5545	4.6800
33	11.7454	21.5034	7.9040	18.1223	4.8672
34	11.9216	20.8515	8.1411	17.6772	5.0619
35	12.1004	20.1898	8.3853	17.2187	5.2643
36	12.2819	19.5183	8.6369	16.7464	5.4749
37	12.4661	18.8366	8.8960	16.2600	5.6939
38	12.6531	18.1447	9.1629	15.7589	5.9217
39	12.8429	17.4425	9.4378	15.2429	6.1585
40	13.0356	16.7297	9.7209	14.7113	6.4049
41	13.2311	16.0062	10.0125	14.1638	6.6611
42	13.4296	15.2718	10.3129	13.5999	6.9275
43	13.6310	14.5265	10.6223	13.0191	7.2046
44	13.8355	13.7699	10.9410	12.4208	7.4928
45	14.0430	13.0021	11.2692	11.8046	7.7925
46	14.2537	12.2227	11.6073	11.1699	8.1042
47	14.4675	11.4316	11.9555	10.5162	8.4284
48	14.6845	10.6286	12.3141	9.8428	8.7655
49	14.9047	9.8136	12.6836	9.1493	9.1161
50	15.1283	8.9864	13.0641	8.4349	9.4808
51	15.3552	8.1467	13.4560	7.6992	9.8600
52	15.5856	7.2945	13.8597	6.9413	10.2544
53	15.8193	6.4295	14.2755	6.1607	10.6646
54	16.0566	5.5515	14.7037	5.3567	11.0911
55	16.2975	4.6604	15.1448	4.5286	11.5348
56	16.5419	3.7558	15.5992	3.6756	11.9962
57	16.7901	2.8377	16.0672	2.7970	12.4760
58	17.0419	1.9059	16.5492	1.8921	12.9751
59	17.2976	0.9600	17.0457	0.9600	13.4941

Factors used in Appendices VIII & IX of *PN* - note only "Factor [5]" is new

Female 60 – married

Age	Factor [1]	Factor [2]	Factor [3]	Factor [4]	Factor [5]
25	10.4615	26.3833	6.2604	21.2472	4.2099
26	10.6184	25.8046	6.4482	20.8958	4.3783
27	10.7777	25.2173	6.6416	20.5339	4.5534
28	10.9393	24.6211	6.8409	20.1611	4.7355
29	11.1034	24.0160	7.0461	19.7771	4.9250
30	11.2700	23.4018	7.2575	19.3815	5.1220
31	11.4390	22.7784	7.4752	18.9742	5.3268
32	11.6106	22.1456	7.6995	18.5545	5.5399
33	11.7848	21.5034	7.9305	18.1223	5.7615
34	11.9615	20.8515	8.1684	17.6772	5.9920
35	12.1409	20.1898	8.4134	17.2187	6.2316
36	12.3231	19.5183	8.6658	16.7464	6.4809
37	12.5079	18.8366	8.9258	16.2600	6.7401
38	12.6955	18.1447	9.1936	15.7589	7.0097
39	12.8860	17.4425	9.4694	15.2429	7.2901
40	13.0792	16.7297	9.7535	14.7113	7.5817
41	13.2754	16.0062	10.0461	14.1638	7.8850
42	13.4746	15.2718	10.3475	13.5999	8.2004
43	13.6767	14.5265	10.6579	13.0191	8.5284
44	13.8818	13.7699	10.9776	12.4208	8.8696
45	14.0901	13.0021	11.3069	11.8046	9.2243
46	14.3014	12.2227	11.6462	11.1699	9.5933
47	14.5159	11.4316	11.9955	10.5162	9.9771
48	14.7337	10.6286	12.3554	9.8428	10.3761
49	14.9547	9.8136	12.7261	9.1493	10.7912
50	15.1790	8.9864	13.1078	8.4349	11.2228
51	15.4067	8.1467	13.5011	7.6992	11.6717
52	15.6378	7.2945	13.9061	6.9413	12.1386
53	15.8724	6.4295	14.3233	6.1607	12.6242
54	16.1104	5.5515	14.7530	5.3567	13.1291
55	16.3521	4.6604	15.1956	4.5286	13.6543
56	16.5974	3.7558	15.6515	3.6756	14.2005
57	16.8463	2.8377	16.1210	2.7970	14.7685
58	17.0990	1.9059	16.6046	1.8921	15.3592
59	17.3555	0.9600	17.1028	0.9600	15.9736

Factors used in Appendices VIII & IX of *PN* - note only "Factor [5]" is new

Male 60 – single

Age	Factor [1]	Factor [2]	Factor [3]	Factor [4]	Factor [5]
25	8.3342	26.3833	4.9874	21.2472	3.5564
26	8.4592	25.8046	5.1370	20.8958	3.6986
27	8.5861	25.2173	5.2911	20.5339	3.8466
28	8.7149	24.6211	5.4499	20.1611	4.0005
29	8.8456	24.0160	5.6134	19.7771	4.1605
30	8.9783	23.4018	5.7818	19.3815	4.3269
31	9.1130	22.7784	5.9552	18.9742	4.5000
32	9.2497	22.1456	6.1339	18.5545	4.6800
33	9.3884	21.5034	6.3179	18.1223	4.8672
34	9.5293	20.8515	6.5074	17.6772	5.0619
35	9.6722	20.1898	6.7026	17.2187	5.2643
36	9.8173	19.5183	6.9037	16.7464	5.4749
37	9.9645	18.8366	7.1108	16.2600	5.6939
38	10.1140	18.1447	7.3242	15.7589	5.9217
39	10.2657	17.4425	7.5439	15.2429	6.1585
40	10.4197	16.7297	7.7702	14.7113	6.4049
41	10.5760	16.0062	8.0033	14.1638	6.6611
42	10.7346	15.2718	8.2434	13.5999	6.9275
43	10.8957	14.5265	8.4907	13.0191	7.2046
44	11.0591	13.7699	8.7454	12.4208	7.4928
45	11.2250	13.0021	9.0078	11.8046	7.7925
46	11.3934	12.2227	9.2780	11.1699	8.1042
47	11.5643	11.4316	9.5564	10.5162	8.4284
48	11.7377	10.6286	9.8431	9.8428	8.7655
49	11.9138	9.8136	10.1383	9.1493	9.1161
50	12.0925	8.9864	10.4425	8.4349	9.4808
51	12.2739	8.1467	10.7558	7.6992	9.8600
52	12.4580	7.2945	11.0784	6.9413	10.2544
53	12.6449	6.4295	11.4108	6.1607	10.6646
54	12.8345	5.5515	11.7531	5.3567	11.0911
55	13.0271	4.6604	12.1057	4.5286	11.5348
56	13.2225	3.7558	12.4689	3.6756	11.9962
57	13.4208	2.8377	12.8430	2.7970	12.4760
58	13.6221	1.9059	13.2282	1.8921	12.9751
59	13.8264	0.9600	13.6251	0.9600	13.4941

Factors used in Appendices VIII & IX of *PN* - note only "Factor [5]" is new

Female 60 – single

Age	Factor [1]	Factor [2]	Factor [3]	Factor [4]	Factor [5]
25	9.8656	26.3833	5.9038	21.2472	4.2099
26	10.0136	25.8046	6.0809	20.8958	4.3783
27	10.1638	25.2173	6.2634	20.5339	4.5534
28	10.3163	24.6211	6.4513	20.1611	4.7355
29	10.4710	24.0160	6.6448	19.7771	4.9250
30	10.6281	23.4018	6.8441	19.3815	5.1220
31	10.7875	22.7784	7.0495	18.9742	5.3268
32	10.9493	22.1456	7.2609	18.5545	5.5399
33	11.1135	21.5034	7.4788	18.1223	5.7615
34	11.2802	20.8515	7.7031	17.6772	5.9920
35	11.4494	20.1898	7.9342	17.2187	6.2316
36	11.6212	19.5183	8.1723	16.7464	6.4809
37	11.7955	18.8366	8.4174	16.2600	6.7401
38	11.9724	18.1447	8.6700	15.7589	7.0097
39	12.1520	17.4425	8.9301	15.2429	7.2901
40	12.3343	16.7297	9.1980	14.7113	7.5817
41	12.5193	16.0062	9.4739	14.1638	7.8850
42	12.7071	15.2718	9.7581	13.5999	8.2004
43	12.8977	14.5265	10.0509	13.0191	8.5284
44	13.0912	13.7699	10.3524	12.4208	8.8696
45	13.2876	13.0021	10.6629	11.8046	9.2243
46	13.4869	12.2227	10.9828	11.1699	9.5933
47	13.6892	11.4316	11.3123	10.5162	9.9771
48	13.8945	10.6286	11.6517	9.8428	10.3761
49	14.1029	9.8136	12.0012	9.1493	10.7912
50	14.3145	8.9864	12.3613	8.4349	11.2228
51	14.5292	8.1467	12.7321	7.6992	11.6717
52	14.7471	7.2945	13.1141	6.9413	12.1386
53	14.9683	6.4295	13.5075	6.1607	12.6242
54	15.1929	5.5515	13.9127	5.3567	13.1291
55	15.4207	4.6604	14.3301	4.5286	13.6543
56	15.6521	3.7558	14.7600	3.6756	14.2005
57	15.8868	2.8377	15.2028	2.7970	14.7685
58	16.1251	1.9059	15.6589	1.8921	15.3592
59	16.3670	0.9600	16.1287	0.9600	15.9736

Factors used in Appendices VIII & IX of *PN* - note only "Factor [5]" is new

Male 65 – married

Age	Factor [1]	Factor [2]	Factor [3]	Factor [4]	Factor [5]
25	8.5604	29.1509	4.7604	22.8566	2.5036
26	8.6888	28.6138	4.9032	22.5535	2.6038
27	8.8191	28.0685	5.0503	22.2413	2.7079
28	8.9514	27.5151	5.2018	21.9197	2.8162
29	9.0856	26.9534	5.3579	21.5884	2.9289
30	9.2219	26.3833	5.5186	21.2472	3.0460
31	9.3603	25.8046	5.6842	20.8958	3.1679
32	9.5007	25.2173	5.8547	20.5339	3.2946
33	9.6432	24.6211	6.0303	20.1611	3.4264
34	9.7878	24.0160	6.2113	19.7771	3.5634
35	9.9346	23.4018	6.3976	19.3815	3.7060
36	10.0837	22.7784	6.5895	18.9742	3.8542
37	10.2349	22.1456	6.7872	18.5545	4.0084
38	10.3884	21.5034	6.9908	18.1223	4.1687
39	10.5443	20.8515	7.2005	17.6772	4.3354
40	10.7024	20.1898	7.4166	17.2187	4.5089
41	10.8630	19.5183	7.6391	16.7464	4.6892
42	11.0259	18.8366	7.8682	16.2600	4.8768
43	11.1913	18.1447	8.1043	15.7589	5.0719
44	11.3592	17.4425	8.3474	15.2429	5.2747
45	11.5296	16.7297	8.5978	14.7113	5.4857
46	11.7025	16.0062	8.8558	14.1638	5.7052
47	11.8780	15.2718	9.1214	13.5999	5.9334
48	12.0562	14.5265	9.3951	13.0191	6.1707
49	12.2370	13.7699	9.6769	12.4208	6.4175
50	12.4206	13.0021	9.9672	11.8046	6.6742
51	12.6069	12.2227	10.2663	11.1699	6.9412
52	12.7960	11.4316	10.5742	10.5162	7.2188
53	12.9880	10.6286	10.8915	9.8428	7.5076
54	13.1828	9.8136	11.2182	9.1493	7.8079
55	13.3805	8.9864	11.5548	8.4349	8.1202
56	13.5812	8.1467	11.9014	7.6992	8.4450
57	13.7849	7.2945	12.2584	6.9413	8.7828
58	13.9917	6.4295	12.6262	6.1607	9.1341
59	14.2016	5.5515	13.0050	5.3567	9.4995
60	14.4146	4.6604	13.3951	4.5286	9.8795
61	14.6308	3.7558	13.7970	3.6756	10.2747
62	14.8503	2.8377	14.2109	2.7970	10.6856
63	15.0731	1.9059	14.6372	1.8921	11.1131
64	15.2991	0.9600	15.0763	0.9600	11.5576

Factors used in Appendices VIII & IX of *PN* - note only "Factor [5]" is new

Female 65 – married

Age	Factor [1]	Factor [2]	Factor [3]	Factor [4]	Factor [5]
25	8.5316	29.1509	4.7444	22.8566	3.0108
26	8.6596	28.6138	4.8868	22.5535	3.1313
27	8.7895	28.0685	5.0334	22.2413	3.2565
28	8.9213	27.5151	5.1844	21.9197	3.3868
29	9.0552	26.9534	5.3399	21.5884	3.5223
30	9.1910	26.3833	5.5001	21.2472	3.6631
31	9.3288	25.8046	5.6651	20.8958	3.8097
32	9.4688	25.2173	5.8351	20.5339	3.9621
33	9.6108	24.6211	6.0101	20.1611	4.1205
34	9.7550	24.0160	6.1904	19.7771	4.2854
35	9.9013	23.4018	6.3761	19.3815	4.4568
36	10.0498	22.7784	6.5674	18.9742	4.6350
37	10.2006	22.1456	6.7644	18.5545	4.8205
38	10.3536	21.5034	6.9674	18.1223	5.0133
39	10.5089	20.8515	7.1764	17.6772	5.2138
40	10.6665	20.1898	7.3917	17.2187	5.4224
41	10.8265	19.5183	7.6134	16.7464	5.6392
42	10.9889	18.8366	7.8418	16.2600	5.8648
43	11.1537	18.1447	8.0771	15.7589	6.0994
44	11.3210	17.4425	8.3194	15.2429	6.3434
45	11.4909	16.7297	8.5690	14.7113	6.5971
46	11.6632	16.0062	8.8260	14.1638	6.8610
47	11.8382	15.2718	9.0908	13.5999	7.1354
48	12.0157	14.5265	9.3636	13.0191	7.4209
49	12.1960	13.7699	9.6445	12.4208	7.7177
50	12.3789	13.0021	9.9338	11.8046	8.0264
51	12.5646	12.2227	10.2318	11.1699	8.3475
52	12.7531	11.4316	10.5388	10.5162	8.6814
53	12.9444	10.6286	10.8549	9.8428	9.0286
54	13.1385	9.8136	11.1806	9.1493	9.3898
55	13.3356	8.9864	11.5160	8.4349	9.7653
56	13.5357	8.1467	11.8615	7.6992	10.1560
57	13.7387	7.2945	12.2173	6.9413	10.5622
58	13.9448	6.4295	12.5838	6.1607	10.9847
59	14.1539	5.5515	12.9613	5.3567	11.4241
60	14.3662	4.6604	13.3502	4.5286	11.8810
61	14.5817	3.7558	13.7507	3.6756	12.3563
62	14.8005	2.8377	14.1632	2.7970	12.8505
63	15.0225	1.9059	14.5881	1.8921	13.3646
64	15.2478	0.9600	15.0258	0.9600	13.8991

Factors used in Appendices VIII & IX of *PN* - note only "Factor [5]" is new

Male 65 – single

Age	Factor [1]	Factor [2]	Factor [3]	Factor [4]	Factor [5]
25	6.6261	29.1509	3.6848	22.8566	2.5036
26	6.7255	28.6138	3.7953	22.5535	2.6038
27	6.8264	28.0685	3.9092	22.2413	2.7079
28	6.9288	27.5151	4.0265	21.9197	2.8162
29	7.0327	26.9534	4.1473	21.5884	2.9289
30	7.1382	26.3833	4.2717	21.2472	3.0460
31	7.2453	25.8046	4.3998	20.8958	3.1679
32	7.3540	25.2173	4.5318	20.5339	3.2946
33	7.4643	24.6211	4.6678	20.1611	3.4264
34	7.5762	24.0160	4.8078	19.7771	3.5634
35	7.6899	23.4018	4.9520	19.3815	3.7060
36	7.8052	22.7784	5.1006	18.9742	3.8542
37	7.9223	22.1456	5.2536	18.5545	4.0084
38	8.0411	21.5034	5.4112	18.1223	4.1687
39	8.1618	20.8515	5.5736	17.6772	4.3354
40	8.2842	20.1898	5.7408	17.2187	4.5089
41	8.4084	19.5183	5.9130	16.7464	4.6892
42	8.5346	18.8366	6.0904	16.2600	4.8768
43	8.6626	18.1447	6.2731	15.7589	5.0719
44	8.7925	17.4425	6.4613	15.2429	5.2747
45	8.9244	16.7297	6.6551	14.7113	5.4857
46	9.0583	16.0062	6.8548	14.1638	5.7052
47	9.1942	15.2718	7.0604	13.5999	5.9334
48	9.3321	14.5265	7.2722	13.0191	6.1707
49	9.4721	13.7699	7.4904	12.4208	6.4175
50	9.6141	13.0021	7.7151	11.8046	6.6742
51	9.7583	12.2227	7.9466	11.1699	6.9412
52	9.9047	11.4316	8.1850	10.5162	7.2188
53	10.0533	10.6286	8.4305	9.8428	7.5076
54	10.2041	9.8136	8.6834	9.1493	7.8079
55	10.3572	8.9864	8.9439	8.4349	8.1202
56	10.5125	8.1467	9.2123	7.6992	8.4450
57	10.6702	7.2945	9.4886	6.9413	8.7828
58	10.8303	6.4295	9.7733	6.1607	9.1341
59	10.9927	5.5515	10.0665	5.3567	9.4995
60	11.1576	4.6604	10.3685	4.5286	9.8795
61	11.3250	3.7558	10.6795	3.6756	10.2747
62	11.4948	2.8377	10.9999	2.7970	10.6856
63	11.6673	1.9059	11.3299	1.8921	11.1131
64	11.8423	0.9600	11.6698	0.9600	11.5576

Factors used in Appendices VIII & IX of *PN* - note only "Factor [5]" is new

Female 65 – single

Age	Factor [1]	Factor [2]	Factor [3]	Factor [4]	Factor [5]
25	7.9686	29.1509	4.4313	22.8566	3.0108
26	8.0881	28.6138	4.5642	22.5535	3.1313
27	8.2094	28.0685	4.7012	22.2413	3.2565
28	8.3325	27.5151	4.8422	21.9197	3.3868
29	8.4575	26.9534	4.9875	21.5884	3.5223
30	8.5844	26.3833	5.1371	21.2472	3.6631
31	8.7132	25.8046	5.2912	20.8958	3.8097
32	8.8439	25.2173	5.4500	20.5339	3.9621
33	8.9765	24.6211	5.6135	20.1611	4.1205
34	9.1112	24.0160	5.7819	19.7771	4.2854
35	9.2478	23.4018	5.9553	19.3815	4.4568
36	9.3865	22.7784	6.1340	18.9742	4.6350
37	9.5273	22.1456	6.3180	18.5545	4.8205
38	9.6703	21.5034	6.5075	18.1223	5.0133
39	9.8153	20.8515	6.7028	17.6772	5.2138
40	9.9625	20.1898	6.9038	17.2187	5.4224
41	10.1120	19.5183	7.1110	16.7464	5.6392
42	10.2637	18.8366	7.3243	16.2600	5.8648
43	10.4176	18.1447	7.5440	15.7589	6.0994
44	10.5739	17.4425	7.7703	15.2429	6.3434
45	10.7325	16.7297	8.0034	14.7113	6.5971
46	10.8935	16.0062	8.2435	14.1638	6.8610
47	11.0569	15.2718	8.4908	13.5999	7.1354
48	11.2227	14.5265	8.7456	13.0191	7.4209
49	11.3911	13.7699	9.0079	12.4208	7.7177
50	11.5619	13.0021	9.2782	11.8046	8.0264
51	11.7354	12.2227	9.5565	11.1699	8.3475
52	11.9114	11.4316	9.8432	10.5162	8.6814
53	12.0901	10.6286	10.1385	9.8428	9.0286
54	12.2714	9.8136	10.4427	9.1493	9.3898
55	12.4555	8.9864	10.7560	8.4349	9.7653
56	12.6423	8.1467	11.0786	7.6992	10.1560
57	12.8320	7.2945	11.4110	6.9413	10.5622
58	13.0244	6.4295	11.7533	6.1607	10.9847
59	13.2198	5.5515	12.1059	5.3567	11.4241
60	13.4181	4.6604	12.4691	4.5286	11.8810
61	13.6194	3.7558	12.8432	3.6756	12.3563
62	13.8237	2.8377	13.2285	2.7970	12.8505
63	14.0310	1.9059	13.6253	1.8921	13.3646
64	14.2415	0.9600	14.0341	0.9600	13.8991

Inland Revenue Contracted-out Employments Group – Pension Sharing on Divorce

July 2000

Background

Pension scheme rights can often be the most valuable part of the couple's assets which need to be considered when a marriage ends. From 1 December 2000 legislation will come into force which will allow divorcing couples the option to share their pension assets as a part of the overall divorce settlement. Apart from the basic State Retirement Pension and survivors pensions, which will not be shareable, it will be possible to share most types of occupational and personal pension rights including those built up in the State Earnings Related Pension Scheme (SERPS).

Pension sharing will be available alongside existing methods of dealing with pension rights on divorce: offsetting and earmarking. The new measure will help to provide courts with a comprehensive range of options for dealing with pensions at the time of divorce. Pension sharing will:

- provide greater flexibility and choice for divorcing couples and the courts;
- allow pension rights to be treated in a way which provides for the fairest overall settlement of assets in each divorce case; and
- increase the opportunity for divorcing couples to achieve complete financial independence through a 'clean break' settlement.

Pension Sharing on Divorce was introduced as part of the Welfare Reform and Pensions Bill and will be available in all divorce and nullity proceedings which begin on or after 1 December 2000. After this date it will be possible for a court to issue a pension sharing order or agreement to the pension scheme or provider as a part of the divorce settlement.

Once a couple decide to go ahead with divorce proceedings a court can order that pension sharing is to apply. The court will issue copies of the pension sharing order or agreement to the pension scheme or provider.

Safeguarded Rights

Rights of a scheme member derived from membership of a contracted-out occupational or Appropriate Personal Pension (APP) scheme which are transferred to the former spouse as a result of a pension sharing order or agreement become 'safeguarded rights' and therefore will be distinguished from the contracted-out rights built up by a member of a contracted-out occupational or APP scheme.

Scheme rules can specify whether all of the accrued rights that are subject to a pension share become safeguarded rights, therefore, safeguarded rights may include some non contracted-out rights. In addition, the safeguarded rights might include safeguarded rights from a previous divorce.

The requirements for safeguarded rights broadly reflect those for contracted-out rights. In particular the government wish to ensure that safeguarded rights (which are wholly or in part financed by rebates of National Insurance contributions, and in the case of APP schemes, tax relief on the employee's share of the rebate) are securely protected and used for the purpose for which they are intended—to provide an income in retirement.

The 'safeguarded' rights will be ringfenced and will be subject to broadly the same conditions that apply to post-1997 salary related contracted-out rights or protected rights. However, schemes will not be required to provide survivors' benefits from safeguarded rights and they will not be tracked by Contracted-out Employments Group (COEG).

A pension in respect of safeguarded rights is required to start being paid between the ages of 60 and 65, unless early payment is appropriate, for example because of ill-health.

As safeguarded rights will not be tracked or monitored by the department, it is important, therefore, that schemes maintain accurate records when a former spouse's rights are preserved in the scheme, transferred or bought out through an insurance policy. Schemes should also keep details of the pension sharing order, as they will need to record the percentage of the share on the member's pension account.

Calculation Services

Occupational pension and APP schemes will be required to provide a valuation of accrued pension rights to enable the courts to decide on the fairest overall settlement of assets.

To assist schemes with this process, the calculation services currently available can be used to request a Guaranteed Minimum Pension (GMP)/ Contracted-out Deduction (COD) calculation at any time during the pension sharing on divorce procedures.

As with the existing Individual Calculation Service, calculations for pension sharing cases will be provided free of charge.

Pension Sharing on Divorce Notification

Where pension rights have been shared, the courts will formally notify the scheme which will, in turn be required to notify COEG. Schemes will have 4 months in which to implement the pension sharing order.

A new form 'Pension Sharing on Divorce Notification' CA2202 (PDF 44K), has been introduced for completion by scheme administrators and providers to notify COEG of the pension share. A copy of this is shown at Annex A. Supplies of the form will be available from 1 November 2000.

As with the existing Individual Calculation Service, calculations for pension sharing cases will be provided free of charge.

On receipt of the notification COEG will update the National Insurance (N.I.) accounts of both the member and the former spouse to show that a 'Pension Share' has occurred.

Details from the CA2202 (PDF 44K) will be held on a database, which can be interrogated to answer any specific enquiries about the pension share itself.

Contracted-Out Deduction

When a member's pension rights are shared with a former spouse, a full COD will always be deducted from the member's Additional Pension under SERPS. The COD will not be reduced to take account of any GMP or protected rights that are subject to a pension sharing order/agreement.

Statements of GMP Liability

The calculation of contracted-out pension rights does not take account of any pension rights shared on divorce, therefore, the full GMP amount will continue to be notified. All statements which show a GMP amount (except for those issued by magnetic media) will include the notation 'The amount quoted does not take account of any pension rights shared on divorce' whether or not a pension share has taken place.

Although pension sharing on divorce will not be implemented until 1 December 2000 this general reminder will start to appear on statements issued from the end of October 2000.

Supervision of Safeguarded Rights

Schemes that opt to hold safeguarded rights after having elected to contract-out will not be required to advise COEG that they intend to start holding safeguarded rights. Instead, all schemes that hold a contracting-out certificate will need to indicate at triennial re-assurance whether or not they hold safeguarded rights. If they do, the schemes will need to confirm that they hold safeguarded rights and meet the prescribed requirements.

Cessation of Contracting-Out

When a scheme ceases to be contracted-out, trustees will have a period of 2 years in which they must make arrangements to secure all safeguarded rights held within the scheme.

Securing Safeguarded Rights

Securing Safeguarded Rights—Salary Related Schemes

Safeguarded rights may be secured by:
- Transfer to a Contracted-out Money Purchase (COMP) scheme or the active COMP part of a Contracted-out Mixed Benefit (COMB) scheme
- Transfer to a Contracted-out Salary Related (COSR) scheme or the active COSR part of a COMB scheme
- Transfer to an Appropriate Personal Pension (APP) scheme
- Purchase of an Annuity
- Preservation within the scheme

Securing Safeguarded Rights—Money Purchase Schemes

Safeguarded rights may be secured by:
- Transfer to a Contracted-out Money Purchase (COMP) scheme or the active COMP part of a Contracted-out Mixed Benefit (COMB) scheme

- Transfer to a Contracted-out Salary Related (COSR) scheme or the active COSR part of a COMB scheme
- Transfer to an Appropriate Personal Pension (APP) scheme
- Purchase of an Annuity
- Preservation within the scheme
- Provision of a pension
- Appropriate policy of insurance

As safeguarded rights will not be tracked or monitored by the Inland Revenue we will not issue calculations or membership lists to the life office/administrator.

Schemes should advise us as soon as all the safeguarded rights held by the scheme have been secured. Details of the individual arrangements are not required.

Approval will be confirmed by the issue of a letter to the scheme.

The Restoration of State Scheme Rights (Deemed Buyback)

Safeguarded rights can not be restored in the State Scheme. They must be secured by some other approved means.

Where scheme trustees intend to secure members' contracted-out rights in the State Scheme, to enable us to calculate the correct Technical Amount for the restoration of their rights in SERPS, the occupational pension scheme should let us know about any members whose contracted-out rights have been shared with a former spouse as part of the divorce settlement.

Further Information

Inland Revenue National Insurance Contributions Office, Contracted-out Employments Group, (Research and Development Team 3), Benton Park View, Longbenton, Newcastle upon Tyne. NE98 1ZZ

Tel: 0191 2250267

Fax: 0191 2250053

Institute of Actuaries Guidance Note 11:
Retirement Benefit Schemes – Transfer Values

Classification

Practice standard

Legislation or Authority

Pension Schemes Act 1993. (c.48).

Pensions Act 1995, (c.26).

Regulations set out in Appendices 1 (the 'Principal Regulations'), 2, 3 and 4.

Matrimonial Causes Act 1973, (c.18).

Family Law (Scotland) Act 1985. (c.37)

Welfare Reform and Pensions Act 1999 (c.30)

London Stock Exchange. *The listing rules* (as updated).

Northern Ireland has its own body of law relating to pensions and to family law. In relation to Northern Ireland, references to the Great Britain legislation contained in this Guidance Note should be read as including references to the corresponding Northern Ireland legislation. The Northern Ireland Regulations corresponding to the Great Britain Regulations are included in Appendices 1, 2 and 4. The Inland Revenue Regulations in Appendix 3 apply to Northern Ireland as well as to Great Britain. Appendix 6 shows the Northern Ireland legislation corresponding to the Great Britain Acts mentioned in this Guidance Note.

Application

Any actuary responsible for the calculation of cash equivalents under the Regulations and other individual transfer values from all types of retirement benefit schemes and to the assessment of benefits in such schemes in respect of incoming transfer payments and pension credits.

This Guidance Note may be used for purposes of the Stock Exchange Listing Rules.

Author

Pensions Board.

Status

Approved under Due Process (Fast Track)

Version   *Effective from*

Version	Effective from
1.0	01.12.85
2.0	01.11.87
3.0	01.07.88
4.0	01.03.90
5.0	01.05.91
5.1	31.03.93

6.0   01.07.94
7.0   06.04.97
7.1   01.03.98
7.2   01.04.98
8.0   01.12.00

1   Introduction

1.1   These guidelines apply to the basis of calculation of cash equivalents under the Regulations (including the treatment of pension debits and credits under pension sharing legislation) and under the listing rules and to the assessment of benefits in retirement benefit schemes in respect of incoming transfer payments.

1.2   The guidelines relate to United Kingdom requirements and conditions.

1.3   The guidelines also apply to other individual transfer values from retirement benefit schemes where no cash equivalent, within the provisions of the Pension Schemes Act 1993, arises and in those cases reference in this Guidance Note to the Regulations should be ignored and references to "cash equivalent" should be read as references to "transfer value".

1.4   This Guidance Note is not intended to inhibit trustees from paying transfer values greater than cash equivalents.

1.5   The guidelines also apply to the calculation of pension costs for the purpose of disclosure in the annual report and accounts of companies in respect of directors of certain UK companies. In such cases it may be necessary to calculate the value of accrued benefits in circumstances in which no entitlement to a transfer value exists. In such cases, the valuation must be consistent with the calculation of transfer values for the scheme concerned subject to paragraph 3.2 below; or (where no transfer values are payable from the scheme) for other schemes of the same employer. For the purposes of this paragraph, no allowance may be made for a reduced cash equivalent (see paragraph 5.2 below) and in particular the guidelines may be used for unfunded schemes. For the avoidance of doubt, Section 4 below would also apply. If benefits are payable from an overseas scheme, the calculation should be consistent with this Guidance Note, taking account of economic conditions in the country concerned.

1.6   The guidelines also apply to the calculation and verification of the value of benefits under a pension scheme for the purposes of divorce proceedings as specified in Regulations (Appendix 4). For the avoidance of doubt, Section 4 below would also apply for the purposes of this paragraph. The calculation of cash equivalents for the purposes of this paragraph must be consistent with the calculation of cash equivalents for the purpose of paying transfer values where an actuarial basis exists for such calculations in the scheme concerned. References to 'deferred pensioners' and 'pensioners' should be taken as including 'pension credit members' and 'pension credit benefit members' respectively, as defined in Section 124(1) of the Pensions Act 1995 and Regulation 2 of the Occupational Pension Schemes (Minimum Funding Requirement and Actuarial Valuations) Regulations 1996 (SI 1996/1536). References to 'members' should be taken as including 'pension credit members' and 'pension credit benefit members'.

2   Purposes of the Guidelines

2.1   The purposes of the guidelines are

(a)   to ensure that members of retirement benefit schemes exercising a right to a cash equivalent can be assured that it fairly reflects the benefits otherwise available (subject to the requirements of Section 4 below),

(b) to ensure that incoming transfers are dealt with consistently with outgoing cash equivalents.

(c) to facilitate consistency in the calculation of pension costs in respect of directors in companies' accounts and

(d) to ensure that pension debits and credits are calculated in accordance with the pension sharing legislation.

3   Standard Basis of Calculation

3.1   It is a fundamental requirement, stemming from the legislation, that a cash equivalent should represent the actuarial value of the corresponding accrued. Such actuarial value should represent the expected cost within the scheme of providing such benefits and should be assessed having regard to market rates of return on equities, gilts or other assets as appropriate.

3.2   Where a cash equivalent is to be calculated in respect of a member who has reached pension age, but whose benefits are not yet in payment, the benefit entitlement to be valued must be that which would apply if payment were to commence immediately. In such cases, and in respect of pensioners, market rates of return may be based on a different asset class from that used for deferred pensioners if the actuary considers that to be appropriate.

3.3   Where a deferred pensioner has a right to exercise an option on terms which are specified in the scheme documentation and are financially disadvantageous to the scheme, account must be taken of the likely cost of such an option on the basis of the assumed probability of deferred pensioners generally exercising the option.

3.4   Guaranteed or statutory increases, both in deferment and after retirement, must be valued as part of the accrued benefit.

3.5   The actuary has to bear in mind that Regulation 8(2) of the Principal Regulations requires that the discretionary grant of additional benefits must be taken into account in certain circumstances unless the trustees direct otherwise. The actuary must therefore establish with the trustees the extent to which they consider it appropriate to make an addition for future discretionary increases to the accrued benefit or for any other benefits granted on a discretionary basis, when calculating its value for transfer.

3.6   In calculating benefits in respect of pension credits or transfer values received by a retirement benefit scheme the actuary must use methods and assumptions which are reasonable and consistent with the methods and assumptions (including any allowance for future discretionary benefits) normally used for outgoing cash equivalents from that scheme. Section 4 below may be taken into account as described in paragraph 4.11. Appropriate adjustment would be required to take account of expected salary increases in cases where 'added years' are to be credited. In cases where the trustees, in accordance with paragraph 3.5, have given a general direction to the actuary that discretionary benefits should *not* be taken into account, then the same principles must be applied to the calculation of the benefits in respect of incoming transfer values and pension credits.

3.7   In the case of both incoming transfers and outgoing cash equivalents, allowance for expenses may be made where appropriate, e.g. to reflect administrative costs incurred, the saving in cost of paying pensions and any relevant costs of sale or purchase of investments.

3.8   Separate values must be quoted of the parts of the cash equivalent which represent benefits in respect of service after 5 April 1997 (other than those relating to voluntary contributions) and, where the payment is to an Appropriate Personal Pension Scheme or to a Contracted-out Money Purchase Scheme, Guaranteed Minimum Pensions (GMPs) under the transferring scheme. These values must be calculated consistently with the calculation of the total cash equivalents, in particular with a consistent assumption as to the expected annual statutory increases in the GMPs.

4   Minimum Cash Equivalent

4.1   In the case of a scheme to which Section 56 of the Pensions Act 1995 applies (the Minimum Funding Requirement (MFR)), the cash equivalent calculated in accordance with Section 3 above shall be increased, where necessary, to the liability which would be calculated in accordance with GN27, as at the effective date of the calculation, in respect of the member (or that part of the member's benefits concerned). A scheme with a 'gilts-matching policy' for deferred pensioners or pensioners must use a gilts-based calculation for the corresponding members in accordance with GN27. The assumptions specified in GN27 may be appropriately modified to take account of individual circumstances, as set out in this section.

4.2   In the case of a scheme to which the 'equity easement' (as described in paragraph 3.14 of GN27v1.4) applies, the equity easement may not be applied to the calculation of minimum cash equivalents for pensioners.

4.3   For the purposes of the calculation of the minimum cash equivalent, the MFR Pension Age must be used for those members who have not yet attained that age.

4.4   The age definition used for the minimum cash equivalent calculations need not be the same as that used for the most recent MFR valuation (if any), but care must be taken to ensure that the calculations are appropriate for the age definition used. In any event the age definition must allow for at least quarter years.

4.5   The mortality assumptions to be used are those set out in GN27. Where scheme-specific mortality might apply, the actuary must use the mortality rates used in the most recent MFR valuation. This does not prevent an actuary using other mortality assumptions, including unisex mortality rates, in the standard basis of calculation.

4.6   Although GN27 sets out a basis for proportions married and age differences between members and their spouses, it is permissible for this purpose to use the actual marital status of the scheme member if this is appropriate. The actuary must have regard to the marital status eligibility requirement for benefit provision under the scheme rules (for example married at date of leaving or married at date of death). Where and only where a spouse's pension would be payable only to a member's current spouse, that spouse's age may be used.

4.7   The same assumptions as those in GN27 must be used for calculating the amount of the scheme member's pension that can be given up for cash at retirement.

4.8   The rates of return to be used are those set out in GN27. For administrative convenience, the MVAs used need not be those applicable on the effective date of the calculation. MVAs may be changed on a regular basis, not less frequently than monthly. The MVAs to be applied in a cash equivalent calculation will be those at the last date of change before the relevant guarantee date.

4.9   The specific allowance for expenses in GN27 is for the closure or wind-up of a scheme.

These expenses are therefore not appropriate for the purpose of calculating minimum cash equivalents. The financial assumptions in GN27 make an implicit allowance for expenses and no further addition therefore should be made by the actuary.

4.10   In most cases the modification of the GN27 assumptions, as set out in this section, to take account of individual circumstances should not produce an aggregate result of the minimum cash equivalents for the whole scheme greatly different from the unmodified MFR cash equivalents. However, if the assumptions used combined with any unusual features of the scheme produce a significant bias, which results in this relationship no longer remaining valid, the actuary must inform the trustees of this and advise them of any implications.

4.11   For an outgoing cash equivalent, the minimum cash equivalent calculated under this Section 4 might exceed the cash equivalent calculated on the standard basis under Section 3. Similarly the benefits in respect of an incoming transfer or pension credit calculated on the standard basis might exceed the transfer credit calculated on the minimum basis. In this situation, the lower benefits, on the minimum basis, may be granted.

5 Departures from the Foregoing Bases of Calculation

5.1 Where an age-related payment by the Board of the Inland Revenue is outstanding, the cash equivalent must first be calculated on the basis of the benefits to which the member would have been entitled had the payment already been made.

The cash equivalent must then be reduced by the amount of the age-related payment, where this is payable to the receiving scheme rather than to the transferring scheme.

5.2 If the immediate payment of a full cash equivalent would reduce the security for the benefits of other members, the actuary should advise the trustees as to any reduced cash equivalent which would be appropriate having regard to the provisions of Regulation 8(4) or 8(6) of the Principal Regulations. The actuary should also advise them that the member's interests might be better served by deferring the taking of a cash equivalent until a later date. Where no reduction is applied, the actuary should draw the implications of this to the trustees' attention.

5.3 In cases where an outgoing cash equivalent is under consideration in respect of a member, in respect of whom a transfer value has previously been received, special care may be needed in the choice of the method of calculation - particularly where 'added years' have been credited - to ensure that the outgoing cash equivalent is, subject to paragraph 5.2, both equitable in relation to, and consistent with, the transfer value received. Except as described in paragraph 5.2, the cash equivalent must not be less than the value of the alternative accrued benefits.

5.4 Special considerations apply in cases where the circumstances of a previous transfer had been such that the assets transferred bore no direct relationship to the leaving service benefits under the previous scheme. Where such cases give rise to an entitlement to the member for a cash equivalent under Chapter IV of Part IV of the Pension Schemes Act 1993, then, for the purpose of paragraph 5.3, the cash equivalent must take account of the preserved benefit which would otherwise have been available had the member actually left service at the previous transfer date.

5.5 However, in cases where the former preserved benefit and/or the cash equivalent were augmented in connection with a full or partial dissolution of the former scheme (either in circumstances where the trustees were obliged to augment benefits in terms of the documents governing the scheme or alternatively at the discretion of the trustees or employer with the objective of enhancing the cash equivalents which would otherwise have been available for the purpose of buying out individual annuity contracts), then, for the purpose of paragraph 5.3, comparison must be made with such higher values.

5.6 If in the actuary's opinion an incoming transfer value would be insufficient to provide minimum statutory benefits (eg a Guaranteed Minimum Pension), the actuary should advise the trustees accordingly.

5.7 Regulation 8(8) of the Principal Regulations requires cash equivalents to be reduced in certain circumstances to less than those which would otherwise apply under this guidance. Such circumstances would include some 'Transfer Club' arrangements.

6 'Partial' Cash Equivalents

6.1 Partial cash equivalents can occur when a transfer is made from a contracted-out to a contracted-in scheme leaving the liability for GMP and post-5 April 1997 Contracted-out Salary Related rights behind. In that circumstance, the whole cash equivalent must be calculated in the normal way and an amount deducted which is calculated consistently in respect of the retained liability.

7   Money Purchase Schemes and Personal Pension Schemes

7.1   Generally the above principles apply to transfers arising out of money purchase schemes and personal pension schemes where the cash equivalents depend on making estimates of the value of benefits. Where all or part of the member's benefits depend directly on the proceeds of an earmarked investment, the corresponding cash equivalents will be the realisable value of that investment, eg the amount of a building society deposit or the cash value of a policy of insurance earmarked for the member. Similarly, if all or part of an incoming transfer value is to be applied to an earmarked investment, the benefit to be granted will depend on the proceeds of the investment.

7.2   In respect of personal pension schemes and other money purchase schemes these guidelines do not apply where cash equivalents depend on rights which do not fall to be valued in a manner which involves making estimates of the value of benefits, since the relevant Regulations make specific rules regarding the calculation of such cash equivalents. They thus do not apply to any personal pension schemes or money purchase schemes which are invested in unit trusts, bank or building society deposits or insurance contracts.

7.3   In relation to transfers to personal pension schemes, for the purposes of giving a certificate under Regulation 6 of the Personal Pension Schemes (Transfer Payments) Regulations 1988 the same principles as outlined in Sections 3 to 5 above must be applied.

8   Presentation

8.1   It is not necessary for each cash equivalent to be authorised separately by the actuary. The actuary may supply tables, for use by the trustees and administrators, for calculating the amount of any cash equivalent payable and the pensionable service or other benefits to be credited for an incoming payment or pension credit. The actuary should specify the circumstances (eg changes in investment conditions or cases involving previous receipt of a transfer value) in which adjustments to the tables or revised rates would apply.

8.2   The actuary is required to certify to the trustees that the method and assumptions being used in the calculation of a cash equivalent are consistent with the legislation. A specimen certificate for this purpose is provided in Appendix A. This should be amended as necessary to make it appropriate for the scheme concerned.

Appendix A

To the Trustees of the [   ] Pension Scheme:

I certify that the methods and assumptions underlying the calculation of cash equivalents for leavers under the [   ] Pension Scheme as specified in the tables and instructions dated [   ] are consistent with:

   (i)   the requirements of Chapter IV of Part IV and Chapter II of Part IV A of the Pension Schemes Act 1993;

   (ii)   *Retirement Benefit Schemes - Transfer values (GN1)* issued by the Institute of Actuaries and the Faculty of Actuaries; and

   (iii)   the methods currently adopted and assumptions currently made in calculating the benefits to which entitlement arises under the Rules of the Scheme for a person who is acquiring transfer credits under those Rules and provide as a minimum an amount consistent with those used for the purposes of Section 57 of the Pensions Act 1995, subject only to appropriate adjustments.

Signed:..   Date:......................

Fellow of the Institute of Actuaries or

Fellow of the Faculty of Actuaries

Appendix 1: Principal Regulations *	GB Reference	NI Reference
The Occupational Pension Schemes (Transfer Values) Regulations 1996 as amended	SI 1996/1847	SR 1996 No 619

Appendix 2: Other Pensions Regulations *

	GB Reference	NI Reference
The Occupational Pension Schemes (Contracted-Out Protected Rights Premiums) Regulations 1987 as amended	SI 1987/1103	SR 1987 No 281
The Personal Pension Schemes (Personal Pension Protected Rights Premiums) Regulations 1987 as amended	SI 1987/1111	SR 1987 No 289
The Personal Pension Schemes (Transfer Values) Regulations 1987 as amended	SI 1987/1112	SR 1987 No 290
The Protected Rights (Transfer Payment) Regulations 1996 as amended	SI 1996/1461	SR 1996 No 509
The Contracting-out (Transfer and Transfer Payment) Regulations 1996 as amended	SI 1996/1462	SR 1996 No 618
The Occupational Pension Schemes (Minimum Funding Requirement and Actuarial Valuations) Regulations 1996 as amended	SI 1996/1536	SR 1996 No 570
The Personal and Occupational Pension Schemes (Protected Rights) Regulations 1996 as amended	SI 1996/1537	SR 1997 No 56
The Occupational Pension Schemes (Disclosure of Information) Regulations 1996 as amended	SI 1996/1655	SR 1997 No 98

Appendix 3: The Inland Revenue Regulations

	GB Reference	
The Personal Pension Schemes (Transfer Payments) Regulations 1988 as amended	SI 1988/1014	

Appendix 4: Family Law Regulations*

	GB Reference	NI Reference
The Divorce etc (Pensions) Regulations 1996 as amended	SI 1996/1676	SR 1996 No 296
	GB Reference	**NI Reference**
The Divorce etc (Pensions) (Scotland) Regulations 1996 as amended	SI 1996/1901(S.153)	
The Pensions on Divorce etc (Provision of Information) Regulations 2000 as amended	SI 2000 No 1048	SR 2000/142
The Pension Sharing (Valuation) Regulations 2000 as amended	SI 2000 No 1052	SR 2000/144
The Pension Sharing (Implementation and Discharge of Liability) Regulations 2000 as amended	SI 2000 No 1053	SR 2000/145

The Pension Sharing (Pension Credit
Benefit) Regulations 2000 as amended   SI 2000 No 1054 SR 2000/146

Appendix 5: Stock Exchange Listing Rules

London Stock Exchange. *The listing rules*
(as updated).

Appendix 6: Northern Ireland Legislation
Corresponding to Great Britain Acts

GB Provision	NI Provision
Pension Schemes Act 1993 (c.48)	Pension Schemes (Northern Ireland) Act 1993 (c.49)
Pensions Act 1995 (c.26)	Pensions (Northern Ireland) Order 1995 (SI 1995/3213 (NI 22))
Matrimonial Causes Act 1973 (c.18)	Matrimonial Causes (Northern Ireland) Order 1978 (SI 1978/1045 (NI 15))
Welfare Reform and Pensions Act 1999 (c. 30)	Welfare Reform and Pensions (Northern Ireland) Order 1999 (SI 1999/3147 NI 11)) Section (of Act) Article (of Order) or Section (of Act)

* The title of the Northern Ireland Regulations are identical to those for Great Britain save
for the insertion of '(Northern Ireland)' after the word 'Regulations and in some instances
where the year may be different this will be indicated by the NI Reference.

November, 2000
To All Members

Dear Member

GN 11: Retirement Benefit Schemes – Transfer Values

Following publication of the regulations covering pensions sharing on divorce, introduced by the Welfare Reform and Pensions Act 1999, the Pensions Board has revised *GN 11: Retirement Benefit Schemes – Transfer Values* Version 8.0 which comes into effect on 1 December 2000 as a Fast track Guidance Note. It is simultaneously being exposed as an Exposure Draft.

Supplements to the Manual of Actuarial Practice are now only being sent to those members who previously requested in writing that this source be continued. If therefore you have requested a posted copy of Guidance Notes, the revised GN11 will be attached to this letter as an A4 document. Otherwise it will be found on the profession's Website at www.actuaries.org.uk/library/map.html.

A copy of GN11 that tracks the changes which have been made since the previous version of GN11 can be found on the Pensions Board Website pages at:

www.actuaries.org.uk/pensions/pensions_gns_track.html

Changes have been made to various paragraphs, both to make explicit provision for pensions sharing and to amend wording which was too restrictive to cover pensions sharing.

The opportunity has also been taken to introduce changes which:

- Remove passages which merely describe the legislation
- Remove unnecessary examples
- Clarify the existing guidance, particularly by the use of 'must' rather than 'should' where guidance is intended to be mandatory.

The regulations provide for trustees to obtain evidence of health of current pensioners, although they do not provide for this evidence to be used in calculating cash equivalents. The profession has taken legal advice on this matter and, as a result, felt it would not be safe to include any provisions within the amended Guidance Note for account to be taken of state of health.

The amendment to the certificate in Appendix A does not indicate that scheme actuaries must issue a new certificate immediately. They should, however, do so before cash equivalents are quoted which exist only under the new legislation, e.g. those for current pensioners or pension credit members.

Legal advice on the draft revised Guidance Note has been obtained and considered and it has been cleared for exposure by the Faculty and Institute Management Committee.

If you have any comments on the Exposure Draft, please send them to Mervyn Bryn-Jones, Secretary of the Guidance Committee of the Pensions Board, at Staple Inn by 1 February 2001. As usual, it would be helpful if you were to co-ordinate these with any comments by colleagues in your organisation.

It is not expected to hold a consultation meeting on this Guidance Note unless specifically requested by members.

Yours sincerely,

Peter Tompkins
Chairman, Pensions Board
24 November 2000

DSS worked examples: pension sharing on divorce and nullity

Illustrative examples of the treatment of a pension debit

This document gives general information and illustrative examples of the operation of pension debits for the purposes of pension sharing on divorce or nullity of marriage. Neither the information nor the examples should be treated as a complete and authoritative statement of the law. The examples illustrate ways in which scheme trustees and managers may interpret the law in different circumstances. It is for scheme trustees and managers themselves to consider whether the examples may be applicable to any particular case or whether another approach would be suitable.

Contents

Pension sharing on divorce

Illustrative examples of the pension debit

Introduction

Pension sharing on divorce or nullity of marriage will come into force on 1 December 2000. The primary objective of pension sharing is to give couples and the courts greater flexibility and choice on divorce or nullity of marriage, by allowing pension rights to be treated in a way which provides for the fairest overall settlement of assets in each case.

Pension sharing will increase the opportunity for divorcing couples to achieve complete financial independence through a 'clean break' settlement because the ex-spouses keep their share of pension rights regardless of changes in the other's personal circumstances following divorce or nullity. In practice this is achieved by a reduction in the pension rights of the scheme member (called a pension debit) and a transfer of pension rights equivalent to the amount of the reduction to the former spouse (called a pension credit).

Section 31 of the Welfare Reform and Pensions Act provides that effect is to be given to a pension debit by reducing a member's pension rights by a percentage specified in the court order or, if the order is in terms of a specified amount, by the percentage that amount represents of the cash equivalent value of the member's rights.

This document gives some illustrative examples of the operation of the pension debit for pension sharing purposes. The examples illustrate ways in which a scheme might interpret the law in different circumstances. It is for the trustees or managers of schemes to consider whether the examples are applicable to any particular case or whether another approach might be more suitable. The examples should not be treated as a complete and authoritative statement of the law.

December 2000
Department of Social Security.

Background Information and Assumptions

1. These examples cannot cover every possible situation where a scheme needs to implement a pension debit in accordance with section 31 Welfare Reform and Pensions Act 1999. As mentioned above, the examples must not be treated as a complete and authoritative statement of the law. The cash equivalent transfer value of the pension rights to which a member would be entitled (the 'relevant benefits' in section 29 of the Welfare Reform and Pensions Act 1999) forms the basis of the pension debit and of the pension credit.

2. In implementing a pension debit a key consideration is which benefits are included as the 'relevant benefits' in the calculation of the cash equivalent transfer value. These will form the 'qualifying benefits' referred to in section 31 of the Welfare Reform and Pensions Act. Since allowance should be made, either explicitly or implicitly, in the calculation for benefits such as any lump sums payable on death for deferred or pensioner members, and benefits to dependants following death, such benefits should be reduced appropriately by a debit.

3. Except for a member in active pensionable service the 'relevant benefits' are broadly all the benefits to which the member is entitled. For a member who is in pensionable service the relevant benefits are those which the member would receive if he or she had left service immediately before the day on which the pension sharing order had come into effect. Hence for a member in pensionable service the debit will be a proportion of the deferred benefits that she or he would

have received if she or he had become a deferred pensioner at the time of the divorce (the 'qualifying benefit'). This means that the situation for implementing debits against members in active pensionable service may have features where the debit and the main scheme benefit behave in slightly different ways – this is covered in example 3.

4. A divorce under Scottish law will see the pension sharing order made in terms of an amount rather than a percentage value. It is expected that schemes may wish to calculate the initial amount of the pension debit by turning the amount into a percentage value by comparing it with the cash equivalent transfer value of the relevant benefits on which the pension share was based. Once this has been done the pension debit can be enforced in the manner shown in these examples. For Scottish divorces where the pension benefits included in the matrimonial property on which the cash equivalent transfer value, and therefore the pension sharing order, was based are not the whole of the pension rights under the scheme the debit should similarly apply only to the rights included in cash equivalent transfer value.

5. Readers should refer to the relevant Inland Revenue Practice Notes, and in particular to PSO Update 62 and subsequent updates, in considering these examples. The examples do not cover situations relating to Inland Revenue maximum benefits where members can rebuild their pension rights following a divorce by virtue of having earnings below one-quarter of the earnings cap.

6. The examples assume that rights in the State Earnings-Related Pension Scheme will generally not be shared where shareable rights exist in a non-state pension arrangement. Where rights in a pension arrangement that is or has been contracted-out on a salary-related basis are shared, the Guaranteed Minimum Pension (GMP) from. The non-state arrangement (after sharing) and the State Earnings-Related Pension Scheme net of contracted-out deduction will probably no longer equal the State Earnings-Related Pension Scheme had the member not been contracted-out. Although this is not covered with a numerical example, scheme administrators may like to be aware of this feature in case their members raise queries about their total benefits.

7. The examples all assume that the member who is subject to the pension sharing order is male. The same principles apply in enforcing a debit against a female member's pension rights.

8. Readers are advised to ensure that they are considering the latest version of the examples in this document by checking in the 'publications' section of the DSS website www.dss.gov.uk. Any comments on the content of the examples may be sent to:

Prakash Raithatha
Pensions Sharing on Divorce Policy Team
Department of Social Security
3rd floor, The Adelphi
1-11 John Adam Street
London WC2N 6HT

E-Mail: pensionsharing@ms41.dss.gsi.gov.uk
Fax: 020 7712 2111.

EXAMPLE 1 – Debit for a pensioner of a defined benefit pension scheme

A pensioner aged 68 with a pension of £10,000 a year is made subject to a pension sharing order. The share to be given to the member's former spouse is 40%. Of the £10,000 a year pension, £1,000 a year represented pre-88 GMP and £500 a year represented post-88 GMP. Other than the GMP elements the whole pension is subject to increases in line with limited-price indexation. Taking the valuations of these different components into account should produce the following result.

At the time of the pension share (age 68)

Total gross pension	£10,000 a year
Debit (= 40% x £10,000)	£4,000 a year
Pension net of debit (= £10,000 – £4,000)	£6,000 a year

Splitting the debit and residual pension into GMP and non-GMP...
The total **gross pension** was split

Pre-88 GMP	£1,000 a year
Post-88 GMP	£500 a year
Thus excess over GMP (= £10,000 – £1,000 – £500)	£8,500 a year

The **debit can be split** in the same proportions

Pre-88 GMP included in debit (= £4,000 x £1,000 / £10,000)	£400 a year
Post-88 GMP included in debit (= £4,000 x £500 / £10,000)	£200 a year
Excess over GMP included in debit (= £4,000 – £400 – £200)	£3,400 a year

Hence the **residual pension after the debit** is made up of

Pre-88 GMP (= £1,000 – £400)	£600 a year
Post-88 GMP (= £500 – £200)	£300 a year
Excess over GMP (= £6,000 – £600 – £300)	
(or = £8,500 – £3,400)	£5,100 a year

In the first year after the pension sharing, assume that the LPI increase is 3.5%. Thus the increase which the scheme must pay on post-88 gmps is 3.0% a year
The **increase on the pension net of debit** is as follows:

Increase on pre-88 GMP	£0 a year
Increase on post-88 GMP (= £300 x 0.03)	£9 a year
Increase on excess over GMP (= £5,100 x 0.035)	£179 a year
Total increase	£188 a year.

EXAMPLE 1A – death of pensioner with debit

Now suppose that the pensioner in example 1 remarries almost immediately after the divorce, but dies aged 70. Retail Prices Index (RPI) increases were 3.5% in the first year (as above) and 2.5% in the second year.

By the **time of death, the pension net of debit** has increased to

Pre-88 GMP (no increases paid by scheme)	£600 a year
Post-88 GMP (increases up to 3% paid by scheme)	
(= (£300 + £9) x (1 + 0.025))	£317 a year
Excess (LPI increases paid) (= (£5,100 + £179) x (1 + 0.025))	£5,411 a year
Total pension net of debit at time of death	£6,328 a year

Under the scheme rules the **spouse inherits a 2/3 rate pension**, ie (= £6,328 x 2/3),	£4,219 a year

Of which a portion is GMP (ignored in this example)
The widow's pension is also affected by the debit because benefits to widows were included in the valuation of the total benefit at the time of the pension share, of which the specified proportion was awarded to the former spouse.

As a **check**, consider the position of the member if there had been no pension debit…
The **pension at time of death** would have been

Pre-88 GMP (no increases paid by scheme)	£1,000 a year
Post-88 GMP (£500 x (1 + 0.03) x (1 + 0.025))	£528 a year
Excess over GMP (£8,500 x (1 + 0.035) x (1 + 0.025))	£9,017 a year
Total	£10,545 a year

And the **spouse's pension with no debit**, two-thirds of this, is £7,030 a year
Ratio of spouse's pension paid after debit (£4,219) to this amount is 60% (= £4,219 / £7,030), as to be expected following a 40% debit.

Any **lump sum benefit** related to the level of the pension (eg 'balance' payments or 'guarantees' in early years of retirement) should be adjusted to reflect the rate of the debit on the same basis, even if they have not explicitly been included in the valuation of pensions in payment.

EXAMPLE 2 – pension debit for deferred pensioner of a defined benefit pension scheme

A deferred pensioner of a defined-benefit scheme aged 50 has a deferred pension, including revaluations to date of divorce, of £10,000 a year. The scheme has a normal pension age of 60. Based on the cash equivalent transfer value (whose value is unimportant in this context), the member is made subject to a debit of 40%, which directly represents a debit of a deferred pension of £4,000 a year.

At divorce at age 50 total gross deferred pension	£10,000 a year
Debit	£4,000 a year

At scheme normal pension age (60)
Increases to deferred benefit in line with statutory revaluation, say 4.1% a year on average (50% over 10 years – **used in all examples**)

Thus total gross pension (= £10,000 x 1.041^{10})	£15,000 a year
Debit (= £4,000 x 1.041^{10})	£6,000 a year
Net pension put into payment (= £15,000 – £6,000)	£9,000 a year

If the deferred pension contained a GMP, **anti-franking** will apply at GMP payment age (65 if member is male, 60 for a woman)
Assume that of the £10,000 pension at age 50, £2,000 was GMP…
Increases to GMP at statutory fixed rate revaluation of 6.25% a year

Gross GMP (= £2,000 x 1.0625^{14})	£4,673 a year
Gross excess over GMP (= £8,000 x 1.041^{10} x 1.035^5)	£14,252 a year
Total **anti-franking minimum gross of debit** (= £4,673 + £14,252)	£18,925 a year

This will generally be higher than the **scheme pension at GMP payment age** – for example this could be (= £15,000 x 1.035^5) £17,815 a year
Therefore **anti-franking** will require a **one-off increase** in the pension-in-payment at GMP payment age.

The calculation of the **cash equivalent transfer value on which the pension sharing order was based should take into account anti-franking**. Thus the debit, calculated as a proportion of that cash equivalent transfer value, is also bound by anti-franking requirements (subject in due course to the new requirements in the Child Support Pensions and Social Security Act 2000 where applicable).

The debit can be split into GMP and excess elements

GMP in debit at age 50 (= 40% x £2,000)	£800 a year
Excess over GMP in debit at age 50 (= 40% x £8,000)	£3,200 a year
At GMP payment age (65)	
GMP in debit (= £800 x 1.0625^{14})	£1,869 a year
Excess over GMP in debit (= £3,200 x 1.041^{10} x 1.035^5)	£5,701 a year

Total debit after allowing for anti-franking (= £1,869 + £5,701)   £7,570 a year
The total debit is still 40% of the gross pension after the effects of
complying with the anti-franking requirements..
The **net pension after allowing for anti-franking at age 65** is   £11,355 a year
thus (= £18,925 – £7,570)

Note that where the scheme revalues GMPS at a fixed rate, the same fixed rate should
be used for the GMP element of the debit for a deferred pensioner as for the gross
benefit. This is because the transfer value, and thus the debit, should have been
calculated on this basis.

EXAMPLE 2A – Commuting pension for lump sum at retirement

At retirement the member in Example 2 may wish to commute part of his pension in
order to provide a lump sum (if the scheme rules allow this). The Inland Revenue
maximum lump sum will depend on whether or not the member has pre-17 March
1987 continued rights or not (ie whether the member is covered by the pre-1987 or
1987-1989 tax regimes or the post-1989 tax regime).

For a **member without continued rights** (post-1989 member)
Pension at age 60 **without debit**   £15,000 a year
Maximum lump sum (= 2.25 x £15,000)   £33,750
If maximum lump sum taken, then maximum residual pension
using Inland Revenue approved commutation factor is
(= £15,000 – (£33,750 / 12))   £12,188 a year

Pension at age 60 **with debit**   £9,000 a year
Maximum lump sum (= 2.25 x £9,000)   £20,250
If maximum lump sum taken, then maximum residual pension
using Inland Revenue approved commutation factor is
(= £9,000 – (£20,250 / 12))   £7,313 a year
The maximum lump sum and the maximum pension where the
maximum lump sum has been taken are 60% of the amount without
the debit.

For a **member with continued rights** (ie who enjoys pre - 1987 limits) the maximum
lump sum could depend on the salary and service as at date of leaving service.
Maximum lump sum without debit say   £39,000
Maximum residual pension if maximum lump sum taken without
  debit (= £15,000 – (£39,000 / 12)),   £11,750 a year
Assuming that the scheme has adopted a 12:1 commutation factor
for all members irrespective of tax regime.
Where the member has a debit, the debit is, in effect, treated as
post-1989 rights, and the maximum lump sum can be calculated on
the better of two bases
Approach one: maximum lump sum
(= £39,000 – (2.25 x £6,000))   £25,500
And maximum pension if maximum lump sum is taken is
(= £9,000 – (£25,500 / 12))   £6,875 a year
Approach two – as if completely under post-1989 regime:
Maximum lump sum (= 2.25 x £9,000)   £20,250
And maximum pension if maximum lump sum is taken is, as before
(= £9,000 – (£20,250 / 12))   £7,313 a year

For further details on calculation of the maximum lump sum and pension where there
is a pension debit, please see the guidance from the Inland Revenue contained in PSO
Update No 62.

EXAMPLE 2B – death during deferment

If the pension scheme **member remarries and dies at age 55**
Assume that **deferred pension revalued to date of death** gross of
debit is $(= £10,000 \times 1.041^5)$ £12,225 a year
Further assume that the scheme pays a 2/3 spouse's pension (and
ignore anti-franking in this case)
Then **gross pension payable to widow** is $(= £12,225 \times 2/3)$ £8,150 a year
Using the same rules for calculating the amount of the debit as for
the main scheme pension gives a **debit at death** of
$(= £4,000 \times 1.041^5 \times 2/3)$ £3,260 a year
And thus a **net pension for the widow** of $(= £8,150 - £3,260)$ £4,890 a year
The debit from the widow's pension is still 40% of the scheme
benefit, as expected.

Any **benefits to other dependants** (eg to children) should also be reduced by the
debit in the appropriate proportion if they are included in the cash equivalent transfer
value on which pension sharing was based.

**EXAMPLE 2C – deferred pensioner choosing to take pension after scheme
normal pension age**

Under regulation 8 of the Occupational Pension Schemes (Preservation of Benefit)
Regulations 1991[1], a preserved pension can come into payment after scheme normal
pension age provided that the value of the late retirement pension is at least as great
as the value of the pension payable from scheme normal pension age. This implies that
schemes must offer increases (enhancements) to deferred pensioner members who
wish to receive their pension after scheme normal pension age, if such postponement
is permitted by the scheme. Inland Revenue restrictions will also apply, meaning that
such postponement of pension will not be possible in all cases.

The following example is based on the assumption that the scheme offers an
increment of 10% a year for each year after the scheme normal pension age that the
benefit is deferred, with allowance for LPI increases as well (at an average of 3.5%
a year over the period in question). Also, that the member in the example 2 chooses
to defer his pension so that it commences at age 65.

Gross pension before debit (for simplicity this does not take into
account anti-franking requirements)
$(= £10,000 \times 1.041^{10} \times 1.035^5 \times (1 + 5 \times 0.10))$ £26,723 a year
The debit, which must be calculated and brought into account
Whenever the main scheme benefits are first put into payment,
Should receive similar enhancements
So the **debit which comes into payment at 65** is
$(= £4,000 \times 1.041^{10} \times 1.035^5 \times (1 + 5 \times 0.10))$ £10,689 a year
The **pension net of debit** is thus $(= £26,723 - £10,689)$ £16,034 a year

**EXAMPLE 2D – other contingencies for deferred pensioners (ill-health or
incapacity pension, voluntary early pension)**

Please see corresponding examples for actives (examples 3D and 3E that follow).

---

1   S.I. 1991/167.

EXAMPLE 2E – deferred pensioner subsequently re-admitted to active membership

At age 52 the deferred pensioner in example 2 is readmitted to active scheme membership, and the 20 years' service on which his deferred pension was based is reinstated. His new salary is £35,000. By scheme normal pension age, 60, his salary has increased to £48,000. He now has 28 years' service.

Gross pension at scheme normal pension age is	
(= 28/60 x £48,000)	£22,400 a year
The **debit**, however, behaves exactly as if he had remained a deferred pensioner, ie from normal pension age it is	
(as in example 2 above)	£6,000 a year
Leaving a **net pension** of (= £22,400 – £6,000)	£16,400 a year

Both scheme pension and debit may receive an increase at GMP payment age (65) as result of the application of anti-franking rules.

The debit is calculated as if he remained a deferred pensioner, because its treatment must be consistent with the calculation of the cash equivalent transfer value on which it was based.

Any cost to the scheme experienced as a result of a deferred pensioner rejoining and having past service counting in full is unaffected by the pension debit.

EXAMPLE 3 – pension debit for active member

A 50-year-old male active member of a defined-benefit scheme with a 1/60ths accrual rate has 20 years' service and a salary of £30,000 a year, giving an accrued (deferred) pension of £10,000 a year. The scheme has a normal pension age of 60. Based on the cash equivalent transfer value, the member is subject to a debit of 40%, which leads directly to a debit of a deferred pension of £4,000 a year.

At age 50	
Total **gross deferred pension as if service terminated at divorce**	
On which cash equivalent transfer value for pension sharing was based	£10,000 a year
Debit	£4,000 a year
At scheme normal pension age (60)	
Salary, say	£48,000 a year
Service	30 years
Thus **gross pension at scheme pension age** (= £48,000 x 30/60)	£24,000 a year
Increases to debit in line with statutory revaluation as if it were a deferred benefit, say 4.1% a year on average (50% over 10 years)	
Debit (= £4,000 x 1.041^{10})	£6,000 a year
Net pension put into payment (= £24,000 – £6,000)	£18,000 a year

Both scheme pension and debit may need to be increased at, GMP payment age, 65 in the case of a man, to meet the anti-franking requirements – the treatment of the debit would be same as in the case of the deferred member in Example 2.

Revaluation of GMP element of debits for active members

In the private sector, schemes will generally choose to revalue the GMP element of a deferred pension in line with fixed rate revaluations. However, there is the option for schemes to revalue the GMP element of deferred pensions in line with section 148 orders as with gmps for those who remain in active service (see section 16 of the Pension Schemes Act 1993). The fixed rate for GMP revaluations is set to approximate the level of future section 148 orders that may be expected.

Schemes may decide to revalue the GMP element of debits in line with section 148 orders for those continuing in active service..

EXAMPLE 3A – commuting pension for lump sum at retirement

At retirement the member in example 3 may wish to commute part of his pension in order to provide a lump sum (if the scheme rules allow this). The Inland Revenue maximum lump sum will depend on whether or not the member has pre-17 March 1987 continued rights or not (ie whether the member is covered by the pre-1987 or 1987- 1989 tax regimes or the post-1989 tax regime).

For a **member without continued rights** (post-1989 member)

Pension at age 60 **without debit**	£24,000 a year
Maximum lump sum (= 2.25 x £24,000)	£54,000

If maximum lump sum taken, then maximum residual pension using Inland Revenue approved commutation factor is

(= £24,000 – (£54,000 / 12))	£19,500 a year

Pension at age 60 **with debit**	£18,000 a year
Maximum lump sum (= 2.25 x £18,000)	£40,500

If maximum lump sum taken, then maximum residual pension using Inland Revenue approved commutation factor is

(= £18,000 – (£40,500 / 12))	£14,625 a year

For a **member with continued rights** (ie who enjoys pre-1987 limits)

Maximum lump sum without debit (= 1.5 x £48,000)	£72,000
Maximum residual pension if maximum lump sum taken without debit (= £24,000 – (£72,000 / 12))	£18,000 a year

Where the member has a debit, the debit is, in effect, treated as post-1989 rights, and the maximum lump sum can be calculated on **the better of two bases**

Approach one: maximum lump sum

(= (1.5 x £48,000) – (2.25 x £6,000))	£58,500
and maximum pension if maximum lump sum is taken is (= £18,000 – (£58,500 / 12))	£13,125 a year

assuming, that the scheme has adopted a 12:1 commutation factor for all members irrespective of tax regime.

Approach two – as if completely under post-1989 regime:

Maximum lump sum (= 2.25 x £18,000)	£40,500
And maximum pension if maximum lump sum is taken is, as before, (= £18,000 – (£40,500 / 12))	£14,625 a year.

EXAMPLE 3B – death of active member with debit

If the member (now earning £39,000 a year) dies at age 55, with 25 years' service...

If the scheme pays a **lump sum** of 4 times salary on death in service, this would be paid as (= 4 x £39,000)	£156,000

With **no reduction** arising from the debit.

If the pension **scheme member has remarried** or is otherwise eligible for a surviving dependant's pension...
Assuming that the scheme pays a spouse's pension of 2/3 of the pension that the member would have received if he had retired at the date of death, based on actual service and salary (ignore anti-franking in this case).

Then the **gross spouse's pension** is (= £39,000 x 25 / 60 x 2/3)	£10,833 a year
Using the same rules for calculating the amount of the debit as for the deferred pensioner member in example 2 gives a **debit** of (= £4,000 x 1.041^5 x 2/3)	£3,260 a year
And thus a **net pension** for the widow of (= £10,833 – £3,260)	£7,573 a year

Any **benefits to other dependants** (eg to children) should also be reduced by the debit in the appropriate proportion.

EXAMPLE 3C – active member choosing to postpone retirement until after scheme normal pension age

Assume the member decides to remain at work until age 65. Assume further that the scheme allows service beyond normal pension age to count as pensionable and to base the final pension on salary at eventual retirement.

At age 65 the member's salary is £60,000 and he now has 35 years' service, the **gross scheme pension** will be   £35,000 a year
Allowing for increments on the debit from age 60 as if it were a deferred pension (say 10% a year) as well as the increases that it would have had had it been in payment (averaging 3.5% a year)
Gives a **debit** of (= £4,000 x 1.041^{10} x 1.035^5 x (1 + 5 x 0.10))   £10,689 a year
Giving a **net pension from age 65** of (= £35,000 – £10,689)   £24,311 a year

If the scheme adopted the more usual approach of ceasing pension accrual at scheme normal pension age and enhancing the pension until it came into payment as if it were a deferred pension, then this example would look just like the deferred pensioner postponing retirement at example 2C.

EXAMPLE 3D – active member taking pension early voluntarily

Assume that at 55, when the member has 25 years' service and a salary of £39,000 a year, he wishes to take voluntary early retirement.

Formally the member leaves with a **short service benefit payable from scheme normal pension age**, 60, of (= £39,000 x 25 / 60)   £16,250 a year

The debit revalued until age 55 is (= £4,000 x 1.041^5)   £4,890 a year
The scheme in fact applies early retirement factors to this pension amount to allow for early payment. These factors are constructed so that the provisions of regulation 8 of the Occupational Pension Schemes (Preservation of Benefit) Regulations 1991 are complied with – ie ensuring that the value of the immediate early retirement benefit exceeds the value of the short service benefit/deferred pension. In this case assume that the factor is a 4% reduction for each year before scheme normal pension age. In addition a check may be needed to ensure that the GMP is covered at GMP payment age, which may lead to early retirement not being an option at some ages (other than this anti-franking is disapplied in the case of such early retirements).

Hence the pension that is put into payment at age 55 is
(= £16,250 x (1 – (5 x 0.04)))   £13,000 a year
The debit, which is a negative deferred pension, should be reduced
in the same proportion, ie to (= £4,890 x (1 – (5 x 0.04)))   £3,912 a year
Thus the net early retirement pension is (= £13,000 – £3,912)   £9,088 a year.

EXAMPLE 3E – active member awarded pension early on ill-health/incapacity

Benefits on ill-health retirement are generally at the discretion of the scheme trustees. In the example below the trustees have decided that the debit is to be applied with no reduction for early payment as would apply in the case of a voluntary early retirement (see example 3D above). Where the trustees of the scheme felt that applying an unreduced debit in such cases resulted in the member experiencing a debit of a considerably higher value than that intended, they may conclude that the appropriate course of action would be to reduce the debit. This might apply particularly to ill-health retirements at young ages where there was no impairment of life expectancy. Trustees may consider that the maximum reduction in debit should ideally be no more than the reduction that would be applied in the case of a voluntary early retirement at the same age.

Assume that at 55, when the member has 25 years' service and a salary of £39,000 a year, the member has to take early retirement on ill-health grounds. The scheme provides a pension based on actual service and salary.

Hence the **gross ill-health retirement pension** from age 55 is   £16,250 a year
(= £39,000 x 25 / 60)
The scheme member's **debit on ill-health retirement** should be   £4,890 a year
(= £4,000 x 1.041^5)
And the **net ill-health retirement pension** after allowing for the   £11,360 a year
debit is (= £16,250 – £4,890)

The same debit could apply where the scheme chooses to pay a higher ill-health retirement pension based, say, on full potential service to scheme normal pension age, with the same flexibility for the debit as described above.

EXAMPLE 3F – active member subsequently becomes deferred pensioner member

Assume that at 55, when the member has 25 years' service and a salary of £39,000 a year, he leaves service with a deferred pension (short service benefit) payable from scheme normal pension age, 60.

The **short service benefit payable from scheme normal pension**
Age, 60, is (= £39,000 x 25 / 60)   £16,250 a year
The **debit**, which is already treated as a negative deferred pension is
(= £4,000 x 1.041^5)   £4,890 a year

Both the actual gross deferred pension and the debit are revalued
using rules for deferred pensions until age 60

At **age 60**
The **gross pension** is now (= £16,250 x 1.041^5)   £19,939 a year
The **debit** is (= £4,890 x 1.041^5)   £6,000 a year
Note that the debit is the same as if the member had been an active
member until age 60, or indeed had been a deferred pensioner
member for the whole period for 50 to 60
Thus the **net early retirement pension** is (= £19,939 – £6,000)   £13,939 a year

This ignores the effect of anti-franking which will apply at 65 if the member is male (at 60, scheme normal pension age, if the member is female).

In order to avoid any problems with the GMP element of the debit growing disproportionately compared with the gross GMP, trustees might decide to revalue the GMP element of the debit in line with section 148 orders while the member remains in active service and by the same fixed rate as the gross GMP in subsequent deferment (ie based on the date of leaving contracted-out employment). Although this may well not be the practice that schemes follow for deferred pensions (and in most cases the debit is treated as a negative deferred pension) trustees might conclude that it should be broadly consistent with the valuation of the debit.

For consideration of further contingencies following leaving service, see Example 2.

EXAMPLE 4 – pension debit for active member of a money-purchase arrangement

These differ from earlier defined-benefit examples in that they are not examples of how the pension put into payment is determined, but rather examples of how the maximum benefits permissible under Inland Revenue rules are determined. The benefits actually put into payment will depend, of course, on the fund available to the member at retirement and annuity rates for the chosen form of annuity at that time.

The examples here cover only active members of defined-contribution schemes. For pensioner members of defined-contribution schemes the principles of application of a debit are similar to those for pensioner members of defined-benefit schemes, and many aspects of examples 1 and 1A are relevant. For deferred members of defined-contribution arrangements, the examples given below for active members generally apply with future contributions being ignored and pre-debit maximum benefit limits taken as appropriate.

A 40-year-old male active member of a defined-contribution scheme has a fund of £80,000. The scheme has a normal pension age of 60. His final remuneration is £30,000 a year and he has 10 years' service. For simplicity, any retained benefits and the earnings cap are ignored. The pension target ('P1') is taken as £20,000 a year (2/3rds of £30,000 a year). The member is subject to a debit of 50%, which leads directly to a reduction of £40,000 in the value of the fund.

At age 40

Total **fund at divorce**	£80,000
Debit (transferred to his (ex-)wife for her to use to provide a pension in a form largely of her own choosing)	£40,000
Notional pension equivalent of debit (= £40,000 / 6.405), where 6.405 is Factor [5] (as defined in the extended tables of factors in Appendix VIII and Appendix IX to Inland Revenue Practice Note IR12(1997)) for a man aged 40	£6,245 a year

At scheme normal pension age (60)

Salary, say	£80,000 a year
Service	30 years
Thus **maximum gross pension at scheme pension age** (= £80,000 x 2/3)	£53,333 a year
Increases to debit in line with statutory revaluation as if it were a defined-benefit deferred pension, say 4.1% a year on average (same assumption as in defined-benefit examples 2 and 3 – equivalent to 50% over 10 years and 125% over 20 years).	
Debit for deduction from maximum (= £6,245 x 1.041^{20})	£14,051 a year
Net maximum pension that could be put into payment (= £53,333 – £14,051)	£39,282 a year.

EXAMPLE 4A – commuting pension for lump sum at retirement

The same principles apply here as in the example for defined-benefit schemes at 3A – ie the maximum lump sum is effectively reduced by 2.25 x the (revalued) debit.

EXAMPLE 4B – death of active member with debit

There are no special issues here. In some cases the scheme will pay a death-in-service lump sum and pensions to dependants (if any) based on salary and service at the time of the member's death. In this case, as with the corresponding example for members of defined-benefit schemes, a death-in-service lump sum will be unaffected by the pension debit, but the maximum dependants' pensions should take account of the pension debit revalued between the date of divorce and the date of the member's death.

EXAMPLE 4C – active member choosing to postpone retirement until after scheme normal pension age

Assume the member decides to remain at work until age 65. Assume further that the scheme allows service beyond normal pension age to count as pensionable and to base the final pension on salary at eventual retirement.

The maximum permissible pension can be calculated on one of two bases. The effect of the debit on the maximum permissible pension must be consistent with the approach used for the gross maximum benefit. (Some members of pension schemes may be restricted as to which of the two approaches can apply to them.)

Approach 1 – late retirement factor applied to pension as at scheme normal pension age

Suppose a factor of 1.42 is used by the scheme to increase the scheme pension at normal pension age to allow for late retirement

The **maximum scheme pension** would be (= £53,333 x 1.42)	£75,733 a year
The **debit** to be taken into account would become (= £14,051 x 1.42)	£19,952 a year
And hence the **maximum pension net of debit** would be (= £75,733 – £19,952)	£55,781 a year

Approach 2 – recalculate the maximum based on salary (and service) at eventual Retirement

At age 65 the member's salary is £100,000, say, so the **maximum gross scheme pension** will be (= £100,000 x 2/3)   £66,667 a year
The debit to be taken into account should be that from age 60 increased in line with statutory revaluation
(= £14,051 x 1.041^5)   £17,178 a year
Giving a **net pension from age 65** of (= £66,667 – £17,178)   £49,489 a year.

EXAMPLE 4D – active member taking pension early voluntarily

Assume that at 50, when the member has 20 years' service and a salary of £50,000 a year, he chooses to take early retirement voluntarily.

The **maximum gross retirement pension** from age 50 is
(= £50,000 x 2/3)   £33,333 a year
The **debit as it affects the maximum pension** should be
(= £6,245 x 1.041^{10} x $(1 - 0.065)^{10}$)   £4,783 a year
Note that in calculating the maximum pension the debit is brought into play with an actuarial reduction as if it were a pension paid before normal retirement age in a defined-benefit scheme.
And the **net maximum pension** after allowing for the debit is
(= £33,333 – £4,783)   £28,550 a year

The factor of 0.065 (compound) for actuarial reduction on early retirement is set by the Inland Revenue for use in these circumstances by money-purchase schemes determining the maximum benefits – such schemes would not generally have cause to use early retirement factors.

EXAMPLE 4E – active member awarded pension early on ill-health/incapacity

Assume that at 50, when the member has 20 years' service and a salary of £50,000 a year, he has to take early retirement on ill-health grounds. The same approach is used here as in voluntary early retirement, with the same 6.5% a year compound reductions factors coming into play.

The **maximum gross ill-health retirement pension** from age 50 is
(= £50,000 x 2/3)   £33,333 a year

The **debit as it affects the maximum pension** should be
(= £6,245 x 1.041^{10} x $(1 - 0.065)^{10}$)   £4,783 a year

Note that since we are defining the way in which the debit affects a *maximum* pension in this case, it is appropriate to treat the person retiring early on ill-health no less favourably than the person retiring early voluntarily, with the debit reduced for early payment. For this reason the reduction in debit should be the same reduction that would be applied in the case of a voluntary early retirement at the same age.

And the **net maximum pension** after allowing for the debit is
(= £33,333 – £4,783)   £28,550 a year.

EXAMPLE 4F – active member subsequently becomes deferred pensioner member

No special issues here.

Table of time limits for provision of information

Information requirements

There are complex information requirements for pension schemes to comply with. This table below sets out some of the more common ones; it is based on a set of tables issued by Abbey National Benefit Consultants.

Who wants the information	What information are they entitled to	When are they entitled to it
Member	Basic information: List 1: (a), (c) to (g)	(a) 1 month of receipt or (b) within 6 weeks if the member has notified the scheme that the information is needed in connection with proceedings or (c) within such shorter period as the court specifies or (d) three months from receipt if request includes request for valuation
Member	Information about valuation of pension benefits (if a deferred member, the cash equivalent on the termination of his pensionable service calculated at the date of the request received, or the guaranteed cash equivalent for defined benefit scheme; if an active member, the cash equivalent calculated on the basis that his pensionable service terminated on the date the request was received)	(a) 3 months of receipt or (b) within 6 weeks if the member has notified the scheme that the information is needed in connection with proceedings or (c) within such shorter time as the court specifies
Member	Information in response to a notification that a pension sharing order or provision may be made: List 1 and List 2	Within 21 days or later date as specified by court

Who wants the information	What information are they entitled to	When are they entitled to it
Spouse	Basic information: List 1: (b)-(g)	Within one month of receipt
Pension scheme	Information required by pension scheme: List 3	Before implementation begins
Beneficiary	Information on death of person entitled to pension credit: List 4	21 days of notification of death.
Court	Information in response to a notification that a pension sharing order or provision may be made: List 1 and List 2	Within 21 days or later date as specified by court
Court	Basic information: List 1	(a) 1 month of receipt or (b) within 6 weeks if the member has notified the scheme that the information is needed in connection with proceedings or (c) within such shorter period as the court specifies or (d) three months from receipt if request includes request for valuation
Court	Information after receipt of sharing order: List 5	21 days of receipt of order, or following implementation period
Court	Information after implementation of sharing order: List 6	21 days of the completion of discharge of liability in respect of the pension credit
Court	Information after earmarking order: List 7	21 days of receipt of order from court

Note: penalty for non-compliance: £200 for any individual case or £1,000 in any other case imposed on trustee or scheme manager.

List 1: Basic information
(a) valuation of pension rights or benefits accrued for a member
(b) statement that valuation will be provided to a member
(c) statement summarising the way in which the valuation is calculated
(d) the pension benefits included in the valuation
(e) whether the scheme offers information to a person with a pension credit other than by offering membership to a divorced spouse of the same scheme
(f) Whether the scheme intends to allow the divorced spouse to become a member of the scheme or to take a transfer value
(g) The schedule of charges to be levied.

List 2: Information in response to a notification that a pension sharing order may be made

(a) Full name and address of the pension arrangement
(b) Whether the scheme is being wound up, and if so (i) the date on which the winding-up commenced and (ii) the name and address of the trustees/administrators dealing with the wind-up
(c) Whether the cash equivalent of the member's pension rights are subject to any deductions
(d) Whether the trustees or administrators are aware of (i) any previous court order (ii) any court order for divorce (iii) any order under Scottish law (iv) any Irish order (v) a forfeiture order (vi) a bankruptcy order (vii) an award on a member's estate
(e) Whether there is any element of the member's rights which are not shareable
(f) If not already provided, whether the charges are to be paid in full or the proportion of charges to be paid
(g) Whether there are any additional charges to be levied and if so the scale of the charges
(h) Whether the member is a trustee of the scheme
(i) Whether the scheme may request information about the member's health from the member if a pension sharing order provision were made
(j) Whether the scheme will enable the transferee to nominate a person to receive the pension credit benefit including any lump sum in the event of their death before coming into payment
(k) Whether the scheme requires any further information (see List 3) before implementation of the order

List 3: Information required by the person responsible for the pension arrangement before the implementation period can begin

(a) In relation to the transferor: (i) all names by which he or she has been known (ii) date of birth (iii) address (iv) NI number (v) the name of the scheme to which the pension order relates (vi) the membership or policy number
(b) In relation to the transferee: (i) all names by which the transferee has been known (ii) date of birth (iii) address (iv) NI number (v) if the transferee is already a member of the pension arrangement from which the pension credit is coming from, then the membership or policy number
(c) Where the transferee is transferring the pension credit to another arrangement: (i) the full name and address of the arrangement (ii) if known the membership number or policy number (iii) the name and all contact details of the person able to discharge the liability (iv) where the rights have arisen from an occupational scheme and where the scheme is being wound up and the rights have been reduced accordingly whether the transferee has indicated he wishes to transfer his pension credit rights (v) any further information required by the receiving scheme

List 4: Provision of information after the death of the person entitled to the pension credit before liability has been discharged

(a) Who the member nominated
(b) Any other person for whom there may be an entitlement
(c) The benefits payable and how those will be levied
(d) Whether there are any charges to be levied from the benefits payable
(e) Full information of the requirements of the nominee in order to enable payment of benefits

List 5: Provision of information after receiving a pension sharing order

(a) A notice of any charges that have not been paid and that implementation will be postponed until the payment has been made
(b) Any further information required by either the pension scheme or person either entitled or authorised to enquire about the pension credit
(c) Notice to the member and spouse of the implementation period

(d) A statement from the pension scheme to the member and spouse explaining why the pension sharing order can not be implemented, perhaps because it requires further information

List 6: Information to be provided after the implementation of a pension sharing order

(a) Issue by the pension scheme of a notice of discharge of liability to the member. Where the pension is not yet in payment, but is affected by the implementation of a pension sharing order, the notice of discharge includes (i) the cash equivalent value of the member's accrued rights (ii) the value of the pension debit (iii) any amount deducted for charges (iv) the cash equivalent value after the charges are deducted (v) the date of the transfer

(b) Issue by the pension scheme of a notice of discharge of liability to the member. Where the pension is in payment, but is affected by the implementation of a pension sharing order, the notice of discharge includes (i) the cash equivalent value of the member's benefits (ii) the value of the pension debit (iii) the amount of the pension before the pension credit is deducted (iv) the amount of the pension after the pension credit is deducted (v) the date of the transfer (iv) any charges being imposed and how they will be recovered

(c) Issue by the pension scheme of a notice of discharge of liability to the spouse. Where the spouse's pension is not in payment, and there is to be an internal transfer the notice of discharge includes (i) the value of the pension credit (ii) any amount deducted for charges (iii) the value of the pension credit after charges are deducted (iv) the date of the transfer (v) any ongoing charges the scheme intends to make (vi) information in relation to membership of the scheme relevant to the pension credit

(d) Issue by the pension scheme of a notice of discharge of liability to the spouse. Where the spouse's pension is not in payment, and there is to be an external transfer the notice of discharge includes (i) the value of the pension credit (ii) any amount deducted for charges (iii) the value of the pension credit after charges are deducted (iv) the date of the transfer (v) details of the pension arrangement to which the credit is being transferred including address, telephone number, reference number, fax number and e-mail address if available

(e) Issue by the pension scheme of a notice of discharge of liability to the spouse. Where the spouse is at or over normal pension age on the transfer date the notice of discharge includes (i) the amount of the pension credit being paid (ii) the date it will be paid (iii) the date of the transfer (iv) any charges being made and how they will be recovered

(f) Issue by the pension scheme of a notice of discharge of liability to the spouse. Where the scheme is being wound up the notice of discharge includes (i) the value of the pension credit rights (ii) any amount deducted for charges (iii) the value of the pension credit (iv) the date of the transfer (iv) any periodical charges to be made and how they will be recovered

List 7: Provision of information after receipt of an earmarking order

Where an earmarking order is made the pension scheme must issue a notice to both parties which includes the following information

(a) Where the pension is not in payment (i) a list of the circumstances in respect of any changes which both parties must notify the pension scheme (ii) the amount of any charges which remain unpaid by either party entitled to the pension rights (iii) how the pension scheme intends to recover the charges (iv) the date when payment is required (either in part or in full) (v) the sum payable by each party (v) whether the sum will be deducted from payments of pension

(b) Where the pension is in payment: (i) the value of the pension rights or benefits of either party with pension rights (ii) the amount of the pension of the party with pension rights after the order has been implemented (iii) the first date when a payment is to be made (iv) a list of the circumstances in respect of any changes which both parties must notify the pension scheme (v) the amount of the pension currently in payment (vi) the amount of the pension which will be payable after the earmarking order is applied (vii) the amount of any charges which remain unpaid by either party entitled to the pension rights (viii) how the pension scheme intends to recover the charges (ix) the date when payments are required (either in part or in full) (x) the sum payable by each party (xi) whether the sum will be deducted from payments of pension.

Appendix II

Glossary

II.1

WORDS	DEFINITION
Accelerated Accrual	Provision by a pension scheme for an accrual rate of greater than one-sixtieth of pensionable earnings for each year of pensionable service. Sometimes described as uplifted sixtieth.
Accrual Rate	The rate at which a pension benefit builds up as pensionable service is completed in a defined benefit scheme.
Accrued Benefits	The benefits of service up to a given point in time. They may be calculated in relation to the current earnings or projected earnings and will include any transfer credits allowed under the scheme.
Accrued Rights	An alternative term sometimes used to describe accrued benefits.
Active Member	A member of a pension scheme who is at present accruing benefits under that scheme in respect of current service.
Actuarial Assumptions	The set of assumptions as to rates of return, inflation, increase in earnings, and mortality, used by the actuary in an actuarial valuation or in other actuarial calculations. Sometimes called 'actuarial basis'.
Actuarial Deficiency	The excess of the actuarial liability over the actuarial value of assets.
Actuarial Increase	An enhancement of pension benefits to compensate for the deferment of pension beyond the normal pension date.
Actuarial Statement	The statement required by the disclosure regulations to be included in the annual report. It must show in the prescribed form the security of the accrued and prospective rights of members and be signed by an actuary.

451

Actuarial Surplus

The excess of the actuarial value of assets over the pension scheme's actuarial liability (see actuarial deficiency).

Actuarial Valuation

An investigation by an actuary into the ability of a pension scheme to meet its liabilities. This is usually to assess the funding level and a recommended contribution rate based on comparing the actuarial value of the assets and the actuarial liability.

Actuarial Value of Assets

The value placed on the pension scheme's assets by an actuary. This can be market value, the present value of estimated income and proceeds of sale or redemption or some other value.

Actuary

An advisor on financial questions involving probability relating to mortality and other contingencies. In the UK this term automatically includes those who are Fellows of the Institute of Actuaries and of the Faculty of Actuaries. Those with other actuarial qualifications may be approved by the Secretary of State for a specific purpose.

Added Year

The provision of extra pension benefit by reference to an additional period of pensionable service in a defined benefit scheme arising from the receipt of a transfer payment, the pay of additional voluntary contributions or through augmentation.

Additional Pension

The earnings-related element of the State Pension over and above the basic pension.

Additional Voluntary Contributions (AVCs)

Contributions over and above a member's normal contributions which a pension scheme member chooses to pay into the scheme in order to secure additional benefits which may be through adding years or through money purchase. These can be within the scheme or through a freestanding scheme (see Free Standing AVCs).

Administrator

The person or persons regarded by the PSO and IRNICO as appropriate as being responsible for the management of a pension scheme. The term is sometimes used also to refer to the person who manages the day to day administration of the scheme.

Allocation

The ability given to the pension scheme member to give up or allocate part of his pension in exchange for a spouse's or dependant's pension.

Annuity

A specified sum, whether immediate or deferred, which may be subject to increases, payable at stated intervals for a number of years and/or until a particular event occurs (most commonly the death of the annuitant).

Appropriate Personal Pension Scheme

An approved personal pension scheme or free standing AVC scheme which is granted an Appropriate Scheme certificate by IRNICO. This enables its members to use it for the purposes of contracting out of SERPS.

Approved Scheme

A pension scheme which is approved by the Inland Revenue under the provisions of the Income and Corporation Taxes Act 1988. The term may include an approved free standing AVC Scheme or a personal pension scheme.

Attachment Orders

A court order ordering a third party to pay to the beneficiary of the order rather than the creditor; see *Pension Attachment Orders*.

Attained Age Method

This is a method of valuing prospective benefits where the actuarial liability makes allowance for projected earnings.

Augmentation

A method by which additional pension benefits are provided in respect of particular members. The cost is usually borne by the pension scheme and/or by the employer.

Band or Banded Earnings

An alternative term for upper band earnings (see below).

Basic Pension

The flat rate state pension paid to individuals who have met the minimum national insurance contribution requirements. A widow, widower or in some cases a married woman may also claim a basic state pension on the contribution record of their spouse.

Beneficiary

A person entitled to benefit under a pension scheme or who will become entitled on the happening of a specified event.

Benefit Statement

A statement or estimate of the benefits which would be payable in respect of an individual.

Bridging Pension

An additional pension sometimes paid from a pension scheme between the scheme member's retirement from employment and his state pensionable age. Once the state pension comes into payment the bridging pension will cease.

Bulk Transfer	The transfer of a group of members from one pension scheme to another usually with an enhanced transfer payment which is higher than the cash equivalent.
Cash Equivalent	The amount which a member of a pension scheme may require to be applied as a transfer payment to another permitted pension scheme under the Pensions Schemes Act 1993, Part IV.
Cash Option	An alternative term for commutation.
Centralised Scheme	A pension scheme operated on behalf of several employers.
Class A, B or C Members	Terms derived from specimen rules issued by the PSO applying to members of occupation schemes who joined during particular periods of time. Different Inland Revenue limits apply to each class. Class A members are members of those schemes established on or after 14 March 1989 and all new members of various schemes joining on or after 1 June 1989.
	Class B members are members of schemes established before 14 March 1989 who joined between 17 March 1987 and 31 May 1989.
	Class C members are those who joined schemes before 17 March 1987.
Closed Scheme	A pension scheme which does not admit new members.
Common Investment Fund	An arrangement through which the assets of two or more pensions schemes which are operated by a single employer or group of employers are pooled for investment.
Commutation	The option that pension scheme members and those with personal pensions have to surrender part or all of the pension payable for an immediate cash sum. In approved schemes this is subject to Inland Revenue maxima.
Contracted-in Pension Scheme	A defined salary or defined contribution pension scheme which provides benefits in addition to those provided in SERPS.
Contracted-out Money Purchase Scheme	Often referred to as COMPS. An occupational money purchase pension scheme which is contracted out from the state scheme.

Contracted-out Protected Rights Premium

Sometimes referred to as COPRP. A type of state scheme premium which until 5 April 1997 could be paid by money purchase scheme contracted out by reference to the provision of protected rights in order to purchase benefits under the state scheme for a member if the scheme ceases to be contracted out.

Contracted-out Rebate

The amount by which the employer's and employee's National Insurance contributions are reduced in respect of employees who have contracted out by virtue of their membership of an occupational pension scheme. It can also mean the equivalent payment made by the Department of Social Security as minimum contributions to a personal pension scheme.

Contracted-out Rights

Rights which emerge under a scheme which is contracted out of the SERPS pension scheme; see *Safeguarded Rights*.

Contracted-out Salary Related Scheme (COSRS)

A defined benefit occupational pension scheme which is contracted out.

Contribution Holiday

A period during which employers and other members contributions are temporarily suspended. This normally happens when the fund is in surplus. The term can sometimes be used to cover situations where contributions continue to be paid but at a reduced rate.

Contributions Equivalent Premium

A type of state scheme premium which can be paid when a member leaves with less than two years' qualifying service (or five years for those who left before 6 April 1988) in return for which the state scheme will take over the obligation to provide his/her GMP.

Contributory Scheme

A pension scheme which requires contributions from active members unless such contributions are temporarily suspended during a contributions holiday.

Controlling Director (20% Director)

A director who, together with his associates, owns or holds 20% or more of the ordinary shares of the employee company. Special restrictions apply to controlling directors who are members of approved pension schemes.

Corporate Trustee

A company which acts as trustee of a pension scheme.

Deferred Annuity	An annuity which starts to be paid at some future date, for example after a stated period has elapsed, or on the attainment of normal pension age.
Death Benefit	Benefit payable to the spouse or dependants of a deceased scheme member, or to that member's estate, on death in service or after retirement. It may take the form of a lump sum, a return of contributions or a survivor or dependant's pension.
Deferred Member	A person entitled to preserved benefits having left a scheme.
Deferred Pensioner	A person entitled to preserved benefits. Deferred pensioners are sometimes referred to as deferred members.
Defined Benefit Scheme	A pension scheme in which the rules specify benefits to be paid.
Defined Contribution Scheme	Another way of describing a money purchase scheme (see below).
Dependant	Someone who is dependent on a member or pensioner or was at the time of death or retirement. For PSO purposes a spouse qualifies automatically as a dependant and a child of the member will always be regarded as a dependant until she or he reaches the age of 18 or ceases to receive full-time education or vocational training.
Disclosure Regulations	Regulations requiring disclosure of information about pension schemes and benefits to scheme members, spouses, beneficiaries and others.
Discretionary Scheme	A pension scheme where the employer selects the employees who are to be offered membership of the scheme. In such schemes the benefits or the contributions may also be decided individually for each member.
Drawdown	See *Income Drawdown*.
Early Leaver	A person who ceases to be an active member of a pension scheme other than on death without being granted an immediate retirement benefit.
Early Retirement	A term used to describe the retirement of a pension scheme member before his normal pension date who received retirement benefits immediately on retirement.

Earnings Cap	A limit introduced by the Finance Act 1989 on the amount of remuneration on which benefits and contributions of Class A members may be based.
Earnings Factor (EF)	A notional amount of earnings used in the calculation of state scheme benefits or GMPs.
Eligible Member	In relation to a qualifying scheme (qv) means a member who has pension credit rights under the scheme.
Equal Access	The term used to describe the requirement that identical entry conditions should apply to each sex – a requirement of the Pensions Act 1995.
Executive Pension Plan or Scheme (EPP)	Occupational Pension Schemes designed for individuals or small groups of senior executives and directors. They are usually money purchase schemes but will normally have a target of providing the maximum pension the Inland Revenue allows. Contributions grow in investment funds earmarked for each scheme member. The employee's or employer's contributions are limited by the Inland Revenue.
Exempt Approved Scheme	An approved pension scheme other than a personal pension scheme which is normally established under irrevocable trusts.
Expression of Wish or Wishes	The means by which a member can indicate a preference as to who can receive any lump sum death benefit. Unless it is subject to a court order the choice is not binding on trustees.
Final Pensionable Earnings/Pay/Salary	The pensionable earnings at or near retirement or leaving service on which the pension is calculated in a final salary scheme.
Final Salary Scheme	A pension where the benefit is calculated by reference to the member's pensionable earnings for a period ending at or before normal pension date or leaving service.
Free Standing Additional Voluntary Contributions (FSAVCs)	Contributions to a pensions contract separate from a company pension scheme made by an active member of that scheme.
Free Standing AVC Scheme	A scheme established by a pension provider who accepts free standing additional voluntary contributions.

Frozen Scheme	A closed pension scheme where no further contributions are payable and scheme members are entitled to preserve the benefits.
Fully Insured Scheme	A pension scheme where the trustees have effected an insurance contract in respect of each member which guarantees benefits corresponding to those promised under the rule.
Funded Unapproved Pension Scheme (FURBs)	FURBs do have assets, and the courts may make a sharing order against the assets, but this will trigger a significant tax charge. See *UURBs* and *SUBURBs*.
Funding Level	The relationship between the actuarial value of assets and the actuarial liability as specified states.
Graduated Pension Scheme	A state earnings related scheme which began on 3 April 1961 and ended on 5 April 1975.
Group Personal Pension Scheme	An arrangement made for the employees of a particular employer to participate in a personal pension scheme on a group basis thereby effecting administrative savings.
Guaranteed Minimum Pension (GMP)	The minimum level of pension which an occupational pension scheme must provide for contracted-out service before 6 April 1987 as one of the conditions of being permitted to contract out. It is available at state pension age and to the widow or widower of the member on his or her death at any time.
Implementation Period	For a pension credit the period of four months beginning with the later of (a) the day on which the relevant order or provision takes effect, and (b) the first day on which the person responsible for the pension arrangement to which the relevant pension order or provision relates is in receipt of (i) the relevant matrimonial documents, and (ii) such information relating to the transferor and transferee as the Secretary of State prescribes by regulations.
Income Drawdown	Allows people up to the age of 75 to take an amount from their personal pensions without having to buy an annuity from an insurance company. A sensible and tax-efficient option, but can prove problematic for spouses, who may have difficulty in arranging for the sharing of such rights.
Indexation	An annual increase in pension benefits, subject to the Pension Schemes Act 1993, s 109 and the Pensions Act 1995, s 51.

Insurance Scheme	A pension scheme where the only long-term investment medium is an insurance policy rather than a managed fund policy.
Late Retirement	The retirement of a member after the normal pension date.
Limited Price Indexation (LPI)	The statutory requirement to increase pensions, once in payment by the lower of 5 per cent per annum or the retail price index.
Lower Earnings Limited (LEL)	The minimum amount approximately equal to the basic pension which must be earned in any pay period before National Insurance contributions are payable.
Managed Fund	An investment contract through which an insurance company offers participation in one or more pooled funds. The term is also used to describe an arrangement where pension scheme assets are invested on similar lines to Unit Trusts by an external investment manager.
Minimum Funding Requirement (MFR)	A requirement introduced by the Pensions Act 1995 that if the value of a pensions scheme's assets is less than its liability the employer must pay additional contributions to restore the funding level. The calculation of assets and liabilities will be determined by the scheme actuary using a prescribed basis.
Minimum Payments	The minimum amount which an employer must pay into a money purchase scheme which is contracted out through the provision of protected rights.
Money Purchase	The name given to pension schemes where an individual member's benefits are determined by reference to the contributions paid into the scheme which will normally be increased by an amount based on the investment return on those contributions. Also known as defined contributions
Net Relevant Earnings	Earnings from non-pensionable or self-employment which are used in determining the maximum contributions to a personal pension or retirement annuity which will qualify for tax relief. Certain business charges and losses can be deducted from them. The percentage of net relevant earnings that can be contributed to a pension and attract tax relief increases with age and is subject since 1989/90 to an earnings cap.

Nil Certificate	A certificate indicating that a transfer value cannot be used to provide lump sum retirement benefits, eg as one from a free standing AVC.
Nomination	The naming by a pension scheme member of the person to whom he wishes any death benefit to be paid. Where this is discretionary and not binding on the trustees it is more commonly called an expression of wish.
Non-Contributory Scheme	A pension scheme which does not require its members to make contributions.
Normal Pension or Retirement Age	The retirement age specified in the contract of employment or pension scheme; it should be distinguished from the state retirement age (currently 60 for women and 65 for men) since it must not discriminate between male and female employees.
Occupational Pension Scheme	A pension scheme organised by an employer or a group of employers or on behalf of an employer or group of employers to provide pensions and other benefits in respect of one or more employees on leaving service or death or retirement. It is governed by the Pensions Act 1995 and defined in the Pension Schemes Act 1993, s 1.
Occupational Pensions Advisory Service (OPAS)	An organisation providing free help and advice to those who have problems concerning their rights under occupational or personal pension schemes. It is grant aided and its service is provided by a network of local volunteer advisers.
Occupational Pensions Board (OPB)	The Board were responsible for dealing with a variety of functions concerned with pension schemes. It was abolished in 1997.
The Occupational Pensions Regulatory Authority (OPRA)	One of OPRA's duties is to insure that transfer payments are made within the statutory time limits.
Opting Out	The decision of an employee to leave or not to join an occupational scheme set up by his employer. Since 6 April 1988 employees have had the right to opt out.
Ordinary Annual Contributions	The contributions payable to an occupational pensions scheme by the employer on a regular basis in accordance and under the provisions of the scheme's documentation.

Outreach Scheme	A pension scheme where the benefit each year of membership is related to the pensionable earnings for that year.
Paid Up Benefit	A preserved benefit irrevocably secured for an individual member under an insurance contract where the premiums have ceased to be payable.
Partially Approved Scheme	A pension scheme only partially approved by the PSO because it provides some benefits which cannot be approved, eg benefits for overseas employees.
Past Service Reserve	A term normally used to describe the present value of all benefits accrued at the valuation date by reference to earnings projected to the dates on which benefits become payable.
Pay As You Go	A version of unfunded pensions schemes (see below) where benefits are paid out of revenue and no monies are put aside to fund future liabilities.
Pension Arrangement	This includes an occupational pension scheme, a personal pension scheme, a retirement annuity contract, an annuity or insurance policy purchased, or transferred, for the purpose of giving effect to rights under an occupational pension scheme or a personal pension scheme, and an annuity purchased, or entered into, for the purpose of discharging liability in respect of a pension credit under the Welfare Reform and Pensions Act 1999, s 21(1)(b) or under corresponding Northern Ireland legislation.
Pension Attachment Order	An attachment order against a pension scheme member's pension payments when they fall due. Commonly known as *earmarking*.
Pension Cost	The cost of providing pensions which is charged to the profit and loss account of the employer's business over the expected service lives or average remaining life of employees in the scheme. This may be more or less than the actual payments made to the pension scheme.
Pension Credit	The amount of money (expressed as a percentage of the CETV (qv)) which the ex-spouse may be awarded in a pension sharing order.
Pension Debit	The amount of money by which a scheme member's rights are reduced. A pension debit will not necessarily diminish the member's rights by the percentage expressed in the order.

Pension Guarantee

An arrangement where on the early death of a pensioner the pension scheme pays a further sum or sums to meet a guaranteed total which may be established by relation to, for instance, the late member's accumulated contributions or a multiple of the pension annual rate.

Pension Mortgage

A mortgage where the lender anticipates paying the capital borrowed on the mortgage from a lump sum commuted from his pension on retirement. There is no formal link and cannot be a formal link between the loan and cash sum.

Pension Schemes Office (PSO)

The Inland Revenue Office which deals with the approval of pension schemes under the tax legislation. Before 1 April 1992 it was called Superannuation Funds Office (SFO).

Pension Sharing Activity

A circular definition: pension sharing activity is activity attributable (directly or indirectly) to the involvement in pension sharing.

Pensionable Earnings

Those earnings on which benefits and/ or contributions are calculated. This may not be the total earnings received as some elements, for example overtime, may be excluded.

Pensionable Service

The period of service taken into account in calculating pensionable benefit. It is defined in the Pension Schemes Act 1993 as far as it concerns preservation, revaluation and transfer payment requirements.

Pensioner Trustee

An individual company with pensions experience appointed in accordance with the requirements relating to the approval of small, self administered schemes (see below) to act as a trustee of such a scheme.

Pensions and Tax Relief at Source (PTRAS)

The system under which contributions to an occupational pensions scheme are deducted from a member's pay before tax is calculated under PAYE. This gives the scheme member immediate tax relief at the highest applicable rate. Relief is also available for contributions to personal pension schemes but at basic rate only. The tax payer has to claim higher rate relief from the Revenue.

Pensions Compensation Board

The body which runs the pension compensation scheme set up under the Pensions Act 1995.

Pensions Ombudsman	The person appointed to deal with complaints against and disagreements with occupational and personal pensions schemes.
Permitted Maximum	The term used in pensions legislation to describe the earnings cap.
Personal Pension Scheme	Schemes normally approved under the Income and Corporation Taxes Act 1988 through which individuals who are non-pensionable employment or who are self-employment can make pension provision. The term is also used to describe free standing AVC schemes.
Practice Notes	Inland Revenue notes which deal with the approval of occupational pension schemes. Recurrent notes are issued as IR12 (1997).
Preserved Benefits	Benefits which arise when an individual ceases to be an active member of a pension scheme and which are payable at a later date.
Projected Accrued Benefit Method	A valuation method which compares the accrued actuarial liability with the value placed on the scheme placed on the scheme assets for valuation purposes. The actuarial liability is based on service up to the valuation date and makes allowance for projected earnings. It is only used in relation to pension scheme surpluses.
Projected Unit Method	An accrued benefits valuation method in which the actuarial liability makes allowance for projected earnings.
Prospective Benefits Valuation Method	A valuation method in which the actuarial liability is the current value of the benefits for current and deferred pensions and dependants and the benefits which active members will receive in both past and future service, less the present value of future contributions payable in respect of current members at the standard contribution rate.
Protected Rights	Benefits under an appropriate personal pension scheme or money purchase contracted out scheme deriving from the minimum contribution or payments.
Qualifying Arrangement	Any pension scheme which is permitted to accept a pension credit (qv); it includes an occupational pension scheme and a personal pension scheme.

Relevant Benefits	The term used in the income tax legislation 1998 and the practice notes to describe the types of benefits within the tax regime governing occupational pension schemes. They cover any type of financial benefit given in connection with retirement, death or termination of service. The definition does not include benefits provided in the event of accidental death or disablement during service.
Retained Benefits	Retirement or death benefits in respect of an employee deriving from an earlier period of employment or self-employment.
Retirement Annuity Contract	A former version of what is now a personal pension, with slightly different tax reliefs and available benefits.
Revaluation	The indexation of benefits or the awarding of discretionary increasing.
Revalued Earnings	The term used to describe index linking of earnings for calculating benefits.
Revalued Earnings Scheme	A pension scheme where the benefits are based on earnings for a given period revalued in direct proportion to a specified index of prices or earnings.
Safeguarded Rights	Contracted-out (qv) rights under SERPS (qv) which are the subject of a sharing order. The benefits which are shared must broadly reflect the benefits under the SERPS scheme, and cannot be converted into any other kinds of benefits.
Scheme Member	In relation to a pension scheme, a person who is or has been in pensionable service under the scheme.
Section 32 Policy	An insurance policy used for buy out purposes.
Secured Unfunded Unapproved Pension Scheme (SUBURB)	A tax-efficient and secure way for a company to provide pension benefits in respect of earnings over the earnings cap (£91,800 in 2000/01). The scheme has no assets, but does carry a charge against the employer's assets as security for the payment of benefits.
Self-Administered Scheme	A pension scheme where the assets are invested by the trustee, an in-house manager or an external investment manager other than wholly by payment of insurance premiums.

Self-Invested Personal Pensions (SIPP)	SIPPs are increasingly attractive to higher earners since they offer the facility of choosing investments (including property), charges by way of fees rather than hidden overheads and the right to income drawdown (qv).
Self-Investment	The investment of a scheme's assets in employer-related investment is now regulated by the pension schemes' office and normally a 5 per cent limit is imposed on employer-related investments. Additional restrictions are imposed on self-investment by small self-administered schemes.
Short Service Benefit (SSB)	The benefit which must be provided for someone who needs a pension scheme only under the preservation requirements of the Pensions Schemes Act 1993.
Small Self-Administered Scheme (SSAS)	A self-administered occupational pension scheme with a small number of members usually fewer than 12.
Stakeholder Pensions	All employers (with five or more relevant employees) must offer access to stakeholder pensions by October 2001; they do not have to make contributions and employees do not have to make contributions. For divorce purposes there is little or no difference with any other kind of personal pension, except that they are available to accept contributions from people without any earnings, such as carers and housepersons.
State Earnings Related Pension Scheme (SERPS)	The additional state pension provision described in more detail at p 19.
State Pensionable Age	The date from which pensions are normally payable by the state scheme. At present this is the 65th birthday for men and the 60th birthday for women. It is being equalised and will be equalised at 65 by the year 2020.
Statutory Scheme	A scheme established by Act of Parliament.
Survivor's Benefit	Pension or lump sum payments made to a scheme member's qualifying dependant in respect of the member's death.
Transfer Credit	The benefits purchased by a transfer payment.
Transfer Day	The day on which any relevant order or provision takes effect.

Transfer Payment

The payment made from a pension scheme to another pension scheme or to an insurance company to purchase a buy out policy in lieu of benefits which have accrued to the member or members concerned to enable the receiving arrangement to provide alternative benefits.

Transfer Value

The amount of a transfer payment which pension scheme trustees are prepared to make to another pension scheme or insurance company.

Trivial Pension

A pension so small it can be commuted in full.

Unapproved Unfunded Pension Scheme (URBS)

See *SUBURBS*. Since there is no money in the scheme it is hard for sharing to apply, and earmarking is the only real way of attaching any rights under the scheme.

Unfunded Scheme

A pension scheme where funds are not set aside so that nil assets are accumulated in advance.

Upper Band Earnings

Earnings between the lower earnings limit and the upper earnings limit on which the additional pension is calculated.

Upper Earnings Limit (UEL)

The maximum amount of earnings approximately equal to seven times the lower earnings limit on which National Insurance contributions are payable by employees.

Valuation Day

The day on which the pensioner becomes subject to the state pension debit.

Vested Rights

These are:
For active members, the benefits to which they would unconditionally be entitled on leaving service;
For deferred pensioners, their preserved benefits;
For pensioners, pensions to which they are entitled.

Winding-Up

The process of terminating a pension scheme. Usually by applying the assets to the purchase of immediate and deferred annuities for beneficiaries or by transferring the assets and liabilities to another pension scheme in accordance with the scheme documentation.

Appendix III

Court forms

III.1

Form A

Notice of [intention to proceed with] an Application for Ancillary Relief

Respondents (Solicitor(s))
name and address

In the	
	*[County Court]
	*[Principal Registry of the Family Division]

Case No. *Always quote this*	
Applicant's Solicitor's reference	
Respondent's Solicitor's reference	

(*delete as appropriate)

Postcode

The marriage of   **and**

Take Notice that

the Applicant intends; *to apply** to the Court for

*delete as
appropriate   *to proceed** with the application in the [petition][answer] for

                                    *to apply to vary:**

☐ an order for maintenance pending suit   ☐ a periodical payments order
☐ a secured provision order   ☐ a lump sum order
☐ a property adjustment order *(please provide address)*   ☐ an order under Section 24B, 25B or 25C of the Act of 1973

If an application is made for any periodical payments or secured periodical payments for children:

- and there is a written agreement made before 5 April 1993 about maintenance for the benefit of children, **tick this box** ☐
- and there is a written agreement made on or after 5 April 1993 about maintenance for the benefit of children, **tick this box** ☐
- but there is no agreement, tick any of the boxes below to show if you are applying for payment:

☐ for a stepchild or stepchildren
☐ in addition to child support maintenance already paid under a Child Support Agency assessment
☐ to meet expenses arising from a child's disability
☐ to meet expenses incurred by a child in being educated or training for work
☐ when either the child **or** the person with care of the child **or** the absent parent of the child is not habitually resident in the United Kingdom
☐ Other *(please state)*

Signed: Dated:
        [Applicant/Solicitor for the Applicant]

The court office at

is open between 10 am and 4 pm (4.30pm at the Principal Registry of the Family Division) Monday to Friday. When corresponding with the court, please address forms or letters to the Court Manager and quote the case number. If you do not do so, your correspondence may be returned.

Form A Notice of [Intention to proceed with] an Application for Ancillary Relief (12.00)   *Printed on behalf of The Court Service*

Form E

Part 2   Financial details   *Capital: Pensions (including SERPS but excluding basic state pensions)*

2.16   Give details of your pension interests.

If you have been provided with a valuation of your pension rights by the trustees or managers of the pension scheme, you must attach it. Where the information is not available, give the estimated date when it will be available and attach the letter to pension company or administrators from whom the information was sought. If you have more than one pension plan or scheme, you must provide the information in respect of each one, continuing, if necessary, on a separate sheet of paper. If you have made Additional Voluntary Contributions or any Free Standing Additional Voluntary Contributions to any plan or scheme, you must give the information separately if the benefits referable to such contributions are separately recorded or paid. Please include any SERPS.

Information about the scheme(s)

Name and address of scheme, plan or policy	
Your national insurance number	
Number of scheme, plan or policy	
Type of scheme, plan or policy *(e.g. final salary, money purchase or other)*	

CETV – Cash Equivalent Transfer Value

CETV Value	
The lump sum payable on death in service before retirement	
The lump sum payable on death in deferment before retirement	
The lump sum payable on death after retirement	

Retirement Benefits

Earliest date when benefit can be paid	
The estimated lump sum and monthly pension payable on retirement, assuming you take the maximum lump sum	
The estimated monthly pension without taking any lump sum	

Spouse's Benefit

On death in service	
On death in deferment	
On death in retirement	

TOTAL value of your pension assets (F)	£0

Pension Sharing Annex under Section 24B of the Matrimonial Causes Act 1973 (Rule 2.70(14) FPR 1991)

In the	
*[County Court] *[Principal registry of the Family Division]	
Case No. *Always quote this*	
Applicant's Solicitor's reference	
Respondent's Solicitor's reference	

The marriage of **and**

Take Notice that:

On ....the court

- made a pension sharing order under Part IV of the Welfare Reform and Pensions Act 1999.
- [varied] [discharged] an order which included provision for pension sharing made under part IV of the Welfare Reform and Pensions Act 1999 and dated ....

This annex to the order provides the person responsible for the pension arrangement with the information required by virtue of The Family Proceedings Rules 1991 as amended.

1. Name of the Transferor: ....

2. Name of the Transferee: ....

3. The Transferor's National Insurance Number: ....

4: Details of the Pension Arrangement and Policy Reference Number:
    (or such other details to enable the pension arrangement to be identified).   ....

5.   The specified percentage value of the
      pension arrangement to be transferred:

*(The specified amount required in order to
create a pension credit and debit should
only be inserted where specifically ordered
by the court).*   ....

In accordance with The Divorce etc.
(Pensions) Regulations 2000 the court
has specified that the benefits shall be
valued as at the following date: ....

Pension Sharing Charges:

(*Delete as appropriate)

It is directed that:

*The pension sharing charges be
apportioned between the parties as
follows: ....
*The pension sharing charges be paid
in full by the transferor.   ....

The court is satisfied that the person responsible for the pension arrangement has
furnished the information required by Regulation 4 of the Pensions on Divorce etc.
(Provision of Information) Regulations 2000 and, that it appears from the information
that there is power to make an order including provision under section 24B (pension
sharing) of the Act of 1973.

THIS [ORDER] [PROVISION] TAKES EFFECT FROM ....

To the person responsible for the pension arrangement:

(*Delete as appropriate)

1.   *Take notice that you must discharge your liability within the period of 4 months
      beginning with the later of:
      • the day on which this order or provision takes effect; or,
      • the first day on which you are in receipt of –
            a.   this [order] [provision] for ancillary relief, including the annex;
            b.   the decree of divorce or nullity of marriage; and
            c.   the information prescribed by Regulation 5 of the Pensions on Divorce
                  etc. (Provision of Information) Regulations 2000.[1]

2.   *The court directs that the implementation period for discharging your liability
      should be determined by regulations made under section 34(4) or 41(2)(a) of the
      WelfareReform and Pensions Act 1999, in that:

---

1   This information is listed at 4.3.4.

Pension Attachment Annex under Section 25B or 25C of the Matrimonial Causes Act 1973
(Rule 2.70(15) FPR 1991)

In the *[County Court] *[Principal registry of the Family Division]	
Case No. *Always quote this*	
Applicant's Solicitor's reference	
Respondent's Solicitor's reference	

The marriage of   **and**

Take Notice that:

On ....the court

- made an order including provision under section [25B][25C]* of the Matrimonial Causes Act 1973.
- [varied] [discharged] an order which included provision under section [25B][25C]* of the Matrimonial Causes Act 1973 and dated ....

  (*delete as appropriate)

This annex to the order provides the person responsible for the pension arrangement with the information required by virtue of The Family Proceedings rules 1991 as amended.

1. Name of the party with the
    pension rights: ....

2. Name of the other party: ....

3. The National Insurance Number
    of the party with pension rights: ....

4. Details of the Pension Arrangement
    and Policy Reference Number:
    *(or such other details to enable the
    pension arrangement to be identified).* ....

5. *The specified percentage of any payment due to the party with pension rights that is to be paid for the benefit of the other party.   ....

*The person responsible for the pension arrangement is required to: ....

*(*delete as appropriate*)

In accordance with The Divorce etc. (Pensions) Regulations 2000 the court has specified that the benefits shall be valued as at the following date: ....

To the person responsible for the pension arrangement:

(*Delete if this information has already been provided to the person responsible for the pension arrangement with Form A or pursuant to FPR 2.70(11))*

1. *You are required to serve any notice under the Divorce etc. (Pensions) Regulations 2000 on the other party at the following address: ....

2. *You are required to make any payments due under the pension arrangement to the other party at the following address: ....

3. *If the address at 2. above is that of a bank, building society or the Department of National Savings the following details will enable you to make payment into the account of the other party (e.g. Account Name, Number, Bank/Building Society/ etc. Sort code):   ....

Note: where the order to which this annex applies was made by consent the following section should also be completed.

The court also confirms:

(*Delete as appropriate)

- *That notice under Rule 2.70(11) of the Family Proceedings Rules 1991 has been served on the person responsible for the pension arrangement and that no objection has been received under Rule 2.70(12).
- *That notice under Rule 2.70(11) of the Family Proceedings Rules 1991 has been served on the person responsible for the pension arrangement and that the court has considered any objection received under Rule 270(12)(b).

Appendix IV

Precedents

IV.1

Pension Sharing Order

It is ordered that:

Provision is made in favour of the Petitioner/Respondent by way of pension sharing pursuant to section 24B of the Matrimonial Causes Act 1973 in accordance with the annex(es) to this order.

Pension Sharing Annex under Section 24B of the Matrimonial Causes Act 1973 (Rule 2.70(14) FPR 1991)

In the *[County Court] *[Principal registry of the Family Division]	
Case No. *Always quote this*	FD 12301
Applicant's Solicitor's reference	MAR/BER032
Respondent's Solicitor's reference	DVD/9324/1

The marriage of   James Brown   **and**   Sarah Brown

Take Notice that:

On   13 March 2001   the court

- made a pension sharing order under Part IV of the Welfare Reform and Pensions Act 1999.
- [varied] [discharged] an order which included provision for pension sharing made under part IV of the Welfare Reform and Pensions Act 1999 and dated ....

This annex to the order provides the person responsible for the pension arrangement with the information required by virtue of The Family Proceedings Rules 1991 as amended.

1. Name of the Transferor: James Brown

2. Name of the Transferee: Sarah Brown

3. The Transferor's National Insurance Number: Y2 34201A

4: Details of the Pension Arrangement and Policy Reference Number: The Equitable Life Personal Pension Plan HG3743892-1

    (or such other details to enable the pension arrangement to be identified).

5. The specified percentage value of the pension arrangement to be transferred: 75%

(The specified amount required in order to create a pension credit and debit should only be inserted where specifically ordered by the court).

In accordance with The Divorce etc. (Pensions) Regulations 2000 the court has specified that the benefits shall be valued as at the following date: 13 March 2001

Pension Sharing Charges:

(*Delete as appropriate)

It is directed that:

~~*The pension sharing charges be apportioned between the parties as follows:~~ ....

*The pension sharing charges be paid in full by the transferor. ....

The court is satisfied that the person responsible for the pension arrangement has furnished the information required by Regulation 4 of the Pensions on Divorce etc. (Provision of Information) Regulations 2000 and, that it appears from the information that there is power to make an order including provision under section 24B (pension sharing) of the Act of 1973.

THIS [ORDER] [PROVISION] TAKES EFFECT FROM 13 MARCH 2001

To the person responsible for the pension arrangement:

(*Delete as appropriate)

1.   *Take notice that you must discharge your liability within the period of 4 months beginning with the later of:

   • the day on which this order or provision takes effect; or,
   • the first day on which you are in receipt of –

      a.   this [order] [provision] for ancillary relief, including the annex;
      b.   the decree of divorce or nullity of marriage; and
      c.   the information prescribed by Regulation 5 of the Pensions on Divorce etc. (Provision of Information) Regulations 2000.[1]

2.   ~~*The court directs that the implementation period for discharging your liability should be determined by regulations made under section 34(4) or 41(2)(a) of the Welfare Reform and Pensions Act 1999, in that:~~

IV.3

Earmarking/Attachment Order

It is ordered that:

Provision is made in favour of the Petitioner/Respondent by way of pension attachment pursuant to section 25B and/or 25C of the Matrimonial Causes Act 1973 and in accordance with the annex(es) to this order.

Pension Attachment Annex under Section 25B or 25C of the Matrimonial Causes Act 1973 (Rule 2.70(15) FPR 1991)

<table>
<tr><td colspan="2">In the

*[County Court]
*[Principal registry of the Family Division]</td></tr>
<tr><td>Case No.
Always quote this</td><td>FD 00374101</td></tr>
<tr><td>Applicant's Solicitor's reference</td><td>MAR/MR</td></tr>
<tr><td>Respondent's Solicitor's reference</td><td>A2P 351</td></tr>
</table>

The marriage of   Edwina Jones   **and**   Robert William Jones

Take Notice that:

On   23.04.01   the court

- made an order including provision under section [25B][25C]* of the Matrimonial Causes Act 1973.
- [varied] [discharged] an order which included provision under section [25B][25C]* of the Matrimonial Causes Act 1973 and dated ....

(*delete as appropriate)

This annex to the order provides the person responsible for the pension arrangement with the information required by virtue of The Family Proceedings rules 1991 as amended.

1. Name of the party with the pension rights: Robert William Jones

2. Name of the other party: Edwina Jones

3. The National Insurance Number of the party with pension rights: YN 374006A

4. Details of the Pension Arrangement and Policy Reference Number: The Tresbury Pension Fund
Ref: 8597321AZ/01

   (or such other details to enable the pension arrangement to be identified)

5. *The specified percentage of any payment due to the party with pension rights that is to be paid for the benefit of the other party.

(a) 50% of the maximum possible sum that can be commuted on retirement and (b) 50% of any death in service payment.

*The person responsible for the pension arrangement is required to:
(*delete as appropriate)*

Pay the sums set out above to Edwina Jones. In the case of (a) above on Robert William Jones' retirement and in the case of (b) following his death in service.

In accordance with The Divorce etc. (Pensions) Regulations 2000 the court has specified that the benefits shall be valued as at the following date:

23.04.01

To the person responsible for the pension arrangement:

(*Delete if this information has already been provided to the person responsible for the pension arrangement with Form A or pursuant to FPR 2.70(11))*

1. *You are required to serve any notice under the Divorce etc. (Pensions) Regulations 2000 on the other party at the following address:

Edwina Jones
Fig Tree Cottage
Oakleaf
Beachshire

2. *You are required to make any payments due under the pension arrangement to the other party at the following address:

Edwina Jones
Fig Tree Cottage
Oakleaf
Beachshire

3. *If the address at 2. above is that of a bank, building society or the Department of National Savings the following details will enable you to make payment into the account of the other party (e.g. Account Name, Number, Bank/Building Society/ etc. Sort code):

N/A

Note: where the order to which this annex applies was made by consent the following section should also be completed.

The court also confirms:

(*Delete as appropriate)*

- *That notice under Rule 2.70(11) of the Family Proceedings Rules 1991 has been served on the person responsible for the pension arrangement and that no objection has been received under Rule 2.70(12).

- ~~*That notice under Rule 2.70(11) of the Family Proceedings Rules 1991 has been served on the person responsible for the pension arrangement and that the court has considered any objection received under Rule 270(12)(b).~~

Appendix V

Addresses

V.1

Note – The information given below in relation to services offered and fees charged is intended for general guidance only.

Actuaries and valuations

The Association of Consulting Actuaries 1 Wardrobe Place London EC4V 5AH 020 7248 3163 www.aca.org.uk provides a useful list of consulting actuaries; handy for establishing SSASs and valuing interests in them.

The professional body is the **Institute of Actuaries** (in Scotland, the Faculty) (Institute of Actuaries, Staple Inn Hall, High Holborn London WC1V 7QJ 020 7632 2100 www.actuaries.org.uk), but they do not generally deal with the public unless there is a complaint about an actuary's service. The Government Actuary's Department is at New King's Beam House, 22 Upper Ground London SE1 9RJ 020 7211 2600 www.gad.gov.uk

Robert Owen, the actuary who advised on some of the numbers in this book is at **Bacon & Woodrow** St Olaf House London Bridge City London SE1 2PE 020 7357 7171.

Keith Popplewell, who wrote the chapter on insurance, is the Managing Director of The Divorce Corporation which offers low cost valuations of pension rights together with full reports in a standard format: **The Divorce Corporation**, 187 Baslow Road, Totley Sheffield S17 4DT (or see the adverts in Family Law) 0114-262 0616 (fax 0114-235 0878).

Advice

See ACTUARIES, FINANCIAL ADVISERS

Compensation

Pensions Compensation Board, Room 501, 5th Floor, 11 Belgrave Road, London SW1V 1RB 020 7828 9794 (fax 020 7931-7239) pays out where there is a deficit in an occupational scheme, there has been dishonesty and the employer cannot make good the deficit. It may be useful where there has been a sharing pension credit but the scheme is insolvent.

Disputes and complaints: company schemes and personal pensions

Office of the Pensions Advisory Service (OPAS), 11 Belgrave Road, London SW1V 1RB 020 7233 8080 offers a useful and free service in relation to disputes about the mismanagement of occupational and personal pensions (www.opas.org.uk).

isputes and complaints: occupational schemes

If OPAS cannot help, more formal complaints about maladministration of an occupational scheme can be made to the **Pensions Ombudsman**, 11 Belgrave Road, London SW1V 1RB, 020 7834 9144. His service is also free. More serious complaints can be made to the **Occupational Pensions Regulatory Authority**, Invicta House, Trafalgar Place, Brighton East Sussex BN1 4BY 01273 627600, fax 01273 627630 www.opra.gov.uk. Information about pension rights can be found by applying to the **Pension Schemes Registry** care of the Occupational Pensions Regulatory Authority PO Box 1NN Newcastle on Tyne NE99 1NN 0191-225 6316.

Disputes and complaints: personal pensions

The Personal Investment Authority Ombudsman Bureau provisionally subsumed into the **Financial Services Authority Ombudsman** service is at 1 Canada Square Canary Wharf London E14 5AZ 020 7538 8860 www.fsa.gov.uk

The Insurance Ombudsman Bureau South Quay Plaza 183 Marsh Wall London E14 9SR 0845 600 6666 can look at personal and group pensions operated by insurance companies, but you would probably be better off with the Pensions Ombudsman or PIA Ombudsmen (www.theiob.org.uk).

Complaints about investment management

Investment Managers Regulatory Organisation 25 The North Colonnade Canary Wharf London E14 5HS 020 7676 3298 www.imro.co.uk

Complaints about financial advice

Personal Investment Authority, 25 The North Colonnade Canary Wharf London E14 5HS 020 7676 3298 www.fsa.gov.uk

Financial advice

A list of financial advisers in your area who charge fees rather than commission (qualified, but not necessarily recommended) is available from the Money Management Register of Fee Based Advisers, **Matrix Data Ltd**, Freepost 22 (SW1565) London W1E 7EZ, provided you send them your address and postcode.

IFA Promotions can also give three members in an area by phoning 020 7971 1177. Lists are also available from **The Society of Financial Advisers**, 20 Aldermanbury London EC2V 7HY 020 7417 4419 www.sofa.org but they are simply that; it is not possible to determined who is suitable for a particular case. Some chartered accountants provide financial advice (the **Institute of Chartered Accountants in England and Wales**, Moorgate Place London EC2P 2BJ 020 7920 8711 (or in Scotland the Institute of Chartered Accountants in Scotland, 27 Queen Street Edinburgh EH2 1LA 0131-225 5673

Solicitors are increasingly providing advice: **The Law Society** 113 Chancery Lane London WC2A 1PL 0171-242 1222 (in Scotland the Law Society of Scotland 26 Drumsheugh Gardens Edinburgh EH3 7YR 0131-226 7411, and especially the highly efficient Solicitors for Independent Financial Advice (SIFA) 01372 721172.

Industry bodies

The National Association of Pension Funds is at NIOC House 4 Victoria Street London SW1H ONX 020 7808 1300 www.napf.co.uk

The Pensions Management Institute is at PMI House 4-10 Artillery Lane London E1 7LS 020 7247 1452 www.pensions-pmi.org.uk

The Association of Pensioneer Trustees, which is involved in the management of small self-administered pension schemes is at JB Trustees 20 Bank Street Lutterworth Leicestershire LE17 4AG 01455 559711

Investment management

The Association of Private Client Investment Managers and Stockbrokers 112 Middlesex Street London E1 7HY provides a list of members.

Solicitors operate the **Association of Solicitor Investment Managers** (ASIM) Chiddingstone Causeway, Tonbridge, Kent TN11 8JX 01892 870065.

Tax

The Pension Schemes Office, changed its name in April 2001 to the **Inland Revenue (Savings, Pensions and Share Scheme Business Group)** but still operates out of its Nottingham offices: Yorke House PO Box 62, Castle Meadow Road, Nottingham NG2 1BG 0115-974 1480 www.inlandrevenue.gov.uk

War pensions

The War Pensions Agency, Norcross, Blackpool FY4 3WP 01253 858858

Legal advice

A list of specialist pensions lawyers is available from the **Association of Pension Lawyers**, c/o Eversheds Senator House 85 Queen Victoria Street London EC4V 4JA 020 7919 4701 www.apl.org.uk

Traded endowment policies/second hand endowment policies (TEPS/SHEPS)

TEPs and SHEPs are the same thing. It may be useful practice to sell such policies rather than surrender them, since insurers generally give poor value for surrenders. Up-to-date lists of dealers in TEPs are published in most of the financial magazines, including Money Marketing, Financial Adviser, Money Management and others.

Appendix VI

At A Glance system of valuation of lost pension

VI.1

A divorce will usually cause a woman to lose the chance of acquiring widow's benefits under her husband's pension. Under s.25B(1)(b) of the Matrimonial Causes Act 1973, these lost benefits are to be taken into account, but often the court has either disregarded them as 'too remote' or invoked them to justify an otherwise unsustainable award.

Regulation 5 of The Divorce etc (Pensions) Regulations 1996 (SI 1996 No. 1676) imposes a requirement on managers or trustees of a pension scheme to specify what proportion of the Cash Equivalent Transfer Value (CETV) of the scheme is attributable to any pension or other periodical payments to which a spouse of the member would be or might become entitled in the event of the member's death.

The information thus provided can be of use in assessing the value of a wife's loss of widow's pension rights. But it should be borne in mind that the proportion specified will merely signify the estimated cost of providing a pension to an average widow of the member. Moreover, the CETV method presupposes a termination of service as at the date of valuation, which limits both service completed and salary to their respective values at that date; whilst s.25B(1)(b) plainly requires consideration of the potential loss in the event that service is completed to normal retirement date.

The method utilised in this Table (which computes the estimated potential value to the wife of the lost benefit on the basis that the husband's pension rights will continue to accrue beyond the divorce until his retirement) is fundamentally different from the statutorily-introduced CETV-valuation method (which assumes that his pensionable service ceases at the valuation date).

The Table uses actuarial techniques to estimate more accurately the value of potentially lost pension rights to the particular wife in question on the basis that the husband works till his anticipated retirement age. The approach in this Table is to work out the widow's pension based on the husband's current pensionable salary and his expected length of service, and then to adjust the resulting figure to give the prima facie lump sum retirement date of buying £1 of widow's pension payable to her on the death of her husband after his retirement. There are three factors that affect the first multiplier: the husband's age at retirement; the age difference between husband and wife; and whether and if so what increases to pension once in payment are provided by his scheme.

The multipliers in Table A cater for:

- five different ages at which the husband may retire, namely 55, 60, 65, 70 and 75

- the age difference between husband and wife ranging from the wife being 10 years younger to 5 years older

- different rates of pension increases once in payment namely 0% p.a. (no increases in payment); 3% p.a.; Limited Price Indexation ('LPI': index-linking up to a ceiling of 5% p.a.); and full index-linking in line with the Retail Prices Index ('RPI').

Simple interpolation may be used for age differences or retirement ages not shown in Table A. Specific actuarial advice should be sought where the age differences or retirement ages are outside the parameters of this table.

The second multiplier (Table B *opposite*) compensates for the payment of the lump sum **now** rather than on the husband's normal retirement date. This discount multiplier takes into account not only expected income and capital growth from such a lump sum, but also expected increases in the husband's earnings, and makes allowance for the possibility of both husband and wife dying before retirement. If the pension is already in payment there is no Table B multiplier.

In summary:

Prima facie lump sum =   Widow's pension x
             Table A multiplier x
             Table B multiplier

It must be emphasised that, having regard to all the inherent uncertainties, the exercise can only produce an approximate estimate of the current value of the likely loss. The result should not be allowed to replace, but only to assist, the exercise of judicial discretion.

Table A

Retirement at age	Husband's age minus wife's age	Multiplier 1 Pension increases			
		0% p.a.	3% p.a.	LPI	RPI
55	10	3.99	9.46	7.04	7.57
55	5	3.30	7.33	5.58	5.97
55	3	3.02	6.52	5.01	5.35
55	0	2.60	5.38	4.20	4.46
55	-5	1.93	3.72	2.98	3.15
60	10	4.60	9.72	7.53	8.02
60	5	3.76	7.46	5.91	6.26
60	3	3.42	6.61	5.28	5.58
60	0	2.92	5.41	4.38	4.62
60	-5	2.12	3.68	3.05	3.20
65	10	5.18	9.80	7.88	8.31
65	5	4.17	7.43	6.10	6.40
65	3	3.76	6.54	5.41	5.67
65	0	3.16	5.30	4.44	4.64
65	-5	2.24	3.53	3.03	3.14
70	10	5.59	9.56	7.96	8.33
70	5	4.40	7.12	6.04	6.29
70	3	3.93	6.21	5.32	5.53
70	0	3.25	4.96	4.30	4.45
70	-5	2.24	3.23	2.85	2.94
75	10	5.72	8.94	7.67	7.97
75	5	4.38	6.49	5.67	5.86
75	3	3.86	5.60	4.93	5.09
75	0	3.13	4.41	3.92	4.04
75	-5	2.11	2.83	2.57	2.63

Table B

Years to retirement	Multiplier 2	Years to retirement	Multiplier 2
0	1.00		
1	0.97	21	0.58
2	0.93	22	0.57
3	0.91	23	0.56
4	0.88	24	0.54
5	0.85	25	0.53
6	0.83	26	0.52
7	0.81	27	0.51
8	0.78	28	0.50
9	0.76	29	0.49
10	0.75	30	0.48
11	0.73	31	0.47
12	0.71	32	0.46
13	0.69	33	0.45
14	0.68	34	0.44
15	0.66	35	0.43
16	0.65	36	0.42
17	0.63	37	0.42
18	0.62	38	0.41
19	0.61	39	0.40
20	0.59	40	0.39

The assumptions

The effect of the pension scheme being used to contract husband out of the state scheme is ignored.

Benefits that may be payable on husband's death in service are ignored.

Husband will receive salary increases not markedly out of line with the rate for non-manual workers.

Husband and wife both in good health (if husband in poor health, value lost will be **greater**; if wife in poor health, **smaller**).

Example below ignores tax: to value **net** pension lost, calculate and utilise widow's pension after tax.

Worked example: male retiring at 65

H is 52 and W is 48. H has 15 years pensionable service to date and will have 28 on normal retirement (when 65). H's current salary is £24,000. Scheme provides for $1/_{60}$th of final salary for each service year and (on his death after retirement) a widow's pension of 50% of the member's pension. Pension increases by 3% p.a. once in payment.

His expected pension at retirement aged 65, based on current salary is

$$^{28}/_{60} \times £24,000 = £11,200 \text{ p.a.}$$

The widow's pension, on this basis, is

$$50\% \times £11,200 = £5,600 \text{ p.a.}$$

Table A multiplier:
(H – W = 52 – 48) = 4 years
and a pension with 3% increases
= (by interpolation) **6.985**

Table B multiplier:
(H = 65 – 52) = 13 years from retirement
= **0.69**

Hence an estimate for the prima facie lump sum by way of compensation is

Widow's pension x Table A multiplier x
Table B multiplier =

£5,600 x 6.985 x 0.69 = **£26,990**

Material reproduced from At A Glance 2000-2001 by kind permission of the Family Law Bar Association. Individual calculations can be carried out using the associated computer program @eGlance. Contact Class Publishing on 020 7371 2119 for details.

DSS Form BR19

VII.1

■ Who can get a Retirement Pension forecast

You can get a Retirement Pension forecast if you are more than 4 months away from state Retirement Pension age when we process your application.

If you are within 4 months of state Retirement Pension age and you have not had a Retirement Pension claim pack, get in touch with your social security office straight away.

■ What your pension forecast will tell you

Basic Pension

This is the part of your state Retirement Pension that is based on the National Insurance (NI) contributions you pay, or are given as credits, during your working life.

Your forecast will tell you in today's money values

• the amount of Basic Pension you have earned already

• the amount of Basic Pension that you can expect at state pension age based on what you have earned already and what you might earn before you retire.

Your forecast will also tell you if there is anything you can do to improve your Basic Pension.

Additional Pension and Contracted-out Deductions (COD)

Additional Pension is the part of your pension that depends on your earnings since April 1978. It is also known as State Earnings-Related Pension Scheme (SERPS).

Some employees are contracted-out of this scheme by their employers or by a personal pension scheme. If this applies to you, we will give you more information in your pension forecast letter.

Your forecast will tell you in today's money values

• the amount of Additional Pension you have earned already

• the amount of Additional Pension you can expect at state pension age based on what you have earned already and what you might earn before you retire.

Graduated Retirement Benefit

This is the part of your pension that depends on the amount of graduated NI contributions you may have paid between 1961 and 1975 when the scheme was in operation.

Your forecast will tell you in today's money values how may units of Graduated Retirement Benefit you have and what they are worth.

If you are widowed or divorced

Your late or former spouse's NI contributions can sometimes be used to help you get a better pension.

Your forecast will tell you in today's money values the amount of pension you can expect by using your late or former spouse's NI contributions, if this will give you a better pension than using your own NI contributions.

■   **What to do now**

Please fill in form BR19 *Application for a Retirement Pension forecast.*

Check that you have answered all the questions that apply to you. And check that you have signed and dated the form.

Please keep these notes for your information.

If you need any help filling in the form, please get in touch with us.

Our address is

Benefits Agency
RPFA Unit
Pensions and Overseas Benefits Directorate
Newcastle upon Tyne
NE98 1BA

This is also the address to send your completed form BR19 to.

If you have a speech or hearing problem, we have a textphone service.

Just ring 0191 218 7280. If you do not have your own textphone system, they are available in some libraries or Citizens Advice Bureau offices.

The textphone service is only for people with speech or hearing problems.

■   **What happens next**

We will send your Retirement Pension forecast to you as soon as we can. If you have filled in **Part 13**, we will send your Retirement Pension forecast to the person or company you have told us about.

When we have received your application form, it may take us up to 40 days to prepare your forecast.

Application forms are subject to security checks if you fill in **Part 13**.

Application for a Retirement Pension forecast

Part 1 - About you

Please tell us about yourself.

National Insurance (NI) number	Letters Numbers Letter
Title	
Requested Title	**?**
Surname	
Other surnames you have used in dealing with the DSS	
Forename	
Other forename(s)	
Date of birth	
Address	
Postcode	
Daytime phone number	

Part 2 - Marital Status

Your Retirement Pension may be affected by a spouse's National Insurance (NI) Contributions.

Please tick the description that applies to you and answer the questions

Single	☐	**Go to Part 5**
Married	☐	**Go to Part 4**
Married but about to get divorced	☐	Expected date of divorce [ ] **Go to Part 3**
Divorced	☐	Date of divorce [ ] **Go to Part 3**
Widowed	☐	Date of widowhood [ ] **Go to Part 3**

Please tick if you are getting

Widow's Pension	☐
War Widow's Pension	☐
Industrial Death Benefit	☐

How much Industrial Death Benefit do you get each week

£ [   ]

Go to Part 3

Application for a Retirement Pension forecast - continued
Part 3 - Marital Status - more information
We need more information if you are 1) Married but about to get divorced, or 2) Divorced, or 3) widowed.

Please tell us about your last spouse here.

Date of marriage

Spouse's surname

Spouse's first forename

Spouse's other forename(s)

Spouse's date of birth

Spouse's National Insurance (NI) number Letters Numbers Letter

Spouse's last known address

Postcode

Part 4 - If you have been married more than once

Were you widowed before April 1978? No ☐ **Go to Part 5**

Yes ☐ What date did you marry your late husband?

What date were you widowed?

What date did you re-marry?

Part 5 - About HM Forces and the Civil Service

Have you ever been in HM Forces or worked for the Civil Service? No ☐ Yes ☐

Part 6 - About Child Benefit

Are you getting Child Benefit? No ☐ **Go to Part 7**

Yes ☐ Is your name the first or only name on the order book or letter about having your money paid into an account?

No ☐ **Go to Part 7**

Yes ☐ What is the date of birth of your youngest or only child?

What is the date of birth of your oldest child if you have more than one child?

Application for a Retirement Pension forecast - continued
Part 7 - About what you are doing now
Please tick all the descriptions that apply to you

A   Working for an employer ☐

B   Working for an employer and getting
    Disabled Person's Tax Credit ☐

C   Self-employed ☐

D   Self-employed and getting Disabled
    Person's Tax Credit ☐

E   Not working ☐

F   Getting Statutory Sick Pay ☐

G   Registering for Jobseeker's Allowance ☐

H   Getting Incapacity Benefit ☐

I   Getting Invalid Care Allowance ☐

J   Getting Severe Disablement Allowance ☐

Part 8 - About NI Contributions

If you have ticked G, H, I or J in Part 7, you do not need to fill in Part 8.

If you have ticked A, B, C, D, E or F in Part 7, we need to know about the NI contributions you are paying.

Please tick all the boxes that apply to you.

Paying full rate NI contributions ☐

Paying married woman's or widow's
reduced rate NI contributions ☐

Paying Class 2 self-employed NI contributions ☐

Paying Class 3 voluntary NI contributions ☐

Not paying NI contributions ☐   If you can improve your Basic Pension by paying Class 3 voluntary contributions, we will tell you about this in your forecast.

Part 9 - About Self-employment

Are you self-employed now?   No ☐
                             Yes ☐   What date did you
                                     become self-employed? [_____]

Have you been self-employed
at any time since 5 April 1975?

                             No ☐   Please give details of your 3 earliest periods of self employment.
                             Yes ☐   From [_____] to [_____]
                                     From [_____] to [_____]
                                     From [_____] to [_____]

Please turn over -->

Application for a Retirement Pension forecast - continued
Part 10 - Living abroad

We need to know if you have ever lived outside the United Kingdom since the age of 16. We use United Kingdom to mean England, Scotland, Wales and Northern Ireland.

Do not include holidays or periods in the armed forces.

Tick the boxes that apply to you.

Australia ☐   Channel Islands ☐

Canada ☐   New Zealand ☐

Any other country or countries ☐   Which countries? ☐

Part 11 - Extra Information

We can also tell you what may happen to your Retirement Pension in different situations. If you want extra information in your forecast, please tick the things you want to know about.

You put off claiming your Retirement Pension past your state pension age ☐

You stop work before you reach your state pension age ☐   Please tell us the date you may stop working

You go to live abroad ☐   Please tell us the country you may go to

You stop paying married woman's or widow's reduced rate NI contributions and start paying full rate NI contributions ☐   Please tell us the date you might change

Please tell us what your annual earnings are now £

Your annual earnings change. Do not include pension income. ☐   Please tell us what they might change to £

Part 12 - Your signature
Please sign and date this form.

Your signature   Date

If you want your Retirement Pension forecast sent to someone else, you must also fill in and sign Part13.

Application for a Retirement Pension forecast - continued

Part 13 - Sending your forecast to someone else

The Department's records are strictly confidential and your Retirement Pension forecast cannot be sent to someone else unless we have your written consent to do so.

If you would like us to send your Retirement Pension forecast to someone else instead of directly to yourself, please fill in the following authorisation.

I authorise the Benefits Agency to send my Retirement Pension forecast to my representative who will act on my behalf and to whom you may diclose any information held on my National Insurance (NI) record which is relevant to my Retirement Pension.

My representative is named below. Use BLOCK CAPITALS.

Their name

Address

Postcode

Daytime phone number   **Please include the standard STD code**

Company reference number, if appropriate

Please sign and date this authorisation.

Your signature   Date

Part 14 - Correspondence address

Is your correspondence address different to your residential address?   Yes [ ]   No [ ]

Correspondence Address

Postcode

Page 5

BR19(P)

Appendix VIII

Pension Sharing on Divorce NAPF
Recommended Scale of Charges[1]

VIII.1

1. Section F of the guide states:

    'One of the Government's key principles for pension sharing is that the parties to the divorce, and not the pension scheme, are responsible for any costs arising from their pension share. This means that costs specifically relating to an individual divorce case, including ongoing administration costs, will be met by the divorcing couple, unless the trustees decide not to make any charges'.

2. The Government has not placed any specific limit on charges. However, the regulations require that all charges made by schemes must be reasonable and linked to the costs associated with each individual case.

3. The NAPF has been concerned that the level of charges could give rise to complaints by the scheme member and/or the ex-spouse, leading to lengthy and costly disputes. In order to try to minimise the likelihood of complaints, the NAPF has, after consulting its Members, devised a recommended scale of charges.

4. The publication of a scale of charges comes with the approval of the Government. In its original consultation document on the Pension Sharing regulations, published in December 1999, the DSS said: *'The National Association of Pension Funds (NAPF) has indicated that it is willing to issue guidance to its Members on charging. The Government welcomes this helpful development'.*

5. The tables set out a range of estimated costs in the case of scheme members who divorce both before and after retirement. The NAPF recommends the adoption of an index-linked flat fee in the range of £750 to £1,000. In addition, schemes should be able to pass on any third party costs such as the supply of medical evidence.

6. It should be remembered that this is a recommended scale of charges. It is neither a maximum nor a minimum. Variations may occur due to the complexity of a particular case or the special features relative to individual schemes. For example, in Scotland, matrimonial property is valued at the 'relevant date'. The relevant date is the earlier of either the date of separation or the date of service of the summons for divorce. The regulations require that where the date on which the request for the valuation was received is more than 12 months after the relevant date, then the date for the purposes of valuing the benefits shall be the relevant date. The cost of providing such an 'historic valuation' could be, in some cases, greater than the NAPF's recommended charge.

7. The pension sharing provisions apply to couples who start divorce or nullity proceedings on or after 1 December 2000. Over the coming months it will be possible to see how pension sharing works in practice. The NAPF consulted its

---

1 Excerpted from *Pensions Sharing on Divorce Made Simple*, NAPF, 2000. © National Association of Pension Funds 2000. All rights reserved. The charges referred to in this appendix are those recommended by NAPF as at November 2000.

Members about the scale of charges and there was broad agreement that they appeared acceptable. The NAPF intends to review the charges once pension sharing is established, in order to ensure that they reflect an accurate picture of charges in practice.

A. Scheme member not yet retired – about to divorce

Procedure	Comments	Estimated cost
i Produce CETV quotation	Standard annual entitlement under disclosure of information regulations	£0
ii Additional CETV quotations		£150 per additional quotation
iii Provision of other information	If under disclosure of information regulations Otherwise, depending on nature of request	£0 from £25 to £75
iv Receipt of pension sharing order or consent order	To cover all administration costs from receipt of pension sharing order to completion of pension payments	up to £750
v Objections to order by scheme	Onus should be on the draftsman of the order to ensure that it is correctly drafted prior to issue.	Scheme to notify member/solicitor that costs for dealing with inoperable orders will be passed on

B. Scheme member retired – Pension in payment – about to divorce

Procedure	Comments	Estimated cost
i Assess the value of the pension in payment, including any contingent benefits	Actual cost dependant on charges incurred for actuarial time	up to £500
ii Administrative cost of collecting and interpreting medical evidence in respect of divorcing couple	It is assumed that the charges for supply of medical evidence will be met by the divorcing couple	Scheme to advise that payment for supply of medical evidence will be the responsibility of the member.
iii Establish a new pensioner record	To cover all administration costs from receipt of pension sharing order to completion of pension payments	up to £750
iv Assuming all documentation is in place, settle a transfer out (instead of iii above)		up to £300
v Establish a new member scheme record (record keeping/tracing reasons etc)		from £25 to £100

Appendix IX

Pension earmarking or sharing and the statutory charge

IX.1

[The following general guidance was provided, in October 2000, by the Legal Services Commission's Policy and Legal Department (Alison Macnair). It is to be followed by more detailed guidance which will be circulated for consultation.]

Basic principles: the charge arises on property that has been *recovered or preserved*.

Property is 'recovered' if the funded client successfully obtains it so that there is a gain for the funded client (see *Hanlon v The Law Society* [1982] All ER 199 at 214 and 215, HL).

Property is 'preserved' if the funded client successfully fends off a claim by someone else to their property so that the funded client keeps all or part of what they regard as their own.

For property to have been recovered or preserved it must have been:

- in issue in the proceedings; or
- obtained under any compromise or settlement arrived at to avoid proceedings or to bring them to an end ('substitution').

To be 'in issue' the property must have been the subject of the proceedings for which funding was granted. The leading guidance on this is in *Hanlon*. Lord Simon said at page 209:

'Property has been recovered or preserved if it has been in issue in the proceedings: recovered by the claimant if it has been the subject of a successful claim, preserved to the respondent if the claim fails. In either case it is question of fact, not of theoretical risk. What has been in issue is to be collected as a matter of fact from the pleadings, evidence, judgment and/or order. I can see no reason for extending the words to items of property, the ownership or possession of which has never been questioned.'

Time of recovery or preservation: The charge will arise when the recovery or preservation takes effect. This is when the former funded client gets the benefit of it, that is, when the payment

- ordered to be made (in respect of the beneficiary of a pension attachment or pension sharing order), or
- made free of the payment or share claimed (in respect of the pension holder)

is in fact made. The recovery or preservation may therefore take place years, even decades, after the final order in the proceedings. But because the recovery or preservation itself does not take place immediately, the Commission does not have to decide to defer enforcement until the payment is in fact made. There are no conditions

496

to be met and interest does not accrue (as happens where enforcement of the charge is deferred on the family home).

When there is a recovery or preservation by reason of a pension earmarking or sharing order, the regional office will first apply the charge to other assets in respect of which the charge arises even if, for example, enforcement is postponed by the charge being registered on the former funded client's home. The Commission is entitled to do so, because it may behave as any other chargee would in order to protect the Community Legal Service Fund's interests: Regulation 95(2) Civil Legal Aid (General) Regulations 1989 and Regulation 51 Community Legal Service (Financial) Regulations 2000.

Exemptions: If the property was recovered or preserved, the charge will arise on it unless property of that nature is **exempt**. There are three potential exemptions affecting shared and earmarked pensions:

- Periodical payments recovered in matrimonial proceedings are always exempt: see Regulation 94(c) Civil Legal Aid (General) Regulations for certificates granted under the Legal Aid Act 1988 and Regulation 44(1)(a) of the Community Legal Service (Financial) Regulations 2000 for certificates granted under the Access to Justice Act 1999 and the Funding Code.

- The first £2,500-worth of property recovered or preserved in proceedings under sections 23(1)(c) or (f), section 23(2) and section 24 of the Matrimonial Causes Act 1973 is exempt: Regulation 94(d) Civil Legal Aid (General) Regulations 1989 and Regulation 44(1)(d) and (2) Community Legal Service (Financial) Regulations 2000.

- Regulation 94(g) of the Civil Legal Aid (General) Regulations 1989 or Regulation 44(1)(h) of the Community Legal Service (Financial) Regulations 2000 both exempt

'Any sum, payment or benefit which by virtue of any provision in, or made under, an Act of Parliament, cannot be assigned or charged.'

This provision applies to pensions preserved after an application for an earmarking order or to a pension share, if (i) the pension itself is unassignable because of a provision in statute or regulations or another form of statutory instrument, and (ii) the prohibition on assignment has not been disapplied by section 166 Pensions Act 1995 or section 44 of WRPA. It does not apply to an earmarked share of a pension because that is an award of financial provision, not a pension itself.

Solicitors' reporting obligations: The Commission's regional offices will be instructed that solicitors will have to report on:

- Whether there has been a recovery or preservation following a claim for an earmarking order or pension share;

- Whether the recovered or preserved payment is exempt. If the funded client's solicitor argues that the property is exempt because of a prohibition against assignment or charging in or under an Act of Parliament they will have to identify the particular provision they claim applies;

- The percentage of the pension payment recovered or preserved;

- Particulars of the trustees, managers or person responsible for the pension affected by the earmarking or sharing order.

Although it may not be straightforward to determine whether the charge arises in a particular case, the funded client's solicitor should be able to give the regional office this information because they should know how the charge will affect the outcome of their client's case.

Protecting the charge: The regional office will protect the charge by writing to the pension trustees, managers or person responsible to tell them that Regulation 87(1) of the Civil Legal Aid (General) Regulations 1989, or Regulation 17(2) and 18(1) of the Community Legal Service (Financial) Regulations 2000 (depending on whether the certificate was granted under the 1988 or 1999 Act), provides that the payment due under the order in the proceedings must be made to the former funded client's solicitor and if they no longer have a solicitor acting, to the Commission. The letter will point to the fact that unless the payment is made to the former funded client's solicitor or the Commission, the payer cannot get a good discharge.

Index

References are to numbered headings. Those prefixed 'S' refer to headings in the Summary and those prefixed 'App' refer to headings in the Appendices.